ARCHAEOLOGY
AND
OLD TESTAMENT
STUDY

ARCHAEOLOGY
AND
OLD TESTAMENT
STUDY

Jubilee Volume of the
SOCIETY FOR
OLD TESTAMENT STUDY
1917–1967

Edited by

D. WINTON THOMAS

OXFORD
AT THE CLARENDON PRESS
1967

Oxford University Press, Ely House, London W. 1

GLASGOW NEW YORK TORONTO MELBOURNE WELLINGTON
CAPE TOWN SALISBURY IBADAN NAIROBI LUSAKA ADDIS ABABA
BOMBAY CALCUTTA MADRAS KARACHI LAHORE DACCA
KUALA LUMPUR HONG KONG TOKYO

© *Oxford University Press 1967*

PRINTED IN GREAT BRITAIN

PREFACE

At a meeting of the Society for Old Testament Study held in January 1964, it was decided that a volume, which should be the fifth of a series, should be published in part celebration of the Society's Jubilee which falls in 1967. In 1925 *The People and the Book*, edited by A. S. Peake, was published; in 1938 *Record and Revelation*, edited by H. Wheeler Robinson; in 1951 *The Old Testament and Modern Study*, edited by H. H. Rowley; and in 1958 *Documents from Old Testament Times*, edited by myself. It was the Society's wish that its Jubilee volume should aim at informing students of the impact of archaeological discovery upon Old Testament study, with reference to selected sites. The Society for the second time did me the honour of entrusting me with the editorship of a volume sponsored by it, and, as previously, I was given complete freedom both to plan the volume and to invite contributors to it.

This volume is not intended primarily for archaeologists—it may, however, hold some interest for them—but for those many students of the Old Testament, whether they be teachers of Scripture in schools, or clergy, or others who are not professional scholars, who wish to know what interest and importance particular sites in Palestine and in other countries of the ancient Near East have for them. The contributions are accordingly not intended to be technical archaeological studies. They attempt rather to relate the archaeological material from the sites as closely as possible to the Old Testament, and to bring out relevant points of interest concerning history, chronology, geography, literature, religion, social life, and so on. Many, if not most, of the sites included in the volume will be familiar by name to Old Testament students, but often it is likely that little more than their names is known to them. This volume aims at providing them with at least some of the information which, it is hoped, will both arouse their interest in these ancient places, and at the same time help them to understand better the role that they have played in the history of ancient Israel and in the life and thought of her people. While the earliest periods are not neglected, the main emphasis falls, as might be expected, upon the period which is covered by the Old Testament. Sometimes the treatment of a site is carried beyond the end of the Old Testament period, up to the Roman period, and occasionally even later.

This volume may in some respects be regarded as a companion volume to *Documents from Old Testament Times*, and there are frequent references in this volume to the earlier one. There the material treated consisted of inscriptions on clay, stone, seals, and coins, and writing on potsherds, papyrus, and leather. In the present volume documents too have their place. No account, for example, of Alalakh, Mari, Nuzi, or Ugarit, could ignore the texts discovered at these sites, nor could the new inscribed material which has in recent years become available from several sites in Palestine, all the more welcome as it is in view of the comparative rarity of such material, be passed over. The chief emphasis in this volume is, however, upon other kinds of material remains unearthed in excavation. As in the earlier volume, attention is directed to discoveries made both in Palestine and in surrounding countries. The sites which have been selected are located in Egypt (two sites), Mesopotamia (four sites), Anatolia (one site), Syria (three sites), and Palestine (fifteen sites and three areas). The weight is thus heavily upon Palestinian sites, as is not unnatural in a volume which is concerned with archaeology and Old Testament study. The land which gave birth to the Old Testament may be allowed the chief voice among the witnesses to her past.

While there are many sites which it would have been desirable to include, considerations of length have imposed a limit on the number that could be included. The sites which have been included, many of them occupied over a very long period of time, bring their own important witness to the history, life, and thought of ancient Israel, and of the peoples who were her near neighbours. Archaeological work at some of the sites goes back a long way in its beginning. In some cases work has been resumed later at these same sites. In other cases the first excavation of a site is of much more recent date. While it may be said that the sites which are included in this volume mostly select themselves, a few have been selected for a special reason. Thus, Nuzi was selected as providing an opportunity for a special study of the Hurrians (the Horites of

the Old Testament); Tell el-Amarna and Thebes for a fresh study
of the Ḫabiru and of the Execration Texts—the latter a highly
important source for Palestinian and Syrian topography and
onomasticon c. 1800 B.C.; and Boğazköy was selected as a basis
for an up-to-date presentation of the Hittites and their civilization.
The articles on the Negeb, Philistia, and Transjordan are designed
to bring together information concerning areas generally less
familiar to students. That there should be some overlap in the
articles—the Ḫabiru and the Hurrians, for example, are frequently
encountered, and many features of everyday life in ancient Israel
recur at different sites—need not cause surprise. The reader may
thereby be made aware that these ancient sites of the Near East
need to be viewed in relation to one another, and that the archaeological information that is derived from excavations at them
requires expert correlation if its significance is fully to be gauged.

The contributors, the majority of whom have either directed,
or participated in, the excavations about which they write, were
asked to adhere to the general plan of the volume, but otherwise
they have been allowed to treat the site or area assigned to them
in their own way, and the views they express are their own. Brief
histories of the excavations of the sites are given, and reference is
made to the individuals and bodies chiefly concerned in them.
The importance of the geographical situation of the site is brought
out, and the identification of it is discussed where necessary. It
may be remarked incidentally that the identification of modern
sites with ancient cities mentioned in the Old Testament is one
of the more significant of the services rendered by archaeology to
Old Testament study. A bibliography accompanies each article,
and a general bibliography is provided in addition. Readers may
often find it useful to consult also the bibliographies in *Documents
from Old Testament Times*.

References to chapters and verses of the Old Testament are
given according to the Massoretic text, but references to the
Revised Version are also given when the numeration differs from
that of the Massoretic text. Names of persons and places which
occur in the Old Testament are normally spelled in the forms as
found in the Revised Version, and quotations in English are from
this version, except where a contributor offers his own translation
of the Hebrew text. The spelling of Egyptian and Mesopotamian

names generally follows that which is found in the revised edition of the *Cambridge Ancient History*. Consistency in the spelling of modern forms of place-names has not been attempted. The system of transliteration followed in the transcription of Hebrew and other Semitic words is normally that which is given in *The Old Testament and Modern Study* (p. xiii). Since some measure of uniformity of chronology is desirable in a volume of this kind, the contributors were requested to work to an outline chronological chart prepared by myself. Opportunity was, however, given to them to depart from it at any point should they wish to do so, and readers will observe that in a few instances dates other than those given in the chart are preferred. The chart in a revised and expanded form is supplied with this volume. The dates given in it, many of them based upon the revised edition of the *Cambridge Ancient History*, must be regarded as approximate only, for, as is well known, on many points of Old Testament and Near Eastern chronology scholars are not agreed, and the dates they propose sometimes differ widely. The chart does not aim at completeness. It is intended only as a guide to the dates, events, and persons specifically referred to in the volume. The illustrations which have been selected include, it is believed, at least some which will be fresh to the reader, and the maps and drawings which accompany some of the contributions will, it is hoped, be found helpful.

My thanks are due to the Society for Old Testament Study for the trust it has placed in me; to the Revd. H. St J. Hart, M.A., B.D., Lecturer in Divinity, University of Cambridge, and Dean of Queens' College, who has kindly prepared the indices, and to the Revd. A. A. Macintosh, M.A., Chaplain of St. John's College, Cambridge, who assisted him; to Mrs. Norma Emerton, M.A., who has translated the French text of Professor Parrot's article, and to Mr. J. H. Eaton, M.A., Lecturer in Theology, University of Birmingham, who has translated the German text of Professor Noth's article; to Mrs. Eleanor Vogel, Archaeological Assistant, Hebrew Union College, Cincinnati, who kindly allowed me to use the research map of Transjordan prepared by her; to Mr. T. C. Mitchell, for undertaking to contribute the article on Philistia at comparatively short notice; to Miss M. R. Munn-Rankin, Lecturer in Near Eastern History, University of Cambridge, to Professor P. R. Ackroyd, and to Professor D. J.

Wiseman, for their advice and help; and to the publishers for their interest and for their skill in the production of the volume. I owe a special debt of gratitude to the contributors to the volume. Some of them are not members of the Society for Old Testament Study, yet they have willingly and generously given of their time and their expert knowledge. Co-operation with so many scholars in different parts of the world has been a great pleasure to me and an exhilarating experience, and their patience and understanding have done much to ease my task. They will, I know, join me in the hope that this volume may not fall too far short of its professed aim, and that it may prove not unworthy of the occasion which it celebrates.

D. WINTON THOMAS

CONTRIBUTORS

P. R. ACKROYD, M.A., M.TH., PH.D., Samuel Davidson Professor of Old Testament Studies, University of London, King's College.

Y. AHARONI, PH.D., Senior Lecturer in Palestinian Archaeology, The Hebrew University of Jerusalem.

W. F. ALBRIGHT, LITT.D., D.H.L., TH.D., Professor Emeritus of Semitic Languages, Johns Hopkins University, Baltimore.

D. R. AP-THOMAS, M.A., B.D., Senior Lecturer in Hebrew and Biblical Studies, University College of North Wales, Bangor.

F. F. BRUCE, M.A., D.D., Rylands Professor of Biblical Criticism and Exegesis, University of Manchester.

R. DE VAUX, O.P., D.TH., École Biblique et Archéologique Française, Jerusalem.

D. DIRINGER, M.A., D.LITT., Reader in Semitic Epigraphy, University of Cambridge, Fellow of University College.

J. A. EMERTON, M.A., B.D., Reader in Semitic Philology, University of Oxford, Fellow of St. Peter's College.

G. M. FITZGERALD, M.A., Field Director, Museum of the University of Pennsylvania Excavations at Beth-shean, 1930–1, 1933.

C. J. GADD, C.B.E., M.A., D.LITT., F.B.A., F.S.A., Professor Emeritus of Ancient Semitic Languages and Civilizations, University of London, Hon. Fellow of Brasenose College, Oxford.

N. GLUECK, PH.D., B.H.L., LL.D., President and Professor of Bible and Biblical Archaeology, Hebrew Union College-Jewish Institute of Religion, Cincinnati.

J. GRAY, M. A., B.D., PH.D., Professor of Hebrew and Semitic Languages, University of Aberdeen.

O. R. GURNEY, M.A., D.PHIL., F.B.A., F.S.A., Shillito Reader in Assyriology, University of Oxford, Fellow of Magdalen College.

KATHLEEN M. KENYON, C.B.E., M.A., D.LIT., F.B.A., F.S.A., Principal, St. Hugh's College, Oxford, Lecturer in Palestinian Archaeology, University of London, 1948–62, Director of the British School of Archaeology in Jerusalem, 1951–63.

M. E. L. MALLOWAN, C.B.E., M.A., D.LIT., F.B.A., F.S.A., Emeritus Professor of Western Asiatic Archaeology, University of London, Director, British School of Archaeology in Iraq, 1947–61, Fellow of All Souls College, Oxford.

B. MAZAR, D.PHIL., D.H.L., Professor of Biblical History and Archaeology of Palestine, The Hebrew University of Jerusalem.

T. C. MITCHELL, M.A., Assistant Keeper, Department of Western Asiatic Antiquities, The British Museum.

M. NOTH, D.TH., Professor of Old Testament, University of Bonn.

A. PARROT, D.TH., Inspecteur général des Musées, Professeur, École du Louvre, Paris.

W. L. REED, B.D., PH.D., Professor of Old Testament, Lexington Theological Seminary, Lexington, Kentucky.

H. W. F. SAGGS, M.A., M.TH., PH.D., Professor of Semitic Languages, University College of South Wales and Monmouthshire, Cardiff.

J. N. SCHOFIELD, M.A., B.D., Lecturer in Divinity, University of Cambridge, Fellow of University College.

OLGA TUFNELL, F.S.A., Member of the Wellcome–Marston Archaeological Research Expedition to the Near East, 1932–3.

C. J. MULLO WEIR, M.A., B.D., D.PHIL., D.D., Professor of Hebrew and Semitic Languages, University of Glasgow.

D. J. WISEMAN, O.B.E., M.A., F.B.A., Professor of Assyriology, University of London.

G. E. WRIGHT, M.A., PH.D., D.D., Parkman Professor of Divinity, Harvard Divinity School, Cambridge, Massachusetts.

Y. YADIN, M.A., PH.D., Professor of Archaeology, The Hebrew University of Jerusalem.

CONTENTS

LIST OF PLATES

LIST OF ILLUSTRATIONS
IN THE TEXT

ACKNOWLEDGEMENTS

THE editor wishes to thank the following for their kind permission to reproduce plates and illustrations:

Plates. A.C.L. Brussels, Pl. I; Messrs. Collins, Pl. II (from M. E. L. Mallowan, *Nimrud and its Remains*, ii, 1966, pl. 321); C. H. Beck'sche Verlagbuchhandlung, Munich, Pl. III (from A. Götze, *Kleinasien*, 1933, fig. 9); the Trustees of the British Museum, Pl. IV; Musée du Louvre, Pl. V; the Department of Archaeology, The Hebrew University of Jerusalem, Pls. VI, VIII, XVII; Palestine Archaeological Museum, Pl. VII; the University Museum, University of Pennsylvania, Pl. IX; Professor Y. Yadin, Pl. X; Jerusalem Excavation Fund, Pl. XI; Palestine Exploration Fund, Pl. XII; the Trustees of the late Sir Henry S. Wellcome, Pl. XIII; Pennarts and Glissenaar, Montfoort, Netherlands, Pl. XIV; the Drew–McCormick Expedition, Pl. XV; *Revue Biblique*, Pl. XVI; The Rockefeller Museum, Jerusalem, Pl. XVIII; Dr. N. Glueck, Pl. XIX.

Illustrations. The Clarendon Press, Figs. 1 and 2; Dr. H. W. F. Saggs, Fig. 3; Professor D. J. Wiseman, Fig. 4; Professor B. Mazar, Fig. 5; Professor Y. Yadin, Fig. 6; Palestine Exploration Fund, Fig. 7; *Revue Biblique*, Figs. 8 and 9; Dr. Y. Aharoni, Fig. 10; Mr. T. C. Mitchell, Fig. 11; and Mrs. Eleanor Vogel, Fig. 12.

ABBREVIATIONS

A.A.S.O.R.	Annual of the American Schools of Oriental Research.
A.f.O.	Archiv für Orientforschung.
A.J.	Antiquaries Journal.
A.J.A.	American Journal of Archaeology.
A.J.S.L.	American Journal of Semitic Languages and Literatures.
Anal. Bibl.	Analecta Biblica.
Anal. Or.	Analecta Orientalia.
Anat. Stud.	Anatolian Studies.
A.N.E.P.	J. B. Pritchard, *The Ancient Near East in pictures relating to the Old Testament*, 1954.
A.N.E.T.	J. B. Pritchard, *Ancient Near Eastern Texts relating to the Old Testament*, 2nd ed., 1955.
A.O.	Archiv Orientální.
A.O.S.	American Oriental Series.
A.P.A.W.	Abhandlungen der preussischen Akademie der Wissenschaften.
A.R.M.	Archives royales de Mari.
A.R.W.	Archiv für Religionswissenschaft.
A.T.	D. J. Wiseman, *The Alalakh Tablets*, 1953 (*A.T.** indicates tablets from Level VII).
A.T.D.	Das Alte Testament Deutsch.
B.A.	The Biblical Archaeologist.
B.A.N.E.	The Bible and the Ancient Near East, ed. G. Ernest Wright, 1961.
B.A.R.	The Biblical Archaeologist Reader.
B.A.S.O.R.	Bulletin of the American Schools of Oriental Research.
B.H.	R. Kittel, *Biblia Hebraica* (3rd ed.).
B.I.E.S.	Bulletin of the Israel Exploration Society.
B.J.P.E.S.	Bulletin of the Jewish Palestine Exploration Society.
B.J.R.L.	Bulletin of the John Rylands Library.
B.O.	Bibliotheca Orientalis.
B.Z.A.W.	Beihefte zur *Zeitschrift für die alttestamentliche Wissenschaft.*
C.A.D.	I. J. Gelb, T. Jacobsen, B. Landsberger, and A. L. Oppenheim, *The Assyrian Dictionary of the University of Chicago*, 1956–.
C.A.H.	The Cambridge Ancient History.

C.M.L.	G. R. Driver, *Canaanite Myths and Legends*, 1956.
Corpus.	A. Herdner, *Corpus des tablettes en cunéiformes alphabétiques découvertes à Ras Shamra-Ugarit de 1929 à 1939*, 1963.
C.R.A.I.	*Comptes rendus de l'Académie des Inscriptions et Belles-Lettres.*
D.O.T.T.	D. Winton Thomas (ed.), *Documents from Old Testament Times*, 1958.
E.A.	J. Knudtzon, *Die El-Amarna-Tafeln*, 1908–15.
EB.	Early Bronze Age.
E.T.	*Expository Times.*
E.Tr.	English Translation.
H.T.R.	*Harvard Theological Review.*
H.U.C.A.	*Hebrew Union College Annual.*
IA.	Iron Age.
I.D.B.	*The Interpreter's Dictionary of the Bible*, 1962.
I.E.J.	*Israel Exploration Journal.*
I.L.N.	*The Illustrated London News.*
J.A.O.S.	*Journal of the American Oriental Society.*
J. As.	*Journal Asiatique.*
J.A.T.	L. H. Vincent and A. M. Steve, *Jérusalem de l'Ancien Testament; recherches d'archéologie et d'histoire*, 1954–6.
J.B.L.	*Journal of Biblical Literature.*
J.C.S.	*Journal of Cuneiform Studies.*
J.E.A.	*Journal of Egyptian Archaeology.*
J.N.E.S.	*Journal of Near Eastern Studies.*
J.O.T.	J. Simons, *Jerusalem in the Old Testament: Researches and theories*, 1952.
J.P.O.S.	*Journal of the Palestine Oriental Society.*
J.R.A.S.	*Journal of the Royal Asiatic Society.*
K.A.I.	Donner, H., and Röllig, W. *Kanaanäische und Aramäische Inschriften*, i, 1962, ii, iii, 1964.
K.A.V.	O. Schroeder (ed.), *Keilschrifttexte aus Assur verschiedenen Inhalts* (= *W.V.D.O.G.* xxxv).
K.S.	A. Alt, *Kleine Schriften zur Geschichte des Volkes Israel*, 3 vols., 1953–9.
LB.	Late Bronze Age.
M.A.M.	*Mission archéologique de Mari*, 1956–9.
MB.	Middle Bronze Age.
M.D.O.G.	*Mitteilungen der deutschen Orient-Gesellschaft zu Berlin.*

M.T.	The Massoretic Text.
N.T.T.	Nieuw Theologisch Tijdschrift.
O.I.C.	Oriental Institute Communications (University of Chicago).
O.I.P.	Oriental Institute Publications (University of Chicago).
O.L.Z.	Orientalistische Literaturzeitung.
O.P.B.I.A.	Occasional publications of the British Institute of Archaeology in Ankara.
Orient.	Orientalia.
O.T.M.S.	H. H. Rowley (ed.), The Old Testament and Modern Study, 1951.
P.E.F.A.	Palestine Exploration Fund Annual.
P.E.F.Q.S.	Quarterly Statement of the Palestine Exploration Fund.
P.E.Q.	Palestine Exploration Quarterly.
P.J.B.	Palästinajahrbuch des deutschen evangelischen Instituts für Altertumswissenschaft des Heiligen Landes zu Jerusalem.
P.J.E.M.	Publications of the Joint Expedition of the British Museum and of the University Museum, University of Pennsylvania, to Mesopotamia.
P.R.U.	Le Palais royal d'Ugarit.
P.S.B.A.	Proceedings of the Society of Biblical Archaeology.
Q.D.A.P.	The Quarterly of the Department of Antiquities of Palestine.
R.	H. C. Rawlinson, The Cuneiform Inscriptions of Western Asia (1861–84).
R.A.	Revue d'Assyriologie et d'Archéologie orientale.
R.B.	Revue Biblique.
R.E.S.	Revue des études sémitiques.
Rev. Arch.	Revue Archéologique.
R.H.A.	Revue Hittite et Asianique.
R.H.P.R.	Revue d'Histoire et de Philosophie religieuses.
R.S.O.	Rivista degli Studi Orientali.
S.A.O.C.	Studies in Ancient Oriental Civilization (Oriental Institute, University of Chicago).
Stud. Or.	Studia Orientalia.
T.L.Z.	Theologische Literaturzeitung.
T.Z.	Theologische Zeitschrift.
U.E.	Ur Excavations (P.J.E.M.), 1927 ff.
U.E.T.	Ur Excavations: Texts (P.J.E.M.), 1928 ff.
Ugar.	C. F. A. Schaeffer, Ugaritica; études relatives aux découvertes de Ras Shamra, 1939 ff.
U.H.	C. H. Gordon, Ugaritic Handbook, 1947.

V.T.   *Vetus Testamentum.*

W.V.D.O.G.   *Wissenschaftliche Veröffentlichungen der deutschen Orient-Gesellschaft.*

Z.A.   *Zeitschrift für Assyriologie und verwandte Gebiete.*

Z.A.W.   *Zeitschrift für die alttestamentliche Wissenschaft.*

Z.D.P.V.   *Zeitschrift des deutschen Palästina Vereins.*

INTRODUCTION

IT is today a truism to say that archaeological investigation in Palestine and in surrounding lands, which, since the end of the First World War has been conducted on an unprecedented scale, has transformed our attitude towards, and our understanding of, ancient Israel and the Old Testament. It is now widely recognized that neither Israel nor the Old Testament can any longer be studied in isolation. Both have been taken out of their position of uniqueness which they were formerly held to occupy, and have found their rightful setting within the wider framework of the ancient Near Eastern world. While this newer way of looking at Israel and the Old Testament—from the outside inwards, so to speak, as we add to the witness of the Old Testament itself the witness also of those neighbouring peoples with which Israel came into contact in the course of her history—may be familiar to students, and while they may be aware that it is archaeological research that has played a major part in bringing about this newer attitude, they are sometimes less clear as to the nature of the contribution which archaeology has to make to Old Testament study, and the kind of service which it can legitimately be expected to perform so far as Old Testament study is concerned. It may accordingly be useful to them if a few general considerations concerning the role of archaeological research in Old Testament study are briefly set out. With such considerations in mind, they may, it is hoped, be the better prepared for what this volume has to offer them.

They may be reminded, first, that as soon as an archaeological discovery is made, the problem of its interpretation at once arises. And concerning material which needs to be interpreted there must always and inevitably be differences of opinion. It should cause no surprise, therefore, that there can be, and frequently is, as much disagreement amongst archaeologists concerning the material they study—concerning the character of an object, its value as evidence, its relationship to other archaeological material, its purpose, and date—as there is among specialists in other fields of study. It is accordingly as fallacious to affirm that 'archaeology says', as if archaeologists always speak with one voice, as it is to affirm, for example, that 'psychology says', as if different schools of psychology do not exist. Both statements are entirely without foundation. As in other fields of Old Testament study, whether it be in the sphere of history, literature, religion, language, or in any other sphere, there are large gaps in the material available for study, with the result that a multiplicity of widely divergent theories arises, so too in the archaeological field a similar situation exists with like results. Archaeological evidence is often fragmentary and disconnected, and is only clothed with significance when the archaeologist has given his interpretation of it. Vigorous debate and divergence of view amongst archaeologists will, and in the nature of the case, must accordingly continue, and few final conclusions must be looked for. Anything like universal agreement will be the exception rather than the rule. The interpretation of archaeological material does not stand still. It calls for constant reinterpretation, particularly in the light of new material that is continually being unearthed. Views that have previously been held, sometimes held for a long time, may later be seen to be erroneous, and may have to be modified, even abandoned. A good example is the long-standing ascription of the Early Bronze Age defences of Jericho to the period of Joshua, a view which cannot be sustained any longer. The archaeological situation as seen today can easily be changed, and changed radically, by tomorrow's discoveries. And tomorrow's discoveries, even if they should by good fortune cast new light on old problems, almost always raise new ones, and thus present a fresh challenge to the interpreter.

The point may next be made that it is not only archaeological evidence which stands in need of interpretation and reinterpretation. The Old Testament itself must be interpreted and reinterpreted on the basis of the most recent research into it, and, as has just been said and as is well known, many and varied interpretations are put upon it. These two kinds of evidence—the internal evidence of the Old Testament and the external evidence of archaeology—thus both need to be interpreted and reinterpreted, and the different use made by Old Testament scholars of the two types of evidence sometimes leads to very different views concerning problems which are central to Old Testament study. As an example may be cited the differing views which have been advanced concerning the date of the Exodus from Egypt and the Settlement in Palestine. We shall return later to this problem of the interpretation of the Old Testament.

It has always been tempting, and still is in some quarters, not only to try to find in archaeological material direct contact with the Old Testament, but also to find in it confirmation of the Old Testament narrative. It cannot be emphasized too strongly or too often, however, that very few archaeological discoveries bear directly upon the Old Testament narrative. In 2 Kings i. 1, iii. 4 f., for example, we read of the revolt of Mesha, king of Moab, against Israel, and we may see in this passage direct contact with the Moabite Stone, and we may note that in this case the archaeological evidence is both confirmatory of the Old Testament narrative and contradictory to it. For, whereas the Old Testament gives us to understand that Mesha's revolt occurred after Ahab's death, the Moabite Stone makes it clear that it took place in the latter years of Ahab's reign. In the Moabite Stone and in the Old Testament the same event is recorded, but the accounts of it differ. The two sources are thus seen to be complementary and mutually explanatory. A further example of direct contact between archaeological discovery and the Old Testament may be seen in the account which Sennacherib gives of his capture of many Judaean towns and villages in Palestine, of his siege of Jerusalem, and of Hezekiah's submission and payment of tribute to him. This account, which is preserved in the Taylor Prism, largely agrees with the account found in 2 Kings xviii. 13–16 (cf. Isa. xxxvi. 1 f.), but in this case too the Old Testament account is supplemented by additional information which the Taylor Prism supplies concerning items of tribute paid by Hezekiah besides silver and gold. Again, the references in the annals of Tiglath-pileser III from Nimrud to Menahem, Pekah, Hoshea, and Jehoahaz of Judah, relate directly to the Old Testament accounts in, for example, 2 Kings xv and xvi, and testify in a striking way to their basic accuracy. A last example to be mentioned here is the direct link which connects the account of Jehoiachin's imprisonment and his daily allowance of food, as recorded in 2 Kings xxiv. 11–15, with the texts found in an underground building consisting of rows of rooms, probably used for administrative purposes, discovered during excavations at the site of ancient Babylon. These texts fill out the Old Testament narrative by specifying the actual amount of rations dealt out to Jehoiachin, who is mentioned by name in the texts, and to his fellow prisoners. Such direct points of contact between archaeology and the Old Testament are, it may be repeated, very exceptional, and when they do occur they are the more striking and valuable. It is to be noted that in the examples which have been given the Old Testament can be brought into relationship with information supplied by inscribed documents. It is those rare occasions when events recorded in the Old Testament are unmistakably referred to in inscribed documents unearthed in excavation that chiefly provide us with examples of direct contact between the Old Testament and archaeological evidence.

From what has been said, it follows that the impact of archaeo-logical discovery upon the Old Testament narrative is mostly of an indirect kind. That this should be the case is indeed only what might be expected. For from the point of view of her powerful neighbours—those who, like the Egyptians and the Assyrians and Babylonians, have left abundant inscriptional remains behind them —Palestine was a small land which merited their interest only in so far as she could be used as a pawn in the struggle between rival empires. The great powers were not interested in the details of her history, or in her way of life and thought and religion. These things, that are of paramount importance to us, to them were of no account. It is not surprising, therefore, that Egyptian and Mesopotamian monuments so rarely relate directly to the Old Testament.

If the direct contribution of archaeology to Old Testament study is, as we have seen it to be, small, it is quite otherwise with the indirect contribution which it makes. This indirect con-tribution is immense and will be abundantly evident throughout this volume. An illustration or two may be given. The first relates to the texts discovered at Nuzi, in Mesopotamia, and at Mari and Alalakh, in Syria, which belong to the Middle Bronze Age, the age of the patriarchs. While these texts provide no evidence at all to establish any of the patriarchs as historical figures, or to make possible the dating with any accuracy of any event recorded in Gen. xii-l, they have rendered much more credible the Old Testa-ment traditions of the patriarchal age by the information they supply concerning the background, especially religious and social, of the age in which the patriarchs lived. Again, the ivories from Samaria can do no more than recall for us in an indirect way Ahab's ivory palace (1 Kings xxii. 39). Yet they bear eloquent testimony to the commercial prosperity of the northern kingdom, and to the luxury enjoyed by the more wealthy classes in Samaria in the reigns of Ahab and later kings. The wealth of ivories from Nimrud, in Mesopotamia, illustrate, in another part of the ancient world, how these expensive luxuries were enjoyed by the kings of Assyria until the end of the eighth century B.C. And, last to be referred to here, the Lachish letters (c. 590 B.C.), while they have no direct bearing upon the book of Jeremiah, or upon the personality of the prophet Jeremiah, yet inform us in a most illuminating way about such matters as the epistolary style which was in vogue among Judaeans in the days of Jeremiah, about the Hebrew language and the kind of script they used, about Hebrew proper names that were current in this period, about the function of a prophet, and about the system of communications that was in operation at the time, including the use of fire signals. These letters demonstrate indeed that the indirect contribution of archaeological material can be hardly less valuable than the direct contribution that it makes. It is well to remind ourselves that, while they throw so much indirect light on the Old Testament, they themselves, like archaeological material in general, need in turn to be interpreted by reference to the Old Testament.

The history of the interpretation of archaeological material in relation to Old Testament study has not infrequently revealed an unhappy tendency to press the archaeological evidence too far, to the point indeed of a claim that archaeology has proved the truth of the Old Testament. The failure to distinguish between the direct and indirect bearing of archaeological evidence on the Old Testament, to which we have just referred, has been a contributory factor in the growth of this tendency. A greater failure, however, has been the failure to distinguish between two quite different kinds of truth—the historical truth of individual statements in the Old Testament and the spiritual truth of the Old Testament. That archaeology can, and does, confirm the truth of individual assertions in the Old Testament is undeniable, and we may be grateful for such confirmation. However, when we speak of the truth of the Old Testament, we surely mean something much more than conformity with the known facts of archaeology, or of history, or of comparative religion. Different levels in Israel's spiritual life are to be distinguished, and it is to what may be broadly called the Canaanite pattern of religion— the type of religion against which the prophets so strongly inveighed—that archaeology chiefly bears witness—to pagan temples and altars, to a multiplicity of gods and goddesses, and to the prevalence of the fertility cult. On Israel's break away from Canaanite belief and practice in all their crudity archaeology is silent. Only in the Old Testament is the record of it preserved. To the central spiritual ideas of the Old Testament—about the one true God, about man, about suffering, and about the kingdom of God—ideas in which is enshrined the profounder truth of the Old Testament—there is no monument in stone or metal. It is usually unsafe to prophesy where archaeology is concerned. We may, however, go so far as to assert that it is in the highest degree improbable that archaeological research will at any time in the future unearth any monument that bears directly upon this profounder truth of the Old Testament, upon those ideas which give to the Old Testament its permanent human value. Moses, Elijah, the great prophets, Ezra—of these significant figures in the history of Israel's religion we hear nothing from archaeology. So far as archaeology is concerned, they might never have existed. The distinctive contribution which the people of Israel made to the history of human achievement is without positive witness so far as material objects are concerned. We may read of it in the pages of the Old Testament; nowhere do we find it embodied in any object made with hands. A large area of the Old Testament thus falls completely outside the scope of archaeological research, and cannot accordingly be tested by external evidence. It may, however, be said that the very absence of material objects constitutes in a negative way testimony to Israel's supreme achievement, to her unique contribution to the spiritual, as opposed to the material, history of mankind.

The very phrase 'confirmation of the truth of the Old Testament', it may be suggested, is not without difficulty, for underlying it there would seem to be the supposition that the Old Testament has been fully understood and rightly interpreted. As has already been said, however, opinions differ greatly as to the way in which it is to be interpreted. It must never be thought that it is an easy task to discover what the Old Testament does in fact say. In the first place, there lies at the back of this problem a preliminary question which needs to be asked. What do we mean when we speak of the Old Testament? Do we mean the Old Testament in Hebrew, or in Syriac, or in Greek, or in Latin? Or do we mean the Authorized Version or the Revised Version, or one of the many modern translations that have been produced in English as well as in other languages in recent years? The answer to these questions is that, if we wish to know what the Old Testament says, we shall not find it in any one of these alone, not even in the Hebrew text itself. For this text has first to be established in its original form, so far as this is possible, by reference to the ancient versions and to Hebrew manuscripts, and when the most likely original text has been established, the most probable meaning of the text has then to be extracted. This too is a difficult task, which must take into account the whole range of Semitic languages and some other languages as well. In the same way the text of the ancient versions in turn needs to be established, both by reference to the Hebrew text and to manuscript authorities, and problems of language arise here also. The most probable original text of the Old Testament can thus only be obtained as the result of a highly complex operation, which involves careful comparison of ancient texts, as well as minute study of linguistic problems. Only when these tasks have been undertaken to the full limit of possibility are we in a position to assert with any confidence what we believe the Old Testament to say. Preconceived notions of what it says or ought to say have thus no place in a genuine desire to seek out its true meaning. To determine its meaning calls both for considerable scholarly equipment, and for long and disciplined labour on the part of the interpreter. If there is a danger of reading too much into archaeological discoveries, too much can be read also into the Old Testament. As often as not, the interpretation of archaeological material depends upon literary sources, and in so far as the Old Testament is one of them, a complicated interrelationship between archaeological material and the Old Testament narrative is set up which defies easy solutions. To claim too much for archaeology is not only to misunderstand the situation, but it is also to overlook the positive contribution which it has to make to

Old Testament study. It is indeed more than this—it is to do a grievous disservice to a field of study to which all students of the Old Testament must feel deeply indebted. We make a grave error if we think that it is the function of archaeology to prove or disprove what we believe the Old Testament to say.

So far we have been considering the differing views of their material which are held by archaeologists, the constant need for the reinterpretation of the material, the problem of the correlation of archaeological evidence and the Old Testament narrative, the lack of positive archaeological witness to the religion of Israel at its highest level, and the claim that archaeology confirms the truth of the Old Testament. From what has been said, it should be clear that archaeology has only a limited contribution to make to Old Testament study. Limited though it may be, its contribution is indispensable. Archaeological evidence, being external to the Old Testament, has a strong prima facie validity. There is a general disinterestedness about it which commends it, it fills gaps in the Old Testament evidence, and it illuminates many things in it. It enables the Old Testament to be more intelligibly understood, for it provides the material from which the background of the life and thought of ancient Israel may be built up slowly bit by bit, so that we may glimpse more clearly the reality behind the events recorded in the Old Testament. Without this essential key to the interpretation of the Old Testament narrative, our understanding of the background of the narrative would be much less full than it is today, and the revolution which has come about in the way in which the Old Testament is studied today, to which reference was made earlier, would not have been possible. Through archaeological research we can appreciate much more deeply today the changing conditions of life in ancient Israel. With its help the stage upon which leading personalities played their part and events of great moment were enacted is brought more vividly before our gaze. We see something too of a humbler way of life, of the problems of living which faced ordinary people, and of their attempts to meet them. It is this background of Israel's life and her way of thinking that archaeology can chiefly be expected to illustrate, and it is with this that the present volume is primarily concerned.

Only brief mention of some of the features that go to make up

this background which are dealt with in this volume can be made
here. Much is heard, for example, of the cities of Palestine, with
their fortifications, gateways, towers, walls, and houses, both of
rich and poor. Domestic furniture and utensils in daily use, and
the arrangements that were made for the storage of food and drink,
receive attention, as do industries, such as the production of wine,
oil, and perfume, and the organization of those who worked in
them into guilds, as well as processes of dyeing, pottery making,
and smelting of copper and bronze. Institutions, such as kingship,
the maintenance of law and order, and armies and warfare, are
considered. The religious life of Canaan bulks large, with its
many gods and goddesses, its temples and altars, with their appropriate furniture, and its sacrificial system, and there is frequent
reference to customs attaching to betrothal, marriage, death, and
burial. Among other matters that are treated are articles of personal adornment—jewellery, beads, and amulets; the arts of architecture, sculpture, painting, and the carving of ivories; language
and phraseology, writing and writing materials, and the development of the Hebrew alphabet; personal and place-names, and
population distribution; seals, weights and measures, and coins;
and the kind of games that were played. The history and life and
thought of Israel's neighbours are delineated, and contacts, sometimes very close—religious, historical, legal, social, literary, and
linguistic—between Israel and these surrounding peoples are
brought out. The volume tells also of the kind of problems which
excavators encounter, and of the way in which they set to work and
record their findings.

   If we were to sum up what has been said, both concerning the
role of archaeology in relation to Old Testament study and the
kind of background to the Old Testament which archaeology makes
it possible to build up, we might say that, if the Old Testament
needs archaeology for its better understanding, archaeology needs
no less the Old Testament for the interpretation of the material
remains which it unearths. If, without the light which archaeology
sheds, the significance of much in the Old Testament would be
missed, so, without the Old Testament, much archaeological
material would go unexplained. Archaeology and the Old Testament together form a mutually interdependent aid for the understanding the one of the other. Yet it can with justice be claimed

for the Old Testament that it is the most indispensable guide to ancient Palestine which exists, providing as it does the cultural, historical, and religious framework to which the material remains which archaeology supplies must be related. To say this is not in any way to denigrate the services of archaeology to Old Testament study. The contribution which archaeological research has made to Old Testament study must evoke from students of the Old Testament both deep gratitude for what it has achieved so far, and provide grounds for a confident hope of further services to come. Yet if our gratitude can be legitimately unbounded, we shall do well not to set our hopes unjustifiably too high. This volume, by providing some indication of what archaeological research has done up to the present time for Old Testament study will, it is hoped, suggest to the reader the kind of contribution it is likely to make in the future. Archaeological research will, we may believe, continue steadily to show that the Old Testament narrative is essentially trustworthy, and that, by its revelation of the religion of Canaan, which Israel found on her entry into the country, and which was a constant temptation to her to apostatize, it will continue to lead to a yet fuller understanding and appreciation of that deeper spirituality to which she in course of time attained, and which in a unique way marked her out from her neighbours, with whom she shared so much, and which gives to the Old Testament its profound and abiding value for mankind.

D. WINTON THOMAS

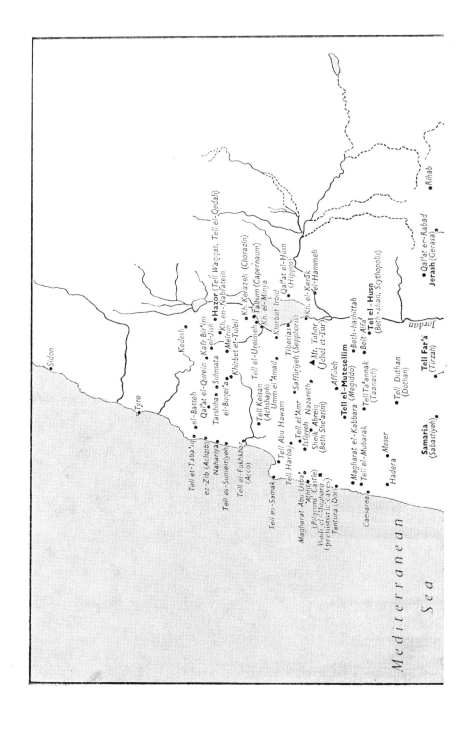

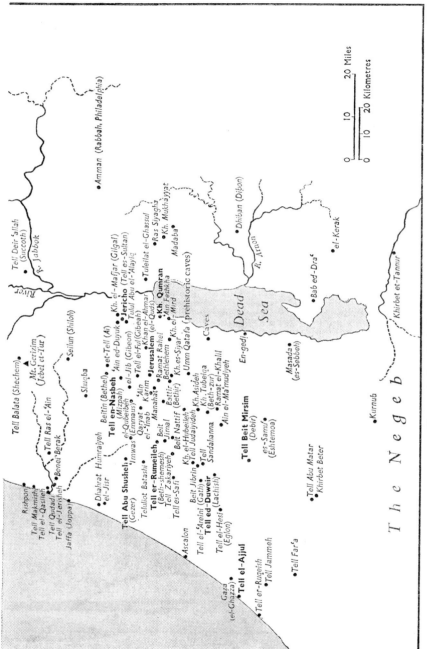

FIG. 1. Archaeological map of Palestine

FIG. 2. Archaeological map of

the Ancient Near East

EGYPT

TELL EL-AMARNA

THEBES

TELL EL-AMARNA

TELL EL-AMARNA is an artificial 'portmanteau' name coined about 1830 by John Gardner Wilkinson, when he combined the name of the village Et-Till, on the right bank of the Nile about 190 miles south of Cairo, with the name of the surrounding district El-Amarna (so called from the Beni ʿAmrān who had settled in this area about 1737). The village name Et-Till was corrupted to Et-Tell—inappropriately, since Tell el-Amarna is not a tell in the usual sense of the term.

Archaeologists had paid some attention to the rock tombs in this neighbourhood in the first half of the nineteenth century, but it was in 1887 that the discovery was made which has given Tell el-Amarna its secure place among the great archaeological sites of the Near East. A peasant woman, digging for nitrous earth formed by the decomposition of mud-brick to use it as a fertilizer, came upon several tablets of baked clay bearing cuneiform inscriptions, comparable to those already known from the Euphrates–Tigris valley. (These were, and still are, the only cuneiform tablets found in Egypt.) The woman naturally knew nothing about cuneiform writing; the tablets were obviously antiquities of a sort, but they did not look specially exciting, and she is said to have sold her interest in the find for ten piastres. A dealer sent some of the tablets to Jules Oppert in Paris; he pronounced them forgeries. There seemed to be no great market for them, so quantities of them are said to have been carried in sacks to Luxor on the backs of camels and donkeys, many of them being ground to dust on the way. However, the significance of the find began to be recognized, and the greater part of the material was acquired by the British Museum (through the interest of E. A. W. Budge) and the Berlin Museum. From the initial find about 350 tablets were preserved, and a few more came to light as a result of excavations by the Egypt Exploration Fund in 1891 under the direction of Flinders Petrie, and by the Deutsche Orient-Gesellschaft between 1911 and 1914.[1]

The standard edition of the tablets—at least of the 358 which were known at the time—is *Die El-Amarna-Tafeln*, by J. A. Knudtzon (1915), which presents the texts in transcription, with German translation, to which O. Weber and E. Ebeling supplied notes and glossary. An English translation was produced by S. A. B. Mercer, *The Tell El-Amarna Tablets* (1939). Soon after Knudtzon's edition appeared, three more fragmentary tablets were identified in Berlin (nos. 359–61); in 1921 six others were published from a Louvre collection (nos. 362–7), yet another from London in 1925 (no. 368), another from Brussels in 1934 (no. 369), while eight more, found in 1933–4 by an expedition sponsored by the Egypt Exploration Fund and directed by J. D. S. Pendlebury, were published several years later by C. H. Gordon in *Orientalia*, xvi, 1947, pp. 1–21 (nos. 370–7). To these a further addition (no. 378) has now to be made, part of the original find. In 1925 the Department of Egyptian Antiquities at the British Museum bought from a Cairo dealer a miscellaneous lot of antiquities, including a slightly damaged clay tablet, now numbered B.M. 50745, which proved to be an 'Amarna' letter, sent by the ruler of Gezer to his Egyptian overlord, probably Akhenaten, protesting his loyalty.[2] This ruler of Gezer, Yapaḥi, was already known as the author of four other Amarna letters to the Egyptian court, nos. 297–300.

The Tell el-Amarna tablets include texts of various kinds—lists of signs and words, and copies of mythological and epic compositions, which are probably scribal exercises designed to give secretaries at the Egyptian court practice in writing cuneiform. But out of the 378 tablets, 356 consist of letters from the archives of Amenophis III and his son Amenophis IV (Akhenaten), kings of Egypt from 1417 to 1362 B.C.—more particularly from the last eight years of the father's reign and the whole range of the son's reign, covering the quarter-century between 1387 and 1362 B.C. The language of all but two of the tablets is Akkadian, which at that time was the language of diplomatic interchange over a great part of the Near East.[3]

But why were the tablets found at El-Amarna? Because El-Amarna marks the site of the city of Akhetaten ('The horizon of Aten'), the new capital built by Akhenaten 300 miles north of his former capital Thebes so that the worship of the god Aten, the sun-disk, might be exclusively cultivated there, far from the dominant influence of Amun, the chief deity of Thebes. The transfer of the capital to Akhetaten was completed in Akhenaten's eighth year (1372–1371 B.C.), but a few years after Akhenaten's death his new capital was abandoned and the court returned to Thebes. When Akhetaten was established as the capital, however, the archives of Akhenaten's earlier years and those of his father's reign were brought there from Thebes, to be housed in the record office of the new city. But why, it may be asked, were they not taken back to Thebes when Akhetaten was abandoned? Perhaps most of them *were* taken back; it is at least arguable that the Amarna documents are those which were inadvertently left behind, to remain undisturbed for over thirty-two centuries.[4]

Of the diplomatic letters over forty belong to correspondence between the Egyptian kings and Asian rulers who were more or less their peers—especially the kings of Babylon, Assyria, Mitanni, and the Hittites. The rest belong to correspondence between the Egyptian court and the vassal rulers of city states in Syria, Phoenicia, and Palestine. The letters in the former category usually mention the Egyptian king by name; those in the latter category do not.

The city states of Syria, Phoenicia, and Palestine had been made tributary to Egypt by earlier kings of the Eighteenth Dynasty. But by the time of the Amarna correspondence the Egyptian grip was slackening; some of the vassals were being attracted into the Hittite sphere of influence, some were being attacked by marauding bands and found it difficult to secure Egyptian aid against them, some were making local arrangements for their own advantage. When writing to the Egyptian king, however, all eloquently protest their loyalty, while some complain of the slanderous reports sent in by their neighbours, and suggest that these neighbours themselves are the real rebels against their Egyptian overlord.

Of the vassal letters fifty-three were sent to the Pharaoh by Rib-adda, the ruler of Byblos in Phoenicia, the Old Testament Gebal.[5] Rib-adda makes repeated reference to a powerful officer of the Pharaoh named Yanḥamu. This Yanḥamu had practically the status and authority of an Egyptian viceroy in Syria; his official title at court was 'royal fan-bearer'.[6] Among his other duties was the supply of grain from a place called Yarimuta for the relief of the Pharaoh's Syrian subjects in time of scarcity.[7] This reminds us of Joseph's function in Egypt, and indeed Yanḥamu, like Joseph, bears a good Semitic name. Yanḥamu and Joseph cannot be identified with each other, but the references to Yanḥamu show how a Semite could attain a position of influence under the Egyptian king (even after the expulsion of the Hyksos), such as that ascribed to Joseph in Genesis. The king's vassals knew that it was politic to stand well in Yanḥamu's favour; thus Rib-adda concludes one letter to the king with the unsolicited testimonial— 'There is no servant like Yanḥamu, a faithful servant to the king!'[8] (Did he expect that Yanḥamu's attention would be drawn to these words?)

i. *The Ḥabiru/SA-GAZ in the Amarna Texts*

Six of the vassal letters are addressed to the king by Abdi-ḥiba, ruler of Jerusalem, who protests his utter loyalty. 'At the feet of my lord,' he says, 'seven times and seven times I fall. . . . Behold, this land of Jerusalem, neither my father nor my mother gave it to me; the mighty arm of the king gave it to me.'[9] But he is distressed by the slanderous reports which his detractors are sending to the king, and also by the menace of people whom he calls the Ḥabiru, against whom the Egyptian officials fail to take effective steps— 'As my lord the king lives, I will say to the commissioner of my lord the king: "Why do you love the Ḥabiru and hate the regents?" '[10] The whole region is being lost to the king—'the Ḥabiru plunder all the king's lands'.[11] Some of the rulers of neighbouring city states, or their relatives, are in league with the Ḥabiru: in particular, Lab'ayu, ruler of Shechem, has surrendered everything to them, or at least his son has done so. Abdi-ḥiba himself is menaced by them—they are actually trying to capture Jerusalem—but other rulers have fared worse—'But now the Ḥabiru are taking the king's cities. My lord the king has no regent left; they are all perishing. Behold, Turbazu has been killed at the city-gate of Zilu: the king held back. Behold, Zimrida of Lachish has been killed by slaves who have joined the Ḥabiru.'[12] Yet the king does nothing, although it is his land and his loyal vassals that are being thus treated. If only the king would send fifty soldiers—if only he would send Yanḥamu—the situation around Jerusalem could be restored; otherwise all the king's territory is lost to him.[13] A little later the situation has deteriorated further; a town, Beth-Ninib, in the region of Jerusalem has fallen to the Ḥabiru. A further insistent plea for military aid is made[14]—with no greater prospect of response than previous pleas.[15]

These letters from Abdi-ḥiba are the only Amarna texts to make explicit mention of the Ḥabiru menace, but it is plain that the people whom Abdi-ḥiba calls the Ḥabiru are those denoted in many of the other texts by the ideograph SA-GAZ—sometimes, especially in letters from Gebal, abbreviated GAZ. Thus, where Adbi-ḥiba accuses Lab'ayu and his family of making common cause with the Ḥabiru, Lab'ayu himself complains that he has been slandered to the king. Evidently Lab'ayu had received a letter from the Egyptian court asking if there was any substance in the accusations. 'The king has written concerning my son', says Lab'ayu. 'I did not know that my son was associating with the SA-GAZ. I have put him into the hand of Addaya [an Egyptian commissioner].'[16] The equation SA-GAZ = Ḥabiru, suggested by the parallel accounts of Abdi-ḥiba and Lab'ayu, is confirmed by much further evidence both in the Amarna correspondence and in other Near Eastern texts of the second millennium B.C.

According to Rib-adda of Gebal, the (SA-)GAZ have been encroaching on the Egyptian empire in Asia since the closing years of Tuthmosis IV (c. 1420 B.C.).[17] Rib-adda has many complaints to make against the Amorite ruler Abdi-aširta, who is taking one city after another in the Egyptian sphere of influence in Phoenicia, and threatening Rib-adda himself. He has detachments of the (SA-)GAZ under his command.[18] After Abdi-aširta's death his aggressive policy is continued by his sons, who, like him, have the aid of the (SA-)GAZ.[19]

One might be tempted to think that SA-GAZ is a general term of abuse, like 'rebels' or 'bandits', and this is supported by the fact that in some Akkadian texts—lexical lists and the like— SA-GAZ is glossed by ḫabbātu 'marauder'. Similarly in a letter from Dagan-takala, ruler of a south Palestinian city state, Pharaoh is asked for help against the SA-GAZ and other 'marauders', where this word ḫabbātu is used.[20] But the SA-GAZ are not always in rebellion against Egypt and her vassals. Sometimes they appear as allies of a ruler loyal to Egypt; thus Biryawaza, Pharaoh's lieutenant-governor in Ube in Syria, speaks of SA-GAZ along

with other followers of his with whom he is marching to keep a
rendezvous with Pharaoh's forces.[21]

ii. *The* 'PR.W *in Egyptian Texts*

From Egypt we have not only the Amarna tablets as a source
of information about the Ḫabiru. Inscriptions in the Egyptian
language belonging to the three centuries between 1450 and 1150
B.C.[22] make reference to people called the '*pr.w*, a term which is
almost certainly equivalent to Akkadian *ḫabiru*. In some of these
texts the '*pr.w* are servants; two inscriptions on tomb illustrations,
for example, from *c.* 1450 B.C. refer to '*pr.w* as straining out wine.[23]
Two papyrus letters from the time of Ramesses II prescribe an
issue of grain for the '*pr.w* who are drawing stone for the great
pylon of the king's house (if this is the meaning of the words describing their work).[24] A papyrus from the reign of Ramesses III,
listing items dedicated to the temple at Heliopolis, includes
'*pr(.w)* along with soldiers, sons of princes, *maryannu*, and 'the
settlers who are in this place'.[25] In an inscription in the Wadi
Hammāmāt, listing men sent by Ramesses IV to quarry there,
mention is made of '800 '*pr(.w)* of the bowmen of '*nt[iw?]*'.[26]

Other Egyptian inscriptions mention '*pr.w* in Asia. The Mem-
phis stele of Amenophis II lists among the booty which he carried
off at the end of his second campaign in Asia "'*pr.w*: 36,000'.[27] The
smaller Beth-shean stele of Sethos I reports an attack on the
nomads of Ruhma by 'the '*pr.w* of Mount Yarumtu together
with the Tayaru'.[28] Grdseloff and Albright identify Yarumtu
with Jarmuth in the tribal territory of Issachar (Joshua xxi. 29).[29]
Papyrus Harris 500 (verso 1:4 ff.), a document of *c.* 1300 B.C.,
records the capture of Joppa by a general of Tuthmosis III, and
tells how the general asked the leading men of Joppa to let the
maryannu bring the horses into the city 'since otherwise, if an
'*pr* passes by, he will steal them'.[30]

From these documents it appears that the '*pr.w* were known
in Syria and Palestine as marauders, but in Egypt as foreign
labourers. This is what we should expect if large numbers of
them were taken as prisoners of war, however generous the discount
we allow on Amenophis II's claim to have captured 36,000 of
them.[31]

iii. *Other Cuneiform Evidence*

In addition to their appearance in the Amarna texts, the Ḫabiru or SA-GAZ are mentioned in a wide variety of other cuneiform documents, in the Sumerian, Akkadian, and Hittite languages, from many parts of Western Asia, dating between the twentieth and twelfth centuries B.C.

In Hittite cuneiform texts from Boğazköy, both from the Old Hittite Kingdom (*c.* 1740–1460 B.C.) and from the Hittite Empire (*c.* 1460–1200 B.C.), references to the Ḫabiru or SA-GAZ appear. In the earlier period they appear once or twice in connexion with a guard-house, perhaps as members of the garrison.[32] Under the empire 'the gods of the SA-GAZ/Ḫabiru' are repeatedly invoked along with other deities in treaties.[33] Two Hittite ritual texts actually mention a god named Ḫabiru;[34] the name appears also as that of a god in a list of deities in the temple of Adad in Asshur,[35] and may be the name of the eponymous deity of the Ḫabiru (unless the identity of the divine name and the group designation is merely coincidental). One text from the period of the Hittite Empire refers to a Ḫabiru settlement in the Kizzuwadna region of south-east Anatolia.[36]

From another Hittite site, Alishar, fifty miles south-east of Boğazköy, comes an Akkadian text, the letter of an Assyrian merchant written at the beginning of the second millennium B.C., which mentions some men of the Ḫabiru 'from the palace of Šalaḫšuwe' who are in custody and for whom a considerable ransom is expected.[37]

In Akkadian texts from Mari, on the Middle Euphrates (eighteenth century B.C.), Ḫabiru soldiers appear as contingents in various armies, or as forming independent military groups on their own, and threatening the security of Mesopotamian towns.[38] One fragmentary letter mentions '3,000 asses of the Ḫabiru'.[39]

When we turn to the texts from the Hurrian state of Nuzi, east of the Middle Tigris (fifteenth century B.C.), we find a different state of affairs. The Ḫabiru are mentioned in over thirty Nuzian documents, but not as armed marauders or mercenary contingents in this or that military force. Here we find them hiring themselves out under contract as household servants—men, women, and families. The majority of these documents come from the household

archives of a Nuzian official named Teḫiptilla; repeatedly mention
is made in them of some member of the Ḫabiru voluntarily
entering his service. Sometimes a Ḫabiru servant will be adopted
as a full member of the household. These Ḫabiru have migrated to
Nuzi from other areas; their names belong to a wide variety of
languages, though the majority seem to be Semitic. It is the
Ḫabiru household servant of Nuzi who presents the closest parallel
from all the Ḫabiru whom we meet in ancient Near Eastern texts
with the Hebrew bondman of Exod. xxi. 1 (see below, p. 12).[40]

The inscriptions unearthed at Alalakh (Tell el-'Aṭshānāh) in
north Syria in 1937–9 and 1946–9 proved to contain further
references to the Ḫabiru, dating from Level VII (eighteenth
century B.C.) and Level IV (fifteenth century B.C.). In these inscriptions the Ḫabiru appear as a military corps or fraternity. From the
earlier of the two levels we have a date formula mentioning 'the
year in which Irkabtum the king, Shenuma, and the Ḫabiru
soldiers made peace'.[41] From the later level comes one inscription
mentioning the Ḫabiru twice in a list of names of which only the
appended professions remain, and eight inscriptions mentioning
the SA-GAZ. Four of these latter give lists of SA-GAZ soldiers;
their names are for the most part non-Semitic, some being recog-
nizably Hurrian.[42]

But the most interesting reference to the SA-GAZ from Alalakh
comes in the inscription on the statue of King Idrimi. In this
Akkadian inscription (also from Level IV) Idrimi, king of Alalakh,
tells how a rebellion forced him to flee south from Aleppo. He
took refuge in north Canaan, in the town of Ammiya, mentioned
also in the Amarna texts, and there he spent seven years among
the SA-GAZ warriors. This may imply that the SA-GAZ warriors of Ammiya had become a more or less settled community
in that area.[43]

The Ḫabiru, then, appear to have been members of a social
group widespread throughout the ancient Near East over several
centuries. According to the circumstances they might hire themselves out as household servants or as mercenary soldiers, or
might organize themselves into bands of freebooters. Only rarely
are they described as having a settled home of their own. Wherever
they are mentioned they are foreigners, frequently, though not
invariably, hostile foreigners. While the term Ḫabiru/SA-GAZ

no doubt had a primary and precise meaning of its own, it came to be used more generally of enemies, or rebels, or simply people whom the speakers or writers did not like—'under certain circumstances it can be used simply as a bad name to call one's enemy'.[44]

iv. *The Hebrews of the Old Testament*

Not unnaturally, speculation was early stimulated on a possible relation between the Ḫabiru/ʿpr.w and the Old Testament Hebrews (Hebrew ʿiḇrîm). Indeed, it was widely maintained that the activity of the Ḫabiru in the Amarna texts should be equated with incidents in the conquest of Canaan by the Israelites under Joshua, since there seemed to be many reasons for dating Joshua about 1400 B.C. Not only was this the dating indicated prima facie by the time note in 1 Kings vi. 1 (where Solomon begins the building of the temple in the 480th year after the Exodus); as recently as 1928–35 it appeared to be archaeologically confirmed by J. Garstang's discoveries on the site of Jericho, which led him to date the fall of the Late Bronze Age city in the reign of Amenophis III.[45]

The term 'Hebrew' (Hebrew ʿiḇrî, fem. ʿiḇriyyāh) is used of the Israelites or their ancestors some thirty-four times in the Old Testament. In the majority of instances, however, it is either applied to them by foreigners or used by themselves when speaking to foreigners. Thus Potiphar's wife complains of the behaviour of 'the Hebrew servant' whom her husband has acquired (Gen. xxxix. 14, 17); and in the closing chapters of Genesis and early chapters of Exodus, 'Hebrew' is the designation regularly used by the Egyptians of the Israelites (Gen. xli. 12; Exod. i. 16,[46] ii. 6 f.), or applied to the latter by the narrator in an Egyptian setting (Exod. i. 15, ii. 11, 13), or used of themselves by Israelites when speaking to Egyptians (Exod. i. 19). Joseph calls Canaan 'the land of the Hebrews' (Gen. xl. 15); Moses repeatedly addresses the Pharaoh in the name of Yahweh, 'the God of the Hebrews' (Exod. iii. 18, v. 3, vii. 16, ix. 1, 13, x. 3).

The same practice recurs later in the context of the Philistine ascendancy. To the Philistines their Israelite tributaries are regularly 'Hebrews' (1 Sam. iv. 6, 9, xiii. 19, xiv. 11, xxix. 3). In one place 'Hebrew' adherents of the Philistines are distinguished

from 'the Israelites who were with Saul and Jonathan', but they
join those Israelites after the Philistines are routed (1 Sam. xiv. 21).[47]
As late as the book of Jonah the Phoenician mariners' question to
the prophet, 'Of what people art thou?' receives the answer, 'I
am an Hebrew' (Jonah i. 8 f.); this may be an imitation of earlier
usage.

In the case-laws of the Book of the Covenant, directions are
given to the Israelites for the treatment of a 'Hebrew servant'
(Exod. xxi. 2); this usage is followed in Deut. xv. 12 ('If thy
brother, an Hebrew man, or an Hebrew woman, be sold unto thee
. . .') and echoed in Jer. xxxiv. 9, 14, where the people of Jerusalem
undertake to set free their Hebrew slaves, male and female (*hā'ibrî
weʰhā'ibriyyāh*). As in Deut. xv. 12, such a slave is a 'brother';
indeed, by Jeremiah's time he is indifferently a brother-Jew
(verse 9) or a brother-Hebrew (verse 14). Originally, however,
there was some special reason why the term 'Hebrew' was regarded
as the appropriate social designation for one who had been bought
as a slave. The parallel with the Ḫabiru servants at Nuzi has been
noticed above (p. 10).

The earliest Old Testament occurrence of the word remains to
be mentioned. In Gen. xiv. 13, when Chedorlaomer and his allies
invade the Jordan valley and lead off a host of captives, a fugitive
carries the news to 'Abram the Hebrew'. A natural inference from
this description of Abram is that the narrative of Gen. xiv is
derived from a non-Israelite source.[48] Whereas the usual LXX
rendering of *'ibrî* is Ἑβραῖος, the LXX version of Gen. xiv. 13
renders *'abrām hā'ibrî* by Ἀβρὰμ ὁ περάτης 'Abram the migrant (or,
one who crosses over)', as though *'ibrî* were cognate with the verb
'ābar 'crossed over'.[49]

Eber (*'ēber*), the great-grandson of Shem, appears in the post-
diluvian genealogies as the eponymous ancestor of the Hebrews
(Gen. x. 24 f., xi. 14 ff.); Shem is called 'the father of all the
children of Eber' (Gen. x. 21), where *beʰnê 'ēber* is equivalent to
'ibrîm, as elsewhere *beʰnê ḥēt* 'the sons of Heth' is to *ḥittîm* 'Hittites'.

It seems quite likely, when we have regard to the contexts in
which the terms appear, that there is some connexion between
the Ḫabiru/*'pr.w* and the Hebrews of the Old Testament. But this
connexion does not amount to complete identity; the most that
can reasonably be said is that the Hebrews of the Old Testament

were one group of the people elsewhere referred to as Ḥabiru/
ʿpr.w, but not necessarily a group specifically mentioned in the
Amarna or other Near Eastern texts. As for the once popular idea
that the Amarna texts provide a Canaanite account of the same
events as are recorded in the books of Joshua and Judges, this is not
really tenable. When we come down to details, we find no points
of contact. For example, the king of Jerusalem threatened by the
Ḥabiru in the Amarna texts is Abdi-ḥiba; the king of Jerusalem
overthrown by Joshua is Adoni-zedek (Joshua x. 1). H. H. Rowley
is completely justified in asserting that 'wherever the names of
persons can be checked, they disagree in the Biblical and in the
Amarna records'.[50] Moreover, the basis for Garstang's calculation
of the date of the destruction of Late Bronze Age Jericho has
been overturned by the more recent excavations on the site directed
by Kathleen M. Kenyon;[51] and while the date of the destruction
of the Late Bronze Age city is problematical, evidence from other
Canaanite sites points with increasing unanimity to the thirteenth
century B.C. as the time when Israel's invasion of Canaan under
Joshua began (during the Nineteenth Dynasty of Egypt).[52]

It should be added that not all scholars who have accepted a
fifteenth-century B.C. date for the Exodus and settlement see an
affinity between the Ḥabiru of the Amarna texts and the followers of
Moses and Joshua. For example, it has been argued that, far from
being identical with, or even related to, the Israelites, the Ḥabiru
were hostile to them, that Cushan-rishathaim, king of Aram-
naharaim (Judges iii. 8), was a Ḥabiru chief from Qusana-ruma in
north Syria, and that his overthrow by Othniel explains the disappearance of the Ḥabiru from our records as a power to be
reckoned with in Western Asia.[53]

H. H. Rowley has argued that if an Old Testament parallel is to
be sought for any of the events reflected in the Amarna correspondence, it should be found in some incidents in the life of Jacob,
especially in the record of Simeon and Levi's attack on Shechem
(Gen. xxxiv).[54] Moreover, if this parallel is acceptable, it follows
that Joseph's career coincides with the later part of the Amarna
age. If the Pharaoh who appointed Joseph as his chief minister
was Akhenaten, this might explain the weakness of Akhenaten's
policy in Canaan, which forms a contrast to the rigidity and strength
of his policy in Egypt.

If his administration was weak in Palestine, it was because it chose to be. . . . The charges of treachery made in some of the letters would not reach the ears of the Pharaoh, or would be offset by the counter-charges, and the support said to be given to the enemy by some of the Pharaoh's own officials would be more easily understandable if those officials knew that they had the connivance of the Pharaoh's chief minister.[55]

This correlation of the Amarna and the Old Testament evidence is tentative at best, but it is not exposed to such conclusive objections as the attempted correlation of the Amarna evidence with the settlement under Joshua.

v. *The Philological Question and the Evidence from Ugarit*

The historical identity and the philological equivalence of Ḫabiru and Hebrew are, strictly speaking, two separate questions. The philological equivalence of Ḫabiru and Hebrew *'ibrî* is possible in so far as Akkadian *ḫ* corresponds to West Semitic ' (*'ayin*) as well as to West Semitic *ḫ* (Hebrew *ḥ*). An alternative proposal was that Ḫabiru meant 'confederate(s)', from the root *ḫbr* (as in Hebron, 'confederation', with which place, indeed, A. H. Sayce connected the Ḫabiru).[56] Egyptian *'pr.w*, however, supported the equivalence with *'ibrî*, so far as the initial radical was concerned, although it raised questions in turn about the middle radical *b/p*.

The publication in 1940 of a text in Ugaritic threw fresh light on this problem. In parallel Akkadian and Ugaritic tax lists of towns required to provide corvée labour for King Niqmad II, contemporary with Akhenaten, the Akkadian *ḫal-bi* [lu] [meš] *SAG-GAZ* 'Aleppo of the SAG-GAZ' has as its Ugaritic equivalent *ḫlb 'prm*.[57] This discovery, if *'prm* = Ḫabiru, which is hardly to be doubted, further confirms the equivalence of Ḫabiru with the ideogram SA-GAZ, here written in an alternative form SAG-GAZ; but, more important still, it confirms that the West Semitic equivalent of Akkadian Ḫabiru had initial *'ayin*, so that Ḫabiru could no longer be associated with *ḫbr* 'confederate'. The *p* of Ugaritic *'prm* linked the word more securely than ever with Egyptian *'pr.w*, but threw doubt on the equivalence with West Semitic *'br*, and so with Hebrew *'ibrî*. But the doubt does not amount to the complete exclusion of the possibility of this last equivalence;

the equivalence could be maintained on the supposition of a local modification of the voiced labial to *p*, or of the unvoiced labial to *b*.

If, on the latter supposition, *'ibri* represents a local modification of *p* to *b*, then a Semitic root *'pr* would have to be envisaged, and Ḫapiru might be a more accurate transcription than Ḫabiru. R. de Langhe suggested a derivation from the root of Hebrew *'āpār* 'dust', as though the Ḫabiru/*'prm* were originally 'dusty ones', that is, 'men of the desert'.[58] Similarly, W. F. Albright recognizes in 'Abram the Hebrew' of Gen. xiv. 13 'a caravaneer of high repute in his time, the chief traditional representative of the original donkey caravaneers of the nineteenth century B.C., when this profession reached the climax of its history'.[59] While this was the primary profession of the 'Hebrews', he agrees that such stateless people 'naturally . . . became freebooters when they could not make a living in their trade'.[60]

It is arguable, on the other hand, that Ugaritic *'prm* represents a local modification from *b* to *p*, in which case we could still derive the word from *'br* and take it to mean primarily people who cross over or pass through—nomads or semi-nomads—but, whichever etymology be preferred, the general picture of their character and activities would not be radically altered. In our own day individual groups of nomads occasionally settle down in particular localities and change their way of life; we need not, therefore, be surprised to find an apparently settled group of Ḫabiru/*'prm* at Aleppo, as the Ugaritic material indicates, or at Ammiya, as the Idrimi inscription indicates, or further north in Kizzuwadna, as attested by a Hittite text from Boğazköy.

We could, then, recognize in the Hebrews of the Old Testament one body of Ḫabiru, bound together by a strong religious tie, who abandoned their former nomadic life and settled in Canaan, with a number of associated groups, at the end of the Late Bronze Age. The linguistic and archaeological arguments for this view are alike inconclusive, but there are a few pieces of evidence in its favour, and the present state of our knowledge permits us to hold it as a provisional working hypothesis.

F. F. BRUCE

NOTES

1. Early accounts of the discovery and disposal of the tablets differ in details; for a judicious summary, see J. A. Knudtzon, *Die El-Amarna-Tafeln*, pp. 1 ff.

2. See A. R. Millard, *P.E.Q.* 1965, pp. 140–3.

3. The two exceptions are nos. 31 and 32, letters between the Egyptian court and Arzawa, in southern Anatolia, written in an Indo-European language now known to be Luwian. Knudtzon recognized the Indo-European character of the language, but so much opposition was offered to his view that he was inclined to retract it (*Die zwei Arzawabriefe: die ältesten Urkunden in indogermanischer Sprache*, 1902; *Die El-Amarna-Tafeln*, p. 1074, note by O. Weber). His first thoughts were vindicated by the decipherment and study of the archives from Boğazköy.

4. Cf. E. F. Campbell, *The Chronology of the Amarna Letters*, p. 53; also the same writer's note in G. E. Wright, *Shechem, etc.*, p. 192.

5. To these must be added eleven letters from the same Rib-adda to other recipients.

6. Akkadian *muṣallil šarri* (*E.A.* 106. 38).

7. Cf. *E.A.* 68. 27 f.; 85. 48 ff.

8. *E.A.* 118. 55 f.

9. *E.A.* 287. 2 f., 25–28; cf. translation by C. J. Mullo Weir, *D.O.T.T.*, p. 39.

10. *E.A.* 286. 16–20. 'Commissioner' represents Akkadian *rābiṣu*, an official subordinate to the 'regent' (Akkadian *ḫazannu, ḫazianu*).

11. *E.A.* 286. 56.

12. *E.A.* 288. 37–44 (*D.O.T.T.*, p. 43).

13. *E.A.* 289. 41–46.

14. *E.A.* 290. 12–18.

15. A different picture of Abdi-ḫiba is given by Šuwardata, ruler of Kilti (in the Hebron region), of whom Abdi-ḫiba complains in *E.A.* 290. 6; Šuwardata accuses Abdi-ḫiba of trying to deprive him of his territory and describes Abdi-ḫiba as a second Lab'ayu.

16. *E.A.* 254. 31–35.

17. *E.A.* 85. 69–73.

18. e.g. *E.A.* 71. 16 ff. Abdi-aširta in his turn complains that he is being slandered, and protests that he is loyally and vigilantly guarding the Pharaoh's interests (*E.A.* 60, 61, 62).

19. *E.A.* 104. 17 ff.

20. *E.A.* 318. 11 f.

21. *E.A.* 195. 24–32. But Biryawaza's conduct is represented otherwise by a neighbouring ruler, who charges him with ruining Pharaoh's lands and handing his cities over to the SA-GAZ (*E.A.* 189 verso, 9 ff., 25 f.).

22. These and other Near Eastern texts referring to the Ḫabiru/SA-GAZ/ʿpr.w are conveniently collected in M. Greenberg, *The Ḫab/piru*, 1955, to which the following references are given.

23. Greenberg, pp. 55 f.

24. Ibid., pp. 56 f.

25. Ibid., p. 57. The *maryannu* were a warrior caste in Western Asia; the word is Indo-Iranian (cf. Vedic *márya* 'young man').

26. Ibid., p. 57.

27. Ibid., p. 56.

28. Ibid., p. 56; cf. translation by J. A. Wilson, *A.N.E.T.*, p. 255. The stele was first published in 1930 by A. Rowe in *The Topography and History of Beth-shan*, i, pls. 42–44.

29. B. Grdseloff, *Une stèle scythopolitaine du roi Séthos Ier*, 1949; W. F. Albright, *B.A.S.O.R.* 125, 1952, pp. 24–32.

30. Greenberg, p. 56.

31. A personal name *pꜣꜥpr* on a scribe's palette, in the Pelizäus Museum at Hildesheim, to be dated *c.* 1150 B.C., seems to mean 'the Ḫabiru man'; ('the Hebrew'?); it belongs to a type adequately attested for the New Kingdom, and suggests that a Ḫabiru could be naturalized in Egypt but retain in his name an indication of his origin (cf. Old Testament Phinehas, Hebrew *pînḥās*, from Egyptian *pꜣnḥsy* 'the Nubian'). Cf. G. Posener, 'Textes Égyptiens', in J. Bottéro, *Le Problème des Ḫabiru*, p. 171.

32. Greenberg, pp. 50 f., 76 f.

33. Ibid., p. 51.

34. Ibid., p. 55 (Boğazköy tablets 5239.7; 6868.2, from H. Otten, *J.C.S.* iv, 1950, pp. 133 f.).

35. Ibid., p. 55 (*K.A.V.* 42. ii. 8–11). See n. 56, below.

36. Ibid., p. 53 (Boğazköy tablet 4889).

37. Ibid., pp. 17 f. (from I. J. Gelb, *Inscriptions from Alishar*, 1935, no. 5, pl. iii).

38. Greenberg, p. 18.

39. Ibid., p. 18 (from C. F. Jean, *Semitica*, i, 1948, p. 22).

40. Greenberg, pp. 23–30; cf. E. Chiera, *A.J.S.L.* xlix, 1932–3, pp. 115 ff.; J. Lewy, *H.U.C.A.* xiv, 1939, pp. 587 ff., xv, 1940, pp. 47 ff.

41. Greenberg, pp. 19 f., from D. J. Wiseman, *The Alalakh Tablets*, 1953, no. 58.

42. Ibid., pp. 20 ff., from Wiseman, op. cit., *passim*.

43. Greenberg, p. 20; cf. S. Smith, *The Statue of Idri-mi*, 1949.

44. E. F. Campbell, *B.A.* xxiii, 1960, p. 14.

45. Garstang himself did not equate the Amarna Ḫabiru with the Hebrews under Joshua—'The original invasion of Canaan by the Hebrew-Israelites under Joshua was . . . distinct both in character and in date from that of the Hebrew-Ḫabiru' (*The Foundations of Bible History, Joshua Judges*, 1931, pp. 256 f.). But some other writers showed no such caution; thus Garstang's popularizer, Charles Marston, speaks of the Old Testament account of the invasion of Canaan as confirmed 'by the Tel el Amarna letters, written at this same period, which mention the Habiru invasion, and even the very name of Joshua' (*The Bible is True*, 1934, p. 268). 'The very name of Joshua' is a reference to one Yashuia,

presumably a Canaanite official in the Egyptian service, mentioned by Mutba'lu, ruler of Gezer, in a letter to Yanḫamu, *E.A.* 256. 18.

46. LXX, Samar., Targ. also in Exod. i. 22.

47. Here LXX has δοῦλοι 'slaves' for 'Hebrews' of M.T.—a confusion of *'brym* and *'bdym*. Similarly in 1 Sam. xiii. 3, where according to M.T. 'Saul blew the trumpet throughout all the land, saying, "Let the Hebrews hear" ', LXX has '. . . The slaves have rebelled'.

48. Cf. E. A. Speiser, *Genesis*, Anchor Bible, 1964, p. 103.

49. Cf. 1 Sam. xxix. 3, where M.T. *'iḇrîm* appears in LXX as διαβαίνοντες and διαπορευόμενοι respectively.

50. H. H. Rowley, *From Joseph to Joshua*, pp. 41 f.

51. Cf. K. M. Kenyon, *Archaeology in the Holy Land*, 2nd ed., 1965, pp. 209 ff.

52. Cf. W. F. Albright, *The Archaeology of Palestine*, 1960, pp. 108 f., and in *Peake's Commentary on the Bible* (ed. M. Black and H. H. Rowley), 1962, p. 51.

53. M. G. Kline, *The Ḫa-BI-ru—Kin or Foe of Israel?*, 1957.

54. *From Joseph to Joshua*, pp. 43 f. Cf. A. T. Olmstead, *History of Palestine and Syria*, 1931, p. 200. Olmstead skilfully weaves the data of the Tell el-Amarna correspondence into a connected narrative (pp. 155–93).

55. *From Joseph to Joshua*, p. 119.

56. A. H. Sayce, *P.S.B.A.* x, 1887–8, p. 495, xi, 1888–9, p. 347; *E.T.* xi, 1899–1900, p. 377, xxxiii, 1921–2, pp. 43 f. In the last-named article he suggested that the god Ḫabiru, mentioned on p. 9, above, was the origin of the Greek Κάβειροι. More securely based was his view that SA-GAZ was not a true ideograph, but a Sumerian loan-word from Akkadian *šaggāšu* 'plunderer' (see the two *E.T.* articles cited above), a view maintained later by B. Landsberger, *Kleinasiat. Forschungen* i, 1930, p. 322, and supported by more recent evidence (cf. Greenberg, pp. 88 ff.).

57. Greenberg, p. 53, from C. Virolleaud, *Syria* xxi, 1940, pp. 123 ff., pl. ii, line 7, pl. viii, line 1, pl. x, line 12. The form SAG-GAZ lends support to the view of Sayce and Landsberger referred to in the previous note. Cf. A. Goetze, *B.A.S.O.R.* 79, 1940, p. 34, n. 14.

58. R. de Langhe, *Les Textes de Ras Shamra-Ugarit et leurs rapports avec le milieu biblique de l'Ancien Testament*, 1948, ii, p. 465.

59. W. F. Albright, *B.A.S.O.R.* 163, 1961, p. 52.

60. Ibid., p. 54.

BIBLIOGRAPHY

i. *Archaeological*

BORCHARDT, L. 'Ausgrabungen in Tell el-Amarna, 1911', *M.D.O.G.* xlvi, 1911, pp. 1–32; 1911–12, ibid. l, 1912, pp. 1–40; 1912–13, ibid. lii, 1913, pp. 1–55; 1913–14, ibid. lv, 1914, pp. 3–39.

FRANKFORT, H., and PENDLEBURY, J. D. S. *The City of Akhenaten*, ii, 1933.

PEET, T. E., and WOOLLEY, C. L. *The City of Akhenaten*, i, 1923.

PENDLEBURY, J. D. S. *et al.*, *The City of Akhenaten*, iii, 1951.

PETRIE, W. M. F. *Tell el-Amarna*, 1894.

ii. *Texts*

BOTTÉRO, J. (ed.). *Le Problème des Ḫabiru*, 1954.

GREENBERG, M. *The Ḫab/piru*, 1955.

KNUDTZON, J. A. *Die El-Amarna-Tafeln*, 1915.

The volumes by BOTTÉRO and GREENBERG include convenient collections of texts relating to the Ḫabiru/SA-GAZ/ʿpr.w/ʿprm from various parts of Egypt and Western Asia.

iii. *Translations*

ALBRIGHT, W. F., and MENDENHALL, G. E. *A.N.E.T.*, pp. 483–90 (selections, with notes).

MERCER, S. A. B. *The Tell El-Amarna Tablets*, 1939.

WEIR, C. J. MULLO. *D.O.T.T.*, pp. 38–45 (selections, with notes).

iv. *General*

ALBRIGHT, W. F. 'The smaller Beth-shan Stele of Sethos I (1309–1290 B.C.)', *B.A.S.O.R.* 125, 1952, pp. 24–32.

—— 'Abram the Hebrew: A new archaeological interpretation', ibid. 163, 1961, pp. 36–54.

—— 'The Amarna Letters from Palestine', *C.A.H.* ii, ch. 20, fasc. 51, 1966.

CAMPBELL, E. F. 'The Amarna Letters and the Amarna Period', *B.A.* xxiii, 1960, pp. 2–22.

—— *The Chronology of the Amarna Letters*, 1964.

—— 'Shechem in the Amarna Archive', Append. 2 in G. E. WRIGHT, *Shechem: The Biography of a Biblical City*, 1965, pp. 191–207.

CASSIN, E. 'Nouveaux Documents sur les Ḫabiru', *J.As.* ccxlvi, 1958, pp. 225–36.

CHIERA, E. ' "Ḫabiru" and Hebrews', *A.J.S.L.* xlix, 1932–3, pp. 115–24.

GARSTANG, J. *The Foundations of Bible History: Joshua Judges*, 1931.

KLINE, M. G. *The Ḫa-BI-ru—Kin or Foe of Israel?*, 1957.

KRAELING, E. G. 'Light from Ugarit on the Khabiru', *B.A.S.O.R.* 77, 1940, pp. 32 f.

—— 'The origin of the name "Hebrews" ', *A.J.S.L.* lviii, 1941, pp. 237–53.

LEWY, J. 'Ḫābirū and Hebrews', *H.U.C.A.* xiv, 1939, pp. 587–623.

—— 'A new parallel between Ḫābirū and Hebrews', ibid. xv, 1940, pp. 47–58.

MEEK, T. J. *Hebrew Origins*, 3rd ed., 1960.

PFEIFFER, C. F. *Tell el Amarna and the Bible*, 1963.

RIEDEL, W. *Untersuchungen zu den Tell el-Amarna Briefen*, 1920.

—— 'Das Archiv Amenophis' IV', *O.L.Z.* xlii, 1939, pp. 145–8.

ROWLEY, H. H. *From Joseph to Joshua* (Schweich Lectures, 1948), 1950.

SPEISER, E. A. 'Ethnic movements in the Near East in the second millennium B.C.', *A.A.S.O.R.* xiii, 1933, pp. 13–54.

THEBES

THEBES became important and famous as the royal city of the great Pharaohs of the Eighteenth Dynasty. The name Thebes is Greek and is first attested in Homer (*Iliad* ix. 381 ff.: 'Thebes in Egypt . . ., which has a hundred gates'). The name of the Boeotian Thebes (*Iliad* iv. 406: 'Thebes of seven gates') has been used to represent an Egyptian expression of some kind. This Egyptian basis of the name can no longer be recovered with certainty; perhaps it is *t ỉp(ε)t as the designation of a part of the Egyptian royal city = Luxor.[1] In fact the city did not have an original native name; it is designated as nỉw.t (nt) ỉmn 'City of Amun' = No (Amon) (Jer. xlvi. 25; Ezek. xxx. 14 ff.; Nahum iii. 8) after the cult of the god Amun which rose to great importance there.

i

The archaeological monuments of Thebes are scanty for the period of the Old Kingdom. There are a few which represent the Eleventh and Twelfth Dynasties, but the great majority come from the great days of the New Kingdom and the periods which then followed. They consist chiefly of temples and tombs, for the city itself, with its palaces and houses of clay brick, has completely disappeared. The great complex of temples in the present village of Karnak and the temple in the middle of the city of Luxor are the chief monuments east of the Nile. On the opposite side of the Nile lie the innumerable tombs; there are the royal tombs hidden in the 'Valley of the Kings', their mortuary temples set on the western edge of the river-plain, and the many tombs of other prominent persons of the kingdom.

While these monuments have long been known, new details are constantly coming to light. From the past half-century two matters deserve mention. The discovery of the tomb of Pharaoh Tutankhamun in the 'Valley of the Kings' by H. Carter in 1922 was a great surprise. Found almost intact, it yielded an astonishing quantity of valuable burial furnishings, which have since been a special treasure of the Egyptian museum in Cairo. Tutankhamun, who put an end to the religious and cultic 'reform' of his father-in-law Amenophis IV (Akhenaten), is not of direct importance for the Old Testament. A significant archaeological enterprise was the survey and excavation of the complex of temple and palace buildings at Medînet Hābu by the Oriental Institute of the University of Chicago. From 1924 the inscriptions of this extensive structure were accurately surveyed with modern methods under the direction of H. H. Nelson, and from 1930 were published in monumental volumes. From 1927 to 1936 excavations took place at Medînet Hābu under the direction of Uvo Hoelscher, who has published the results in five volumes. The main construction of Medînet Hābu comes from Pharaoh Ramesses III. This Pharaoh succeeded in repulsing from Egypt the 'Sea Peoples', especially the *prst* (Philistines) and *ṯkr*. He had this victory portrayed with figures and inscriptions in Medînet Hābu.[2] The consequence of the repulse of the *prst* and *ṯkr* from Egypt was their settlement in the Palestinian coastal plain at the beginning of the twelfth century B.C. Thus the records of Ramesses III take us into the immediate vicinity of the settlement of the Israelite tribes in Palestine.

ii

Important for Syria and Palestine in the second millennium B.C., and so for the presuppositions of the history of Israel, is the discovery of a distinct category of Egyptian texts known as the Execration Texts, which first came to light in Thebes. In the spring of 1925 H. Schaefer and K. Sethe bought a series of potsherds from a dealer in antiquities in Luxor for the Berlin museum; they bore hieratic inscriptions and were said to have come from a tomb in western Thebes. Some further pieces of the same kind were subsequently passed on by the same dealer—they had belonged to the widow of a fellah in western Thebes. Finally it transpired that in its older collections of unknown origin the Berlin museum already possessed some pieces from the same complex of discoveries. Sethe thereupon provided the standard treatment and publication of this first collection of Execration Texts, 289 inscribed fragments in all.

Some time later this first discovery was matched by another. This consisted not of clay sherds but of small clay figures roughly

PLATE I

Clay figurine with execration text
(Copyright A. C. L. Brussels)

representing the upper part of the human body in the form of a prisoner, and again bearing Execration Texts in hieratic script (Pl. I). In 1938 A. Capart found pieces of this kind in the Parisian antiquities market and acquired them for the Musées Royaux d'Art et d'Histoire in Brussels. Similar pieces had already been in the possession of the Egyptian museum in Cairo for some time; they had been found in 1922 in Saḳḳara, lying on the ground in a brick sepulchre north of the mortuary temple of Teti. It could thus be reckoned as probable that the Paris pieces had also come from Saḳḳara. Publication by G. Posener soon followed (in all, twenty-four figurines).

Both these discoveries appear to be far exceeded by a very recent discovery, of which only preliminary reports are so far available. In Mirgissa, some 15 kilometres south of Wadi Ḥalfa on the left bank of the Nile, discovery has been made of a small settlement of the Middle Kingdom, a cemetery reaching back to the Second Intermediate Period, and a fortification. A pit was discovered nearby in the level floor of the desert. Inside the pit and lying beside a very large number of uninscribed potsherds were found *in situ* no less than 3,600 inscribed fragments of about 70–100 clay pots bearing Execration Texts. In the same vicinity were found three clay figurines of human form buried in the sand; still unbroken, they were inscribed with Execration Texts similar to those from Saḳḳara. J. Vercoutter reported on this discovery to a gathering of the Paris Academy.[3]

In the Execration Texts actual or potential enemies of Egypt are enumerated according to a more or less stereotyped scheme. The pots and figurines were evidently used in an act of sorcery; the breaking or burying signified the magical destruction of these enemies. While the enemies are sometimes internal Egyptian adversaries of the régime, more often they are foreign foes. Three groups of the latter are especially prominent, namely Nubians, Asiatics, and Libyans. Within these groups are listed primarily rulers, with their names and domains, but we also meet particular elements of population and occasionally some special categories of persons.

The dating of these texts is still uncertain. It is generally acknowledged that the Sethe texts are older than those of Posener, perhaps by about a century (the chronological arrangement of the texts from Mirgissa is not yet decided). There is also agreement on the general placing of the texts in the early centuries of the second millennium B.C. Since Sethe's early dating of his texts in the period of the Eleventh Dynasty (c. 2133–1991 B.C.) has proved to be untenable,[4] a dating in the second half of the period of the Twelfth Dynasty, that is, in the nineteenth or early eighteenth century B.C., might seem to meet the case. The Posener texts might then belong to the beginning of the period of the Thirteenth Dynasty (c. 1786–1633 B.C.).[5]

The Execration Texts are of interest for the Old Testament from various points of view. The rite of the destruction of internal and external enemies through an act thought to be magically effective is not entirely without analogy in the Old Testament.[6] Mention may be made of the symbolic act of breaking an earthen jar performed by the prophet Jeremiah in connexion with an oracle of doom against Jerusalem and Judah (Jer. xix. 1–13); also of the series of oracles of doom directed by the prophets against foreign peoples (e.g. Amos i. 2–ii. 16). There is, indeed, no question of Old Testament dependence on the Egyptian execration rites, but only of a very vague comparability. In the case of the Execration Texts it seems likely that, when the names of the enemies had been inscribed, the magical destruction was accomplished with a silent act. In the case of the prophets, however, the names of the enemies (of Yahweh) appeared in the spoken word, while of 'sacramental acts accompanying words like Amos i. 2–ii. 16',[7] we in fact hear nothing. The Execration Texts are connected with the Old Testament only by the general and widespread conception of the effective commination and destruction of enemies.

More important is the value of the Execration Texts as sources for the situation in Syria and Palestine c. 1800 B.C. The lists of 'Asiatic' rulers, domains, and peoples[8] afford some insight into the conditions of this region. Noteworthy here are first the names of places cited in the lists, and then the names of rulers.

With regard to the names and designations of places, the fundamental task is correct identification; only when this is assured can the cause and significance of the mention of precisely these places be considered. Unfortunately, however, it is only in a very limited number of cases that the identification is obvious enough to be accepted without serious reserve. In general there is no great difficulty in recognizing the Syro-Palestinian originals behind these names, which have been written according to the Egyptian rules for the transcription of foreign words. The difficulty is that a great many Syro-Palestinian place-names are not unequivocal, since the same name was often used for a number of places and in very different districts. Only by an insight into the context and purport of the relevant document can we decide in a particular instance which place is intended. Nevertheless, there are some cases in which the Execration Texts offer unambiguous testimony. Thus the names Ashkelon and Jerusalem occur in the Sethe and in the Posener texts (it is the earliest literary attestation of the name Jerusalem); the more abundant Posener texts have also the names Shechem, *pḥlm* (the later Pella), Hazor, Tyre, Acco; the 'people' of Byblos are already named in the Sethe texts. The occurrence of these and other places in the Execration Texts occasions no great surprise; their existence at the beginning of the second millennium B.C. has either been demonstrated already by archaeology or is at least very probable on general grounds. All the same, the citation in the Execration Texts affords welcome literary witness to the existence and designation of the place in question.

It is important to establish the field of vision within which the places that are named lie. First and foremost is the coast of Palestine and Syria, which was accessible from Egypt by sea; the part which is represented probably extends as far as the northern end of the Lebanon, if '*ꜣ-q-tm*[9] is correctly identified with the Irqata of the Tell el-Amarna tablets and the present Tell 'Arqa, north-east of Tarablus, as is very likely. Coastal places further north seem to lie outside this field. In the interior Palestine features almost alone, being represented by isolated cities and settlements. Among these is especially Jerusalem;[10] in the Posener texts we also find Shechem, the district of the upper Jordan valley (with *pḥlm*, Hazor, and probably Laish), and probably also the extreme south of Syria (with Bosra, etc). Though attractive in itself, the identification of *qꜣqꜣm*[11] with the familiar Qarqar (Tell Qerqūr) in the central Orontes valley[12] falls too far outside the framework to be accepted; in any case, the root *qrqr* seems to have been often used in the formation of place names (cf. Judges viii. 10).

Consideration of the few identifiable places gives rise to several questions which unfortunately cannot be answered with certainty.

Do the places that are named belong to an area of Egyptian suzerainty, or do we meet here hostile princes and peoples outside the
limit of the Egyptian sphere of power? Is the execration accordingly
directed against rebellious subjects or against external enemies
who were an actual or potential menace to Egypt? The Execration Texts themselves provide no answer. Only by reference to the
general situation under the later Pharaohs of the Twelfth Dynasty
can it be regarded as probable that these are places and districts
within the sphere of Egyptian power. A comparison of the Sethe
texts with those of Posener would then give evidence of an extension of this sphere in the hinterland, for the localities in the upper
Jordan valley and in southern Syria are found exclusively in the
Posener texts and are completely absent from the older Sethe
texts. The question then arises, why these particular places, with
their rulers, are listed, while others are not. Even the series of
places along the coast of Palestine and Syria between Ashkelon
and Irqata is by no means complete. The selection of places in
the interior of Palestine (and southern Syria) seems quite arbitrary; there is no recognizable system. One misses, for example, the
old and important cities in the Palestinian plain of Jezreel. Did
the 'author' of the Execration Texts only cite places, mostly with
their rulers, which were known to him more or less by chance?
In itself, this would not be impossible. But the citing of rulers'
names which could not have been invented suggests rather that
actual knowledge of conditions in Palestine and Syria lies behind
the Execration Texts. In this case the probability must be admitted
that the rulers and places mentioned were actually rebellious and
consequently subjected to the ceremony of magical execration.
The obedient and submissive rulers and places would then have no
place in the Execration Texts. In favour of this interpretation one
special point can be adduced. The ruler of the well-known city
of Byblos is not named; there is mention only of 'the (people) of
Byblos'[13] and of 'the tribes of Byblos'.[14] The ruler of Byblos, as is
known from other sources, was a loyal subject, or even viceroy, of
the Egyptian Pharaoh at the time in question, and so had no place
in the Execration Texts; on the other hand, the territory of Byblos
probably contained refractory persons or tribes who would be
included in the execration of the Pharaoh's enemies. Against the
acceptance of an actual situation in the subjected area of Palestine

and Syria as the basis of the Execration Texts can be set the fact that, apart from the extra material in the Posener texts, the two groups of texts show considerable agreement, although separated from each other by a fairly long interval; they would thus seem to be more stereotyped than actual in their composition. One must reckon with the possibility, however, that there existed inveterately rebellious places and districts.

The most surprising and important contribution of the Execration Texts to the illumination of Syro-Palestinian conditions in the nineteenth–eighteenth centuries B.C. lies in the names of the rulers. What was at once clear from the publication of the Sethe texts was confirmed by the Posener material and by all the special researches connected with these publications[15] the rulers' names are not only thoroughly Semitic, but belong chiefly to a distinct type of name formation, which was already known from the cunei- form tradition of Mesopotamia and then established ever more thoroughly by the publication of the cuneiform texts from Mari. Personal names of this kind were remarkable in the region of Mesopotamia, since they were clearly different in their manner of formation from the native Akkadian personal names, and so were evidently borne by a population which did not belong to the old Mesopotamian stock but represented a stratum of later immi- grants. Such personal names first make their appearance sporadi- cally in Mesopotamia in the time of the Third Dynasty of Ur, they become more frequent in the Isin-Larsa period, and then appear in great numbers especially among the rulers of the First Dynasty of Babylon and the kingdom of Mari. The Mari texts have provided by far the greatest number of such names.[16] These names are significant for the Old Testament because a series of particularly old Israelite personal names belong to the same type of name formation. A long and still unfinished discussion has arisen over the problem of the appropriate designation of the owners of these names. Account has to be taken of the fact that through the Egyptian Execration Texts names of this kind are attested for Syria and Palestine in the nineteenth–eighteenth cen- turies B.C., and that an element of population is thus exhibited which, on the evidence of kindred personal names, was connected in its origins with the contemporary non-Akkadian immigrant population of Mesopotamia.

Hence there arises the historical question of the origin of these people, and with this again is connected the question of the appropriate designation. Seen from the point of view of Mesopotamia, the owners of these names can with some justification be designated 'West Semites' as distinct from the 'East Semitic' Akkadians. Whether this designation can be meaningful also for the Syro-Palestinian owners of the names, however, is very doubtful. The question here is whether the rulers named in the Execration Texts belonged, with their adherents, to the ancient and perhaps even primeval population of Syria and Palestine. The solution of this question would be very important. Unfortunately, the Execration Texts do not give sufficient information to allow a certain answer. Even so, a striking circumstance is perhaps significant in this connexion. In the older Sethe texts there are often several rulers specified for one and the same territory, while in the Posener texts for the same districts we have only one, sometimes two. Hence it can be concluded[17] that the owners of these names were immigrants also in Syria and Palestine at the beginning of the second millennium B.C., seizing power at first in several groups in the older, larger territories, until there gradually emerged a 'normal', more stable order, where once more the central cities had usually only one ruler at a time. If this judgement is correct, we have to reckon with an immigration into Syria and Palestine like that into Mesopotamia, albeit somewhat later. In Syria and Palestine we should then have to take account of an earlier, already Semitic, population, for various cities, which very probably reach back at least into the third millennium B.C., such as the 'Phoenician' ports, already have Semitic names. This earlier population would be designated 'Canaanite' in accordance with the usage which has become customary. The rulers and peoples of the Execration Texts, however, should then probably be thought of as having immigrated from the east, just as their kinsfolk in Mesopotamia probably had come from a western direction. The designation 'West Semites' would thus be unsuitable for Syria and Palestine.

For the immigrants of the beginning of the second millennium B.C. the designation 'Amorites' has established itself in many quarters, and can perhaps be justified by way of the Mesopotamian use. For want of a better and less ambiguous name this designation may be accepted, provided that it is understood as a matter of convention, and that premature connexions are not claimed with the Old Testament 'Amorites', whose name is probably derived in quite a different fashion from the Akkadian word *amurrū*. With the people of the Execration Texts we have the first appearance in Syria and Palestine of the migratory movement to which, on the evidence of the affinity in personal names, the incoming Israelites also later belonged.

iii

The Egyptian Thebes has also provided the majority, including the largest, of those lists of place-names which are very informative for Palestinian and Syrian topography in the period of the Egyptian New Kingdom, the period shortly before the settlement of the Israelite tribes. These lists have in fact been known for more than half a century; only a few smaller representatives of this category have been added through new discoveries outside Thebes. But in the understanding of these lists many important advances have been made in recent decades.

Pharaoh Tuthmosis III was, so far as is known, the first to portray his victorious campaigns outside Egypt in a stereotyped form in reliefs, having himself represented as a single combatant who slays captive enemies with his mace, while a deity leads to him long rows of further captives in bonds. These latter captives are shown with the upper part of the body, the hands bound behind the back (there is a certain similarity with the figurines of the Execration Texts from Saḳḳara and Mirgissa, which are about half a millennium older). The trunk of these prisoners is replaced by a kind of cartouche, which is formed by a schematically represented ring of city walls; in each cartouche is set the name of a city in hieroglyphic script. The captives thus represent the populations of the cities which the Pharaoh conquered on his campaigns. These representations were placed by Tuthmosis III on various pylons of the temple of Karnak; subsequently pylons, but also temple walls and occasionally columns, continued to be the favourite positions. The Pharaoh certainly desired to spread his fame among his contemporaries and among subsequent generations. But one may suspect an influence from a belief in the magical effect of such representations in sanctuaries, like the effect associated in a different way with the Execration Texts. Here it would be

a question not of magical destruction of enemies, but only of sub-
jugation of foreign cities and their inhabitants, to be magically
assured and guaranteed by the representation. The example of
the great Tuthmosis was followed by later Pharaohs, especially
Sethos I, Ramesses II, and Ramesses III. The last Pharaoh from
whom such a representation is preserved is Sheshonq, the contemporary of the kings Jeroboam of Israel and Rehoboam of Judah.

The scientific study of these lists has been made much easier
by a new edition, comprehensive and synoptical, which J. Simons
has made on the basis of earlier publications and some new photographs, not on the basis of an original re-examination. The question which above, all, needs to be answered concerns the origin and
composition of the lists. From Tuthmosis III onwards the lists were
arranged, as a rule, in two parts; they have an 'Asiatic' and an
'African' part, which face each other in corresponding fashion,
perhaps on the twin towers of a pylon. Here we see the schematism
which governs the whole composition. In later examples of the
type a mixture of Asiatic and African names occasionally appears;
this is hardly to be explained from some actual situation, but as
due to the neglect and decay of the old arrangement.

Only the Asiatic parts are of interest for the Old Testament;
only these parts have been taken into account in the new edition
of J. Simons and have become the subject of various studies.
According to the best preserved of the accompanying inscriptions
and to the evident sense of the representations as a whole, these
lists are connected with the numerous campaigns of the Pharaohs
of the New Kingdom (and also Sheshonq) into Palestine and
Syria, by means of which the Egyptian suzerainty over this
region in the period shortly before the Israelite conquest was
founded, consolidated, and occasionally restored. The very many
Palestinian and Syrian places which are listed by name give an
actual picture of the settlement of the country. The lists thus
present a prime source for the topography of this region in the Late
Bronze Age (only the Sheshonq lists stand apart in time, belonging
to the tenth century B.C.).

So far as the names are legible—the lists are, in general, fairly
well preserved, except for some from Ramesses II which are
very difficult to read—the original Palestinian and Syrian place-
names can be recognized with relative ease and assurance, being

reproduced according to the rules of Egyptian 'group-writing';[18] the transposition of the names into a different system of pronunciation and writing has naturally caused some ambiguities. The actual locating of the places is often difficult because of the use of the same place-name many times over in Palestine and Syria (the same problem has been noted for the Execration Texts). Nevertheless, a basis of certain or at least very probable identifications affords insights into the structure of the lists.

It has been shown[19] that even the external arrangement of the individual names in the lists is not arbitrary but is of material significance. The construction in shorter and longer lines standing one upon another, as also the difference in the direction of the rows (expressed by the direction in which the stereotyped profiles of the prisoners are facing), signify that the lists have been arranged with an eye to content. The position of the individual names within the lists must therefore always be taken into account in their explanation. One element in these lists, which is usually indicated by its position and is also readily distinguished by its contents, is a compilation of conventional names of foreign (Asiatic) peoples and cities; being more or less traditional, this is not of particular interest, since it bears no special relation to the actual background of the relevant lists.

What is important, however, is the series of names which are not conventional, and are indeed sometimes peculiar. As a rule these names constitute the main part of the lists. An essential observation here is that in various parts of various lists there appear series of place-names, which unambiguously are the stations along a particular route arranged in correct sequence. This leads to the working hypothesis that the lists generally, even where particular proof is no longer possible, rest upon records of such stations. But since the accompanying inscriptions and the manner of presentation establish the relation of the lists to the Pharaohs' campaigns in Palestine and Syria, it is a short step to conclude that the lists in their essential parts represent the campaign routes of the Pharaohs' armies, or particular detachments, by enumeration of the conquered or besieged places. It is known that the Pharaohs of the New Kingdom had diaries kept on their campaigns giving exact accounts of the daily movements of their troops (cf. especially the 'annals' of Tuthmosis III). The lists can thus be understood as extracts from such diaries, being compilations of the places mentioned in them.

Yet this working hypothesis cannot be expected to provide the key for the solution of all the riddles presented by the Pharaonic lists. Even where the hypothesis seems in general to be obvious, we must recognize that, for one reason or another, the diaries occasionally included places which were not involved in the movements of troops and which were thus inappropriate in the records of campaign stations. One must ask especially whether the hypothesis can be applied equally to all the Pharaonic lists. It seems to hold good for the 'Palestine lists' of Tuthmosis III and for the lists of Sethos I.[20] For other lists the more general question arises as to how far they are really original, and how far they have imitated older lists. It is certain that Ramesses II in part simply copied and appropriated the lists of his father Sethos I. It is also certain that the great list of Ramesses III on the pylon of Medînet Hābu is at least in parts compiled from copies of older lists (Tuthmosis III, Ramesses II). An independent and original example occurs again with the list of Sheshonq I; unfortunately preserved only fragmentarily, it is of particular interest for the Old Testament since it deals, not with the pre-Israelite Palestine and Syria, but with the Palestine of the early Israelite monarchy.

Work on the Pharaonic lists is still by no means completed, quite apart from the fact that new accessions of material may bring new questions and new possibilities of solution. Above all, there is still needed a thorough analysis of the great 'Syrian list' of Tuthmosis III which is attached to the 'Palestinian list' of Tuthmosis III on the eighth pylon of Karnak. Fruitful possibilities of comparison are offered by the rich fund of place-names in the texts from Ugarit and Alalakh and perhaps also Mari. W. Helck has, indeed, devoted much labour to this Syrian list and has proposed an interesting thesis which deserves serious consideration; he argues that it is 'compiled in reverse order'[21] that is, it cites the places in the opposite order to which they were reached by the troops, so that to interpret them historically we must read them in reverse. But it is not yet settled whether this is generally true, or whether perhaps it is true for particular parts of the list. The great list of Ramesses III also awaits fundamental study. It must be established more exactly than hitherto how far it contains borrowings from older lists, and how far possibly original material. With this is linked the question how far it should be adduced in the reconstruction of older lists, the originals of which are no longer completely preserved. There is no doubt that more work on the Pharaonic lists will prove worth while and will be likely to yield further results for the topography of Palestine and Syria.[22]

M. NOTH

NOTES

1. Cf. A. H. Gardiner, *Ancient Egyptian Onomastica*, ii, 1947, pp. 25* f.

2. His historical inscriptions have been translated into English by W. F. Edgerton and J. A. Wilson. For details of this and other works referred to in the notes, see the Bibliography.

3. Further preliminary communications have been made by him and by A. Vila in *Journal des Savants*. Some of the texts are translated in *A.N.E.T.*, pp. 328 f.

4. Cf. P. Montet, *et al.*

5. So W. Helck, p. 53.

6. Cf. A. Bentzen.

7. Ibid., p. 87.

8. Sethe sections e and f; in Posener the corresponding E and F.

9. Sethe e 22; Posener E 54.

10. Sethe e 27/28, f 18; Posener E 45.

11. Posener E 56.

12. Considered very guardedly by A. Alt, p. 31, n. 1.

13. Sethe f 2.

14. Posener E 63.

15. By W. F. Albright, M. Noth, W. L. Moran, and A. Goetze.

16. Cf. now especially the great collection and study of these names from Mari by H. B. Huffmon.

17. Cf. Alt, pp. 36–39.

18. Cf. W. F. Albright, *The Vocalisation of the Egyptian Syllabic Orthography*.

19. Cf. M. Noth.

20. The latter case is disputed by W. Helck, p. 203.

21. 'Rückläufig zusammengestellt', p. 150.

22. This article has been translated from the German text of Professor Noth by Mr. J. H. Eaton, M.A., Lecturer in Theology, University of Birmingham.

BIBLIOGRAPHY

ALBRIGHT, W. F. 'The Egyptian Empire in Asia in the twenty-first century B.C.', *J.P.O.S.* viii, 1928, pp. 223–56.

ALBRIGHT, W. F. *The Vocalisation of the Egyptian Syllabic Orthography* (A.O.S. v, 1934).

ALT, A. 'Herren und Herrensitze Palästinas im Anfang des zweiten Jahrtausends. Vorläufige Bemerkungen zu den neuen Ächtungstexten', *Z.D.P.V.* lxiv, 1944, pp. 21–39.

BENTZEN, A. 'The ritual background of Amos i 2–ii 16', *O.T.S.* vii, 1950, pp. 85–99.

BORÉE, W. *Die alten Ortsnamen Palästinas*, 1930.

DUSSAUD, R. 'Nouveaux renseignements sur la Palestine et la Syrie vers 2000 avant notre ère', *Syria*, viii, 1927, pp. 216–33.

—— 'Nouveaux textes égyptiens d'exécration contre les peuples syriens', ibid. xxi, 1940, pp. 170–82.

EDGERTON, W. F., and WILSON, J. A. *Historical Records of Ramses III. The Texts in Medinet Habu.* Vols i/ii (S.A.O.C. No. 12, Chicago, 1936).

GOETZE, A. 'Remarks on some names occurring in the Execration Texts', *B.A.S.O.R.* 151, 1958, pp. 28–33.

HELCK, W. *Die Beziehungen Ägyptens zu Vorderasien im 3. und 2. Jahrtausend vor Chr.* (Ägyptolog. Abh. 5, Wiesbaden, 1962).

HOELSCHER, U. *The Excavations of Medinet Habu*, vols. i–v (O.I.P. xxi, xli, liv, lv, lxvi, 1934, 1939, 1941, 1951, 1954).

HUFFMON, H. B. *Amorite Personal Names in the Mari Texts: a Structural and Lexical Study*, 1965.

KEES, H. 'Thebai (Ägypten)', *Paulys Realencycl. der class. Altertumswiss.*, zweite Reihe, zehnter Halbband, 1934, pp. 1553–82.

MONTET, P. 'Pays et princes redoutés des Égyptiens sous la XIIIᵉ dynastie', *Kêmi*, i, 1928, pp. 19–28.

MORAN, W. L. 'Mari notes on the Execration Texts', *Orient.* xxvi, 1957, pp. 339–45.

NELSON, H. H. *Medinet Habu. Epigraphic Survey*, vols. i–vi (O.I.P. viii, ix, xxiii, li, lxxxiii, lxxxiv, 1930, 1932, 1934, 1940, 1957, 1963).

NOTH, M. 'Die syrisch-palästinische Bevölkerung des zweiten Jahrtausends v. Chr. im Lichte neuer Quellen: 2. Die Herrenschicht des 19./18. Jahrhunderts', *Z.D.P.V.* lxv, 1942, pp. 20–34.

—— 'Die Wege der Pharaonenheere in Palästina und Syrien. Untersuchungen zu den hieroglyphischen Listen palästinischer und syrischer Städte: I. 'Die konventionellen Namenzusammenstellungen', II. 'Die Ortslisten Sethos I', ibid. lx, 1937, pp. 183–239.

—— III. 'Der Aufbau der Palästinaliste Thutmoses III', ibid. lxi, 1938, pp. 26–65.

—— IV. 'Die Schoschenkliste', ibid. lxi, 1938, pp. 277–304.

—— V. 'Ramses II. in Syrien', ibid. lxiv, 1941, pp. 39–74.

POSENER, G. *Princes et pays d'Asie et de Nubie. Textes hiératiques sur des figurines d'envoûtement du Moyen Empire*, 1940.

SETHE, K. *Die Ächtung feindlicher Fürsten, Völker und Dinge auf altägyptischen Tongefässscherben des Mittleren Reiches* (*A.P.A.W.*, No. 5, 1926).

SIMONS, J. *Handbook for the study of Egyptian Topographical Lists relating to Western Asia*, 1937.

VERCOUTTER, J. 'Textes exécratoires de Mirgissa', *C.R.A.I.*, 1963, pp. 97–102.

VILA, A. 'Un dépôt de textes d'envoûtement au Moyen Empire', *Journal des Savants*, 1963, pp. 135–60.

VINCENT, L. H. 'Les Pays bibliques et l'Égypte à la fin de la XIIᵉ dynastie égyptienne', *Vivre et Penser* ii = *R.B.* li, 1942, pp. 187–212.

MESOPOTAMIA

BABYLON

NIMRUD

NUZI

UR

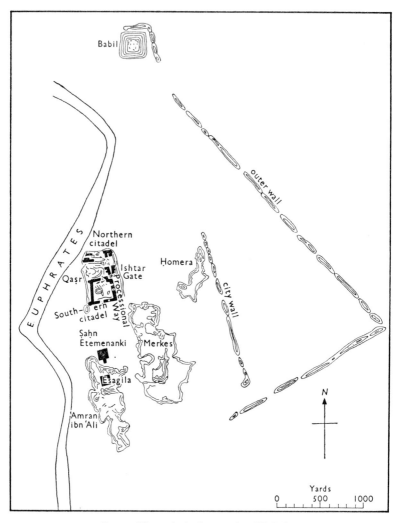

FIG. 3. The principal mounds of Babylon

BABYLON

THE Old Testament story of the tower of Babel, together with reports in classical sources, ensured early attempts at the identification of Babylon. The area in which to seek was suggested by the traditional attachment of the name Babil to a mound 6 miles north-east of Hillah, although some early travellers arbitrarily proposed the identification of the remains of the tower of Babel with Aqarquf near Baghdad.[1] The ancient city of Babylon finally proved to be represented by a number of mounds in the area approximately $1\frac{1}{2}$ to $2\frac{1}{2}$ miles to the south of Babil, the principal mounds being known as Qaṣr, ʿAmran ibn ʿAli, Merkes, and Ḥomera (Fig. 3).

The ancient ruins in the neighbourhood of Hillah, including not only Babil and the area immediately south of it in which the inner city of Babylon ultimately proved to lie, but also Birs Nimrud 8 miles south-west of Hillah, were visited and described by pilgrims, and later by tourists, from an early period. The first extant account of value is that of Benjamin of Tudela, who visited the area in the twelfth century.[2] He correctly associated the Babylon of Nebuchadrezzar with the ruins north-east of Hillah, though he identified the tower of Babel with Birs Nimrud, actually the remains of the ziggurat of Borsippa.[3] The first modern traveller to identify and describe the ruins of Babylon was Pietro della Valle, who visited the area in 1616.[4]

Even after the correct identification of the approximate site of Babylon, the relationship between the impressive ruins of Birs Nimrud, the mound Babil, and the ruins immediately south of Babil, continued to present a problem. The Danish explorer Carsten Niebuhr, who visited the Hillah area in 1765, proposed to solve the problem of the relationship by postulating a greater Babylon which included Birs Nimrud:[5] the hypothesis is disproved by cuneiform evidence, in which Borsippa and Babylon are always distinguished.

The ruins of Babylon had long been used as a quarry for building materials for Hillah, and in the course of such digging not only the ubiquitous inscribed bricks but also occasionally other antiquities had come to light, usually, if not of metal, to be cast away by the Arabs as worthless. Reports of such objects reached J. de Beauchamp, Vicar-General of Babylon, who visited the Hillah area on several occasions from 1784. In consequence he undertook a minor excavation, and subsequently published a memoir,[6] which was influential in directing attention to the possibility of productive excavation at Babylon.[7]

The few antiquities obtained from Babylon prior to 1811 were all, with a partial and limited exception in the case of those of de Beauchamp, casual surface finds or the result of random native digging. Organized excavation, directed to investigation of a site rather than disinterment of antiquities, first took place during a visit in 1811 by C. J. Rich, the East India Company's Resident in Baghdad. Rich made a careful survey of the ruins of Babylon, and employed ten men to excavate at Babil and Qaṣr. A second visit followed in 1817 to elucidate certain details of topography. The results of both visits were published as memoirs.[8]

With the beginning of large-scale excavation at various Mesopotamian sites from 1842 onwards, attention inevitably turned again towards Babylon. A. H. Layard proposed to excavate at Babylon on a scale comparable with his work in the north, but was prevented by the disturbed state of the country from achieving more than a few trial trenches in Babil, Qaṣr, and 'Amran ibn 'Ali, in late 1850.[9]

A French expedition under F. Fresnel, with J. Oppert as epigraphist, was formally engaged in excavation at Babylon from 1852 to 1854, though little sustained digging took place and results were slight.[10] During the succeeding forty-five years Babylon was frequently visited by Assyriologists, some of whom undertook small digs, but no results of importance were achieved.

The major work on the excavation of ancient Babylon was begun in 1899 under the leadership of the German architect Robert Koldewey, sponsored by the Deutsche Orient-Gesellschaft, and continued under him without a break until 1917, when the British occupation of Mesopotamia finally compelled its cessation.[11] More recently some small excavations have been undertaken by H. Lenzen[12] and, in connexion with work of restoration, by the Iraqi Department of Antiquities.

Excluding Babil, the major part of the ruins, representing the city within the inner walls at the time of Nebuchadrezzar, lies within a zone of about a mile from north to south by three-quarters of a mile from east to west. The actual area of ancient Babylon was slightly greater than the dimensions of the more conspicuous ruins would indicate, since the arm of the Euphrates, which in antiquity flowed approximately through the centre of the city, has since shifted westwards to cover part of the western sector of Babylon. The inner city wall, remains of which are still visible, defines the eastern boundary of the city and includes an area south of Ḥomera which is not marked by prominent mounds. The total area of the city is considerably less than the figure given by classical authors.[13] In addition to ruins already mentioned, there are traces of ancient canals, and considerable remains of an outer defence wall (see below). Babil has proved to be the remains of a palace, or fortress, of the Neo-Babylonian kings, sited north of Babylon at the northern end of the outer defence wall.

These extensive ruins, of which, despite Koldewey's work, only a small proportion has been excavated, have during past centuries been extensively plundered for building materials. Partly in consequence of this, much of the surface now presents an appearance of such chaotic disorder that it is strongly evocative of the prophecies of Isa. xiii. 19–22 and Jer. l. 39 f., the impression of desolation being further heightened by the aridity which marks a large part of the area of the ruins.

Old Testament tradition associates Babylon with Erech and Accad,[14] with the implication that it was one of the earliest of the cities of Babylonia. A corresponding view of the venerable antiquity of Babylon was current in Babylon itself in the period after Hammurabi,[15] but is not in accordance with archaeological or contemporary literary evidence. Direct archaeological evidence, and the evidence of cuneiform texts from the period before Hammurabi, provide no indication of an important status for the city comparable with that enjoyed in the third millennium B.C. by Erech, Kish, Nippur, Ur, Sippar or, later and more transitorily, by Accad.[16] Onomastic considerations may also indicate that Babylon was not amongst the earliest founded cities of Babylonia, for it alone amongst the great cities apparently bore a Semitic name.[17]

Whilst Koldewey's excavations revealed some data for all

occupation levels from Old Babylonian (c. 1894–1595 B.C.) to Parthian (c. 539–331 B.C.), their main importance lay in the extensive evidence they yielded for the topography of Babylon in the Neo-Babylonian period (c. 625–539 B.C.): only isolated remains were found from periods earlier than the Sargonid (c. 721–612 B.C.). Though this was partly due to modern circumstances, in that a rise in the water-table limited the possibility of deep excavation, it also in part accurately reflected historical developments in the first millennium B.C. As a result of the deliberate destruction of the capital by Sennacherib, relatively little can have remained of pre-Sargonid Babylon above ground level in the central area of the city. Esar-haddon, Ashurbanipal, and Nabopolassar all undertook rebuilding, but the most considerable building activity was that of Nebuchadrezzar. His work is almost everywhere evident, indicating that he could with considerable justification have uttered the words attributed to him in Dan. iv. 27, R.V. 30.[18]

The city was defended in the Neo-Babylonian period by a powerful system of walls, whose virtual impregnability in terms of ancient warfare gives added point to Jeremiah's prophecies of their destruction.[19] The city wall proper was of double construction, with a countermure 21 feet thick and provided with towers at intervals of about 60 feet. The outer component of the wall, 12 feet thick, lay 23 feet from the countermure, and was also provided with towers. Outside this double wall was a fosse, lined with baked bricks and bitumen, and kept filled from the Euphrates. This primary defence system completely circumvallated the city on both sides of the river. A further defence system to the eastern, and more ancient and important, part of the city was provided by an outer wall, also of double form, running approximately south-east from the Euphrates a mile and a half north of the city and turning south-west to rejoin the Euphrates 250 yards south of the city.

The mound Qaṣr, in the northernmost part of the city, proved to contain the ruins of two citadels, the Ishtar Gate, with part of the Processional Way, and the associated defence systems. The remains of the larger citadel are mainly of Nebuchadrezzar, though there are parts of it which are earlier, and it also received additions under subsequent rulers. It lay between the city walls at its north and a canal at its south, and was of considerable size, the greatest length (east to west) being nearly 340 yards and the greatest width (north to south) about 220 yards; in these dimensions the western fortifications by the river are not included. Basically the plan was that of five principal complexes built round courtyards lying on an east–west axis.

North of the most easterly courtyard, in the part of the citadel complex nearest the Ishtar Gate, was found a structure consisting basically of a narrow passage with a row of seven narrow vaulted chambers leading off on both sides, the whole being below the level of the main palace. This structure was enclosed in a wall which was distinct from the outer wall of the citadel. To the south and west, enclosed within a further wall, was a series of small rooms, in one of which was a well of unique form, with three shafts. Koldeway and others have assumed this vaulted building to have been the sub-structure of the 'Hanging Gardens' of Babylon, for which the well provided irrigation.[20] Whether or not this conclusion is justified, it is clear that the subterranean chambers were used for some administrative purpose. This is established by the discovery there of about 200 cuneiform tablets[21] of the period from the tenth to the thirty-fifth year of Nebuchadrezzar, dealing with ration issues: it is amongst these that documents referring to Jehoiachin of Judah (see below, page 45) occur.[22]

North of the principal citadel, just outside the city walls and opposite the Ishtar Gate, Nebuchadrezzar built a new citadel, with powerful fortifications to its north. Within this building were found monuments (statues and inscriptions, the majority unassociated with Babylon in origin) of various periods from the Third Dynasty of Ur onwards. The part of the building containing these monuments has been called a 'museum',[23] but the description rests upon a mistranslation of a text:[24] more probably it was a storehouse for booty carried away from conquered peoples to Babylon.[25]

East of the northern fortifications was the beginning of the Processional Way[26] and the approach to the Ishtar Gate. This gate, one of eight great gates in the city walls, comprised a barbican projecting 65 feet beyond the two pairs of towers which flanked the road where it passed through the city walls. The walls of the whole gate were faced with alternate rows of bulls and dragons, in brick relief or enamel.

The Processional Way represented part of the course taken during the New Year Festival, for it was along this route that the king led Marduk and Nabu out of the city to the Akitu House north of the Ishtar Gate:[27] it is possible that Deutero–Isaiah was satirizing such a procession in xlvi. 1.[28] Southwards the Processional Way led past the ziggurat Etemenanki to the great Marduk temple Esagila.

The remains of the ziggurat Etemenanki were, when Koldewey began excavation, marked not by a mound but by a depression known as Ṣaḥn ('basin'), south of Qaṣr. This ziggurat had been partially dismantled in antiquity by Alexander in preparation for a proposed rebuilding,[29] and had been plundered in more recent times for building materials. Sufficient remained to establish that the dimensions of the base were 298 feet square, comprising an inner core of 200 feet square of unbaked clay, enclosed in a shell of baked brick 49 feet thick. Three broad staircases converged to the south face of the ziggurat. For details of the higher parts of the structure there is available, besides the reports in classical authors, a cuneiform tablet giving detailed dimensions.[30] This permits the calculation that the ziggurat, of seven stages, reached a total height of 295 feet, possibly an ideal figure.

Immediately south of the Ṣaḥn depression, the mound ʿAmran ibn ʿAli was excavated to reveal the remains of Esagila, the principal temple of Babylon, closely related to Etemenanki. The shrine of Marduk, associated with chapels of other gods including Nabu, stood in an enclosure some 470 yards by 240 yards. In addition to Esagila, a number of other temples were identified in the city and excavated in whole or in part. Over fifty temples or chapels in Babylon are known from cuneiform documents,[31] but most have not yet been identified. This plethora of temples, taken together with discoveries by Koldewey in the streets of Babylon and the cuneiform evidence, provides an interesting comment upon Jeremiah's indictment (1. 38)—'it is a land of graven images, and they are mad upon idols'. Over 6,000 figurines were found,[32] though some of these were of periods subsequent to Jeremiah. In addition to these, ten street altars were discovered, all of the period from Esar-haddon to Nabonidus.[33] According to the cuneiform description of Babylon, these represented only a very small proportion of the spots in the city at which images were likely to be in evidence, since there were, in addition to the temples, '300 daises of the Igigi gods and 1200 daises of the Annunnaki gods', as

well as '180 open-air shrines for Ishtar' and over 200 socles for
other deities.[34]

East of Etemenanki, the group of mounds known as Merkes
proved to conceal principally the remains of private dwellings,
and attested the fullest range of occupation levels found at Babylon,
extending from the First Dynasty to the Parthian period.[35]
Homera was found to consist principally of the rubble removed
from Etemenanki by Alexander and his successors in preparation
for proposed rebuilding: there was also a Greek theatre in this
area.

Babylon, though less important as a source of cuneiform
material than Nineveh, particularly in relation to literary texts,
has yielded texts to be numbered in thousands, the greater part
from illicit digging. The principal categories represented are
bricks, foundation cylinders, administrative, legal, and business
documents, chronicles, astronomical texts, and letters. There are
also small groups of tablets concerned with literary texts or omen
literature, and isolated examples of texts in several religious
categories. Chronologically the tablets range from the Old Babylonian to the Seleucid period (c. 311–95 B.C.). Many texts from
Babylon remain unpublished.

The cuneiform material with the most direct relationship to
Old Testament studies consists of four tablets[36] listing rations of
corn and oil for '[$^m i$]a-'u-kīnu king of ^{mat}ia-[a-ḫu-du] and [x]
sons of the king of ^{mat}ia-a-ḫu-du and 8 ^{amel}ia-a-ḫu-da-a-a',[37]
for '^{m}ia-ku-ú-ki-nu son of the king of ^{mat}ia-ku-du and five sons
of the king of ia-ku-du',[38] and for '[^{m}ia]-'-ú-kīnu king of ^{mat}ia-
a-ḫu-du and [x sons of the king] of ^{mat}ia-a-ḫu-du'.[39] A date, the
thirteenth year of Nebuchadrezzar, is extant on only one of the
four tablets; the termini of the group of tablets of which they are
a part are the tenth and the thirty-fifth years of Nebuchadrezzar.
Ia'u-kīnu of Iāḫudu (and variant spellings) can only be Jehoiachin
of Judah. Other Old Testament Hebrew names represented in
these texts are Gaddiel (^{m}ga-di-'-ilu) and Shelemiah (^{m}šá-lam-ia-
a-ma).[40] The description of Jehoiachin in one tablet as 'son of
the king of Judah' may, if not a simple lapsus calami, indicate an
ambiguity, or a change at some point in time, in the view taken
by Nebuchadrezzar of the status of Jehoiachin.

Other recently published texts from Babylon shed some light on political events in Nebuchadrezzar's capital in the early years of Jehoiachin's captivity, and offer the possibility of an interpretation of the historical setting of Jer. xxviii. 2 ff., in which Hananiah in the fourth year of Zedekiah, that is, in 594 B.C., prophesied the overthrow of Nebuchadrezzar within two years. A chronicle speaks of an insurrection in Babylonia in Nebuchadrezzar's tenth year (595–594 B.C.),[41] whilst a juridical text shows a decision being made near the end of Nebuchadrezzar's eleventh year (594–593 B.C.) concerning the property of a man who had been executed in Babylon for high treason.[42] There is no specific evidence to connect such disturbances in Babylonia with Hananiah's prophecy, but the instance of Merodach-baladan's embassy to Hezekiah[43] does provide a precedent for an intriguer in Babylonia attempting to secure support from abroad, and the possibility cannot be excluded that opponents of Nebuchadrezzar in Jerusalem were aware of circumstances elsewhere apparently threatening his continued rule.[44] It is clear that Jeremiah's evaluation of the consequences of rebellion against Nebuchadrezzar (xxvii. 16 f.) were more in accordance with the political realities of the situation in Babylon than those of Hananiah.

Amongst other Neo-Babylonian kings mentioned, or possibly mentioned, in the Old Testament, the one who has gained most stature from recent publications is Neriglissar (Nergal-shar-uṣur, possibly Nergal-sharezer of Jer. xxxix. 3, 13, one of Nebuchadrezzar's principal officers at the siege of Jerusalem). A newly published chronicle[45] shows Neriglissar to have personally led a major campaign in Cilicia in 557–556 B.C., and establishes him as a general of considerable ability.

Further evidence has also appeared to elucidate the activities of Nabonidus. It has long been recognized that cuneiform material from Babylon and elsewhere has clarified the position of Belshazzar 'king' of Babylon, who deputized for his father Nabonidus during his prolonged absence in Tema.[46] The new evidence substantially amplifies the details of the circumstances in which Nabonidus left his capital: it occurs in the form of three stelae, two of Nabonidus himself and one of his mother, found at Harran in 1956.[47] These texts show Nabonidus' departure to have been the result of a mutiny amongst the citizens of Babylon, Borsippa, Nippur, Ur, Erech, and Larsa against his plan to rebuild the temple of Harran in a manner which would indicate that the Moon-god Sin held supremacy in the pantheon.[48] The same texts also offer some indications of the probable fate of a part of the Jewish people. It is clear that at least part, and possibly a large proportion, of the troops accompanying Nabonidus to Arabia were from the western countries of his empire,[49] and the troops accompanying him must have been the nucleus of the six colonies which Nabonidus established at oases in western Arabia.[50] It is striking that at the time of the Hegira five of these oases were already occupied by Jews.[51] The origin of the Jews in these places has long been the subject of speculation, but it is now a reasonable conclusion that their ancestors were placed there as colonists by Nabonidus.

A text inscribed at Babylon, though transmitted in antiquity to Calah (Nimrud), gives details of a siege of Babylon in the reign of Tiglath-pileser III which provides a parallel to the circumstances of the siege of Jerusalem by Sennacherib (2 Kings xviii. 17–36). In 732 B.C. the throne of Babylon had been usurped and the capital occupied by a Chaldaean prince, Ukin-zer, who was ultimately overthrown by Assyrian military action.[52] The document concerned is a letter to Tiglath-pileser from two Assyrian officials before the arrival of the Assyrian army.[53] They reported that they had stood before the Marduk gate[54] to negotiate with Ukin-zer's representatives within the city. As at the siege of Jerusalem, the Assyrian officials then attempted to bypass the city rulers and, by offering favourable terms, to treat with the citizens direct: they sought to persuade the Babylonians, who were standing with Ukin-zer's representatives, to act independently and to open the gates, offering the inducement of Assyrian recognition of the Babylonians' special privileges.[55] Just as in the case of Jerusalem, however, the ruling party in Babylon seems to have prevented any direct verbal reply by the Babylonians, for the Assyrian officials report—'They would not parley with us; they kept sending us messages.'[56]

The most celebrated archaeological find associated with a king of Babylon, the stele bearing the greater part of the laws of Hammurabi, was neither discovered at Babylon nor, probably, originally sited there. The stele, of diorite, 7 ft. 4 in. high, was found in three pieces by the French expedition at Susa in December

1901 and January 1902. There were also found some further laws
on fragments of diorite, probably parts of a duplicate monument.
Other objects excavated nearby bore inscriptions proving them
to have been removed from Sippar, and there is no internal evidence in the text of the main stele which conflicts with the hypothesis of such an origin for it.[57] Further fragments of laws on clay
tablets, some of them from Babylon itself, recognized in museum
collections or excavated since the publication of the main stele,
have permitted the restoration of about half the missing sections
of the text.[58]

The origin and purpose of the laws of Hammurabi,[59] and of
written law in general in the ancient Near East, have been clarified
by the discovery of several earlier collections of laws, antedating
those of Hammurabi by up to nearly two and a half centuries.
Parts of four such collections, two in Sumerian and two in Akkadian, are now known; of these, one collection, the so-called 'Old
Assyrian Laws',[60] is not only very fragmentary but also stands
apart from other groups in that the extant sections deal solely with
administrative procedures amongst merchants, and so will not be
discussed here.

Of the other laws, the oldest collection is that of Ur-Nammu
(2113-2096 B.C.), founder of the Third Dynasty of Ur.[61] The
laws are preserved on one tablet of eight columns, in poor condition, datable to the early post-Sumerian period.[62] There is no
conclusive internal evidence as to the nature of the original of
which the text of the table is a copy, but it could have been a
stele corresponding to that on which Hammurabi's laws occur. A
prologue outlines the mythological and historical circumstances
in which Ur-Nammu became king, and then states that, having
secured the boundaries of his city, Ur-Nammu instituted internal
reforms in the interests of the economically weak: his activities
included regulation of weights and measures, abuses of which are
frequently a matter of concern in the Old Testament. The precise
manner in which the succeeding paragraphs of laws were introduced is uncertain, owing to a break. It is estimated that there may
originally have been twenty-two laws,[63] of which five are largely
intelligible in the extant text. One of the extant laws concerns
trial by ordeal in case of accusation of witchcraft, another the
return of a slave to his master, and the other three penalties for

infliction of personal injury. These latter are of particular interest in that they prescribe not the *lex talionis*, as in the laws of Hammurabi and the Old Testament, but the payment of specified weights of silver.

The second group of Sumerian laws are those of Lipit-Ishtar, king of Isin (1932–1906 B.C.), approximately a century and a half earlier than the laws of Hammurabi. The extant copies of these laws, all of the early post-Sumerian period, are contained on seven clay tablets or fragments, six of them from Nippur, the other of unknown provenance:[64] four of them bear extracts from the laws made for scribal purposes, whilst the other three are parts of a single large tablet which originally bore the complete text. The text begins with a prologue of about 100 lines, similar in form to, though shorter than, that which introduces the laws of Hammurabi. It refers to the status of Ninisinna as tutelary deity of Isin, and the selection of Lipit-Ishtar by the gods An and Enlil to establish justice in the land. As in the case of the Ur-Nammu laws, a break has destroyed the evidence as to the manner in which the laws were introduced. Of the laws themselves, the first half are entirely lost except for a few traces; about two-thirds of the remainder can be restored, giving thirty-eight laws legible in whole or in part. The laws are followed by an epilogue, much damaged but preserving sufficient text to indicate that it was of similar import to the epilogue following the laws of Hammurabi, and to establish that the Lipit-Ishtar laws were also originally inscribed on a stele. The extant laws are grouped according to subject-matter and deal with hire of boats, orchards and waste land, slavery, inheritance and marriage, and damages for injury to hired oxen. There is nothing in the extant part of the laws to indicate whether the *lex talionis* or a monetary fine was applied in cases of personal injury.

The third group of laws antecedent to Hammurabi are the laws of Eshnunna, a state in the Diyala region which flourished between the fall of the Third Dynasty of Ur and the rise of Hammurabi to paramountcy. The laws, in Akkadian, are preserved on two tablets, one almost complete, excavated in 1945 and 1947 at Tell Abu Ḥarmal, a small mound on the outskirts, now in the suburbs, of Baghdad.[65] The name of the ruler who promulgated the laws is lost.[66] The tablets themselves can be dated archaeologically to not later than the reign of Dadusha, an early contemporary of

Hammurabi. A comparison of divergences between the two versions of the text, particularly in relation to the orthographic
systems, establishes that the form of the text of one is substantially
older than that of the other, and that both forms of the text go
back to an archetype older than either. The original laws, though
they cannot at present be dated to a particular reign, were thus
substantially older than the laws of Hammurabi.

The text is introduced by a seven-line date formula relating to
an unidentified year. Then follows a tariff of prices[67] of corn, oil,
wool, salt, spice and copper, rates of hire for wagons and boats,
and wages for various classes of agricultural worker. Set within
this framework of price regulation are three laws, two concerning
responsibility in certain mishaps with boats, and the third defining
the liability of a hired harvester in the event of breach of contract.
The first and second laws are interpolated after the statement of
rates of hire for boats, and the third after the clauses on wages of
harvesters and winnowers.

The remaining laws concern the following subjects: trespass and
housebreaking, business transactions, bride-money, loans, unlawful distraint, betrothal and marriage, defloration of a slave-girl,
children reared by foster-parents, responsibility for deposited
property, limitations upon rights of sale and purchase, assault,
slavery, injury from animals or a collapsing wall, divorce, and neglect of duty by a house-guard. The total number of clauses, including the tariff of prices and rates of hire and laws only fragmentarily
preserved, is sixty.

Approximately three-quarters of the laws of Eshnunna are
parallel to clauses of the laws of Hammurabi. There are some provisions in the Eshnunna laws which are paralleled quite closely in the
laws or practice of the Old Testament but not at all, or less directly,
in the laws of Hammurabi. The provisions referred to concern the
following subjects: death as the accepted penalty for housebreaking at night (*Laws of Eshnunna*, § 13; Exod. xxii. 1, R.V. 2);
a suitor's service to the potential father-in-law to gain a bride
(*L.E.*, § 25; Gen. xxix. 18); penalty for defloration of a slave-girl
(*L.E.*, § 31; Lev. xix. 20 f. [the nature of the penalty differs in the
two cases]); an oath to be taken by the depositary in the event of
loss of goods on deposit (*L.E.*, § 37; Exod. xxii. 6 f., R.V. 7 f.);
right of original owner to repurchase his property (*L.E.*, § 39;

Lev. xxv. 29); division of loss between owners in event of one man's ox killing another's (*L.E.*, § 53; Exod. xxi. 35). In the penalties for personal injury arising from assault, the laws of Eshnunna are basically in agreement with the Ur-Nammu laws, against the laws of Hammurabi and of the Old Testament, in specifying not the *lex talionis* but a fine; there is, however, at the end of the section dealing with personal injuries a broken clause which appears to prescribe that in the more serious cases the aggressor shall be subject to trial in addition to the prescribed fine.

Not only the earlier origin in time of the laws of Eshnunna but also considerations of form point to their being more primitive than the laws of Hammurabi: logical grouping of subjects is much less marked in the Eshnunna laws than in those of Hammurabi, and whilst in the latter all clauses, including those dealing with rates of hire, are in a standard form, with the hypothetical activity introduced by *šumma* 'if' in a protasis and the consequence indicated in an apodosis, in the laws of Eshnunna the forms are more variable, about a quarter of the clauses occurring in the form of a direct statement or prohibition.[68]

The divergences of the laws of Eshnunna from the laws of Hammurabi in content and form are instructive. One of the more significant differences relates to the tariff of prices found in the earlier laws. There is in the laws of Hammurabi no list of commodity prices, but there does occur a list of rates of hire of animals and equipment and of rates of pay, corresponding, in subject-matter but not in form, to similar lists in the laws of Eshnunna. In the latter documents these lists of rates of hire and pay are closely associated with commodity prices, which are placed at the very beginning of the laws. The position of the list of commodity prices, taken together with other evidence pointing to the setting up of stelae specifically concerned with price regulation,[69] provides support for the view that stelae bearing collections of laws were a direct development from monuments inscribed with royal edicts regulating prices. The position of the first three laws (see above), intrusive within a section dealing with rates of hire, is explicable on the hypothesis that these laws represented decisions upon disputes arising from the application of the primitive tariff, which were eventually incorporated in a revised edition of the edict governing prices.

This view of the origin of written royal law in Mesopotamia postulates an economic basis for the practice. This is consistent with the well-attested attempts of ancient Mesopotamian kings, from the time of Urukagina (*c.* 2400 B.C.) at least, to provide economic regulators for their lands. The 'justice' (*mišarum*) which kings claim to have established was primarily economic justice, and consisted in a decree, normally in a king's first full regnal year, aimed at liberating citizens from the burden of debt to which they had become subject during the previous reign. The practice became regular at the time of Hammurabi, and an example of such a decree, promulgated by Ammi-ṣaduqa, Hammurabi's fourth successor, is known.[70] A possible reflection of a similar practice in the Hebrew kingdoms has been pointed out, and evidence adduced to suggest that the *yāšār* for which good kings were commended contained an economic element comparable with that of the *mišarum* act of Mesopotamian kings.[71]

H. W. F. SAGGS

NOTES

1. For references, see S. A. Pallis, *Early Exploration in Mesopotamia*, 1954, p. 6.

2. M. N. Adler, *The Itinerary of Benjamin of Tudela; critical text, translation and commentary*, 1907, pp. 42 f.

3. It may be noted that the certainty that Birs Nimrud was not the ziggurat of Babylon does not necessarily involve the conclusion that it could not have been the structure remembered in Hebrew tradition as the tower associated with Babel.

4. Original Italian edition, *Viaggi di Pietro della Valle il Pellegrino . . . Diuisi in tre parti*, parte i, 1650, pp. 713–20, in 'Lettera 17. da Baghdad De' 10. e 23. di Decembre 1616'. French translation, *Les Fameux Voyages de Pietro della Valle*, seconde partie, 1662, pp. 50–55. Unger's statement (*Babylon, die heilige Stadt*, 1931, p. 4) that Pietro della Valle 'hielt die grosse Ruine des Tempelturms, der in Birs Nimrud . . . existiert, für den "Turm zu Babel"' appears to be incorrect. Pietro della Valle specifically says (Italian edition, parte i, p. 720; French edition, seconde partie, p. 55) that he could not at the time of his visit be made to understand that there was anything worthy of a visit beyond Hillah, although his Arab guides attempted to inform him about the tomb of Ezekiel at Kefil, on the route to which Birs Nimrud lies. He does in his account of ruins refer (Italian edition, p. 713) to 'la Torre di Nembrotto, nella città di Babilonia, ò Babèl, come infin' hoggi questo luogo si chiama', but it is reasonable to suppose that this was also a consequence of his inadequate

Arabic, which led him to take the term Birs Nimrud ('Torre di Nembrotto') employed by his guide, attempting to tell him about other ruins in the area, as an alternative designation for Babil.

5. S. A. Pallis, op. cit., pp. 7 f.

6. *Journal des Sçavans*, décembre 1790, pp. 797–806; translated into English in *The European Magazine and London Review* xxi, 1792, pp. 338–42.

7. See S. A. Pallis, op. cit., pp. 29 f., iv, letter of East India Company of 18.10.1797.

8. *Mines de l'Orient*, iii, 1813, pp. 129–62, 197–200, republished as *Memoir on the Ruins of Babylon*, 1815. *Second Memoir on the Ruins of Babylon*, 1818. The two memoirs are referred to by Byron in *Don Juan* (written in 1818), Canto the Fifth, LXII. Ten years after Rich's second visit further excavations were undertaken on the Qaṣr, on a slightly larger scale, by Robert Mignan; see R. Mignan, *Travels in Chaldaea*, 1829, pp. 189–92.

9. See unpublished Layard Papers 38939, p. 39 (19 July 1849), 'If I have time and means at my command I intend to dig out as much as I can of old Babylon'; 38946, p. 17 (31 March 1851), 'The disturbed state of the country rendered all my attempts to visit the ruins of southern Babylonia and to excavate on the site of Babylon unavailing.' See also A. H. Layard, *Discoveries in the Ruins of Nineveh and Babylon*, 1853, pp. 494 and 502–9.

10. J. Oppert, *Expédition scientifique en Mésopotamie exécutée par ordre du Gouvernement, de 1851 à 1854*, i. *Relation du voyage et résultat de l'expédition*, 1863.

11. Published in *M.D.O.G.* iii, 1899, to lxxix, 1942, *passim*, and in *W.V.D.O.G.* i, 1901, ii, 1901, iv, 1904, xv, 1911, xxxii, 1918, xlvii, 1926, xlviii, 1930, liv, 1931, lv, 1932, lix, 1938, lxii, 1957. See also R. Koldewey, *Das wieder erstehende Babylon*, 4th ed., 1925.

12. *Sumer* xii, 1956, p. 92, xv, 1959, p. 39; *A.f.O.* xviii, 1957–8, pp. 174 f.

13. Herodotus, *The Histories*, I. 178. Strabo, XVI. i. 5 = *The Geography of Strabo* (Loeb Class. Libr., E. Tr. by H. L. Jones), 7, pp. 197 ff. Diodorus Siculus, II. vii. 3 = *Diodorus of Sicily* (Loeb Class. Libr., E. Tr. by C. H. Oldfather), i, p. 372.

14. Gen. x. 10.

15. See L. W. King, *Chronicles Concerning Early Babylonian Kings*, ii, 1907, p. 8, lines obverse 18 ff., a chronicle of the Cassite period which attributed the downfall of Sargon of Agade to his sacrilegious conduct in despoiling Babylon for the benefit of the new capital Accad.

16. See C. J. Gadd, *Babylonia, c. 2120–1800 B.C.* (= *C.A.H.*, rev. ed. of vols. i and ii, ch. xxii, 1965), p. 12. The earliest historical reference to Babylon is in a year-formula of Shar-kali-sharri, *c.* 2250 B.C.; see *Reallex. d. Assyr.* ii, 1938, p. 133, col. 1, c. Contemporary documents give the names of governors of the city under the Third Dynasty of Ur; see D. O. Edzard, *Die 'Zweite Zwischenzeit' Babyloniens*, 1957, p. 122, n. 637.

17. I. J. Gelb, *Journ. of the Instit. of Asian Studies* i, 1955, pp. 1–4, argues that Bāb-ilim represented a popular etymology of a non-Semitic name.

18. On the possibility of Nebuchadrezzar having used Aramaic, see R. A. Bowman, *J.N.E.S.* vii, 1948, p. 76.

19. Jer. l. 15, li. 44, 58. It may be noted that the prophecies were not fulfilled.

20. The nature of the vaults agrees with the description in Strabo, XVI. i. 5, but according to Strabo irrigation was from the Euphrates and not from wells.

21. *M.D.O.G.* xxi, 1904, p. 6.

22. The subterranean chambers are not to be taken as dungeons in which Jehoiachin and others were confined (2 Kings xxv. 29); records of ration issues would be kept in the storekeeper's offices, not with the prisoners.

23. E. Unger, *Babylon, die heilige Stadt*, 1931, p. 224.

24. The passage adduced by Unger (*supra*) does not necessarily refer to this building; for its translation in context, see *C.A.D.* iii, p. 22, 2′.

25. Cf. 2 Kings xxiv, 13 ff.

26. Akkadian *Ai-ibūr-šabû* 'Let the adversary not prevail'.

27. A. G. Lie, *The Inscriptions of Sargon II King of Assyria*; part i, *The Annals*, 1929, pp. 56, 58, lines 384 ff.

28. The carrying of gods from a doomed city is attested in the Neo-Babylonian period in D. J. Wiseman, *Chronicles of Chaldaean Kings*, 1961, p. 50, line 6, p. 52, lines 19, 21.

29. According to Strabo, XVI. i. 5, the ziggurat had earlier been partially demolished by Xerxes I.

30. For references and edition, see E. Unger, op. cit., pp. 237 ff.

31. Ibid., pp. 136–63. But see W. L. Moran, *Anal. Bibl.* xii/iii, 1959, p. 257.

32. *W.V.D.O.G.* xlvii, 1926, pp. 11, 17, 24, 29, 133 *et passim*, and R. Koldewey, *Das wieder erstehende Babylon*, 1925, pp. 271–9.

33. E. Unger, op. cit., pp. 120 f.

34. *W.V.D.O.G.* xlviii, 1930, Taf. 82, col. III. For a new fragment of the text concerned, see W. L. Moran, 'A new fragment of DIN.TIR.KI = *Bābilu* and *Enūma Eliš* vi. 61–66', *Anal. Bibl.* xii, 1959, *Studia Bibl. et Orient.*, iii, *Oriens Antiquus*, pp. 257–65.

35. *W.V.D.O.G.* xlvii, 1926, p. 4.

36. E. F. Weidner, *Mél. syr. offerts à monsieur René Dussaud*, 1939, ii, pp. 922–35.

37. Ibid., p. 925, text B, obv. II, line 38.

38. Ibid., p. 926, text C, rev. II, lines 17 f.

39. Ibid., p. 926, text D, lines 20 f.; p. 925, text A, obv. line 29, also gives the name *ᵐia-'-ú-kīnu*, but the name of the country is lost.

40. Both names in text A; see E. F. Weidner, op. cit., p. 927. The Akkadian form of Gaddiel, with non-doubling of -d-, agrees with LXX rather than with M.T. spelling (Num. xiii. 10).

41. D. J. Wiseman, op. cit., p. 72, lines 21 f. The immediately following expedition to collect tribute in the west in the same year (ibid.,

lines 23 f.) indicates, if not active rebellion, at least that the political stability of the area was in doubt.

42. E. F. Weidner, *A.f.O.* xvii, 1954–6, pp. 1–9.

43. 2 Kings xx. 12 f.; Isa. xxxix. 1 f.; 2 Chron. xxxii. 31. On Merodach-baladan's embassy to Hezekiah, see most recently J. A. Brinkman, 'Merodach-baladan II', *Studies Presented to A. Leo Oppenheim*, 1964, pp. 31 ff.

44. Another hint of a possible attempt to instigate action against Nebuchadrezzar (three years later) is given in an Egyptian papyrus, which mentions an expedition (not specifically noted as hostile) of Psammetichus to Phoenicia; see F. K. Kienitz, *Die polit. Gesch. Ägyptens vom 7. bis zum 4. Jahrh. vor der Zeitwende*, 1953, p. 25.

45. D. J. Wiseman, op. cit., pp. 74 ff., B.M. 25124.

46. R. P. Dougherty, *Nabonidus and Belshazzar; a study of the closing events of the Neo-Babylonian empire*, 1929.

47. C. J. Gadd, *Anatol. Stud.* viii, 1958, pp. 35–92. A fourth stele of the same group was known earlier; ibid., p. 35.

48. *Anatol. Stud.* viii, 1958, pp. 56 ff., H2, A and B, col. i, lines 5–27.

49. C. J. Gadd, op. cit., p. 85.

50. *Anatol. Stud.* viii, 1958, p. 58, col. i, lines 24 ff.; p. 60, col. ii, lines 8 ff.; and pp. 62 ff., col. iii, lines 14 ff.

51. C. J. Gadd, op. cit., pp. 85–88.

52. For the most recent summary, see p. 11 f. in J. A. Brinkman, op. cit.

53. *Iraq* xvii, 1955, pp. 23 f., letter I.

54. In the northern part of the eastern wall; see E. Unger, op. cit., p. 69.

55. *Iraq* xvii, 1955, pl. iv and p. 23, letter I, lines 17 f. Collation (April 1965) establishes the reading as *(amel)ki-din-nu-ut-ku-nu a!-na!* [*k*]*a!-'!-un a-na DIN.TIR.KI al-la-ka*, 'I come to Babylon to confirm your citizen privileges'.

56. Ibid., lines 21 f.

57. G. R. Driver and J. C. Miles, *The Babylonian Laws*, i, 1952, p. 29.

58. Ibid. ii, 1955, pp. 1 f.; D. J. Wiseman, *J.S.S.* vii, 1962, pp. 161–72.

59. For the most recent detailed discussion of the origin and purpose of the 'code' of Hammurabi, see F. R. Kraus, 'Ein zentrales Problem des altmesopotamischen Rechtes: was ist der Codex Hammu-rabi?', *Genava* viii, 1960, pp. 283–96. Kraus argues that the 'code' is in its existing form a literary rather than a legal document.

60. Edited in G. R. Driver and J. C. Miles, *The Assyrian Laws*, 1935, pp. 376–9.

61. For publication, see S. N. Kramer, *Orient.* xxiii, 1954, pp. 40–48, with appendix by A. Falkenstein, pp. 48–51.

62. S. N. Kramer, op. cit., p. 40.

63. Ibid., p. 41.

64. For publication, see F. R. Steele, *A.J.A.* lii, 1948, pp. 425–50.

65. For most recent publication, see A. Goetze, *The Laws of Esh-nunna* (= *A.A.S.O.R.* xxxi), 1956.

66. The frequently reproduced statement, based on the *editio princeps*, that the laws were those of King Bilalama, derives from a faulty restoration.

67. A. Goetze, op. cit., pp. 24 ff., regards them as maximum rather than absolute prices.

68. In their extant sections both the laws of Ur-Nammu and those of Lipit-Ishtar show consistency by the introduction of clauses by *tukum.bi*, approximately the Sumerian equivalent of *šumma*.

69. V. Scheil, *Mél. épigraph.* (= *Mémoires de la mission archéologique de Perse*, xxviii, 1939), pp. 4 ff., text 3. See also C. J. Gadd, *C.A.H.*, rev. ed., ii, ch. v, 1965, p. 18.

70. Published and edited in F. R. Kraus, *Ein Edikt des Königs Ammi-ṣaduqa von Babylon*, 1958.

71. D. J. Wiseman, *J.S.S.* vii, 1962, pp. 167 f.

BIBLIOGRAPHY

DOUGHERTY, R. P. *Nabonidus and Belshazzar; a study of the closing events of the Neo-Babylonian empire*, 1929.

DRIVER, G. R., and MILES, J. C. *The Babylonian Laws*, 2 vols., 1952, 1955.

GOETZE, A. *The Laws of Eshnunna* (= *A.A.S.O.R.* xxxi), 1956.

KOLDEWEY, R. *Das wieder erstehende Babylon*, 4th ed., 1925. (An English translation of the first edition is published as *The excavations at Babylon*, 1914.)

KRAUS, F. R. *Ein Edikt des Königs Ammi-ṣaduqa von Babylon*, 1958.

OPPERT, J. *Expédition scientifique en Mésopotamie exécutée par ordre du Gouvernement, de 1851 à 1854*, i. *Relation du voyage et résultat de l'expédition*, 1863.

PALLIS, S. A. *Early Exploration in Mesopotamia* (= *Det Kongelige Danske Videnskabernes Selskab, Historisk-filologiske Meddelelser*, bind 33, nr. 6), 1954.

RICH, C. J. *Memoir on the Ruins of Babylon*, 1815.

—— *Second Memoir on the Ruins of Babylon*, 1818.

SAGGS, H. W. F. *The Greatness that was Babylon*, 1962.

UNGER, E. *Babylon, die heilige Stadt nach der Beschreibung der Babylonier*, 1931.

NIMRUD

IT may seem surprising that many persons who are familiar with the name Nineveh, the most famous city of Assyria, have hardly heard of Nimrud and would find it difficult to define. Indeed, until recently there were some authorities on Old Testament studies who thought that these two places were synonymous. Perhaps the comprehensive publication in 1966 of *Nimrud and its Remains* has helped to set Nimrud in its proper perspective.[1]

The reason for the undeserved obscurity which has for so long enshrouded the site of Nimrud is in the main due to an accident of history. In the Old Testament the books which are intimately concerned with Assyria, especially Kings, Chronicles, and Isaiah, as well as the prophets Amos, Hosea, Micah, and Nahum, are particularly interested in events which occurred after the middle of the eighth century B.C., when Nineveh was about to become the most important political centre in the east and Nimrud was on the decline. Old Testament writers were not bent on relating the history of Assyria *qua* history; they were primarily interested in expounding the means which God used to enlist Assyria as an instrument for the punishment of Israel and Judah for their sins and abominable practices (Amos vi. 1—'Woe . . . to them that are secure in the mountain of Samaria'; Isa. x. 5—'Ho Assyrian, the rod of mine anger, the staff in whose hand is mine indignation'). The direct intervention of Assyria in Israelite affairs did not, however, begin to be a daily and permanent menace before the reign of Tiglath-pileser III (*c.* 745–727 B.C.) known as Pul in 2 Kings xv. 19, who resided on the site of Nimrud, and was one of the last Assyrian kings to use it as his main residence. His successors for the most part lived either at Nineveh, or elsewhere. Earlier Assyrian kings residing in the same city had, indeed, conducted military campaigns in western Syria and Palestine, notably Ashurnasirpal II (*c.* 883–859 B.C.), Shalmaneser III (*c.* 859–824 B.C.), and Adad-nirari III (*c.* 810–782 B.C.), but they did not go beyond the exacting of tribute, capturing prisoners, and sacking cities—the period of more or less direct administration and active interference in politics was still to come.

It is, however, not only historically that the memory of the place has been clouded, but philologically also. Nimrud, correctly pronounced Nimrood, is often casually referred to as Nimrod, partly because in this country we are apt to think of a popular musical composition by Elgar, or a famous race-horse, and partly because from the Old Testament we retain a memory of Gen. x. 9 —'Like Nimrod a mighty hunter before the Lord', whereas Nimrud itself is never mentioned. Yet we may not be wrong in connecting these two not altogether dissimilar names, for archaeology has revealed that in ancient times the site was dedicated by the Assyrians to Ninurta, sometimes written Nimurta, originally a Sumerian god whom Ashurnasirpal II made, so to speak, the patron saint of his city. The great ziggurat or temple-tower, the ruins of which still dominate the plain from afar, together with a temple at its foot, were among the first buildings erected in honour of that divinity. Since Ninurta was a god of the chase, and carvings of hunting scenes as well as lions, both in relief and in the round, abounded, and since some of them were still visible in the soil long after the city was a ruin, there is little difficulty in understanding how Ninurta or Nimurta remained enshrined in the human memory as Nimrud, and was eventually assimilated to Nimrod of the Old Testament and the mythological hero associated with Abraham in the Koran.

This strange genealogy is fortified in its relation to the ancient site by a passage in Gen. x. 1–12 where the hero is associated with the city:

Now these are the generations of the sons of Noah, Shem, Ham and Japheth; and unto them were sons born after the flood. . . . And the sons of Ham; Cush, and Mizraim, and Put, and Canaan. . . . And Cush begat *Nimrod*: he was the first to be a mighty one in the earth. He was a mighty hunter before the Lord: . . . And the beginning of his kingdom was Babel, and Erech, and Accad, all of them in the land of Shinar. Out of that land he went forth into Assyria, and builded Nineveh, and Rehoboth-Ir, and *Calah*, and Resen between Nineveh and *Calah* (the same is the great city).

The names Nimrod and Calah have been italicized in order to emphasize the connexion between the two, a real one, although the author of this passage in Genesis may hardly have been aware of it. But he was adumbrating historical traditions which contained a hard core of truth, and these he resolved into a number of broad and simplified generalizations, in order to explain the diversity of races and peoples that populated the world, in accordance with the current anthropological notions.[2]

We have already seen that the equation Nimrod–Nimrud is philologically acceptable, and to these factors may be added Calah, for this is obviously the Old Testament name for Assyrian Kalḫu which is the standard appellation for the place noted in all the cuneiform inscriptions found there. The authors of Gen. x. 1–12, moreover, were evidently aware that the principal cities of Assyria were an ultimate offshoot of more ancient Babylonia (Sumer and Akkad), and here too their concepts were sound inasmuch as the urban civilization of Assyria was in general based on Sumero-Babylonian traditions.

Apart from Nineveh, which is mentioned in this same passage, we know nothing about Rehoboth-Ir and Resen, and excavation alone can solve this problem.[3] Asshur, the old religious capital, figures merely as one of the sons of Shem in Gen. x. 22; there is no mention of Dur-sharrukin, founded by Sargon II (c. 722–705 B.C.), or of Tarbasu, the royal seat of the crown prince. These omissions and the laconic references to the known cities serve to show, as we have already remarked, that the Old Testament writers were not interested in the history of Assyria per se, and it says much for the renown of Calah that it is once mentioned. In no other passage of the Old Testament can the apparently similar names Halah, Calneh, Calno, be satisfactorily identified with Calah-Nimrud.[4] But in Mic. v. 5, R.V. 6, we are perhaps justified in seeing a direct reference to Calah-Nimrud as an essential part of Assyria—'they shall rule the land of Assyria with the sword, and the land of Nimrod with the drawn sword'. Is this a reflection of the fact that Nimrud was once the greatest military installation of Assyria?

We may now ask what is known archaeologically about Nimrud before considering the special bearing which some of the discoveries made there have upon the Old Testament. First we may consider its situation and then the expeditions which have revealed some of its history.

Nimrud lies about 20 miles south of Mosul, on the east bank

of the river Tigris, which in antiquity washed the city walls, but now flows about 2 miles to the west. The core of the city was enclosed by a perimeter of great mud-brick walls about 4¾ miles in length, comprising within them nearly 900 acres of ground. At the south-west angle of the walled perimeter the acropolis was built, over an area of about 65 acres, again heavily defended by high walls, most of which are now concealed under huge turf embankments.

The choice of the site, though no doubt primarily dictated by the fact that it was a convenient staging post, a day's march on the southward road from Nineveh, was also reinforced by other considerations. It lay along the bank of the Tigris—the life-line of Assyria; there was a ford across the river; there was good hunting, and good agriculture, for a tract of country estimated at 25 sq. km., served by a canal down to the Zab, was capable of intensive cultivation. An elaborate system of irrigation had already been organized early in the ninth century B.C.

Our intimate knowledge of Nimrud is the result of more than a century of excavation, beginning with Austen Layard, who dug the place intermittently, on a considerable scale, between 1845 and 1851 while concurrently excavating Nineveh. Most of Layard's work was confined to the acropolis where he concentrated primarily on the excavation of the ziggurat and a series of temples and palaces. His outstanding discovery was the palace of Ashurnasirpal II, of which he excavated the central block comprising the state apartments and the great throne room. Here he unearthed a series of vividly carved gypsum bas-reliefs which represented the triumphs of Assyria in war, as well as a number of stone colossi, winged bulls, lions and *lamassu* figures, part human part animal, which guarded the portals. After the close of the Great Exhibition of 1851 in Hyde Park, some of the sculpture was obtained by the Crystal Palace Company, and the world at large was startled by these great stone phantoms, resurrected nightmares which the people of ancient Israel must have seen in their dreams when they were beset by the cruel might of Assyria.

It was, however, the discovery by Layard in December 1846 of the Black Obelisk[5] of Shalmaneser III which eventually brought home to the public the close bearing which the remains at Nimrud had on passages in the Old Testament. For on this great monument, now conveniently to be seen in the British Museum, one of the panels illustrates Jehu, king of Israel, kissing the feet of the king of Assyria to whom he had brought tribute. Although 1 Kings xix. 16 calls Jehu the son of Nimshi (incidentally contemporary of Hazael, king of Damascus, 2 Kings xiii. 22), in the Assyrian inscriptions he is referred to as 'the son of Omri', while Israel generally appears as 'the land of the house of Omri'. In fact it was Jehu who had brought the dynasty of Omri to an end, but to the Assyrians it was the older dynastic name that counted, an interesting discrepancy from the Old Testament where Omri was of no great account; though on the Moabite Stone Mesha, king of Moab, had recognized him as a powerful oppressor.

Another monarch, this time Hazael, who was the contemporary of Jehu, and king of Damascus, has been recorded also at Nimrud. One recent discovery is a fragment of ivory veneer found in a hall (T. 10) of the palace of Shalmaneser III, in the outer town of Nimrud. The name seems to be preceded by the letter *n* and would, if so, almost certainly be parallel to another ivory fragment from Arslan Tash, inscribed *mr'n hz'l* 'Lord Hazael'.[6] Interesting as is this confirmatory evidence from outside sources of a king whose dynasty had clashed with Assyria, it is no less significant that the chamber in which it was found was a hall built by Shalmaneser III, packed with mutilated ivories which had been cast into it after the final sack of the city. As many of these ivories are known to have been made in Syrian workshops, it would appear without a doubt that some of them had been acquired in the latter half of the ninth century B.C., including probably many fine specimens of the chryselephantine cloisonné or champlevé work which have been so frequently found at Nimrud. The famous Old Testament city of Hamath is also named, on another clay label from the same building, and a third fragment of veneer bears writing in the Old Hebrew script which may perhaps be read 'from King Gdl'.[7] Other evidence proved decisively that until the end of the eighth century B.C., ivories, many of them chryselephantine, were being acquired by successive kings of Assyria who filled their houses with the expensive luxuries which were so frequently condemned by the puritanical prophets of Israel and Judah.

One other document, which belongs to the ninth century B.C., also contains a passage of cuneiform inscription which records an echo of Israelite practice; this is the celebrated sandstone stele set up by Ashurnasirpal II outside his palace in the fifth year of his reign (879 B.C.). This monument, inscribed back and front with 154 lines of Assyrian cuneiform, contains an inventory of the principal buildings, including palaces and temples as well as the zoological and botanical gardens, within the city of Calah—Assyrian Kalḫu. At the top of the stele the king is depicted in full ceremonial robes, surmounted by the symbols of the principal gods of Assyria—a dignified commemoration of the five years' work which he had completed on his refounded city, to which he had added an expensive canal. Much of the labour had been provided by prisoners obtained in his north Syrian campaigns, although no Israelite cities are mentioned. There is, however, an echo of the Old Testament in the concluding paragraph of this long inscription which describes the feast given to the people of Calah and to many distinguished visitors, a total of 69,574 persons in all. The concluding lines run—'The happy people of all the lands together with the people of Kalḫu for ten days I feasted, wined, bathed, anointed and honoured them and then sent them back to their lands in peace and joy'.[8]

When we compare this passage with the description of Solomon's feast held to celebrate the completion of his temple at Jerusalem, the parallel is remarkable. In 1 Kings viii. 65 we read—'So Solomon held the feast at that time, and all Israel with him, a great congregation, from the entering in of Hamath unto the brook of Egypt, before the Lord our God, seven days. . . . On the eighth day he sent the people away, and they blessed the king, and went unto their homes joyful and glad of heart. . . . ' These two great feasts, held within a century of one another, illustrate a common oriental practice, the giving of what is familiarly termed in the west a 'house-warming party', to mark the inauguration of a new building. There can be little doubt also that the occasion was used for the taking of an approximate reckoning of the local population—normally an unpopular measure, but doubtless overlooked by the populace when a feast was provided.[9] One exceptional feature of the festival held at Calah on this occasion is that on the stele we have full details of the menu, vast dishes of meat and wild fowl, vegetables, spices, fruit, not forgetting the roasted barley cakes (*gubibate*), still served in the district today and known by a not altogether dissimilar name (*kubbeh*). Ample portions of wine and of beer were also provided.

The importance of this inscription from Nimrud is that it has been the first to provide a basis for an approximate calculation of the population within the Nimrud district in the early ninth century B.C. The problem has been discussed elsewhere,[10] and it must suffice to say here that the inhabitants of the district are not likely to have been much less than 100,000 in all. A century and a half later the numbers were probably much increased when the army was mustered in the outer town, in and around the precincts of Fort Shalmaneser, as we shall see below. These figures for the fifth year of Ashurnasirpal's reign (879 B.C.) we may compare with the statement in the book of Jonah—'And should not I have pity on Nineveh, that great city; wherein are more than a hundred and twenty thousand persons who do not know their right hand from their left, and also much cattle' (iv. 11).

Thus it will be seen that the complementary figures, given both from Old Testament and cuneiform records, concerning Calah and Nineveh, provide ample justification for the fears of Israel and Judah on account of the overwhelming military might of Assyria, which in its homeland alone, in the eighth and seventh centuries B.C., contained also other populous centres such as Asshur, Dur-Sharrukin (Khorsabad), Tarbasu, Keremlais, and Karakosh.

The long course of excavations at Nimrud has yielded to many expeditions further evidence with a direct bearing on the Old Testament, and here we should recall that, following on the work of Layard, both W. H. Loftus (1854–5), Hormuzd Rassam (1854 and 1878), and George Smith (1872–3) added their quota from the site. But the most comprehensive campaigns were conducted under the auspices of the British School of Archaeology in Iraq in 1949–63, in a series of no less than thirteen expeditions.[11]

Very soon after the inception of the latter campaigns it was discovered that the NW. palace of Ashurnasirpal II, in which, as we have seen, Layard had excavated the state apartments, covered a far greater amount of ground than had previously been demonstrated, and that there were in addition two more wings, one on the north side which had been devoted to the administration, and one on the south to the domestic quarters. The whole complex covered no less than 6 acres of ground.

It was in the northern administrative wing that a most important set of cuneiform documents was found, written for the most part, if not entirely, in the reigns of Tiglath-pileser III (Pul of the Old Testament) and Sargon, the conqueror of Samaria. The chamber which contained them, numbered ZT. 4 on the Palace plan, was evidently the chancery. We were fortunate in finding the scribal benches, and, against them, the little square burnt-brick compartments which must once have served as filing cabinets.[12] Here again we were brought through the Assyrian records into intimate contact with Israel and Judah in the latter half of the eighth century B.C., when the Assyrian imperialists were thrusting through Syria and Palestine which they now aspired to control, either directly or indirectly, towards the frontiers of Egypt itself.

Tiglath-pileser III was indeed already known from Layard's discoveries to have had a palace of his own at Calah, overlooking the river, on the western side of the acropolis, and some fine bas-reliefs, carved to his order, are now principally in the British Museum.[13] The remains of his annals, inscribed upon stone, and originally set up in his palace, were also found by Layard. In addition, George Smith found in 1873 a broken tablet in the 'SE Palace of Nimrud' (subsequently identified as a religious complex properly called Ezida, and comprising the Nabu and other temples), recording this same king's campaigns down to 731 or possibly 730 B.C. It is perhaps not altogether surprising that this text (K 3751) had later been incorporated within the great collection of Ninevite tablets; but when we come to dig again in the acropolis we noted that Smith's own writing was still clearly legible on the tablet, identifying the building in which he had found it at Nimrud. Moreover, from Smith's description we were eventually able to identify the office in which it was found—room NTS 10, an office which for the sake of light opened directly on the great entrance courtyard of Ezida.[14] Other fragments of these historical annals were also found by us elsewhere in the same building, and in one to the north of it, named the Governor's Palace.[15]

Among the many items of interest which recur in these catalogues of Assyrian triumphs is the reference to Damascus as the broad (territory of the house) of Hazael which was evidently a dynastic name for a line of

Damascene kings, since more than one Hazael is known: there is also a mention of Israel in the form 'the house of Omri', as it had long ago been called in the annals of Shalmaneser III. In this context we also hear about an alliance between a contemporary Hiram of Tyre with Rezin of Damascus, and an Assyrian expedition to Israel in 732 B.C. when Hoshea was set on the throne in place of Pekah.[16] On a tablet ND. 400 from the Governor's Palace we had already been told about the defeat of the King of Gaza; here we learn that he came to Calah and presented his tribute personally. Assyria had now reached the frontiers of Egypt and was later to acquire considerable booty from that country.[17]

Apart from the royal annals, the recent excavations at Nimrud have enriched our knowledge of the reign of Tiglath-pileser III by the discovery of an extensive collection of letters from the king's governors, some of them stationed in Phoenicia. Of particular interest to students of the Old Testament are documents from the chancery, ZT. 4 of the NW. Palace, describing the troubles which beset His Majesty's Commissioners of Inland Revenue in Tyre and in Sidon, and the trade-war with Egypt which was competing with Syria at the time for the timber of Lebanon, a country which was then also producing wine.[18] Other documents indicate that emissaries received at the court of Assyria in this and in the subsequent reign included Egyptians or Arabs, Moabites, Ammonites, and Edomites. These and the annals of Tiglath-pileser III, which include references to Menahem (written *me-nu-hi-me*), to Pekah, Hoshea, and Jehoahaz of Judah,[19] are a remarkable confirmation on the Assyrian side of the basic accuracy of the corresponding Old Testament records (2 Kings xv and xvi, for example). Yet, as we have seen, Calah does not figure in the relevant Old Testament passages, because the Judaean chroniclers had no interest in Assyrian history as such: their records on this subject were perhaps the more reliable in that they were wholly objective.

These Assyrian annals, letters, and reports, recovered from no less than four different buildings in Calah-Nimrud, together with the majestic bas-reliefs from his palace, sufficiently attest the authority of this king and the veneration with which he was regarded, for he it was who restored the fortunes of the empire after a period of more than three and a half decades during which the power of Assyria had been eclipsed by that of Urartu, ancient Armenia. These attestations of his work at Nimrud are therefore the best

possible verification of the passage in 2 Kings xv. 19 f. where
this monarch is mentioned by his Babylonian name—'Pul the
king of Assyria came against the land; and Menahem gave Pul a
thousand talents of silver, that he might help him to confirm his
hold of the royal power. Menahem exacted the money from Israel,
that is from all the wealthy men, fifty shekels of silver from every
man, to give to the king of Assyria.' This was evidently the price
which was exacted by the enemy for every able-bodied man as a
ransom from being press-ganged into military service. And we
may confidently justify this interpretation inasmuch as fifty shekels
of silver was approximately the price of a first-class slave in
Assyria at the time. Reckoning also that a thousand talents of silver
was the equivalent of 3 million shekels, we are entitled to conclude
that the fighting force available to Menahem of Israel was a maximum of 60,000 men—a number which at this time would have
been much inferior to that which could have been mustered by
Assyria.

For the military manpower available in the latter half of the
eighth century B.C. we have one remarkable, laconic, and dramatic
document which was discovered by us in Fort Shalmaneser, a vast
arsenal situated in the south-east corner of the outer town: this is
a docket which is a record of inspection of 36,242 bows, most, if
not all, of which had probably been imported from north-western
Syria.[20] Since the bowmen in the Assyrian army can hardly have
amounted to more than a third of the striking force, it seems not
improbable that a figure not far short of 100,000 men would have
been available for war against Israel.

It is, therefore, hardly surprising that five years after the death
of Tiglath-pileser III, Samaria, the great capital city of Israel,
fell before the onslaught of Assyrian arms. The Old Testament
reference to this event occurs in 2 Kings xvii. 3 ff. where the three-
year siege is correctly ascribed to Shalmaneser V (c. 727–722
B.C.) as is corroborated by the Babylonian Chronicle. Not until
720 B.C. did Sargon return to deport its people and rebuild it as
the centre of a new province, Samerina.[21] From the Assyrian side
various versions of these events were incorporated on a series of inscribed prisms which Sargon deposited in Asshur and in Nineveh,
together with correlative texts in Khorsabad. Some fragmentary
examples of this series were also found at Nimrud—the completest

of them, known as prism D, was found in the chancery of the NW. Palace, and incidentally records that 27,280 captives were taken. Thereafter Sargon restored the city and placed an Assyrian governor in strict control of it.

Interesting as are the events described in these long texts, it is perhaps the passage concerning Babylon which carries one of the most memorable echoes of the voices in the Old Testament. Sargon relates that the

approach [to] Babylon . . . was not open, its road was not passable . . . [in] the inaccessible tracts, thorn thistles, and jungle prevailed . . . jackals assembled in their recesses and huddled together (?) like lambs . . . [The] settlements . . . had lapsed into ruin. . . . Over their cultivated ground channel and furrow did not exist, [but] it was woven over with spiders' webs. Their rich meadows had become like a wilderness, their cultivated grounds were forlorn of the sweet harvest song, grain was quite cut off. The jungle I cut down, the thorn and thistles with flames I burned, the Aramaeans, a plundering race I slew with arms; as for the lions and wolves, I made a slaughter of them.[22]

Those familiar with the Old Testament will at once recall many passages which reflect the word-painting and imagery of this thrilling Assyrian poem. The description of Babylon overgrown with thorn and thistle is almost the verbal equivalent of Gen. iii. 18 and Hos. x. 8, Assyrian *gissu daddaru* being exactly matched by the Hebrew *ḳôṣ wedardar*—'Thorns and thistles shall it bring forth to thee', says Genesis. Not less striking are the parallel descriptions of Babylon in Jer. l. 39, li. 37—'wild beasts and jackals shall dwell in Babylon', and Isa. xiii, xiv, xv, and xvi (the lament for Moab; xvi, 10—'And joy and gladness are taken away from the fruitful field; and in the vineyard no songs are sung'). Out of the component fragments of our Nimrud prisms, found in 1952–3, we have recovered the authentic voice of the prophets, and here comes the assurance that the words we read about Babylon and Moab in the Old Testament 'represent a current poetical *koine* taken out of the mouths of the dwellers in the countryside from Palestine to Assyria'.[23]

The chamber which yielded prism D produced another remarkable document which can also be dated to Sargon's reign. This was a baked clay cylinder completely restored from three separate pieces, found on different days in the rubbish fill; it was inscribed to the order of Marduk-apal-iddina (*c.* 721–710 B.C., Merodach-baladan of Isa. xxxix. 1; cf. 2 Kings xx. 12) then king of Babylon, a Chaldaean sheikh who had aimed at uniting with Hezekiah, king of Judah, in an anti-Assyrian coalition—a policy which Isaiah astutely discouraged.[24] The boastful text recovered from Nimrud describes how the Assyrian had been driven out of Akkad. Fortunately, however, Sargon, who overcame his enemy, had captured this piece of defamatory propaganda from the city of Erech and substituted an 'improved' version of his own.[25] This discovery demonstrates how this Chaldaean, a thorn in the side of the flesh to four successive kings, beginning with Tiglath-pileser III and ending with Sennacherib, had wielded enough effective power to figure so prominently in the book of Kings and in Isa. xxxix.

After the reign of Sargon, who used Calah as his base while founding his new capital Dur-Sharrukin (Khorsabad), the political direction of affairs was transferred to Nineveh, and another chapter could be written describing the impact of that city on the authors of the Old Testament.

Sennacherib (*c.* 705–681 B.C.), Sargon's son and successor, rebuilt the city of Nineveh and erected a building which he named 'The Palace without a Rival'.[26] The ground plan of the so-called SW. Palace was uncovered by Layard, and the walls were lavishly adorned with triumphal reliefs. It is remarkable that the focal point of these reliefs was an inner chamber (XXXVI)[27] depicting the surrender of Lachish which this monarch evidently regarded as the climax of his campaigns, thus inevitably emphasizing his failure to invest Jerusalem. He was murdered 'as he was worshipping in the house of Nisroch his god' (2 Kings xix. 37), probably the temple of Ishtar which was adjacent to the Palace.

Esar-haddon (*c.* 681–669 B.C.) to the end of his life retained a fearful memory of the dread days of uncertainty which ensued after that event, and in the part of his last will and testament referring to his succession nominated Ashurbanipal to be king of Assyria, and Shamash-shum-ukin (*c.* 668–648 B.C.) king of Babylon after him. For this purpose he caused a series of tablets to be inscribed, known as 'The Vassal Treaties' and had copies of them deposited at Calah.[28] The nomination of his sons was accompanied by the enactment of a dramatic ceremony in Ezida, at which the nobles, the army, and various princes of Iran were bidden to

PLATE II

Ivory bed-head, partly restored (Nimrud). The six panels depict warriors and magical trees (84 × 56 cm.)

swear oaths of loyalty to them. Fearful curses were invoked on transgressors of the oath. In this way Calah has reflected the impact which the murder mentioned in the book of Kings made upon the court of Assyria.

The evidence recovered from Nimrud suggests that Esar-haddon was intending to make Calah his capital rather than Nineveh, for he built a new palace on the acropolis which he lined with reliefs, and in the outer town enlarged the southern wing of the great arsenal which he began refacing with magnificent blocks of ashlar masonry.[29]

This building, known as Fort Shalmaneser and referred to by Esar-haddon as the arsenal, was originally built by Shalmaneser III, and was completely excavated for the first time by a series of expeditions conducted by the British School of Archaeology in Iraq between 1957 and 1963. The full account of it has now been published.[30] Here there were traces of occupation from the time of its foundation in the ninth century B.C. until the two successive sacks in 614 and 612 B.C. which brought to an end both Calah and the whole of the Assyrian Empire.

In Fort Shalmaneser, at Nimrud, the greatest collection of ivories ever found has been recovered. These pieces, many of them chryselephantine, superbly carved and of great beauty, were purely ornamental and were for the most part applied as veneer. Some of the panels which had formed bed-heads and chair-backs could be completely reconstituted; they had been dismantled, smashed, and abandoned in the first great sack of 614 B.C., effected by a combination of the Babylonians and the Medes. Calah, then a repository for much ancient treasure, is not specifically mentioned in the Old Testament since it was no longer the capital; it was Nineveh that symbolized the fall of the empire—'Woe to the bloody city!', 'Nineveh is laid waste' (Nahum iii. 1–7). We find perhaps a more direct bearing on Calah in Amos iii. 15—'. . . and the houses of ivory shall perish, and the great houses shall come to an end'; similarly in vi. 4 we have 'those who lie upon beds of ivory, and stretch themselves upon their couches'. How vividly this curse was recalled to our minds when we were excavating the great chamber known as SW. 7, where in the year 613 B.C. a last desperate attempt had been made to reconstitute the royal beds before a second sack, a year later, put an end to all these hopes (Pl. II).[31] That Old

Testament references to ivory houses were not unjustified is borne out by another discovery made on the acropolis in a building known as the 'Acropolis Palace', where one of the walls had been covered with an ivory screen which rose to a height of about $1\frac{1}{2}$ metres above the floor, thus vividly recalling 'the ivory house which he (Ahab) built' (1 Kings xxii. 39).[32]

The latest inscribed ivory among the vast collection of Nimrud fragments is a scarab of the Pharaoh Taharqa whose statues Esar-haddon set up at the Nebi Yunus, the arsenal of Nineveh, in 671 B.C.[33] This is the Tirhakah, king of Ethiopia (2 Kings xix. 9), and doubtless the ivory was acquired after the Assyrian conquest of Egypt; indeed from the seventh century B.C. we have evidence of Egyptian names at Nimrud.

One last example of a connexion with the Old Testament needs recalling: it is an ostracon, inscribed in ink, in Aramaic, with a list of Hebrew and Phoenician names, the only example of the kind discovered at Nimrud. Possibly this was a list of foreign workmen employed by the arsenal in the seventh century B.C.; it is evidence of the mixture of peoples that lived in Calah at the time.[34] Aramaic was becoming the *lingua franca* and the writing of it duplicated Assyrian. This fragment of an inscribed potsherd vividly illustrates the cosmopolitan character of the city at the time and reminds us that, even in the heart of Assyria, Jews were employed by the government.

M. E. L. MALLOWAN

NOTES

1. M. E. L. Mallowan, *Nimrud and its Remains*, 2 vols., illustrated, 1966.

2. It is generally recognized that the genealogies in Genesis are composite and that variant sets of traditions have been registered in chapters v and x; see, for example, Theodore H. Robinson, 'Genesis', *Abingdon Bible Commentary*, 1929, p. 227.

3. On Rehoboth-Ir, see G. Dossin, *Le Muséon* xlvii, 1934, p. 108, for a solution which is by no means convincing; W. F. Albright, *Recent Discoveries in Bible Lands*, 1955, p. 71, suggests that this is not a proper name, but has the meaning of 'open-places'—*piazzas*. On Resen, see *The New Bible Dictionary*, 1962, p. 1085; for these references I am indebted to Professor D. J. Wiseman. Identification with Selamiyah, near Nimrud, a few miles to the north of it, seems unlikely, because no Assyrian remains have been detected there so far; this place was pros-

perous in the medieval period. Ras al-'Ain in north Syria on the upper Khabur is too far distant. Hammam Ali on the west bank of the Tigris between Calah and Nineveh is a possibility.

4. None of these names has any good claim for identification with Calah. In Isa. x. 9 and Amos vi. 2 Calno and Calneh may be read as Kullania, possibly Kullan Köi near Arpad; see *A.J.S.L.* li, 1935, pp. 189 ff.

5. C. J. Gadd, *The Stones of Assyria*, pp. 147 f. with reference to the illustrations.

6. Mallowan, op. cit., p. 598, and pl. 582.

7. Ibid., pls. 577 Gdl and 578 Hamath.

8. Ibid., pp. 57–83, and pl. 27. *Editio princeps* and translation by D. J. Wiseman, *Iraq* xiv, 1952, pp. 24–44.

9. E. A. Speiser, *B.A.S.O.R.* 149, 1958, pp. 17–25, demonstrates the unpopularity of the census both from the evidence of the Old Testament and the Mari texts and from the evidence of ritual precautions that were concurrently taken. Thus, see 2 Sam. xxiv. 10—'And David's heart smote him after that he had numbered the people. And David said unto the Lord, I have sinned greatly in that I have done: . . .' A devastating pestilence followed this census, perhaps because the proper precautions had not been taken. The writing down of a name seems to have been reckoned as rendering a person liable to a call from the Underworld.

10. In the Schweich Lectures delivered to the British Academy in 1955. The printed version is now being prepared.

11. Mallowan, op. cit., pp. 13–19, gives a list of the institutions which supported these expeditions, notably the Metropolitan Museum of Art, New York. The writer has been the over-all director throughout and from 1957 onwards David Oates was the principal Field Director.

12. Ibid., pp. 172 f., and pl. 106.

13. R. D. Barnett and M. Falkner, *The Sculptures of Tiglath-Pileser III*, 1962.

14. Mallowan, op. cit., p. 237, and pl. 194.

15. Ibid., p. 349 n. 16 for a list of these tablets with provenance of each.

16. See for the reference *D.O.T.T.*, pp. 53–58.

17. Quoted from Mallowan, op. cit., p. 239.

18. Ibid., p. 174. These difficult tablets have been admirably published in a series of articles by H. W. F. Saggs, *Iraq* xvii, xviii, xx, xxi, xxv, xxvii.

19. *D.O.T.T.*, pp. 55 ff.

20. Mallowan, op. cit., pp. 406, 602. This tablet fragment, ND. 10082, was found in room NW. 21 situated within a wing of the arsenal which may have been used by the armourers.

21. The sequence of events has been convincingly demonstrated by H. Tadmor, *J.C.S.* xii, 1958, pp. 22–42. For other possible interpretations and references to the relevant texts see *D.O.T.T.*, pp. 58–63.

22. C. J. Gadd, *Iraq* xvi, 1954, pp. 173 f. Translation of this paragraph is quoted from p. 193.

23. Quoted from the Schweich Lectures delivered in 1955 on 'Assyria and the Old Testament'.

24. Mallowan, op. cit., p. 175, and pl. 107.

25. C. J. Gadd, *Iraq* xv, 1953, pp. 123–34.

26. D. D. Luckenbill, *The Annals of Sennacherib* (*O.I.P.* ii, 1924).

27. R. Campbell Thompson and R. W. Hutchinson, *A Century of Exploration at Nineveh*, 1929, plan 3.

28. D. J. Wiseman, *The Vassal Treaties of Esarhaddon*, 1958; Mallowan, op. cit., pp. 241 f.

29. Ibid., pp. 466 f., and pl. 379.

30. Ibid., chs. xvi, xvii.

31. Ibid., pp. 409 f.

32. Ibid., pp. 293 ff., and pl. 264.

33. Ibid., p. 599, and pl. 583.

34. Ibid., p. 407 and n. 54 with reference to J. B. Segal, *Iraq* xix, 1957, p. 139.

BIBLIOGRAPHY

Iraq i–xxviii, 1934–66.

LAYARD, A. H. *The Monuments of Nineveh*, 2 vols., 1849–53.

—— *Nineveh and its Remains*, 2 vols., 1950.

—— *Discoveries in the Ruins of Nineveh and Babylon*, 1853.

MALLOWAN, M. E. L. *Nimrud and its Remains*, 2 vols., 1966.

RASSAM, H. *Assur and the Land of Nimrod*, 1897.

SMITH, G. *Assyrian Discoveries: an account of explorations and discoveries on the site of Nineveh, during 1873 and 1874*, 1875.

THIELE, E. R. *The Mysterious Numbers of the Hebrew Kings*, 1951.

NUZI

Nuzi,[1] modern Yorghan Tepe, about 9 miles south-west of Arrapḫa, modern Kirkuk, in the eastern hill-country of ancient Assyria, was excavated (1925–31) by the American Schools of Oriental Research in Baghdad, first with the Iraq Museum and later with Harvard University, under the direction of E. Chiera, R. H. Pfeiffer, and R. F. S. Starr. The settlement, originating before 3000 B.C., had, c. 2200 B.C., an Akkadian population and was called Gasur, but by 1500 B.C. its name was Nuzi and its population mainly Hurrian. The ruins, including a temple in seven levels, a palace, with some painted rooms, and many private houses, contained pottery and other small objects. Most important, however, were some 4,000 cuneiform tablets[2] dating c. 1500–1400 B.C. and written in Akkadian influenced by Hurrian vocabulary and idioms. These and a few similar tablets from Arrapḫa comprised, besides administrative documents, family archives of juristic character which interest Old Testament students because some of the social customs and situations they record resemble unexpectedly those of Israel, especially in the patriarchal period.

As in Israel, the common people were not without defence against corrupt and venal rulers; several tablets[3] demonstrate the impeachment of the mayor of Nuzi.

A curious legal fiction at Nuzi was nominal 'filial adoption' of a purchaser of land by its seller, presumably to satisfy some obsolescent religious taboo or legal restriction against transfer of land outside the family; modern scholars term this 'sale-adoption'.[4] Israel also, for social and religious reasons, disapproved of and tried to control land alienation (cf. 1 Kings xxi. 3; Isa. v. 8; Mic. ii. 2; Num. xxvii. 7–11, xxxvi. 2–9; Lev. xxv. 23–28).[5] Genuine filial adoption[6] of a stranger, sometimes a slave, by a childless couple to tend them in old age and perform their funeral rites in return for the inheritance, was common in Nuzi,[7] as in Babylonia and Assyria, and although evidently rare in Israel, it is mentioned in Gen. xv. 2 ff., where Abraham contemplates as heir his slave Eliezer. Often in these lands, if there were daughters but no sons, a poor, landless man was, as son-in-law, adopted into sonship, giving his personal services instead of a bride-price and joining his wife's family. Such apparently were the marriages of Moses (Exod. ii. 21, cf. ii. 16, iii. 1), Jarha (1 Chron. ii. 34 f.), and Barzillai (Ezra ii. 61; Neh. vii. 63). Jacob's marriage to Leah and Rachel resembles in some features this (*errebu*) type. It was usually stipulated that if brothers of the wife were subsequently born they should share, ranking preferentially, with the adopted son-in-law, and one Arrapḫa tablet,[8] besides featuring this, echoes in several ways the story of Jacob. It runs as follows:

> Tablet of adoption belonging to Našwi, son of Aršenni. He has adopted Wullu, son of Puḫišenni. As long as Našwi lives, Wullu shall provide food and clothing; when Našwi dies, Wullu shall become heir. If Našwi has a [natural] son, he shall share the estate equally with Wullu, but Našwi's son shall take Našwi's gods. He has also given his daughter Nuḫuya in marriage to Wullu, and if Wullu takes another wife, he shall forfeit the lands and houses of Našwi. Whoever defaults shall pay one mina of silver and one mina of gold. [Names of five witnesses and the scribe follow.]

The parallels with the Old Testament are not exact. In the pastoral setting of the Genesis story written contracts and witnesses are not mentioned, but Jacob, in marrying Laban's daughters, undertook prescribed duties (Gen. xxix. 15–18, 27 f.), and was apparently envisaged as Laban's prospective heir,[9] since no sons of Laban appear in the story until twenty years later (xxxi. 38, 41), when they plot to have Jacob sent away (xxxi. 1 ff.). Foreseeing this, Jacob had arranged his own departure with a suitable recompense from the estate, but his wives protest about Laban—'he hath sold us, and hath also quite devoured our money', using an idiom (*akālu kaspa*) found often in Akkadian texts and sometimes at Nuzi,[10] and referring here probably to the bride-price frequently set aside, in whole or in part, at Nuzi and elsewhere, as a reserve for the bride in case of widowhood or divorce.[11]

The reference in the Arrapḫa tablet to Našwi's 'gods', probably portable figurines, assigned in preference to a natural son, is paralleled where Rachel (Gen. xxxi. 34 f.) appropriates her father's 'gods' (xxxi. 30, 32; called 'teraphim' in verses 19, 34), obviously not from sentimental reasons, but probably to safeguard her husband's future leadership of the family. Other Nuzi texts[12] also refer to such family 'gods', sometimes[13] debarring from access to them a son by 'sale-adoption'. No Babylonian or Assyrian contract has been found to mention them, so this is a unique link between Nuzi and the patriarchs. A further parallel is Laban's parting injunction to Jacob (Gen. xxxi. 50) and Našwi's similar requirement of Wullu not to take another wife; this is quite a common feature in marriage contracts of Nuzi,[14] as of Babylonia and Assyria.

Another Nuzi text,[15] besides instancing adoption of a son-in-law as prospective heir, with reservation in case of a subsequent natural son, and the prohibition of an additional wife, provides further links with the patriarchal stories, as the following excerpts show:

> Tablet of adoption belonging to [Zike], son of Akkuya. He has given his son Šennima for adoption to Šuriḫi-ilu. . . . If Šuriḫi-ilu has a [natural] son, he as principal son shall take a double share; Šennima shall then be next in order and take his due share. As long as Šuriḫi-ilu lives, Šennima shall serve him; when Šuriḫi-ilu dies, Šennima shall become heir. Kelimninu has been given in marriage to Šennima. If Kelimninu has children, Šennima shall not take another wife; but if Kelimninu does not bear children, Kelimninu shall acquire a woman of the land of Lullu for marriage to Šennima and Kelimninu may not send away the offspring. . . . Yalampa is given as handmaid to Kelimninu. . . .

This text recalls Gen. xvi. 1 ff. where the childless Sarai gives her handmaid Hagar to Abraham and adopts the offspring, Ishmael, as her own. Similarly, Rachel and Leah relinquished their handmaids Bilhah and Zilpah as concubines to Jacob and legitimized their children (Gen. xxx. 4, 9). When Sarah, after the birth of her natural son, Isaac, subsequently drove out Ishmael (Gen. xxi. 10), she was contravening the custom of Nuzi, as well as of Babylonia and probably also of Assyria. The practice of presenting a bride with a handmaid is found again in the case of Rebekah (Gen. xxiv. 61); perhaps Hagar and Abigail's five handmaids (1 Sam. xxv. 42) were similarly acquired. Concubinage, common in Nuzi, Babylonia, and Assyria, continued in Israel beyond patriarchal times (Judges xix. 9; 2 Sam. iii. 7). Polygamy, permitted in Nuzi and Assyria, but abnormal in Babylonia, was practised in the patriarchal period by Jacob, Lamech (Gen. iv. 23), and Esau (Gen. xxviii. 9); later, except in the case of kings (1 Kings xi. 3; 2 Chron. xi. 21; Gideon imitated royal custom, Judges viii. 30), it is mentioned

only of Elkanah (1 Sam. i. 2), but Deut. xxi. 15 ff. suggests that it
was not uncommon.

Another parallel to Zike's document is the inheritance of a
double share by the principal son, normally the eldest natural son,
as is definitely prescribed in Deut. xxi. 15 ff. This was usual in
Nuzi[16] and Assyria but not in Babylonia. An eldest son in Israel
might, however, be demoted like Reuben (Gen. xlix. 3 f.) and
Shimri (1 Chron. xxvi. 10); so also at Nuzi.[17]

The Old Testament cites instances of a father's death-bed
blessing and last wishes (Gen. xxvii, xlviii. 15 f., 20, xlix; 1 Kings ii.
1–9, cf. i. 1–37); such testamentary dispositions, written or oral,
were common in the ancient Near East; an example is found in a
Nuzi text,[18] part of which states:

> Tarmiya spoke thus before the judges: 'My father Ḫuya was ill and
> lay in bed: then my father seized my hand and said to me: "My other
> sons, being older, have acquired wives but you have not acquired a
> wife, so I give you herewith Ṣululi-Ištar as your wife".' . . . The wit-
> nesses of [Tarmiya] were examined before the judges and the judges
> spoke to Šukriya and Kulaḫupi—'Go and take the oath of the gods
> against the witnesses of Tarmiya.' Šukriya and Kulaḫupi shrank from
> the gods, so Tarmiya won in the lawsuit and the judges assigned the
> female slave, Ṣululi-Ištar, to Tarmiya. . . .

This document shows the judicial respect for a verbal death-bed
testament,[19] just as Isaac, Rebekah, Jacob, and Esau all regarded
Isaac's death-bed pronouncements as binding (cf. Gen. xxvii,
especially verse 33). The juridical use of an oath, characteristic
also of Babylonia and Assyria, is found in Gen. xxiv. 3, xxvi. 28;
Exod. xxii. 11; 1 Sam. xiv. 24; Neh. v. 12; while Deut. xxi. 1–10
reinforces it by the symbolic breaking of an animal's neck. An
ordealistic significance is attached in the Nuzi text[20] to taking the
oath 'before the gods', presumably before divine images, as in
Exod. xxii. 7 f. (R.V. 8 f.: 'before God', originally 'before the gods'
as the plural verb shows); 1 Kings viii. 31 f. ('before thine altar in
this house'); cf. also Exod. xxi. 6, where a man engages himself
before God to be a slave. Another Nuzi,[21] and Babylonian,[22]
ordeal was to plunge in a river; this was virtually impracticable
in Palestine, but Num. v. 16–31 prescribes a water-drinking
ordeal.

Many scholars conjecture a parallel to Esau's sale of his birthright (Gen. xxv. 33) in a Nuzi tablet[23] where a man sells his brother an orchard, or garden, for three sheep; this apparently unequal transaction may conceal a birthright exchange. Irregular transactions may have sometimes been legalized at Nuzi by including a pair of shoes,[24] since one document[25] transfers to a woman, as a dowry, land in exchange for animals, together with a pair of shoes and a garment; another[26] arranges the sale of a girl for a garment and a pair of shoes. The references in Amos ii. 6, viii. 6 to buying or selling the poor 'for a pair of shoes' may signify unlawful transactions, but Ruth iv. 7 cites an early, antiquated Hebrew custom of attesting a bargain by handing over a shoe, and frequently at Nuzi a sale of land is confirmed by the seller lifting his own foot and placing the buyer's foot on the soil;[27] cf. also Ps. lx. 10, R.V. 8, cviii. 10, R.V. 9—'upon Edom will I cast my shoe' (a token of appropriation). A different symbolic usage is implied in Deut. xxv. 9 f., where a rejected widow removes judicially her brother-in-law's shoe.

Many Nuzi tablets[28] state that they were written 'in the gate' (of a town or temple, sometimes named); this accords with the early Hebrew practice of conducting legal business in the town gate, a frequented place where witnesses were available (for example, Gen. xxiii. 17 f.; Ruth iv. 1–11). Collective public responsibility for a crime, exemplified, for example, in Gen. xxxiv and Deut. xxi. 1–9, appears also at Nuzi.[29] As in Israel (Num. xxvi. 55 f.; Joshua xviii. 2–10; Ps. xvi. 6) land was sometimes apportioned by lot.[30] It has been suggested[31] that the *kašku*-portion of the crop of a field, reserved for the mortgager in some Nuzi mortgage (*titennūtu*) contracts, may have some ideological relationship to the 'corner' (*pē'āh*) of the field reserved for the poor in Israel (Lev. xix. 9 f., xxiii. 22).

Sometimes at Nuzi a brother arranged for his sister's marriage,[32] her father presumably being deceased. This may be a relic of primitive fratriarchal family organization, but both in Nuzi and in Israel the family was fundamentally patriarchal.[33] Rebekah's marriage was arranged by her brother Bethuel (Gen. xxiv. 24–53); the only reference to her father (verse 50) is probably a later gloss; the phrase 'her mother's house' (verse 28) implies that her father was dead. In Gen. xxxiv Dinah's brothers share with her father in planning her marriage (verses 11, 13). In 1 Sam. xx. 29 David's

brother may be exercising a fratriarchal right in summoning to a
family sacrifice.

In Nuzi, as in Israel (Exod. xxi. 7–11), a bride was sometimes
acquired by a man for optional marriage to himself or to one or
other of his sons;[34] one tablet enjoins that a certain woman may
be remarried ten times.[35] Exod. xxi. 9 prescribes that such a bride
must be treated 'after the manner of daughters'; some Nuzi tablets
require that she shall be treated 'like a daughter of Arrapḫa';[36] an
Assyrian contract has 'like his daughter, an Assyrian'. In the Old
Testament (cf. Ezek. xvi. 39; Hos. ii. 3) an unfaithful wife could
be driven naked from her house; some Nuzi texts[37] prescribe this
punishment for a widow who remarries. At Nuzi, and in Assyria,
the finger,[38] in Israel the hand, of a woman was cut off if she
seized a man's sexual organ in a brawl (Deut. xxv. 11 f.).

Some Nuzi texts designate by the term *ḫapiru* (or *ḫabiru*?)[39]
certain foreigners, from Asshur, Akkad, or elsewhere, usually with
Akkadian, rarely Hurrian, names, who accepted voluntary servitude or labour with a private individual or with the state. Whatever
the original sense of the term, at Nuzi it seems virtually to mean
'destitute immigrant'. It recalls the references to 'Hebrew' slaves
in Exod. xxi. 1–6; Deut. xv. 12–18; Jer. xxxiv. 9, 14, and the
'Hebrews', apparently mercenaries, in the service of the Philistines (1 Sam. xiv. 21). In the Old Testament the term 'Hebrew'
is sometimes applied, chiefly by foreigners, to Israelites, including
the patriarchs (for example, Abraham, Gen. xiv. 13; Joseph, Gen.
xxxix. 14, cf. xl. 15; Exod. i. 15.). In Israel (cf. Lev. xxv. 39, 47),
as at Nuzi, ordinary citizens sometimes sold themselves or their
children into temporary servitude for loans of money or for other
reasons,[40] but Israelite law, like Babylonian, prescribed a maximum period for such servitude (Lev. xxv. 10; Deut. xv. 12). Some
slaves at Nuzi, as in Babylonia, were tattooed on the forehead;[41]
in Israel a slave's ear was sometimes pierced (Exod. xxi. 6; Deut.
xv. 17).

Many Nuzi personal names, Semitic or other, resemble phonetically names found in the Old Testament, either Israelite[42] or non-
Israelite.[43] Some Nuzi terms[44] and idioms[45] recall Hebrew ones;
the Hebrew word for 'breastplate' (*širyōn*) seems to be a loan-word
from Hurrian *zariam*, a kind of leather equipment for warriors
and horses, perhaps body-armour.[46] Nuzi texts sometimes cast

light on obscure Old Testament passages.[47] The name Naḫmuliel in the Hurrian story of the Flood, a fragment of which was found at Boğazköy, may be the prototype of the Hebrew Noah.[48]

The Nuzi—especially as distinguished from other Mesopotamian—parallels to Israelite, particularly patriarchal, customs suggest the possibility of cultural and other connexions between early Israel and the Hurrians. The Hurrians were a non-Semitic, non-Indo-European people of agglutinative speech who, in the early third millennium B.C. overflowed from their home in the region of Lake Van in Armenia southwards and westwards, establishing small isolated groups of peaceful settlers as far apart as Nippur in central Babylonia by 2300 B.C., and Kanesh in Cappadocia by 2000 B.C. In the eighteenth century B.C. Hurrian raiding parties clashed with Šamši-Adad of Assyria and Zimrilim of Mari. Military expansion soon after 1700 B.C., motivated probably by Indo-Iranian pressure from the east, settled Hurrians in large numbers in Alalakh by 1650 B.C. and in Ugarit and Qatna by 1500 B.C. In upper Mesopotamia they founded before 1500 B.C. in the valley of the Khabur the state of Mitanni, ruled by a small caste of Indo-Iranian chariot warriors called *mariannu*. By 1450 B.C. Mitanni was the leading Mesopotamian power, controlling even Assyria for a time, and including Nuzi and Arrapḫa in its jurisdiction. Its strength was weakened by Tuthmosis III of Egypt (*c.* 1504–1450 B.C.) but it maintained friendly relations by treaties and royal intermarriages with Tuthmosis IV, Amenophis III, and Amenophis IV, acting as a counterbalance to Assyria, Babylonia, and the Hittites, until the growing might of Suppiluliumas, the Hittite king, led to internal dissensions, and *c.* 1350 B.C. Mitanni was absorbed into the Hittite empire. Hurrian power thereafter centred in Urartu, around Lake Van, until its virtual extinction by Assyria in the seventh century B.C.

The Hurrians mediated Assyro-Babylonian culture to the Hittites and influenced Assyrian art and architecture. The longest extant Hurrian text is a Tell el-Amarna letter,[49] but little has survived of their literature. The Mitannian pantheon contained Assyrian, Hittite, Iranian, and Hurrian deities, but almost nothing is known of the cult.

Hurrian penetration into Palestine apparently never occurred on an organized scale, but infiltration of small independent groups took place during the second millennium B.C., sometimes under Indo-Iranian leadership. Several Tell el-Amarna letters[50] (fourteenth century B.C.) were written by a governor of Jerusalem whose name, conventionally read as Abdi-ḫepa, means 'servant of Ḫepa', and Ḫepa was the Hurrian mother-goddess. The El-Amarna letters also locate in Palestine several persons with Indo-Iranian names,[51] such as Biridašwa of Yenoam, Biridiya of Megiddo, Šuwardata of Keilah(?), and Yašdata, probably of Taanach. Cuneiform documents of the same period found at Taanach (Tell Taʿannak)[52] cite Hurrian names; others from Shechem[53] contain foreign names that may be Hurrian.

For some time after the expulsion of the Hyksos invaders from Egypt (c. 1550 B.C.) the Egyptians called Syria and Palestine Ḫor (ḫr), and since the Hyksos included Semites and non-Semites it is conjectured that this name is derived from Hurrian, or partly Hurrian, settlements in these lands.[54] The name of the Old Testament Horites (Hebrew ḥrym), formerly explained by scholars as meaning 'cave-dwellers', is phonetically the Hebrew equivalent for Hurrians. The Horites are described in Gen. xiv. 6 as resident in Seir (Edom) as early as the time of Abraham, and Deut. ii. 12, 22 states that they were expelled from there by the Edomite descendants of Esau. It is quite likely that some Hurrians settled in Edom, and some of the Horite personal names preserved in the Old Testament (Gen. xxxvi. 20–39; cf. 1 Chron. i. 38–53) seem to be of Hurrian origin.[55]

The names of two other Palestinian peoples, the Hittites (ḥtym) and the Hivites (ḥwym) are, however, in Hebrew so similar to that of the Horites (ḥrym) that interchange of the names has sometimes occurred through scribal error. Zibeon is called in Gen. xxxvi. 2 a Hivite, but in xxxvi. 20 a Horite. In Gen. xxxiv. 2 and Joshua ix. 7, where the Hebrew text mentions Hivites, the LXX calls them Horites; on the other hand, where the LXX of Isa. xvii. 9 speaks of Hivites, the Hebrew text probably originally read Horites (ḥrym now corrupted to the meaningless ḥrš). In Joshua xi. 3, where the Hebrew text mentions 'the Hittites . . . and the Hivites under Hermon', the LXX reads 'the Hivites . . . and the Hittites under Hermon'.

In view of the Tell el-Amarna and parallel evidence of Hurrians in Palestine, it is curious that the Old Testament never includes

Hurrians, or Horites, in the lists of Palestinian peoples conquered by the Israelite invaders; it is also noticeable that the Hittites, frequently mentioned in such lists, are not known from any extra-biblical source, including their own records, to have ever settled in Palestine.[56] Probably, therefore, the Old Testament writers sometimes use the term Hittite vaguely as a general designation for northern non-Semitic immigrants, including, doubtless, Hurrians. The term is used in a more strictly ethnic, or rather political, sense in 1 Kings x. 29, xi. 1 and 2 Kings vii. 6 to denote neo-Hittite peoples of the ninth century B.C. outside Palestine. Abraham's purchase of the field of Machpelah at Mamre (Hebron) from 'Ephron the Hittite' (Gen. xxiii) seems to have followed Hittite legal procedure,[57] so perhaps Hittites had settled there, but several personal names from that region in the time of Joshua (Joshua xv. 14: Anak, Ahiman, Sheshai, Talmai) have exact affinities with Hurrian names,[58] whereas no names of Hittite or proto-Hittite (Hattic) type have been certainly identified in the Old Testament.[59]

The frequent mention of Hivites in Old Testament lists of conquered peoples suggests a numerous and widespread national group. They are located specifically at Shechem (Gen. xxxiv. 2), Gibeon (Joshua ix. 7, xi. 19), Mount Lebanon (Judges iii. 3), and Hermon (Joshua xi. 3), and apparently also in north or central Palestine (cf. 2 Sam. xxiv. 7), which are all places where remnants of Hurrian invaders, as well as other peoples, could readily have settled; Hurrian names were actually found in cuneiform documents at Shechem. Speiser has suggested[60] that in Judges ix the tension between Abimelech and the Shechemites had Hurrian racial implications because his mother was a Shechemite while his father was a Semite (Judges ix. 1). Verse 28 stresses that the Shechemites were descendants of Hamor who is described in Gen. xxxiv. 2 as a Hivite (LXX Horite), and Gen. xxxiv. 14 ff. shows that the Shechemites of that period were uncircumcised and so probably not Semites. Since Hivites are unheard of outside the Old Testament, their equation with Hurrians, or a particular group of Hurrians, seems plausible. Speiser[61] regards the name 'Hivites' as probably an invention of later Hebrew writers to distinguish the (Palestinian) Hurrites from the (non-Hurrian) Horites of Edom; this may be so, even if the Horites were also Hurrians.

Other names of Palestinian conquered peoples may also refer

G

to Hurrians. One of the Tell el-Amarna letters[62] mentions an envoy of the Hurrians, not necessarily a Hurrian, named Perizzi. The name Girgashite has been tentatively connected with a people called by the Hittites Qaraqiša,[63] whose locality and race are unidentified. The Jebusites, who inhabited Jerusalem at the time of King David, may have been Hurrians;[64] an earlier Jerusalem governor, Abdi-ḫepa, bore a Hurrian name, and the name of Araunah 'the Jebusite' (2 Sam. xxiv. 16 ff.), also given as Ornan (1 Chron. xxi. 15 ff.), has no apparent Semitic affinities, but Speiser would connect it with a Hurrian word meaning 'ruler' which often occurs in Hurrian personal names.[65] Perhaps the name of Uriah 'the Hittite', whose home was apparently in Jerusalem (2 Sam. xi. 1 ff., etc.), is also to be connected with this word. The Avvim (ʿwym), a people expelled from Gaza by the Philistines (Deut. ii. 23), have been doubtfully associated with the Hurrian personal name Ḫu(w)ya.[66]

There is, however, probably no need to postulate a direct influence of Hurrian communities on Israelite law and custom, whether in Palestine or in Mesopotamia. It is, especially on a large scale, unlikely. Firstly, the customs of Nuzi, in so far as they differ from those of the Assyrians and Babylonians, need not be exclusively or even characteristically Hurrian but could have been borrowed from, or shared with, Semitic neighbours, since it is known that there was contact at least as early as 1700 B.C. between north-western Semites ('Amorites') and Hurrians both in Mesopotamia and in eastern Assyria,[67] and part of the fifteenth-century population of Nuzi was ḫapiru. Secondly, in the Hyksos invasions, Hurrians and Semitic 'Amorites' probably entered Palestine together, as they certainly did when, in the period of the Tell el-Amarna letters, they seized control of some Palestinian towns. It is reasonable to conclude, therefore, that, before and during the period of the Israelite conquest, many customs of Mesopotamian origin, often similar to those of Nuzi, were observed in various urban centres of Syria and so called 'Canaanite' towns of Palestine. There is no custom common to Nuzi and Israel of which this might not be true. Thirdly, whether the 'Hebrew' patriarchs were caravan traders[68] or semi-nomadic pastoral sheikhs or both, it is understandable that they would conform in some respects to similar patterns. We need not wonder, then, that both the patriarchal narratives and the Book of the Covenant often exhibit customs and phraseology found also at Nuzi, and in Assyria and Babylonia. The Nuzi documents do not mention any Old Testament incident or personage, nor do they indicate with certainty that any of Israel's ancestors ever lived in or visited Mesopotamia.[69] Their fifteenth-century provenance cannot accurately date patriarchal traditions since the customs they portray may have originated much earlier and may have persisted in Palestine until the monarchical period. They reveal, however, that the social customs, much of the terminology, and many of the personal names in the Pentateuch and elsewhere in the Old Testament were those current in parts of the Near East during the second millennium B.C., and to that extent they validate Israelite tradition. They also, by their wealth of detailed cases and individual situations, greatly widen and deepen our insight into the daily life and the social and personal problems of the Israelites and their neighbours in Mesopotamia, Syria, and Palestine.

C. J. MULLO WEIR

NOTES

1. Or possibly Nuzu or Nuza; cf. E. A. Speiser, *J.A.O.S.* lxxv, 1955, pp. 52 ff.

2. Cited here as G, Hv, Hix, JEN, or SMN, followed by a number; cf. the Bibliography.

3. Cf. *A.A.S.O.R.* xvi, 1936, pp. 59–75.

4. e.g. G. nos. 11, 34, 51; *J.A.O.S.* xlvii, 1927, p. 37 (JEN 1), 39 (JEN 52); *A.A.S.O.R.* xvi, 1936, pp. 82 ff.

5. Cf. H. Lewy, *Orient.* xi, 1942, pp. 1 ff., 209 ff., 297 ff. On land-tenure in the Old Testament, cf. K. H. Henrey, *P.E.F.Q.S.* 1954, pp. 5 ff.

6. On all types of adoption at Nuzi, cf. E.-M. Cassin, *L'adoption à Nuzi*, 1938; on adoption in Israel, cf. S. I. Feigin, *J.B.L.* i, 1931, pp. 186 ff.

7. e.g. G 9; *A.A.S.O.R.* x, 1930, p. 30 (Hv 60); *J.A.O.S.* xlvii, 1927, p. 40 (JEN 59).

8. G 51 (*A.N.E.T.*, pp. 219 f.).

9. His adoption as a son would explain Laban's claim to be owner of Jacob's family and property (Gen. xxxi. 43; cf. xxix. 19—'Abide with me').

10. Cf. *A.A.S.O.R.* x, 1930, p. 64 (Hv 11); C. H. Gordon, *Z.A.* xliii, 1935, p. 158 n.

11. On marriage gifts in Nuzi and Israel, cf. I. Mendelsohn, *B.A.* xi, 1948, 3, pp. 26–29.

12. Cf. G 5 (a redraft of Našwi's will); M. Greenberg, *J.B.L.* lxxxi, 1962, pp. 239 ff.

13. JEN 89, 216.

14. Cf. *A.A.S.O.R.* x, 1930, p. 60 (Hv 80), xvi, 1936, p. 105 (SMN 768); *Anal. Or.* xii, 1935, pp. 171 f. (Hix 24).

15. Hv 67 (*A.N.E.T.*, p. 220).

16. Cf. G 5.

17. Cf. *A.A.S.O.R.* x, 1930, p. 39 (Hv 21).

18. SMN 2134 (*A.N.E.T.*, p. 220).

19. Cf. E. A. Speiser, *J.B.L.* lxxiv, 1955, pp. 252 ff.; he refers also to Hix 34.

20. Cf. also G nos. 27, 28, 35; *A.A.S.O.R.* xvi, 1936, p. 119 (SMN 2027); *Iraq* vii, 1940, pp. 132 ff.

21. Cf. *A.A.S.O.R.* xvi, 1936, pp. 119 (SMN 1110), 120 (SMN 251); A. E. Draffkorn, *J.B.L.* lxxvi, 1957, pp. 216 ff.

22. Cf. Codex Hammurabi, Sections 2 and 132.

23. JEN 204 (Cassin, op. cit., p. 230).

24. Cf. E. A. Speiser, *B.A.S.O.R.* 77, 1940, pp. 15 ff.

25. *A.A.S.O.R.* x, 1930, p. 66 (Hv 76).

26. Ibid., p. 63 (Hv 17).

27. Cf. E. R. Lacheman, *J.B.L.* lvi, 1937, 53 ff.; he cites Hv 58, etc.

28. e.g. G nos. 27–30, 48–51; *A.A.S.O.R.* x, 1930, 63 (Hv 26); cf. E. A. Speiser, *B.A.S.O.R.* 144, 1956, pp. 20 ff.

29. Cf. C. H. Gordon, *R.A.* xxxiii, 1936, pp. 1 ff.; *B.A.* iii, 1940, p. 11. He cites JEN 125; cf. also JEN 337.

30. Cf. E. A. Speiser, *J.A.O.S.* lv, 1935, pp. 439 f.: at Nuzi apparently by shaking arrows out of a quiver (JEN 196). Cf. Ezek. xxi. 21.

31. Cf. E. A. Speiser, *J.A.O.S.* lii, 1932, pp. 365 f.

32. Cf. *A.A.S.O.R.* x, 1930, pp. 58 (Hv 79), 59 (Hv 80), 61 (Hv 25), xvi, p. 106 (SMN 768).

33. Cf. C. H. Gordon, *J.B.L.* liv, 1935, pp. 223–31.

34. e.g. *A.A.S.O.R.* x, 1930, pp. 58 (Hv 79), 60 (Hv 80).

35. Ibid. xvi, 1936, p. 84 (SMN 2016).

36. Ibid., p. 96 (SMN 2037); see also G 12. Cf. Gen. xxxi. 15 (Laban's daughters)—'Are we not counted of him strangers?'

37. Ibid. x, 1930, p. 50 (Hv 71); cf. also JEN 444.

38. Cf. C. H. Gordon, *J.P.O.S.* xv, 1935, p. 32 (Hv 43).

39. e.g. JEN 452, 459 (*A.N.E.T.*, p. 220); cf. J. Lewy, *H.U.C.A.* xiv, 1939, pp. 587 ff.

40. Cf. *A.A.S.O.R.* xvi, 1936, pp. 109 f. (ten years, SMN 365), 112 (twenty years, SMN 2089), 110 f. (a son for five years, SMN 2082, 2078).

41. Cf. E.-M. Cassin, *R.A.* lvi, 1962, pp. 57–80.

42. Cf. J. Lewy, *R.E.S.* 1938, pp. 49–75; H. L. Ginsberg and B. Maisler, *J.P.O.S.* xiv, 1934, pp. 258–65.

43. e.g. Toi (king of Hamath, 2 Sam. viii. 9 f.), Arioch (Gen. xiv. 9),

Shamgar (Judges iii. 31); cf. *R.A.* xxiii, 1926, pp. 73 (G 53), 80 (G 31, etc.; G 28, etc.).

44. e.g. *ḫupšu* (Hebrew *ḥopšī*, with a slightly different meaning); cf. E. R. Lacheman, *B.A.S.O.R.* 86, 1942, pp. 36 f.

45. Cf. E. A. Speiser, ibid. 72, 1938, pp. 15 ff., on 1 Sam. i. 24.

46. Cf. F. R. Kraus, *V.T.* viii, 1958, pp. 107 f.

47. Cf. O. Eissfeldt, *A.P.A.W.* cv. 6, 1960, on 1 Sam. xxv. 29 and Song iv. 2.

48. Cf. E. A. Speiser, *Mesopotamian Origins*, 1930, pp. 160 f.

49. *E.A.* 31.

50. Ibid. 280, 282, 285–90.

51. Cf. *C.A.H.* ii, 1924, p. 331. Widia, of Ashkelon, and Tadua, seem to be Indo-Iranian or Hurrian names.

52. Cf. W. F. Albright, *B.A.S.O.R.* 94, 1944, pp. 12–27.

53. Cf. ibid. 86, 1942, pp. 28–31.

54. Cf. E. A. Speiser, *A.A.S.O.R.* xiii, 1933, p. 27.

55. e.g. Dishon and Dishan (Gen. xxxvi. 20 f.); cf. Daysenni and Taysenni (*R.A.* xxiii, 1926, pp. 74, 81); Horite names are also found in Judah and the Negeb (cf. 1 Chron. ii) where Hurrian settlements might be expected; cf. H. L. Ginsberg and B. Maisler, *J.P.O.S.* xiv, 1934, pp. 243–65.

56. But the eighth-century annals of Sargon II of Assyria call the people of Ashdod Hittites (*A.N.E.T.*, pp. 286 f.).

57. Cf. M. R. Lehmann, *B.A.S.O.R.* 129, 1953, pp. 15–18.

58. Cf. R. de Vaux, *R.B.* lv, 1948, p. 326, n. 1. Hebron was an ancient centre of Anakim (Joshua xi. 21, xiv. 15).

59. But Hittites are distinguished from Hivites in Gen. xxxvi. 2 and Exod. xxiii. 28; cf. also Gen. x. 15 ff. Some at least of the 'Hittite' names in Gen. xxvi. 34, xxxvi. 2, appear to be Semitic.

60. *I.D.B.* ii, 1962, p. 665.

61. Ibid., p. 645.

62. *E.A.* 28; cf. 27.

63. Cf. W. F. Albright, *J.P.O.S.* xv, 1935, p. 189.

64. Ezek. xvi. 3, 45, claims a Hittite stratum in early Jerusalem.

65. *ewri* and *erwi* (Ugaritic *'wrn*); cf. E. A. Speiser, *A.A.S.O.R.* xx, 1941, p. 218. 2 Sam. xxiv. 16 spells the name *ḥ'wrnh*; verse 18 has *'rnyh*.

66. Cf. *A.A.S.O.R.* xiii, 1933, p. 30, n. 67. There was also a town *'wym* near Beth-el (Joshua xviii. 23).

67. Cf. J. Laessøe, *People of Ancient Assyria*, 1963, p. 147, n. 2.

68. Cf. C. H. Gordon, *J.N.E.S.* xvii, 1958, pp. 28 ff.; W. F. Albright, *B.A.S.O.R.* 163, 1961, pp. 36–54.

69. Cf. M. Noth, *V.T. Supp.* vii, 1960, pp. 270 f.

BIBLIOGRAPHY

i. *Excavations*

STARR, R. F. S. *Nuzi. Report on the Excavations at Yorghan Tepa near Kirkuk, Iraq,* i, 1939, Text; ii, 1937, Plates and Plans.

ii. *Cuneiform Texts*

CHIERA, E., *et al. American Schools of Oriental Research. Joint Expedition with the Iraq Museum at Nuzi*, i–vi, 1927–39. (Cited as JEN.)

—— *Harvard Semitic Series*, 1929–62 (continuing), v, ix, x, xiii–xvi, xix (sometimes cited as *Excavations at Nuzi*, i–viii). (Vols. v and ix, which are of special interest to Old Testament students, are cited as Hv and Hix.)

GADD, C. J. 'Tablets from Kirkuk', *R.A.* xxiii, 1926, pp. 49–161. (Cited as G.) Other texts are cited as SMN (Harvard University Semitic Museum, Nuzi Section).

iii. *Transliterations and Translations*

CASSIN, E.-M. *L'adoption à Nuzi*, 1938.

CHIERA, E., and SPEISER, E. A., 'Selected "Kirkuk documents" ', *J.A.O.S.* xlvii, 1927, pp. 36–60.

GORDON, C. H. 'Nuzi tablets relating to women', *Anal. Or.* xii, 1935, pp. 163–82.

—— 'Fifteen Nuzi documents relating to slaves', *Le Muséon*, xviii, 1935, pp. 113–32.

PFEIFFER, R. H., and SPEISER, E. A., 'One hundred new selected Nuzi texts', *A.A.S.O.R.* xvi, 1936.

SAARISALO, A. 'New Kirkuk documents relating to slaves', *Stud. Or.* v, no. 3, 1934.

SPEISER, E. A. 'New Kirkuk documents relating to family laws', *A.A.S.O.R.* x, 1930, pp. 1–73.

—— 'New Kirkuk documents relating to security transactions', *J.A.O.S.* lii, 1932, pp. 350–67, liii, 1933, pp. 24–46.

iv. *The Hurrians*

LAESSØE, J. *People of Ancient Assyria, their Inscriptions and Correspondence* (E.Tr. F. S. Leigh-Browne), 1963.

O'CALLAGHAN, R. T. 'Aram Naharaim', *Anal. Or.* xxvi, 1948.

SPEISER, E. A. 'Introduction to Hurrian', *A.A.S.O.R.* xx, 1941.

v. *General*

DE VAUX, R. 'Les Patriarches hébreux et les découvertes modernes', *R.B.* lvi, 1949, pp. 22–36.

GORDON, C. H. 'Biblical Customs and the Nuzi tablets', *B.A.* iii, 1940, pp. 1–12.

ROWLEY, H. H. 'The Patriarchal Age', *B.J.R.L.* xxxii, 1949–50, pp. 48–79.

SPEISER, E. A. 'Nuzi', *I.D.B.* iii, 1962, pp. 573 f.

—— 'Ethnic movements in the Near East in the second millennium B.C.', *A.A.S.O.R.* xiii, 1933, 13–54.

TOURNAY, R.-J. 'Nouzi', *Dict. de la Bible* (ed. L. Pirot, A. Robert, H. Cazelles), *Supp. vi*, 1960, pp. 646–74 (with bibliography).

UR

ONE of the oldest and most revered cities of ancient Babylonia, Ur had a history extending over more than two millennia, continuing a pre-history probably as long;[1] its life ended in an age of gradual but finally completed disappearance some time between the fourth century B.C.[2] and the beginning of our era. Even after that it enjoyed a modest survival in Jewish and Christian tradition thanks to the repute of being the birthplace of Abraham. It has always been physically marked by the greatest extant monument of antiquity that its country can boast, the still-impressive brick tower raised by the city's most powerful dynasty. Until the middle of last century this pile had been only the wonder of passing travellers,[3] for it was distinguished from a thousand similar tells in the Near East by being clearly the ruin of a single building, not the mere accumulated debris of many generations. The tradition was not associated with the standing monument until the latter, Tell el-Muḳayyar, was identified as marking the site of Ur. This discovery was made, after 1856, by H. C. Rawlinson,[4] who was by that time able to read the inscriptions on bricks and foundation records brought from the ruin; the immediate source was a foundation text[5] of Nabonidus, copies[6] of which had been found at the corners of the tower.

The site of Ur is in Lower Iraq, more than 6 miles from the right bank of the Euphrates in its present course, and about an equal distance from the modern Turkish foundation of Naṣiriyyah;[7] its geographical position[8] is given as approximately lat. 31° N. and long. 46° E. Ancient Ur was not one of the most extensive cities of its period. The greatest length of the ruins is about 1,200 metres, their breadth about 675 metres.[9] Estimates of the population, which doubtless varied greatly in times of prosperity or decay, must be hazardous—an average of 24,000 has been deduced[10] from density of housing in the domestic quarter.

Modern exploration of Ur began with the visit of W. K. Loftus[11] in 1850, on his way to Warka. The impulse had been given by the sensational discoveries of Botta and Layard in Assyria, and the first work was carried out in 1853–4 by J. E. Taylor, then British Vice-Consul at Baṣrah. He confined himself[12] mostly to the ziggurat and to a prominent ruin south-east of this, afterwards revealed to be the important state building called É-dubla-maḫ;[13] he also explored graves in a 'tomb-mound',[14] afterwards found to be of the Kassite and later periods. 'Múgeyer', when Taylor was excavating, was still not known to be Ur, but, despite this interesting revelation soon made, the lack of monumental finds and the difficulty of access caused the southern Babylonian sites to be generally avoided, and nothing more was done at Ur until towards the end of the First World War, when the British Museum was able to resume the long-neglected exploration.

Its first representative was R. C. Thompson who made a few soundings in 1918 before passing on to Eridu, where his work was of more importance.[15] Shortly afterwards H. R. Hall not only made certain discoveries at Ur itself,[16] both upon the ziggurat and in buildings and tombs nearby, but observed and excavated the little mound called Al-'Ubaid,[17] 4 miles from the main site. Here he found the remains of an isolated temple which had existed from pre-historic times down to the 'classical' Sumerian (Third Early Dynastic) Period (c. 2600–2370 B.C.). It was here too that, apart from the temple itself and its remarkable decorations, the first inscriptional evidence was later found of the First Dynasty of Ur,[18] already known from the Sumerian king-list, and this opened a new perspective into an era of Babylonian history hitherto regarded as semi-legendary, revealing that, on the contrary, it belonged to a high civilization already well known from discoveries elsewhere.

In 1922 began the celebrated series of excavations[19] conducted jointly by the British Museum and the University Museum of Pennsylvania, and directed from the first by C. L. Woolley; these continued every year until 1934. Part of the work in one season was devoted to continuing the excavation of Al-'Ubaid,[20] but otherwise attention was almost wholly confined to Ur itself, where discoveries were made so numerous and remarkable that no short account of them can possibly be given in the space available here. The ziggurat and its surroundings were thoroughly explored,[21] and many buildings with ancient names were uncovered and identified by the inscriptions of their builders[22] upon bricks, tablets, clay cones, and stone objects. The development of these buildings could often be followed through the course of the city's history. Most of them lay within a sacred area, called from the beginning a *temenos*, which varied in shape and extent through succeeding ages.[23] In the New Babylonian period, at least, it was a vast enclosure containing or adjoining not only the ziggurat, but a number of temples and secular establishments; its wall passed over the old tombs of the Third Dynasty kings, and the (still longer forgotten) burials constituting the 'Royal Cemetery'. The thickly populated quarter of private streets, chapels, and houses[24] (which yielded the greatest part of the literary resources of Ur) lay outside this enclosure, and so did the great buildings called by the excavators 'Palace of Bel-shalṭi-Nannar'[25] and the 'Harbour Temple'. The latter was placed 'on the eastern bank of the canal-basin at the north end of the city',[26] while another area, called Diqdiqqah, partly explored, was also connected with the navigations.[27] There was a harbour too on the west side of the city,[28] testifying again to the importance of inland and external water-borne trade[29] to the prosperity and to the very existence of Ur.

Tradition had not much to tell about the history of Ur—indeed all material which could be described as literary is extremely disappointing in this respect. The numerous royal inscriptions which have been found do not add very much to historical information, being concerned almost wholly with the building activities of pious kings. The, evidently very long, pre-history of Ur is, of course, entirely a modern discovery, save in so far as the native scribes had knowledge of 'Kings before the Deluge', reigning for fabulous thousands of years in cities which did not include Ur, though its neighbour Eridu was first in the list.[30] These dim figures of hoary antiquity, and probably some of those in the fantastically long 'First Dynasty of Kish' which followed the Deluge, may perhaps be regarded as embodying a Babylonian idea of pre-history. More concrete is the modern archaeologists' classification of artefacts, especially the pottery, which can now be seen following a succession of styles, earlier to later, designated by conventional labels, derived from the sites where they were first observed. Those which principally concern Ur (disregarding still earlier varieties)[31] are called 'Ubaid, Uruk, and Jamdat-Naṣr—the first so named from Al-'Ubaid, close to Ur, mentioned above. Pottery and other objects of the 'Ubaid class were abundant in the lowest levels at Ur itself, remains of the later periods less so.[32] The interest of these nethermost strata resides especially in the claim made by the excavator that a three-metres-thick layer of 'clean water-laid sand' separating them 'must be . . . the deposit left by the great Flood',[33] that is, the Flood described in the Eleventh Tablet of the Gilgamesh Epic and thence, in part derivatively, as is variously allowed,[34] in the book of Genesis.

This claim, one of the 'sensations' of the Ur discoveries, has given rise to a great deal of discussion, archaeological and scientific, much complicated by the discovery, at about the same time, of similar 'flood deposits' at other ancient Babylonian sites, Kiš and Šuruppak. The point fixed historically, if the word can be properly used, is that Gilgamesh, whose real existence as a king of Uruk need no longer be doubted, was both contemporary with the end of the First Kish Dynasty (before 2500 B.C.)[35] and lived, according to the story, some indefinite number of generations after Ziusudra of Šuruppak, hero of the Deluge, who was himself the last, or son of the last,[36] 'king before the Deluge'. The tradition can therefore be claimed as consistent with itself, but how to reconcile it with the 'flood deposits' at Ur and the other cities is more questionable. It has been possible to demonstrate stratigraphically that in the different places these deposits belong to different ages, and this, in view of the prevalence of flooding at all times down to the present in Lower Iraq, is no more than natural. Moreover, it is clear that the picture of a universal catastrophe engulfing all mankind, as presented both by the Gilgamesh Epic and in the Old Testament account, is an exaggeration of whatever limited disaster it was which so impinged upon posterity. Nor, indeed, was this idea of universality general in Babylonian belief, for not only does the Epic make the hero of the Flood a specifically local king of Šuruppak, but later tradition[37] also told of the famous Flood of antiquity as 'the Flood which was in Šuruppak'. It seems clear, in fact, from the stratigraphical evidence that, among all the 'flood deposits', that which has been found on the site of Šuruppak has the best claim to fit[38] the situation as the legend preserves it. The main stratum at Ur, on the contrary, appears much too early for this reasonably defined historical context.

It may be accepted, then, that material evidence certainly exists of a great flood, or rather several great floods, having occurred in the early ages of Babylonian reminiscence, and that one of these flood-deposits, found on the site of Šuruppak, where tradition located the event, does in fact correspond well enough with the historical situation of the characters figuring in the story. But the deposit at Ur, the most imposing in bulk, and that which started the theory, is not likely to have been that which was laid down by the 'Great Flood' itself; and this was in no case, wherever it happened, a world-wide or even country-wide destruction, however deep the impression it made upon the minds of contemporaries, and however enduring and far extended its memory.

An obvious parallel has long been observed[39] between the generations from Adam to Noah (Gen. iv. 17 f. and the longer list in Gen. v) and the Sumerian 'Kings before the Flood', both lines ending in the hero and survivor of that calamity. The well-known names of these legendary kings, preserved by Berossus, were restored and confirmed as authentic by the recovery of their original forms through a king-list published[40] first in 1923. More information about them, and especially about their even more famous 'sages' (*apkallū*), the amphibians Oannes and his successors, who brought civilization to mankind during the reigns of these kings, has lately been published[41] from a tablet of Uruk, and this has again brought striking confirmation of the Hellenistic historian's perfect acquaintance with the traditional lore of his country. None of these kings is said to have reigned at Ur, and the 'sages', in the list from Uruk, are simply attached to the kings, without local ascription. But Ur had its place in the tale of these giants of old; its representative was one named Lu-Nanna, who was nevertheless not a character of pre-history, but lived in the reign of Šul-gi, second and greatest king of the Third Ur Dynasty. These famous counsellors (*ummanū*), whose title and office came to be that of 'vizier', continued long after the Flood, for the last of them was none other than the celebrated Aḥiḳar, who held this position under Esar-haddon, last but one of the kings of Assyria. As concerns Lu-Nanna himself, some obscure, but evidently significant, action is ascribed to him in the Ištar-temple of Šul-gi;[42] he was the possessor of a valuable medical prescription;[43] and above all he was remembered as the poet or transmitter of the myth concerning the ancient half-divine King Etana, of which considerable remains are still extant.[44] There is another list[45] of seven *apkallū*: clay figures of these were to be moulded and buried at the head of a sick man's couch, with their names written each upon their left hip. The first was called 'Day of Life, offspring of Ur',[46] this being perhaps Lu-Nanna, who possessed potent healing arts, for the prediction 'he will live' was regularly used of a patient's recovery.

The legendary figures thus described may serve as an introduction to the early, but otherwise partly unrecorded, personages associated, by their own inscriptions, with the 'Royal Cemetery'; for no account of Ur could be imagined which did not include some notice of the most famous discovery made there.[47] Any repeated description of these treasures could not possibly find room here, but a little more can now be said of the original possessors who carried these riches to their graves, and whose descendants had the art or good fortune to keep those graves mostly unplundered until they passed into oblivion.[48] The names of these possessors, among whom Meskalamšar[49] and the 'queen'[50] are the best known, still remain elsewhere unfound, whereas Mesannipada and his son A'annipada, evidently almost contemporaries of the unknowns, were preserved, the former, at least, by tradition as belonging to the First Dynasty of Ur, and had already been discovered in the inscriptions at Al-'Ubaid. It was clear from the beginning[51] that all of these belonged to the same historical period as the line of Ur-Nanše and his successors at Lagaš (Tello), that period being the apogee of Sumerian civilization, known to modern scholars as the Third Early Dynastic. The Sumerian king-list was compiled from local records;[52] the case of Ur seems to show that the edition was eclectic, and that it was incomplete, or exclusive, is proved by the omission of Lagaš itself, which, by evidence of the original inscriptions of its most powerful ruler Eannatum, was plainly entitled to claim the 'kingship' over the land.[53] Mesannipada of Ur was granted that title as founder of the First Dynasty, and the extent of his sway has now been illustrated by the reported discovery[54] of his name at Mari, the distant outpost of Sumerian culture on the Middle Euphrates. Similarly, there had appeared at Ur the inscription[55] of a daughter of a king of Mari whose name is written AN.BU;[56] a person so named figures in the king-list as heading a dynasty of Mari, which counts as the eleventh after the Flood, whereas the First Ur Dynasty is the third after the Flood, and thus formally much earlier. There is no proof that AN.BU and Mesannipada were in fact contemporaries, but should this turn out to be the case it would be an extreme instance of that disregard for chronological order, in the modern sense, which has often been observed in the arrangement of the king-list. Close relations between Ur and Mari were long continuing, for in a later age Ur-Nammu, the principal builder of the ziggurat, took a wife from Mari.[57]

What has principally given to Ur its age-long interest within the traditions of Western Asia and of Europe has been its fame as the birthplace of Abraham; yet it must be owned that no actual proof exists to assure us that the celebrated 'Ur of the Chaldees' was the place indelibly marked by Tell el-Muḳayyar. This part of the tradition takes its place in an immense discussion, the complexity of which has only been increased by the great discoveries, literary and archaeological, of the last hundred years. The factual existence of Abraham himself, his origin, his social condition, his family and descendants, his history, his chronology, especially as viewed against the background of the famous chapter Gen. xiv, a possible connexion between him and the ubiquitous (as they are now seen to be) Ḥabiru, which leads into the general debate who and what these were[58]—all such topics and a host of corollary questions have given rise to a vast literature of learning and opinion[59] which stuns the mind by its bulk, and yet perpetually disappoints by its failure to reach firm conclusions. Nor is it much to be expected that future discovery will shed new light upon this perplexity. Abraham and the patriarchs of Israel were unknown to the Babylonian scribes, and even the tablets of Ugarit, which entered so dramatically on to the Old Testament scene, have not after all, as once believed, anything to tell about the father of Abraham and his supposed origin from the south,[60] although they do include the name, not the personality, of Abram.[61]

Fortunately, it is only one fraction of the patriarchal story which needs be considered here—was Abraham born, or so reputed, at the spot now called Tell el-Muḳayyar? Was this 'Ur of the Chaldees' (a phrase which has given all its magic to the name), or must we look for this place rather in the north-west, the neighbourhood of Harran, upon which so much of Abraham's life centres? Traditions of respectable antiquity exist in favour of both places,[62] which prove only that the Old Testament description occasioned as much uncertainty in ancient as in modern readers.

The continuing impossibility of reaching a decision upon this question has been brought out by a recent resumption of the debate in form.[63] The geographical problem, intractable in itself, is inseparable from the chronological problem of the lifetime of Abraham, for it is common ground that the attested appearance of the Kaldu in southern Babylonia is considerably later than the vaguely accepted but unprovable dating of Abraham as belonging to the earlier part of the second millennium B.C. This belief, subsidiary arguments notwithstanding, has still to be founded principally upon the partly impossible, partly unfixed chronologically, comparisons of the oriental monarchs of Gen. xiv with identifiable or conceivable figures of oriental history.[64] That 'Chaldaeans' were ever recognized as present in the north is unlikely.[65] If Abraham lived about the time of the First Dynasty of Babylon, the Babylonian Ur was not then 'of the Chaldees' (the qualification would have to be considered an anachronism);[66] if his time was later, the Babylonian Ur was, in the later second millennium B.C., of little importance, and the northern orientation of the Abraham stories would then correspond better with the historical situation, and a northern Ur might be more probable—but it could still not be 'of the Chaldees'.

In the reputed travels of Abraham the weakest link, assuming his southern origin, is the stage Muḳayyar to Harran.[67] Any real reason for this migration can scarcely be found in the oft-mentioned common devotion of these two cities to the worship of the Moon-god; indeed, the later stories of Abraham as the first to reject and ridicule the heathen cult in which his father traded[68] would suggest the strongest reason for not removing from one of its centres to the other, although, it is true, the opposite motive might have prevailed with Terah, by whom (Gen. xi. 31) the move was actually made. No doubt communication between the two cities by the Euphrates route was active at all times, but there is no particular evidence of a special trade relation at the supposed date of Abraham[69]—assuming, again, that Abraham was specifically a trader.[70]

It may be, after all, that the best indication in favour of the southern Ur is the local tradition which survived, for it is decidedly stronger and more detailed here than in the north. One account has it that Abraham was born at Kutha in the reign of the tyrannical

Nimrod who persecuted him,[71] and the name of that site, Tell Ibrāhīm, is evidence of this abiding belief.[72] Another account was that the patriarch was born at Warka, whence his father afterwards removed to Kutha; this was the tradition to which Rawlinson referred[73] when seeking to identify the site of Ur. Late, vague, and inaccurate as these stories are—for they do not, oddly, include the name of Ur itself—they may embody a genuine folk memory attached to definite places, and deserve a degree of credit. But the main support of this tradition is that, in earlier centuries, both Eupolemus, or an imitator, and Josephus[74] applied without hesitation to Abraham an allusion which they found in Berossus himself. Even if this was unintended by Berossus, as doubtless it was, the tradition of the pious sage's birth in south Babylonia cannot be questioned, and the name of Kamarinê applied to his birthplace fits both the dedication of Ur and the strong Arab ingredient in the people who came to dwell there.[75] Contrasting with all this, in the north we find nothing traditional but the attachment to Urfa, of uncertain date, highly improbable in itself—for Urfa (Edessa) as such was a much later foundation, and it is not known what may have occupied its site before[76]—and now generally abandoned.[77]

For a city of its age and fame Ur is not rich in history. This is only to say that its records which have come down to us are very deficient in this respect. Of the three dynasties which were known to have held sway from it over the land singularly little is now to be learned. The First, which may be assumed, from the remains of its wealth, to have been the most brilliant, flourished in an age when writing was only beginning to be used for recording actions; the Second is a mere shadow;[78] the Third is only too amply attested, but in a host of documents which permit very little to be gathered,[79] even by inference, about the doings and fortunes of kings who were magnificent at home and not unsuccessful abroad. Even the material remains of this dynasty are comparatively few and, apart from the ziggurat, not very impressive. Thereafter Ur can be discerned intermittently playing a part through the vicissitudes of the 'national' fortunes, but it was never again in the lead, and appears never to have fully recovered from its great destruction at the end of the Third Dynasty.[80] Its abiding problem was clearly water-supply, both for subsistence and for navigation.[81]

Only in occasional intervals of effective government, able and ready to devote the required resources to the work of maintenance, was this necessity supplied. Generally it does not seem that the city's trade or prosperity were seen as of sufficient importance to justify such exertions. The last Babylonian kings, for political and economic reasons, made a considerable effort to revive the languishing city. They were ill-rewarded (for Ur was one of the centres taking part in the revolt[82] which drove Nabonidus into his long exile at Tema), and unsuccessful. With the Persian conquest came a short restoration and even some return of prosperity[83] under Cyrus, who was to be the last official builder at Ur; he instituted his new order with inscriptions[84] which recall the exordium of his general proclamation in Ezra i. 2a. Under some of his successors a certain life remained;[85] the city perhaps still existed when Eupolemus, in the second century B.C., had at least heard of it as Kamarinê.[86] After that all is silence but for echoes of the name of Abraham.

C. J. GADD

NOTES

1. According to two 'Carbon 14' dates from about the beginning of settlement at Ur, one from Tepe Gawra (W. F. Libby, *Radio-carbon Dating*, 2nd ed., 1955, p. 82), the other from Warka (*Science* cxxvi, 1957, p. 198); I am obliged to Mr. T. C. Mitchell for the latter.

2. See *U.E.T.* iv, 1949, Intro. p. 5.

3. W. K. Loftus, *Travels . . . in Chaldaea and Susiana*, 1857, pp. 127 ff.; H. R. Hall, *A Season's Work at Ur*, 1930, pp. 70 ff.

4. It is, nevertheless, not easy to find his unequivocal statement of this. None of the places cited by Loftus, op. cit., p. 131, contains it; nearest is the *Proceedings of the Royal Geograph. Soc.* i, 1857, p. 47, 'Mugeyer . . . is most probably the Ur of the Chaldees of Gen. xi . . . there was a palace here, on the bricks of which occurs the name Chedorlaomer'. The last is certainly incorrect, but it is not clear to what inscription he referred.

5. The difficulty of being sure about the identity of Ur was probably to interpret the 'ideogram' with which its name is always written. In 1853 Rawlinson was already reporting to the *Thirtieth Annual Meeting of the Royal Asiat. Soc.* (p. xix) that he had found 'the ideographs for Warka or Erech, Accad or Kaskar, Calneh or Niffer'. The earliest publication of a reading *ú-ri*, and then only in an adjectival form, appears to have been that of the tablet K. 4338a in II *R.* 45 and 46 (part of the IV Tablet of the series called ḪAR-ra: *ḫubullu*, see B. Landsberger, *Material. z. sumer. Lex.* v, 1957, pp. 143 ff.): this was in 1866.

6. B.M. Dept. of W. Asiat. Antiq., nos. 91125–8; *Guide to the Bab. and Assyr. Antiq.*, 3rd ed., 1922, pp. 141 ff. and pl. xxxviii.

7. S. H. Longrigg, *Four Centuries of Modern Iraq*, 1925, pp. 308, 313.

8. H. R. Hall, *U.E.* i (*Al-'Ubaid*), pp. 6 f.; T. Jacobsen, *Iraq* xxii, 1960, pl. xxviii.

9. General plan of the town by A. S. Whitburn, *A.J.* x, 1930, pl. xxxiii; contour map by F. L. W. Richardson, *A.J.* xii, 1932, pl. lviii. J. E. Taylor (*J.R.A.S.* xv, 1854, p. 260) gives the circuit of the walls as 2,946 yards. By contrast, Warka measures 3,030 metres north to south and 2,140 metres east to west; J. Jordan and C. Preusser, *Uruk-Warka*, 1928, p. 6, and Tafel I.

10. H. Frankfort (*The Town-Planning Review* xxi, 1950, p. 104) reckoned Ur as of about the same size (150 acres) and population (24,000) as the city of Asshur; this reference I again owe to Mr. T. C. Mitchell. For comparison, Roman London has been reckoned as containing 330 acres and perhaps 25,000 inhabitants; R. G. Collingwood, *The Archaeology of Roman Britain*, 1930, p. 92.

11. Op. cit., pp. 127 ff.; H. R. Hall, op. cit., pp. 77 ff.

12. *J.R.A.S.* xv, 1854, pp. 260 ff.

13. *U.E.* viii, 1965, references on p. 112; *A.J.* v, 1925, pp. 376 ff.; H. R. Hall, op. cit., p. 88; C. L. Woolley, *Excavations at Ur*, 1954, p. 202.

14. *A.J.* vi, 1926, pp. 385 ff.; *U.E.* ix, 1962, pp. 52 ff.; H. R. Hall, op. cit., p. 89.

15. *Archaeologia* lxx, 1920, pp. 101 ff.; *U.E.* i, 1927, p. 5.

16. H. R. Hall, op. cit., pp. 77 ff.

17. *U.E.* i, chs. i–iii; Hall, op. cit., pp. 229 ff.; P. Delougaz, *Iraq*, v, 1938, pp. 1 ff.; Seton Lloyd, *Iraq* xxii, 1960, pp. 29 ff.

18. *U.E.* i, pp. 61, 126; *A.J.* iv, 1924, p. 330.

19. The only continuous narrative of the work as a whole is still to be found in the preliminary reports published annually in *A.J.* iii, 1923 to xiv, 1934, but the official publication, divided into the two series of *Ur Excavations* (*U.E.*) and *Ur Excavations: Texts* (*U.E.T.*), is now (1965) approaching completion: see the table facing title-page of *U.E.* viii. There is a good summary account in C. L. Woolley, *Excavations at Ur*, 1954.

20. *A.J.* iv, 1924, pp. 329 ff.; *U.E.* i, chs. iv ff.

21. *U.E.* v, 1939.

22. *U.E.T.* i, 1928 (*Royal Inscriptions*).

23. Plans of the *temenos* in its historical development are given for the Third Dynasty in *A.J.* xiv, 1934, pl. xlix; for the Old Babylonian Period in *A.J.* x, 1930, pl. xxx; for the Kassite Period ibid., pl. xxxi and *U.E.* viii, pl. 47; for the New Babylonian Period in *A.J.* x, pl. xxxii and *U.E.* ix, pl. 60, and ch. ii.

24. *A.J.* vii, 1927, pp. 386 ff.; xi, 1931, pp. 359 ff.

25. *A.J.* x, 1930, pp. 319 ff.; *U.E.* ix, pp. 41 ff. The name, which should be read En-nigaldi-Nanna, is hardly justified by the use of some Nabonidus bricks apparently left over from a different building.

26. *A.J.* x, 1930, pp. 320 ff.; *U.E.* ix, p. 35.

27. *A.J.* v, 1925, pp. 18 ff.; T. Jacobsen, *Iraq* xxii, 1960, pp. 181 ff.

28. *A.J.* x, p. 318.

29. A. L. Oppenheim, *J.A.O.S.* lxxiv, 1954, pp. 6 ff.; M. Lambert, *R.S.O.* xxxix, 1964, pp. 90 ff. The vocabulary mentioned above (n. 5) lists a ship of a special design or rig called a 'ship of Ur' (A. Salonen, *Wasserfahrzeuge in Babylonien*, 1939, p. 52). This was probably a sea-going dhow, since ships of the oversea lands Magan and Meluḫḫa also occur in the list: see *C.A.H.* i², ch. xix (fasc. 17, 1963), pp. 25, 39.

30. T. Jacobsen, *The Sumerian King-list*, 1939, pp. 57 ff.; J. J. Finkelstein, *J.C.S.* xvii, 1963, pp. 39 ff.; see below, n. 40.

31. W. Nagel, *Berliner Jahrb. für Vor- und Frühgeschichte*, i, 1961, ii, 1962; Seton Lloyd, *Iraq* xxii, 1960, pp. 23 ff.; A. L. Perkins, *The Comparative Archaeology of Early Mesopotamia*, 1949.

32. *U.E.* iv, 1956, chs. ii, iii; Joan Oates, *Iraq* xxii, 1960, pp. 32 ff.

33. *A.J.* x, 1930, p. 334; *U.E.* iv, pp. 15 ff.

34. A. Heidel, *The Gilgamesh Epic and Old Testament Parallels*, 1945, especially pp. 224 ff.

35. *C.A.H.* i², ch. xiii (fasc. 9, 1962), p. 20.

36. J. J. Finkelstein, *J.C.S.* xvii, 1963, pp. 43 f.

37. R. C. Thompson, *Assyrian Medical Texts*, 1923, no. 105, line 22; W. G. Lambert, *J.C.S.* xvi, 1962, p. 72.

38. The whole question of the flood-deposits, and which of them is most likely to have been that of Ziusudra's (and Noah's) Flood, has recently been examined with great care by M. E. L. Mallowan, *Iraq* xxvi, 1964, pp. 62 ff.; his conclusions are summarized there on p. 81.

39. See, most recently, E. A. Speiser, *Genesis* (The Anchor Bible, 1964), pp. 35 f.

40. S. Langdon, *Oxford Editions of Cuneiform Texts*, ii, pp. 2 ff.; and see above, n. 30.

41. J. van Dijk, *Vorläufiger Bericht über die . . . in Uruk-Warka unternommenen Ausgrabungen* (Abh. d. Preuß. Akad. d. Wiss., Phil.-hist. Kl.), xviii, 1962, pp. 44 ff.

42. W. G. Lambert, *J.C.S.* xi, 1957, p. 7; E. Reiner, *Orient.* xxx, 1961, p. 10.

43. 'Secret of Lu-Nanna, the sage of Ur'; W. G. Lambert, loc. cit., p. 7, n. 27; E. Reiner, loc. cit., p. 8.

44. Translated by E. A. Speiser, *A.N.E.T.*, pp. 114 ff.

45. See H. Zimmern, *Z.A.* xxxv, 1924, pp. 151 ff.

46. *C.A.D.* vi (Ḫ), p. 168a, translates, however, 'spirit of life, born *on the roof*', which, in this context, seems perverse.

47. *U.E.* ii (*The Royal Cemetery*), 2 vols., Text and Pls., 1934.

48. Together with the custom of human sacrifice at burials, which it seems impossible to deny in this unique case; see C. J. Gadd, *Iraq* xxii, 1960, pp. 51 ff.

49. Or Meskalamdug.

50. Long called Šub-ad, which was a mere rendering of the signs.

A proposal to read the name as Semitic, Pù-abi (I. J. Gelb, *Glossary of Old Akkadian*, 1957, pp. 12, 210) would have far-reaching implications; see E. Sollberger, *J.C.S.* xvi, 1962, p. 41; *U.E.T.* viii, Intro. p. 1.
51. *U.E.* i (Al-'Ubaid), 1927, pp. 138 ff.
52. T. Jacobsen, *The Sumerian King-list*, 1939, pp. 167 ff.
53. *C.A.H.* i², ch. xiii (fasc. 9, 1962), pp. 26 ff.
54. G. Dossin, *C.R.A.I.* 1965, p. 405.
55. *U.E.T.* i, 1928, no. 12.
56. T. Jacobsen, op. cit., p. 103, n. 189.
57. M. Civil, *R.A.* lvi, 1962, p. 213; *C.A.H.* i², ch. xxii (fasc. 28, 1965), 5.
58. They are presented, in recent literature, as 'dusty' men, travelling ἐν στροφάλιγγι κονίης kicked up by the hooves of their donkey-caravans; see E. Dhorme, *Rev. historique* ccxi, 1954, p. 261; R. Borger, *Z.D.P.V.* lxxiv, 1958, pp. 121 ff. What is known about the Ḥabiru, in the various times and places where they appear, has been summed up in two comprehensive works, J. Bottéro (ed.), *Le Problème des Ḥabiru* (*Cahiers de la Société asiatique*, xii), 1954, and M. Greenberg, *The Ḥab/piru*, 1955.
59. No better guide to and through this barren labyrinth can be found than the full and authoritative article 'Patriarches' by H. Cazelles, *Supp. au Dict. de la Bible*, fasc. 36, 1961, cols. 82 ff. See also O. Eissfeldt, *C.A.H.* ii², ch. xxvi (fasc. 31, 1965), pp. 5 ff.
60. G. R. Driver, *C.M.L.*, p. 5; A. S. Kapelrud, *The Ras Shamra Discoveries and the Old Testament*, 1965, pp. 16 f.; Cazelles, loc. cit., col. 97.
61. C. F. A. Schaeffer, *Ugar.* iv, 1962, p. 43 (two persons named *abrm*, in Cyprus and in Egypt).
62. Quoted by T. G. Pinches in Hastings *Dict. of the Bible*, iv, 1902, pp. 835 ff.; cf. H. W. F. Saggs, *Iraq* xxii, 1960, p. 200. There is also a good discussion of the locality by G. R(awlinson?) in W. Smith (ed.), *Dict. of the Bible*, iii, 1893, pp. 1596 ff. It has been suggested elsewhere (by J. B. Segal, *Edessa and Harran*, 1963, pp. 21 f.) that belief in the birth of Abraham at Urfa is no older than the eighth–ninth centuries of our era.
63. By C. H. Gordon, *J.N.E.S.* xvii, 1958, pp. 28 ff.; H. W. F. Saggs, loc. cit. A rejoinder by Gordon appears in *Hebrew and Semitic Studies presented to G. R. Driver* (ed. D. Winton Thomas and W. D. McHardy), 1963, pp. 75 ff. See also W. F. Albright, *B.A.S.O.R.* 163, 1961, p. 44.
64. A recent review of these again by W. F. Albright, loc. cit., pp. 49 ff. 'Amraphel' is still the stubbornest; another emendation is there suggested.
65. Saggs, loc. cit., pp. 205 ff.; Gordon in *Studies . . . Driver*, pp. 82 f. The idea in *Recueil É. Dhorme*, 1951, p. 245, 'Le mouvement qui amène la famille d'Abraham . . . se rattache à la migration chaldéenne au début du second millénaire' is scarcely established as historically convincing by the section which precedes.
66. Saggs, loc. cit., p. 205.
67. *Recueil É. Dhorme*, pp. 212 ff.
68. J. Hamburger (ed.), *Real-Encyclop. des Judentums*, 1896, Abt. i, p. 30; C. J. Gadd, *History and Monuments of Ur*, 1929, pp. 181 ff.

72421

69. W. F. Albright, *B.A.S.O.R.* 163, 1961, pp. 45 f.

70. This question has been especially prominent in the recent discussions.

71. See n. 68, above.

72. G. Le Strange, *The Lands of the Eastern Caliphate*, 1905, pp. 68 f.

73. *J.R.A.S.* xii, 1850, p. 481. Dr. W. N. Arafat has informed me that *Ṭirāz al-Majālis* was written by a late (died 1069/1659) Arabic author Al-Ḥafāǧī. The value of his compilation is said to consist in its preserving extracts from older works lost or undiscovered.

74. P. Schnabel, *Berossos und die babylon.-hellenist. Literatur*, 1923, pp. 68, 268 (40).

75. B. Moritz, in *Paul Haupt . . . Anniversary . . . Volume*, 1926, pp. 204 ff.; *U.E.T.* i, no. 192 (U. 6900), *U.E.* ix, pp. 31 and 114 (U. 7815); E. Burrows, *J.R.A.S.* 1927, pp. 795 ff. (U. 7815, 7819, 6900); W. K. Loftus, *Travels . . . in Chaldaea and Susiana*, p. 233.

76. J. B. Segal, *Edessa and Harran*, 1963, pp. 7, 22.

77. Cazelles, loc. cit., col. 99. But Gordon (*Studies . . . Driver*, p. 83) is inclined to uphold it.

78. See *C.A.H.* i², ch. xix (fasc. 17, 1963), p. 21.

79. Ibid., ch. xxii (fasc. 28, 1965), pp. 4, 12, 25.

80. For the general history of the city the writer may be permitted to refer to his book *History and Monuments of Ur*, 1929, although it would now require extensive revision; also to *C.A.H.* i², chs. xiii, xix, xxii, and ii², ch. v.

81. A. L. Oppenheim, *J.A.O.S.* lxxiv, 1954, pp. 6 ff.; T. Jacobsen, *Iraq* xxii, 1960, pp. 174 ff.; J. Jordan and C. Preusser, *Uruk-Warka*, pp. 3 f. See also above, n. 29.

82. *Anatol. Stud.* viii, 1958, pp. 58 f., col. i, lines 19–22.

83. *U.E.* ix, pp. 2, 7 f., 25.

84. *U.E.T.* i, nos. 194, 307.

85. Ibid. iv, Intro. p. 5; M. Lambert, *R.S.O.* xxxix, 1964, p. 109.

86. See above, p. 95.

BIBLIOGRAPHY

(Additional to works quoted in the footnotes)

BARTON, G. A. *The Royal Inscriptions of Sumer and Akkad*, 1929.

BEER, B. *Leben Abrahams nach Auffassung der jüdischen Sage*, 1859.

BÖHL, F. M. Th. 'Die Tochter des Königs Nabonid', *Symbolae . . . P. Koschaker dedicatae*, 1939, pp. 151 ff.

CHRISTIAN V. *Altertumskunde des Zweistromlandes*, i, 1940.

CONTENAU, G. *Manuel d'archéologie orientale*, i–iv, 1927–47.

EDZARD, D. O. *Die 'zweite Zwischenzeit' Babyloniens*, 1957.

GADD, C. J. 'Seals of ancient Indian style found at Ur', *Proceed. of the Brit. Acad.* xviii, 1932, pp. 191 ff.

—— 'En-an-e-du', *Iraq* xiii, 1951, pp. 27 ff.

GADD, C. J. 'Two sketches from the life at Ur', ibid. xxv, 1963, pp. 177 ff.

GARELLI, P. (ed.). *Gilgameš et sa Légende*, 1960.

GELB, I. J. 'The early history of the West Semitic Peoples', *J.C.S.* xv, 1961, pp. 27 ff.

GOETZE, A. 'Šakkanakkus of the Ur III Empire', ibid. xvii, 1963, pp. 1 ff.

GÜTERBOCK, H. G. 'Die historische Tradition und ihre literarische Gestaltung bei Babyloniern und Hethitern bis 1200.' Erster Teil, *Z.A.* xlii, 1934, pp. 1 ff.

HALLO, W. W. 'The Royal Inscriptions of Ur: a typology', *H.U.C.A.* xxxiii, 1962, pp. 1 ff.

HILPRECHT, H. V. *Explorations in Bible Lands*, 1903.

JONES, T. B., and SNYDER, J. W. *Sumerian Economic Texts from the Third Ur Dynasty*, 1961.

KRAMER, S. N. *The Sumerians: their history, culture, and character*, 1963.

KRAUS, F. R. 'Provinzen des neusumerischen Reiches von Ur', *Z.A.* li, 1955, pp. 45 ff.

KUPPER, J.-R. *Les Nomades en Mésopotamie au temps des rois de Mari*, 1957.

LEEMANS, W. F. *Foreign Trade in the Old Babylonian Period*, 1960.

LEGRAIN, L., and WOOLLEY, C. L. Articles descriptive of the excavations and discoveries in *The Museum Journal*, Philadelphia, from 1923 onwards.

MERCER, S. A. B. *Sumero-Babylonian Year-Formulae*, 1946.

OPPENHEIM, A. L. *Catalogue . . . Wilberforce Eames Collection . . . Tablets of the time of the Third Dynasty of Ur*, 1948.

PARROT, A. *Archéologie mésopotamienne*, i, 1946.

—— *Sumer*, 1960.

—— *Nineveh and Babylon*, 1961.

SCHNEIDER, N. *Die Zeitbestimmungen der Wirtschaftsurkunden von Ur III*, 1936.

SMITH, S. Translation of texts in WOOLLEY, C. L. 'Babylonian prophylactic figures', *J.R.A.S.* 1926, pp. 695 ff.

SOLLBERGER, E. 'Notes on the early inscriptions from Ur and El-Obed', *Iraq* xxii, 1960, pp. 69 ff.

SPEISER, E. A. 'The Epic of Gilgamesh', *A.N.E.T.*, pp. 72 ff.

THUREAU-DANGIN, F. *Die sumerischen und akkadischen Königsinschriften*, 1907.

UNGNAD, A. 'Datenlisten', in *Reallex. der Assyr.*, ii, 1938, pp. 131 ff.

VAUX, R. DE. 'Les patriarches hébreux et l'histoire', *R.B.* lxxii, 1965, pp. 5 ff.

ANATOLIA

BOĞAZKÖY

BOĞAZKÖY

BOĞAZKÖY is a village which has given its name to the adjacent site of the Hittite capital Hattusa, about 100 miles east of Ankara (the new official name, Boğazkale, is not generally current in archaeological circles). The site is an unusual one, consisting of an area of no less than 419 acres (167·7 hectares), rising 300 metres from its most northerly point, just above the village, to its summit at Yerkapu in the south; beyond this the ground falls away a little, only to rise again to merge with the range of hills extending far to east and west. On either side the site is bounded by valleys, that to the east, indeed, being a precipitous gorge (from which the modern village derives its name, 'Gorge Village'), while the western valley is more open. To the north, at the foot of the range of hills, lies a wide undulating plain giving an uninterrupted view of the next line of hills some 20 miles to the north. Two miles away across broken ground is Yazilikaya, a rocky outcrop fashioned by the Hittites into an open-air shrine and adorned with a frieze of bas-reliefs representing the leading figures of the pantheon.

The first western traveller to visit the site of Hattusa was Charles Texier, who in 1834 was able to inspect the massive ramparts round the upper part of the city, the ruins of the great temple, now known as Temple I, on the lower slopes, and the rock-carvings of Yazilikaya.[1] In 1893-4 Ernest Chantre, another French archaeologist, found there clay tablets inscribed with cuneiform script in an unknown language,[2] and it was realized that excavation within the area of this ancient city would be likely to yield rich rewards. The concession was secured by the German Assyriologist, Hugo Winckler, who in 1906, 1907, 1911, and 1912 conducted excavations there together with Theodore Macridy Bey on behalf of the Ottoman Museum at Istanbul, with funds supplied by the Deutsche Orient-Gesellschaft (an expedition sponsored by the German Archaeological Institute and directed by Otto Puchstein was simultaneously at work during 1907 on an investigation of the buildings and architecture).[3] About 10,000 fragments of tablets were recovered, and from those written in Akkadian it was immediately apparent that the excavators had found the royal archives of the Hittite kings of the fourteenth and thirteenth centuries B.C. The Hittite language, in which most of the documents were written, was deciphered in 1915 by the Czech scholar, B. Hrozný,[4] and the publication and translation of the archives in the years since the end of the First World War, mostly by German scholars, has resulted in the revelation of the history and civilization of this ancient Bronze Age kingdom, one of the great powers of its time.

In 1931 the excavations were reopened by K. Bittel on behalf of the Deutsche Orient-Gesellschaft and the German Archaeological Institute, and, apart from an interruption of twelve years caused by the Second World War, have continued to the present day. Work has been mainly concentrated on the citadel, Büyükkale ('Great Fortress'), which has yielded the following stratification:

Levels I–II: post-Hittite, so-called Phrygian.

Level III: the Hittite Empire (c. 1400–1200 B.C.)

Level IV: 'Old Hittite', subdivided into four building levels, a–d.

Level V: pre-Hittite (reached only in isolated spots).

New archives of tablets were discovered, and the buildings in which they had been housed were carefully recorded.

Outside Büyükkale the excavation of two large buildings, one of them the so-called Temple V in the upper city, was completed, and a section of living quarters in the lower city, north of Temple I, was opened up. In the lower levels of this area documents were found which showed that in the pre-Hittite period an Assyrian merchant colony had been situated there. Excavations were also carried out on the great rock of Büyükkaya, across the gorge from the main city, and in front of the shrine of Yazilikaya, where a temple had been constructed in the heyday of Hittite civilization. Finally, an overhanging rock near the road to Yazilikaya was found to have been used throughout the whole history of the site, from the Assyrian colony period to the end of the Empire, as a burial ground, cremation and inhumation being apparently practised concurrently.[5]

i. *History*

The texts reveal that Anatolia in the Middle and Late Bronze Ages was populated by a mixture of peoples. The Hittite language, in which most of the texts are written, is Indo-European in structure, and presumably represents the language of the dominant aristocracy of the kingdom; it is of great philological interest, preserving as it does certain archaic features which were lost in the cognate languages. Luwian, which seems to have been spoken in the south and west of Asia Minor, and Palaic, which was at home in an undefined area in the north, were languages related to Hittite. Totally unrelated, however, either to these or to each other, were Hattic and Hurrian. The former seems to have been the language of the original population, and there are indications that it was no longer spoken at the time we are considering. Hurrian, on the other hand, was the speech of an eastern people known from Mesopotamian sources, and a comparatively recent arrival on the Anatolian scene. The Indo-European peoples must have entered Anatolia some time during the third millennium B.C., either by way of the Caucasus or across the Bosphorus, since the homeland of these peoples is known to have been to the north of the Black Sea; but archaeology has not yet produced any unambiguous evidence for their arrival in the country. This was a prehistoric movement of populations for which written evidence cannot be expected. The original extent of the Hattian population can also only be surmised. It is from them that the country received the name of Hatti, which in turn gave rise to the Old Testament Heth and the English Hittite. The ancient place-names suggest that they inhabited principally the northern and central parts of Anatolia.

The Hittite kings claimed descent from one Labarnas, king of Kussar, who is said to have made conquests as far as the sea coasts. The earliest texts, however, date from the reign of his successor, Hattusilis I, who seems to have been the first king to rule from Hattusa. Under him we already find many cities of the Anatolian plateau assigned to princes of the royal blood. In his third year Hattusilis had to repel an invasion of the Hurrians from across the Euphrates, and for the rest of his reign he was occupied with wars in the direction of Syria. Final victory there was left to his successor, Mursilis I, who defeated Aleppo, proceeded on down the Euphrates and overthrew Babylon itself, bringing to an end the First Dynasty of Babylon in 1595 B.C., a feat of arms which was remembered with pride by later generations. On returning home, however, Mursilis was murdered by his brother-in-law, Hantilis, and for a period of several generations a series of palace revolutions brought discredit on the royal house. These disturbances were probably not unconnected with external events, for, although at first the reign of Hantilis appears to have been prosperous, he was obliged to fortify the capital, and towards the end of his reign the kingdom began to feel the pressure of new enemies from the north and east. Under his successors Hittite fortunes rapidly deteriorated and most of the outlying provinces were lost. The rich coastal plain of Cilicia in particular was invaded and occupied at this time by a Hurrian dynasty and became for several centuries the domain of a powerful rival kingdom named Kizzuwadna, the history of which is as yet largely unknown. Thus, after a brief period of expansion into northern Syria, the Hittites were thrown back once more to the north of the Taurus Mountains, and although *c.* 1525 B.C. King Telepinus restored order in the kingdom, reforming the laws and entering into treaty relations with the kings of Kizzuwadna, Hittite affairs would at that time have been of little concern to the inhabitants of the Syrian plains, who now fell under other masters, as the conquering pharaohs of the Eighteenth Dynasty of Egypt and the Hurrian kingdom of Mitanni contended for supremacy. The population of Syria and Palestine was deeply penetrated by Hurrians during this century.

About 1450 B.C. a new dynasty, in which the dynastic names Tudhaliyas and Arnuwandas are prominent, rose to power in Hattusa and Hittite fortunes began to revive. One of the first of these rulers, a Tudhaliyas, succeeded in breaking through once more into Syria and reconquering Aleppo, but his success was short-lived, and it was only in the fourteenth century that the Hittites eventually emerged as a world power. King Suppiluliumas led his army eastward across the Euphrates, passed through the territory of Mitanni, and recrossed into Syria, defeating there the army of the king of Kadesh and so acquiring northern Syria as a Hittite province. By the end of his reign Mitanni had been reduced to vassalage, Hittite princes ruled in Aleppo and

Carchemish, and the king of Kizzuwadna had sent his tribute to Hattusa. Suppiluliumas must also have reduced the kingdom of Arzawa in the west of Anatolia to submission, but the settlement did not outlast his death, and the conquest of Arzawa was the main achievement of his successor, Mursilis II. Egypt at this time was ruled by kings without military ambitions and the Hittite Empire in Syria was firmly consolidated. When at last in 1300 B.C. the ambitious Ramesses II once again challenged the Hittites by leading an army up from the coast into the interior of Syria, he suffered a surprise attack beneath the walls of Kadesh, and was forced, despite great personal valour, to retreat, thus failing to shake the hold of the Hittites on the territory. During the following years the tense relations between the two great powers gradually improved, and in 1284 B.C. Hattusilis III and Ramesses II concluded a treaty of peace by which the demarcation line between the Hittite and Egyptian spheres of influence was fixed by mutual agreement just south of Damascus.

With political stability Hittite civilization now reached its peak of prosperity. Hattusilis and his successor, Tudhaliyas IV, were able to concentrate on works of peace and religious reforms. However, new enemies were threatening on their frontiers, Assyria in the east, powerful barbarians in the west. Tudhaliyas was obliged to lead Hittite armies eastward against Assyria and may even have met his death in the campaign, while in the west, it seems, he was unable to prevent an adventurer named Madduwattas from conquering most of his more distant provinces. We know the names of two more Hittite kings, but the records suddenly come to an end, and about 1200 B.C. the Hittite kingdom was overwhelmed by the great mass migrations associated with the 'Peoples of the Sea' in the Egyptian annals. Excavation has shown that the city of Hattusa went up in flames and probably remained uninhabited for some considerable time. The Phrygian settlement which eventually arose on the site was extremely modest and can hardly be identical with the Pteria of Herodotus I. 76, 'the strongest city of all that region', as was formerly supposed.[6]

ii. *Hittite Civilization*

The Hittites were a tough, highland nation with a mainly agricultural economy. Trade was limited, though the rich metallic ores present in the Taurus ranges were a valuable asset which they used to good effect.[7] Their kings seem to have lived in modest style in their massive stone palace on the citadel at Hattusa, and there is no evidence of luxury.

The Hittite laws reveal a patriarchal society in which the husband 'takes' his wife and can dispose of his children by sale.[8] However, the independent position of the queen, who retained her office even after the death of the king, and the prominence of a goddess in the pantheon, suggest that there had been an earlier matrilineal society in Anatolia, vestiges of which survived into Hittite times.

The organization of the state was feudal in character. From the earliest times authority was delegated by means of an oath of fealty to the king; important offices were sometimes held as fiefs with hereditary rights, and as new provinces were conquered the system was extended to them, local princes being summoned to Hattusa and sworn in as vassal kings of the conquered territory, often receiving a Hittite princess in marriage. The 'treaty' in which such a relationship was embodied consisted essentially in the obligations imposed on the vassal (Hittite *išḫiul*) and the oath by which he accepted them; it was a type of transaction with a long Mesopotamian tradition, but it is only in the Hittite archives that a number of such treaties and oaths of fealty have been recovered in a good state of preservation. The earliest is a fragment of an oath sworn by a band of Ḫabiru engaged in military service to one of the early kings,[9] and several treaties of these early kings with the independent state of Kizzuwadna are attested, though poorly preserved. It is under the Empire, beginning with King Suppiluliumas, that our knowledge of these treaties is most complete. They conform to a fairly consistent pattern—(i) the preamble, giving the name and titles of the Great King as author of the treaty; (ii) the historical prologue, summarizing the past benefits conferred on the vassal by his suzerain; (iii) the stipulations themselves, detailing the obligations imposed on the vassal in return for the favours he has received; (iv) provision for deposit in the temple and periodic public reading; (v) the list of gods as witnesses; (vi) the curse and blessing formula. The Hittites were able to adapt this form to special circumstances, as when terms were imposed on a group of barbarian chieftains, or when the other contracting party was either a royal prince or a potentate of equal status with the Hittite king (the so-called parity treaty). For the latter situation there is a well-known example in the thirteenth-century treaty drawn up between Hattusilis III and Ramesses II, where the act consists essentially in a double *išḥiul* and a double oath, clearly an adaptation of the scheme developed for vassal treaties, though a different form of parity treaty seems to be attested by a fragment of an early treaty with a king of Kizzuwadna.[10] Vassal treaties in the form outlined above have also come to light at Ugarit, and the influence of this form of treaty has even been traced in the covenant of Yahweh with the Israelites embodied in the Decalogue.[11] In the Hittite Empire the personal character of the vassal relationship resulted in a certain instability and led to frequent revolts on the death of the sovereign.

The king was both commander-in-chief of the Hittite army and supreme high priest of the realm; his duties in these two capacities must have given him little leisure, for the summer was usually spent in campaigning, while the many religious festivals in different parts of the country must have filled the winter months. Though deified at death, and protected from defilement by elaborate taboos, he was never actually regarded as divine during his lifetime.

Hittite religion, as we find it in the texts, presents an appearance of great complexity. The pantheon, summed up in the phrase 'the thousand gods of the Land of Hatti', contains a vast number of divinities, many of whom are little more than names to us. This complexity, however, is somewhat artificial. The texts present the official religion of the capital, an attempt to create a national cultus based on the innumerable local cults of the Anatolian cities, while recognizing the individuality of the local deities.

As befits a mountainous country, the prevalent deity in Hittite Anatolia was a Storm or Weather God, known under various names. To the Hurrians he was Teshub, to the Hattians Taru, to the Hittites themselves he seems to have been known most widely as Tarhu, Tarhun, or Tarhunt.[12] His sacred animal was the bull and he was sometimes even represented as a bull himself, as on the bas-relief showing a scene of worship from Alaca Hüyük (Pl. III). Cults of the Storm God are attested for a great number of Anatolian cities, and not least for the Syrian city of Aleppo. It was thus natural that the supreme high god of the state was named the Storm God of Hatti; he is the real king of the Land of Hatti, the king himself merely his viceroy. Almost equally prominent, however, in the state documents is the 'Sun-Goddess of [the city] Arinna', evidently the goddess of a single cult-centre, not yet located with certainty, elevated to a supreme position as special protectress of the queen, who is even in some way identified with her at death. As mentioned above, this phenomenon has a strong suggestion of a primitive matriarchy. The character of this Sun-Goddess is not yet fully elucidated; she has distinctly chthonic associations and apparently little connexion with the physical sun.[13] The solar deity was in fact a god, named Istanus. In the state pantheon the Storm God and the Sun-Goddess are husband and wife, with two sons, a daughter, and a granddaughter.

All these leading deities belong properly to the original Hattian stratum of the population. In the temple rituals, however, and particularly in personal names, Hurrian deities are very prominent. Here the leading goddess, wife of Teshub, is Hebat or Hepat, and their son is Sharruma or Sharma. Ancient Sumerian deities, such as Ea, entered the Hittite pantheon by this channel. The cult of these deities was introduced into the Hittite capital at a comparatively late date, but so prominent did they become that they were officially identified with their Hattian counterparts, and their names were given to the figures representing the national pantheon in the shrine at Yazilikaya. This fostering of the Hurrian element in the religion is probably connected with the origin of the dynasty which came to power in the fifteenth century.

Springs and mountains were frequently deified and figure as minor deities in the lists. This tendency is also exemplified by the many Hittite rock-sculptures of a religious nature, which are either near a spring or on a mountain peak.[14]

The cult of the gods is the subject of by far the largest number of texts in the Hittite archives. We have the prayers spoken by members of the royal family, instructions for festivals and ceremonies, mostly conducted by the king and queen, and records of divination by which the divine will was ascertained on matters of moment. Magical rituals, usually of a private nature, and ascribed to a particular author, are also numerous. Of special interest to students of the Old Testament are some of the prayers, with their

PLATE III

Hittite king and queen worshipping bull (Alaca Hüyük)

conception of sin; national disasters are attributed to divine anger
resulting from a sin committed by the speaker's father, for which
the speaker himself, though guiltless, is willing to make atone-
ment.[15] There is even a passage oddly reminiscent of the prayer of
Abraham in Gen. xviii. 23 ff.[16] On the other hand, there is no
abject submission to divine caprice. The Hittite kings themselves
showed a strong sense of justice and fair dealing in relation to their
subjects, and, if they felt that their gods had lapsed from their
own high standards, they did not hesitate to address them with
robust resentment and criticism.[17]

iii. *The Hittites and the Old Testament*

Canaan (Palestine) was always outside the boundaries of the
Hittite Empire and was recognized by the Hittites as Egyptian
territory. It is unlikely, therefore, that the Israelites ever came into
contact with the Hittites of the second millennium B.C.; the possible connexion of the legendary 'Tidal king of Goiim' (A.V. 'of
nations', Gen. xiv. 9) with the Hittite royal name Tudhaliyas is
entirely conjectural.[18] After the downfall of Hattusa and the great
popular migrations at the end of the Bronze Age, Syria and eastern
Anatolia split up into a number of petty kingdoms, some retaining
much of the earlier Hittite traditions, others purely Aramaic, and
the name 'Land of Hatti' was applied by neighbouring countries
to the whole Syro-Palestinian region as a geographical term. It was
at this time that Solomon imported horses from Egypt and sold
them to the 'kings of the Hittites and the kings of Syria' (2 Chron. i.
17), and the reputation of these 'kings of the Hittites' was formidable enough to inspire panic in the army of Ben-hadad, king of
Damascus (2 Kings vii. 6 f.). The ancient city of Hattusa (Boğazköy) had, however, long since ceased to be a Hittite metropolis.
The centre of gravity of this 'Neo-Hittite' world was at Carchemish on the Euphrates, where successive dynasts adorned their
palace with elaborate monumental inscriptions in 'Hittite' hieroglyphs and sculptures showing a mixed Hittite-Assyrian style.
This 'hieroglyphic' script had been invented and used to a limited
extent by the Hittites of the second millennium B.C.; but the
language of the Neo-Hittite inscriptions is not Hittite but a form
of Luwian.

Yet individuals described as Hittites appear in the Old Testament from the time of Abraham, who bought the cave of Machpelah from Ephron 'the Hittite', to that of David and Solomon, who took 'Hittite' wives. The accounts of the Hebrew settlement in Canaan also contain frequent references to the Hittites among the tribes whom they found already living in the country. Taken at their face value, these references present a difficult problem. Only one instance is known of subjects of the king of Hattusa emigrating to Egyptian territory;[19] the reference is difficult to understand, and it is quite uncertain whether these people from the Hittite city of Kurustama settled in Canaan, as has been suggested, or in Egypt itself. That they could ever have formed a significant proportion of the Canaanite population is obviously unlikely. Moreover, it is a striking fact that all Hittites mentioned by name in the Old Testament (with the possible exception of Uriah, whose wife, Bath-sheba, was taken by David) bear good Semitic names.[20] More probably, therefore, the term 'Hittite' in these instances has no ethnic significance but is to be understood in a general sense, almost equivalent to 'native', derived from the late use of the name Hatti as a geographical term for the whole of the Levant.[21] The references to the Hittites as one tribe among many during the Israelite settlement could be due to a misunderstanding by the redactor.

O. R. GURNEY

NOTES

1. C. Texier, *Description de l'Asie Mineure*, i, 1839, pp. 209 ff.

2. E. Chantre, *Recherches archéologiques dans l'Asie occidentale, Mission en Cappadoce, 1893–4*, 1898.

3. H. Winckler and O. Puchstein, *Smithsonian Report*, 1908, pp. 677–96; O. Puchstein, *Boghasköi, die Bauwerke*, 1912.

4. B. Hrozný, *M.D.O.G.* lvi, 1915, pp. 17–50.

5. For a recent summary of the excavations in the various parts of the site and full bibliography, see F. Fischer, *Die hethitische Keramik von Boğazköy*, 1963, pp. 14–27. A brief summary in English without bibliography was given by H. G. Güterbock, *Archaeology* vi, 1953, pp. 211–16.

6. C. Texier, op. cit., pp. 221 ff., followed by W. M. Ramsay, *The Historical Geography of Asia Minor*, 1890, pp. 29–33, and J. Garstang, *The Land of the Hittites*, 1910, pp. 32 ff., 197; but cf. S. Przeworski, *A.O.* i, 1929, pp. 312 ff., and K. Bittel, *Boğazköy-Hattuša*, i, 1952, pp. 30 f.

7. A. Goetze, *Kleinasien*, pp. 119 f.

8. V. Korošec, *Reallex. der Assyr.* ii, 1938, p. 293.

9. The problem of the *'Apiru* (cuneiform *Ḫa-pí-ru*, *Ḫa-bir-a-a*, Ugaritic *'-p-r*) and their possible equation with the Biblical *'ibrîm* (Hebrews) has been revitalized by W. F. Albright, who maintains that the original meaning of the word was 'the dusty ones', a nickname for the donkey caravaneers of the second millennium B.C., who turned to banditry or service as mercenaries when they were unable to ply their trade; see *B.A.S.O.R.* 163 (1962), pp. 52–54, and *C.A.H.* ii², ch. xx, pp. 14–20 (fascicle 51). Other recent interpretations have been 'resident alien' (J. Lewy, *H.U.C.A.* xxviii, 1957, pp. 1–13) and 'people who have rejected and withdrawn from their society' (G. E. Mendenhall, *B.A.* xxv, 1962, p. 71). Cf. also R. Borger, *Z.D.P.V.* lxxiv, 1958, pp. 121–32.

10. H. Otten, *J.C.S.* v, 1951, pp. 129 ff.

11. G. E. Mendenhall, *B.A.* xvii, 1954, pp. 50–76. S. R. Külling, *Zur Datierung der 'Genesis P-Stücke', namentlich des Kapitels Genesis XVII*, 1964, traces the same influence in the covenant with Abraham in Gen. xvii; but cf. Mendenhall, op. cit., p. 62.

12. E. Laroche, *R.H.A.* xvi, 1958, pp. 88 ff.

13. See J. G. Macqueen, *Anatol. Stud.* ix, 1959, pp. 171 ff.; H. G. Güterbock, *Neuere Hethiterforschung*, ed. G. Walser, 1964, pp. 54 ff., especially pp. 58 f.

14. R. D. Barnett, *B.O.* x, 1953, pp. 77 ff.; H. G. Güterbock, *Anatol. Stud.* vi, 1956, pp. 53 f.

15. O. R. Gurney, in *Myth, Ritual and Kingship*, ed. S. H. Hooke, 1958, p. 111.

16. O. R. Gurney, *Annals of Archaeology and Anthropology* (Liverpool), xxvii, 1940, p. 31, with commentary, p. 109.

17. Ibid., p. 27.

18. F. M. Böhl, *King Hammurabi of Babylon in the Setting of his Time*, 1946, p. 17; W. F. Albright, *A.J.S.L.* xl, 1924, pp. 132 ff.; F. Cornelius, *Z.A.W.* lxxii, 1960, pp. 1 ff.

19. E. Forrer, *P.E.Q.*, 1936, pp. 190–209, 1937, pp. 100–15.

20. M. Vieyra, 'Parallèle hurrite au nom d'Urie "le hittite" ', *R.H.A.* v, 1939, pp. 113–16.

21. See L. Delaporte, *R.H.A.* iv, 1938, pp. 289–96.

BIBLIOGRAPHY

AKURGAL, E. *The Art of the Hittites*, 1962.

BITTEL, K. *Die Ruinen von Boğazköy*, 1937.

—— and NAUMANN, R. *Boğazköy-Hattuša I. Architektur, Topographie, Landeskunde und Siedlungsgeschichte*, 1952.

CAMBRIDGE ANCIENT HISTORY, ii, rev. ed. (in press).

CAVAIGNAC, E. *Les Hittites* (L'Orient ancien illustré), 1950.

CONTENAU, G. *La Civilisation des hittites et des hurrites du Mitanni*, 2nd ed., 1948.

DELAPORTE, L. *Les Hittites* (L'Évolution de l'Humanité), 1936.

GOETZE, A. *Kleinasien*. Kulturgeschichte des alten Orients, Abschn. iii. 1, 2nd ed., 1957. (Part of I. MÜLLER, *Handb. der Altertumswissenschaft*.)

GURNEY, O. R. *The Hittites*, rev. ed., 1966.

GÜTERBOCK, H. G. 'Hittite Religion', in *Forgotten Religions*, ed. V. Ferm, 1949.

—— 'Hittite mythology', in *Mythology of the Ancient World*, ed. S. N. Kramer, 1961.

OTTEN, H. 'Das hethitische Felsheiligtum von Yazilikaya', *Das Altertum*, ii, 1956, pp. 141–50.

VIEYRA, M. *Hittite Art*, 1955.

SYRIA

ALALAKH

MARI

UGARIT (RAS SHAMRA)

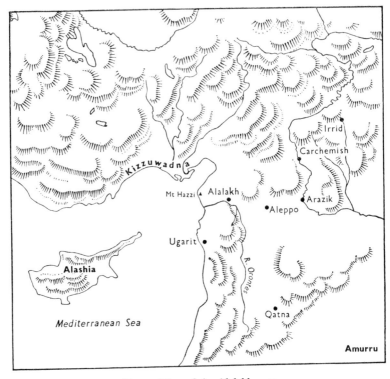

Fig. 4. Map of the Alalakh area

ALALAKH

SIR LEONARD WOOLLEY, searching in 1935 for a site which might yield evidence of the cultural connexions between the Mesopotamian and East Mediterranean civilizations, chose Tell el-'Aṭshānah in the 'Amq plain of north-west Syria, now Açana in Hatay, Turkey. This was a large oval ruin mound (750×300 metres) which overlooked the river Orontes and the main routes leading from the Mediterranean port of Al-Mina via Antioch to the Lebanon and eastwards to Aleppo and the river Euphrates. Excavations were sponsored by the British Museum, with the support of the Ashmolean Museum, the Royal Geographical Society, the British School of Archaeology in Iraq, and of private donors, and were undertaken in 1937–9 and 1946–9.[1]

Seventeen occupation levels were traced which may be dated from c. 3100–c. 1200 B.C. In the earliest was found some Khirbet Kerak ware known from Palestine and a temple site (XVI) in the north-western quarter of the town close to the colonnaded royal palace and fort. These early levels (for example, XIV) show affinities with the equivalent Ur and Nineveh levels, and doubtless came under the influence of the great conquerors and traders Sargon of Agade and Naram-Sin from Babylonia. The best-preserved remains were the early vaulted temple and walled courtyard (XII, c. 2400 B.C.), the latter with a glacis-type construction known also from Palestine.[2]

The main archaeological discoveries were made in two distinct levels (VII and IV), in both of which archives of inscribed tablets, totalling 457 texts, were found.[3] In the earlier Level VII, dated to the end of the eighteenth century B.C., and therefore about half a century after the Mari texts and corresponding to the latter part of the First Dynasty of Babylon, the palace of Yarimlim at this city, named Alalakh, was cleared. The state-rooms were decorated with frescos, and the towered city gate was of typical eastern Mediterranean workmanship. The whole complex had been destroyed by the fire which marked the end of this occupation level. This was followed by a 'dark age' of about two centuries (Levels VI–V) in which polychrome pottery like that from Megiddo X–IX and a single 'Union Jack' motif, also common in Palestine *c.* 1600 B.C., were found. With Level IV a new palace, ascribed by the excavator to King Niqmepa, employed a more 'Hurrian' type of construction with its grand staircase and single-columned entrance as well as the local technique of using rough stones for the lower courses, aligned and bonded by carefully dressed corner-stones supporting courses of wood interspersed with mud-brick, also found in Palestine.[4] Here too archives were found in the palace which was destroyed by fire, although the occupation of other quarters remained unchanged. In Level III the temple was found burnt and rebuilt on non-Hittite lines while the fortress-palace continued in use.[5] Buildings, seals, and tablets show that the Hittites were in command.[6]

The chronology of Alalakh is the subject of much discussion and is not yet finally settled. However, despite the use made of the evidence of the texts and discoveries to support varying systems of chronologies of Mesopotamia and the ancient Near East, this in no way invalidates the general comparisons made with the patriarchal period in Hebrew history which is itself still no more closely defined. Thus for the main periods to which reference is made here, Levels VII and IV, the dates *c.* 1720–1650 and 1550–1473 (or 1483–1370) B.C. cover the main theories at present proposed.[7]

i. *The Political Environment*

Alalakh came into the hands of a west-Semitic ruling family when, after a revolt against Abba'el (or Abban),[8] son of Hammurabi of Yamhad, whose capital was Aleppo, one of his brothers was given the city in exchange for Irrid, east of Carchemish (*A.T.** 1). This was an act of Abba'el's generosity and free will[9] and the gift was confirmed in a treaty or 'covenant'-text. Like the later Hittite covenants this outlines the historical circumstances, stipulations, and the witnesses, and invokes curses upon any who should break its terms. This is an early witness to a literary genre which continued with no basic change throughout the ancient Near East, including Palestine, for two millennia.[10] The act of exchanging towns and villages either to maintain a natural frontier or as payment for international obligations occurs in other texts (*A.T.**

52–58). They have been compared with the later treaty between Solomon and Hiram of Tyre whereby the former gave twenty villages bordering Tyre in exchange for wood and 120 talents of gold supplied for the construction of the Jerusalem temple (1 Kings ix. 11).[11] Yarimlim was followed by his son Ammitakum whose long reign was contemporary with four kings of Aleppo.[12] He styled himself 'King of Alalakh', but before the end of his rule there are signs of the break up of the kingdom of Yamhad which at this time controlled Syria from the Euphrates to Qatna and the Mediterranean.[13] By a daughter of the governor of Apishal, Ammitakum had a son Hammurabi whom he appointed his heir. In the presence of his overlord, Yarimlim of Yamhad, 'he decreed the destiny of his house, estates, land and all that he had, in the same way as his father had appointed him . . . he appointed Hammurabi his son'. The transaction was effected by an oral statement: 'Hammurabi is my son . . . the [other] sons which the daughter of Nawar-adal, the vizier, bore him shall have no claim. Hammurabi is the rightful owner of my city and he is [the master of] my house. Moreover, he is the servant of Yarimlim, my lord.' This transaction was witnessed by all the high officers of state, the vizier, secretary, commander-in-chief, mayor, judge, cup-bearer, and scribe, and dated to the year Yarimlim defeated Qatna (*A.T.** 6). With this oral deposition may be compared the need to avoid rivalry among the princes which evoked a public statement naming Solomon his heir by the aged David (1 Kings i. 17, 20, 30–36). It is possible that, despite this will, Ammitakum was in fact soon followed by another son Irkabtum,[14] in whose reign peace was made with the Ḫabiru-warriors under Shemuba (*A.T.** 58). His rule ended when the palace at Alalakh was sacked and burned (end of Level VII), an event usually attributed to the Hittite Mursilis I about the time of his conquest of Aleppo.[15]

In the intervening 'dark age', for which there are no documents to furnish any details, the Mitanni state with its Indo-Aryan rulers must have taken over. Texts from Level IV once more provide a clear picture. A base found *in situ* at this level exactly fitted a statue recovered from a pit (Level III) beneath the floor of the Level I temple (*c.* 1200 B.C.).[16] The inscription[17] on the statue of Idrimi (Pl. IV) is in the form of a speech[18] in which he, as youngest son of Ilimilimma (I)[19] of Aleppo, tells how the family fled after a popular revolt and took refuge with maternal relations at Emar. After a time he refused to remain a passive exile, so taking his horse, chariot, and squire, he passed through the desert to Canaan, where in Ammiya he found fellow refugees from Aleppo, Niʿ, and Amae[20] in Syria. For seven years he stayed among the semi-nomadic *ḫabiru* until, guided by omens, he won sufficient support to mount an expedition which crossed by boat to the foot of Mount Hazzi (Cassius). This was Mukish-land in which lay Alalakh as capital of a territory now more limited than in earlier times. 'In a single day and like one man the people rallied to me', wrote Idrimi. He was reconciled to his brothers, and after seven years was ready to plead with Parattarna, the Great King of the Hurrians, on the grounds of a former treaty and family loyalty. Thus he regained his kingdom. Indeed, he extended it by an unopposed expedition into Hittite territory before handing over to a son Adad-nirari after he had ruled for thirty years.[21] With the spoils of this campaign Idrimi claims to have built a palace, probably the imposing edifice of thirty-three rooms around three courtyards ('Palace of Niqmepa')[22] which was the principal architectural discovery from this period.

Idrimi's adventures,[23] which are unusually said to have been written by the scribe Sharruwe, have several points in common with the Old Testament. The story is told in a free-flowing narrative style without parallel in such texts from Mesopotamia and Egypt, and can only be compared with parts of Genesis and especially with the story of David.[24] The latter fled to maternal relatives in Moab (1 Sam. xxii. 3 f.) as did Absalom (2 Sam. xiii. 37). Winning support from refugees he inquired of Yahweh before attempting to regain his lost kingdom (2 Sam. ii. 1–4, v. 1, 3). Following a welcome from the majority of the people, David was also reconciled with his family and neighbours before extending the kingdom by armed force. He too used the spoils of war for the construction of a royal palace.[25] Moreover, the repeated seven-year periods, the emphasis on divination, and the reconciliation of the hero with brothers are strikingly like elements in the Joseph narrative (Gen. xl. 1), showing that such motifs in biographical writing were current at least as early as the sixteenth century B.C.[26] The role of the Ḥabiru (SA–GAZ) at Alalakh is of interest since among lists of such semi-nomads one document names

PLATE IV

Statue of Idrimi, king of Alalakh

a Canaanite (Sharniya) from Ammiya.[27] These *ḫabiru* sometimes placed themselves at the service of local chiefs, as perhaps did the Hebrew Abraham (Gen. xiv. 13). Their forces were drawn from many localities, and included varying professions and even slaves. Some owned chariots, for one tablet lists a total of 1,436 *ḫabiru* of whom eighty owned or drove chariots (*A.T.* 183).[28]

Idrimi made treaties with his neighbours. One, with Pilliya of Kizzuwadna (Cilicia), reaffirms regulations laid down earlier by Parattarna and survives as an agreement (literally 'a bond') for the mutual seizure and extradition of fugitives; in this it is probably an extract of a treaty with many provisions (*A.T.* 3). If anyone other than the owner seizes the fugitive, then a payment of 'the equivalent of' his value[29] had to be made, 500 shekels of copper for a male and double that sum for a female. Extradition rights are also covered in a long treaty made by Niqmepa with Ir-Teshub of Tunip—'If anyone from my territory shall enter your territory, you shall not pay attention to him but will write and give me information. If he stays in your country you shall seize [him] and hand him over to me' (*A.T.* 2). In both treaties the mayor and five elders or responsible men[30] have to give the news[31] concerning activities in their town. According to 1 Kings ii. 39 f. Shimei was allowed to enter Philistine territory to search for his two runaway slaves and Achish returned them on demand. This would imply the existence of a mutual treaty with extradition rights negotiated between Gath and Judah by Solomon, perhaps to remove the possibility of anyone emulating David's action in his flight from Saul (1 Sam. xxvii. 5 ff.).[32] Such treaty stipulations also throw light on the Deuteronomic prohibition of the extradition of fugitive slaves (Deut. xxiii. 16 f., R.V. 15 f.).[33] One text describes the procedure by which three such slaves were handed back by the authorities in Aleppo before witnesses in return for a receipt (*A.T.* 101).

At this time (Level IV) north Syria was dominated by Mitannian kings, Parattarna, Saussha(ta)tar, and Shutarna, to whom the local rulers of Alalakh owed allegiance. The non-Semitic Hurrians (Old Testament Horites) had already been established as part of the population in the eighteenth century B.C. to judge by personal names,[34] and by the time of Niqmepa were in the majority.[35] The early Hurrian 'occupation' of the city, when compared with Mari and Ugarit, may be due to its location on the main thrust south-wards which was to influence Palestine (Egyptian *Huru*) also. Hurrians are found at Tell Ta'annak and at Shechem.[36]

The subsequent history of the city is only illuminated by a few references in external sources. Niqmepa was followed by Ilimi-limma II, and it may have been in his reign that Tuthmosis III took tribute from Alalakh (Egyptian *irrḫ*) as, according to the Semnah stele, did Amenophis II. In the clash between the great powers it was inevitable that the kingdom of Mukish should fall to the Hittites owing to its geographical position. Following intrigues by its ruler Ituraddu, the Hittite Suppiluliumas recaptured the city and inaugurated a period of Hittite control which lasted till the beginning of the twelfth century B.C.[37] Alalakh was then destroyed by the 'Sea-Peoples' and ceased to be a major settlement.

ii. *Economic and Social Conditions*

In the earlier texts the ruler of Alalakh styled himself Governor (literally 'Man') and only later as 'King',[38] a title common throughout the area in all periods. He ruled personally as an autocrat, sitting in judgement in the palace on any lawsuits brought before him. Oral decisions were made and then incorporated in an agreed written and witnessed contract. These included cases relating to a citizen's status or property (for example, *A.T.** 8). Cases in which the king himself was concerned came before his overlord, either the king of Yamhad in the earlier period, as the dispute with the priest over the sheep promised to the temple by Yarimlim on his accession (*A.T.** 10), or, later, before the kings of Mitanni who were asked for decisions on the status of members of their kingdom or on inter-state boundaries (*A.T.* 13–14). The Yamhad rulers would not allow Ammitakum to sell villages they granted him without their consent (*A.T.** 79), otherwise he was free to exchange, sell, or give away villages and land (*A.T.** 56, 126). By this means the king, aided by the chief merchant Irp-Adu, his son Shamshi-Adu, and the city treasurer, Pentammu, won control of much of the property in his area.

Slavery played an important part in providing the palace with domestic and agricultural workers, though for the latter corvée labour was largely relied upon.[39] Slaves were recruited from prisoners of war (*asiri*), given daily rations by the palace, and from defaulting debtors. The king would grant loans in silver needed as capital in agricultural and other operations on the security of the debtor himself, his wife, or children. Such a pledge was a 'stand-in' (*mazzazanutum*) who for the money was required to 'dwell in the house of the king' (*A.T.** 18–27), his service being the equivalent of interest due on the loan.[40] The debtor was thus the 'slave' of the king (*A.T.** 32. 11) and received no wages. Similar legal overtones might apply to the Old Testament phrase 'to dwell in the house of the king' (cf. Pss. xxiii. 6, xxvii. 4) and could explain David's anxiety not to dwell with Achish (1 Sam. xxvii. 5). Such debtors could not be freed at any time of general amnesty or release which was decreed periodically at Alalakh (*A.T.** 65) as in Israel.[41] No date is specified in these texts for the reimbursement of a loan; the debtor had 'to repay the money during his lifetime' (*A.T.** 20, 47, 50), and 'when he repays the money to the royal palace he may go wherever his heart desires' (*A.T.** 21). The average value of a male slave at Alalakh in the fifteenth century B.C. was about 25 shekels of silver (or 5½ talents of copper)—the female being worth approximately double—and this may be compared with an average of 40 shekels at Ugarit and 30 shekels a little later in Israel. While no more than three slaves are listed as belonging to any one master, it would seem that as many as ten to fifty persons could be given as presents to another ruler (*A.T.* 224). Since the king at Alalakh would pay off debts owed by one citizen to another, it will be seen that there was an increasing general indebtedness to the 'merchant princes' in the palace. Such an exercise of kingship in Syria would be surely known to the Israelites, quite apart from Samuel's counsel when they demanded a like institution (1 Sam. viii).

The social structure of Alalakh in the eighteenth century B.C. was typical of Mesopotamia at the time with its freemen, semi-free dependants, owing service and dues in kind to the palace, and slaves. This was replaced, under Hurrian influence, in the fifteenth century by a distinctive class system. Thus the king could grant the status of '(chariot-)warrior' (*maryannu*) to a citizen and this would be hereditary (*A.T.* 15). Such a position appears to have involved religious obligations also, and the person so honoured could be a freed slave.[42] This class, estimated at thirty-four persons in a population of 2,500, was required to provide chariots and carts with horses or oxen for military or corvée purposes. Below these were 'freemen' (*eḫele*), without specific feudal obligations, who included a wide range of palace and other officials as well as some skilled craftsmen. The major part of the population, classed as 'rural retainers' (*ṣabē namē*) were subdivided in the census-lists into 'Haneans'—mainly horse- and ox-owners—and *ḫupšu*, who owned lands and vineyards (*A.T.* 211), dwelt in houses as tenants of the king (*A.T.* 186, 16–20), or owned private property; while the majority of references are in lists of householders where they predominate numerically (*A.T.* 186, 187, 202), the latter would seem to be tenant-farmers with certain feudal obligations, free-born 'coloni' and not slaves, and can thus be compared with the Hebrew *ḥopšī* who preferred bondage with economic security to liberty with its attendant risks.[43] These too were free from certain taxes (cf. 1 Sam. xvii. 25) and worked willingly for their masters (Exod. xxi. 5 f.; Deut. xv. 16 f.).

More than 100 of the Alalakh tablets are devoted to lists, primarily of persons by name according to their status or location. Some lists specify persons by their weapons, as, for example, the 'archers' who also played an important part in chariot warfare.[44] Others name the inhabitants of towns and their subordinate villages (cf. Joshua xv. 32 ff., xviii. 9 ff.), or houses allocated by lot (*purina*, cf. 1 Chron. xxiv. 7–19). From such detailed lists emerges a picture of a busy town and religious centre serving a predominantly agricultural community. Merchants, smiths, woodworkers, weavers, dyers, potters, jewellers, and entertainers form a close-knit society.

Local customs, amply reflected in these texts, can help in the interpretation of incidents recorded in the Old Testament. Thus at Alalakh marriage was a civil affair before witnesses and recorded in a written contract.[45] The bridegroom 'asked' the father for his daughter as bride (*A.T.* 17. 4; cf. Gen. xxvi. 7; 2 Chron. xi. 23), bringing a voluntary (betrothal) gift (*nidnum*). Thus when Shatuwe asked Apra for the hand of his daughter 'he brought a betrothal gift in accordance with the custom of the city of Aleppo' (*A.T.* 17, 5–6). In the same way and neighbourhood Isaac, through Eliezer, gave choice presents to his future brother and mother-in-law (Gen. xxiv. 53). Shechem, possibly a Hurrian, offered Jacob a 'betrothal-gift' (*mattān*) as well as a 'bride-gift' (Gen. xxxiv. 12). At Alalakh the 'bride-gift' (*tirḫatu*) was given to, and retained by, the bride's family. In one case, contrary to the usual custom of it being a token sum, this amounted to 200 shekels of silver and 30 shekels of gold (*A.T.* 93). As in Mesopotamia, the bride's father gave her a dowry (*šeriktu*) which she usually kept on widowhood or divorce. One marriage contract runs—

If Naidu [the bride] should hate Irihalpa [the husband] and continually harass him, the *tirḫatu* of the young girl he shall withhold, but whatever was apportioned her of her father's property she shall take. However, if he shall mistreat the girl [literally 'drag her by the nose'], then he shall return the *tirḫatu* and whatever she brought from her father's house as her portion [that is, her dowry] she shall take and go free (*A.T.* 92, 6–14).

Since polygamy was practised, the marriage contract sometimes defined the position of other wives. 'If either [wife], Akap-kiashe or Zilip-Nanua, gives birth [to a son], he may not marry a third wife. Should both of them fail to give birth, then he may take a third wife. [This is] a royal judgement' (*A.T.* 91, 24–31). Other contracts rule that if the wife 'fails to give birth in seven years he may take a second wife' (*A.T.* 93, 94). If this was in Jacob's first contract it might explain the need to wait a further seven years for Rachel (Gen. xxix. 18, 27). This restriction was doubtless imposed to spare the girl the indignity of a rival wife or need to provide a concubine (cf. 1 Sam. i. 6; Gen. xxx. 1 ff.). Similarly, Laban made Jacob swear not to take other wives besides his daughters, since his departure for Canaan would take him to an area where other customs prevailed (Gen. xxxi. 50).

There is some evidence that the father had the right to disregard the law of primogeniture and choose the son to be designated 'first-born'.[46] 'If Naidu does not give birth to a son, then the daughter of his brother, Iwashura, shall be given Irihalpa [as wife]. If another wife of Irihalpa gives birth to a son first and afterwards Naidu gives birth to a son, the son of Naidu alone shall be the first-born' (*A.T.* 92, 15–19). This practice, also known from Ugarit and Nuzi, seems to have been common in Palestine where Abraham annulled Ishmael's position on the birth of Isaac to Sarah (Gen. xxi. 10 ff.), and Jacob chose Joseph instead of Reuben

(Gen. xlviii. 14, 22, xlix. 3 f.; cf. 1 Chron. v. 1 f.) and Ephraim instead of Joseph's eldest son Manasseh (Gen. xlviii. 13 f.). This custom was subsequently abrogated by the Deuteronomic legislation (Deut. xxi. 15 ff.). It must be assumed that at Alalakh, as in Palestine and Mari,[47] the eldest son was given an additional share to cover the cost of maintaining the aged parent and the funerary expenses. It was for this reason, as much as to ensure the perpetuation of the family name and property rights, that a childless person might adopt a son, as Abraham did Eliezer (Gen. xv. 2 ff.). Conversely, as at Nuzi, a man might adopt another as 'father'. Thus Tulpuri took the king Ilimilimma as father in return for lifelong support. Should Tulpuri die, all he possessed goes to Ilimilimma provided he has not mistreated him (*A.T.* 16).

It is also noteworthy that in a fifteenth century B.C. case an evil-doer was put to death and his property came into the palace (that is, was confiscated), the king being responsible for satisfying any outstanding creditors.[48] Such action is reminiscent of Ahab's action against Naboth (1 Kings xxi). In another case king Yarimlim acquired the village of Nashtarpi from a woman Tattaya who claimed that it was hers by her father's will. The king argued that this had been wrongfully given her and she thereupon asked that 'Yarimlim should smite my head' which he did before three witnesses and the village came into the possession of the palace (*A.T.** 11). This symbolic act with its legal significance may well denote either a show of disapproval or a transference of responsibility by the action of a higher authority.[49] It has greater force than the idiom 'to lay upon the head' which means 'to put the responsibility on' a person, as in 'his sins shall be laid upon his own head' (*A.T.* 2. 52; cf. 1 Sam. xxv. 39). Another symbolic act here, as at Mari, is 'to seize (or let go) the hem of the garment' which denotes the giving of unreserved submission to (or defection from) a person (*A.T.** 456, 45–57), which may imply that David's act in cutting off the 'wing' or hem of Saul's garment was an act of rebellion for which he was later repentant (1 Sam. xxiv. 4 f., R.V. 3 f.).[50]

Another typical Syrian custom is perhaps to be seen in transactions for the purchase of real estate where, above the normal payments by silver and grain, an 'additional payment' was made, sometimes in kind as, for example, '2 oxen, 1 length of cloth and 1 spear as additional (equalizing) payment' (*A.T.** 78, 7 f.).[51]

Wheat, jars of wine, honey, and oil were also used for these and normal payments, and are indicative, as at Ugarit and Mari, of a way of life in the west not common in lower Mesopotamia. Since land as a saleable commodity is described as 'soil' or 'dust' (*epiru*, Hebrew *'āpār*), the Syrian Naaman may well have considered the gold, silver, and cloth given to Gehazi as an 'additional payment', though his master had refused anything for the token soil he wished to remove to the Rimmon temple (2 Kings v. 17–23). In this connexion it should be noted that temple land at Alalakh may have been called the '*epiru* of Ishtar' (*A.T.** 58, 15). Payment by lengths of cloth or garment was common (cf. Gen. xxiv. 53; 2 Kings v. 5, cf. vii. 8), as also by 'pots of oil' (*A.T.** 52–58). The prophet's widow provided by Elisha with an unusual supply of oil would have had no difficulty in disposing of it locally in direct barter for anything from real estate to food (2 Kings iv. 7). As in the Hebrew texts, the specified weight could be unexpressed as well known, for example, '100 (shekels) of silver' (cf. Gen. xx. 16). In the fifteenth century B.C. copper by the talent (*qaqqaru*) took the place of the rarer silver for normal transactions. Large quantities ('10,000 (*ribbat*) of silver') were prescribed in the penalty clauses of contracts to express a prohibitive expense.[52] Two scales of weight, the larger twice that of the smaller as in Palestine, were in use, weights varying according to the locality ('the weight of Alalakh' (*A.T.* 46, 48) or 'of Aleppo' (cf. Gen. xxiii. 16).

In this agricultural community viticulture played its part as did sheep farming.[53] Horses, domesticated or pet gazelles, and possibly camels were rare.[54] Kings employed donkeys both for caravan and personal use.

iii. *Culture and Religion*

In each of the main periods of Alalakh's prosperity, as witnessed by the texts, at least five scribes were at work among the estimated population of about 2,500. They were adequately trained in Akkadian, perhaps at a main city such as Aleppo, where they learned the Babylonian cuneiform script which they wrote in a typical western provincial style.[55] The accepted Babylonian scribal techniques and forms of documents were adapted to local use, the north-west Semitic dialect being marked by numerous Hurrian loan-words.[56] As at Ugarit, legal judgements recorded 'before the king . . .' were prefaced by 'from this day . . . (for ever)' and emphasize the legal terminology current in the Deuteronomic legislation.[57] In this connexion it is to be noted that one event recorded in the form of a 'treaty' or 'covenant' might be copied out in its various parts or associated documents, so that the absence of any one part of an assumed formula is no proof that the literary form did not exist, or was not in continued use, from the early second millennium B.C. onwards. Thus the summary of the agreement whereby Abban deeded Alalakh to Yarimlim (*A.T.** 1) was followed by the same scribe at the same time making a document outlining the religious obligations (here the offerings of birds, kids, lambs, oil, and manna to be made in the temple on behalf of the king). The latter also ends with curses 'if you . . . the god Adu/ Teshub will deliver you into the hand of your enemy. If you enter the temple of the goddess Ishtar with hands unwashed you will [invalidate what you have done]' (*A.T.** 126). Yet another text by an identical hand records the payments by the king (Yarimlim) towards this temple endowment (*A.T.** 127). Similar extracts from fuller treaties can be seen in the Idrimi-Pilliya text already quoted. Tradition and precedent were considered of much importance, continuity of authority being underlined by the use of a royal 'dynastic' or predecessor's seal.[58] The art, represented by the seals and architecture, shows that combination of Anatolian and Mesopotamian elements in a local tradition which characterizes Syria throughout its history.[59]

The religious life of Alalakh is unfortunately only incidentally reflected in the texts and archaeological remains. The god IM (Adu or Teshub) and his wife Hepat, whose principal seat was in Aleppo (*A.T.** 63), were probably represented in the main temple found in the excavations at each main period of occupation. The latter was, however, dedicated to the goddess Ishtar (the reading of whose name is not always certain, being sometimes possibly an ideogram for Ishhara or even Hepat), who is invoked in the treaties and contracts from the eighteenth century B.C. onwards and claimed the king of Alalakh as her 'special possession'.[60] Personal names imply the adoration also of the moon-god Sin (Hurrian *Kušaḫ*), the sun-god Shamash (*Saps*), Ea, Enlil, Aia, Irra, and Sharru, as well as such west-Semitic deities as Baʻal, Malik, and Lim. Hurro-Hittite gods common in the later onomastica include Aštapi, Hamani, Kiaše, Kumuḫ, Kupapa, and Šauška. A general invocation of 'the gods above and the gods beneath' was not forgotten (*A.T.** 126, 127).[61] A festival of Ishtar in the months of *utithi* and *hiari* involved the dedication and sacrifice of sheep (*A.T.* 346). When Abban swore a solemn oath ('by the life of the god') to Yarimlim, he cut the neck of a lamb (saying): 'So [be done to me] if I take back what I have given you . . .' (*A.T.** 455. 40–46); the expression, with its imprecation understood but not expressed, is the same as the Hebrew phrase 'God do so to thee and more also if . . .' (1 Sam. iii. 17, etc.). Divination from sheep's entrails or liver was practised and a model employed for this purpose was found in the palace ruins.[62] The movement of birds and even their fighting was used, as were astronomical observations, to predict the future.[63] Oxen were also sacrificed (*A.T.* 54. 16) and libations poured out (for the dead?, *A.T.** 57, 60).

Until the discovery of the Alalakh tablets the history of Syria in the eighteenth and fifteenth centuries B.C. was virtually unknown. Although the finds made there, especially of the tablets, do not bear directly upon the Old Testament, they provide a valuable source of comparative material, as do the texts from neighbouring Mari and Ugarit (Ras Shamra). History, customs, language, religion, and general culture can be viewed in detail at a site and period more closely allied to the patriarchs' homeland and activities than was hitherto possible.

D. J. WISEMAN

NOTES

1. C. L. Woolley, *Alalakh*, p. 6; *A Forgotten Kingdom*, pp. 17 ff.; cf. R. D. Barnett, *Journ. of Hellen. Studies* lxxvii, 1957, pp. 356 ff.

2. C. L. Woolley, op. cit., p. 50.

3. Texts published in D. J. Wiseman, *The Alalakh Tablets*, 1953; *J.C.S.* viii, 1954, pp. 1–30; xii, 1958, pp. 124–9; xiii, 1959, pp. 19–33, 50–62; also S. Smith, *A.J.* xix, 1939, pp. 38–48. Text references are given according to publication nos. (*A.T.*), Level VII tablets being distinguished by *. A few additional fragments remain unpublished.

4. *P.E.Q.*, 1960, pp. 57 ff.

5. C. L. Woolley, op. cit., pp. 397 ff.

6. For Hittite texts, see n. 56; C. Picard, *Rev. Arch.* xv, 1940, pp. 97 f. for the Hittite temples.

7. M. B. Rowton, *C.A.H.* i/vi, 1962, pp. 43, 60; W. F. Albright,

B.A.S.O.R. 127, 1952, pp. 28–36; 146, 1957, pp. 26–34; A. Goetze, ibid., 146, 1957, pp. 20–26; *J.C.S.* xi, 1957, pp. 56–61, 63–73. See also B. Landsberger, ibid., viii, 1954, pp. 51–61.

8. The grandson of Yarimlim of Yamhad, the powerful contemporary, according to the Mari texts, of Hammurabi of Babylon and father-in-law of Zimrilim of Mari. The reading of the name as Abba'el rather than Abban can be questioned in the light of contemporary names ending *-a-an*.

9. Literally 'in the love of his heart he gave it'; S. Loewenstamm, *B.I.E.S.* xx, 1956, pp. 13–16.

10. Evidence summarized in J. A. Thompson, *The Ancient Near Eastern Treaties and the Old Testament*, 1963; contrary D. J. McCarthy, *Treaty and Covenant*, 1963, pp. 168 ff., which does not allow for variety of documents (see pp. 123, 130) and thus requires different forms of covenant in the first millennium B.C.

11. D. J. Wiseman, *Journ. of the Trans. of the Victoria Institute* lxxxii, 1956, p. 124; C. Fensham, *J.B.L.* lxxix, 1960, pp. 59 f.

12. J.-R. Kupper, *C.A.H.* ii/i, 1963, p. 34.

13. Ibid., p. 36.

14. Most commentators consider that Irkabtum ruled in Yamhad (H. Klengel, pp. 141 ff., see Bibliography), but he may also have been co-regent with the aged Yarimlim.

15. A. Goetze, *B.A.S.O.R.* 146, 1957, pp. 24 ff.; or to Hattusilis I (M. B. Rowton, *C.A.H.* i/vi, p. 42).

16. C. L. Woolley, *A Forgotten Kingdom*, p. 122.

17. S. Smith, *Statue of Idri-mi*, 1949, and reviews in *J.C.S.* iv, 1950, pp. 226–31; *R.A.* xlv, 1951, pp. 151–4.

18. D. J. Wiseman, *Syria* xxxix, 1962, p. 186.

19. That is, 'God is verily my god'.

20. The place of Balaam's origin (Num. xxii. 5); cf. *B.A.S.O.R.* 118, 1950, p. 15, n. 13.

21. S. Smith, *Statue of Idri-mi*, pp. 86–88.

22. C. L. Woolley, *Alalakh*, pp. 130 ff.; *A Forgotten Kingdom*, pp. 105 ff.

23. 'Toils' (*manaḥāte*), or possibly 'wanderings' (cf. Hebrew *nûaʿ*; Gen. iv. 12; 2 Sam. xv. 20).

24. A. L. Oppenheim, *J.N.E.S.* xv, 1955, pp. 199 f.

25. G. Buccellati, *Bibbia e Oriente* iv, 1962, pp. 95–99.

26. W. F. Albright, *B.A.S.O.R.* 118, 1950, pp. 14 ff.

27. *A.T.* 181. 9. Canaanites (ᴸᵁ *Ki-in-a-ni*) Pa-a-la-ia (Baʿalia), his wife (Zamtaru) and son (Akiya) are named in *A.T.* 48. 4–7; also Yampali in *A.T.* 158. 35 and Lahaše in *A.T.* 188. 8.

28. D. J. Wiseman, in J. Bottéro, *Le Problème des Habiru*, 1954, pp. 32–42.

29. The term *mištannu* explains Deut. xv. 18 (*mišneh*) used of a man who has served 'the equivalent of' a hired servant for six years. Also Jer. xvi. 18 ('I will recompense the equivalent of their iniquity'), since the

interpretation 'twice as much' would stigmatize Yahweh as unreasonable (M. Tsevat, *H.U.C.A.* xxix, 1959, p. 125).

30. Literally 'good man' (*A.T.* 2. 27, 3. 38). This description is found also in Deut. xix. 12, cf. xxi. 1–9; Joshua xx. 4; in the Talmud (Meg. 26a–27a, M. Tsevat, op. cit., p. 126), and in the New Testament (1 Tim. v. 17; Titus. i. 8).

31. *basāru* is used of passing on factual information, whether good or bad news (cf. Hebrew *bāśar*, 1 Sam. iv. 17; 1 Kings i. 42).

32. C. Fensham, op. cit., pp. 59 f.

33. I. Mendelsohn, *I.E.J.* v, 1955, pp. 65–72.

34. *A.T.*, p. 9; J.-R. Kupper, op. cit., pp. 36 f.; cf. I. J. Gelb, *J.C.S.* xv, 1961, p. 40. This makes the presence of Syrians (*bʰnē ḥēṭ* in Gen. xxiii. 3) far from anachronistic. Personal names from Level VII include Abinahmi (*A.T.** 455. 13), cf. Abinoʿam (Judges iv. 6; *J.A.O.S.* lxxiv, 1954, p. 227, n. 35); Aiabi (= Job) and Sapsi (= Shamash), cf. Samson (ibid., p. 231).

35. Estimated at more than half the population.

36. *B.A.S.O.R.* 94, 1944, pp. 12–27; E. A. Speiser, *Journ. of World History* i, 1953–4, pp. 322 ff. (Unesco, Paris).

37. The Hittite texts (n. 56), *P.R.U.* iv. II. A. 13; K. A. Kitchen, *Suppiluliuma and the Amarna Pharaohs*, 1962, p. 43.

38. The method of writing by ideogram (LUGAL) makes it uncertain whether this was sometimes read as Hurrian *ewiri* 'lord' or west-Semitic *malku* 'chief' (cf. such names as Bitta-LUGAL also written in full as Bitta-ma-al-ki, *A.T.* 94. 11 f.).

39. The term *masi* (Hebrew *mas*; Joshua xvii. 13; 1 Kings v. 27) is used.

40. I. Mendelsohn, op. cit., pp. 65–72; H. Klengel, *Acta Antiquae Acad. Scient. Hungaricae*, xi, 1/2, 1963, pp. 1–15.

41. For the *andurarum* (Hebrew *dʰrôr*), see J. Lewy, *Eretz-Israel* v, 1958, pp. 21 ff., and D. J. Wiseman, *J.S.S.* vii, 1962, p. 168.

42. S. Loewenstamm, *I.E.J.* vi, 1956, p. 220.

43. I. Mendelsohn, *B.A.S.O.R.* 139, 1955, pp. 9 ff.; cf. 83, 1941, pp. 36 ff.

44. Designated *s/šananu* (on the confusion of sibilants at Alalakh, cf. A. Goetze, *J.C.S.* iv, 1950, p. 227, and *R.A.* lii, 1958, pp. 137 ff.). On this term, see *A.T.*, p. 11, n. 4; W. F. Albright on Ps. lxviii. 18, in *Interpretationes ad Vet. Test. . . . S. Mowinckel*, 1955, pp. 2 ff. The Egyptian *snny* is perhaps to be translated 'bowman' rather than as chariot warrior armed with bow (R. Schulman, *Military Rank, Title and Organisation in the Egyptian New Kingdom*, 1964, pp. 59–62). It may well be a loan-word from Syria (cf. Ugar. *tnn*).

45. I. Mendelsohn, *Essays on Jewish Life and Thought presented in honor of S. W. Baron*, 1959, pp. 351–7.

46. I. Mendelsohn, *B.A.S.O.R.* 156, 1959, pp. 38 ff.

47. Gen. xlviii. 22; *A.R.M.* viii. 1, 1958, pp. 2, 181.

48. *A.T.* 17; see S. Lowenstamm, *I.E.J.* vi, 1956, p. 225. The designation *bēl mašikti* could refer to law-breaking or murder (B. Landsberger,

J.C.S. viii, 1954, p. 60, n. 129), or insurrection against the king (Idri-mi Statue, 4; *R.A.* xliv, 1950, p. 151, n. 2).

49. But cf. Ps. cxli. 5, where the action indicates judicial disapproval. The phrase 'to smite the cheek' in the Laws of Hammurabi (cf. 'strike the head' in the parallel Hittite law) probably has a like legal significance. If so, this could explain the official striking of Jesus (John xviii. 19–23) in disapproval as of a false witness (cf. also Matt. v. 39, Luke vi. 29). The corresponding Hebrew phrase occurs in Ps. iii. 8, R.V. 7; 1 Kings xxii. 24; Lam. iii. 30.

50. The word used is *qarnu* 'horn', a synonym for *sissiktu* 'fringe' (*J.C.S.* xii, 1958, p. 129), and thus Hebrew *ḵānāp̄*. The custom may well have lingered on and thus explain the woman's act in Matt. ix. 20.

51. *teknetum* (*A.T.* 52. 13, 53. 10, 54. 13, 57. 29). Cf. *J.A.O.S.* lxv, 1955, p. 197.

52. Thus the Hebrew *ribbō* need not be a later (Aramaizing) form of *reḇāḇāh* (M. Tsevat, op. cit., p. 127). Similarly, the dry measure *parisi* (Old Babylonian *paras*) may be related to the later *perēs* (Dan. v. 28).

53. There are lists of vineyards (*A.T.* 207–11) giving the yield (207) or size of holding (⅛–3 'acres' (*iku*); 211). The term *šukuku* used of vine- and olive-yards (*A.T.* 87. 14–15, 88. 3–4) may be compared with *mesūkāṭô* in Isa. v. 5. The agricultural seasons may be reflected in the local month names (Tsevat, op. cit., p. 128). Sheep appear to have been imported, 28,800 being sent from Carchemish (*A.T.* 349).

54. Tame gazelles were later kept in Palestine, judging by the tax imposed by Solomon (1 Kings v. 3, R.V. iv. 23); see Tsevat, op. cit., p. 128. The presence of the domesticated camel at this early period (*A.T.** 269, 59) has been questioned (*J.C.S.* xii, 1959, p. 29), but it was known at Ugarit, *c.* nineteenth century B.C. (*B.A.S.O.R.* 160, 1960, pp. 42 f.).

55. See D. J. Wiseman, *Syria* xxxix, 1962, pp. 180–7 for some aspects of the Babylonian influence at Alalakh. The style of script is similar to that known from Ugarit and the Gilgamesh fragment from Megiddo (*'Atiqot* ii, 1959, pp. 121–8, pl. xviii).

56. On the grammar, see J. Aro, *A.f.O.* xvii, 1956, pp. 361–5. Hittite texts, a letter (*A.T.* 125), and an oracular inquiry investigating the displeasure of a deity (*A.T.* 454) come from later levels (II–III) as do the Babylonian lexical texts.

57. *A.T.* 15; cf. Deut. iv. 4, xi. 26, xxvi. 16; Ps. cxv. 18; *I.E.J.* vi, 1956, p. 222. The phrase 'for ever' (*ana daria*) is in other legal documents *urram šeram*, literally 'today and tomorrow', with which has been compared the Hebrew 'tomorrow and the day after (tomorrow)'; see J. J. Rabinowitz, *J.N.E.S.* xiv, 1955, pp. 59 f.

58. Thus the seal used in Level IV named Abban, the true founder of the city state (*A.T.*, p. 6). This seal describes the king as *sikiltu* of the god (see note 60).

59. W. Nagel and E. Strommenger, *J.C.S.* xii, 1958, pp. 109–22.

60. *sikiltu* (cf. Hebrew *segullāh*), discussed by M. Greenberg, *J.A.O.S.* lxxi, 1951, pp. 172 ff.

61. Cf. the interesting designation 'the heavens above and the earth beneath' in describing territory in its totality (*A.T.** 55; cf. Deut. iv. 39; Joshua ii. 11).

62. C. L. Woolley, *Alalakh*, pp. 250–7.

63. A. L. Oppenheim, *Ancient Mesopotamia*, 1964, p. 209.

BIBLIOGRAPHY

KLENGEL, H. *Geschichte Syriens in 2. Jahrtausend v.u.Z. Teil I— Nordsyrien*, 1965.

KUPPER, J.-R. *North Mesopotamia and Syria* (*C.A.H.* ii/i), 1963.

SMITH, S. *Alalakh and Chronology*, 1940.

—— *The Statue of Idri-mi* (O.P.B.I.A., no. 1), 1949.

WISEMAN, D. J. *The Alalakh Tablets* (O.P.B.I.A., no. 2), 1953.

WOOLLEY, C. L. *A Forgotten Kingdom* (Pelican Books), 1953.

—— *Alalakh. An Account of the Excavations at Tell Atchana in the Hatay, 1937–1949* (Reports of the Research Committee of the Society of Antiquaries of London, no. xviii), 1955.

MARI

THE city of Mari is situated on the right bank of the Euphrates, not far from Abu Kemal; it is in the Arab Republic of Syria, about 25 kilometres north of the Iraq frontier. Today it bears the Arabic name of Tell Ḥarîri. Since December 1933 this site has been excavated by a French expedition led by the writer, who conducted his sixteenth season there in 1966. Inscriptions found in the temple of Ishtar enabled Tell Ḥarîri to be definitely identified with Mari in January 1934.

Before these excavations began, the city of Mari was known from various cuneiform texts[1]—the chronological tablets from Nippur and Kish; the Oxford prism; the statue of Itur-Shamash in the British Museum; the records of the campaigns of Sargon (middle of the third millennium B.C.) and of Naram-Sin, kings of Agade; the account of the foundation of the dynasty of Isin (end of the third millennium B.C.) by Ishbi-Irra, 'the man of Mari'; the annals of the thirty-third and thirty-fifth years of the reign of Hammurabi, king of Babylon (c. 1792–1750 B.C.), mentioning his capture of Mari, followed by its destruction; and finally the relief of Shamash-resh-uṣur, the Assyrian governor of Mari.

This rather limited information has been enlarged beyond all expectation by the excavations. First, they have enabled us to locate the city exactly, whereas, though it was previously thought to be on the Middle Euphrates, somewhere between Deir ez-Zor and Anah, on an area extending over some 300 kilometres, it had actually never been found. Moreover, the excavations laid bare a capital city of unsuspected splendour. It had several great periods of prosperity, especially one corresponding exactly to the period of the patriarchs, and of Abraham in particular. This indicates its importance with respect to the Old Testament. Mari has much to offer towards a better knowledge of the Old Testament, but the first thing to notice is that the city appears in the history of Mesopotamia. This links it with the Old Testament because, according to Genesis, Mesopotamia was the country of origin of Terah and Abraham.

Mari had two great periods of activity and splendour, the earlier one being in the first half of the third millennium B.C. In France we call this period 'pre-Sargonic' because it comes before Sargon, the founder of the dynasty of Agade; British and American scholars use the term 'Early Dynastic'. The second period was at the beginning of the second millennium B.C., when the powerful kings Iaḫdunlim and Zimrilim, who had restored the city from a state of ruin, were defeated by their ambitious rival, Hammurabi of Babylon. These two periods are illustrated at Mari by impressive buildings. From the first period date the pre-Sargonic palace (discovered in 1964 and still in course of excavation), the archaic ziggurat, and the temples of Ishtar[2] (known as Astarte to the Semites in the Old Testament period), Shamash, Ninhursag, Ishtarat, Ninni-Zaza,[3] and of Dagan with its statues of kings such as Lamgi-Mari, Itur-Shamagan, and Iblul-il. The second period is represented by an enormous palace where Zimrilim, the last king of Mari, lived;[4] it forms a single block of buildings with an area of over $2\frac{1}{2}$ hectares, and it contains more than 300 rooms and courtyards. These buildings were not empty. The temples contained statues and statuettes, placed by the worshippers at the foot of the altars. The palace possessed statues, paintings, and a library, which we shall mention later because of the light they shed on the world of the Old Testament. After or between these two periods of independence Mari was the vassal of the empires which were then at the zenith of their power—the empire of Agade (middle of the third millennium B.C.), the Third Dynasty of Ur (end of the third millennium B.C.), and the Assyrian empire (second and first millennia B.C.). Mari had been one of the greatest capital cities of the ancient world, but just before the Christian era it had been reduced to the little village of Merrhan. Several centuries later it had completely lost its name, and was known only as Ḥarîri.

The population of Mari was basically Semitic, and thus totally different from the people of south Mesopotamia, who were of Sumerian origin. For this reason our knowledge of the customs and beliefs of the people of Mari is of the greatest importance for our understanding of the world of the Old Testament. Cultic practices are an example of this. The ancient temples at Mari were built in the form of a house; this means that the gods were thought to need dwellings similar in arrangement to those of men. We note that in later times Solomon's temple at Jerusalem was called *beṭ Yahweh*, literally 'the house of Yahweh'; in our opinion, this was a reminiscence of earlier times. It is known that the Canaanite cults made great use of *'ašêrîm* (wooden poles) and *maṣṣēḇôṭ* (stone stelae). There is a perfect illustration of this at Mari.[5] In the court-yard of the temple of Ninni-Zaza stood a *maṣṣēḇāh* around which the worshippers walked in procession. At the foot of the temple of Dagan (beginning of the second millennium B.C.) two *'ašêrîm* were erected on stone altars intended for libations, judging by the holes cut in them. Now, in the Old Testament, Judges vi. 25 tells how Gideon cut down the *'ašêrāh* which was *upon* the altar dedicated to Baal. The text refers to a definite event, which is again illus-trated by archaeology. We also know that there was a regulation directing that the altars of Israel must be made of earth (Exod. xx. 24); this is exactly the case of most of the altars at Mari (Pl. V), and the long vessels buried in the earth indicate that libations were poured out at the foot of the altar. Similarly, libations formed part of the cult in Israel, as shown by the reference, for instance, to the Israelite sanctuary at Mizpah (1 Sam. vii. 6). Finally, the Book of the Covenant (Exod. xx. 24) orders sacrifices of 'sheep and oxen', which were also known at Mari. Several small statues re-present worshippers holding sheep or goats in their arms, which they have brought for sacrifice; while on the terrace of the temple of Dagan a pit full of the bones of animals which had been sacri-ficed was dug up.

The city of Mari possessed a ziggurat, or perhaps two, as well as its sanctuaries. It is well known nowadays that the story of the tower of Babel (Gen. xi. 1–9) was directly inspired by one of these tiered buildings, which were common in Mesopotamia.[6] It has now been shown that these enormous buildings, which were con-structed entirely of unbaked bricks (clay bricks dried in the sun), with occasional layers of reeds mixed with bitumen, formed a base for a temple built at the top. The god entered this upper temple after his voyage in heaven, then went in procession down the long flights of steps to the lower temple where he lived. His stay there brought fertility to the land. The unbaked brick ziggurats nearly always had a facing of baked bricks cemented together with bitu-men, to give strength and to protect them against erosion. The Old Testament preserves an extraordinarily exact description of

PLATE V

Earthen altars in temples (Mari)

these buildings—'They had brick for stone, and slime [marg. bitumen] had they for mortar' (Gen. xi. 3); it is accurate in every detail. The name of the city, Babel (Gen. xi. 9), is even more explicit; it is based on the Akkadian *bâb-ili* meaning 'gate of god'. It was in fact the gate by which the god came to earth. Unfortunately, erosion has been so severe at Mari that nothing is left of the upper temple; but the lower temples remain, both dedicated to Dagan, the great fertility god, in the third to the second millennium B.C.

In the palace, dating from the second millennium B.C., there was a large mural painting;[7] it provides a particularly relevant illustration to the Old Testament. This painting, which we named 'The Investiture', was found *in situ* in courtyard 106; it was taken down and brought to the Louvre, where it is now on view. In the centre stands the king of Mari, to whom the goddess Ishtar is giving the emblems of power in the presence of the gods. This scene is surrounded by trees, animals, and goddesses. Some of the details remind one of the Old Testament story of Eden (Gen. ii–iii),[8] which relates, among other things, that the garden of Eden was watered by a river with four tributaries (Gen. ii. 10), that two trees were there, the tree of the knowledge of good and evil (ii. 17) and the tree of life (iii. 22), and that, after the fall of man, Yahweh placed cherubim to guard the way to the tree of life (iii. 24). It is rather surprising that the picture from Mari seems to retain the same memory. Beneath the investiture, two goddesses hold a vase each, out of which pours a flow of water in four streams. On both sides of the central scene two different trees are represented; one is a palm-tree bearing bunches of dates to which men are climbing. The other, which has very stylized branches, cannot be definitely identified, but it is noteworthy that it is obviously guarded by three cherubim who are keeping watch. It must be admitted that this garden, which has been planted, watered, and guarded, does not lack features which relate it to the garden of Eden in Genesis.

The palace of Mari was destroyed by the soldiers of Hammurabi, who reigned at Babylon in the eighteenth century B.C. This is exactly the period in which many Old Testament scholars date the patriarchs, particularly Abraham, the first patriarch. For this reason the written documents of Mari have an important contribution to make. During the excavation of the residence of Zimrilim, we were fortunate enough to discover the city and state archives, some 25,000 cuneiform tablets.[9] Amongst them are economic, legal, and diplomatic texts;[10] the latter are the least numerous, but we suspect that in some respects they are the most valuable. They come from reliable sources, for they are letters sent to the court at Mari by officials, neighbouring kings, members of the royal family, and ambassadors—all eye-witnesses or well-informed reporters of events about which they were warning the king. One could not wish for better correspondents. There is no doubt about the authenticity of the information, nor about its date in history; the period is certainly the first quarter of the second millennium B.C. As mentioned above, this is the period in which the patriarchal epic must be dated, and in particular two of its most important episodes—the departure from Ur, the journey from Ur to Harran and the stay in Harran (Gen. xi. 31).

Although some scholars would differ, we consider that 'Ur of the Chaldees' (Gen. xi. 28), Abraham's birthplace, is the Sumerian city of Ur in southern Mesopotamia, which was excavated by C. L. Woolley from 1922 to 1934.[11] It was pre-eminently the city of the moon-god, Nannar-Sin, to whom a magnificent three-tiered zig-gurat was dedicated. There are two possible routes from Ur to Harran: one way follows the Euphrates upstream, and then the Balikh; the other way follows the Tigris upstream until above Nineveh, where it leaves the Tigris to cross the Ğezireh. In our opinion the Mari tablets indicate that the first route is more likely. These tablets do not, of course, mention Abraham by name, but they refer to events which fit in very well with what we know from the Old Testament. Several times the Mari letters mention the Ḫabiru, whom many orientalists connect with the Hebrews, and above all a tribe called the Benjaminites[12] (some Assyriologists read the name as Iaminites) which sounds unmistakably like the Old Testament tribe. These peoples were migrating from south to north; at any rate, they are all mentioned as being to the north of Mari. *Bene-iamina* means 'sons of the right hand' or 'sons of the south', so one would expect them to live to the south of Mari. There is no doubt that this people's homeland was in southern Mesopotamia, as their name shows, and that they migrated to northern Mesopotamia. One group even arrived at Harran; the text which gives us this information is as follows—'Asditakim and the kings of Zalmaqum on the one hand, and the *suqaqu* and the Elders of the Benjaminites on the other hand, have made a treaty in the temple of Sin at Harran.' We also know that Harran was a centre of the cult of the moon-god, Sin, and that places of pilgrimage were often stopping-places for caravans. The mention of Harran and Ur together is thus strikingly explained,[13] but the mention of the Benjaminites being at Harran is even more striking.

But there is yet more to come. The tablets give an unflattering picture of the Ḫabiru and the Benjaminites; both are described as plunderers and robbers. We seem to hear an unmistakable echo of this opinion in the blessing of Jacob—'Benjamin is a wolf that ravineth: in the morning he shall devour the prey, and at even he shall divide the spoil' (Gen. xlix. 27). However, it must be clearly understood that this mention in the tablets proves that a group of nomads or semi-nomads already called Benjaminites existed before the patriarch Jacob, who can hardly be dated before the seventeenth century B.C.[14] The descendants of these ancient Benjaminites kept up the same traditions; they were always men of war (cf. Judges xx. 16; 1 Chron. xii. 2), and in the seventh to sixth centuries B.C. they still used beacons to pass on information, as they had done in the eighteenth century B.C. (cf. Jer. vi. 1, where *maśʾēt* means 'fire signal'). One tablet from Mari clearly speaks of this— 'All the Benjaminites have raised the torch. From Samânum to Ilum-Muluk, from Ilum-Muluk to Mishlân, all the Benjaminite cities of the Terqa region have raised the torch in response.' Some of the Benjaminites who lived on the banks of the Middle Euphrates had already crossed the river and were migrating westwards, towards the Orontes valley. It could hardly be more obvious that this is the second stage of the patriarchs' journey, taking them from Harran to the land of Canaan (Gen. xii. 5).

Some other texts from Mari are also worthy of note. On several occasions some of them report the death of a *dâwîdûm*. There is some disagreement about the translation of this word (G. Dossin thinks of a *dâwîdûm* as an important person, perhaps a military leader),[15] but it is quite certain that this word is philologically related to King David's name and is definitely connected with warlike deeds. So it is interesting to observe that, when Jesse of Bethlehem named his son David (1 Sam. xvi. 18 f.), he was placing him under the protection of an important person who was valiant in war and who died in battle.

In several places the Old Testament uses language based on the cuneiform tradition. Thus Gen. xxiv. 10 speaks of 'the city of Nahor', the father of Terah; this appears at Mari as *Nakhur*, with Itur-asdu as governor. The name *Laba-an* also appears, though not, of course, the Old Testament character of the same name who was the brother of Rebekah and the son of Nahor (Gen. xxiv. 29, xxix. 5). It is easy to recognize the *Aramu* of Mari as Aramaeans, and this makes sense of the description 'Aramaean' which follows Laban's name (Gen. xxv. 20, xxviii. 5, xxxi. 20, 24), and also of the related liturgical formula from the Mosaic period—'A wandering Aramaean was my father' (Deut. xxvi. 5). Many scholars have tried to see in this formula a projection into the past of a state of affairs which is inconceivable before the twelfth century B.C. It is becoming more and more obvious that the Old Testament accounts of the patriarchs fit in perfectly with our archaeological knowledge of the beginning of the second millennium B.C., and only imperfectly with any more recent period. In the words of H. G. May, cited by H. H. Rowley—'Absolute scepticism towards the patriarchal narratives as historical records is difficult to maintain today in the light of the materials contemporary with the patriarchal period made available as a result of archaeological research'.[16]

The Mari tablets have given new insight into the origins of prophecy in Israel; this has been observed by A. Lods, M. Noth, W. von Soden, and E. Jacob. At Mari we find the conception of a god, especially Dagan, who reveals himself spontaneously, without being asked.[17] The god is imperative; he says—'Go, I *send* you, so that you may *speak* to Zimrilim in these words'. This formula is strictly identical with the one used by the great prophets of Israel—'I do *send* thee unto them: and thou shalt *say* unto them, Thus saith the Lord God' (Ezek. ii. 4). A. Lods was the first to observe[18] that not only the form but often the content, too, of the Mari oracles corresponds with the revelations made known by various *nᵉbî'îm* in Israel. At Mari, as in Israel, the god commanded that an order should be given to the king, and spoke to him like a suzerain to his vassal. At Mari, as in Israel, the prophetic word had to express criticism or a reprimand; then it was not very welcome, but that was a matter of no concern. As

M. Noth has emphasized, these similarities cannot be accidental,[19] and so far they have been found nowhere else in the entire Near East. What has come to light is, therefore, the prehistory of prophecy.

Thousands of proper names occur in the Mari texts, and they shed new light on many Old Testament names, both in the patriarchal age and later. This rich supply has received the attention of several scholars.[20] The meaning of many expressions which were previously obscure has been brought to light. For instance, 'cut a covenant' (Gen. xxxi. 44; 1 Sam. xxiii. 18; 1 Kings v. 26, R.V. 12) becomes clear when it is compared with 'cut the ass' (of a covenant) found in several of the Mari tablets.[21]

The excavations at Mari have played an important part in what H. H. Rowley has called 'The Rediscovery of the Old Testament', referring to the revolution in exegetical methods which is due largely to archaeological research. We may expect the contribution of Mari to go on increasing, since each season we unearth new finds and our information increases year by year.[22]

ANDRÉ PARROT

NOTES

1. *Mari, une ville perdue*, 1945, pp. 226–8.
2. *M.A.M.* i. *Le Temple d'Ishtar*, 1956.
3. Ibid. iii, *Les Temples d'Ishtarat et de Ninni-Zaza*, (1967).
4. Ibid. ii, *Le Palais*, 1958–9.
5. A. Parrot, *V.T. Supp.* i (Congress Volume, Copenhagen, 1953), pp. 112–19.
6. A. Parrot, *Ziggurats et Tour de Babel*, 1949; *La Tour de Babel*, 2nd ed., 1954.
7. A. Parrot, *M.A.M.* ii. *Le Palais. 2. Peintures murales*, 1958.
8. A. Parrot, *Le Musée du Louvre et la Bible*, 1957, pp. 9–12.
9. In course of publication under the title *Archives royales de Mari*, since 1946.
10. For the diplomatic archives, see G. Dossin, *Syria* xix, 1938, pp. 105–206.
11. A. Parrot, *Abraham et son temps*, 1962; C. L. Woolley, *Excavations at Ur*, 1954.
12. G. Dossin, *Mél. syr. offerts à M. René Dussaud*, ii, 1939, pp. 981–96.
13. E. Dhorme, *R.B.* xxxvii, 1928, pp. 367–85, 481–511, xl, 1931, pp. 364–74, 503–18, and *Recueil Edouard Dhorme*, 1951, pp. 191–272; R. de Vaux, *R.B.* liii, 1946, pp. 321–48, lv, 1948, pp. 321–47, lvi, 1949, pp. 5–36, lxxii, 1965, pp. 5–28.
14. For the discussion of the reading of this name, see A. Parrot, *Abraham et son temps*, 1962, pp. 44 f.

15. For the interpretation of this name, A. Parrot, loc. cit. p. 47.
16. H. G. May, *J.B.L.* lx, 1941, p. 113, cited by H. H. Rowley, *B.J.R.L.* xxxii, 1949, p. 4.
17. M. Noth, ibid. xxxiii, 1950, pp. 194–206.
18. A. Lods, *Studies in O.T. Prophecy presented to Professor T. H. Robinson*, ed. H. H. Rowley, 1950, pp. 103–10.
19. M. Noth, loc. cit., p. 199.
20. M. Noth, *Geschichte und A.T.* (*Festschrift* A. Alt), 1953, pp. 127–52.
21. M. Noth, *Ann. de l'Instit. Philol. et d'Hist. orientales et slaves*, xiii, 1953, pp. 433–44; G. Dossin, *Syria* xix, 1938, pp. 108 f.
22. This article has been translated from the French text of Professor Parrot by Mrs. Norma Emerton, M.A., of Oxford.

BIBLIOGRAPHY

i. *Excavations*

Preliminary reports in *Syria* xvi, 1935, pp. 1–28, 117–40, xvii, 1936, pp. 1–31, xviii, 1937, pp. 54–84, 325–54, xix, 1938, pp. 1–29, xx, 1939, pp. 1–22, xxi, 1940, pp. 1–29, xxix, 1952, pp. 183–203, xxx, 1953, pp. 196–221, xxxi, 1954, pp. 151–71, xxxii, 1955, pp. 185–211, xxxix, 1962, pp. 151–79, xli, 1964, pp. 3–20, xlii, 1965, pp. 1–24.
Definitive publications. *Mission archéologique de Mari.* i. *Le temple d'Ishtar*, 1956, ii. *Le Palais*. *1. Architecture*, 1958; *2. Les Peintures murales*, 1958; *3. Documents et monuments*, 1959; iii. *Les Temples d'Ishtarat et de Ninni-Zaza* (in the press).

ii. *Archives*

Archives royales de Mari, under the direction of A. PARROT and G. DOSSIN. Vols. i, iv, v (G. DOSSIN), ii (CH. F. JEAN), iii, vi (J.-R. KUPPER), vii (J. BOTTÉRO), viii (G. BOYER), ix, xii (M. BIROT), xi (M. BURKE), xv (J. BOTTÉRO and A. FINET); G. DOSSIN, 'Les Archives épistolaires du palais de Mari', *Syria* xix, 1938, pp. 105–26; 'Les Archives économiques du palais de Mari', ibid. xx, 1939, pp. 97–113; 'Signaux lumineux au pays de Mari', *R.A.* xxxv, 1938, pp. 174–86; 'Benjaminites dans les textes de Mari', *Mél. syr. offerts à M. René Dussaud*, ii, 1939, pp. 981–96.

iii. *General*

GIBSON, J. C. L. 'Light from Mari on the Patriarchs', *J.S.S.* vii, 1962, pp. 44–62.
KUPPER, J.-R. *Les Nomades en Mésopotamie au temps des rois de Mari*, 1957.
PARROT, A. *Mari, une ville perdue*, 1945.
—— *Mari* (Éditions Ides et Calendes), 1953.
—— 'Les Tablettes de Mari et l'Ancien Testament', *R.H.P.R.* xxx. 1950, pp. 1–11.
—— *Abraham et son temps*, 1962.

UGARIT

UNTIL 1928 the large mound of Ras Shamra (about 70 acres) near the Syrian coast, about 25 miles south of the mouth of the Orontes, was just another of the many ruin mounds of Syria, potentially rewarding in the disclosure of the succession and interrelation of cultures in the corridor between Mesopotamia, Anatolia, and Egypt. The proximity of Cyprus, visible on a clear day, suggested the further probability of contacts with Crete under the Minoan sea-kings and with Mycenaean Greece and the Aegean. All these expectations were realized, but the unique significance of the site was unsuspected till the clearance of a tomb-vault in hewn stone, accidentally discovered by a peasant, roused the interest of R. Dussaud, the late distinguished Curator of Oriental Antiquities at the Louvre, at whose instance an expedition was mounted, under C. F. A. Schaeffer, to Minet el-Beida, the sea-shore settlement where the tomb was found, and to the neighbouring mound of Ras Shamra, which was soon identified, thanks to documentary discoveries, with ancient Ugarit, already known as an important city in Canaan from the Tell el-Amarna tablets (c. 1400 B.C.),[1] and from the political correspondence in the Mari tablets (c. 1700 B.C.).[2] Since then twenty-eight campaigns have not exhausted even the Late Bronze Age at Ras Shamra nor, happily, the energy and resource of Schaeffer, who, even when the Second World War closed excavations, and called him to military service, produced his magisterial conspectus of cultural relations of the various archaeological stations in the Near East in the third and second millennia B.C.,[3] for which Ras Shamra provided an admirable key.

Ras Shamra is peculiarly associated with the sensational discovery of voluminous cuneiform texts, administrative, religious, and literary, of which those in Akkadian and in the new Canaanite alphabetic script are the most numerous and significant. The pioneer work of decipherment and interpretation will ever be honourably associated with the names of C. Virolleaud[4] and R. Dussaud[5] respectively, and even if their initial opinions have since modified, many of their inspired insights have stood the test of criticism. But even apart from the texts, which are the most significant archaeological discovery of our time for the elucidation of the subject-matter of the Old Testament, Ras Shamra, with its strategic situation and ubiquitous contacts, would have been outstanding in Near Eastern archaeology, thanks to the wealth of evidence from the site and the versatile interest of Schaeffer in relating it to neighbouring regions.

Restriction of space and the interests of Old Testament scholarship demand that our study be limited to the apogee of the culture of Ras Shamra in the last two centuries of her history, from about the middle of the fourteenth century B.C. to the early part of the twelfth century B.C., when her collapse, like that of most of the flourishing coastal sites of Syria and Palestine and of the empire of her overlord, the Hittite king, coincided with the coming of the 'Sea Peoples' including the Philistines familiar in the Old Testament. At that time Ugarit was an impressive city with its stone-built palace of 10,000 square yards, with its host of officials and feudal retainers of various degree around the royal family, its foreign diplomats and wealthy merchants, its higher quarter crowned by the temples of Baal and Dagon with their cultured clergy with their libraries of literary texts, its comfortable and spacious urban residences, its busy port thronged with resident merchants and shipping with interests in Egypt, Cyprus, Crete and the Aegean, Byblos, Tyre, Acco, Ashdod and Ashkelon, all attested in business records from the southern adjunct of the palace[6] —to say nothing of merchants from Anatolia, who are often mentioned in the political correspondence of the Hittite kings and their viceroys in Carchemish in the 'Foreign Office' of the palace, which is one of the great discoveries of Ras Shamra.

The significant new cultural development at Ras Shamra and other sites in Syria and Palestine in the first phase of the Middle Bronze Age was undoubtedly a consequence of the sedentarization of the Amorites after the disturbances of the last three centuries of the third millennium B.C. The only conspicuous monuments of this period so far excavated are the temple of Baal on the acropolis, which Schaeffer feasibly dates to the twenty-first century B.C., and that of Dagon, about 50 yards to the south-east, somewhat more massively and simply constructed on the same general plan and orientation,[7] which may be earlier. These are the earliest examples of the tripartite temple of outer court with the great altar, inner court or hall, and inmost shrine; cf. *ḥāṣēr, hêḵāl,* and *dᵉḇîr* of Solomon's temple. The founding of these temples, with the cult of Baal, which predominated in the religion of Ras Shamra and, indeed, the whole of Canaan until the destruction of Ras Shamra, marks the beginning of the known Canaanite historical period at the site.

Probably also from the same period, Baal himself is depicted in a striking near life-size relief on a stele from the temple,[8] which represents his characteristic features and activities as known from the Baal myth in the alphabetic texts from the residence of the chief priest of the temple. A warlike figure, bearded and striding out in the warrior's short kilt, with a helmet garnished with horns of the bull, his cult-animal, he wields a mace in his right hand, the weapon in his conflict with the tyrant waters of chaos in the myth,[9] and in his left he holds a spear with the point grounded. The spear-haft is crooked and branched, representing either forked lightning of the early winter storms, in which Baal in the myth is particularly active, or a cedar tree, which he brandishes in a certain passage of the myth describing his moment of triumph.[10] Two registers of undulations under the figure are regarded by Schaeffer as the Egyptian hieroglyphic ideogram for a mountain region,[11] but they may be an adaptation of the hieroglyphic sign for water, reflecting the title of Baal in the myth 'He who Mounteth the Clouds' (*rkb 'rpt,* cf. *rōḵēḇ bāᶜᵃrāḇôt,* Ps. lxviii. 5, R.V. 4; for the general conception, cf. Deut. xxxiii. 26; Pss. xviii. 11, R.V. 10, lxviii. 34, R.V. 33, civ. 3) and his victory over Sea-and-River (cf. Ps. xciii. 3 f.). The double row of undulations may symbolize the upper and lower waters of Semitic cosmology. A small figure which stands before Baal, facing the same way, with hands upraised and palms outwards, suggests a priest mediating the blessing of Baal, but, in view of the antiquity of the sculpture, it may depict the king in his sacral office,[12] the kings Krt and Dn'el in the legends being *ex officio* priestly mediators of the blessing of their god in nature[13] (cf. Ps. lxxii. 6 f.; Isa. ix. 5, R.V. 6, xi. 6–9).

Two other male figures, the one, unfortunately fragmentary, holding the Egyptian *was* sceptre of well-being and the *ankh* symbol of life,[14] and the other with features indeterminate, but horned and wearing a curious head-dress, either foliage or an

ostrich plume,[15] were also found near the Baal temple. The short
sceptre of the latter in the form of a crook is the symbol of Osiris,
the dying and rising god of vegetation in Egypt, whose crown is
characterized by a double ostrich plume, which is added to the
crown of the dead Pharaoh, who was assimilated at death to
Osiris. Schaeffer compares the former to the representation of
Seth in the Four Hundred Year Stele of Ramesses II at Tanis,[16]
suggesting that the god is Mot,[17] the power of Death and Sterility,
the inveterate enemy of Baal in the Ras Shamra myths.[18] A later
stele from the Baal temple, however, also an Egyptian dedication,
represents Seth of Sapuna, that is Saphon, the mountain seat of
Baal in the myths, so that both figures represent Baal in his various
characters, as giver of life and well-being,[19] like Osiris the dying
and rising god of vegetation, and, in the case of the first relief,
Baal as the god of thunder and winter rain—Hadad, as he is
termed in the myths—an active warrior, god in his eternal struggle
to maintain Order against Chaos. The female figure in another
fragmentary relief with spear and *ankh* sign and enfolded by wings[20]
is almost certainly Anat, the sister and associate of Baal in the
myths, where she is the most active goddess in the fertility cult,
and in one of which she accomplishes a journey on the wing.[21] The
ankh sign in her hand reflects her fertility function and her role in
the myths as the champion of Baal when he is in eclipse in the
underworld as the dying and rising vegetation god, while the spear
well accords with her warlike character exemplified in a text[22]
where she annihilates her adversaries in a veritable blood-bath.
There is so far no representation of Dagon, but his cult in the
other temple is attested by two votive stelae (*skn* and *p gr*; cf. Lev.
xxvi. 30, with *double entendre*) dedicated to him found by the
temple. The cult of Baal was certainly established by the time of
the Twelfth Dynasty of Egypt, several of the representatives of
which dedicated statuary to the temple, the inscriptions on which
have survived. The furniture of the cult has not survived, but
a magnificent gold bowl[23] and patera[24] in repoussé work, which we
regard as of provincial Mycenaean work, which were found in
a cache near the temple, were probably used in the cult. The
temples were finally destroyed at the beginning of the twelfth
century B.C.

Western influences are apparent at Ras Shamra from *c.* 1900

B.C. in distinctive Cretan pottery[25] and a type of masonry tomb with access through a stepped corridor,[26] which developed into the symmetrical tombs with finely hewn stone,[27] which recall, but with distinct local peculiarities,[28] the corbel-vaulted tombs of Mycenae. The Mycenaean settlement in this lucrative trade terminal intensified in the Late Bronze Age, when Mycenaean and Cypriot pottery forms predominate and Mycenaean provincial art developed, best attested at Ras Shamra in the repoussé work on the gold patera and bowl from near the Baal temple, and in the beautiful ivory relief on the lid of an unguent casket from Minet el-Beida[29] depicting the Mother-goddess, with Cretan features and dress, offering heads of corn to two rampant caprids. This is a significant sculpture as it seems a variant on the motif of two caprids similarly flanking a date-palm on a distinctive painted pottery found most abundantly in the vicinity of Tell el-'Ajjul in Palestine.[30] The Minet el-Beida sculpture suggests that the tree corresponds to the Mother-goddess, and is in fact the tree of life. The association between tree and goddess (Canaanite Ashera, as we now know from the Ras Shamra texts) explains the significance of the 'ašērāh, which might be either a natural or a stylized tree at local Canaanite sanctuaries, so abominated in the Old Testament.

The presence of these wealthy Mycenaean merchants with their contacts with Crete and Egypt was probably conducive to the comfort and elegance of domestic building in Ugarit of the Late Bronze Age, which was remarkable in contemporary Canaan. The most distinctive feature is the finely built family vault below the ground story or courtyard of the dwelling-houses and in a separate compartment of the north side of the palace. A remarkable feature in those tombs was an aperture to permit the dead access to libations, for which a jar was provided at the aperture,[31] and other such provisions were made both within and without the tomb.[32] Bottomless jars communicating with small pits by the tombs may also have served for the libation, or for blood from sacrifices to the dead. Such installations are also attested in Crete and Cyprus.[33] Schaeffer has cited convincing evidence from Hesiod for such a rite in the myths of the daughters of Danaos, who spent their time pouring water into bottomless jars.[34] This is generally explained as a frustrating task in punishment for the murder of their husbands, but it may be the eventual rationalization of a primitive fertility rite, of which Hesiod is apparently aware. Though this myth in conjunction with the Cretan prototype of the corbel-vaulted masonry tombs of Ras Shamra indicates western affinities, the rite of libation to the dead was widely practised beyond the influence of the Aegean, the most remarkable analogy being actually from Israelite Samaria,[35] which may give a new point to the insistence on the confession of the Israelite peasant, when he presented his tithes, that nothing of the crop had been offered to the dead (Deut. xxvi. 14).[36]

The recognition of Aegean settlements in the Late Bronze Age on the coast of Syria and at Tell Abu Hawam by the mouth of the Kishon in Palestine opens up the interesting possibility of the mutual influence of Aegean and Semitic traditions, for example, the myth of Perseus and Andromeda, which is localized at Jaffa, and the Canaanite myth of Astarte, the bride of the tyrant Sea, which is extant in an Egyptian version,[37] and perhaps also the Greek myth of Typhon,[38] the power of Chaos, which may be associated with a local myth of the god of Mount Saphon on the northern horizon of Ras Shamra before he was displaced by Baal,[39] who is known in the Ras Shamra myths as the champion of Order against Chaos. Of more interest for Old Testament study is the possibility of the influence of the Herakles myth on the Samson saga.[40]

The exigencies of this study oblige us to pass over the splendour of the great stone-built palace, which in its superficial extent of over 10,000 square yards[41] is by far the largest palace excavated in the Near East outside Mesopotamia. It was actually the administrative centre as well as the residence of the royal family, and contained the archives of the realm, the voluminous administrative texts in Akkadian and the vernacular being systematically, and for the student very conveniently, grouped in the various government departments—the fiscal business of the provincial regions in compartments by the main, western entrance, the business of the city concerning dues to and from various classes and individuals in the city and palace in the eastern archive by the entrance to the palace from the city, and legal matter of conveyance of property, royal gifts, and investiture with feudal status, in which the king was personally involved, in the central archive. The south archive was exclusively devoted to foreign correspondence in affairs of state,

particularly with the Hittite overlords and their viceroys in Carchemish, and with other states in north Syria such as Amurru,
with whom at least one of the kings of Ugarit, Ammištamru II,
intermarried, as is indicated by a dossier on his divorce, apparently
for adultery, 'the great sin',[42] for which he was able to insist on
the death penalty (cf. Deut. xxii. 20 f.; Lev. xx. 10) even after the
lady had effected her escape to the court of her brother, the king of
Amurru.[43] In this case it is interesting to note that the obligation
of the king of Amurru to avenge the blood of his sister was dis-
charged by the payment of blood-money by Ammištamru at the
instance of the Hittite king Tudhaliyas IV, the overlord of both.[44]
In addition to these palace archives further discoveries of the same
nature have been made in a large building south of the palace-
complex, styled by Schaeffer 'the little palace', where a number of
texts are reported dealing with commercial relations.[45] In addition, a number of texts were recovered, still in the palace baking-
oven in court V of Schaeffer's plan, which are reported to attest
contacts with such well-known places as Byblos and Tyre on the
Syrian coast, and Acco, Ashdod, and Ashkelon in Palestine.[46] All
these administrative departments had their apprentice scribes,
whose exemplars and exercises have been recovered,[47] including
specimens of the local cuneiform alphabet,[48] the earliest alphabet
in the history of man.

The Hittite correspondence in the south archive of the palace
has a peculiar interest. In reporting to the Pharaoh on the state of
affairs in Syria in the Tell el-Amarna tablets, Abimilki of Tyre
reports that half of Ugarit, or perhaps of the palace, has been
destroyed by fire and half of it has disappeared,[49] which Schaeffer
relates to the great conflagration of the site, with evidence also of
earthquake, which is dated in the reign of Akhenaten, whose
scarabs were found both below and above the layer of destruction,
and which is the basis of his great *Stratigraphie Comparée*.[50] In the
same letter Abimilki states that the Hittites are not in Ugarit,
though the implication is that they might have been expected.
The Hittite correspondence now discovered at Ugarit specifically
documents the Hittite advance in north Syria with vassal treaties
with various north Syrian principalities, including those in the
region mentioned in the Amarna correspondence. These tablets
in Akkadian cuneiform are carefully sealed with the seals of the

Hittite kings Suppiluliumas I, Mursilis II, Hattusilis III, Tudhaliyas IV, and their viceroys Initešub and Talmitešub in Carchemish, and name the kings of Ugarit from Niqmad II to Hammurabi between *c.* 1365 B.C. and the beginning of the twelfth century B.C.[51] They thus permit a fairly accurate relative chronology of the last six kings who reigned in Ugarit, and they are a valuable supplement to the Tell el-Amarna tablets and to the Hittite archives of Boğazköy. Of particular interest to Old Testament scholarship is the fact that in the treaty of Suppiluliumas I with Niqmad II,[52] and more particularly in that of Mursilis II with Niqmepa,[53] we have a fine example of the conventional form of vassal treaties in the Late Bronze Age, the recognition of which in the Hittite archives of Boğazköy by V. Korošec[54] has had such fruitful impact on form criticism of passages in the Old Testament relating to the Covenant.[55] The Hittite domination, firm, if scrupulously just and even considerate, lasted till the fall of both Ugarit and the Hittite Empire in the early part of the twelfth century B.C., with a brief interlude under the rebel Arḫalbu,[56] when apparently the Pharaoh Horemheb was able to take the offensive against the Hittites in north Syria and reassert Egyptian influence at Ugarit, where fragments of alabaster vases with his cartouche were found in the palace, and perhaps the Egyptian votive stele to Seth of Sapuna (*v. supra*, p. 148) was dedicated by one of his 'treasurers'. In view of this situation the fragments of an alabaster vase depicting the wedding of a prince, described in hieroglyphics as 'Niqmad Prince of Ugarit',[57] with an Egyptian princess, apparently one of the daughters of Akhenaten, to judge from elements of Amarna art,[58] introduces a note of real drama. In thus giving his daughter to a foreign prince, which in the days of Amenophis III was stated to be never done,[59] the Pharaoh was surely making a last desperate effort to retain control of this important and very wealthy Canaanite metropolis in face of the encroachment of Suppiluliumas.

With the synchronisms with Hittite chronology and royal deeds from the central archive in the palace of Ugarit, which cite the king and name his father, the evidence for the succession at Ugarit from Niqmad II, the contemporary of Suppiluliumas I (*c.* 1380–1346 B.C.), to Hammurabi ('*mrp* in alphabetic cuneiform), the contemporary of Suppiluliumas II (*c.* 1225 B.C.), is complete.

Besides these ruling kings, including Ammištamru I (*v. supra,*
n. 1), the dynastic seal of the kings of Ugarit, used also on some of
those tablets, names 'Yaqaru the son of Niqmad, king of Ugarit'.
He is actually named in a fragmentary king-list so far unpublished
but intimated by Schaeffer,[60] and estimated by him to have contained no fewer than thirty names. Reckoning on the basis of about
200 years for the last eight kings of Ugarit, we may propose a date
in the sixteenth century B.C. for Yaqaru, which might coincide
with his investment by one of the early Pharaohs of the Eighteenth
Dynasty in their campaigns to 'the inverted river' Euphrates after
the expulsion of the Hyksos in the sixteenth century B.C. In this
connexion it may be recalled that Addunirari of Nuḫašše in north
Syria evidently traced his dynasty back to the anointing of his
grandfather by Tuthmosis III.[61] Nougayrol dates the glyptic of
the seal to the nineteenth or eighteenth century B.C. on the
analogy of Mesopotamian glyptic.[62] This to be sure is probably
too early for Yaqaru, but his seal may be adapted from an earlier
family seal or heirloom, the earlier figures named in the fragmentary king-list being not ruling kings but ancestors of the royal
house, the lengthy pedigree having its analogy in Arab tribal
genealogies. The name Yaqaru is also attested in a royal deed in
Akkadian.[63] This may be, as Nougayrol suggests, the proper name
of the founder of the dynasty used as a title by his successors, as
among the Hittites, in Mitanni, and apparently also in Alalakh,[64]
or in Judah, where no successor of David bore this personal name,
but all identified themselves with the founder of the dynasty, as is
suggested by the Psalms, where the king is referred to as 'David'.
But since there is no other known reference to any of the reigning
kings of Ugarit by the name, the deed is probably a relic from the
actual reign of Yaqaru.

The dynastic seal has a further significance. The motif has been
demonstrated, on the evidence of Mesopotamian seals, to be that
of homage to the deified king.[65] There is a striking parallel in the
neighbouring kingdom of Alalakh, where in the Late Bronze Age
king Niqmepa uses a seal of Abba'el the Mighty King, son of
Šarri-il the Servant of Tešub, the Peculiar Possession[66] of Tešub'.[67]
In the glyptic on the seal Abba'el triumphs over a prostrate enemy
and receives the sign of life (*ankh*) from a horned goddess, possibly Anat. The peculiar association of king and god is significant

in view of the conception of the king in Israel as the son of God
(Ps. ii. 7; Isa. ix. 5, R.V. 6;[68] 2 Sam. vii. 14). This theme is further
expressed in a remarkable ivory relief on the central panel of
a series of sixteen from a couch, or bed, from the royal apartments
in the palace, depicting a winged goddess, probably Anat, suckling
a pair of youths,[69] probably a single person here depicted in
duplicate for the sake of symmetry. This is surely the heir apparent,
who is described in the Legend of King Krt among the literary
texts of Ras Shamra as one

> Who sucks the milk of Aterat,
> Who sucks the breast of the Virgin (Anat).[70]

In this connexion the new king-list seems, at first sight, to offer
significant new data for the conception of divine kingship in
ancient Canaan, since the royal names are prefaced by *'il* 'god'.
But as this applied apparently only to dead kings, the evidence
probably carries us no further than the cult of the dead ancestor
(*'il'ib*) already attested at Ras Shamra in texts and in grave installations (*v. supra*, pp. 149 f.).

The cosmopolitan life of this wealthy Levantine entrepôt of
international trade, which was courted by both Hittites and Egypt,
is reflected in the many inscriptions, which are the most striking
of the many great discoveries at Ras Shamra. Inscriptions of
greater and less content have been found in five scripts and no less
than seven languages. Inscriptions on Egyptian monuments by
the Baal temple and on smaller fragments in the palace are in
hieroglyphics. The association of the Semitic population with
Mesopotamia from the third millennium B.C. is reflected in
Sumerian, which was, however, the dead language of liturgy in the
Late Bronze Age, for which lexicons and syllabaries with the
vernacular in alphabetic script, Akkadian syllabic cuneiform, and
in certain cases Hurrian equivalents, were necessary.[71] In the
extreme north of Syria the Hurrians were numerous, as the nomenclature of the administrative texts indicates, and there are texts
wholly in the Hurrian language in the local alphabetic script. In
Akkadian and vernacular texts Hittite words intrude, while in the
seals of the Hittite rulers in their political correspondence in the
south archive Hittite hieroglyphics were used. Finally, a linear
script with Cypriot affinities was attested sparsely in a few letters

on painted Mycenaean pottery and in a short inscription on a silver bowl from the vicinity of the temples on the acropolis,[72] and latterly in tablets from the wealthy residential quarters just east of the palace,[73] and in two from the 'small palace',[74] where significantly they were found with official fiscal records in alphabetic cuneiform. With the discovery of these tablets at Ras Shamra and similar tablets recently found in the last phase of the Bronze Age at Khirbet Deir 'Alla in the Jordan Valley,[75] a new problem is set in Near Eastern archaeology. In the present state of the evidence, however, such a find, while interesting evidence of a permanent western element in the population of Ugarit, is of uncertain significance since the script has not yet been deciphered.

Of most direct relevance to the study of the Old Testament are the great number of administrative texts from the palace, and the myths, sagas, and ritual texts from the libraries of two priests in the neighbourhood of the temple of Baal on the acropolis, both dated later than the great destruction of Ugarit *c*. 1365 B.C. The former are vital for the study of Canaanite society and institutions; the latter, of epic style and often approaching epic proportions, comprise a substantial torso of the literature of Canaan on the eve of the Hebrew settlement in Palestine.

The administrative texts, in conjunction with the legends of the ancient kings Krt and Aqht, permit the study of the development of the institution of kingship from its primitive origin, when the king was personal leader in war, priest, dispenser of fertility (cf. Ps. lxxii. 6; Lam. iv. 20), and judge (cf. 2 Sam. xv. 2), to the devolution of his authority in the Late Bronze Age. By then the priesthood had devolved upon fourteen families,[76] and his military function on professional soldiers in a feudal order. One of these, 'iwržr, was apparently a high-ranking baron in command of a frontier area.[77] The order was based on chariot tactics introduced into Western Asia by the Aryans *c*. 1800 B.C.; hence the title of the chief military order *mrynm*, known as a Sanskrit word from the 'charioteers' (*maryas*) of the war-god Indra. These were the 'knights', who had 'squires' (*n'rm*, cf. 2 Sam. ii. 14; 1 Kings xx. 15) and other retainers, with estates to maintain their studs. Many of the royal deeds from the palace deal with grants of this status and its perquisites, with the burdens to the palace waived or adjusted,[78] as Saul, on a smaller scale, was prepared to make immune (*ḫopši*) the family of the man who would take up the challenge of Goliath (1 Sam. xvii. 25). The same texts reveal an order *mur'u* attached to high-ranking officers and to the crown-prince. The precise significance of this term is uncertain, but it may correspond to the personal retinue which Adonijah affected to support his pretensions to the throne (1 Kings i. 5). Another order is *mudu* (Akkadian), defined as 'the king's *m*.' and 'the queen's *m*.'. Nougayrol proposes that this term means 'familiars',[79] which might suggest 'the king's friends' of 1 Chron. xxvii. 33. The civilian subjects of the realm were organized by localities, or by guilds of professions or trades for state levies in money, produce, or day labour of man or beast of burden,[80] a much milder corvée than Solomon applied in Israel. Fiscal tablets also attest the distribution of the produce levied on the various districts to the court and palace retainers,[81] which recalls Solomon's fiscal provision (1 Kings iv. 7 ff.).

In Ugarit, as in all other states great and small in the Near East in the second millennium B.C., there were *ḫabiru*, or SA-GAZ.[82] First known at Ugarit in a fiscal text in Akkadian cuneiform[83] and in two others in alphabetic cuneiform,[84] where they are called '*prm*,[85] and are associated with a part of the town *Ḫalbu*, they are named in several other texts. The most interesting, if perhaps the most problematic, of these is a royal grant of land where it is stated 'the *ḫabiru* shall not enter his house'.[86] In the context certain immunities are granted, and the reference may be to the exemption from quartering *ḫabiru* on the property. Alternatively, the clause may prohibit the harbouring of *ḫabiru*, who might make a baron unduly powerful. A significant contribution to the problem of the *ḫabiru* is the agreement with king Niqmepa under the seal of Hattusilis III to extradite subjects or fugitive slaves of Ugarit who should seek refuge in the territory of 'the *ḫabiru* of the Sun', that is, the Hittite king.[87] Thus the *ḫabiru*, known from other treaties of the Hittite kings with north Syrian states as a distinctive community, with its own gods, and from domestic archives from Nuzi (fourteenth century B.C.) as aliens of various origin, were an alien class, settled in separate cantonments and districts where they might be effectively controlled, and, if necessary, recruited.[88] Such a concentration of the settlement of this alien class was highly advisable, since they were a potentially dangerous element among whom an exile might recruit a following to support his ambitions, as in the case of Idrimi from the neighbouring state of Alalakh in the late sixteenth or fifteenth century B.C., who records how he found refuge in the territory of the SA-GAZ south of the kingdom for seven years until he was able to return and establish himself on the throne of Alalakh.[89] The Ras Shamra texts do not further define the status of the *ḫabiru*, but, in view of their status as resident aliens, there is no reason to suppose that that was other than among the Hittites or at Nuzi, where, though not slaves, and in individual cases able to rise high in mercenary servitude, they were still an underprivileged class, who might, as at Nuzi, opt for the security of the slave by binding themselves to service for a stated period, an institution which Hebrew law in the Book of the Covenant seems to visualize (Exod. xxi. 2–6).

No law code has come to light at Ras Shamra, and though there are many legal texts, these relate largely to feudal administration, and have the form of absolute royal decrees. There are, however, cases which are evidently governed by an objective legal tradition, where the king is cited as witness and guarantor of the transaction, to which his personal seal is often affixed. Marriage contracts apparently refer to a regular legal convention, the bride-price being the capital of husband and wife while the marriage obtained, but reverting to the wife in the event of divorce.[90] Deeds of adoption are attested, one such[91] being possibly a case of sale-adoption, where a creditor for the sum of 500 shekels acquires the title to succeed to the property of his adoptive mother. In an interesting text[92] a slave-girl, Iliyawa, is emancipated in view of marriage, the redemption price being at once her purchase price and the bride-price to her master as head of the household to which she had belonged. This deed and others attest anointing as a rite of emancipation, a piece of evidence which indicates that the significance of the rite was not the conferment of a special *mana*,[93] nor the delegation of authority,[94] but separation from a former status and association,[95] which best explains the anointing of inanimate objects, such as the priestly vestments (Exod. xxix. 21) and the tabernacle and its furniture (Exod. xxx. 26–29), as is indicated by the use of the verb *ḳidēš* 'sanctified' as a synonym of *māšaḥ* 'anointed'. The convention of slavery for debt was also known, as in Israel (Exod. xxi. 7; 2 Kings iv. 1; Isa. l. 1; Neh. v. 5; cf. Code of Hammurabi, §117). There is a record, for instance, of the redemption by one *'ewrkl* of certain persons from the people, or merchants, of Beirut, with the stipulation that they should incur no obligation (*'unṯ*) until they had reimbursed *'iwrkl*.[96] Our interpretation of this interesting text is that they should not incur further debts on the security of their persons, to which *'iwrkl* had a prior claim, until their ransom price was paid. Perhaps the pledge of a debtor's cloak in Hebrew law (Exod. xxii. 26; cf. Amos ii. 8), which could be of little practical value to the creditor, was a guarantee of the prior claim of his creditor to acquire him as a slave, the cloak symbolizing the person.

Social conventions, on which customs and probably Canaanite law were based, are further implied in the literary texts. These relate to the ritual seclusion at birth[97] (cf. Lev. xii), death and mourning,[98] to marriage ceremonial[99] with the involvement of the bride's whole family, and to blood-revenge. These are expressed in the mythological texts, the anthropomorphism of which entitles us to see here a faithful reflection of actual conventions in Canaanite society.[100]

The chief mythological texts concern four subjects, Baal's triumph over Chaos,[101] his struggle against Death and Sterility,[102] the Birth of the Dawn and Evening Star,[103] and the marriage of Nikkal and the Moon-god.[104] The last exemplifies the details of the marriage transaction, and probably relates to an actual marriage of a bride, who is named at the end of the text. The third, which contains both myth and rubrics, relates to a spring ceremony, possibly one where a communion meal confirms the association of peasants and migrant nomads in their summer grazing, the rather broad sexual myth relating to the *connubium* of the two groups and the reunion of the nomads with their *ṣadîka* wives, to which there may be a certain analogy in the association of the Hebrew nomads and the Moabite women at Baal-peor (Num. xxv. 1 ff.; Hos. ix. 10).

In the Baal mythology three fragmentary texts describe how Order in nature is menaced by the insolence of 'Sea the Prince and River the Ruler' against whom 'the divine assembly' (cf. Pss. lxxxii. 1, lxxxix. 6 ff., R.V. 5 ff.; Isa. xiv. 13) is apparently powerless. Baal, however, engages the unruly waters and eventually prevails, so gaining his 'eternal kingship'. This is the local Canaanite variant of the myth of Cosmos and Chaos, best known in the Babylonian myth *enuma eliš*, the leading motifs of which it exhibits. The theme and imagery recur in the Old Testament in passages in the Prophets relating to God's kingship and judgement or rule, and in the Enthronement Psalms, notably Ps. xciii. The various indications of the association of such passages with the autumnal New Year suggest a similar association of the Canaanite myth, though in the fragments cited there is no conclusive proof.

The rest of the Baal mythology reflects the tension between fertility and sterility in the peasant's year. The chief themes are the death of Baal, the vengeance of his sister Anat, his resurrection, the building of his 'house', and his final victory over Death. Baal, primarily the god manifest in the rains and storms of winter, is here the local variation of Mesopotamian Tammuz, Egyptian Osiris, and Greek Dionysus, which suggests its relation to seasonal rituals. Anat's mourning for the dead Baal suggests the weeping for Tammuz by the women of Jerusalem, presumably in the sixth month (Ezek. viii. 14); her vengeance on Death and Sterility, cutting him with a sickle, winnowing him, parching him with fire, grinding him, and so on, obviously suggest the Hebrew rite of the first sheaf (Lev. ii. 14); the building of the 'house' of Baal in the season of heavy rains suggests the analogy of the dedication of Solomon's temple in the seventh month, Ethanim, the 'regular rains' (1 Kings viii. 2). This was also the season of the Feast of Tabernacles in Israel. The ascendancy of Baal at this season, who is acclaimed as 'our king, over whom none has pre-eminence', and the establishment of his 'house' as a symbol of his lordship, are themes which immediately evoke the analogy of the establishment of the house of Yahweh (Isa. ii. 2; Mic. iv. 1), whose kingship is also established through conflict (e.g. Pss. xlvi, xciii, etc.).[105] The functional nature of these Baal myths as the verbal counterpart to seasonal rituals in the fertility cult[106] has been disputed, and we freely admit that they are the end-product of a long period of elaboration and have an intrinsic literary value.[107] The relations between the vicissitudes of Baal and the peasant's year, however, to which we have referred, seem too obvious to be ignored.

The legends concerning the two ancient kings Krt and Dn'el have also a direct bearing on Old Testament study. Both, without prospect of an heir, receive, like Abraham, assurance of issue. Dn'el's son is described with relation to his social duties, an important text for sociological study. The vicissitudes of Krt and his marriage and provision of an heir have a similar value, to be fully realized by detailed study.[108] The Dn'el text, like the Krt text, is fragmentary, though substantial, and is similarly to be appreciated. Dn'el's son Aqht receives a bow from the divine craftsman, which, intended for gods, excites the envy of Anat, who, using her allurements to secure it, is repulsed by Aqht with scorn, but then strikes him down. His blood violently shed and uncovered by the earth occasions sterility (cf. Gen. iv. 11 f.; Num. xxxv. 33), the drought being described in practically the same terms as in David's curse on the mountains of Gilboa on the death of Saul (2 Sam. i. 21). The association of the primitive king with fertility in nature may be noted, as also in the Krt text. Dn'el then performs certain rites of imitative magic to transmit fertility, fondly anticipating his son Aqht gathering in the harvest, an instance of dramatic irony on the part of the poet. Learning subsequently that the slain man is his own son, Dn'el recovers his remains, mourns, and buries the body. Underlying the myth may be the personification of the genius of the corn, which was ceremonially killed to make the new crop available for public use; cf. the dismemberment of Mot (Death and Sterility) in the Baal myth, and the slaughter of Saul's seven sons at Gibeon (2 Sam. xxi. 8 ff.), where tradition has associated a local harvest rite of desacralization, probably long obsolete in its gruesome original form, with an historical event.[109]

Detailed study of these texts reveals numerous striking points of contact with the Old Testament, and their value for Old Testament study is manifold. They document the Canaanite fertility cult by which the Hebrews were influenced, and against the grosser aspects of which their prophets reacted. The legends document the institution of kingship and social practices and values in the Canaanite environment of Israel, both subjects being available for study in their historical development in the administrative and legal texts from the palace.

We must, however, emphasize the discretion of Israel in her use of the heritage of Canaan. The theme of Baal's triumph over the tyrant waters, for instance, was readily appropriated and developed as the theme of the kingship of God in the New Year Festival, to which it probably originally related. That of the vicissitudes of Baal as a dying and rising god, on the contrary, remained simply a literary influence, which did not influence Hebrew thought. What is significant in the Hebrew legacy from Canaan is what Israel appropriated and what she ignored, and how she adapted what she borrowed. In each particular the new matter emphasizes the distinctive ethos of Israel.

The language and imagery of the texts enhances the appreciation of nuances in the Old Testament, particularly in the Prophets, Psalms, and the book of Job, in instances too numerous for citation here.[110] The Ras Shamra texts are of great value for the appreciation of the literary conventions of dramatic narrative, which so often in the Old Testament is reminiscent of poetic saga. They are also of value for textual criticism. Many words in the Old Testament, formerly regarded as suspect and rejected as *hapax legomena*, have been found in several contexts in the Ras Shamra texts, the rather rigid parallelism fixing the meaning beyond all doubt, so that the Massoretic text is often supported. In certain doubtful passages in the Old Testament the Ras Shamra texts suggest emendation, but a careful listing of the evidence has convinced us that such cases are notably fewer than those where the standard Hebrew text is corroborated.

J. GRAY

NOTES

1. J. Knudtzon, *Die El-Amarna-Tafeln*, 1908–15 (hereafter *E.A.* 45. 35; 89. 51; 126. 6; 151. 55–58). In *E.A.* 45 the fragmentary name (*m*)*istu* may now be restored in the light of administrative texts from the palace of Ras Shamra as Ammištamru. *E.A.* 46, 47, and 48 are also most probably from Ugarit, as the clay and the writing indicate (O. Weber, *E.A.* ii, p. 1097).

2. A. Parrot, *Syria* xvi, 1935, pp. 1117, xvii, 1936, p. 1, xviii, 1937, p. 54, xix, 1938, p. 1. G. Dossin, ibid., xviii, 1937, p. 74.

3. *Stratigraphie comparée et chronologie d'Asie Occidentale*, 1948.

4. For Virolleaud's decipherment, see *C.R.A.I.*, 1930, p. 265; cf. H. Bauer, *Vossische Zeitung*, clxxxii, 4 June 1930, and E. Dhorme, *R.B.* xxxix, 1930, pp. 571–7, who reached roughly the same conclusions independently.

5. For Dussaud's interpretation of the Ras Shamra literary texts see particularly *Les Découvertes de Ras Shamra (Ugarit) et l'Ancien*

Testament, 1937, 2nd ed., 1941, and on religion, *Les Origines Cananéens du Sacrifice Israélite*, 2nd ed., 1941.

6. Reported by J. C. Courtois, *Bible et Terre Sainte*, 69, Dec. 1964, pp. 10 f. The letter from the king of Tyre is published by Virolleaud in *P.R.U.* v, 1965, 59 (RS 18. 31), pp. 81 ff.

7. C. F. A. Schaeffer, *Ugar.* i, 1939, fig. 9.

8. Ibid. ii, 1949, pl. xxiii.

9. A. Herdner, *Corpus des tablettes en cunéiformes alphabétiques découvertes à Ras Shamra-Ugarit de 1929 à 1939*, 1963 (hereafter *Corpus*), 2, iv = C. H. Gordon, *Ugaritic Handbook*, 1947 (hereafter *U.H.*), 68.

10. *Corpus*, 4 (II AB), vii, 41 = *U.H.* 51, vii, 41, *ktǵẓ. 'arz. bymnh* 'when the cedar is brandished in his right hand'.

11. Schaeffer, op. cit., pp. 128 f.

12. Ibid., pp. 129 f.

13. *Corpus*, 16 (II K), iii = *U.H.*, 126; *Corpus*, 19 (I D), 61 ff. = *U.H.* 1 Aqht, 61 ff.

14. Schaeffer *Ugar.* ii, pl. xxii. 3.

15. Ibid., pl. xxii. 2.

16. Ibid., fig. 36.

17. Ibid., pp. 49–130.

18. *Corpus*, 4 (II AB), vii–viii = *U.H.* 51, vii–viii; *Corpus*, 5 (I AB) = *U.H.* 67; *Corpus*, 6 (I AB) = *U.H.* 49.

19. The symbols of the god, however, are those held by the god Mekal ('the Annihilator') in the Late Bronze Age stele at Beth-shean (A. Rowe, *The Topography and History of Beth-shan*, 1930, pl. xxxiii), where the god, as is apparent from the gazelle horns on his helmet, is Resheph, the god who slew men in mass by war or plague. The *ankh* and *was* symbols are not incongruous with this character, since he holds the power of life as well as death, and is associated with the life-giving fertility goddess in the famous stele of Qodšu in the British Museum (J. Gray, *The Canaanites*, 1964, pl. 20).

20. Schaeffer, *Ugar.* ii, pl. xxiii. 1.

21. *Corpus*, 10 (IV AB), 10–11 = *U.H.* 76, ii. 10–11.
tš'u. knp. btlt. 'n(t)   The Virgin Anat raises the wing
tš'u knp. wtr. b'p   She raises the wing and wheels in flight.

22. Herdner, *Corpus* 3 (V AB) = *U.H.*, 'nt ii.

23. Schaeffer, *Ugar.* ii, pl. i.

24. Ibid., pls. ii–v.

25. Ibid. i, 1939, pp. 22, 53 ff., figs. 42, 43, 44.

26. Ibid., fig. 49.

27. Ibid., pls. xvi f.

28. Schaeffer notes particularly the rectangular plan and stepped *dromos* (entrance corridor), the niches and apertures for offerings to the dead, and the T-shaped keystone, which occasionally finishes off the corbel-vaulting, ibid., pp. 90 ff.

29. Ibid., pl. i.

30. J. Gray, op. cit., figs. 40, 42–44. It was known also in Syria.

31. Schaeffer, *The Cuneiform Texts of Ras Shamra-Ugarit*, 1939, pl. xxx.

32. Ibid., pls. xxviii, fig. 1; xxix, figs. 2 and 3.

33. C. Picard, *Les Religions pré-helléniques*, 1948, pp. 166, 235.

34. Schaeffer, op. cit., pp. 54 ff., figs. 12 f.

35. E. L. Sukenik, *Ḳedem* ii, 1945, pp. 42–58 (in Hebrew). A. Parrot has adduced impressive textual and material evidence from Mesopotamia, Egypt, and Syria, in the fourteenth, thirteenth, and eighth centuries B.C., and from Jewish communities in the Hellenistic age (Tobit iv. 17; Ecclus. vii. 33), of which Luke xvi. 19–24 is probably a reminiscence (*Le 'Refrigerium' dans l'au-delà*, 1937).

36. This passage, however, may refer to the rite underlying the funerary offering to the dead Baal in *Corpus*, 6 (I AB), i. 18–29 = *U.H.* 62, 18–29. We are not convinced by any of the Ras Shamra passages cited by H. Cazelles, *R.B.* lv, 1948, pp. 54–71, in support of his thesis that the Old Testament passage refers to an offering to Mot, treated on this occasion as an Adonis figure.

37. A. H. Gardiner, *Studies Presented to F. Ll. Griffiths*, 1932, pp. 74–85.

38. Cf. G. Zunz, *Museum Helveticum*, viii, 1951, pp. 12–35, who contends that Ṣaphon was actually the name of the god before the advent of the Semitic Baal-Hadad, when it became merely the name of the mountain. It must be added, however, that Ṣaphon has all the appearance of a genuine Semitic word, being connected possibly with the root *ṣāpāh* attested in Hebrew as 'kept a look out' (so O. Eissfeldt, *Baal Zaphon, etc.*, 1932, pp. 17 f.) and 'overlaid', perhaps a reference to the high mountain overlaid by clouds. A reminiscence of an originally independent local god, however, may be *bʿl ṣpn* mentioned in the new ritual text RS 24. 253, which mentions also *bʿl 'ugrt*.

39. In the stele dedicated by the Egyptian fiscal agent Mami in the temple of Baal in the late Bronze Age the god is called 'Seth of Sapuna'. The Egyptians regarded Seth as the inveterate enemy of Osiris, the vegetation deity, whose functions correspond to those of Baal, and they associated him with the Asiatic Hyksos, who overwhelmed Egypt c. 1750 B.C., as evidenced by the Four Hundred Year stele set up by Ramesses II at Tanis. This is not to say, however, that Seth was, like Typhon, a god of Chaos, but simply denotes from an Egyptian point of view Baal, the chief god of the invading Hyksos.

40. Common features are the killing of a lion by the hero with his bare hands, menial service to a weaker enemy, and betrayal by a woman. C. F. Burney considers that the Samson saga was also influenced by the Gilgamesh epic (*The Book of Judges*, 1930, pp. 391–403). In his day the chief difficulty in admitting the influence of the west was the date, but with the new evidence of Mycenaean settlement on the coast of the Levant, and conceivably even at Jaffa near Samson's home, the thesis is much more feasible.

41. For a plan of the palace in 1955, see *P.R.U.* i, 1955, pl. i.

42. RS 17. 116; 16. 270; 18. 06; 17. 459; 17. 372 A; 17. 228; 17. 450 A; 17. 318, *P.R.U.* iv, pp. 129–46. On the nature of 'the great sin' as adultery, see W. L. Moran, *J.N.E.S.* xviii, 1959, pp. 280 f.

43. RS 17. 372 A; 17. 228; 17. 318.

44. Ibid. and RS 17. 82.

45. Reported by J. C. Courtois, op. cit., pp. 10 f. Some of these are now published by Virolleaud, *P.R.U.* v, 1965, 119–23, pp. 144 ff.

46. See n. 5.

47. e.g. Virolleaud, *Reprise des Fouilles à Ras Shamra* (ed. C. F. A. Schaeffer), 1955, pp. 22 ff.

48. Schaeffer, ibid., p. 10, fig. 4.

49. *E.A.* 151. 55–57. The text is ambiguous. Knudtzon (ad loc.), Virolleaud (*La Légende Phénicienne de Danel*, 1936, p. 51), and S. A. B. Mercer (*The Tell El-Amarna Tablets*, 1939, ii, p. 497) take it to refer to the city of Ugarit as the fortress of the Pharaoh. W. F. Albright takes it to refer to the palace of the king of Ugarit (*J.E.A.* xxiii, 1937, p. 203).

50. Even apart from the Amarna reference, the level of destruction and earthquake at Ras Shamra is accurately dated in the reign of Ak-henaten. The synchronism between the various archaeological stations in the Levant by means of the earthquake, however, is a useful working hypothesis, without being conclusive. For instance, there is no evidence of the earthquake at this time at Byblos.

51. Schaeffer, op. cit., pp. 42–51; J. Nougayrol, *P.R.U.* iv, 1956, pp. 29–210. The international situation, known from the Tell el-Amarna tablets and the Hittite archives of Boğazköy, reconstructed by Nougayrol in the light of this new evidence (op. cit.), is amplified by a study by E. Laroche, *Ugar.* iii, 1956, pp. 1–160, where the Hittite seals are well illustrated and their legends studied in detail, and, in a wider historical context, by M. Liverani, *Storia di Ugarit*, 1962.

52. *P.R.U.* iv, pp. 48–52.

53. The full content of this vassal treaty may be recovered from fragments of copies, especially RS 17. 338 (*P.R.U.* iv, pp. 85 f.) and RS 17. 353 (*P.R.U.* iv, pp. 88 ff.). The former begins with a recapitulation of the historical events, which have established the relationship between vassal and suzerain, continues with the claim to absolute allegiance, with detailed demands, citing in a fragmentary passage various gods as witness of the oath of fealty, and stating finally that the vassal treaty is duly recorded. The latter text contains the list of the gods invoked in the imprecation. This pattern, with the exception of the two last features, is reproduced in the Decalogue and, so far as the imprecations are concerned, in the Twelve Adjurations relating to the sacrament of the Covenant in Deut. xxvii. 15–26.

54. *Hethitische Staatsverträge, ein Beitrag zu ihrer juristischen Wertung*, Leipz. Rechtswissenschaftl. Stud., Heft 60, 1931.

55. G. E. Mendenhall, *Law and Covenant in Israel and the Ancient Near East*, 1955; K. Baltzer, *Das Bundesformular*, 1960; W. Beyerlin, *Herkunft und Geschichte d. ältesten Sinaitraditionen*, 1961; H. von Revent-

low, *Gebot und Predigt im Dekalog*, 1962; J. Stamm, *Der Dekalog im Lichte d. neueren Forschung*, 1962; D. J. McCarthy, *Treaty and Covenant*, 1963.

56. The fragmentary copies of the vassal treaty RS 17. 338, 2–3, RS 17. 353, 2, and RS 17. 407, 2 make it plain that the accession of Niqmepa was a restoration by the Hittite king.

57. Schaeffer, *Ugar.* iii, p. 164 (citing the reading of J. Vandier) and fig. 118.

58. Ch. Desroches-Noblecourt, *Ugar.* iii, pp. 180–220.

59. *E.A.* 4, 6 f.

60. *A.f.O.* xx, 1963, pp. 214 f.

61. *E.A.* 51, 4 ff.

62. Nougayrol, *P.R.U.* iii, pp. xli f.

63. RS 16. 145, *P.R.U.* iii, p. 169.

64. S. Smith, *A.J.* xix, 1939, p. 38.

65. E. D. van Buren, *Z.A.* li, 1955, pp. 92 ff.

66. *zigiltu*; cf. *'am s^{e}ğullāh* (Deut. vii. 6, xiv. 2, xxvi. 18) and *s^{e}ğullāh* expressing the same conception of 'a peculiar people' (Exod. xix. 5; Mal. iii. 17; Ps. cxxxv. 4).

67. S. Smith, *A.J.* xix, 1939, p. 38, pl. xviii. 3.

68. Accepting the view of Alt, *K.S.* ii, 1959, pp. 217 f., von Rad *T.L.Z.* lxxii, 1947, col. 216, and O. Kaiser (*Der Prophet Jesaia*, A.T.D., 1960, pp. 93 f.), that the passage gives the royal titulary, reflecting the conception of the adoption of the king as the son of God in terms of the Davidic Covenant in 2 Sam. vii. 14, cf. Ps. ii. 7, we would refer the titles to Hezekiah, not, however, at his accession, as these scholars do, but at the moment when he was singled out from the rest of the royal family as heir apparent or co-regent with his father, which we date in 729 B.C. in accordance with the confusing chronology in Kings; see the writer's *I and II Kings*, 1963, p. 73.

69. Schaeffer, *Reprise des fouilles de Ras Shamra-Ugarit*, 1955, pl. viii.

70. *Corpus*, 15, ii. 25–27 = *U.H.* 128, ii. 25–27.

71. F. Thureau-Dangin, *Syria* xii, 1931, pp. 255 f., xiii, 1932, pp. 233–41.

72. Schaeffer, *Ugar.* iii, pl. ix*a*.

73. Ibid., pp. 228 ff.

74. Ibid., fig. 204*a*, *b*; pl. viii*a*, and, for a general study of the script, O. Masson, ibid., pp. 233–50.

75. H. J. Franken, *V.T.* xiv, 1964, pp. 377 ff.

76. Herdner, *Corpus* 113 = *U.H.* 400, vi. 21 ff.

77. RS 16. 402, *P.R.U.* ii. 12.

78. Nougayrol, *P.R.U.* iii, pp. 22–176.

79. Ibid., p. 234.

80. e.g. Herdner, *Corpus* 65 = *U.H.* 108, etc.

81. *P.R.U.* ii. 87–93.

82. J. Bottéro, *Le Problème des Ḫabiru*, 1954.

83. *P.R.U.* iii, p. 189 (RS 11. 790).
84. Herdner, *Corpus* 67. 70 = *U.H.* 110, 112.
85. The spelling explodes Dhorme's view (*La Religion des Hébreux Nomades*, 1937, pp. 81 f.) that *ḫabiru* is derived from *ḫbr* meaning 'confederates', and makes the equation *ḫabiru*/Hebrew *'ibrîm* more feasible; cf. H. H. Rowley, *P.E.F.Q.S.* 1940, pp. 90–94.
86. *P.R.U.* iii, p. 105 (RS 15. 109).
87. RS 17. 238.
88. Liverani, op. cit., p. 89.
89. S. Smith, *The Statue of Idri-mi*, 1949, pp. 14 ff.
90. *P.R.U.* iii, pp. 54 ff. (RS 15. 92).
91. Ibid., pp. 64 f. (RS 16. 200).
92. *P.R.U.* iii, pp. 159 f. (RS 16. 261).
93. W. R. Smith, *The Religion of the Semites*, 3rd ed., 1927, pp. 383 ff.
94. E. Kutsch, *Salbung als Rechtsakt im A.T. und im Alten Orient*, B.Z.A.W. lxxxvii, 1963, pp. 33–70.
95. Ibid., pp. 16–33.
96. *P.R.U.* ii, p. 6 (RS 11. 730).
97. *Corpus* 23 (SS), 65 ff. = *U.H.* 52, 65 ff.
98. *Corpus* 5 (I AB), vi, 8–25 = *U.H.* 67, vi. 18–25; *Corpus* 6 (I AB), i. 18–29 = *U.H.* 62, 18–29.
99. *Corpus*, 24 (NK) = *U.H.* 77.
100. This is the basis of A. van Selms's *Marriage and Family Life in Ugaritic Literature*, 1954.
101. *Corpus*, 2 (III AB), i = *U.H.* 137; *Corpus* 2 (III AB), iii = *U.H.* 129; *Corpus*, 2 (III AB), iv = *U.H.* 68.
102. *V. supra*, n. 18.
103. *Corpus*, 23 (SS) = *U.H.* 52.
104. *Corpus*, 24 (NK) = *U.H.* 77.
105. A. S. Kapelrud, *N.T.T.* 1940, pp. 38–88; 1960, pp. 241–85; W. Schmidt, *Königtum Gottes in Ugarit und Israel*, B.Z.A.W. lxxx, 1961.
106. This view was strenuously opposed by the late R. de Langhe, *Myth, Ritual and Kingship*, ed. S. H. Hooke, 1958, pp. 130 ff.
107. W. Baumgartner, *T.Z.* iii, 1947, pp. 89 ff., emphasizes the aesthetic character of the Ras Shamra myths in their extant form, while admitting that aesthetic interests stand side by side with religious interests.
108. e.g. C. Virolleaud, *La Légende de Keret, roi des Sidoniens*, 1936; R. de Langhe, *Les Textes de Ras Shamra-Ugarit et leurs rapports avec le milieu biblique de l'A.T.* 1945, ii, pp. 67–147; J. Pedersen, *Berytus*, vi, 1941; H. L. Ginsberg, *B.A.S.O.R.*, Supp. Studies 2–3, 1946; *A.N.E.T.*, pp. 142–9; G. R. Driver, *C.M.L.*, pp. 2–5, 28–47; J. Gray, *The Krt Text in the Literature of Ras Shamra*, 1955, 2nd ed., 1964.
109. H. Cazelles, *P.E.Q.* 1955, pp. 165–75, admits the connexion in this incident with the death of Mot as a harvest sacrifice, but emphasizes the historical aspect of the case as admitting the Gibeonite claim to the rights of the *lex talionis* against Israelites. A. S. Kapelrud, *La Regalità*

sacra, 1959, pp. 294–301, too admits the religious aspect of the incident, but emphasizes its political aspect, David astutely using the pretext of the case of the Gibeonites against the house of Saul to transfer his responsibility in the famine to them, thus making ritual punctilio ancillary to political expediency.

110. A detailed study of such cases will be found in ch. vi of the writer's *Legacy of Canaan*, 1957, 2nd ed., 1965.

BIBLIOGRAPHY

AISTLEITNER, J. *Die mythologischen und kultischen Texte aus Ras Shamra*, 1959.

—— *Wörterbuch der ugaritischen Sprache* (ed. O. Eissfeldt), 1963.

DRIVER, G. R. *Canaanite Myths and Legends*, 1956.

DUSSAUD, R. *Les Découvertes de Ras Shamra (Ugarit) et l'Ancien Testament*, 2nd ed., 1941.

EISSFELDT, O. 'Ras Shamra und Sanchuniathon', *Beitr. z. Religionsgesch. des Altertums*, Heft 4, 1939.

—— 'El im ugaritischen Pantheon', *Berichte über die Verhandlungen der sächsischen Akademie der Wissenschaften zu Leipzig*, Phil.-hist. Klasse, Band 98, Heft 4, 1951.

GASTER, T. H. *Thespis*, 1950.

GINSBERG, H. L. 'Ugaritic Myths and Legends', *A.N.E.T.*, pp. 129–55.

GORDON, C. H. *Ugaritic Handbook*, 1947.

—— *Ugaritic Literature*, 1949.

—— *Ugaritic Manual*, 1955.

GRAY, J. *The Legacy of Canaan, V.T.* Supp. v, 1957; 2nd ed., 1965.

—— 'Texts from Ras Shamra', *D.O.T.T.*, pp. 118–33.

—— *The Canaanites*, 1964.

KAPELRUD, A. S. *Baal in the Ras Shamra Texts*, 1952.

—— *The Ras Shamra Discoveries and the Old Testament* (E.Tr., G. W. Anderson), 1962.

LANGHE, R. DE. *Les Textes de Ras Shamra-Ugarit et leurs rapports avec le milieu biblique de l'Ancien Testament*, 1945.

LIVERANI, M. *Storia di Ugarit*, 1962.

NOUGAYROL, J. *Le Palais Royal d'Ugarit* (ed. C. F. A. Schaeffer), iii, 1955, iv, 1956.

POPE, M. *El in the Ugaritic Texts, V.T.* Supp. ii, 1955.

SCHAEFFER, C. F. A. *Ugaritica*, i, 1939, ii, 1949, iii, 1956, iv, 1963.

—— *The Cuneiform Texts of Ras Shamra-Ugarit*, 1955.

VIROLLEAUD, C. Articles on the Baal myth, etc., *Syria* xii, 1931 ff.

—— *La Légende phénicienne de Danel*, 1936.

—— *La Légende de Keret, Roi des Sidoniens*, 1936.

—— *Le Palais Royal d'Ugarit* (ed. C. F. A. Schaeffer), ii, 1957, v, 1965.

—— *Légendes de Babylone et de Canaan*, 1949.

PALESTINE

BETH-HACCHEREM

BETH-SHEAN

BETH-SHEMESH

DEBIR

EN-GEDI

GIBEON

HAZOR

JERICHO

JERUSALEM

LACHISH

MEGIDDO

MIZPAH

SAMARIA

SHECHEM

TIRZAH

THE NEGEB

PHILISTIA

TRANSJORDAN

BETH-HACCHEREM

WHEN excavations began at the tell of Ramat Raḥel, half-way between Jerusalem and Bethlehem, in 1954, it was an unknown site, without name and history.[1] Five seasons of excavations, terminating in 1962,[2] have revealed the history of a Judaean settlement unique in some respects, which illuminates several passages in the Old Testament. We believe now that this was the Old Testament Beth-haccherem, the residence of a district governor in the days of Nehemiah (Neh. iii. 14), and that this was the very place where King Jehoiakim built his magnificent palace, so vehemently denounced by Jeremiah (Jer. xxii. 13–19). However, before surveying the historical problems connected with the site, we will first describe briefly the results of the excavations, with the emphasis on the earlier periods.

i. *The Strata of Settlement*

The ancient site of Ramat Raḥel is called today *khirbeh* 'ruin' and not *tell* 'mound' by the Arabs, because, though one of the highest points on the Jerusalem–Bethlehem road, the hill rises gradually and the ancient debris is quite shallow. Its size and depth are very moderate as compared with most other excavated mounds. Its built-up area does not exceed 2–3 acres in most periods, and the depth of ancient debris is generally only 5–6 feet. Though we were able to recognize seven strata of occupation, not all the site was occupied in the different periods, and usually not more than two or three layers were preserved one on top of the other. The shallow debris is also due to the principal building material of the hilly area, namely stone, which was for the most part reused by the settlers of later periods. For this reason many of the ancient walls were completely dismantled, sometimes only foundation trenches remaining. It is a common feature at Ramat Raḥel that the floors of Byzantine cellars are lower than the remaining adjacent Iron Age floors. It is, therefore, no wonder that the earlier strata are in a bad state of preservation, and that the description of them and their history emerged only slowly and incompletely.

The first settlement at Ramat Raḥel was founded in the ninth or eighth century B.C., perhaps from its very beginning as a royal citadel, surrounded by gardens and vineyards. One of the later kings of Judah enlarged and completely rebuilt the royal edifice, transforming it into a large citadel with a magnificent palace, which was destroyed at the end of the period of the First Temple. After this destruction the royal edifice was never rebuilt, but the site was resettled in the latter part of the sixth or the early fifth century B.C. Again it was no common settlement but rather a citadel, from which a wealth of unique stamped jar handles from the Persian period was recovered. This stratum was destroyed during the third century, and after an interval the site was again occupied, now for the first time by common dwellings and workshops. This settlement flourished mainly during the Early Roman (Herodian) period and was destroyed with the capture of Jerusalem in A.D. 70. Most of the site lay again in ruins for more than a hundred years, and only during the third century were some new buildings erected, according to the stamped tiles, by the Roman Tenth Legion, established in Jerusalem up to the end of the third century. During the fifth century a large church and monastery were built at the site, well known from Byzantine sources as the Kathisma Church. They were destroyed during the seventh century, and a small village of the Early Arab period was the last settlement at the site until the modern Qibbutz. The following numeration has been given to these seven strata:

Stratum	*Date*	*Type of settlement*
I	Seventh–Eighth centuries A.D.	Arab village
II	Fifth–Seventh centuries A.D.	Kathisma Church.
III	Third–Fifth centuries A.D.	Installations of the Roman Tenth Legion.
IVa	First century B.C.–First century A.D.	Jewish settlement.
IVb	Fifth–Third centuries B.C.	Citadel of the Persian period.
Va	*c.* 600 B.C.	Judaean royal citadel.
Vb	Eighth–Seventh centuries B.C.	Judaean citadel and village.

ii. *The Later Strata*

A very short outline of the finds of the later strata, which are outside the scope of this book, may suffice. The latest poor village is of no interest, nor does the Byzantine church add much to the many churches of this period so far discovered in Palestine. The identification of it with the Kathisma Church (The Church of the Seat), built c. A.D. 450 by a rich Jerusalem woman near Mary's traditional resting place on her way to Bethlehem, is conclusively attested through the preservation of its name. Below the western slope of the mound, beside the old Jerusalem–Bethlehem road, there is an ancient well called by the Arabs Bir Qadismu, obviously derived from the Greek *Kathisma*. At this period no regular settlement existed at the site. No common buildings were discovered besides the church, the monastery, and its store-rooms and farm installations.

The well-built structures of the Roman Tenth Legion were for the most part reused in the Byzantine period. They comprised a bath-house and a large villa with a peristyle court. It is interesting to note that most of the Roman and Byzantine structures were erected on foundations of the Iron Age citadel in spite of the gap of about a thousand years between them. On the other hand, the large open courtyard remained mainly as a courtyard also in the later periods. It is clear, therefore, that the old solid walls were still standing above the ground, and it seemed worth while to use them at least as foundations.

The Jewish settlement from the end of the period of the Second Temple was quite small and unimportant. Of more interest are some burial caves, one of which, with its rich contents, had already been excavated in 1931 by B. Mazar and M. Stekelis.[3] This cave, and others, belong probably to this period. However, one of them, discovered on the slope below the Roman villa, can hardly be earlier than c. A.D. 200, a date based on glassware and terracotta lamps found in it. On the other hand, the type of burial, and especially the ossuaries, leave no doubt that this too was a Jewish grave. This late date in the immediate vicinity of Jerusalem is surprising; however, this problem also is beyond our present scope.

iii. *Seal Impressions of the Persian Period*

The actual character of the site in the Persian period (Stratum IVb) remained enigmatic even after the fifth season of excavation. In spite of all our efforts we were unable to uncover a single preserved room or floor of this period. Two main reasons apparently account for this fact. First, our work was concentrated mainly in the area of the Iron Age palace, which was left in ruins during the Persian period, and secondly, in the other sections Byzantine building operations have destroyed almost all the earlier remains. Nevertheless, this stratum yielded a wealth of most interesting material for the Old Testament scholar, namely, over 300 seal impressions on jar handles. Most of them were found in pits and heaps scattered over the debris of the old palace. Their date can, therefore, be fixed only tentatively in the fifth–fourth centuries B.C. They belong probably to a new citadel, erected beside the ruins of the older one, and they come mainly from refuse pits, scattered during levelling operations of later periods.

Most of these seal impressions are the usual types of Hebrew and Aramaic stamps, known from other sites of the Persian province of Yehud (Judah), though they have nowhere been found in such a large quantity and with so many variations. They belong to the fiscal authorities of Yehud; some bear various forms of the name of the province (*yhd*), sometimes abbreviated, and others the name Jerusalem (*yršlm*) between the points of a pentagram. Some have also designs of animals, mainly lions, also known from other places.

Several types, however, are altogether new. Besides the common *yhd* stamps appear also stamps with *yhwd* written *plene*. Another stamp reads *yhwd/ḥnnh* 'Yehud/Ḥaninah', similar to the Yehud/ Uryo stamp discovered in Jericho.[4] Both men are apparently functionaries, probably priests, acting in the fiscal administration of the province. The most interesting, however, are the *pḥw'* stamps, as we have called them. Several have merely the inscription *yhwd/pḥw'*, but two others, preserved in several specimens, include also names. One reads *yhwd/yhw'zr/pḥw'*, and the second *l'ḥzy/pḥw'*.

We can offer only a tentative interpretation of these inscriptions, which deserve thorough examination by epigraphists, linguists, and historians. Like the other *yhd/yhwd* stamps, there seems hardly any doubt that these stamps too are connected with the fiscal authorities of the Jewish province, concentrated around Jerusalem and the temple. If our reading *pḥw'* is correct,[5] it can be interpreted in one of the following ways. First, it could be an Aramaic-Hebrew form of the word *pḥwh* = province (from the root *pḥḥ*,

Akkadian *pāḥātu*), meaning 'governor' or 'governorship'.[6] On this interpretation Yehoezer and Aḥzai might have been functionaries in the fiscal administration of the province. Or secondly, it could be the Aramaic emphatic state of the word *pḥh* 'the governor'. It is true that in the approximately contemporary Elephantine papyri we find the word *pḥt*' instead of our *pḥw*'.[7] This, however, can be explained as a dialectic back formation from the plural *pḥwt-pḥwwt* (as attested in the Old Testament in Ezra viii. 36; Neh. ii. 7, 9).[8] According to this interpretation, which seems the most probable, the inscriptions read 'Yehud, the governor'; 'Yehud, Yehoezer, the governor'; 'belonging to Aḥzai the governor'.

If this is correct, then we have here the first epigraphic evidence from Palestine for a governor of Judah under Persian rule. The importance of this new information may be considerable, especially as we possess extremely little knowledge of Judah during the Persian period. From the Old Testament we know of three Jewish governors—Sheshbazzar, Zerubbabel, and Nehemiah—who ruled the province at various times at the end of the sixth and during the fifth centuries B.C. A fourth governor, Bagohi, who ruled in Judah after Nehemiah at the end of the fifth century B.C., is known from the Elephantine papyri.[9] His name is definitely Persian, but it was in use also among the Jews who returned from exile in Babylonia (in the form Bigvai; cf. Neh. vii. 19). It has been generally accepted that after Bagohi only Persian governors ruled in Judah, and that the autonomy of the province was limited to religious matters. Most of the Ramat Raḥel stamps belong apparently to the fourth century B.C., judging by the shape of the pottery found together with them. Do we have here epigraphic evidence for the continuance of Jewish governors in Judah during the fourth century B.C.? The name Yehoezer is especially common in priestly families in the post-exilic period. Does this perhaps foreshadow the situation in the Hellenistic period, when the secular and priestly administration of Judah was concentrated in one and the same hand?

This wealth of seal impressions connected with the fiscal authorities of the province have to be taken into consideration when evaluating the settlement at Ramat Raḥel. In spite of our poor knowledge about this stratum, we may deduce from them that in this period the site was not a village but most probably an administrative centre.[10] We shall return to this point when we discuss the identification and history of the site.

iv. *The Iron Age Citadels*

Unquestionably the most important discoveries at Ramat Raḥel in connexion with Old Testament studies were made in the two earliest strata which belong to the Iron Age. Actually not much is known about the earliest settlement (Stratum Vb), as most of it was levelled up by the extensive constructions of the late Iron Age stratum (Va). In its centre there probably stood a strong citadel, judging from the few foundations which escaped destruction. This citadel, however, was quite small; beneath part of a building of the later citadel an agricultural terrace was found, indicating that there had been no earlier structures here, but that the area had been under cultivation.

On the outskirts of the later citadel remains of a simple private house were discovered. Its narrow walls stood in striking contrast to the massive structures of the following period, which led to its complete destruction. What remained of it was deliberately filled with stones and covered over. Among the few preserved pieces of pottery two jar handles were discovered, bearing the impression of a Hebrew seal with the inscription *šbn'/šḥr* '[belonging to] Shebna [son of] Shahar'. Identical seal impressions are known from two other Judaean sites—Lachish and Mizpah (Tell en-Naṣbeh). They provide excellent stratigraphic correlation, and their distribution at these various sites, at quite a distance from each other, raises again the question of the purpose of this type of stamps. Are they really 'private stamps', belonging to private landowners, as is generally assumed? There are some other seal impressions with Hebrew names which are found again at other Judaean sites, like Beth-shemesh and Tell Beit Mirsim (Debir). But the most surprising discovery was a double-stamped jar handle, bearing side by side a royal stamp and a 'private stamp', with the inscription *lnr'/šbn'* 'belonging to Nera [son of] Shebna'. The question arises as to whether these 'private stamps' on jar handles may not have belonged actually to royal functionaries or beneficials, and have been used for a similar purpose as the royal stamps. Both appear on the same type of vessel with similar shape and colour.[11]

We come next to the question of the royal seal impressions, one of the oldest and most discussed problems in Palestinian archaeology. The more than 150 additional stamps of this kind, so common at most sites in Judah, contribute towards the understanding of their purpose and date in two ways. First, the double-stamped jar handle mentioned above stands in contrast to the royal potters theory. It is true that for the first time a 'private stamp' has been found beside a royal seal impression (with the two-winged disk and the inscription *lmlk/ḥbrn*). Though apparently exceptional, it must, however, be taken into consideration. A 'private seal' was kept and impressed in the same workshop in which the royal jars were manufactured. It is clear, therefore, whatever their purpose was, that they were not meant to indicate the place or name of the potters' workshop. Secondly, the various types of the royal seal impressions have been dated by scholars in the eighth–seventh centuries B.C. Opinions differ mainly on the question when they were first used, while it is generally agreed that they continued to be used until the end of the period of the First Temple. The reason for this vague dating is that at all the tells where such impressions have been found no stratigraphic break during the seventh century B.C. was detected, as these cities were apparently prosperous and relatively peaceful. At Ramat Raḥel there appears a distinct break near the end of the seventh century B.C. when the new citadel was constructed. The astonishing fact is that the royal seal impressions belong exclusively to the earlier citadel, and most of them were found in fills of the new constructions, where older material was dumped. It is, therefore, obvious that these seal impressions were *not* in use at the end of the monarchy. On the same types of jar handles various rosette stamps appear in the later stratum. It seems, therefore, that, with the abolition of the royal stamps, the rosettes took their place.

In the Ramat Raḥel report we have dealt more fully with this problem,[12] and we here summarize our conclusions. The four names found on the sealings are those of royal administrative centres; the seal impressions date from the late eighth and early seventh centuries B.C. (the period of Hezekiah and Manasseh), and they went out of use before the time of Josiah (*c.* 640–609 B.C.) who reigned over a much larger kingdom than their area of distribution.[13] These conclusions agree well with the finds at Lachish, and they may help also in the much-debated question of the date of the destruction of Level III. Most of the royal seal impressions were found in this level at Lachish, and a few in Level II. A late date for the destruction of Level III, such as the first campaign of Nebuchadrezzar (598–597 B.C.), is, therefore, out of the question. The later citadel of Ramat Raḥel was undoubtedly constructed before this date, and, as has been noted, the royal seal impressions went out of use earlier. On the other hand, a date 701 B.C. (Sennacherib) for the destruction of Lachish III fits in excellently with the distribution of the royal stamps at this site.

v. *The Late Iron Age Palace*

The royal seal impressions provide also a *terminus a quo* for the construction of the later citadel. The date of the two winged impressions can hardly be raised higher than the early part of the seventh century B.C., and may well go back to the middle of that century. As has been noted, the later citadel at Ramat Raḥel post-dates their disappearance, and it is obvious, therefore, that its construction belongs to the latest phase of the Iron Age.

The early citadel probably lay in ruins, because none of it was repaired and reconstructed, but entirely new structures were erected. Tremendous efforts were put into the new edifices, and the entire hill was reshaped by fillings up to 3–4 metres in height.[14] The inner citadel was enlarged to an area of about 50 × 90 metres, and its main buildings were shaped in a manner used only in royal palaces. It was surrounded by a large lower citadel, 4–5 acres in size, fortified by a strong wall. Though only trial excavations were carried out in the area, there remains little doubt that it was composed almost in its entirety of open spaces without any buildings, part of it being artificially levelled. It was obviously a fortress, not a town, built for some specific purpose. Its large dimensions argue against its being built merely to protect the inner citadel. We may conjecture that it was an army camp, perhaps mainly for chariots, which served as a huge military stronghold near Jerusalem, on the main highway leading to the south.

The inner citadel, though much smaller, has all the appearances of a royal palace, the first discovered in Judah. It is surrounded by a casemate wall of excellent construction. Its main building flanked the west. Another large building in the northern section served apparently for household purposes and for storage. Its south-eastern corner was occupied by a large and smoothly paved court-yard. The double-piered gate was in the centre of the eastern wall, paved with huge blocks of limestone, blackened and cracked by fire. Near it, among broken storage jars, a stamped jar handle was found with the inscription *l'lyqm n'r ywkn* 'belonging to Eliakim, steward of Jokin'. Identical seal impressions have been found at Beth-shemesh and Tell Beit Mirsim. W. F. Albright is probably correct in assuming that Eliakim was a functionary of King Jehoiachin, shortened to Jokin, as in Assyrian inscriptions.[15] He was the son of King Jehoiakim, and was taken into exile by the Babylonians in 597 B.C. after a short reign of three months. This seal impression gives a *terminus a quo* for the destruction of the citadel in 598–597 B.C., and, if Albright is right, even later during his captivity. Thus it is obvious that the citadel was destroyed by Nebuchadrezzar *c.* 587 B.C., or, at the earliest, during his first campaign in 598–597 B.C. The traces of fire give evidence of the extent of the destruction.

The palace suffered almost complete dismantling as a result of later building activities, but several sections of the casemate wall are well preserved. Its outer wall was built with a line of well-laid headers. Parts of the gate and the inner wall facing the courtyard were constructed of well-smoothed ashlar masonry, laid with stretchers and headers alternately, resembling closely the royal buildings at Samaria. Among the debris and in the walls of later buildings four complete Proto-Aeolic capitals were found, in addi-tion to fragments of at least three more, one of them being smaller and carved on both sides. This is the first time that capitals of this kind have been found in Judah. Two similar capitals have been discovered recently by Kathleen M. Kenyon in Jerusalem, and others are known from royal buildings in the northern kingdom, at Samaria, Megiddo, and Hazor; one was found on the surface at Medeibi in Transjordan. The similarity of craftsmanship and decoration at all these sites is striking, and the relatively late date of the Ramat Raḥel palace is a warning against their use as evidence for accurate dating. It seems that these techniques, borrowed from Phoenicia, underwent very little change from the time of Solomon down to the end of the monarchy.

The finds in most of the rooms were rather poor, because most

were destroyed below floor level. Mention should be made, however, of two unique finds made in a store-room of the northern
building among a heap of common late Iron Age pottery. The first
are several beakers of the so-called 'Assyrian Palace Ware', discovered for the first time in Palestine. They give some evidence of
the luxury and use of imported vessels in the royal household. The
second, still more interesting, is a jar fragment painted in black
and red, with a drawing of a bearded man with curled hair, seated
on a high, decorated chair (Pl. VIa). He is dressed in an ornamented
robe with short sleeves, and his hands are in an outstretched position, the right above the left. Comparison with similar motifs in
Near Eastern art shows that the figure depicted is a king. It recalls
the Assyrian style of the eighth–seventh centuries B.C., but the
potsherd is of local ware. It must be the work of a local artist who
fully mastered the materials and techniques involved. It is a unique
drawing of its kind, still more interesting as it was found in the
palace of one of the kings of Judah.

The most striking find, however, was made near the north-west
corner of the palace, namely, a heap of debris containing fragments
of small columns and capitals. After they were rearranged, a row
of small columns appeared, decorated with a drooping petal motif
and topped by small capitals of the Proto-Aeolic type, joined
together at the edges of the volutes. To the best of our knowledge
no similar architectural features have been found in Palestine or
adjacent countries, except a frieze decorated with a similar pattern
which was found at Ramat Raḥel in the course of the preliminary
survey.[16]

Their usage, however, is completely clear when they are compared with a common motif in Phoenician ivory plaques, examples
of which are known from excavations in Palestine, Syria, and
Assyria, for example, at Samaria, Arslan Tash, Nimrud, and
Khorsabad.[17] This plaque, known as 'the woman in the window',
shows the head of a woman in the frame of a window, the lower
part of which has a railing of three or four columns of the same
shape as those under discussion. It is therefore clear that our rows
of decorated columns are the balustrades of windows, which con-
stituted a remarkable part of the royal architecture at Ramat
Raḥel. The ornamented window adorning the façade of the royal
palace with the queen looking out is a common motif in the Old

PLATE VI

a. Sherd with drawing of bearded king (Beth-haccherem), *c.* 600 B.C.

b. Balustrade of windows of royal palace (Beth-haccherem), *c.* 600 B.C.

Testament (cf. Judges v. 28; 2 Sam. vi. 16; 2 Kings ix. 30; Prov. vii. 6). Yet it seems probable that these very windows are mentioned in the Old Testament, and this brings us to the question of the identification of the site.

From the beginning it seemed improbable that a place of such importance and so near to Jerusalem should not be mentioned in the Old Testament. The royal buildings of the Judaean kings stood inside the city of Jerusalem, and we frequently hear about them from the days of Solomon onwards. The building of the splendid palace at Ramat Raḥel was certainly no routine matter, and we should expect an allusion to it in the Old Testament. Furthermore, the choice has been narrowed down to one of the last kings of Judah, as we have seen that a date earlier than the middle of the seventh century B.C. is out of the question.[18]

To the best of our knowledge we have in the Old Testament only one allusion to the building of a magnificent palace by one of the last kings, by Jehoiakim (609–597 B.C.), the son of Josiah and the father of Jehoiachin, whose name is mentioned in the seal impression described above. Jeremiah denounced his activities in the following words:

Woe unto him that buildeth his house by unrighteousness, and his chambers by injustice; that useth his neighbour's service without wages, and giveth him not his hire; that saith, I will build me a wide house and spacious chambers, ('lywt = upper stories), *and cutteth him out windows; and it is cieled with cedar, and painted with vermillion* [Jer. xxii. 13 f.].

This description fits in every respect the palace at Ramat Raḥel. It was a royal citadel and palace into which unusual efforts in labour and craftsmanship were put. It clearly existed in Jeremiah's day, and could not have been built long before. The single phase of occupation, and the absence of any traces of repair or rebuilding, indicate its short duration. Jeremiah does not indicate where the new palace was built,[19] but it is difficult to believe that the last kings of Judah built several palaces of this kind, and therefore the identification seems fairly certain.

The balustrade (Pl. VI*b*) too fits exactly the description of Jeremiah. On top of the capitals are holes into which, as appears from the ivories, wooden beams were fitted (cieled with cedar!),

and on the stones there remained traces of red paint (vermilion!).
Of course, other palaces were probably likewise decorated, but the
palace at Ramat Raḥel is essentially similar to that described by
the prophet. It is hardly surprising that Jeremiah singled out the
conspicuous ornamented windows, which evidently decorated the
façade of the main building.

Another passage in Jeremiah states that Jehoiakim 'sat in the
winter house' (xxxvi. 22), from which we may conclude that the
palace at Ramat Raḥel was his summer house. We may conjecture
also its name, and suggest its identification with Beth-haccherem
'the house of the vineyard'. Since the earliest level is composed of
a fortress surrounded by terraced gardens and houses, it may be
supposed that here was the summer residence of the kings of
Judah, within the royal vineyards, around which lay the houses of
vine-dressers and farmers.

The references in the Old Testament to Beth-haccherem support this identification. It is mentioned for the first time in the
district of Bethlehem in Joshua xv. 59 (as Karem, preserved only in
the LXX, xv. 59a). Its foundation in the ninth or eighth century
B.C. agrees well with the generally accepted date for this Judaean
district list. Jeremiah mentions Beth-haccherem in his description
of an enemy approaching Jerusalem from the south—'and blow
the trumpet in Tekoa, and raise up a signal on Beth-haccherem'
(vi. 1). No place could better suit this description than Ramat
Raḥel, which was an important royal and military stronghold in
the days of Jeremiah, situated on a high hill on the road to Tekoa,
easily visible from Jerusalem. In the days of Nehemiah, Beth-
haccherem was the residence of a district governor (Neh. iii. 14),
which may explain the abundance of seal impressions from this
period. The place is mentioned also in the Mishnah and in two of
the Dead Sea scrolls.[20] This is the period of the Jewish settlement
at the end of the period of the Second Temple, and from these
sources we may conclude only its immediate proximity to Jerusalem. This is the last reference to Beth-haccherem. The Roman
installations and the Kathisma Church evidently did not preserve
the ancient name.

The citadel of Ramat Raḥel gives us not only some idea of
a Judaean royal palace, discovered and excavated here for the
first time, and illuminating one of the prophecies of Jeremiah; it

raises also interesting historical questions which we can only briefly mention in conclusion. What were the reasons for the gigantic effort in building this large citadel and magnificent palace during the short eleven years of Jehoiakim's reign, frequently shaken by international affairs? Are these fortifications to be connected with his unsuccessful revolt against Babylon which brought about the end of his reign? Jehoiakim was put on the throne by the Egyptians and he encountered much popular resentment in Jerusalem, which he violently suppressed (cf. 2 Kings xxiv. 4; Jer. xxii. 17). Did he secure this stronghold overlooking Jerusalem in order to sweep down on the city in case of an uprising? At any rate the strong and tragic personality of this king is vividly illuminated, and the uncompromising opposition of Jeremiah can be better understood.

Y. AHARONI

NOTES

1. Its Arab names Khirbet Ṣaliḥ and Khirbet Abu Bureik do not go back to antiquity; Ramat Raḥel is the modern name of a Qibbutz (collective settlement) inhabiting the area today. Its Hebrew name means 'Hill of Raḥel' and recalls the traditional tomb of Rachel nearby.

2. The first season was a trial excavation on a small scale under the auspices of the Israel Department of Antiquities and the Israel Exploration Society. Their results were published in *I.E.J.* vi, 1956, pp. 102–11, 137–57. The work ceased for four years during which the author participated in the Hazor excavations, and was renewed in 1959 under the auspices of the Hebrew University, co-operating with the two institutions mentioned above. For the last three seasons (1960–2) the University of Rome joined the Israeli institutions as a half-partner. The main assistants of the author were M. Kochavi, of the Hebrew University, and A. Ciasca, of the University of Rome. The results have been published in two volumes: *Excavations at Ramat Raḥel, Seasons 1959 and 1960*, 1962; *Seasons 1961 and 1962*, 1964.

3. B. Maisler (Mazar) and M. Stekelis, *Qobeṣ (Mazie Vol.)*, 1935, pp. 4–40 (in Hebrew).

4. P. C. Hammond, *P.E.Q.* 1957, pp. 68 f.; N. Avigad, *I.E.J.* vii, 1957, pp. 146–53.

5. F. M. Cross has suggested to me the reading *pḥr'* 'the potter'. This seems, however, difficult to accept for the following reasons. First, the Aḥzai stamp may be read *pḥr'*, granted that the letters *w* and *r* are similar in the Aramaic script of this period; this reading is, however, very difficult in the Yehoezer stamp. Here the letter under discussion is exactly like the *w* in both upper lines, while it is remarkably different from the *r* and *d*

(virtually identical letters) which appear in them. In the *yhwd/phw'* stamp the *w* is clear and the reading *r* seems impossible. Secondly, I cannot find a plausible explanation for 'Yehud the potter' if his name is not mentioned. Still more difficult would be 'belonging to Aḥzai, the potter'. The *lāmed possessivus* argues strongly against this interpretation, as a potter would hardly stamp vessels designated for others as *belonging to him*.

6. L. Koehler and W. Baumgartner, *Lex. in Vet. Test. Libros*, p. 757.

7. A. Cowley, *Aramaic Papyri of the Fifth Century B.C.*, 1923, p. 252.

8. Cf. Y. Kutscher, *Tarbiṣ* xxx, 1961, pp. 112–19 (in Hebrew).

9. Cowley, op. cit., pp. 111, 123.

10. F. M. Cross has suggested to me that they could belong to a pottery workshop, manufacturing jars for tax collection. Even then it seems more probable that this was situated at some administrative centre rather than in an unimportant village or on an uninhabited hill.

11. This theory has now been strengthened by the discovery of three 'private seals' at Arad in the archive of a royal functionary; see p. 400.

12. *Seasons 1959 and 1960*, pp. 51–56.

13. The argument that they went out of use before the days of Josiah is not based on stratigraphical considerations, but mainly on their limited distribution and the limited number of seals from which the impressions were made, which points to their relatively short duration.

14. In these artificial fills beneath the floors most of the royal seal impressions were found.

15. *J.B.L.* li, 1932, pp. 77–106.

16. Maisler and Stekelis, op. cit., pp. 14, 27 ff.; pl. 3.

17. See, for example, *A.N.E.P.*, no. 131.

18. After the early seasons I conjectured that it could be the palace of the leprosy stricken Uzziah (cf. 2 Chron. xxvi. 21) which was probably outside the city. However, with the continuation of the excavations it became obvious that a date in the eighth century B.C. is untenable.

19. Could the concluding words of the prophecy ('cast forth beyond the gates of Jerusalem', Jer. xxii. 19) perhaps be connected with the location of the palace, particularly as they did not materialize?

20. Cf. *Seasons 1959 and 1960*, p. 50.

BIBLIOGRAPHY

AHARONI, Y. 'Excavations at Ramath Raḥel, 1954, Preliminary Report', *I.E.J.* vi, 1956, pp. 102–11, 137–57.

—— *Excavations at Ramat Raḥel, Seasons 1959 and 1960*, 1962; *Seasons 1961 and 1962*, 1964.

BETH-SHEAN

THE excavations at Beth-shean[1] were begun in 1921 by the
Museum of the University of Pennsylvania. The first Field
Director was C. S. Fisher, who was in charge for three
seasons until 1923, when he resigned. His chief assistant, A. Rowe,
started work again in 1925, and remained Field Director till the
season of 1928. The present writer took over for 1930, 1931, and
1933, after which the University Museum discontinued the excavations.

The site has a long history. At one point a sounding to virgin
soil was dug down for 70 feet through eighteen main occupation
levels, and pottery of the Chalcolithic period was found dating
from about the middle of the fourth millennium B.C. Successive
phases of the Early Bronze Age are well represented, as is the
Hyksos occupation (at Level X), but these strata lie outside the
purview of this chapter.

In the late Bronze Age Beth-shean became an important stronghold of the Egyptian Empire, especially under the Pharaohs of the
Nineteenth and Twentieth Dynasties, from Sethos I to Ramesses
III. It seems that a garrison of mercenaries akin to the Philistines
was installed in the fortress after the defeat of the invading 'Sea
Peoples' by Ramesses III early in the twelfth century B.C., and
remained in occupation after his death, when Egyptian authority
had broken down. The relations between the 'Sea Peoples' and
the native Canaanite population during the following century are
not recorded, but Beth-shean was in alliance with the Philistines
who, after their victory on Mount Gilboa, exposed the bodies of
Saul and his sons on the city wall (1 Sam. xxxi. 10, 12). Thanks to
David's victories, Solomon was able to incorporate Beth-shean,
along with Taanach and Megiddo, in the district allotted to Baana
(1 Kings iv. 12). It figures among the conquests of Sheshonq
(Shishak of the Old Testament), but the period of the Israelite
monarchy is very poorly represented within the area that has so far
been excavated.

In the Hellenistic period Beth-shean came to be known as

Scythopolis ('City of the Scythians'), possibly from a contingent of Scythian cavalry in the army of Ptolemy II,[2] but surely not from occupation by Scythian invaders in the sixth century B.C., as was formerly supposed. Under the Seleucids, in the second century B.C., Beth-shean acquired the additional name of Nysa, to which Dionysiac legends were attached; the primitive name nevertheless remained on the lips of the 'barbarian' natives and has survived to this day in Arabic as Beisān. After having been in Jewish hands from the time of John Hyrcanus (135–104 B.C.), Scythopolis enjoyed great prosperity during the Roman period as the only city of the league called the Decapolis that lay west of the Jordan, and likewise in later centuries as a Christian city and bishopric, enlarging its boundaries far beyond the mound, now called Tell el-Ḥuṣn, which was the nucleus of the ancient settlement. In A.D. 636 the Byzantine forces were defeated, and thenceforth the city gradually lost the importance it had held for so long.

This importance was undoubtedly due to its position at the meeting place of frequented highways. It lies in the valley of the Jalud, a perennial rivulet which flows into the Jordan through a gap in the mountains at the eastern end of the fertile plain of Jezreel. It thus had access to the Mediterranean coast by tracks across the plain, to north Syria by way of the west coast of the Sea of Galilee, and by the Jalud valley to the Jordan fords and a highway to the south. Though actually situated about 350 feet below sea level, Tell el-Ḥuṣn occupies a dominant position on a promontory between the Jalud on the north and a converging valley on the south-east, high above the Jordan and commanding a wide prospect, justly described by Fisher as a beautiful and majestic situation. The ruins of Beth-shean-Scythopolis cover a wide area within which a number of mosaic floors and a Roman theatre of the second or third century have been cleared in recent years by the Antiquities Department of Israel.

But as a matter of course the excavations begun in 1921 were directed in the first place to the imposing tell—*tertre gigantesque et solitaire*, as L. H. Vincent described it—and secondarily to the slopes on the opposite side of the Jalud, honeycombed with tombs that range in date from the Middle Bronze to the Byzantine Age. Disentangling the history of Beth-shean proved to be no easy task, and it was somewhat unfortunate that the excavations were put in hand so early in the period of the British Mandate after the First World War. In 1921 study of the pottery sequence in Palestine had not been carried far enough to make the absolute dating of successive levels easily discernible. For various reasons it has not yet been possible completely to publish the results of the excavations, so with reference to the tombs and to many of the occupation levels only brief preliminary reports have appeared. Moreover, many of the dates originally proposed have been shown to require correction. It is therefore very gratifying to know that Mrs. Frances James has been able to work in the University Museum and in Jerusalem on the finds from Beth-shean, and that her forthcoming work[3] will undoubtedly throw a great deal of fresh light on the Israelite strata. The present writer is greatly indebted to Mrs. James for the information which she has generously put at his disposal.

The tell, incorporating the debris of eighteen occupation levels, stands on a spur that slopes steeply on all sides except the west, where a more gentle incline makes it possible to reach a ruined gateway at the north-western angle of an outer circuit wall of Byzantine, or perhaps later, masonry. From this gateway a paved road, from which some house walls have been cleared away, leads to the highest point of the tell, about 260 feet above the river Jalud. Any idea of clearing the whole tell layer by layer was soon abandoned, and all the excavations that we are concerned with took place in a small acropolis area, the Summit.

Levels I and II represented the Arab and Byzantine periods, the latter providing an interesting example of geometrical planning, a circular church with an apse towards the east. Beneath its paved floor the platform of debris made it difficult to work out the stratification of Hellenistic and Roman remains in Level III. In it was a hoard of silver tetradrachms of Ptolemy Philadelphus (285–247 B.C.), but the main feature of this level was what remained of a peripteral temple, at first thought to be Hellenistic, but more probably Roman, of which the foundation trenches cut through Level IV into the mud-brick walls of Level V. In an adjoining cistern there were column drums from this temple and a marble head, perhaps representing Dionysus. To the period of Stratum III belongs a sarcophagus from the cemetery north of the

Jalud bearing the name Antiochus (son of) Phallion; this may possibly be the Phallion whose brother was Antipater, the father of Herod the Great.

The Iron Age pottery from Level IV awaits publication in Mrs. James's work mentioned above, but she has kindly informed me that occupation seems to have lasted only from *c.* 815 to *c.* 700 B.C., followed by a long period of desertion before the Hellenistic period. Only a few figurines, formerly regarded as evidence of Scythian occupation, have suggested the possibility that under the Persians a hill-top shrine, of which no trace was found, stood on the tell.

It is disappointing that so little information should be forthcoming about the Israelite period, but the excavated area produced only insignificant buildings at Level IV, with quantities of intrusive material from cisterns and wall foundations of later date. Level V presented a very different picture. It was the latest, and thus the first to be reached, of five strata which contained substantial buildings and an informative variety of objects, and which have thereby made a contribution to our knowledge of Canaanite religion and civilization as they were when they confronted the invading Israelites.

The results obtained from the five Levels IX to V have been fully described in Rowe's volumes. An unfortunate decision on the part of Fisher, misled by having found on Level V Egyptian monuments originally set up at lower levels, led to the designation of successive levels by the names of Egyptian rulers whose reigns did not in fact correspond to the dates of the strata. This maladjustment has to be borne in mind by readers studying the published material. An acceptable scheme was proposed in 1937 by W. F. Albright, who assigned Level IX ('Thothmes III') to the late fourteenth century B.C., Level VIII ('Pre-Amenophis') to the fourteenth–thirteenth centuries, Level VII ('Amenophis III') to the thirteenth century, Level VI ('Seti I') to the twelfth century, and Level V ('Rameses II' or 'Rameses III') to the twelfth–tenth centuries.[4] No doubt greater precision would be attainable if more of the tell were ever to be excavated and more material made available for the further study that these strata deserve.

The earliest of the succession of buildings on the Summit dedicated to the service of religion—in a tradition which may be said to culminate in the Byzantine church—stands at Level IX, which is separated from the underlying Middle Bronze Age stratum by a layer of debris that may well represent an occupation subsequent to the conquests of Tuthmosis III. Here the excavations uncovered, not a temple in the strict sense, but rather a sacred precinct with some characteristics of a Canaanite high place. Whether any part of the area was roofed over is quite uncertain; at all events it seems to have been set apart mainly for animal sacrifices. An altar stood near the entrance from a courtyard into an inner sanctuary in which were two more altars, one of them recorded as having on it the bones of a young bull. A stone hearth in an enclosure further to the east contained charred remnants of horns and bones. A corridor at a slightly higher level, running along the south side of the area, was perhaps a separate shrine; there was a large altar near the western end of it, and at the east a small chamber containing a miniature *maṣṣēḇāh*, or standing stone, conical in shape, on a base of unhewn stones. Close by this primitive emblem, or personification, of the native deity lay the corresponding tribute of an alien civilization in the form of a stone panel of Egyptian character with an inscription naming the god Mekal, Lord of Beth-shean. This votive stele is dedicated on behalf of Amen-em-Apt, a builder, by his son Pa-Ra-em-Heb, and depicts both of them standing in adoration before the god, who is seated on a throne holding in his right hand the *crux ansata* and in his left a sceptre, symbols of life and welfare. He is bearded and wears a close-fitting tunic, a necklace of beads, and a tall conical head-dress with two streamers depending from it at the back; two gazelle horns project over the god's forehead. These features are associated in art with a god of war and pestilence, Resheph, and make it probable that Mekal is to be identified with him.[5]

The numerous small objects scattered about the precinct bear witness to the diverse influences to which Palestine was subject: a fine amethyst scarab of Sesostris I (*c.* 1971–1928 B.C.) among others, a seal and a faience bowl with hieroglyphs, faience beads, and a typically Egyptian head from a small basalt statue. One of several leaf-shaped gold pendants had incised upon it the figure of a goddess, Astarte or Anat, nude, but wearing an Egyptian head-dress and holding the *was* sceptre; other finds were clay plaques of female deities, with a mould for making them, a bronze figurine coated with gold leaf, and the figure of a man in ivory inlay. A bowl fragment with a snake in high relief and a cylindrical stand are early examples of forms which in later centuries become common; among Late Bronze Age pottery fragments the Cypriot milk bowl indicates Aegean contacts. Northern influences appear in a dagger of a form represented in Hittite sculpture and in the numerous 'Hurrian' or 'Mitannian' cylinder-seals from Level IX. A particularly fine example of sculpture in relief is a basalt panel, about three feet in height, with the upper register depicting two animals —one certainly a lion, the other apparently a mastiff—confronted on their hind legs, and the lower showing the lion as he moves away unconcernedly while the mastiff attacks his flank (Pl. VII). There is nothing to show where exactly the panel had originally been set up, and it seems doubtful whether any symbolical meaning can be attributed to it. Both animals, but especially the lion with the star-shaped tuft on his shoulder, have much in common with those on fourteenth-century B.C. gold vessels from Ras Shamra,[6] and with several from the tomb of Tutankhamun, in particular a lion cub of carved wood overlaid with gold.[7]

Above the ruins of the precinct sacred to Mekal, Level VIII consisted of a street with houses that were in no way remarkable. The objects found included Egyptian scarabs, Mitannian cylinder seals, and pottery with Aegean affinities, thus carrying on the traditions of the preceding stratum. Since Level VIII dates in all probability from about the time of Sethos I, we may now advert to the two stelae which he set up in Beth-shean, although both of them had been removed by successive generations, the larger being found lying on Level V, the other still higher up, defaced by being used as a door-sill.

The former contains an account of military operations in the first year of Sethos' reign. On being informed that the enemy at Hamath, in alliance with Pella, was threatening, or perhaps had already captured, Beth-shean, and was besieging Rehob, the king sent one division of his army, that of Amen, entitled 'Powerful Bows', to Hamath, another, that of Ra, entitled 'Many Braves', to Beth-shean, and a third, that of Sutekh, entitled 'Many Bows', to Yenoam, with the result that the enemy was defeated. Pella, across the Jordan, is well known; Rehob was probably a short distance south of Beth-shean; Hamath and Yenoam are possibly to be

PLATE VII

Combat between dog and lion (Beth-shean), fourteenth century B.C.

located in northern Palestine, but it is not certain how far afield these three army corps, which are known also from other sources, were dispatched.

The other stele of Sethos I was in poor condition and difficult to read. Rowe had noted a mention of the 'Apiru and studied the text in collaboration with W. F. Albright, by whom it was finally published,[8] though not before a version by B. Grdseloff had appeared.[9] The date is broken off, but this stele must refer to a later operation—a punitive expedition lasting two days, by a force that included chariotry, against the 'Apiru (distinguished by a determinative sign as warriors) who, in alliance with Tayaru tribesmen, were attacking the nomads of Ruhma, presumably in the neighbourhood of Beth-shean. The interest of this monument lies in its mention of the 'Apiru, or Ḥabiru, who play so many different roles in the history of Western Asia and whom it seems impossible completely to dissociate from the Hebrews.

The occupation of Level IX probably came to an end in some such period of disturbance as preceded the reign of Sethos I, but whatever the exact date of Level VIII may be, it seems that Level VII, originally thought to be the Amenophis III Level, must be associated with the Nineteenth Dynasty. This includes the reign of Ramesses II, who set up a stele in his ninth regnal year recording the homage paid to him by Asiatic rulers at Per-Ramessu, his capital in the Delta. This stele was later moved, with those of his father Sethos I, up to Level V.

In Level VII stood the earlier of two temples, laid out on almost identical lines, dating respectively from the century of the Exodus and the reign of Ramesses III, times when Egypt dominated and the imitative Canaanite culture in Beth-shean was open to influence from all sides but was not yet in contact with Israel. It will be sufficient to describe only the later and better preserved of the two similar temples, the one on Level VI, with its walls of sun-dried brick resting partly on the ruins of the earlier one. The main sanctuary was nearly 50 feet long from north to south, and almost equally wide at its northern end, but narrowing to the south; the entrance to it was through two antechambers at the southern end, the inner one entered from the west, the outer through a doorway on its northern side. Two basalt column bases in the sanctuary indicated that a roof had covered the northern part, within which a low altar of brick stood at the floor level. Beyond this a flight of seven steps led to an upper chamber, flanked by two store-rooms and containing another altar, part brick, part limestone. The floor of this altar chamber was coloured blue; on it lay the figure of a hawk, life-size and wearing the crown of Upper and Lower Egypt. In ground plan these two temples resemble certain shrines at Tell el-Amarna, but even if the latter may owe something to Asiatic influence, it is not now possible to regard them as of later date than the buildings of Beth-shean.

Before reverting to the level of the earlier temple, we may note in passing the surprising fact that no remains of a town wall have appeared in the excavations along the edge of the tell (except the late stone wall on the uppermost level), perhaps because of erosion caused by the steepness of the slope towards the south. However, at Level VII a substantial gate-tower, or *miḡdôl*, protected the approach to the Summit from the western slope. This was a rect-angular edifice containing five rooms and remains of a stairway, with two projecting towers to guard the entrance; its brick walls were strengthened by a core of large stones. An adjoining building may have been the residence of the governor or the commander of the garrison.

At the same level there were numerous small finds such as scarabs and faience or glass amulets representing the cobra and other typically Egyptian subjects; the Hathor head-dress appears on clay plaques and on an ivory fragment. A limestone panel about 15 inches high shows a worshipper standing before a female goddess who holds an *ankh* symbol and a sceptre and has on her head a high crown above two horns—a typical goddess of fertility and perhaps the consort of Mekal. A socketed axe-head, like the dagger from Level IX, is shaped like one represented on a relief at Boğazköy, and a Hittite cylinder-seal was found, as well as one attributed to the period of the First Dynasty of Babylon, and a great number of Mitannian seals. Some imported pottery, My-cenaean in character, may have reached Palestine from Cyprus.

The temple on Level VI has been described above. From inscriptions now known to come from this level we learn that it dates from the reign of Ramesses III, under whom the authority of Egypt was restored, and that there was an Egyptian of high rank, named Ramesses-Wesr-Khepesh, serving under him. Besides the temple there was another large building comprising a hall nearly 30 feet square with small rooms round it and a principal entrance through a forecourt on the west side. A peculiarity of this level was the use of limestone for door-sills (seven of them were found *in situ*) and for door-jambs with hieroglyphic inscriptions, although the walls were of the usual sun-dried brick on rough stone foundations. Two column bases about 5 feet in diameter lay at the entrance from the forecourt. After the destruction of the building there followed a period, presumably brief, of reoccupation, characterized by insignificant walls.

Hardly any typically 'Philistine' vases have been found at Beth-shean, but at Level VI there were lentoid flasks and stirrup vases like those found in tombs from the neighbouring cemetery with the so-called anthropoid sarcophagi.[10] These are clay coffins with a lid at one end on which a face is modelled, either of a somewhat grotesque type with indications of a head-dress, or with smaller and perhaps womanlike features. With them were Egyptian amulets, beads, and *ushabti* figures. Similar coffins have been found at other sites in Palestine (with Philistine pottery at Tell el-Far'ah, probably Sharuhen, south-east of Gaza), and in Egypt, whence this burial custom was obviously derived. It seems to have been introduced by the Philistines and others of the 'Sea Peoples' who provided mercenaries in the Egyptian forces.

At Level VI objects of interest—apart from the Horus hawk on the temple floor and the hieroglyphic inscriptions already mentioned—were comparatively few, but they include a small glass plaque on which a Babylonian deity, bearded and horned, and a worshipper are represented, and two bronze objects—a tripod, with a rope-pattern circular top and supports terminating in volutes, of a class found in Greece, Crete, and Cyprus, and a smaller stand with a bowl-shaped top. Neither of these seems out of place in a stratum of the twelfth century B.C. Below a cistern that had broken through the floor level above, and so of doubtful provenance, were two fragments bearing hieroglyphic inscriptions, one of limestone with traces of three men's heads incised on it, the other a small basalt stele dedicated by a certain Hesi-Nekht to 'Antit Lady of Heaven and Mistress of all the Gods'—yet another Canaanite deity depicted like Astarte with Egyptian symbols.

Level V, which now remains to be described, contained many

noteworthy features—a gateway with 'Israelite' masonry, and two of the buildings published in Rowe's volume[11] (the others being those on Levels VI and VII), as well as the larger stele of Sethos I, that of Ramesses II, and the statue of Ramesses III. It was due to these Egyptian monuments, of which we have already made mention, that the name of Ramesses II[12] came to be attached to this Iron Age level.

After the death of Ramesses III, Egypt gradually lost control of Palestine, and the buildings on Level VI were probably in ruins by the beginning of the eleventh century B.C., a plausible date for the earliest phase of Level V with its two temples. The southern temple, close to the present edge of the tell, was built directly over that of Ramesses III, but differed from it in orientation and ground plan. It measured over all about 50 feet in width, and consisted of a hall about 26 feet wide, with a row of chambers or magazines on either side and an entrance at the west end; the eastern part of the building, where an altar might originally have stood, had been destroyed by a cistern dug down from a late level. Six stone bases for roof supports ran the length of the hall in two rows about 7 feet apart, making it seem possible that light was obtained from a clerestory. Each of the two centre bases had a foundation deposit laid beside it—a jug with gold ingots and a few silver ornaments at the north, and a pot with silver ingots and objects at the south.

On the other side of a corridor stood the northern temple, a plain building, not perfectly rectangular in plan, about 40 feet in length from west to east by 27 feet in width. The entrance was at the south-west corner; to prevent passers-by from obtaining a view of the interior the southern wall ran on westward for a short distance and then turned north. Four stone bases for roof supports rested on the lowest floor level, but above them was a solid flooring which extended over the whole building, making it obvious that a thorough reconstruction had taken place, and that what may be called the first phase of Level V had come to an end. For a later phase of this level the period of the Israelite monarchy is indicated by the presence of ninth-century B.C. pottery and by the masonry in the gateway at the north-west of the Summit with stones drafted on only two or three edges. Equally typical was the row of stone pillars that ran down the middle of a room close to the gateway. The royal stelae and statue were apparently set up, and perhaps venerated, at a time when Egypt was no longer in a position to command loyalty in Palestine. Eventually they were treated with scant respect; thrown down from their bases, they were found lying outside the temples, one stele over the other, and the statue broken in two.

The circumstances in which the occupation of Level V came to an end are obscure. Rowe has emphatically stated that there was no evidence of a conflagration, but substantial buildings were replaced by the mean constructions of Level IV, with the disappointing result that we are left with practically no information about Beth-shean in the period of the divided monarchy.

On the other hand, abundant material was forthcoming at Level V, presumably from an early phase, dominated either by 'Sea Peoples' or by Canaanites. Some of the finds are Egyptian, and these may have been brought from one of the lower levels— fragments of yet another royal stele and of a statue, and the private stele of one Amen-em-Apt, the same name as appears on the Mekal stele from Level IX. There were also some scarabs—one Hyksos, one of Tuthmosis III—and a handsome cylinder-seal depicting a standard, raised over two bound captives, with Ramesses II shooting an arrow at it, and on the other side a god, who is named Seth, although he bears a gazelle head on his brow like Resheph or Mekal.

Clay figurines of Astarte and a bronze one of a seated god are common native types, but the characteristic of Level V is the great number of cult objects of which the fragments were scattered in and around the two temples, some beneath the upper floor of the northern temple. Rowe has treated of these objects from every aspect with his customary thoroughness,[13] but the ruined buildings provide no evidence as to what role the objects played in Canaanite rites and ceremonies. A few fragments were found, as at Levels VI and VII, of the so-called *kernoi*, hollow rings supporting six or seven small vases; but the typical cult object is the stand with two handles, open at top and bottom, and described as cylindrical, though widening out to a bell-shaped base. Stands of this form had been known for many centuries, since the First Dynasty of Egypt (founded *c.* 3100 B.C.), the third millennium B.C. at Asshur, and Middle Minoan Crete (*c.* 2000–1600 B.C.), and seem to have been put to various uses. At Beth-shean they were evidently connected with a cult in which doves and snakes were prominent; most of them have triangular or rounded apertures, in each of which a bird is sitting and up to which spotted snakes are crawling. Even more remarkable are two models of buildings with doors and windows—shrine houses—which seem dedicated to the same cult, since they display similar snakes, together with nude female figures and, in one case, a lion.

These features all point to the conclusion that it was the goddess of fertility—Anat or Antit, or by whatever name she might be invoked—whose cult predominated when Beth-shean first fell to the invading Israelites.

G. M. FITZGERALD

NOTES

1. Spelt Beth-shan in 1 Sam. xxxi, 10, 12.
2. M. Avi-Yonah, *I.E.J.* xii, 1962, pp. 123–34.
3. F. W. James, *Beth-Shan at the beginning of the First Millennium B.C., a study of Levels V and IV.*
4. *A.A.S.O.R.* xvii, 1938, pp. 76–79.
5. L. H. Vincent, *R.B.* xxxvii, 1928, pp. 512–43.
6. C. F. A. Schaeffer, *Ugar.* ii, 1949, pp. 1–48, pls. i–xi.
7. Howard Carter, *Tut-ankh-Amen*, i, 1923, pl. lxviii.
8. *B.A.S.O.R.* 125, 1952, pp. 24–32.
9. *Une stèle scythopolitaine du roi Séthos Ier*, 1949.
10. W. F. Albright, *A.J.A.* xxxvi, 1932, pp. 295–306; G. E. Wright, *B.A.* xxii, 1959, pp. 54–66.
11. *Beth-shan II, i.*
12. Ibid.
13. Ibid., ch. vi.

BIBLIOGRAPHY

FitzGerald, G. M. *Beth-shan II, ii, The Four Canaanite Temples of Beth-shan. The Pottery*, 1930.
—— *Beth-shan III, Excavations 1921–1923; The Arab and Byzantine Levels*, 1931.
—— 'Excavations at Beth-shan', *P.E.F.Q.S.*, 1931, pp. 59–70; 1932, pp. 138–48; 1934, pp. 123–34.
Rowe, A. *Beth-shan I, The Topography and History of Beth-shan*, 1930.
—— *Beth-shan II, i, The Four Canaanite Temples of Beth-shan. The Temples and Cult Objects*, 1940.
—— and Vincent, L. H. 'New light on the evolution of Canaanite temples as exemplified by restorations of the sanctuaries found at Beth-shan', *P.E.F.Q.S.*, 1931, pp. 12–21.

BETH-SHEMESH

THERE are several different cities named Beth-shemesh ('House or Temple of the Sun') in the Old Testament, but the present article is concerned only with the one that stood on the site of the modern Tell er-Rumeileh by 'Ain Shems ('Spring of the Sun' in Arabic). It lies on the south side of the valley of Sorek near the western end of the Shephelah almost due east of, and about 20 miles from, Jerusalem. The position is important, because it is close to the route leading up from Philistia and the coastal plain in the west, through the valley of Sorek, to the Judaean hill country and Jerusalem in the east; it also lies just to the west of a road running northwards from Hebron.

The city does not play a very prominent part in the Old Testament. According to 1 Sam. vi, when the Philistines sent the ark back to the Israelites, its first resting place was Beth-shemesh. Considerably later it was the scene of Amaziah's defeat by Jehoash;[1] and 2 Chron. xxviii. 18[2] records that it was among the cities captured by the Philistines in the time of Ahaz. Otherwise, Beth-shemesh appears only in lists.[3] The city is doubtless to be identified with Ir-shemesh ('City of the Sun') in Joshua xix. 41, where it is allotted to the tribe of Dan, in contrast to other passages[4] in which it is reckoned to belong to Judah, probably according to a later system. It has been suggested that Beth-shemesh is also to be identified with Mount Heres (Judges i. 35; *heres*, like *šemeš*, means 'sun'), but the identification is disputed.[5]

The first excavations were carried out on behalf of the Palestine Exploration Fund in 1911 and 1912 under the direction of Duncan Mackenzie. The second series of archaeological campaigns was sponsored by Haverford College, Pennsylvania, and directed by Elihu Grant. Grant distinguished six different strata, and his analysis of the excavations, worked out in collaboration with G. E. Wright, has been adopted in the following account.

Very little can be said about the history of Beth-shemesh in the early period, represented by Stratum VI. No trace has been discovered of buildings in this stratum, but the pottery appears to justify the conclusion that the city was founded *c.* 2200 B.C., and that the stratum covers approximately 500 years. The same type of evidence suggests that the population was small in the earlier part of the period but that it increased in Middle Bronze Age II A.

Stratum V is dated *c.* 1700–1500 B.C. and thus comes from the age at the beginning of which the Hyksos dominated Egypt and during which the Egyptians, after expelling them, fought several campaigns in Palestine. The city was fortified in the late seventeenth or sixteenth century B.C.: there was a wall with massive stones, some nearly a metre thick, in the lower part and smaller stones higher up—the width of the wall varies between 2·20 and 2·40 metres; and Mackenzie excavated a great gate in the southern wall of the city. The breaches found in the wall were probably made in the attack that destroyed the city at the end of the period of Stratum V, though they are possibly to be dated in the period of Stratum IVa. This attack, which caused a layer of burnt debris, has been plausibly attributed to one of the Egyptian military expeditions after the expulsion of the Hyksos, and perhaps took place in the reign of Amenophis I (*c.* 1546–1526 B.C.) or of his successor Tuthmosis I (*c.* 1525–1512 B.C.).

A short part of the city wall was used as one side of a large house which was presumably the home of a wealthy citizen. The lower layers of the house's outer walls were made of stone, above which mud brick was probably used, and the floor and the inside of the walls were lined with lime. Apart from this building, all that has been found of houses in this stratum are the remains of a few rooms and walls. One room of the large house had a storage jar in the corner; another means of storage common in the period was a bin consisting of a small square structure of stone with a floor of lime or beaten earth. A different aspect of life is illustrated by the discovery of two gaming boards, one of which may, however, come from Stratum IV. The game, which originated in Mesopotamia and spread to Egypt, was also known in other parts of Palestine: playing figures and parts of boards have been found at Tell el-'Ajjul and at Tell Beit Mirsim. A teetotum was spun, and the number of holes in the side that fell uppermost determined a player's moves.[6]

Several tombs from this period have been discovered. Like those of later periods, they were hollowed out of the rock, and one at least of them makes use of a natural cave. The dead were laid in the tombs with pottery and other objects, such as a dagger and scarabs, beside them. The entrance to one tomb led into a room of the large house, but it was probably no longer in use and was blocked up when the house was built. Two jars containing children's bones were found in rooms elsewhere in the city; the excavators think it unlikely that they were foundation sacrifices.

Stratum IV, which comes from c. 1500–1200 B.C., is divided into two periods by a destruction c. 1425 B.C., probably in a campaign of Amenophis II. It is uncertain who was responsible for a further destruction at the end of the Late Bronze Age; it may have been the Philistines, though the disaster may have taken place too early for this, or the Egyptians, or perhaps the invading Israelites. Whether or not the Israelites under Joshua sacked Beth-shemesh, Stratum IV belongs to the Canaanite city in the centuries immediately before their entry into the land.

Beth-shemesh flourished in the Late Bronze Age. The city wall of Stratum V was repaired, and buildings were well constructed. A new large house was built in Stratum IVa on the site of the old one, and the remains of another large building have been discovered in Stratum IVb. The latter is of particular interest, because it contained furnaces for smelting copper—evidence of industrial activity at the time. In contrast to Stratum V, many cisterns were found; they were rendered waterproof with a cement made from lime, and the introduction of this technique enabled people to store large quantities of water and must have made a great difference to their life. For the storage of grain, small square bins continued to be used, but round silos, usually lined with stone, were introduced as well.

Other signs of prosperity have been found, such as a hoard of jewellery and a diorite bowl, and a fragment of a second, made in Egypt something like twelve or fifteen hundred years before. Among the many objects from this stratum, several are of religious interest: two small bronze representations of the god Resheph and fragments of others, and a clay plaque of a nude goddess; there is also a Mycenaean pottery fragment of a goddess. It may here be noted that representations of fertility goddesses not only appear in Stratum IV, but continue to be found as late as Stratum IIc. However, the form of the representations changed as time passed:

pillar-type figurines began to appear in the Iron Age and became more popular than plaques.[7] Two tombs, both outside the city wall, belong to Stratum IV, and they contain earthenware and other objects, such as scarabs, ivory amulets, and beads. The pottery from this period includes Mycenaean ware, some of it imported from Cyprus.

Two texts from Stratum IV deserve special mention. The first is an ostracon which is usually dated between the fifteenth and thirteenth centuries B.C., though W. F. Albright[8] has suggested a date *c.* 1100 B.C., well into the Iron Age. On the ostracon are characters closely resembling those of the proto-Sinaitic inscriptions, but there is not yet general agreement about the decipherment of the text.[9] The second is a tablet written in the alphabetic cuneiform used at Ugarit.[10] However, some letters are written in an unusual way and, in contrast to all but a very few of the texts from Ugarit, the writing runs from right to left; in this the Beth-shemesh tablet agrees with an inscription on a bronze knife found on Mount Tabor.[11] Having noted that the texts running from right to left have other peculiarities in common, A. Herdner has suggested[12] that a modified form of the Ugaritic alphabet was developed and used in Canaan. Whether or not this is so, the Beth-shemesh tablet testifies that the use of alphabetic cuneiform was not entirely restricted to the city of Ugarit. The interpretation of the text is disputed, but some believe it to be magical in character. It is probably to be dated in the fourteenth or thirteenth century B.C.

Stratum III, from the beginning of the Iron Age, *c.* 1200–1000 B.C., belongs to the period of the Judges, during which the Israelites were settling down in the land. The presence of much pottery that is probably Philistine might suggest that Beth-shemesh was occupied by the Philistines, but it appears from 1 Sam. vi. that the city was Israelite at the time. The Philistine pottery is evidence of the powerful influence exerted on the Israelite inhabitants by the people in the coastal plain who were culturally more advanced. The destruction at the end of the period probably occurred in the wars between the Philistines and the Israelites in the time of Saul or perhaps David.

The first Israelite city of Beth-shemesh shows a marked decline from the finest days of the Canaanite occupation in the Late

Bronze Age. The city wall was badly repaired, and buildings were not well constructed. The most impressive building excavated was a house with a courtyard, perhaps belonging to a local person of importance. It has been suggested that this house and similar buildings in other Israelite cities 'were not aristocratic mansions, like the Canaanite buildings whose place they sometimes take, but were occupied by several smaller families, grouped around a patriarchal head';[13] the suggestion is interesting, though such interpretations of archaeological evidence must be advanced with caution. Round silos were discovered in this stratum, as in the preceding one, and cisterns continued to be used for storing water. Now, however, there was also a large well for the water-supply. Furnaces for the smelting of bronze were found, but iron was beginning to come into use, primarily for weapons and jewellery. Iron sickles had not yet displaced the ancient tools made of flint blades attached to wooden handles. As has been noted, Philistine influence was dominant in pottery, and indeed Philistine pottery was superior to native Israelite ware; a small amount of Cypriot pottery was imported, in contrast to the larger quantities of the preceding stratum.

The city was rebuilt fairly soon after its destruction at the end of Stratum III. There is general agreement that Stratum II began *c.* 1000 B.C. and ended *c.* 587 B.C. with Nebuchadrezzar's invasion of Judah, that the stratum is to be divided into three periods, and that the city was fortified during only the first two periods. However, different opinions have been expressed about the precise dates of the periods. Grant and Wright in 1939 proposed the following dates: *c.* 1000–950 B.C. for Stratum IIa, *c.* 950–825 B.C. for IIb, and *c.* 825–586 B.C. for IIc. The city of Stratum IIb clearly ended in general destruction, but Grant and Wright were not willing to commit themselves to a choice among the various occasions on which this may have happened. They were uncertain whether there was general destruction at the end of Stratum IIa, but they detected some evidence of devastation. The city walls of Stratum IIa, which differed in construction from those of earlier strata, are one of the subjects involved in the controversy over chronology. They were casemate walls, the inner wall being about 1·10 metres thick and the outer wall, 1·50 to 2 metres away, varying between 1·40 and 1·60 metres. Among the houses excavated were two of great size and importance. One of them, built on the site of the large house of Stratum III, was erected in Stratum IIa and continued to be used in later periods. Its size has suggested that it was not the dwelling of a private citizen, but was connected with the administration of the city.[14] This view of its purpose would account for the presence nearby of an enormous silo, of which the depth was 5·70 metres and the other dimensions 7·50 and 6·50 metres respectively; here taxes in kind were perhaps collected and stored. Albright[15] has drawn attention to the similarity between the casemate walls of Beth-shemesh and those at Tell Beit Mirsim, which is such as to suggest to him the probability that they were built under the same supervision; similarly, the large building can be compared to a structure at Lachish which was perhaps also used as a government granary.[16] Albright and Wright believe that these buildings and casemate walls can be dated to the time of David. This dating has been made the basis of a theory by F. M. Cross and Wright[17] who suggest that the division of Israel into administrative districts in the time of Solomon was preceded by a similar division of Judah by David. In the article in which the theory is advanced, Wright modifies the chronology of Stratum II that he had proposed in 1939. He now maintains that there was a gap in the occupation of Beth-shemesh throughout most of the ninth century B.C., and that this explains why the city is not mentioned in Joshua xv which, he thinks, contains a list compiled in this century; Stratum IIb is to be dated entirely in the tenth century B.C., and the city was probably destroyed in Shishak's campaign of 918 B.C.[18] He thinks that, after this destruction, it remained unoccupied until the later part of the ninth century B.C.

This theory has been challenged by several Israeli scholars,[19] partly because of their dating of certain types of pottery, and partly because they take a different view of the casemate walls. The excavation of similar walls at Hazor, and Y. Yadin's acute discovery[20] that contemporary walls of this kind existed at Gezer (which, if 1 Kings ix. 16 f. is to be taken at its face value, did not come into Israelite hands until Solomon's reign) and at Megiddo, lead them to think that the casemate walls at Beth-shemesh were built in Solomon's time, and that Stratum IIb is therefore later than Wright's revised dating. Y. Aharoni suggests the following chronology: *c.* 1000–925 B.C. for Stratum IIa, *c.* 925–795 B.C. for IIb, *c.*

795–750 B.C. for the gap in occupation, and *c.* 750–587 B.C. for IIc. The year 795 B.C. is chosen because Aharoni thinks that the battle at Beth-shemesh between Jehoash and Amaziah, recorded in 2 Kings xiv. 11 ff. and 2 Chron. xxv. 21 ff., took place in that year. Wright has replied[21] briefly to the criticisms of his revised chronology, and general agreement on the question has not been reached. It may be added that the difference over chronology makes no difference to the assertion of Grant and Wright that no trace has been found of the Assyrian campaigns in Judah in the late eighth century B.C., although Mackenzie had earlier believed that there was evidence that the city suffered severely from Sennacherib's army *c.* 701 B.C. Nor does there seem to be any trace of the Philistine capture of the city recorded in 2 Chron. xxviii. 18.

This stratum contains evidence of Israelite life in the period of the monarchy. The Philistine pottery that was so prominent in Stratum III disappears, and there is much Israelite earthenware of differing kinds. There are also vats for dyeing, and a number of olive and grape presses, which suggests that the production of olive-oil and the making of wine were important industries. Evidence of copper forging has been found in Stratum IIa, and iron was used more extensively than in the preceding period. In particular, two uses of iron for agricultural purposes may be noted. First, an iron sickle, which may, however, come from Stratum III, is an example of a tool that was at last rendering the use of flint sickle blades obsolete. Secondly, although two small bronze plough points have been found, there are a greater number of larger iron points. The latter tool must have led to a great improvement in the farming of the land.[22] Another change in this period is that, although the well of Stratum III continued to be used in periods a and b of Stratum II, a large cistern was dug, probably in the eighth century B.C., and Grant and Wright believe that it was the principal source of water in the dry season for the city of Stratum IIc. Two further comments may be made on the buildings. In the first place, there is evidence in Strata IIa and IIb for the practice of constructing walls with strengthening pillars within them. Secondly, it is interesting to note that a cigar-shaped stone, probably used for a religious purpose at an earlier period, was degraded to the status of building material for a house.

A number of tombs outside the city have been excavated, varying in date from the late tenth to the early sixth century B.C. As in earlier periods, they were hollowed out in the rock, and use was sometimes made of natural caves. They normally contained a ledge or ledges for the bodies, and the entrance was closed with a stone seal against which another stone was rolled.

Some of the pottery has been stamped by seals bearing Hebrew names. Of particular historical interest is a jar handle labelled 'belonging to Eliakim, the [se]rvant of Yaukin'.[23] The same seal was used for a jar handle found at Beth-haccherem and for two jar handles found at Tell Beit Mirsim, and Albright has pointed out[24] that Yaukin is probably to be identified with King Jehoiachin who was deposed and deported to Babylon in 597 B.C.[25] The jar handles must come from a time when he was a prisoner, and are interesting evidence that his property was not confiscated or appropriated by his successor Zedekiah but was administered on his behalf.

Stratum I, the latest layer of Beth-shemesh, is of little interest to the student of the Old Testament, except for its testimony to the devastation brought to the land by Nebuchadrezzar in the sixth century B.C. The city was never rebuilt, though there is evidence, chiefly coins and pottery, that a few people lived on the site in Hellenistic and Roman times.

J. A. EMERTON

NOTES

1. 2 Kings xiv. 11, 13 = 2 Chron. xxv. 21, 23.

2. The Chronicler is probably drawing on an old source other than the books of Kings. Cf. M. Noth, *Überlieferungsgeschichtl. Studien*, 1943, p. 142.

3. Joshua xv. 10, xxi. 16 (cf. 1 Chron. vi. 44, R.V. 59); 1 Kings iv. 9.

4. Joshua xv. 10 and 2 Kings xiv. 11 (= 2 Chron. xxv. 21), and, by implication, Joshua xxi. 16. Cf. F. M. Cross and G. E. Wright, *J.B.L.* lxxv, 1956, pp. 202–26; B. Mazar, *I.E.J.* x, 1960, pp. 65–77; cf. also the articles in *V.T.* by Y. Aharoni and Z. Kallai-Kleinmann mentioned below, p. 205, n. 19.

5. Cf. Mazar, op. cit., p. 67.

6. Cf. W. F. Albright, *The Archaeology of Palestine and the Bible*, 1932, pp. 87 f.; *Mizraim* i, 1933, pp. 130–4; *A.A.S.O.R.* xvii, 1938, pp. 48 f.

7. The Beth-shemesh representations of fertility goddesses are among those discussed by J. B. Pritchard, *Palestinian Figurines in Relation to Certain Goddesses known through Literature*, 1943.

8. G. E. Wright (ed.), *The Bible and the Ancient Near East*, 1961, p. 358. In a discussion of this text and others in the same script (*P.E.Q.*, 1937, pp. 180–93), S. Yeivin has pointed out that Grant does not describe precisely where the ostracon was found, and that it is therefore difficult to date it from its archaeological context.

9. G. R. Driver, *Semitic Writing*, rev. ed., 1954, p. 101, regards the ostracon 'as unlikely ever to be deciphered'. For attempts to translate the text, see H. Grimme, *A.f.O.* x, 1935–6, pp. 270–7; Yeivin, op. cit., pp. 188 ff.; B. Maisler, *J.P.O.S.* xviii, 1938, pp. 290 f. Cf. also F. M. Cross, *B.A.S.O.R.* 134, 1954, pp. 15–24.

10. Cf. W. F. Albright, *B.A.S.O.R.* 53, 1934, pp. 18 f.; ibid. 173, 1964, pp. 51 ff. An anonymous note, perhaps by E. F. Weidner, *A.f.O.* ix, 1933–4, p. 358, draws attention to an Assyrian inscription running from right to left. The suggestion that texts were written in this way in order to puzzle the unlearned might account for the Beth-shemesh tablet, which may be magical, but seems less appropriate for the Mount Tabor dagger (cf. the next footnote).

11. Cf. Yeivin, *Ḳedem* ii, 1945, pp. 32–41 (in Hebrew), VIII (English summary); Albright, *B.A.S.O.R.* 99, 1945, p. 21.

12. *Syria* xxv, 1946–8, pp. 165–8. On the basis of texts running from right to left, C. Virolleaud advances a more far-reaching and controversial theory that the Phoenician alphabet came into existence under the influence of that of Ugarit: *C.R.A.I.*, 1960, pp. 85–90. It should be noted that a text in alphabetic cuneiform found recently at Taanach runs from left to right, although some letters show affinities in form to those of the texts running the other way; cf. D. R. Hillers, *B.A.S.O.R.* 173, 1964, pp. 45–50.

13. Albright, *The Biblical Period from Abraham to Ezra*, 1963, p. 46.

14. It is unlikely that it was a temple, although this theory was held at one time.

15. *A.A.S.O.R.* xxi–xxii, 1943, pp. 11, 13 f.

16. Ibid., pp. 22 ff. Cf. G. E. Wright, *B.A.* i, 1938, p. 28, and E. F. Campbell and D. N. Freedman (ed.), *B.A.R.* ii, 1964, p. 303; *J.N.E.S.* xiv, 1955, p. 188; *V.T.* v, 1955, p. 99.

17. *J.B.L.* lxxv, 1956, pp. 202–26, especially pp. 215 f., 225 f.

18. For a different view of Shishak's treatment of the cities of Judah, cf. Mazar, *V.T. Supp.* iv, 1957, pp. 57–66. In the editorial chronological chart Shishak's date is given c. 945–924 B.C.

19. Y. Aharoni and R. Amiran, *I.E.J.* viii, 1958, pp. 171–84; Aharoni, *B.A.S.O.R.* 154, 1959, pp. 35–39, and *V.T.* ix, 1959, pp. 225–46; Z. Kallai-Kleinmann, *V.T.* viii, 1958, pp. 134–60. Cf. Mazar, *I.E.J.* x, 1960, p. 70.

20. *I.E.J.* viii, 1958, pp. 80–86; *B.A.* xxiii, 1960, pp. 62–68, reprinted in Campbell and Freedman, op. cit., pp. 240–7.

21. *B.A.S.O.R.* 155, 1959, pp. 13–29, especially pp. 14, 28 f.

22. Cf. Albright, *The Biblical Period etc.*, p. 105.

23. Cf. *D.O.T.T.*, p. 224.

24. *J.B.L.* li, 1932, pp. 77–106; cf. *B.A.* v, 1942, pp. 49–55, reprinted in G. E. Wright and D. N. Freedman (ed.), *B.A.R.* i, 1961, pp. 106–12. For Beth-haccherem, see p. 179.

25. 2 Kings xxiv. 12, cf. xxv. 27–30.

BIBLIOGRAPHY

GRANT, E. *Beth Shemesh* (*Palestine*). *Progress of the Haverford Archaeological Expedition*, 1929.

The following five works are numbers 3–5, 7–8, respectively, of the series, *Biblical and Kindred Studies* (Haverford College, Haverford, Pennsylvania):

GRANT, E. *Ain Shems Excavations* (*Palestine*) *1928–1929–1930–1931*, *Part I*, 1931; *Part II*, 1932.

—— *Rumeileh being Ain Shems Excavations* (*Palestine*), *Part III*, 1934.

—— and WRIGHT, G. E. *Ain Shems Excavations* (*Palestine*), *Part IV* (*Pottery*), 1939.

—— Ibid., *Part V* (*Text*), 1939.

MACKENZIE, D. *P.E.F.A.* i, 1911, ii, 1912–13.

DEBIR

i. *Identification of the Site*

AFTER a horseback trip through southern Palestine in the
spring of 1924, I proposed identifying the most impressive
site we had studied, Tell Beit Mirsim, with Old Testament
Kiriath-sepher or Debir. Basic to my identification was the fact
that this was the only site near the point where the Shephelah,
hill country proper (Hebrew *har*), and the Southland (Negeb)
meet, which seemed to fit the requirements of Old Testament
tradition. At the same time it was the most important unidentified
mound of the entire area south and south-west of Hebron, though
still undoubtedly within the boundaries of Judah. The pottery
which covered the top of the site seemed to end with the close of
the monarchy of Judah, and numerous sherds of earlier ware were
strewn on the slopes of the prominent mound. The excavations
which followed in 1926–32 have made it certain that the stratigraphic history of the site coincides extremely well with Old
Testament references to Debir. Furthermore, investigation of surrounding areas has proved that no other unidentified site in the
whole region occupied by the sixth district of Judah, to which
Debir belonged, could possibly compete with it in size and location.[1]

According to our Old Testament data, the town had been occupied by the Canaanites whose king resisted Joshua and perished
with his subjects when the town was destroyed (Joshua x. 38). The
capture of Debir by Othniel, Caleb's nephew, is mentioned again
(Joshua xv. 16 ff.; Judges i. 11 ff.). That it was a 'royal city', that is, a
fortified town with its own prince and with smaller towns and villages dependent on it, may be surmised from the fact that all other
Canaanite towns listed in Joshua x were either certainly or probably
fortified towns with their own princes. Judging from the evidence
uncovered by J. L. Starkey and his colleagues at Lachish, that
town was definitely destroyed after the fourth year of Merneptah.
A striking confirmation of the antiquity of the story of the occupation

of the Debir area is preserved in Joshua xv. 18 f. = Judges i. 14 f. This passage is adapted from an older poem, though there are obvious gaps in the continuity; it can be turned into excellent mixed verse (3+3, 3+3, 3+3+3, 2+2+2). Repetitive style and archaisms guarantee its antiquity. I suspect that the original poem dealt with events preceding the capture of Debir and not following it, as suggested by the preserved text.

The basins (*gullôt*) in question are obviously to be identified with the 'wells' below and above Tell Beit Mirsim, which are neither springs nor wells in the ordinary sense, but are underground basins fed by springs under the accumulated alluvium which now fills the floor of the valley to the depth of over 20 metres. Tell Beit Mirsim is now about 1,630 feet above sea level and is far too high above the water-table to permit digging any true wells. This is undoubtedly why the term *gullôt* 'basins' was used, wherever they may have been located.

Whatever the exact relation between the roles of Joshua, Caleb, and Othniel may have been, it is clear that we are dealing here with authentic oral tradition going back to the period when western Judah was conquered by the Israelites. It is no accident that we invariably found, both in soundings and in area excavation, remains of destruction levels wherever we penetrated below the stratum containing early Philistine pottery into a Late Bronze Age stratum. Furthermore, the new settlers utilized old house walls wherever possible as foundations for new structures, however different the new plan might be in detail.

Probably even more significant is the fact that we found on the edge of our excavation in the south-west the collapsed roof of a large burned building, presumably a temple. Just outside it was an ancient pit containing bones of sacrificial animals, into which the destroyers of the Late Bronze Age town had hurled a crude stone lion and a stone basin with the head and forepaws of a lioness and the bodies of lion cubs in high relief around the rim. Such contemptuous disposal of sacred Canaanite objects which were too heavy for easy removal certainly suggests deliberate destruction by Israelites, especially since somewhat similar defacement of an idol was found in a Canaanite temple from the end of Late Bronze Age Hazor. Both these destructions are fixed by pottery in the second half of the thirteenth century B.C.

Under the monarchy Debir appears as a town in the sixth district of Judah (Joshua xv. 49) as well as one of the Levitic cities of Judah and Simeon (Joshua xxi. 15). The towns of the sixth district, as far as known, all lie south and south-west of Hebron. Excavations show that Tell Beit Mirsim had been occupied during three successive phases of Iron Age I and during most of Iron Age II, coming down to the time of the final destruction by the Chaldaeans c. 589–587 B.C. During the latter part of the Iron Age it was a flourishing town, surrounded by reasonably strong fortifications and occupying about 3½ hectares.

The correspondence between our data is so close that it is, in my opinion, highly probable that Tell Beit Mirsim is the site of ancient Debir. At the same time, I recognize that only those who know the Shephelah and the adjacent hill-country as I do after many years of constant exploration can realize the strength of our evidence where there is no direct epigraphic attestation of the identification. Whether Tell Beit Mirsim is Debir or not, it must be emphasized that there is not a single other suitable site within the entire area required for the location of Debir by our geographical and topographical data.

ii. *The Excavation of the Site*

The four campaigns of excavations at Tell Beit Mirsim lasted two months each in alternate years (1926, 1928, 1930, 1932). During three of these campaigns we were able to dig in the summer because of the location of the site high above the Shephelah proper and exposed to refreshing breezes which usually began about mid-morning and lasted until the late afternoon. All four campaigns were under the joint auspices of the American Schools of Oriental Research in Jerusalem and the Xenia Theological Seminary. Since the American Schools of Oriental Research had scarcely any funds in those days, over half of the cost of the four campaigns was borne by Dr. Melvin Grove Kyle himself and his friends. The first campaign was essentially a series of soundings for the purpose of determining the nature of the site; the following three campaigns were organized according to the methods of C. S. Fisher, with surveyors and Egyptian foremen trained by him and secured through his mediation. He assisted us notably by participating in our planning as well as by giving advice on many occasions.

While more precise methods of recording profiles and stratigraphic details were later introduced by Sir Mortimer Wheeler
and especially by Kathleen M. Kenyon, the loss was much less
than might have been expected. In the first place, we were always
on hand to investigate details of the dig as they appeared, and to
study the pottery as it was emerging from the ground. In the
second place, there was comparatively little building with mud-
brick, stone being the principal building material. Where we had
brick walls preserved *in situ*, they had generally been covered with
white plaster which was clearly visible as soon as we reached the
Bronze Age stratum in question. Most important was the fact that
destruction levels were generally continuous and could be traced
without serious interruption both on the vertical sides of the excavation and on the floor of areas being dug. Only in periods and areas
of sparse occupation was there room for uncertainty about the
attribution of given buildings to strata and phases. We took a
great many photographs of the sides of our excavation in order to
have a permanent record of the clues to stratification preserved
in them; most of these photographs were not clear enough for
reproduction, but a number were subsequently published in the
excavation reports. Of paramount importance, however, was the
fact that we were in constant touch with other archaeologists
and excavations under way in order to compare our pottery groups.
When the pottery of the four campaigns was published, especially
in 1932 and 1933, our chronology became standard. It is true that
severe criticisms against the pottery chronology were levelled by
even such a great scholar as the late L. H. Vincent,[2] but these
criticisms were quickly disproved by the results of excavation at
such sites as Megiddo, where the same sequence of Middle Bronze
Age occupations was found as at Tell Beit Mirsim.

In our interpretation of the site we were extremely cautious. One
serious mistake was natural enough in 1924, when we identified
stone posts projecting above the surface of the mound in the north-
west quadrant as ancient *maṣṣēḇôṯ* belonging presumably to a
sanctuary. In 1926 this proved to be entirely wrong, since the
stone posts were structural elements in private houses and had
nothing to do with cult. Otherwise, I do not recall a single published interpretation of any significance which proved to be in
error.[3]

iii. *Results of the Excavation*

In the red earth at the bottom of our excavation in the south-east quadrant and elsewhere, we found pottery remains (some whole or substantially whole vases and many fragments) belonging to EB IIIB. We called these deposits Stratum J. In this case it has been possible to date the pottery by similar pieces from the tombs of the Sixth Egyptian Dynasty to about the twenty-third century B.C. [4] This pottery certainly precedes any of Kathleen M. Kenyon's Early Bronze–Middle Bronze Age (EB–MB) ware. It was found in red earth because J was the first settlement after the covering of trees and brush had been burned off; occupation was too short to permit accumulation of black earth, containing burned and otherwise oxidized organic material.

We found no remains anywhere on the site belonging to the early part of Kathleen M. Kenyon's EB–MB period, which has been provisionally classified by Ruth Amiran as Phases B and C of her Middle Bronze Age I. On the other hand, there were extensive remains from the latter part of this transitional period, both of accumulated debris and of pottery artifacts. The town had been fortified at that time, and remains of house walls as well as fallen mud-brick walls were found. There were also storage caves with entrances lined with stone. The pottery belonged entirely to Ruth Amiran's Phase A of MB I, to which, in my present opinion, the designation MB I should be applied, leaving Phases B and C to be included in EB IV, unless one wishes to follow P. Lapp's recent suggestion to call this period 'Intermediate Bronze Age'. My original date for the two phases of this period, found in Stratum I and H, respectively, H being later than I, was roughly between 2100 and 1900 B.C. This date I have recently lowered to between c. 2000 and 1800 B.C., but there is no apparent reason why the MB settlement of Stratum I should antedate the nineteenth century B.C. The main difference in pottery styles between I and H, which were separated by a semi-continuous burned level, was that true envelope jar handles appeared in I and apparently not in H. Otherwise the ceramic differences between them were relatively small. The lower date for the end of the stratum follows my recent demonstration that levels G–F of Tell Beit Mirsim and contemporary pottery elsewhere all date from the eighteenth century B.C., coming to an end about 1700 B.C. (see below). MB I was known at the time of our excavation only from Jericho, where it had been called 'Spätkanaanitisch' by C. Watzinger. Since our excavation at Tell Beit Mirsim this pottery has been found in increasing quantities, both in western and eastern Palestine, until now it is one of the best known of Palestine.

This highly distinctive ware is found particularly on trade routes along the edge of the desert in eastern Palestine, in the Jordan and Dead Sea Valley, in the watershed ridge of western Palestine, and also scattered over hundreds of sites in southern Palestine and Sinai. Note particularly that it occurs at points along the caravan routes between Palestine and Egypt, where no other pottery, earlier or later, is found.[5]

Strata G–F, though marked by two different phases of construction, separated from one another by a continuous area of burned debris, exhibit the same pottery and cannot be separated from one another by more than a few years. The date can now be fixed by my recent demonstration that the so-called royal tombs of Byblos (I–IV) all date from the eighteenth century B.C. and contain native pottery of the same types as G–F.[6] Wherever we dig under early Hyksos *pisé* ramparts, the latest pottery under them is precisely of this period—MB IIA (the MB I pottery of Kathleen M. Kenyon). Strictly speaking, this period was only the first phase of MB II, which lasted in Palestine down to the end of the sixteenth century B.C., and there is no reason to assign it a duration of more than two centuries.

Ruth Amiran has shown that the ultimate source of the caliciform pottery of I–H is to be found in the pottery of Mesopotamia during the Akkad period (twenty-fourth to twenty-third centuries B.C.),[7] whereas it is quite clear today that the MB II pottery has its closest points of contact in the Aegean region, spreading later to Syria and finally to Mesopotamia.

The following two strata, E–D, are early and late Hyksos respectively. Stratum E probably began about 1700 B.C. with *pisé* revetments added in places to the fortifications of G–F. The city walls were later enormously strengthened by the addition of a polygonal stone revetment in the style of the 'battered' wall of Jericho, best preserved south of the East Gate. As far as the MB II revetment is preserved, it is much less massive than the walls of Jericho

and Shechem. After three campaigns of deep excavation in the
south-east quadrant, we concluded that the evidence is quite
adequate to distinguish four successive phases of E and D, but not
five, as first thought. E 1 was characterized by a deposit of *terre
pisée* near the East Gate of the city. The battered stone wall came
in E 2. Two successive phases of E and two of D were distinguished
as we analysed the remains of patrician houses, but it was found
difficult to determine whether the earlier E phase was contemporary with the *pisé* rampart. Owing to the fact that no intact MB II
burials were found at Tell Beit Mirsim—chiefly because we
decided against starting a search for tombs which might lead to
systematic spoliation of tombs by the natives—all our extensive
pottery of Middle Bronze Age II comes from residential quarters
and can therefore be used directly to refine our pottery chronology
by stratigraphic as well as stylistic considerations.

In view of the comparative poverty of other strata at Tell Beit
Mirsim, the concentration of wealth in Strata E–D was quite
extraordinary; it corresponds to a similar situation in other excavated Palestinian towns of the period. The most interesting single
find was a well-preserved patrician house of Stratum D, probably
built about 1600 B.C., not long after a similar patrician house
excavated by M. E. L. Mallowan at Chagar Bazar in northern
Mesopotamia—another illustration of the north Mesopotamian
provenience of a substantial part of the Hyksos invaders.[8]

As we learn more about Hyksos chronology and especially about
the comparative archaeology and art of this period, it is becoming
possible to date more precisely. Many scarabs of Hyksos princes
have been found in MB II sites in Palestine. In Stratum E 2 we
found a secondary scarab of the first known Semitic Hyksos ruler,
Ya'qub. This scarab naturally gives only a *terminus ante quem*, but
it does prove that this phase is later than the early seventeenth
century B.C. After the invasion of Egypt by non-Semitic Hyksos
about the middle of the seventeenth century B.C., the Hyksos
empire became more extensive—and much richer. Since the overwhelming mass of their non-Egyptian followers must have been
northwestern Semites who spoke Canaanite dialects, it is not
surprising that the chieftains became very wealthy, and that much
of this wealth passed over into the mode of life of their followers.
Tell Beit Mirsim illustrates the extent to which it could affect

the everyday life of a chieftain's retainers in a provincial fortress town.

The date of Stratum D must now be reduced substantially, since it has become increasingly clear in recent years that the end of Hyksos rule in Egypt did not come until after the eleventh year of Amosis,[9] which would fall after *c.* 1540 B.C. according to W. Helck (1962), after *c.* 1545 B.C. according to R. A. Parker (1964), and after *c.* 1550 B.C. according to E. Hornung (1964). It follows that the three-year blockade of Sharuhen (Tell el-Far'ah in southern Palestine) could not have taken place until after the middle of the liberator's reign. In other words, the invasion of Palestine itself and the destruction of Tell Beit Mirsim, Jericho, and many other fortified towns of Palestine, could not well have taken place before the last few years of Amosis. Since some sites in the Coastal Plain seem to have surrendered without resistance and were therefore not destroyed, it is clear that the use of MB IIC pottery continued down to about the end of the sixteenth century B.C., when it gave way to Late Bronze Age I. The best single LB I. type for comparative chronological purposes in this period is the bichrome panelled ware which was at the height of its use just before the fall of Megiddo *c.* 1469 B.C. Its span is, therefore, to be placed between *c.* 1500 and 1450 B.C., contrary to some recently expressed views.

Stratum D (MB IIC) was completely destroyed and the site was then abandoned for a comparatively long time. Not only was there a complete break in town planning and a general levelling off, but storage pits were dug into the remains of the MB II town well below the floor levels of the earliest LB occupation. When the site was reoccupied, it was much less important, relatively speaking, than it had been—possibly because of shifting trade routes. In any event, the people of C continued to employ the massive stone revetment which, because of its 'batter' and the fact that most of it had been buried under the ruins of the mud-brick superstructure of the city wall, just as at Jericho, needed only to be cleaned to be a very effective defence. Apparently, as at Jericho, the outer walls of houses built at the edge of the mound above the battered wall served as a surrogate for a rampart of their own. At particularly vulnerable points, especially near the East Gate, new stone foundations of vertical walls were laid. Owing to the location of Tell

Beit Mirsim there was, of course, incomparably less erosion from wind and water than at Jericho. The reoccupation of the city in LB probably took place well after *c.* 1400 B.C., since no sherds which could be definitely attributed to LB I were found on the site. The first phase of Stratum C was very badly preserved, and though evidently destroyed by a conflagration, most of the houses were presumably fragile in construction and did not survive the destruction, which may be tentatively placed about the middle of the fourteenth century B.C. A somewhat earlier or later date is, however, not excluded. In the LB debris of Tell Beit Mirsim some thirty sherds from as many different Late Helladic IIIB vases were discovered, all dating between the middle of the fourteenth century and *c.* 1240–1230 B.C. Most of them came from certain or probable C 2 levels or deposits; not a single piece could be dated with any plausibility to C 1. Two dated scarabs turned up in C debris; one of Tuthmosis IV (*c.* 1425–1417 B.C.) and the other of Amenophis III (*c.* 1417–1379 B.C.). These scarabs can be taken only as giving *tempora post quem* since they may have been brought in later.

Town C 2 must have been destroyed quite late in the thirteenth century B.C., as indicated by the close resemblance of its latest ware to the corresponding ware from the end of the Canaanite occupation of Lachish, which could not have preceded the fourth year of Merneptah. A date for the destruction of C 1 before the latter part of the reign of Ramesses II (1304–1238 B.C.) is also excluded by a secondary scarab of this Pharaoh. The importation of Late Mycenaean pottery (Late Helladic IIIB) into Palestine and Syria was abruptly stopped by the first great invasion of the 'Sea Peoples' before the fifth year of Merneptah, so there is full agreement between the dating of the Mycenaean pottery from C 2 and the end of the occupation.

The following Israelite occupation appears in three phases of Stratum B and two phases of Stratum A, which extended from *c.* 1225 B.C. to *c.* 589–587 B.C. Since the Israelite town of Stratum B was very thinly occupied and much space was taken up by grain pits, it was difficult to establish any general stratification which carried conviction. We finally decided to base our chronology on pottery sequences and to refer isolated buildings and grain pits to these phases. The first phase, B 1, was fixed by the fact that in several silos we found no Philistine ware but only pottery of degenerate Late Bronze Age type, without any imported ware at all. The duration of this phase may be roughly set between 1225 and 1175 B.C. The following phase, B 2, was dated by quantities of characteristic Philistine pottery of the type now so well known from sites in the Philistine plain and the surrounding areas. This pottery is now known to be very closely related to the local type of Late Helladic III C1 which A. Furumark found at Sinda and C. F. A. Schaeffer found at Enkomi near Salamis in north-eastern Cyprus. This phase of Philistine pottery was replaced before 1000 B.C. by a derived type of painted pottery, emphasizing purple spirals, first isolated by B. Mazar at Tell Qasile near Tel-Aviv. The latter type of pottery has not hitherto been found in Israelite territory proper, probably because the Philistine Empire ceased to exist after c. 1020 B.C., and so the new ware was not exported into the hill-country.

The third and final phase of Stratum B at Tell Beit Mirsim was entirely post-Philistine and was represented largely by hand-burnished pottery and by bowl profiles, and so on, of characteristically tenth-century B.C. type in subsequently excavated sites. Stratum B seems to have been destroyed by Shishak during his campaign in Palestine in the fifth year of Rehoboam, which I should date c. 918 B.C.[10] Some loci attributed to B 3 in my first reports on Tell Beit Mirsim may now be assigned to A 1, in the ninth century B.C., as shown by their pottery content. Another point which must rest *sub judice* is the attribution of the original casemate wall. This type of construction seems to be first documented by the first fortress of Gibeah, built probably by the Philistines in the late eleventh century B.C., though this is disputed by some.

Arguing from considerations of territorial geography and history, I have long attributed the casemate walls of Tell Beit Mirsim and Beth-shemesh to the reign of David, preferably to the early part of his reign before he had begun to establish his empire. This view, however, has been opposed by Y. Aharoni, arguing from the striking similarity of the wall of Tell Beit Mirsim to the Solomonic casemate wall excavated by Y. Yadin at Hazor. In my opinion, this argument is rather weak, since there is no good reason to limit such a rough style of construction to a single reign.

It seems scarcely probable that Solomon would fortify towns well
inside the frontier of his empire. David, on the other hand, before
his final defeat of the Philistines might easily try to protect his
narrower frontiers from Philistine incursions.

A I constructions dated from the ninth and eighth centuries B.C.;
there were no indications of destruction by fire. By the seventh
century B.C. the town was certainly so full of dwellings that there
was barely room for narrow lanes and none at all for grain pits.
The town of this period was remarkably well preserved, and seems
to have been continuously occupied, with only minor destruction
of parts of its fortification in one of Sennacherib's invasions of
Judah and again in 598 B.C. (see below). There was scattered rebuilding, and the prevailing type of house was characteristic of
Jewish towns of the period. No patrician houses were discovered.
The principal industry was spinning, weaving, and dyeing
woollen cloth, suggesting that it may have been included in an
association or guild of woollen manufacturers which extended to
other towns as well. Such craft associations or guilds are mentioned,
as is well known, several times in the list of the clans of Judah in
I Chron. ii and iv.

The latter part of Tell Beit Mirsim's history was elucidated
by our analysis of the successive phases of construction at the
West Gate, where we distinguished four main phases, α, β, γ, and δ,
counting from the top. The analysis was carried out by A. H. Det-
weiler, now associate dean of the College of Architecture of Cornell
University, in constant consultation with me. A recent attempt to
alter details of our extremely careful surveys and elevations in order
to fit an arbitrary reconstruction of the West Gate and Tower is
totally unacceptable. Before one reinterprets, one must be sure
of one's data! In 1932 we completed the excavation of the West
Tower, begun in 1926, distinguishing four successive phases. The
two final phases coincided with corresponding phases in the construction of adjacent houses inside the town, the uppermost of
which probably followed a partial destruction of the fortifications
after Judah's revolt against the Chaldaeans in the time of Jehoiachin.
In this uppermost level were found two identical jar handle stamps
which I compared with a similar stamp from Beth-shemesh,
finding that it had been made by the same seal or a precise replica
of it. In the 1962 campaign at Ramat Raḥel, Y. Aharoni discovered

a fourth identical stamp. The inscription reads 'belonging to Eliakim, steward of Yaukin'. That Yaukin was indeed king Jehoiachin was immediately recognized by L. H. Vincent and was proved by the subsequent publication of Babylonian ration lists from c. 592 B.C.[11] There have been doubts expressed concerning the translation of na'ar by 'steward', but they should be removed by the fact that Ziba, Saul's steward, is described after Saul's death as his na'ar in 2 Sam. ix. 9 f., xix. 18, R.V. 17. Ziba is not only 'na'ar of Saul' and 'na'ar of the house of Saul'; he is also in charge of all the property which had been Saul's, and is credited with having fifteen sons and twenty slaves himself. It thus becomes obvious that Eliakim, who must himself have been a man of great substance, was the steward of Jehoiachin's property while Jehoiachin was in Babylonian captivity. The Babylonian texts listing the rations paid to him, the royal princes, and other important Jews, call him explicitly 'king of Judah'. These clear-cut facts prove conclusively that the three sites of Tell Beit Mirsim, Beth-shemesh, and Ramat Raḥel near Jerusalem were destroyed by the Chaldaeans in 589–587 B.C.

iv. *Chief Points of Old Testament Interest*

Since the most significant results of our work from the standpoint of Old Testament research have had to be discussed in connexion with the account of the excavations, they will be listed briefly.

1. The location of Debir (Kiriath-sepher) has probably been fixed; personally I regard it as virtually certain.

2. The period to which the traditions of Abraham may be assigned has been set in the nineteenth century B.C. This attribution will presumably remain controversial for some time to come.

3. Tell Beit Mirsim has contributed to our understanding of the feudal society established in Palestine by the Hyksos invaders, and still dominant at the Conquest.

4. Tell Beit Mirsim has contributed substantially to fixing both date and nature of the Israelite conquest of Canaan. My present date for the conquest of the Shephelah is about 1234–1230 B.C.

5. Tell Beit Mirsim has contributed greatly to our better understanding of life in the period of the Judges.

6. Tell Beit Mirsim has given us the most complete picture of town life in Judah in the last century before the Exile.

7. Tell Beit Mirsim has been in some ways decisive in proving that the views of Kosters, Torrey, and more recent scholars, on the nature of the events which took place in Judah between *c.* 598 and 585 B.C. are radically false, and that Old Testament tradition is quite correct.

W. F. ALBRIGHT

NOTES

1. I am giving a much fuller treatment of the topographical arguments in the account of the site and its excavation being prepared for a volume edited by B. Mazar.

2. *R.B.* xlii, 1933, p. 468, xlviii, 1939, p. 487, n. 1.

3. Ibid. p. 487, n. 2, where Père Vincent objected to my demonstration that the floor of the main hall of a large house in G had been *lowered* when the house was repaired. He might have compared the *Odyssey*, Book xxii, where Ulysses 'scraped the floor of the great hall with spades', after the slaughter of the suitors. The key point is that the latest floor level in the hall was *lower* than the foundation of the walls around it!

4. See especially *B.A.S.O.R.* 168, 1962, pp. 40 f.

5. See ibid. 163, 1961, pp. 36–40 for a survey. P. Lapp's discoveries at Mirzbaneh and Bab edh-Dhraʿ in the Jordan and Dead Sea valleys are notably enlarging our material for 'Intermediate Bronze' (EB IV and MB I).

6. See ibid. 176, 1964, pp. 38–46, and 178, 1965, pp. 38–43.

7. *I.E.J.* x, 1960, pp. 204–25.

8. New material has come to light since *A.A.S.O.R.* xvii, p. 28, n. 2.

9. See C. F. Nims, *Thebes of the Pharaohs*, 1965, p. 199, n. 2.

10. The Egyptian chronology here depends on the Old Testament synchronism, and the latter should be adjusted to suit the extant Phoenician chronology; cf. my discussion in *Mélanges Isidore Lévy*, 1955, pp. 1–9.

11. See my discussion in *B.A.* v, 1942, pp. 49–55.

BIBLIOGRAPHY

ALBRIGHT, W. F. *The Excavation of Tell Beit Mirsim. I. The Pottery of the First Three Campaigns (A.A.S.O.R.* xii), 1932.

—— *The Excavation of Tell Beit Mirsim IA: The Bronze Age Pottery of the Fourth Campaign* (ibid. xiii, pp. 55–127), 1933.

—— *The Excavation of Tell Beit Mirsim. II. The Bronze Age* (ibid. xvii), 1938.

ALBRIGHT, W. F., and KELSO, W. F. *The Excavation of Tell Beit Mirsim. III. The Iron Age (A.A.S.O.R.* xxi–xxii),1943.

ALBRIGHT, W. F. *The Archaeology of Palestine and the Bible,* 1932, pp. 63–126.

—— *The Archaeology of Palestine* (Pelican Books), 1949.

—— 'Researches of the School in western Judaea', *B.A.S.O.R.* 15, 1924, pp. 4 f.

—— 'The excavations at Tell Beit Mirsim', ibid. 23, 1926, pp. 2–14.

—— 'The second campaign at Tell Beit Mirsim (Kiriath-sepher)', ibid. 31, 1928, pp. 1–11.

—— 'The third campaign at Tell Beit Mirsim', ibid. 39, 1930, pp. 1–10.

—— 'The fourth joint campaign of excavation at Tell Beit Mirsim', ibid. 47, 1932, pp. 3–17; *A.J.A.* xxxvi, 1932, pp. 556–64.

—— 'The American excavations at Tell Beit Mirsim', *Z.A.W.* xlvii, 1929, pp. 1–18.

—— 'The Second Campaign at Tell Beit Mirsim', *A.f.O.* v, 1929, pp. 119 f.

—— 'The Third Campaign at Tell Beit Mirsim', ibid. vii, 1931, pp. 56 ff.

—— 'The Third Campaign at Tell Beit Mirsim and its historical results', *J.P.O.S.* xi, 1931, pp. 105–29.

—— 'Archaeology and the date of the Hebrew Conquest of Palestine', *B.A.S.O.R.* 58, 1935, pp. 10–18.

—— 'The Israelite conquest of Canaan in the light of archaeology', ibid. 74, 1939, pp. 11–23.

—— 'The seal of Eliakim and the latest preëxilic history of Judah, with some observations on Ezekiel', *J.B.L.* li, 1932, pp. 77–106.

KYLE, M. G. *Excavating Kirjath-sepher's Ten Cities,* 1934.

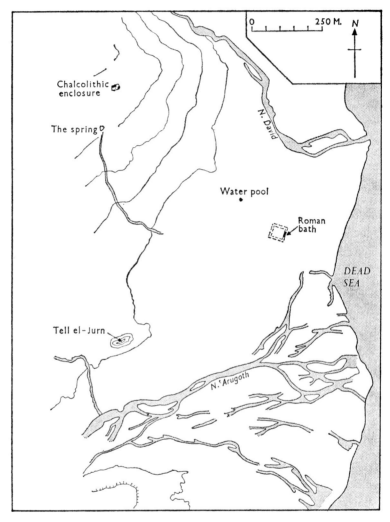

FIG. 5. Plan of the En-gedi area

EN-GEDI

THE oasis of En-gedi on the western shore of the Dead Sea was, at various periods, a flourishing settlement in the Judaean desert. The Hebrew name '*Ên-gedî*, which remarkably was never forgotten over the centuries—in Arabic it is ʿAin Jidî—is actually the name of the perennial spring which flows from a height of about 700 feet above the Dead Sea. The name En-gedi is known as early as the beginning of the Hebrew monarchy. The waste land along the western shore of the Dead Sea was called the En-gedi desert, and the En-gedi 'strongholds' (Hebrew *mᵉṣâḏôt*), where David and his men hid from King Saul, were apparently enclosed camps at the almost inaccessible tops of the mountain crags (1 Sam. xxiv. 1–8, R.V. xxiii. 29–xxiv. 7).

However, there is no proof that there was a permanent settlement in En-gedi in the tenth century B.C. From the archaeological evidence it can be concluded that the settlement of En-gedi, which is mentioned several times in the Old Testament (Joshua xv. 62; Ezek. xlvii. 10; Song of Sol. i. 14; 2 Chron. xx. 2), was not established until the seventh century B.C. In later sources En-gedi (Greek 'Εγγαδδί, Latin *Engaddi*) is often mentioned as an economic and administrative centre at various times, and it was famous particularly as a place where fine dates and rare spices were grown. The literary sources, the archaeological evidence, and the recently discovered documents in the cave of Naḥal Ḥever, combine to form an intelligible picture of the occupational history of the oasis, beginning with the last phase of the kingdom of Judah and continuing up to the Byzantine period, when En-gedi was still, according to Eusebius, 'a great Jewish village'.

Archaeological interest in En-gedi began in April 1949, when a small expedition, headed by the present writer, began a systematic survey in the oasis, and made a trial dig at Tell el-Jurn, an elongated narrow hillock rising above the valley in the northwestern part of the oasis. It became clear that the settlement of Tell el-Jurn played an important role in the history of En-gedi, especially in Old Testament times. Following the initial survey came other surveys, at first directed by Y. Aharoni, and later by J. Naveh, which filled out the picture. The investigation of building remains, terraces along the mountain slopes, reservoirs, and aqueducts, demonstrated that in ancient times the inhabitants of En-gedi had developed an efficient irrigation system and advanced techniques for collecting water, and that agriculture was intensively pursued there. In certain periods a central authority dealt with the upkeep of the terraces and the water system, and also with the security of the population, by means of a network of strongholds and watch-towers placed at strategic points.

Following these surveys, three seasons of excavations were carried out in 1961–2 and in March 1964. They were all sponsored by the Hebrew University of Jerusalem and the Israel Exploration Society, and were led by I. Dunayevski and the present writer, with Trude Dothan participating. The principal work was done at Tell el-Jurn, but an interesting building complex of the Chalcolithic period on the terrace above the spring, as well as an Israelite watch-tower near the spring, and a Roman bath near the sea-shore, were also excavated.

Tell el-Jurn was by nature easy to defend, but the very narrow top of the hill (about 80 feet) made it inconvenient for a large settlement. It was essential, therefore, when the settlement began to spread out, that terraces should be constructed on its slopes, on which buildings could be erected. An important result of the excavations at Tell el-Jurn was the discovery of the oldest settlement (occupational period V), which represents the period of Josiah, king of Judah, and his successors, until the destruction of the kingdom of Judah and the abandonment of southern Judah (c. 582 B.C.). This settlement was built on the top of the hill and on the terraces along its slopes. Several structures and their courtyards on the terraces along the northern and southern slopes which were uncovered are remarkable for their specific character and for the wealth of finds unearthed in them. Especially interesting is the series of large pithoi (jars) up to a metre in height and characterized by the coarse texture of the clay, which were found grouped closely together in the courtyards. Besides these pithoi there was an abundance of pottery and also basalt utensils and implements of bronze, iron, and bone, as well as clods of asphalt from the Dead Sea. Especially remarkable amongst the pottery are jars—some with

PLATE VIII

Installations and ovens connected with perfume industry (En-gedi)

the impression of a rosette on the handles—jugs, decanters, perfume juglets, cooking-pots, bowls, and lamps, most of them characteristic of Iron Age II in Judah. Several rare types were found.

Altogether the finds in the courtyards, which have been uncovered *in situ* under a layer of ash, appear to have served special industrial needs, probably the perfume industry, which in ancient times required only simple operations. Along the street to the north of the buildings, installations, including ovens, have been found, and they too appear to have some connexion with the perfume industry (Pl. VIII). It seems that it was the cultivation and production of balm which brought about the economic importance of the oases on the banks of the Dead Sea, including the agricultural complex of Qumran-'Ain Feshkha, En-gedi, and Zoar. Particularly instructive is the information in Josephus, Pliny, and other writers, on the cultivation of opobalsamum, known also from Talmudic sources as '*aparsāmôn*, which thrived only in this region. Opobalsamum was held to be a most expensive and desirable perfume. A Talmudic source alludes to an old tradition that 'the poorest of the land', whom Nebuchadrezzar's general left behind as vinedressers (Hebrew *kôremîm*) in Judah (Jer. lii. 16) after the destruction of Jerusalem, were indeed the balm('*aparsāmôn*)-gatherers from En-gedi to Ramtâ (Shabb. 26, 1). Very instructive also is the Talmudic tradition that, after anointing oil was hidden away by King Josiah, kings were anointed with '*aparsāmôn* oil. We may, therefore, suppose that, during the reign of Josiah, En-gedi became a royal estate, its inhabitants being employed mainly in the growing and manufacture of balm. The workshops were located in the settlement of Tell el-Jurn, and the perfumers were apparently organized in a guild, after the model of the linen, metal, and pottery manufacturers in Judah (cf. 1 Chron. iv. 21 ff.). It is quite possible that after the destruction of Jerusalem the Babylonian authorities attempted to continue the production of balm for their own advantage, but this went on for a short time only.

On a ribbed jar handle unearthed in the ashes of period V was found a seal impression which contains a double-winged symbol and a short inscription. The four Hebrew characters may be read *lmrt* 'belonging to mrt' (or 'to nrt'), or *lmr*' 'belonging to mr''. *Mr*' may be the official Aramaic title *mârê*' 'lord, sovereign', and the reference could be to King Nebuchadrezzar. In the buildings of period V some objects of special interest have been found in-cluding Hebrew epigraphic material. They include a seal bearing the name *ṭbšlm*,[1] and alongside the script geometric designs, one of them resembling the plan of the building in which it was found. In the same building a pot was discovered covered with an oil lamp, and inside was a hoard of silver ingots of different shapes, which must have served as a form of currency, namely, as 'silver, current money with the merchant' (Gen. xxiii. 16), used before the inven-tion of coins. In another place was found a small quadrilateral seal with the Hebrew inscription *l'ryhw 'zryhu* 'belonging to Uriyahu [son of] Azaryahu'.[2] In yet another place was found a jar with the inscription *lpṭyhu* 'belonging to Putiyahu', a hybrid Egyptian-Hebrew name, like Putiel (Exod. vi. 25). Worthy of mention also are the three dome-shaped stone weights with a sign represent-ing the royal shekel, accompanied by the numbers 1, 4, and 8 respectively. Weights of this particular type have come to light at various sites in Judah, and they all belong to the last phase of the kingdom of Judah. The finds from this period include also some imported vessels, fragments of alabaster juglets, an Egyptian scarab, a comparatively substantial amount of women's jewellery, such as rings, ear-rings, and beads, as well as various types of bronze and iron arrows. All these finds testify to the growth of En-gedi by the end of the kingdom of Judah, and to her connexion with the capital and centres further afield.

This ancient settlement on Tell el-Jurn was completely destroyed and abandoned after a conflagration. In its place a new settle-ment (occupational period IV) was built at the beginning of the Persian period, probably in the time of Zerubbabel. During the Persian period the settlement extended far beyond the limits of that of the Israelite period. In the area north of the tell the excava-tions have not yet reached the boundary of the settlement or any wall which may have encircled it. The buildings of this period are characterized by their size and relatively solid workmanship. Of particular interest is the large building discovered north of the tell below a deep layer of debris. Over 22 feet of the west wall of this building have been uncovered, as well as a shorter section of the south wall. Further excavations are needed to trace the complete plan of the building. The excavations in the trench running west of the building mentioned above have revealed an oven and a silo and numerous pottery fragments. This pottery is generally characteristic of Stratum IV, with some admixture of sherds of Stratum V. Several finds deserve special mention—an Aramaic ostracon, which can be dated to the Persian period; jar handles stamped with the word *yhd, yhwd*, and one with *yh*; a sherd with the seal impression *b'*, all in Aramaic script; and a jar handle with a seal impression showing a roaring lion. In addition, a considerable amount of fifth- and early fourth-century B.C. Attic sherds, as well as sherds decorated with wedge-shaped and round impressions, have been found. Since the pottery complex contains no later admixtures, it is possible to determine the pottery types at En-gedi during the Persian period. Taking into consideration the Attic ware and the epigraphic material, as well as the absence of later fourth-century B.C. pottery, we may fix the date of the destruction of this settlement at the first half of the fourth century B.C. En-gedi was, however, a prosperous settlement in the time of Nehemiah and Bagoas, governors of Judah, and there is no doubt that it belonged at that time to the province of Judah.

After the destruction, or rather the abandonment, of this settlement, most certainly by Arab tribes, a fortress was erected on the top of Tell el-Jurn. This fortress (occupational period III) was probably built in the third century B.C., if we may judge from the Hellenistic pottery and from the evidence of some Ptolemaic coins. Moreover, we have testimony to a settlement in En-gedi at this time in Ecclesiasticus, where the famous dates of this oasis are mentioned (xxiv. 14). We do not know when this fortress, whose purpose was apparently to guard the royal estate, became prosperous. Only by supposition can we fix the date in the reign of John Hyrcanus (135–104 B.C.), who conquered Idumaea, and apparently annexed the oases on the western shore of the Dead Sea and added them to the estates of the Hasmonaeans. But this occupational period (III) is essentially that of Alexander Jannaeus (103–76 B.C.). This was certainly an important period in the growth and development of En-gedi. Judging from the many coins found in the vicinity of Tell el-Jurn and over the whole oasis, as well as from tombs investigated by N. Avigad at Wadi Sudeir, En-gedi reached the peak of its development in the days of Alexander Jannaeus. It appears that the Hasmonaean king gave special attention to the economic development of the Dead Sea region.

We cannot determine the precise date of the destruction of this fortress, but in view of the fact that no pottery and coins from the period of Herod the Great have been discovered at Tell el-Jurn, we may surmise the period of the Parthian invasion and the war of the last Hasmonaeans against Herod, that is, in the years 40–37 B.C.

The next occupational period (II) is represented by a strong fortress on Tell el-Jurn, surrounded by a wall of large stones, two metres thick, strengthened by a rectangular tower elaborately planned and executed at the western end of the hill, outside the wall of the fortress. The date of the fortress and the tower is proved by pottery of the first century A.D. En-gedi was an important settlement and the centre of a toparchy in the period of the Herodian dynasty (Josephus, *Wars*, iii, 3.8) and was destroyed in A.D. 68 (*Wars*, iv, 7.2). It is an amazing fact that no remains have been found at Tell el-Jurn from the second century A.D., including the period of Bar-Kokhba. Moreover, even the remains from the third to the fifth centuries A.D. (occupational period I) witness to the poor and temporary structures and agricultural terraces, not to the great Jewish village Engaddi mentioned by Byzantine authors. Nevertheless, coins which have been found in various places in the oasis testify to the existence of a settlement there in the second century A.D., as well as in the third to the fifth centuries A.D., alluded to also by later authors. Moreover, the Greek documents found recently by Y. Yadin in the cave of Naḥal Ḥever, which belong to the period of Roman rule preceding the Bar-Kokhba revolt, explicitly mention En-gedi as an estate and village of the emperor; and indeed letters of Bar-Kokhba found in the same cave are addressed to heads of his military government in En-gedi. In view of these facts, we may surmise that in the Herodian period the settlement's centre moved from Tell el-Jurn to the plain northeast of the tell, and perhaps reached the sea-shore. Concrete evidence of this settlement has been recently discovered in the plain between Naḥal David and Naḥal 'Arugoth, about 600 feet west of the sea-shore.

In the third season our expedition uncovered a portion of a Roman bath, which probably formed part of a much larger complex, consisting probably of a central courtyard surrounded by various structures. Six bronze coins found in a hole of a doorjamb reused as a building stone indicate the date of the bath. The earliest is of Titus, with the legend *Judaea capta*, and the latest was minted in Ashkelon in A.D. 117. The pottery and fragments of glass vessels fit well into the span of time indicated by the coins, namely, after the destruction of Jerusalem and before the Second Revolt. Very instructive is the fact that many stones were taken from older buildings, apparently from the Herodian period, and were reused here. They include twelve Dorian capitals, stones decorated with rosettes, an amphora, and clusters of graves. Further excavations are needed to trace the complete plan of the building complex, including the bath, and to throw more light on the history of En-gedi in the Herodian, Roman, and Byzantine periods.

In the second season of excavation (1962) a well-planned enclosure, some sort of a *temenos*, on the terrace above the spring, about 450 feet to the north, was unearthed. The whole complex, which belongs to a late stage of the Chalcolithic Age (*c*. 3300–3200 B.C.), testifies to a period of remarkable architectural ability and high efficiency. It contains several structures built of stones laid in rough courses—one main building on the north, a smaller building on the east, a gate-house facing the En-gedi spring on the south, and an additional gate on the north of the smaller building, facing the spring of Naḥal David. Stone walls connect these four structures to make a single unit. At the centre of the large courtyard, surrounded by the structures and walls, stands a little round structure built of small stones which might have a cultic significance.

The main building on the north, about sixty feet long, was presumably a sanctuary. The doorway to this quadrangular building is located in the middle of the long wall which faces the courtyard. As in the other structures, the stone socket of the door has remained intact. Opposite the doorway there is a fenced-off depression in the shape of a hoof, which might be interpreted as an altar. We found therein remains of animal bones, sherds, and ashes, as well as a most interesting model of a bull laden with a pair of churns. Noteworthy also are the stone benches in the middle of the hall, and the regularly arranged rows of small depressions at the two ends of the building, containing animal bones, horns, sherds, and a large amount of ash. The pottery which was discovered in the various structures and in the courtyard are clearly related to the final phase of the Ghassulian culture, well known from the excavations at Teleilat Ghassul, and in the region of Beer-sheba. We know, indeed, that in this phase the Ghassulian culture spread extensively in the arid areas of southern Palestine, including the Negeb and the Judaean desert. The Chalcolithic enclosure at En-gedi is apparently a sacred place—a conclusion drawn from the plan of it, the various installations, and the pottery, which seems to be characteristic of cultic vessels, as well as from the absence of flint tools and kitchen utensils. A shrine similar in its plan to the main building in the En-gedi enclosure was also discovered in a late Chalcolithic level at Megiddo. In all probability we may assume that the En-gedi enclosure was the central sanctuary of the shepherds and villagers of the Judaean desert and its oases. Nothing is known about the settlement of this period in En-gedi, and the oasis must be further explored before further light will be shed on this problem.[3]

B. MAZAR

NOTES

1. Cf. the name Ṭobšillem in Lachish ostracon I, line 2 (*D.O.T.T.*, p. 213). The name is not found in the Old Testament.

2. Cf. the Old Testament names Uriah (e.g. 2 Sam. xi. 3 f.) and Azariah (e.g. 2 Kings xv. 6).

3. The fourth season of excavation was carried out in the autumn of 1964. It is intended to publish a preliminary report on the work in the near future.

BIBLIOGRAPHY

MAZAR, B. 'Excavations at the oasis of Engedi', *Archaeology* xvi, 1963, pp. 99–107.

—— DOTHAN, T., and DUNAYEVSKY, I. 'En Gedi, Archaeological Excavations 1961–62', *B.I.E.S.* xxvii, 1963, pp. 1–134 (in Hebrew).

—— and DUNAYEVSKY, I. 'En-Gedi, Third Season of Excavations, Preliminary Report', *I.E.J.* xiv, 1964, pp. 121–30. (Published in Hebrew in *B.I.E.S.* xxviii, 1964, pp. 143–52.)

GIBEON

i. *The Problem of Relevance*

THE task of assessing the results of an excavation for their relevance to a study of the Old Testament is not an easy one. Obviously, many of the discoveries made during the course of any excavation may have only a very indirect bearing on an understanding of the Old Testament references to the city under excavation. Furthermore, the archaeological evidence uncovered at ancient Gibeon (el-Jîb) may be said to have relevance in many instances at the points of supplementing the mass of information previously available from other Palestinian sites that have been excavated. In general, the archaeological evidence from Gibeon must be considered with similar evidence from such cities as Jericho, Shechem, Lachish, Tell Beit Mirsim, and others, for the substantial contribution all have made to a better understanding of the daily life of the people who lived during Old Testament times. Modern knowledge of the fortifications, burial customs, industrial endeavours involving the manufacture of wine and the conservation of water, and the construction of houses, has been enhanced by the excavations at el-Jîb.

The use of caution in seeking to explicate the significance of the archaeological evidence from el-Jîb for an understanding of the ancient Gibeonites is most appropriate. Questions regarding the theological ideas that may have motivated the burial practices at Gibeon, the source and meaning of the tradition that the sun stood still at Gibeon (Joshua x. 12 f.), the cultural process whereby the Gibeonites became Hebrew to the extent of supplying the great high place where Solomon worshipped and where he offered his prayer for wisdom (1 Kings iii. 4–9), the significance of the tradition that Gibeon produced the prophet Hananiah who spoke to Jeremiah, the priests and the people in the temple in Jerusalem, are ones for which the excavations have provided no answers.

In this matter of relevance, J. B. Pritchard, director of the excavations and author of all the official reports of the results, has been a model of the scholarly approach which deals with the problem of relevance in a properly cautious and conservative manner. The context in which the significance of the excavations at Gibeon should be appraised for its value to Old Testament studies is provided by Pritchard's statements:

Obviously the methods of archaeological science can neither prove nor disprove the major themes which the Bible asserts. Archaeology is able, however, to lay bare evidence that is useful in interpreting and evaluating the accounts of events narrated in the Bible. . . . Fortunately we have been able to establish a bridge between these literary references and the actual remains found at el-Jib. . . . No small part of the fascination that the work at el-Jib has held for us has been the interlacing of archaeological with biblical evidence . . . the results at el-Jib have in a remarkable degree been congenial to the literary accounts preserved in the Bible. In addition to these significant correspondences there have been discovered details about industry, commerce and daily life which illuminate and supplement the written tradition.[1]

It is evident that the relevance of the excavations is to be found in a clarification of the references to Gibeon in the Old Testament, rather than in the confirmation of specific dates or in the proof of Old Testament doctrines.

Ancient Gibeon, occupying approximately 16 acres, like other Palestinian sites that have been investigated, has been only partially excavated, but the main strata and most promising regions of the city were cleared. In view of the fact that the recent series of excavations have been completed, that the results have been promptly and attractively published, and that it is unlikely that further work at the site will be undertaken for some years to come, the resources are at hand for an evaluation. However, the materials are so extensive that the present study can do little more than touch upon a few points that are considered important.

ii. *The Excavations*

Prior to 1955 investigations at Gibeon were limited to surface exploration and to the accidental discovery of a tomb in which there was a rich deposit of Iron Age pottery, beads, scarabs, bronze rings, and toggle-pins.[2] In 1955 Pritchard made a study of the site, located about 8 miles north and slightly west of Jerusalem,

Jordan, and laid plans for a campaign to be completed over a period of several years.

Five seasons were conducted during the summers of 1956, 1957, 1959, 1960, and 1962. The University Museum of the University of Pennsylvania was the principal sponsor and is the repository for the share of finds allocated to the expedition by the Jordan Department of Antiquities; the remainder have been acquired for the Jordan Archaeological Museum in Amman. During the first two seasons the Church Divinity School of the Pacific, in Berkeley, California, was a joint sponsor. The American Schools of Oriental Research in Jerusalem co-operated by providing housing for the staff, work-room facilities, and equipment for use in the field. The Jordan Department of Antiquities, through its successive directors, G. Lankester Harding, Said Dura, and Awni Dajani, co-operated in the arrangements and made available the services of several of the members of their staff.

The successful completion of each campaign and the prompt publication of the results are due chiefly to the ability and experience of Pritchard, whose qualifications included the directing of the excavations at Tulûl Abū el-'Alayiq (Herodian Jericho), work at Dhîbân (Old Testament Dibon), and an involvement of many years in teaching and publishing in the field of Palestinian archaeology. The excavations were well financed and equipped, and were staffed by forty supervisors, representing several nationalities, many of them working more than one season, thereby helping to maintain a continuity so essential to an efficient operation.[3] Day labourers from el-Jîb, sometimes numbering more than 150 in one season, and specialists from Jericho, acquired considerable skill in digging with the result that careful attention was given to stratigraphy.

Among the principal discoveries may be listed the great pool (Pl. IX), the water tunnels, the collection of inscriptions and royal stamps, the winery, the fortifications of the city, the necropolis, and a number of houses and storage rooms. Before proceeding to a discussion of the relevance of this material for Old Testament studies, it may be appropriate to discuss briefly the archaeological features of each, reserving until later the questions of chronology.

The great pool measures 37 feet in diameter and 82 feet in depth. Cylindrical in shape with perpendicular sides cut in the bed-rock which appears near the present surface at the north sector of the tell, the pool has a spiral stairway consisting of seventy-nine steps formed of the bed-rock remaining when the pool was cut. During the course of the first two seasons the pool was discovered and completely excavated, a very considerable achievement. Although prior arrangements with land-owners made it necessary to fill in many other sectors excavated, in order that farming might be resumed at the site, the pool has been kept open, standing today, as it must have stood in ancient times, as a spectacular monument of the city. Although there is no way of determining water levels when the pool was in use, there is no reason to doubt that it was an important feature of the water system of the city. Similar to pools that have been observed in north Arabia, this one must have been used for the storage of rain-water, or for ready access to the water-table.

An impressive stepped water tunnel, the lower section of which had been previously recorded, located in the vicinity of the pool, was completely cleared. The rock-cut tunnel was found to extend upward from the spring, feeder tunnel, and cistern room, in such a way as to enable the inhabitants to bring water from the spring below in time of siege without being exposed to an enemy. Some indication of the remarkable engineering ability involved in the cutting of the tunnel may be seen in the fact that it penetrates a vertical distance of 80 feet and extends a distance of 167 feet; it has ninety-three steps and in its walls were fashioned niches to hold the oil lamps providing light for the 'drawers of water' (Joshua ix. 27).

A collection of inscriptions and royal stamps on jar handles is an important contribution to Near Eastern epigraphy. Of the total of sixty-one jar handles in which inscriptions were incised with archaic Hebrew script, a total of thirty-one contained all the letters, or a recognizable part, of the word *gb'n* 'Gibeon'.[4] In addition, more than eighty handles were found that were stamped with *lmlk* 'to the king', or royal seal. Common Old Testament names such as Azariah, Amariah, Hananiah, and Neriah, as well as such place-names as Hebron, Socoh, and Ziph, appear in the inscriptions and stamps.

An industrial area, designated by the excavators as the winery, was cleared. Located in the sectors both north and south of the

PLATE IX

The great pool (Gibeon)

pool, the installation contained numerous winepresses, fermenters, and sixty-three cellars capable of serving as cool storage places for large wine jars. The winery, occupying more than 1,100 square yards, contained many cuttings in the limestone, some of the cellars being more than 7 feet deep and equipped with stone covers; the entire installation was capable of storing wine in jars to the amount of 25,000 gallons (U.S.). It was not until the area had been completely excavated, wine jars, ceramic funnel, and stoppers had been discovered, and until a comparison had been made with the modern winery of the Trappist monastery in Latrun nearby, that the function of the Gibeonite installation was determined. Although some of the cellars had been reused in the Roman period as tombs, and in Byzantine and modern times as cisterns, there is no doubt that the manufacture of wine was an important feature of the economy of Gibeon in Old Testament times.

The defences of the city were uncovered at numerous points, and sections of two impressive stone walls which encircled the city at different periods were exposed. No traces of the city walls that could be dated to the Early, Middle, or Late Bronze periods were found, although the remains of house walls, pottery, and tombs indicate that the city was occupied during those periods. By taking account, not only of the age of the debris located near the bases of these city walls, but also the other evidences in the city reflecting the degree of affluence which would have made such immense city walls possible, Pritchard concluded that the construction of the earlier wall 'may reasonably be placed sometime within the 12th century B.C.' and that the later wall was in existence during the tenth century B.C. and continued in use until the end of the seventh century. The later wall, the better preserved of the two, was a very substantial and well-constructed stone wall of which segments totalling about 134 metres were excavated. The average thickness of the wall was approximately 4 metres; it is estimated that the circumference of the fortification was 954 metres.

A necropolis, situated west of the city and about half-way down the rock scarp, was excavated during the campaigns of 1960 and 1962. Fifty-five tombs were cleared; forty-nine of them contained pottery, skeletal remains, scarabs, and other artefacts. Only a few of the tombs had escaped the ravages of time, having been broken into by modern farmers, or silted up by the water which flows down the tell during the rainy seasons. The sizes of the tombs varied considerably, but they were remarkably similar in plan. Each consisted of a cylindrical shaft cut vertically into the bed-rock and having an average diameter of 1·13 metres and a depth which varied from 1 to 4 metres. Doorways, averaging 0·74 metre high by 0·59 metre wide and constructed so that they could be sealed by one large stone or several smaller ones, opened from the side of the shaft into the burial chambers, there being one doorway for each tomb.

This uniformity of plan, together with the fact that more than one-half of the tombs contained artefacts dating to the Middle Bronze I period, suggests that all the tombs were originally cut during that period. It is probable that the tombs were used over a fairly long period; however, comparative studies of the pottery point to a date in the twenty-first and twentieth centuries B.C. as the period of the first burials. Several centuries later these same tombs were reused, in some cases being cleared, and in others the earlier burials being pushed aside. Pritchard reports two periods of such reuse, one dated roughly to the seventeenth century B.C. (Middle Bronze Age IIB), and the other to the fifteenth–fourteenth centuries B.C. (Late Bronze Age). One tomb in the necropolis was reused during the Roman period when it was converted into a columbarium, probably at the same period that a group of wine-cellars in the city was converted into a large tomb containing a columbarium, and graves cut in the floor and walls of an elaborate tomb for which access was provided from the surface by a series of steps. The Early Bronze Age and the Iron Age cemeteries have not been discovered, but evidence of burials during those periods came from a cave located on the east side of the city.

A number of houses were excavated in the area south-west of the great pool and others near the city walls at the west side of the tell. Frequent rebuilding through the centuries and the shallowness of the debris remaining when the city was abandoned account for their poor state of preservation. One house with pillars was found to be associated with the earlier of the city walls, having been partially destroyed by the construction of the later city wall. It is clear that Gibeon was a thriving city during the Iron Age I and Iron Age II periods containing well-constructed stone houses, ovens, and the typical assortment of household utensils including lamps, hand grindstones, metal implements, and pottery jars and bowls of various types. For a good description of a comparatively elaborate house located near the great pool and containing three rooms built around an open courtyard, see Pritchard's *Gibeon, Where the Sun Stood Still*, pp. 105–8. The house was in use during the first half of the seventh century B.C. and was, no doubt, typical of the houses during that period. The extent and characteristics of the housing areas during the Bronze Ages are less clear, but evidence for settlements in these periods was detected in the occupational debris at a number of points.

iii. *Identification*

It has been implied in the preceding description of the results of the excavations that el-Jîb is to be identified with ancient Gibeon. As early as 1838 Edward Robinson proposed this identification on the basis of a brief visit to the site. He was led to this conclusion by a similarity between the Arabic name Jîb and the Hebrew Gibeon, and also by Josephus's references to the location of the city. Although most scholars accepted Robinson's identification, there remained some doubt because of a reference in the *Onomasticon* of Eusebius which seemed to place Gibeon four Roman miles west of Beth-el, a location excluding el-Jîb as a possibility. The question remained open as late as 1953 when the late A. Alt, who had previously proposed Tell en-Naṣbeh as the site of Gibeon, withdrew this suggestion in the light of the results of the excavations at Tell en-Naṣbeh and proposed instead the village of el-Bireh, located near the modern road east of Ramallah.[5]

A result of the excavations at el-Jîb, certainly a point of relevance for Old Testament studies, has been the solution of the problem of the location of Gibeon. W. F. Albright's observation, based upon his study of the inscribed jar handles from el-Jîb, has been generally accepted—'Since many of them are inscribed with the name "Gibeon", there can no longer be any doubt that the site has been correctly identified.'[6] When the jar handles were first discovered, Pritchard was properly cautious in speculating about their probable use, even raising a question as to the possibility that the name Gibeon on them might simply indicate that they had been shipped to el-Jîb from a Gibeon located elsewhere. However, the discovery of the winery with its numerous cellars, winejars, more than forty clay stoppers, and a clay funnel, supported the view that the inscribed handles were from winejars which had originally been in use in Gibeon (el-Jîb) and had been returned to be re-filled. 'The theory that the inscriptions were means for identifying returnable containers seems to be the more tenable one.'[7] In view of the tradition in Joshua ix. 4, which pictures the Gibeonites as approaching Joshua taking with them '. . . worn-out sacks upon their asses, and wineskins, worn-out and torn and mended . . .', it is also possible that none of the inscribed jar handles bearing the name Gibeon has been found elsewhere because wine was transported in wineskins. In any case, the name Gibeon, and the personal name of the manufacturers such as Hananiah, Amariah, Azariah, and so on would serve as labels of certification.

Further confirmation of the identification of el-Jîb with Gibeon may be found in certain geographical and chronological considerations. The location of Gibeon, north of Jerusalem and accessible to the city, as it was in the time of David, Solomon, and Jeremiah, and south-west of Ai, near enough to it to give credibility to the tale of the Gibeonite deception of Joshua, commend the identification of Gibeon with el-Jîb. The periods of occupation at el-Jîb are in accordance with those periods alluded to in Old Testament tradition as having been ones of habitation by the Gibeonites.

iv. *Chronology*

As suggested in the preceding discussion, the results of the excavations have relevance for an understanding of the chronological history of the city, both by furnishing a background for the Old Testament record and by filling in the gaps which exist in the chronology of Gibeon. It is clear, for example, that Gibeon had been in existence many centuries before its first contact with the Hebrews at the time of Joshua. The city was one of considerable wealth and importance during the age of the patriarchs, Abraham, Isaac, and Jacob. Although the military strength of Gibeon at that period is not apparent in the results of the excavations, its location, natural strength, and membership in the league of Hivite cities would have been sufficient reason for Abraham to avoid the city.

There are forty-five references to Gibeon and the Gibeonites scattered through eight books of the Old Testament (Joshua, 2 Sam., 1 Kings, 1 and 2 Chron., Neh., Isa., and Jer.). The events referred to in these passages span a period from the time of Joshua in the thirteenth century B.C. to the period of the rebuilding of the wall of Jerusalem in the fifth century B.C., when the men of Gibeon are mentioned in a list of people who helped with the rebuilding of the wall (Neh. iii. 7). Gibeon is remembered by the Old Testament writers chiefly in connexion with unusual events that took place there, or visits there by important people. Thus, there are gaps in the literary history of the city which can now be filled in with some details provided by the excavations. This is true for the period of almost four centuries between the time of Solomon in the tenth century B.C. and Jeremiah in the sixth. Although the Old Testament writers make no reference to Gibeon during this long period, the archaeological results show that the city was a flourishing community, defended by a strong city wall, skilled in the art of water conservation, and engaged in commerce with its neighbours, especially through its winery.

The traditions of the Old Testament mention Gibeon as being in existence during four historical periods, namely, those of Joshua, David, Solomon, and Jeremiah. Although the dates of these traditions are obviously later than the persons and events described (see, for example, Isa. xxviii. 21), their accuracy need not be doubted as far as the archaeological evidence is concerned. However, because of its long and continuous history, Gibeon presents a special problem to the literary critic who is concerned about dating and testing the authenticity of the Old Testament traditions. There are no signs of general conflagration or destruction at Gibeon to mark sharp transitions between chronological periods. Furthermore, the monuments at Gibeon such as the great pool, the stepped water tunnel, the fortifications, and the winery, continued in use for several centuries; hence their existence does not help to date, except in a general way, the events alluded to in the Old Testament.

Because of the paucity of archaeological evidence from the Late Bronze Age, the results of the excavations do not help to solve the problem of the date of the Conquest. However, the existence of a strong city wall constructed sometime within the twelfth century

B.C. (see above) suggests that the covenant between the Hebrews and the Gibeonites provided the conditions of peace so essential to such building activity.

The 'pool of Gibeon' is referred to as the scene of a gruesome contest between the forces of Abner, Saul's military leader, and those of Joab, leader of David's forces (2 Sam. ii. 12–17). About four centuries later another conflict took place between the forces of Johanan and Ishmael who met at 'the great pool which is in Gibeon' (Jer. xli. 12; the M.T. reads: 'the great waters that are in Gibeon'). As noted above, it is difficult to determine the date of the great pool; therefore, it cannot be certain that either or both of these events took place at the great pool of el-Jîb. Pritchard's dating of the original construction of the pool is based on its association with the water tunnel and city wall: '. . . the construction of the pool may be placed somewhere within the twelfth and the eleventh centuries.'[8] If this is correct, as it seems to be, it is likely that the pool was still open at the time of David. It is at least possible that the pool was still known in the time of Jeremiah, especially since the use of the wine cellars as late as the seventh century B.C. near the pool might have made its presence known and even useful to the industrial establishment.

In the time of Solomon, Gibeon was the place where the king went to offer sacrifices and where he made his famous prayer for wisdom (1 Kings iii. 4–14). The report refers to 'the great high place' (habāmāh hagᵉdôlāh) and to the altar. A later tradition reports that David left 'Zadok the priest, and his brethren the priests, before the tabernacle of the Lord in the high place that was at Gibeon...' (1 Chron. xvi. 39; cf. 2 Chron. i. 3, 13). As we have seen above, the excavations at el-Jîb have demonstrated that Gibeon was an important city in the time of David and Solomon. However, no traces were found of the cultic installation that can be linked with these events. This may be explained by the fact that the Gibeonite sanctuary may rest in one of the areas not excavated. Another likely possibility, suggested by Pritchard, is that the high place and the altar were associated with 'the mountain of the Lord' at Gibeon (2 Sam. xxi. 6), and that all three are to be located, not at Gibeon, but near Gibeon on Nebi Samwil, a conspicuous peak one mile to the south.[9]

v. *New Light on Gibeonite Culture*

It may be predicted that the published reports of the excavations
will continue to provide scholars with important research materials
for an understanding of the culture of Gibeon. Space permits no
more than a brief allusion to the direction which such research
may take, but a few suggestions may be appropriate. It is already
apparent that the epigraphic materials from Gibeon are very important for a study of the palaeography of ancient Hebrew.[10]
Although scholars are not in agreement as to whether this material
is to be dated in the seventh–sixth or in the sixth–fifth centuries
B.C., the inscribed jar handles have provided significant details
regarding the characteristic shapes of Hebrew consonants and a
list of common Hebrew names.

It is of more than passing interest that the Gibeonites should be
remembered as a people who preferred negotiation to war, and that
the archaeological evidence should demonstrate the continuous
history of the city without the usual marks left by the ravages of
war. When the Old Testament tradition refers to the 'elders' of
Gibeon (Joshua ix. 11), we may now, with the support of archaeological evidence, visualize these city officials as persons who were
resourceful in the art of government, no doubt responsible in
part for the material remains of the high degree of culture which
existed at Gibeon.

Several Hebrew words take on a new dimension or meaning
in the light of these discoveries. An example is the word *'ôṣār*
which should be translated 'cellars' in I Chron. xxvii. 27 where we
read: '. . . and over the produce of the vineyards for the wine-
cellars was Zabdi the Shiphmite.' We can now envision a typical
wine-cellar and appreciate the economic importance of officials
engaged in the supervision of work connected with a winery.
Knowing of the importance of the winery in Gibeon, and that
Jeremiah's opponent at once time was Hananiah the 'prophet,
which was of Gibeon' (Jer. xxviii. 1), we can sense the reality of
the tradition which pictures Jeremiah as a supporter of the Rechabites who abstained from the drinking of wine (Jer. xxxv. 1 f.).
Is it possible that the conflict between a true prophet and a false
one involved economic as well as theological factors?

The word *gdr* which appears on the inscribed jar handles from el-Jîb, always following the name Gibeon, appears a number of times in the Old Testament where it has been variously translated as 'wall', 'fence', or 'hedge' (Num. xxii. 24; Isa. v. 5, etc.).[11] It now appears that *gdr* may have a meaning like the French *clos*, meaning a section of a vineyard, a walled enclosure or vineyard. The custom of 'beating out wheat in the winepress, to hide it from the Midianites' (Judges vi. 11) becomes understandable in the light of the knowledge of Gibeon's winepresses. Located inside the city where the breezes could not operate as they did on the hill-top threshing-floors, the use of the winepress in threshing was an exercise in extreme fear.

No doubt scholars will continue to find new meanings in old concepts and additional points of relevance for Old Testament studies in the results of the excavations at Gibeon, and the city will hold a place of importance on the roster of Palestinian sites whose secrets have been unlocked by the spade of the archaeologist.

W. L. REED

NOTES

1. *Gibeon, Where the Sun Stood Still*, pp. 22 f.

2. Awni K. Dajani, *Ann. of the Dept. of Antiquities of Jordan*, ii and iii. It was reported that the tomb is located on a slope east of the spring; it contained 500 ceramic vessels, was discovered in 1949, and was excavated by the Department of Antiquities in 1950.

3. The subjective nature, but its basis in first-hand observation, of this favourable evaluation of the leadership and the staff is apparent in the fact that the present writer served as a supervisor in 1959 and 1962, and assisted in Berkeley during the summer of 1961 with the preparation of the materials from the winery for publication.

4. Twenty-seven examples of the name Gibeon found on jar handles during the seasons of 1956 and 1957 are published by Pritchard in *Hebrew Inscriptions and Stamps from Gibeon*. Four additional specimens of this type were found in 1959 and published by him in *B.A.S.O.R.* 160, 1960, pp. 2–6.

5. For an excellent discussion of the history of the problem of the identification of Gibeon, see Pritchard, *Gibeon, Where the Sun Stood Still*, pp. 24–29.

6. *B.A.S.O.R.* 159, 1960, p. 37.

7. Pritchard, *Gibeon, Where the Sun Stood Still*, p. 51.

8. Ibid., pp. 71 f.

9. Ibid., p. 39. For the reading *b^ehar* 'on the mountain' for M.T. *b^eḥîr* 'chosen', see S. R. Driver, *Notes on the Hebrew Text of Samuel*, pp. 351 f.

10. See Bibliography for the excellent article by Cross.

11. Pritchard, *Gibeon, Where the Sun Stood Still*, pp. 48 f.; it is also possible that *gdr*, at first read *gdd*, may be a personal name, Gedor, as it is in 1 Chron. viii. 31, ix. 37.

BIBLIOGRAPHY

AVIGAD, N. 'Some notes on the Hebrew inscriptions from Gibeon', *I.E.J.* ix, 1959, pp. 130–3.

CROSS, F. M. 'Epigraphical notes on Hebrew documents of the eighth–sixth centuries B.C. The inscribed jar handles from Gibeon', *B.A.S.O.R.* 168, 1962, pp. 18–23.

PRITCHARD, J. B. (*i*) Preliminary reports of the excavations and evaluations of the results in:

   B.A. xix, 1956, pp. 66–75, xxiii, 1960, pp. 23–29, xxiv, 1961, pp. 19–24.

   B.A.S.O.R. 160, 1960, pp. 2–6.

—— (*ii*) Final reports of the excavations in each season (Museum Monographs, The University of Pennsylvania):

   Hebrew Inscriptions and Stamps from Gibeon, 1959.

   The Water System of Gibeon, 1961.

   The Bronze Age Cemetery at Gibeon, 1963.

   Winery, Defenses and Soundings at Gibeon, 1964.

—— (*iii*) *Gibeon, Where the Sun Stood Still, The Discovery of the Biblical City*, 1962.

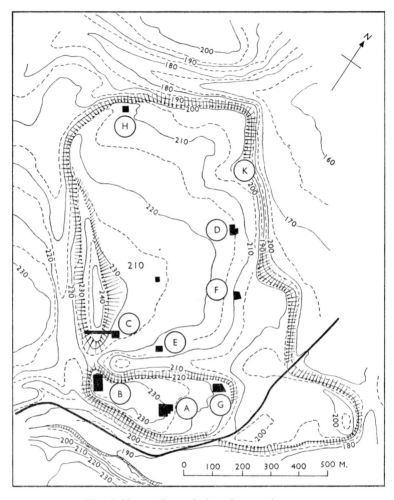

Fig. 6. Hazor: General plan of excavation areas

HAZOR

HAZOR was a large Canaanite and Israelite city in upper Galilee. Its location was first identified by J. L. Porter[1] with Tell el-Ķedaḥ (also known as Tell Waḳḳaṣ), some 14 kilometres north of the Sea of Galilee and 8 kilometres south-west of Lake Huleh (co-ordinates 2032; 2691). Today's Qibbutz 'Ayelet Hašaḥar lies at the foot of the tell. This identification was again proposed in 1926 by J. Garstang,[2] and since then it has been generally accepted.

Hazor is first mentioned in the Egyptian Execration Texts (the Posener Group).[3] It figures prominently in the archive of Mari; not only is it the only Palestinian city mentioned in these documents but it ranks in importance with such large centres of commerce as Yamḥad and Qatna. Caravans travelled between Babylon and Hazor,[4] and it is mentioned also in connexion with the important trade in tin.[5] It is further mentioned in a Babylonian Dream-book, again together with important centres of commerce and administration, such as Mari, Ḥalab, and Qatna.[6]

Hazor is frequently mentioned in Egyptian documents of the New Kingdom—in the city lists of Tuthmosis III[7]—as well as in the important Papyrus Hermitage 1116A[8]—and of Amenophis II and Sethos I. The role of Hazor in the Tell el-Amarna letters is of particular interest. Hazor's king is the subject of several letters[9] from which we can infer, on the one hand, that his activities extended far beyond his own city, and on the other that the city was exposed to certain unrest, caused by the Ḥabiru. It is interesting to note that the king of Hazor is called *šarrum* 'king'[10] unlike most other rulers mentioned in these letters, a title which he assumes even in one of his own letters to the Pharaoh.[11] The latest occurrence of Hazor's name in Egyptian documents is in Papyrus Anastasi I, probably dating from the time of Ramesses II, where mention is also made of a nearby river.

In the Old Testament Hazor is referred to on a number of occasions; the first of these is concerned with the conquests of Joshua (Joshua xi. 10–13). Especially noteworthy are the following words—'And Joshua turned back at that time, and took Hazor, and smote the king thereof with the sword: for Hazor beforetime was the head of all those kingdoms . . . and he burnt Hazor with fire. . . . But as for the cities that stood on their mounds, Israel burned none of them, save Hazor only; that did Joshua burn.' Here, then, is an exact description of the role of Hazor at the time of the Conquest.[12] Later, Hazor is mentioned in connexion with Deborah's wars in the prose version preserved in Judges iv—'And the Lord sold them into the hand of Jabin king of Canaan, that reigned in Hazor; the captain of whose host was Sisera, which dwelt in Harosheth of the Gentiles' (verse 2). The important problem of the relation between the Joshua story and that of Judges, and what light has been shed on it by the excavations, will be discussed in the chronological summary.

In 1 Kings ix. 15 it is pointed out that Hazor, together with Megiddo and Gezer, was (re)built by Solomon. From 2 Kings xv. 29 it is known that Hazor, along with other Galilean towns, was conquered by Tiglath-pileser III, most probably in 732 B.C. This is the last historical reference to Hazor in our sources, except for the brief mention in 1 Macc. xi. 67, which states that Jonathan camped, while he fought against Demetrius (147 B.C.), on the plain of Hazor. According to Josephus (*Ant.* v. 199) Hazor lay 'over the Lake Semechonitis', that is, Lake Huleh.

i. *The Site and History of the Excavations*

The site is composed of two distinct elements (*a*) the tell proper, covering about 30 acres and reaching a height of 40 metres, above the surrounding plain, (*b*) a large rectangular 'enclosure' to the north of the tell, about 175 acres in area (1,000×700 metres). On the west this 'enclosure' is bounded by a very large rampart of beaten earth and a deep fosse, while on the other sides it is limited by a steep slope reinforced by supporting walls and glacis. On the south a deep fosse separates the enclosure from the tell. Several trial soundings were made by Garstang in 1928 under the patronage of Sir Charles Marston. Though the results were not published in detail,[13] Garstang was able to offer the following conclusions: in the 'enclosure', called by him the 'camp area', 'in L.B.A. (Late Bronze Age) there appears to have been only a surface occupation, in tents or huts, which was brought to a close by a general conflagration'. Furthermore, he concluded that 'the complete absence of Mykenaean specimens, as of Jericho, suggests a date of destruction about 1400 B.C.', a date which he attributed to the conquest of Joshua. As will be seen below, both these cardinal conclusions have been proved incorrect in the light of our excavations. Garstang further made several soundings on the tell proper. Here 'layers of burning were traced . . . associated with Cypriote pottery (LBA i), but the occupation seems to have continued, less intensively, until towards the end of L.B.A. ii. Thereafter ensued a considerable gap in which specimens of E.I.A. were conspicuously absent; but in E.I.A. ii the city sprang again to life, with traces of Solomonian work including stamped bricks, and a building supported by a row of square stone monoliths, possibly a stable (cf. Megiddo).' As will be seen later, here Garstang's chronological conclusions appear to have been more accurate, although he attributed the pillared building incorrectly to Solomon.

During the years 1955–8 the James A. Rothschild Expedition, under the direction of the writer, excavated on the site, on behalf of the Hebrew University, with the aid of the Palestine Jewish Colonization Association, the Anglo-Israel Exploration Society, and the Government of Israel.[14] During the twelve months of the four seasons of excavations several areas (indicated by Roman letters) were excavated, both on the tell and in the 'enclosure'. The latter proved to be nothing less than a lower city throughout its entire history. Due to the large distances between the areas of excavation, separate strata numbers (indicated by Arabic figures) were assigned in each area. These were later synchronized with the strata of the tell, and an over-all strata scheme (indicated by Roman numerals) is offered in the table at the end of this article.

Because of the abundance of finds directly relevant to Old Testament study, let us first describe briefly the outstanding ones in each area, whether buildings or objects, pointing out their interest for Old Testament study; only later will we try to present the over-all picture of the site, emphasizing the chronological conclusions and their bearing on Old Testament problems. We shall begin our description with the results of the excavations in the lower city (the 'enclosure').

ii. *The Lower City*

Area C is located on the south-western corner of the lower city, adjoining the earthen rampart. It was here that we discovered the first indications that the 'enclosure' was indeed a proper city throughout its history, that is, from its foundations in the MB IIB period up to its downfall in the LB IIB period. Stratum 4 is the lowest level in the area and dates to the beginning of the MB IIB period, the period of the first fortifications and ramparts of the lower city. A jar bearing an Akkadian inscription, incised before firing and giving the name of the vessel's owner, most probably belongs to this level, since it was discovered directly over the foot of the beaten-earth rampart.[15] Stratum 3 was destroyed by conflagration. The pottery dates its fall at the end of the MB IIC period. Many infant burials in jars were found beneath the floors of the houses. Stratum 2 lies atop a thick layer of ash (of the destruction of Stratum 3) and represents the city inhabited during the LB I period.

Stratum 1b represents the period of Hazor's zenith in the LB period. A small broad shrine was discovered at the foot of the rampart's inner slope. A niche in the western wall contained a number of small stelae and statues, found in the context of the next stratum (see below). Benches for offerings line the walls. Nearby are several large houses, including a potter's workshop with all its installations, evidently serving the shrine. Of special note are a pottery cult mask, similar to one found in Area D, from the potter's workshop, and a silver-plated bronze standard, bearing the relief of a goddess who is holding snakes. The local and imported (Mycenaean IIIA) pottery places the level in the LB IIA period, and this must be the city of the Tell el-Amarna correspondence. Stratum 1a is basically a reconstruction of the previous city; the structures of 1a are similar to those of 1b in the main, particularly the public buildings. As Stratum 1a is close to the surface, the preservation of its buildings is rather poor; modern ploughing and erosion have destroyed considerable parts of its remains. The stelae shrine of 1b was reconstructed here, and most of its accessories were found placed *in situ* as reinstalled—a row of small top-rounded and plain basalt stelae, except for the central one which bears a bas-relief of two hands, outstetched upwards towards a divine lunar symbol—a crescent and a disk. A basalt statuette of a seated male figure with an inverted crescent pendant on his breast—its head deliberately broken off and lying on the floor—was placed on one side of the row of stelae. A small lion's orthostat, probably from the entrance of the previous shrine, was found below the stelae in secondary use, as a support for one of the stelae. Near the shrine a store-room was found in which a score of similar stelae, some unfinished, was found scattered. This shrine is unique, and is perhaps the only one from Palestine representing the true Old Testament *maṣṣēḇôt*.[16] Mycenaean IIIB sherds, together with local pottery, indicate clearly that this city was destroyed before the close of the thirteenth century B.C., when occupation in the lower city came to an end.

Areas D, E, and 210 are located at various spots within the lower city and, besides the many finds made there, are important in confirming that the entire area of the 'enclosure' was a real city from the MB IIB period to the close of the LB IIB period. The following are some of the significant finds made in these areas. In Area D most rich MB IIB–C graves came to light, as well as LB I and II building remains containing Mycenaean vessels. Among the finds should be mentioned a part of a thirteenth-century B.C. jar bearing a proto-Canaanite inscription written in paint (*[bʿ/ʾ]tt*). Area E enriched our knowledge of the pottery of the LB I period. From it we have a number of pieces unparalleled in Palestine but resembling LB I types from Anatolia. Area 210, which is merely a trial sounding at the centre of the lower city measuring 5 × 5 metres, proved that the sequence of strata here is the same as that found in Area C. Here too a large number of infant burials in jars was found beneath the floors of Stratum 3. Area F brought to light buildings and installations from all the phases of occupation in the lower city. A unique find, attributed to Stratum 4, are the rock-cut tombs and the elaborate network of tunnels connecting them. The usual plan of these tombs consists of large rectangular shafts, from the bottom of which hewn caves in varying shapes branch off. The shafts are interconnected by the tunnels. The tombs were found empty and had probably been rifled in antiquity.

In Stratum 3 (MB IIC) was found an extensive palace of rectangular plan and very thick walls. Its channel system was connected to the older tunnel network, now definitely adapted for drainage. In Stratum 2 (LB I) a part of the palace was reconstructed, others being left in disuse. A number of burials nearby contained a rich collection of bichrome ware. A basic change in the nature of the area took place in Stratum 1b (LB IIA) when it assumed a cult character. A stone altar—a large ashlar stone, 2·4 metres long, 0·85 metres wide, and 1·2 metres high, taken from the MB II palace—was found. It shows a depression for the draining of the sacrificial blood into the channel network of the previous periods. Around the altar, structures were found containing alabaster incense vessels and other ritual objects. A considerable quantity of animal bones was also found. A large tomb belonging to this stratum contained hundreds of vessels among which was a substantial number of beautiful Mycenaean IIIA vessels as well as a scarab of Tuthmosis IV. The tomb served for burials during the entire period of Stratum 1b in the fourteenth century B.C.[17]

Area H lies at the northern edge of the lower city. Here a series of four large superimposed temples came to light. These were situated against the inner face of the earthen rampart, similar to the shrine in Area C. No building came to light in Stratum 4, the phase in which the rampart was erected, because, during the building of the oldest temple discovered (Stratum 3, MB IIC), the entire area was levelled and filled up to the edge of the rampart.

The temple of Stratum 3 consisted of a broad hall on the north side of which was a small rectangular niche, a sort of 'holy of holies'. The remains of two basalt capitals, or bases, indicate that in the centre of the room stood two columns supporting the roof. On either side of the wide entrance in the south, two square areas were evidently the foundations of two towers flanking the entrance of the hall. To the south of the hall was a raised platform, to which several steps of well-dressed basalt led up. The entire area around the temple was paved with tiny cobble-stones, almost resembling a mosaic. In several respects this temple serves as a prototype of those found in Shechem[18] and in Megiddo Stratum VIII, though in Hazor the temple consists of a broad rather than a long hall.

The temple of Stratum 2 is the same as that of the former, though the floor has been raised. The major modifications were made around the temple in an area which actually formed a closed court, cobble-paved on the south, with a large open space further south paved with cobble-stones. Passage from the open space into the court was made through a broad propylaeum. Within the court a large rectangular *bāmāh* and several smaller altars were found. Near the *bāmāh*, where the sacrificial animals were slaughtered, a unique drainage channel had its inlet; this drain was made up in part of disused incense stands. On the other side of the court a pottery kiln, still containing a large number of votive bowls, was discovered. East of the main *bāmāh* was found a pile of broken ritual vessels—a sort of dump—including unique clay models of livers for priestly divination. One of these bore an Akkadian inscription mentioning various evil omens. The liver is from the sixteenth or fifteenth century B.C. and is further evidence of close ties with Babylonia.[19] Another find from the open area worthy of mention is a hammered bronze plaque delicately depicting in relief a Canaanite dignitary wrapped in a long robe.[20]

The temple of Stratum 1b is perhaps the most important one from the point of view of Old Testament study. Its plan differs essentially from that of the two earlier structures, though it was partly built on their foundations. It now comprised *three* major elements following each other from north to south, with the doorways on a single axis leading to each chamber in succession. It is very similar in plan to the temple of Solomon and is unique in Palestine. It is the oldest 'prototype' of the Solomonic temple ever found. The *porch* was the main addition to the previous structure and was south of the temple; two pillars were placed within the porch, near the inner entrance (their bases were reused in 1a; see below). The *hall* was essentially identical with the porch of the previous temples. The *holy of holies*, a broad room—also similar to that of the previous temples—has a rectangular niche in its northernmost part. Two bases found in the centre of the room bore (wooden?) columns to support the roof. The most important feature in temple 1b from an architectural viewpoint and with regard to the influences upon it, is the row of well-dressed basalt orthostats forming a dado around the interior of the porch and the holy of holies. This is the first time that such technique has been found in Palestine, and it is without doubt evidence of northern influence, as it closely resembles such elements found at Alalakh[21] and other sites. On the other side of the entrance to the porch stood a basalt orthostat of a lion in relief. However, only one lion has been found, buried in a pit specially dug near the entrance,[22] where a small basalt obelisk was also found. No traces of fire were evident in this temple and the finds were relatively scarce. It is most likely that the majority of the ritual vessels found in Stratum 1a originally furnished this phase.

The temple of Stratum 1a is identical with the previous one, restored, like the shrine in Area C, with minor repairs. The floor of the holy of holies was raised and two new column bases were found resting on it. The hall was enlarged at the expense of a side room to the east, and the porch was reconstructed in such a manner that it is difficult to discern whether it was roofed over or open and walled in. Before the entrance, leading into the hall, two round bases were found in situ. Their location would lead to the belief that they had no functional purpose and that they were evidently of a ritual nature, such as Jachin and Boaz in Solomon's temple.

The important discoveries in this temple are the numerous ritual vessels, which most probably originated in the temple of Stratum 1b. Amongst these should be mentioned a basalt incense altar in the form of a square pillar, on one side of which appears in relief the divine symbol of the storm-(sun-)god—a circle with a cross at its centre; a sort of large, round basin, like the 'sea' of Solomon's temple, also of basalt, found next to the altar; several libation tables, and a deep basalt bowl, with a beautifully carved running spiral on its exterior; a statuette of a seated figure, probably a king, and a great number of cylinder seals of the 'Late Mitannian' type; a scarab bearing the name of Amenophis III, found on the floor, a phenomenon known from other thirteenth-century B.C. temples, as at Beth-shean and Lachish. A most important find was made outside the area of the temple proper, namely, fragments of a statue of a deity which had stood on a base, in the form of a bull, and on its chest a divine symbol identical with that appearing on the incense altar mentioned above. The temple was destroyed in a violent conflagration.

Area K is located on the north-eastern edge of the lower city, not far from the northernmost corner. In this area a series of city gates was found, ranging from the founding of the lower city down to its final destruction by fire. The plan of these gates is extremely interesting, but their discussion falls outside the scope of the present article. It is sufficient to say that, except for the gate of Stratum 4, all subsequent gates, from Stratum 3 to 1a, had the plan of the 'classical' MB IIB–C gates (Megiddo, Shechem, etc.), that is, in the gate passage three pairs of pilasters narrowed the width of the opening to 2 metres. On either side of the passage stood a large tower, but only the one on the south, which was divided into two interconnected chambers, was excavated. To the gate of Stratum 3 (MB IIC) belongs a true casemate wall, the earliest of its type found hitherto in Palestine. It should be noted that the cobbled floor of the latest gate was covered by a thick layer of ashes.

iii. The Upper City

Three areas were excavated within the upper city, that is, the southern tell; Area A in the centre, Area B on the western edge, and Area G on the eastern edge.

Area A, in the centre of the tell, was the site of Garstang's trial excavation; he found there a row of columns and assigned them to a stable of the time of Solomon (see below Stratum VIII). In one section of Area A we reached bed-rock, and we have therefore a clear section of the levels of occupation in the upper city from the first settlement onwards. The number of strata in the upper city is indicated by Roman numerals, which coincide with the over-all numbers of the strata in Hazor as indicated in the table below.

Strata XXI–XIX. Immediately above bed-rock, building remains from three EB strata were found. In Strata XX–XIX a large number of sherds of Khirbet Kerak ware (EB III) was found. Stratum XXI contained some pottery datable to the end of EB II. No proper buildings were found in Stratum XVIII which contained typical MB I pottery. This conforms to the situation in most Palestinian sites of this period, indicating a semi-nomad occupation (see below in the final section dealing with the chronological summary).

Strata XVII–XVI, corresponding to Strata 4–3 in the lower city and representing the MB IIB–C periods respectively, are in fact two floors of a large building of palatial character. East of this area, in a sectional trench, a massive wall assigned to these two strata was discovered; it is 7·5 metres thick and built of plastered brick on a stone foundation. This wall probably protected the inner part of the upper city. Much of this wall remained in the LB periods. Together with its moat, the wall was reused in Solomon's fortifications (see below, Stratum X) and formed a sort of inner defence of the acropolis.

In Stratum XV (parallel to Stratum 2 in the lower city—LB I) were found portions of a large palace built mostly of brick. Amongst the typical LB I sherds found was a number of bichrome ware vessels. In Stratum XIV (parallel to Stratum 1b—LB IIA) mainly portions of a large palace and a paved court came to light. Entrance to the court was effected by means of a stairway. Nearby a fragment of a lioness orthostat was found. This orthostat is very similar to the one discovered in temple 1b in Area H. One of the doorways of the palace was lined with orthostats identical with those of the same temple. All the above finds, and the pottery, definitely prove the contemporaneity of this stratum with 1b in the lower city.

Stratum XIII, the last LB level on the tell, corresponds to Stratum 1a in the lower city. The destruction evidenced by this level brought an end to Canaanite Hazor in the thirteenth century B.C. After a certain gap, and definitely above the accumulation of debris of Stratum XIII, was found a settlement at the beginning of the Iron Age (Stratum XII). This was of semi-nomadic character, consisting mainly of deep silos, hearths, and foundations for tents or huts. The pottery is typical of the twelfth century B.C. and closely resembles that found at similar poor settlements in upper Galilee (see further below—Summary).

Stratum X represents the rebuilding of Hazor as a fortified city. The major features are a casemate wall and a large gate with six chambers, three on either side, and two towers flanking the passage-way (Pl. X). On the basis both of stratigraphy and pottery, this level is to be assigned to the Solomonic period. The identity of plan of the gate and the wall with such Solomonic structures at Gezer[23] and Megiddo[24] confirms this dating conclusively. Two phases (Xa and Xb) were discernible in this level. The wall and gate seem to have defended the acropolis proper. Stratum IX, which is also divided into two phases and shows a certain decline in the buildings, belongs to the period between Solomon and the rise of the Omrid dynasty. This city was destroyed by fire.

The major feature of Stratum VIII, in which extensive building

PLATE X

Aerial view of Area A (Hazor). Left: Solomonic gate and casemate wall. Centre: pillared building (Stratum VIII). Top right: private building (Strata VI–V)

activity is evident, is a large storehouse, down the centre of which run two rows of pillars. The rooms of the earlier casemate wall were now used only as store-rooms. The northern of the two rows of pillars is the one uncovered by Garstang and mistakenly assigned by him to Solomon and considered by him to be a stable. The general layout of these buildings differs entirely from the structures of Strata X–IX, and the construction of this city is a distinct turning-point in the history of Israelite Hazor, representing most probably the enterprise of the house of Omri. The pillared storehouse continued in use in Stratum VII though the floor had been repaired over the debris of the fallen roof of Stratum VIII. The public buildings of the previous levels were not reused in Stratum VI; the entire area became a residential quarter, including workshops. There is evidence that this city was destroyed by earthquake, probably the one which occurred in the days of Jeroboam II (cf. Amos i. 1). In one of the houses part of a storage jar was found bearing an incised Hebrew inscription denoting the owner's name (*lmkbrm* 'belonging to Mkbrm'). In Stratum V most of the buildings from the previous stratum were reconstructed. The city met its destruction by a conflagration, traces of which were evident throughout the ruins. This destruction was final for Hazor as a fortified Israelite city, and is to be attributed to the conquests of Tiglath-pileser III. Almost nothing was found of Strata IV–I (see below, Area B).

Garstang had excavated in Area B and discovered the remains of a large building which he did not publish in detail. Most of this area was occupied in the Israelite period by a large citadel which was left as found after our excavations. Therefore most of our knowledge of the older periods stems from the evidence of only a small sector east of the citadel. Here Bronze Age remains in rather poor condition were discovered. Generally the stratification agrees with that achieved at Area A and will not be discussed here.

Stratum XII. The traces of the first Israelite settlement, poor as it was, were found over the ruins of the last Canaanite occupation, from the LB IIB period, as in Area A. In character it is identical with that in Area A—silos, tent and hut foundations, and suchlike. The traces of Stratum XI were found mostly in Area B, and the remains indicate that at one phase later than XII, though earlier than the establishment of Solomonic Hazor, an additional *unfortified* occupation did exist here at several spots. In contrast to Stratum XII, which still had a semi-nomadic character, Stratum XI shows definite traces of a more permanent settlement. The main feature of this level is a sort of *bāmāh*, or shrine, near which were found incense vessels and a cache of bronze offering objects in a jar. Among the latter were a number of weapons and a male deity figurine. The stratigraphy and pottery place this stratum in the eleventh century B.C.

In Strata X–IX the remains of the city built by Solomon are clearly preserved, consisting mainly of a casemate wall which encircles the tell. On the western edge the fortifications were extended to form a sort of bastion; because of the later structure of Stratum VIII above, it was not possible to ascertain its exact plan. Traces of Level IX were found here too, though so faint that a general plan was unobtainable. The main feature of Stratum VIII was a large citadel which spread over almost this entire excavated area. The building of this edifice, in Stratum VIII, marks a turning-point in the character of Israelite Hazor, just as in Area A. The citadel measures 21 × 25 metres, with a wall about 2 metres thick. Nearby a number of buildings, evidently serving the administration of the citadel, was recovered. The wall coming from the east was the former casemate wall, now filled with earth and stones, forming a solid construction typical of all Palestinian cities beginning early in IA II.[25] The large citadel built in the first half of the ninth century B.C. continued in use through the entire Israelite period, till in Stratum V it was destroyed down to its very foundations. Of special interest is the entrance into the citadel, which was quite grand and ornamented with proto-Aeolic capitals similar to those found at Samaria.

In the first phase of Stratum V radical changes are evident. To meet the approaching Assyrian menace the citadel was further strengthened by an additional offsets and insets wall. Some of the surrounding buildings had to be destroyed in the process, the wall being constructed directly over their ruins and joined up with the older wall. In this phase two buildings of the four-room type were added, probably to replace the ones which had been destroyed. The destruction of the citadel was final and the whole area was covered with a layer of ash and debris about 1 metre thick. Noteworthy among the finds from this period are an ivory pyxis with a 'tree of life', and several Hebrew inscriptions on jars (*lpkh smdr* 'belonging to Pekah-semadar' (a type of wine? Cf. Song of Sol. ii. 13, vii. 13).[26] Could this refer to King Pekah in 'whose' stratum the jar was found? The other inscription is *ldlyw* 'belonging to Delayo'.

After the destruction of the citadel there appeared a temporary unfortified settlement (Stratum IV), remains of which were found immediately over the ruins of the citadel and the city wall. This occupation may be assigned to the end of the eighth century B.C. and belonged probably to the Israelite inhabitants returning after the fall and sack of the city. In Strata III, II, and I were found fortresses of the Assyrian, Persian, and Hellenistic periods respectively.

Area G is located on the northern edge of the eastern terrace of the tell. It provided important information on the extent of the upper city in the various periods and the fortifications in this sector. Special mention should be made of a fine stone wall with battered slopes and moat of the MB IIB–LB period. Of the Israelite period should be mentioned a postern in the city wall which was blocked during Stratum V, evidently in the course of strengthening the fortifications against the Assyrians (cf. above, Area B, Stratum V).

iv. *Summary*

The results of the excavations at Hazor make possible a clear reconstruction of the history of the site and the nature of its unique occupation. Furthermore, it is possible to relate the rich archaeological findings to much of the data of the written sources, the Old Testament included.

It is clear now that the first settlement in Hazor in EB II was confined to the tell proper. This occupation continued to the end of EB III. The tell was resettled in MB I after a gap in EB IV. However, this settlement appears to have been of a seminomadic character, similar to many sites in Palestine. The great decisive change in Hazor started with MB IIB, when the huge lower city was founded, together with a well-fortified acropolis on the tell. It appears that no settlement existed in Hazor in the MB IIA period.

These facts raise two interesting problems relating to MB chronology.

1. *The mention of Hazor in the Execration Texts*

This group of texts is dated differently by various authorities throughout the nineteenth century,[27] while the end of the MB I phase is generally placed at *c.* 1900 B.C. If we attribute these texts to the MB I settlement of Hazor, one must either raise the date of the Execration Texts (Posener Group) to the very end of the twentieth century, or lower the date of the end of MB I well into the latter part of the nineteenth century.[28] If, on the other hand, the reference to Hazor and its chief is to a proper city rather than to a semi-nomadic settlement, then the unavoidable conclusion is that one must lower the date of the Posener Group well into the MB IIB period. This brings us to the problem of Hazor and Mari.

2. *Hazor and Mari*

As has been stated above, Hazor plays an important role in the economy of the period reflected by these letters. This can refer only to Hazor after the establishment of its huge lower city, which was founded not earlier than the very beginning of the MB IIB period. If we accept the date of *c.* 1750 B.C. for the beginning of this period, then the unavoidable conclusion is that Albright's dating in the latter part of the eighteenth century is the only one acceptable to the Mari correspondence.[29]

The lower city flourished throughout the LB periods, being alternately destroyed and rebuilt. Excavations at various locations scattered over the entire lower city prove that it should no longer be termed 'enclosure' or 'camp area'. The city reached its zenith in the fourteenth century B.C.—the Amarna period—when it was the largest city in area and population in all the land of Canaan. However, the greatest contribution of the excavations to Old Testament study is related to the vexed problem of 'Joshua–Judges'. The excavations have shown in a decisive manner that the great Canaanite city was destroyed by fire, and was never rebuilt, in the second part of the thirteenth century B.C., that is, at a period when Mycenaean IIIB pottery was still current. This destruction must be attributed to the one described so minutely in the book of Joshua.[30] Furthermore, evidence of the greatest importance for the understanding of the process of Israelite settlement are the remains of Stratum XII. These—clearly belonging to the twelfth century B.C., when Hazor ceased to be a true city and

essentially identical with other remains of the Israelite settlements
in upper Galilee—indicate that the bulk of these settlements, still
of semi-nomadic character, occurred *after* the fall of the great
cities and provinces of Canaan. The theory[31] that the archaeological
evidence of the Galilee survey supports the view of a peaceful infiltration of the tribes of Israel, prior to the destruction of the
Canaanite cities—at least as far as Hazor is concerned—seems,
therefore, to collapse. More than that—the fact that no true city
actually existed in the mound of Hazor in the twelfth or eleventh
century B.C. eliminates the possibility of shifting the description in
Joshua xi and placing the events mentioned there within the time
frame of Deborah's activities. Those scholars who still maintain
such a theory will have to place Deborah well in the thirteenth
century B.C., a date which must be considered hard to accept.
Thus we have to conclude that the true historical kernel relating
the Deborah war is embedded in her song, which deals with
Sisera and the war in the valley of Jezreel, and to assume that in
Judges iv there is a *later* effort to interrelate Sisera with Jabin.

The meagre Israelite occupation in the twelfth–eleventh centuries B.C. was replaced in the Solomonic period by a large and
well-fortified city. The possibility of identifying the structures and
finds from Stratum X with Solomon is not only a good example of
how Old Testament data can play an important role in field archaeology in the Holy Land, but, and this is more important, it enables
us now to fix the pottery sequence of the first centuries of the first
millennium B.C. with much greater accuracy.[32] This was further
aided by the rapid destructions and rebuilding of Israelite Hazor
between the Solomonic period and the final destruction of the
city in 732 B.C.

The dating of the strata at Hazor in the lower and upper cities,
and the correlation between them, is given in the following table:

Upper city	*Lower city*	*Period*	*Remarks*
I		Hellenistic (second cent. B.C.)	Citadel.
II	No longer settled.	Persian (fourth cent. B.C.)	Citadel and small settlement.
III		Assyrian (seventh cent. B.C.)	Citadel.

Upper city	Lower city	Period	Remarks
IV		Eighth cent. B.C.	Unfortified Israelite settlement.
V		Eighth cent. B.C.	Destruction by Tiglath-pileser III, 732 B.C.
VI		Eighth cent. B.C.	City of Jeroboam II, destruction by earthquake.
VII	No longer settled	Ninth cent. B.C.	Reconstruction of parts of City VIII.
VIII		Ninth cent. B.C.	Omrid dynasty.
IX		End of tenth and beginning of ninth cent. B.C.	Conflagration (destroyed by Ben-hadad I?).
X		Mid-tenth cent. B.C.	City of Solomon.
XI		Eleventh cent. B.C.	Limited Israelite settlement.
XII		Twelfth cent. B.C.	Temporary Israelite settlement, semi-nomadic.
XIII	1a	Thirteenth cent. B.C.	Destruction in the second half of the thirteenth cent. B.C. by Joshua.
XIV	1b	Fourteenth cent. B.C.	The Amarna period.
XV	2	Fifteenth cent. B.C.	Tuthmosis III–Amenophis II.
XVI	3	Seventeenth to sixteenth cents. B.C.	Destruction by conflagration (Amosis?).
XVII	4	Eighteenth to seventeenth cents. B.C.	Foundation of lower city c. mid-eighteenth cent. B.C. (MB IIB).
XVIII		MB I	Semi-nomadic settlement. Destroyed or deserted c. 1850 B.C.
XIX XX	Not yet founded	EB III	Khirbet Kerak ware.
XXI		EB II–EB III	Built on bed-rock.

Y. YADIN

NOTES

1. J. L. Porter, *Handbook for Travellers in Syria and Palestine*, pp. 414 f.

2. J. Garstang, *Joshua Judges*, 1931, pp. 381–3.

3. G. Posener, *Princes et Pays d'Asie et de Nubie. Textes hiératiques sur des figurines d'envoûtement du Moyen Empire*, 1940, no. E 15.

4. *A.R.M.* vi, no. 23; 78.

5. Ibid. vii, no. 236.

6. A. L. Oppenheim, *Trans. Amer. Philos. Soc.* xlvi, 1956, p. 313. For this document, as well as the documents from Mari and their bearing on the position of Hazor, see A. Malamat, *J.B.L.* lxxix, 1960, pp. 12 ff.

7. For this and the other lists mentioned below, see most conveniently *A.N.E.T.*, p. 242.

8. W. Golénischeff, *Les Papyrus hiératique Nos. 1115, 1116A et 1116B de l'Ermitage Imperiale à St. Peterbourg*; cf. C. Epstein, *J.E.A.* xlix, 1963, pp. 49–56.

9. *E.A.* 148, 227, 228, 256a.

10. Ibid. 148.

11. Ibid. 227; cf. also Malamat (*supra*, n. 7), p. 19.

12. Against Malamat's view (op. cit., p. 19) who maintains that the expression ' "For Hazor beforetime was the head of all those kingdoms" testifies to the former greatness of this city founded in the Middle Bronze Age'. While there is no doubt, as the Mari documents show, and the excavations have proved (see below), that Hazor had already achieved its greatest dimensions in the MB IIB period, it is similarly clear from the results of the excavations that Canaanite Hazor had maintained its large area down to its downfall in the thirteenth century B.C. It seems to me, therefore, more natural to assume that 'beforetime' refers to the Conquest period from the narrator's point of view.

13. Op. cit., loc. cit.

14. Senior members of the staff were Y. Aharoni, Ruth Amiran, M. Dothan, Trude Dothan, I. Dunayevsky, Claire Epstein, and J. Perrot.

15. Cf. the study of P. Artzi and A. Malamat, *Hazor II*, pp. 115 f. The name should be read $^m I\check{s}$-me-ilam^d, and, as pointed out by Malamat (op. cit., *supra*, n. 7, p. 18), the main interest lies in the fact that the first element (*išme*) of the name is Akkadian rather than the west-Semitic form *iasmaḫ*.

16. On the various views concerning the interpretation of this shrine, see W. F. Albright, *V.T. Supp.* iv, 1957, pp. 242 ff.; K. Galling, *Z.D.P.V.* lxxv, 1959, pp. 4–13. For a detailed description of this shrine, see *Hazor I*, pp. 83 ff.; pls. xxvii–xxxi, clxxx.

17. For a detailed description of the finds, see *Hazor II*, pp. 127 f.

18. On these, see now G. E. Wright, *Shechem*, 1965, pp. 80 ff.

19. On this liver model, see now B. Landsberger and H. Tadmor, *I.E.J.* xiv, 1964, pp. 201 ff.

20. See *Hazor III–IV* (pls.), pl. cccxxxix.

21. Cf. C. L. Woolley, *Alalakh*, 1955, pp. 82 ff. The similarity between Hazor's temples and those of Alalakh is evident also in their general plan and inventory.

22. The lion's orthostat too resembles in style those of Alalakh, although far superior in execution. Cf. *Hazor III–IV* (pls.), pl. cxx; *Alalakh*, pl. xlix.

23. Y. Yadin, *I.E.J.* viii, 1958, pp. 80 ff.

24. Y. Yadin, *B.A.* xxiii, 1960, pp. 62 ff. For a more detailed discussion, see Yadin, *The Kingdoms of Israel and Judah*, Jerusalem, 1961, pp. 66 ff. (in Hebrew).

25. The same phenomenon was found at Megiddo; see Yadin, op. cit. (*supra*, n. 23). On the possible military reason for this change at this period, see Yadin, *The Art of Warfare in Biblical Lands*, 1963, p. 289.

26. For the discussion of this inscription and others found at Hazor, see *Hazor II*, pp. 70 ff.

27. On the date of this group of texts, see now also G. Posener, in *Syria and Palestine* (*C.A.H.*, rev. ed. of vols. i and ii, 1965).

28. As suggested recently by W. F. Albright; cf. *B.A.S.O.R.* 176, 1964, p. 44, and their previous bibliography.

29. In a postgraduate seminar, recently conducted by N. Avigad, B. Mazar, and myself, on the subject of MB chronology, the following synchronization was suggested by Mazar (generally based on Sidney Smith's chronology): The Execration Texts and the Mari Texts are to be placed at the beginning of the eighteenth century, and both refer to Hazor of the MB IIB period. The beginning of the MB IIB period is to be raised, according to this suggestion, to *c.* 1800 B.C. Although it appears that there was no proper settlement in the MB IIA period on the tell, it should be noted that the MB strata here were reached in narrow trenches only. It is possible, therefore, that the few MB IIA sherds encountered may represent a larger settlement than was assumed It is my intention to investigate this very important problem–amongst others–in the forthcoming fifth season of excavation planned for the summer of 1967.

30. Cf. W. F. Albright, *J.B.L.* lxxv, 1956, pp. 172 f.

31. e.g. Y. Aharoni, *Antiquity and Survival*, ii, 1957, p. 149. On these problems, see most recently O. Eissfeldt, *The Hebrew Kingdom* (*C.A.H.*, rev. ed. of vols. i and ii, 1965, p. 23).

32. On some of these problems, see most recently Kathleen M. Kenyon, *Bull. No. 4 of the Inst. of Archaeology* (University of London), 1964, pp. 143 ff.

BIBLIOGRAPHY

i. *Identification and Excavations*

GARSTANG, J. *Joshua Judges*, 1931, pp. 381 f.

GRAY, J. 'Hazor', *V.T.* xvi, 1966, pp. 26–52.

PORTER, J. L. *Handbook for Travellers in Syria and Palestine, 1875*, pp. 414 f.

YADIN, Y. *I.E.J.* viii, 1958, pp. 1–14, ix, 1959, pp. 74–88.

YADIN, Y., AHARONI, Y., AMIRAN, R., DOTHAN, T., DUNAYEVSKY, I., and PERROT, J. *Hazor I–II* and *III–IV* (pls.), 1959–64.

ii. *The Shrine in Area C*

ALBRIGHT, W. F. *V.T. Supp.* iv, 1957, pp. 242–58.

GALLING K. *Z.D.P.V.* lxxv, 1959, pp. 1–13.

iii. *The Conquest of Hazor by the Israelites*

MAAS, F. *Von Ugarit nach Qumran*, B.Z.A.W. lxxvii, 1958, pp. 105–17.

YADIN, Y. Deliberations on the Book of Joshua (*Proceedings of the Bible Circle at the home of D. Ben-Gurion*), Jerusalem, 1961, pp. 234 ff. (in Hebrew).

iv. *The Status of Hazor in the Canaanite Period*

MALAMAT, A. *J.B.L.* lxxix, 1960, pp. 12 ff.

v. *Israelite Hazor*

YADIN, Y. *I.E.J.* viii, 1958, pp. 80 ff.; *B.A.* xxiii, 1960, pp. 62 ff.

JERICHO

THOUGH the prominent part that Jericho plays in the account of the entry of the Israelites under Joshua into Palestine has been the reason that has attracted archaeologists to the site for nearly a hundred years, it will be seen (p. 271f.) that denudation has removed nearly all deposits belonging to the second half of the second millennium B.C., and thus direct evidence concerning the entry of the Israelites is scanty. The main interest of the site for Old Testament studies is the evidence concerning the background against which the story of the entry of the Israelites took place and the culture and environment of the peoples amongst whom the Israelites settled. Since the newcomers to a very large extent absorbed this culture, information concerning it has a real bearing on Old Testament studies.

The site of ancient Jericho can with certainty be identified as Tell es-Sulṭân, on the western outskirts of the modern town (Pl. XI). Though there are other tells in the neighbourhood, none have the importance of Tell es-Sulṭân, and they mostly appear to be late in date. The decisive factor in identifying the site is, however, its situation at the source of the copious perennial spring of 'Ain es-Sulṭân, control of the waters of which would be essential for all early occupation. The tell today stands to a maximum height of 70 feet above the surrounding plain, a much eroded elongated oval covering an area of some 10 acres.

The history of the excavation of Jericho begins almost a hundred years ago. Captain (later Major-General Sir Charles) Warren sank some shafts on the tell in 1867 in the course of his explorations on behalf of the Palestine Exploration Fund.[1] Two of them came to light during the course of the 1952–8 excavations, remarkable well-like affairs penetrating to a depth of some 30 feet. Though one was sunk right through the Early Bronze Age town wall, and the other cut well into the Pre-Pottery Neolithic levels of the sixth millennium B.C., Warren's conclusions were that nothing was to be found on the site, for archaeological methods of the time could not recognize such remains. The first large-scale excavations were carried out by an Austro-German expedition in 1907–9. The line of the wall surrounding the summit was traced, a considerable area of the uppermost levels at the northern end of the mound was excavated, and a deep trench was cut across it from east to west. By the time of these excavations the importance of pottery for dating purposes was becoming recognized, but unfortunately the excavators preferred their own pottery chronology to that being built up by Père Vincent and others, so that their dating of successive building periods is unreliable. Their deep trench did in fact penetrate into the Pre-Pottery Neolithic levels, but these were not recognized.

The next excavations were on an even larger scale. They were carried out from 1930 to 1936 by John Garstang on behalf of the Neilson Expedition of the University of Liverpool. He devoted much attention to the mud-brick town walls of which the line following the crest of the mound on the north, west, and south sides had been traced by the previous expedition, and through which he cut a number of trenches. He assigned them to four stages, two to the Early Bronze Age, one to the Middle Bronze Age, and one to the Late Bronze Age. The destruction of the latter by fire and earthquake he assigned to the time of the Israelite attack. This was, as will be seen, a completely erroneous identification, for the defences in question belonged to the Early Bronze Age. His interpretation of structures and tombs as providing evidence of continuous occupation down to c. 1400 B.C. was also erroneous, since pottery of this period was at that time not clearly distinguished. A very important result of this expedition was the identification in a deep trench at the north end of the mound of the Pre-Pottery levels underlying the Bronze Age remains.

These excavations were followed by another series between 1952 and 1958, sponsored by the British School of Archaeology in Jerusalem, the Palestine Exploration Fund, and the British Academy, with collaboration in some seasons from the American Schools of Oriental Research and the Royal Ontario Museum, and directed by the present writer. In these the sequence of occupation of the site, from its first occupation to its final abandonment, was examined in a number of soundings in all parts of the mound, and it is on this evidence that the account is based.

The earliest stages do not concern Old Testament studies, for they are purely prehistoric. From Mesolithic beginnings *c.* 8000 B.C. a Proto-Neolithic stage developed into a full Neolithic town by *c.* 7000 B.C. This town was succeeded by another, still in the Pre-Pottery Neolithic stage, in the course of the seventh millennium B.C., which continued well into the sixth millennium. This first urban stage in Palestine, however, did not last. The succeeding culture at Jericho, the Pottery Neolithic, is that of dwellers in flimsy, partly sunk huts, who were probably semi-nomadic.

It was only in the Early Bronze Age, starting at the end of the fourth millennium B.C., that Palestine began to assume the appearance of the country which the Israelites entered, with numerous small towns occupying strategic positions. Jericho, like the rest of the towns, was a closely built-up settlement, within town walls following the crest of the mound built up by the remains of the successive layers of earlier occupation. Though the Early Bronze Age did not directly make any contribution to the culture of the Old Testament period beginning in the second millennium B.C., it is necessary to describe the Early Bronze Age defences, owing to the erroneous ascription of them to the period of Joshua, to which reference has already been made, for it has appeared in the literature for some thirty years.

These Early Bronze Age defences had in fact a very complex history. In a period of time ranging from perhaps *c.* 3000 B.C. to *c.* 2300 B.C.[2] there were very many rebuilds. Some were refacings, or rebuildings of superstructures on existing foundations. Others were complete rebuildings, with new foundations laid on the levelled-over debris of the earlier wall. It is very likely that some repairs were local, and that the same sequence would not be found everywhere. Some of the collapses were clearly the result of earthquake, some apparently because the foot of the wall was eroded by rain and wind, and some were certainly caused by fire, presumably in the course of enemy attack. The most complete sequence was obtained in a cut through the defences on the west side, where seventeen successive stages were identified. Fourteen of these were on the same line. The last three were 7 metres in advance, with the foundations of the fifteenth very clearly cut into the debris overlying the fourteenth; two later rebuilds were superimposed on the top of this wall on the new line. This advance of the walls down the slope is found all round the site, thus creating two parallel lines.

PLATE XI

General view of the site of Jericho

This was interpreted by the earlier excavators, from lack of observation of the stratification, as a double wall; this it certainly is not,
for the inner wall was abolished when the outer was built. The outer
wall was destroyed by fire. Again, this cannot be ascribed to the
period of Joshua, as previously suggested. Not only is the stratigraphical evidence quite clear that even the later of the two lines
of wall is Early Bronze Age, but in two places it is destroyed by a
house of the Intermediate Early Bronze–Middle Bronze period,[3]
which in turn is in both places sealed by the plaster-faced bank
of the Middle Bronze Age defences, which was not recognized by
the earlier excavators. The double wall of the Late Bronze Age
simply does not exist.

A further piece of evidence from the remains of the fourth and
third millennia B.C. has significance for the Old Testament period.
Both for the end of the fourth millennium and the end of the third,
excavation has produced evidence that Jericho was a point of
entry of nomadic tribes. Joshua told his spies 'Go view the land,
and Jericho' (Joshua ii. 1). Whatever degree of factual record is
accorded to the account in the book of Joshua, this is a perfectly
reasonable proceeding for the leader of any group of invaders or
infiltrators coming in from the east, for Jericho's position opposite
the main ford over the lower Jordan, defending the main passes
up out of the Jordan valley, and controlling a vital water-supply,
meant that it was a point of vantage for all invaders. The full
Early Bronze Age was preceded by a series of nomadic incursions.
The Jericho evidence shows them arriving as separate groups of
people whose nomadic character is indicated by the fact that there
is little structural evidence of their occupation, though their
presence is amply testified to by their tombs. As these groups penetrate further into the country, they mingle and merge, and only in
Jericho can their separate identity be recognized.[4] A very similar
process went on at the end of the Early Bronze Age. The urban
civilization of this period was destroyed by nomadic invaders, again
identifiable as separate tribal groups from their burial customs, which
again become mixed and altered as they penetrate further into the
country. Jericho was an important gateway for thousands of years.

It is in fact with this break-up of the Early Bronze Age civilization that we first make contact with the Old Testament period. The
infiltrating Israelites found the Amorites in the hill-country and

the Canaanites on the coasts and in the plains (Num. xiii. 29). The nomadic invaders who were responsible for the destruction of the Early Bronze Age towns of Palestine were the Amorites. Syria as well as Palestine suffered nomadic invasions in the last centuries of the third millennium B.C., and here the evidence is clear that the nomads were the Amorites.[5] The archaeological evidence provides the connexion between these invaders in Syria and those in Palestine.[6] The evidence from every site in Palestine is the same; town life is abruptly destroyed, and the succeeding occupation is that of nomadic groups. The evidence is particularly clear at Jericho. Reference has already been made to the destruction by fire of the final Early Bronze Age town wall. The house of the Intermediate Early Bronze–Middle Bronze period that was built on its ruins does not immediately succeed it, for there is an appreciable period during which the Early Bronze Age ditch was silting up, with, in its silt, pottery of the new type, and during which period the newcomers were still presumably living in tents. When houses do appear, they are flimsy and ill planned, quite unlike those of the preceding phases.

The Jericho tombs provide even stronger evidence both of the complete break between the period and the Early Bronze Age and also that the newcomers were nomads, organized in tribal groups. During the Early Bronze Age, burials had been in communal tombs, which contained up to 300 successive burials. Suddenly the practice of individual burial appears, with some rare cases of tombs with two bodies, with the result that during the 1952–8 excavations, in contrast to seventeen tombs of which the nine excavated tombs contained some 469 burials covering a period of about 800 years, 346 tombs were located containing 356 burials covering a period of about 400 years. Moreover, the tombs fall into seven well-defined groups characterized by differing burial practices, which can best be explained as evidence of allied but not identical groups living side by side. The nomadic character of the groups is suggested especially by the practice of burying disintegrated skeletons, which must be derived from the custom of bringing dead people back to ancestral burial places which were only visited at intervals during seasonal migrations.

The break at the end of the period of occupation of these nomadic Amorites is shown by the Jericho evidence to have been as sharp as was the break that marked their arrival. Round about 1900 B.C. they were submerged beneath a new wave of immigrants, though a sense of identity must have remained in those towns which were still called Amorite some 500 years later, while in Transjordan they apparently withstood the newcomers.

West of the Jordan, however, the culture brought by these newcomers completely superseded that of the nomadic Amorites. To this culture can be given the name of the second of the chief elements in the population found by the Israelites, the Canaanites. It is the culture found the whole length of the Syro-Palestinian coast in the second millennium B.C., and it probably first developed in an area centred on Byblos.[7]

From the point of view of Old Testament studies, the importance of this culture that appears at the beginning of the Palestinian Middle Bronze Age is not only that it belongs to a group of the inhabitants who preceded the Israelites. The archaeological evidence is clear that the culture introduced c. 1900 B.C. lasted until at least 1200 B.C. and was thereafter only gradually modified. It therefore well overlaps the period of the entry of the Israelites, and this entry on archaeological evidence makes no obvious cultural impact. The Israelites, therefore, absorbed the more sophisticated culture that they found in the towns and villages that they occupied.

Circumstances at Jericho have been peculiarly favourable for the preservation of evidence concerning the culture of the Middle Bronze Age. A continuous succession of town levels, though excavated, and indeed surviving, only in a small area, showed the continuous development from c. 1900 B.C. in artefacts, such as pottery, which is evidence of the basic continuity of culture. An important change in methods of fortification is evidence of how foreign ruling aristocracies could impose themselves without altering the existing culture, for the appearance of a type of defence based on a sloping bank instead of a free-standing independent wall is probably to be ascribed to the Hyksos,[8] and the Jericho evidence is emphatic that there is no cultural break.

The successive layers of houses, moreover, end with one violently destroyed by fire. A violent destruction always leaves more archaeological evidence than a peaceful abandonment, for the contents of houses are buried beneath the debris of collapse. Further, a destruction by fire preserves walls by hardening them and some organic materials by carbonizing them, whereas otherwise they would have decayed. The destruction of this final stage of Middle Bronze Age Jericho early in the sixteenth century B.C., probably connected with the expulsion of the Hyksos from Egypt, has therefore left very clear evidence of the town of that period, and the archaeological evidence is clear that the towns found by the Israelites two or three centuries later would have been very similar. The general layout of the town was indeed not unlike that of towns that today, like the Old City of Jerusalem, admirably retain their medieval characteristics. Cobbled streets ascend the slope of the mound in shallow steps. Opening on to the streets are single-roomed shops and store-rooms. Living quarters and industrial installations were on the first floor, and in the debris of collapse caused by the fire were found the objects from the upper floor, such as a plethora of querns which must indicate a milling establishment, probably associated with the grain found calcined in jars in the store-rooms at street level. The wealth of objects recovered from this destruction level was considerable.

The unique contribution of Jericho to the knowledge of this Canaanite culture is not, however, from the remains on the town site, for destruction levels have been found elsewhere. Only at Jericho, however, has so much complementary evidence been found in the tombs. This is due to the fact that in the tombs at Jericho organic matter has been preserved to a degree not hitherto found elsewhere in Palestine. It was the custom of the Middle Bronze Age inhabitants of Jericho to bury with the dead a considerable amount of furniture and personal possessions. In fact, one may reasonably conclude that the equipment provided for the dead was the equipment they required during life, and the tombs therefore give evidence of the normal household furnishings of the period. From this one can say that the equipment of the average household in Jericho was simple. The ordinary family sat and slept on rush mats on the floor, but without exception they possessed a long, narrow table, with two legs at one end and one at the other, from which they ate. Only the important members of the community possessed wooden stools, and a few had wooden beds, or slept on a dais raised from the floor. If provision for the dead is a criterion, food, mainly joints of sheep or goat, was lavish, as was drink in great jars provided with dippers for ladling it out. Vessels used for eating and drinking were entirely of pottery. The dead had usually their personal provision of toilet equipment, combs, and juglets probably holding oil or perfume, often placed in rush baskets.[9] The bodies were usually placed in the tomb clothed with a loose garment ordinarily secured on the shoulder or chest with a pin. Ornaments were very few.[10]

The picture given of Middle Bronze Age Jericho is that of simple villagers. There is no suggestion at all of luxury. Gold is at a minimum, a very few mountings of scarabs and so on, though some disappearance of valuable objects may be accounted for by subsequent robbing; the archaeological evidence, however, does not suggest that this was common.[11] It was quite probable that Jericho at this time was something of a backwater, away from the contacts with richer areas provided by the coastal route. It can, however, be reasonably taken as typical of all except the most important towns of the period.

The simplicity of the culture is one important conclusion. The other is the complete absence of any evidence in the tombs of interest in religion. The provision made for the dead is entirely for physical needs and not for needs of the soul. This emphasis is particularly striking in contrast with contemporary Egyptian practice. The objects placed in the Jericho tombs, scarabs, alabasters, faience vessels, and the style of the wooden furniture, show often clear Egyptian influence, but the basic conception of the needs of life after death is utterly different.

Most of the evidence concerning Middle Bronze Age Jericho has survived because the destruction that brought it to an end was followed by a period of abandonment. The ruins of the burnt town were covered by wash-layers in which the burnt material from upper levels was gradually spread down the slope. The latest burials in the tombs were not disturbed by the pushing aside of ancestral remains to make place for the latest member of the family.

The existence of this period of abandonment was not realized at the time of the 1930–6 excavations, largely because evidence concerning the pottery of the later sixteenth–early fifteenth centuries B.C. was lacking, and only became available with the publication of the Megiddo evidence.[12] The erroneous dating of the Beth-shean levels, which associated vessels characteristic of the fourteenth century B.C. with the period of Tuthmosis III (early fifteenth century B.C.), was used to date Jericho levels and tombs, with most unfortunate results. Moreover, the implications of the stratification both on the town site and in the tombs was not understood. It was therefore claimed that both town and tombs showed continuous occupation from the Middle Bronze Age down to c. 1400–1380 B.C. It must be strongly emphasized that the stratification of the town site shows a period of abandonment, and that the complete absence of pottery of the second half of the sixteenth century and of the fifteenth century B.C. makes it clear that the site was abandoned during this period. The presence of scarabs, within this period, such as that of Tuthmosis III, cannot be used as an argument against this evidence, for objects of this nature may well be heirlooms.

Jericho, therefore, was abandoned for a lengthy period after a destruction at the end of the Middle Bronze Age. It is reasonable to infer that this destruction was associated with the disturbances caused by the expulsion of the Hyksos from Egypt, at a date which modern views on chronology tends to put at about 1560 B.C.; the destruction might be caused either by Egyptian retaliatory forays against their Asiatic enemies or by the groups dispersed from Egypt. During the period of abandonment the ruins of the town suffered the depredations of rain and wind, which covered the Middle Bronze Age houses in the low-lying area towards the spring on the east side with entirely characteristic layers of wash. Elsewhere nothing even as late as the Middle Bronze Age survives, but to what extent this was the result of this particular period of abandonment is not clear, for the erosion may have been completed at a later date. It is at any rate clear that it happened before about the eighth–seventh century B.C.

The evidence is equally clear that this does not mark the end of Bronze Age Jericho, and that there was certainly a town for a time in the Late Bronze Age. Proof of this can be adduced in the first place from the tombs. Garstang found five tombs, originally Middle Bronze Age, which were reused for burial in the Late Bronze Age II.[13] A considerable number of burials were made in these tombs, and there are no doubt others not found. The stratification on the town site is equally definite. Above the layer of wash over the Middle Bronze Age houses on the eastern slopes of the mound a portion of a Late Bronze Age house was found in 1954.[14] Very little of it indeed survives immediately beneath the modern surface. Surrounding the surviving area, the modern surface layers had cut into the Late Bronze Age floor, and near-by storm-gulleys filled with Iron Age material had cut well below the level. But this poor remnant showed firm evidence that there had been a Jericho in Late Bronze Age II. Of the defences of the period, which from the Old Testament record should have been those of the town attacked by the Israelites under Joshua, it is quite clear that nothing can survive. The summit of the Middle Bronze Age bank, already described, only survives at one point of the circuit, with the bare foundations of the city wall on top of it. Obviously, the defences of any later period have completely vanished.

The dating evidence for this final Bronze Age stage at Jericho is not very great. In the 1952–8 excavations very little Late Bronze Age pottery was found on the tell. A single juglet lay on the surviving fragment of floor beside a small clay oven. It is of fourteenth- rather than thirteenth-century B.C. type, but cannot be closely dated. In the 1930–6 excavations rather more pottery was found on the tell, and there were more satisfactory groups from the tombs. It would seem that reoccupation took place about the beginning of the fourteenth century B.C., and that the terminal date seems to be somewhat after the middle of that century. It must be admitted that evidence for the close dating of pottery of this period is lacking. It would, however, be reasonable to say that there is nothing characteristic of the thirteenth century B.C.

Current scholarship prefers a date for the Exodus in the thirteenth century B.C. In the view of the writer it is impossible to associate the destruction of Jericho with such a date. The town may have been destroyed by one of the other Hebrew groups, the history of whose infiltrations is, as generally recognized, complex. Alternatively, the placing at Jericho of a dramatic siege and capture may be an aeteological explanation of a ruined city. Archaeology cannot provide the answer.

A question that many visitors to the site ask is why lengthy periods of abandonment occur, as the excavations have shown very clearly, at a site which, as again excavations have shown, was so extremely favourable for a settlement. One of those periods of abandonment is that between the destruction of the Late Bronze

Age town and its reoccupation hundreds of years later. The answer is that more than nature was required to enable the land round the spring of 'Ain es-Sultân to support the population of a town. The flourishing oasis of Jericho today is dependent on irrigation, and all the evidence points to the fact that the ancient settlements similarly had an irrigation system. When a violent destruction interrupted the maintenance of the irrigation channels, the extremes of the Jericho climate would within a year or so cut back the oasis to the immediate vicinity of the spring, as photographs taken during the Turkish period show. Automatically the area ceased to be able to support a town.

The Old Testament record states that Jericho was abandoned from the period of the entry of the Israelites until the time of Hiel the Beth-elite (1 Kings xvi. 34), who can be assigned to the period of Ahab. Excavations on the tell have produced little evidence of such a ninth-century B.C. occupation, though one tomb[15] provides some evidence for this period. It was only in the seventh century B.C. that there is evidence of sufficiently large-scale occupation to suggest that Jericho once more had become a town. This town came to an end at the time of the Babylonian destruction at the beginning of the sixth century B.C., and was the last town on the ancient site. Herodian and Roman Jericho was a mile to the south and dependent on the waters of the Wadi Qelt. Arab, Crusader, Medieval, and Turkish Jericho returned to the waters of 'Ain es-Sultân, but were situated a mile to the south-east of the ancient site. Modern Jericho has its centre here, but has spread up to the foot of Tell es-Sultân.

KATHLEEN M. KENYON

NOTES

1. *Underground Jerusalem*, 1876, p. 195.

2. Work has still to be completed to establish the date of the earliest walls; they certainly do not belong to the very beginning of the Early Bronze Age. For the terminal date, I am in disagreement with the editorial chronology in placing the end of the Early Bronze Age as late as *c.* 2100 B.C.

3. A terminology preferable to Middle Bronze Age 1 of the editorial chronology.

4. See K. M. Kenyon, *Archaeology in the Holy Land*, 2nd ed., 1965, p. 97; *Jericho I*, 1960, pp. 4–10, *II*, pp. 4–6.
5. *C.A.H.* i, ch. xxi, § iv.
6. K. M. Kenyon, *Amorites and Canaanites* (Schweich Lectures 1963), 1966, pp. 36 ff.
7. Ibid., pp. 54 ff.
8. Ibid., pp. 65 ff.
9. For details, see *seriatim Jericho I* and *II*.
10. *Jericho II*, Appendix D.
11. Ibid., pp. 578 f.
12. P. L. O. Guy and R. M. Engberg, *Megiddo Tombs* (O.I.P. 33, 1938); G. Loud, *Megiddo II: Seasons of 1935–1939* (O.I.P. 62, 1948).
13. The reason why the use of these tombs cannot be interpreted as a continuous process is discussed in *P.E.Q.*, 1951, pp. 114 ff., and in K. M. Kenyon, *Digging up Jericho*, 1957, pp. 234 f.
14. Ibid., p. 261.
15. *Jericho II*, pp. 482–9.

BIBLIOGRAPHY

GARSTANG, J. *Annals of Archaeology and Anthropology* (University of Liverpool), xix, 1932, pp. 3 ff., xx, 1933, pp. 3 ff., xxi, 1934, pp. 99 ff., xxii, 1935, pp. 143 ff.
—— and GARSTANG, J. B. E. *The Story of Jericho*, 1948.
KENYON, K. M. *P.E.Q.* 1952, pp. 62 ff.; 1953, pp. 81 ff.; 1954, pp. 45 ff.; 1955, pp. 108 ff.; 1956, pp. 67 ff.; 1957, pp. 101 ff.
—— *Digging up Jericho*, 1957.
—— *Excavations at Jericho*, i, 1960, ii, 1965.
SELLIN, E., and WATZINGER, C. *Jericho*, 1913.

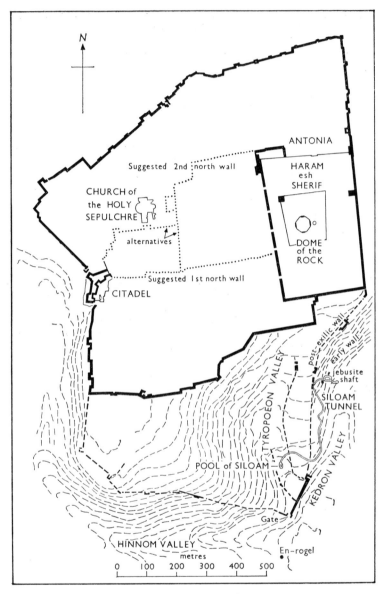

FIG. 7. Map of Jerusalem

JERUSALEM

'B Y far the most famous city of the ancient east'—so was Jerusalem extolled by the elder Pliny (*longe clarissmaa urbium orientis—Hist. Nat. v. 15*). In the mosaic map in the floor of the sixth-century church at Madeba—as in other Christian maps of ancient times—Jerusalem is the centre of the world. It was, and is, the most sacred city to Jew and Christian and almost as high in veneration to the Muslim. Unlike most other ancient sites there is still today a Jerusalem, even though on at least two occasions the city has been demolished and left desolate. After falling, it has risen again on the ruins of former days, quite literally. Partial destructions and local rebuildings have alternated continually throughout the thousands of years of occupation on this site down to the present day, but owing to the continuity of settlement there has never been any doubt about the identification of Jerusalem.[1]

The name first occurs as Urusalim in the Tell el-Amarna letters, then as Urisalimmu in the Assyrian records of Sennacherib in an historical context, though it is found as early as the nineteenth–eighteenth centuries B.C. in the Egyptian Execration Texts.[2] These forms are almost identical with the Hebrew and Aramaic *yᵉrûšālaim* and *yᵉrûšālēm*, and they have the same meaning—'the foundation of (the god) Salem (Prosperer)'.[3]

In addition to the form Beth-Shalem also found in the Tell el-Amarna letters, there is the abbreviation Salem (Hebrew *šālēm*) in Gen. xiv. 18 and Ps. lxxvi. 3 (R.V. 2). The land of Moriah (Gen. xxii. 2) is equated with Jerusalem under the name Mount Moriah in 2 Chron. iii. 1; and it is designated by the cryptic term Ariel in Isa. xxix. 1 f. There is perhaps the possibility that Bezek (Judges i. 4) refers to Jerusalem—if that is so, then its king, no doubt with propagandist exaggeration, claims overlordship over seventy other city states (Judges i. 5–8). At least part of the settlement was called (Stronghold of) Zion and City of David (2 Sam. v. 7, etc.), and the Roman city, built by Hadrian in A.D. 135 to replace the one destroyed so completely by Titus sixty-five years previously, for a time bore the name Aelia Capitolina.

How important was Jerusalem in ancient times? The site certainly lies almost athwart the north–south route along the backbone of Palestine. From west to east the fairly gradual slope up from the Mediterranean sea to the watershed then makes an abrupt plunge down to the Jordan rift valley, so that, according to some authorities,[4] at least for east–west traffic Jerusalem is not well placed. But although there are good approaches from the west to Hebron and to Bethlehem, from both one must then come north to Jerusalem in order to pass around the Dead Sea; the most direct route from the west to Jericho and the east, however, runs some ten or twelve miles north of Jerusalem itself, past Michmash, Beth-el, and Ai.[5]

The reason for choosing this site for settlement may, therefore, have been primarily defensive. The location of the earliest city was on a narrow spur of limestone jutting south-east from a cluster of somewhat higher hills, so limiting the defence works necessary to a wall across the comparatively narrow northern neck of the spur to hinder attack from higher ground, and to some means of safeguarding the natural water-supply bubbling out half-way along the foot of the spur on its south-eastern flank and anciently known as Gihon (1 Kings i. 33). Only one other spring or well in the vicinity of Jerusalem is known, and that is down on the floor of the Wadi en-Nâr which unites the three valleys of Jerusalem and drains them to the Dead Sea; its name was En-rogel (2 Sam. xvii. 17). The modern names of these supplies are respectively Umm ed-Daraǧ ('Mother of Steps'—a reference to the present means of access) or The Virgin's Fountain for the former, and Bir Ayyub ('Job's Well'—after a Muslim legend) for the latter. Two spurs of land were in course of time occupied, an eastern and a western.

The eastern spur or ridge rises sharply from the Kidron ravine (2 Sam. xv. 23, etc.), also called the Valley of Jehoshaphat (Joel iv. 2, R.V. iii. 2), on the east, and the central valley, called by Josephus the Tyropoeon ('Cheese-makers') Valley on its west— the ancient name of this valley has been lost. In early times it was deep and steep sided but is now largely filled in by up to sixty feet or more of debris. Between this central valley and the Valley of (the Sons of) Hinnom (Joshua xv. 8, etc.) rises the western spur, much broader and considerably higher than the eastern but not so easy to defend from the north, and without a natural water-supply. A glance at a contoured map shows the two spurs forming together a shape like a lobster claw, the eastern ridge representing the thinner, movable, member.

The area enclosed by the medieval Turkish walls of the present-day Old City corresponds roughly to the Byzantine city and to the Roman Aelia Capitolina, but only the southern portion of this area can ever have been part of Old Testament Jerusalem, whose centre was on the eastern ridge southward of the temple area, the present Haram esh-Sherif. The cramped nature of the site (8 or 9 acres only), and the steep fall on every side but the north, made it easy to defend and, in the days of bow-shot range, its inferiority in height compared with the surrounding hills was not such an insuperable drawback as it has appeared to Josephus and some others who have been responsible for transferring the name Mount Zion and even City of David to the present guide-book site on the knoll at the south end of the western ridge, whose tip shows no sign of occupation before New Testament times; whereas city walls going back to the Middle Bronze Age (*c*. 1800 B.C.) have been located on the eastern ridge[6]—most often referred to as Ophel, though there are grounds for restricting this name in strict accuracy to a slight eminence protruding into the Kidron ravine slightly south of the temple area.[7]

Christian pilgrims from the West have shown interest in, and recorded reputed remains of, Biblical Jerusalem ever since the days of Constantine; but systematic archaeological investigation in Palestine is scarcely more than a century old and has, more often than in most places, suffered bedevilment from the non-coincidence of opportunity and ability. Two individuals, an American theological college professor, Edward Robinson (1794–1863), and a German architect working in Jerusalem, Conrad Schick (1822–1901), did a great deal of valuable, mostly individual, investigation and remarkably scientific recording; but they were not primarily archaeologists. It was the Palestine Exploration Fund, inaugurated in 1865, which gave the great impetus to systematic archaeological investigation by its encouragement and employment of such notable explorers as Charles Wilson, whose ordnance survey of the city dates from 1864, and two army engineers, Charles Warren and C. R. Conder, who took up the same work, three folio volumes of their researches being published in 1865.[8] Other books dealing with the work of these men in excavating Jerusalem during the years 1867–70 and later were published between 1871 and 1884. They are still of fundamental importance.

In 1877 the Deutsche Verein zur Erforschung Palästinas was founded, and in 1881 Herman Guthe conducted investigations for this German society on the south-east hill, whose importance for the early history of the city was beginning to be realized. A more satisfactory and much more extensive series of campaigns was thereafter undertaken for the Palestine Exploration Fund by the American F. J. Bliss from 1894–7, with the help of A. C. Dickie for two years to draw up the plans.[9] But archaeological methods were still far from perfect, and the determination of the age of discoveries—particularly walls—was often little more than guess-work, owing to comparative neglect of the new science, developed by Flinders Petrie, mainly in Egypt, of dating buildings and levels of occupation from the type of pottery found associated with them. The outdated tunnelling or burrowing methods forced on Charles Warren by the circumstances of his day had also far too long a life under his successors, with the sad consequence that in some cases all the evidence for an accurate dating by more modern techniques has been destroyed for ever.

Discoveries made by Bliss and Dickie include remains of defensive walls around the southern edge of the western ridge and across the mouth of the central valley, in addition to numerous traces of streets and of ancient waterworks.

It would be needless to mention the 1909–11 borings and tunnellings on Ophel by Montague Parker under the guidance of a Scandinavian crystal-gazer but for the fortunate liaison with the local École Biblique et Archéologique de St. Étienne whose brilliant and experienced archaeologist L. Hugues Vincent was allowed to study and record the data unearthed in this fantastic scrabble for the hypothetical lost treasure of Herod's temple—or maybe it was that of Solomon! Vincent published the results of his researches in 1911[10] and, amongst other work, gave a competent treatment of the complex water channels dug by the ancient inhabitants to utilize the waters of the Gihon spring. These researches and the results of other investigations carried out by himself and by others are brought together in the massively erudite book published by him at the very end of his long life, with the assistance of A. M. Steve,[11] which, though inevitably suffering in some places from theories which should have been discarded in the light of recent research, remains, with the work of J. Simons, already referred to, the most comprehensive synthesis of the archaeological, topographical, and historical investigations of Old Testament Jerusalem published to date, though both will inevitably be outdated and need correction in places by the results of subsequent expeditions.[12]

Vincent's work on the water system in 1911 was extended by the French army captain Raymond Weill who shed further light on the mutual relationship of these water channels as the result of a campaign in 1913–14 and again in 1923–4. He published the results separately, in 1920 and in 1947, but both volumes bear the same title.[13] His main aim was to find the tombs of David and his successors. He found a number of tombs at the southern apex of Ophel, which may indeed be remains of the royal necropolis, but the depredations of Roman stone quarriers make identification hazardous.

In 1923–4 the Palestine Exploration Fund again launched a campaign in Jerusalem under the leadership of R. A. S. Macalister, assisted by J. Garrow Duncan. They excavated an area near the north central section of Ophel, on the eastern edge, nearly above Gihon. About 400 feet of defensive walls were uncovered here but, owing to neglect of pottery dating, a massive tower and ramp crowning the ridge were assigned to David and the Jebusites instead of to the Maccabees and Herod.[14] The expedition did, however, also discover walls and a gulley, partly artificial, running across the northern end of the south-eastern hill which are much older and may mark the northern limits of the city in the time of David (see below, p. 286).

After the days of Warren comparatively little attention had been directed towards the seemingly shallow central or Tyropoeon valley. In 1927 J. W. Crowfoot and G. M. FitzGerald began to open a trench across this valley from east to west on behalf of the Palestine Exploration Fund and the recently established British School of Archaeology in Jerusalem. Excavation soon showed that, although there was only a slight rise in the occupation level on the top of the ridge, even since David's time, the present shallowness of the central valley was due to the accumulation over the ages of up to 60 feet of debris. The original valley in fact continues under the south-western corner of the Haram area, right across the present walled city and out at about the Damascus Gate. Crowfoot was fortunate in finding within his area of excavation a massive gateway opening from Ophel on to the central valley at a point almost opposite to the Maccabaean tower overlooking Gihon on the other, eastern, side. Crowfoot's gate also had clearly been in use in the Maccabaean period, but there was no positive evidence to show how early a gate had existed there. There is no proof, therefore, that this was the line of the western wall of the Israelite city or, if it were, that there was a gate here then,[15] but it seems quite likely.

The technically most up-to-date excavations in Jerusalem on a large scale are the series commenced in 1961 for the British School of Archaeology in Jerusalem by Kathleen M. Kenyon, with R. de Vaux for the École Biblique et Archéologique de St. Étienne, and A. D. Tushingham for the Royal Ontario Museum. The annual series of campaigns is planned to finish in 1967 but, although important new discoveries and corrections of old deductions have already been published[16], the full results will inevitably not be available for some time after the excavating itself has been concluded.[17]

Long before history proper begins, there were men in and around Jerusalem, where their flint arrow-heads and scrapers have been found. Some, who lived in a cave under Mount Zion,[18] have left there their kitchen pots of Early Bronze Age I.[19]

Occupation, at least of the site, in the third millennium B.C.[20] gives a very respectable antiquity to a city which was, therefore, already old when, as we are told in Gen. xiv. 18, the patriarch Abraham was visited by and paid a tithe to Melchizedek, king of Salem. We cannot prove by archaeology that this event happened, or that Salem was in fact Jerusalem, but as a place-name it is a quite natural abbreviation and is used as such in Ps. lxxvi. 3 (R.V. 2); also ṣedeḳ is found elsewhere as an element of royal names in Jerusalem (cf. Joshua x. i). Jerusalem in those days seems to have been an Amorite city (cf. Joshua x. 5).[21] The Amorites were a nomadic Semitic people who apparently settled down in Palestine to found the prosperous towns of the Middle Bronze Age II, after bringing the Early Bronze Age to an abrupt end by conquest and

PLATE XII

a. Walled Jerusalem. The trench down Ophel's steep eastern flank revealed in 1962 early city walls a little above the spring Gihon (under smaller flat roof, bottom centre). The Tyropoeon lies behind the houses of Ophel's flat crest; its original continuation up under present city wall is marked by dip in skyline

b. Corner of Jebusite/Davidic wall (centre) of Jerusalem. Wall on upper right, seventh century B.C.

continuing their non-urban mode of life for the two centuries designated MB I.[22]

The Kenyon excavations of 1961 and following years discovered the town wall of MB II (c. 1800 B.C.) on the steep eastern slope of Ophel, some 160 feet down from the crest of the ridge (Pl. XIIa). One reason for having the wall so low on the slope was to safeguard the perennial water-supply from the spring Gihon at the foot of the slope. The spring itself was too far down the hill to be included within the city walls, but the water was led back under the hill by means of a horizontal tunnel behind the spring, and then tapped by a vertical shaft at the end of a curiously erratic passage whose entrance was within the city wall—the famous shaft discovered by Warren in 1867 and more fully surveyed for the Parker mission in 1909–11 by Vincent, who witnessed the successful attempt of a daring young member of the mission to climb up this shaft with the assistance of a Welsh miner.[23] This exploit was undertaken to prove that this could have been how Joab pierced the city's defences, as so enigmatically recorded in 2 Sam. v. 6 ff. and 1 Chron. xi. 4 ff.; which was a theory accepted by many commentators even when the mouth of the shaft was still thought to be outside the city wall! (But see below, p. 286.) That this tunnel and shaft already existed before the capture of Jerusalem by David is certain, and the MB II wall already mentioned served for him and his successors until superseded by its seventh century B.C. replacement slightly higher up the slope.[24]

Several other schemes for the protection or more efficient utilization of the waters of Gihon can still be traced. What is perhaps the earliest of all, a short 5-feet-deep trench leading the water of the spring straight out into a natural rock basin, lost its function when the dam was built across its inner end to back up the water into the tunnel leading back under Warren's shaft. This dam would also have been necessary to send the water along two canals running mainly along the surface of the slope, which have been traced for some distance southwards, the lower of the two for about 175 feet, at which point it directed its waters down the slope. Canal II ran all the way along the eastern slope from the spring, through a tunnel bored through the southern apex of the ridge and into the old reservoir now called Birket el-Hamra, which has become a flourishing orchard. This was clearly an irrigation canal, for water could be drawn off through small apertures in its outer wall and thus irrigate the gardens in the valley below. This canal, and a link between it and Hezekiah's tunnel (see below), were blocked up during the late monarchy, judging by pottery found there, and the occasion may have been the Assyrian emergency when Hezekiah 'stopped all the fountains, and the brook that flowed through the midst of the land' (2 Chron. xxxii. 4),[25] because in the reign of his father Ahaz the prophet Isaiah is thought to be referring to this canal and its slow-moving irrigation water when he complains that 'this people hath refused the waters of Shiloah that go softly' (Isa. viii. 6). Just how old these canals are we do not know. Canal I must be older than Hezekiah, and on the basis of Eccles. ii. 6 it has been suggested that it is even as early as Solomon.[26] Presumably Canal II could have been built by Hezekiah to replace Canal I, though the piece of hydraulic engineering especially associated with his name and referred to twice in the Old Testament (2 Kings xx. 20; 2 Chron. xxxii. 30; and, most explicitly, in Ecclus. xlviii. 17) is the tunnel which today bears his name and still conducts the waters of Gihon through to the west side of Ophel. Hezekiah's engineers began from each end, utilizing much of the early tunnel which fed Warren's shaft, but no one has been able yet to explain satisfactorily the curious S-course taken by the tunnel, which meant digging out over 1,700 feet of rock instead of the 1,000 feet or so along the direct line.[27]

However, the workers were so proud of their achievement that they prepared a smooth surface on the side of the tunnel some 20 feet in from the tunnel exit, to record their feat,[28] but only the lower half of the inscription was ever cut, beginning apparently in the middle of a sentence.[29]

The purpose of the tunnel is obvious—to keep the water from the besieger and make it safely available to the besieged—but at present the line of the defence wall on the west is not known. A wall across the open end of the central valley would make sense only if it continued and enclosed the south-western hill but, as we have said above (p. 279), no signs of occupation earlier than the time of Herod Agrippa have been found there. Consequently Kathleen M. Kenyon has suggested[30] that the pool of Siloam into which Hezekiah's tunnel debouched was originally a very large underground rock-cut reservoir whose roof at some period has caved in. The scarp from which the rock must have split has clearly been artificially trimmed, for half the overflow channel can still be seen, undercutting the foot of the scarp, showing that originally it was bored through solid rock.[31] This may solve one mystery, but another turned up almost simultaneously. Some 24 feet beneath the road level at the mouth of the central valley was found a complex of Iron Age II tunnels apparently about on the level of the bottom of Birket el-Hamra but, apart from being clearly intended to carry water, their precise purpose may never be discovered, not even if the Iron Age II dam across the mouth of the valley can at some time be excavated—its approximate position is now known, since the massive Herodian dam and the earlier Hellenistic one behind it are both based on Iron Age II material which must have been kept *in situ* by an Iron Age II dam lower down the valley, possibly seen by Bliss but by no one since.[32] But it would seem that this dam, like the later ones, did not form part of the city's defences.

The advisability of treating the whole complex of water systems based upon Gihon as a whole has caused a break in our chronological treatment. Some centuries before David—during the fourteenth century B.C.—we know from correspondence discovered in the colonial office archives of Tutankhamun's father-in-law Akhenaten at Tell el-Amarna that the ruler of Jerusalem was called Abdi-ḥiba. Maybe it was he who so badly needed more room that he built houses even on the steep eastern slopes of Ophel, so extending the area of habitation by a strip as much as 55 feet wide.[33] Remains of the occupation terraces have often been reported as defence works by earlier investigators. David, or his immediate successors, seems to have had to rebuild these terraces. A very massive supporting wall, probably Davidic, was discovered on this slope in 1964 and is a good contender for the title of 'Millo' ('Fill'), which, we are told, was the outermost part of the city repaired by David (2 Sam. v. 9; 1 Chron. xi. 8). Apparently the work again had to be renewed by Solomon (1 Kings ix. 15, 24, xi. 27) and by Hezekiah (2 Chron. xxxii. 5). The Kenyon excavations have revealed clear evidence of the frequent rebuildings made necessary on these slopes after the havoc wrought by the winter rains and, maybe, also by the occasional earth tremor.

The northern defences of the ancient city must have depended entirely on artificial constructions, and the line of this wall seems now to have been found, running across the neck of Ophel from east to west[34] (see also above, p. 281). Whether the wall actually found in 1962 was Jebusite (LB) like the lowest deposits to the south, that is, behind it, or early Israelite (Iron Age I) is not clear, but, at least, it seems to have continued as the northern limit of habitation until the ninth century B.C., and the whole of the present-day walled city, including the Haram or temple area, was therefore outside and to the north of the city of David—a city which was almost certainly coterminous with that of the Jebusites whom David conquered.

In passing, we may note that there is no archaeological or extra-biblical evidence for the name Jebus applied to Jerusalem in two passages (Judges xix. 10f; 1 Chron. xi. 4f.). It was so designated apparently to distinguish in the story between pre-Israelite and Israelite occupation—especially where the inhabitants are guilty of 'Canaanite' crimes. It very possibly had no real currency, but was simply coined from the name of the tribe called Jebusites who lived there (Joshua xviii. 28).

Once David had conquered Jerusalem we hear no more of Jebus and little of the Jebusites; the new king named the stronghold he had captured the City of David. Whether the two passages (2 Sam. v. 6–9; 1 Chron. xi. 4–8), which together record all we know of the conquest, will ever be satisfactorily made to elucidate the method of capture is doubtful. The key word *ṣinnôr* (2 Sam. v. 8) rendered 'watercourse' (R.V.) or 'watershaft' (R.S.V.)—found elsewhere only in Ps. xlii. 8 (R.V. 7) and there translated as 'waterspouts' (A.V., R.V., 'cataracts' R.S.V.)—would probably refer more naturally to a wash-out or floodwater gulley than to Warren's shaft mentioned earlier (p. 283), and accepted by many as the surprise route exploited by the agile and daring Joab. Simons[35] distinguishes between Stronghold of Zion which became City of David, the name for the fortified south-eastern ridge, on the one hand, and Jerusalem, a term of wider significance, inclusive of unwalled suburbs, on the other. Though fourth-century Christian tradition has transferred the name Mount Zion to the south-west hill, just as an earlier age, in Israel, had transferred it to the temple area, there is little doubt that this name, particularly in the form Stronghold of Zion (2 Sam. v. 7) originally referred to the south-eastern ridge 'Ophel' in the broader sense (see above, p. 279), the site of the Jebusite and subsequent Davidic occupation. The difficulty in the way of discovering buildings to prove this on the south-east ridge lies in the shallowness of deposits over most of the hill, unwanted debris having been pushed over the edge, and good building material reused. The location of David's palace (2 Sam. v. 11; 1 Chron. xiv. 1), if we may accept that the house of David in Neh. xii. 37 refers to it and not to his mausoleum, lay somewhere near the southern apex of Ophel, whereas 'the upper house of the king' (Neh. iii. 25) would appear to lie at the other, northern end of the ridge. We are never told that this latter was Davidic, and it was more probably the palace originally built by Solomon as part of his extensive complex of royal edifices (1 Kings iii. 1, vii. 1, 8) in this quarter. Some very well-cut blocks and a proto-Ionic pilaster capital typical of Israel's most prosperous period have been found tumbled below the crest of the ridge above Gihon and show that a very important building of the period of the monarchy once stood on the ridge hereabouts.[36] A massive casemate wall of approximately Solomon's time has been uncovered along the eastern crest of the ridge, running south from the northern boundary of the Davidic city, and it may well have formed part of an acropolis or royal quarter—the city wall itself at this period would be lower down the slope by the testimony of the portion uncovered above Gihon.[37]

Another link with the Davidic period is the possible site of the royal necropolis at the south end of Ophel. Several rock-cut 'tombs' were discovered by Weill here, which is where we would expect the royal necropolis to be, if it were near 'the stairs that go down from the city of David' (Neh. iii. 15 and see below, pp. 291f.); here David and his twelve immediate successors were buried 'in the city of David' (1 Kings ii. 10, etc.). But the area has been used as a quarry by Roman stone-cutters, and even the remaining tombs are badly mutilated, making definite identification of any one as a tomb quite impossible. King Uzziah's bones at some period were removed from his tomb—which was not within the royal cemetery (2 Chron. xxvi. 23, as against 2 Kings xv. 7)—and placed in an ossuary, the plaque from which, bearing the inscription 'Hither were brought the bones of Uzziah, king of Judah. Not to be opened!', somehow found a home in a Russian museum on the

Mount of Olives.[38] No king after Ahaz is recorded as having been buried in the city of David; Manasseh and Amon were buried in the 'Garden of Uzza', apparently in the palace grounds and thus very near the temple area (cf. Ezek. xliii. 7 f.). The popular guidebook 'Tomb of David' on the south-west hill has no more basis in history than the location there of Mount Zion. The 'Tombs of the Kings' near St. George's Cathedral are those not of Israelites at all but of the first century A.D. royal house of Adiabene in Lower Armenia. The late Hellenistic 'Tomb of Absalom' in the Kidron valley cannot be the memorial raised by David's son of that name (2 Sam. xviii. 18); nor is it really likely that the name has migrated from across the valley where, on the opposite slope, somewhat to the north of Gihon, a ritual complex of some sort, complete with two stone pillars (maṣṣēḇôṯ)—perhaps memorials (cf. 2 Sam. xviii. 18)—and possibly an altar, has been uncovered, associated with a quantity of pottery dated c. 800 B.C. which had been carefully walled up in a cave alongside.[39] This shrine may more likely have been one of those 'high places of the gates (or, satyrs)' mentioned in the account of Josiah's reform (2 Kings xxiii. 8).

David's son Adonijah planned a coup with a gathering at En-rogel (1 Kings i. 9), which is the perennial well now called Bir Ayyub ('Job's Well'), situated where the convergent Kidron, Tyropoeon, and Hinnom valleys become the Wadi en-Nâr (see p. 278), under half a mile (1 Kings i. 41) from the spring Gihon, where Solomon was hastily anointed in order to forestall his older brother (1 Kings i. 38). At this, Adonijah, fleeing from his feast at the stone Zoheleth (unidentified, in spite of many attempts), seeks sanctuary in the Tabernacle (1 Kings i. 50, cf. ii. 28) which was presumably still inside the City of David (2 Sam. vi. 12, 20) near David's palace (2 Sam. vi. 16). This site was quite distinct from that on which Solomon built the temple (2 Chron. iii. 1) and which had been bought by David with some such end in view (2 Sam. xxiv. 21, 24). From its original use as Araunah's threshing-floor, and from the detail in the story that the plague was stayed before it struck the city itself (2 Sam. xxiv. 16), it is clear that the temple site was outside the Jebusite and Davidic city limits. The obvious site is, therefore, the one on the traditionally indicated hill, which has been almost completely covered with the gigantic podium raised upon it by Herod the Great and later rulers.[40]

Nothing of the hill itself remains visible except the rock summit which gives its name to the Dome of the Rock, and which tradition identifies with Abraham's intended sacrifice of Isaac (Gen. xxii. 9). Owing to the tenacity of tradition regarding sacred spots—even through changes of religion—it is very probable that this rock's sanctity goes back to the days of Solomon, or even David, but if so, it would also be reasonable to suppose that an extension of the city wall to the north to enclose the new temple complex would also have been undertaken by Solomon (1 Kings iii. 1, ix. 15). The Iron Age II occupation levels found to the north of the ancient Jebusite/Davidic north wall (see above, p. 286, Pl. XIIb) support this conclusion; but the exact course of the wall is not yet known; probably the present Haram area extends over and beyond it on north, west, and east. It is very unlikely that Solomon enclosed any of the western ridge. The 'Ophel Wall' discovered by Warren, running along the crest of the Kidron slope from the Davidic city northward towards the temple area, might be part of Solomon's wall, though the discoverer regarded it, probably on insufficient evidence, as pre-Israelite.[41]

What traces of Solomonic and other building operations lie beneath the vast podium of the temple area is unknown; all traces of the Old Testament temple remain invisible. Whatever lingering tradition lies behind the name 'Solomon's Stables' given to a large vaulted cellar in the south-eastern corner of the temple area, there is nothing Solomonic about the present large hall whose floor is in places almost 100 feet above bed-rock.[42]

Traces of a possibly early east to west wall slightly south of modern David Street have been found,[43] and this might be the wall of which Jehoash of Israel demolished 200 yards 'from the gate of Ephraim unto the corner gate' (2 Kings xiv. 13; 2 Chron. xxv. 23), when he took Amaziah of Judah down a peg. If that is so, the Corner Gate may have stood roughly where David Street now begins,[44] though the whole question of the extent of the city to the north-west is not yet adequately answered archaeologically. Some evidence is provided, though, by a rough wall of the Iron Age built on bed-rock some 50 or 60 feet east of the present Turkish city wall;[45] and this could conceivably be on the line from the above Corner Gate to form the western boundary of Jerusalem as expanded under the (later) monarchy. Where this wall turned east again to join up with the old wall of the Davidic city is not yet known, but it did not enclose the lower promontory of the south-western hill as still shown on most plans.

When we come to the reigns of Ahaz and Hezekiah in the eighth century B.C. we have the problem of locating 'the conduit of the upper pool, in the high way of the fuller's field' (Isa. vii. 3, xxxvi. 2 = 2 Kings xviii. 17). In both cases it seems that the site is one on a natural approach route to Jerusalem, but the description also makes it clear that it was adjacent to a good water-supply—which narrows down the available sites considerably. The 'fuller's field' would be where woollen cloth was stretched on frames after being fulled—consolidated and cleansed by being trodden in water with *neṭer* (washing soda) and ashes of the soda plant *bôrît* (Jer. ii. 22; Mal. iii. 2) as detergents.[46] En-rogel (see above, p. 278) is sometimes translated 'Fuller's Well' (a different word here from that used in the passages in Isaiah and Kings), but a site there would not suit the events on either of the occasions mentioned above. The only other source of sufficient water for fulling would be Gihon, conse-quently the Upper Pool is sometimes[47] located at or near the spring head; this is possible, if the conduit led *from* the pool, but scarcely so if it led *to* the pool, as there would then be no point in telling Isaiah to go to the *end* of such a short conduit (Isa. vii. 3); nor would there be much sense in specifying that Isaiah should stand by a conduit if, at that point, it flowed into a pool; either, then, the conduit did not at that time flow into a pool or, if it did, there must have been some particularly noteworthy feature near the lower end of the conduit. The Upper Pool cannot, *ex hypothesi*, have been the Pool of Siloam if that was made by Hezekiah to receive the waters of Gihon via his famous tunnel (Hezekiah was Ahaz's son). But if, *in some form*, the Pool of Siloam antedated Hezekiah, in spite of 2 Kings xx. 20, and this pool were fed by Canal II (see above, pp. 283 f.), then this proto-Pool of Siloam could have been the Upper Pool, and the Lower Pool (Isa. xxii. 9) could then quite easily be the modern Birket el-Hamra nearer the mouth of the central valley, and whose basin was once considerably deeper.[48] If, as has been recently suggested, the Pool of Siloam was originally underground (see above, p. 284), a reference to the conduit, rather than the pool, would be understandable. It would seem, therefore, that the fuller's field should be located near the mouth of the central valley, and then possibly Sennacherib's envoys stood on the lower end of the south-western hill (Isa. xxxvi. 11, 13). Archaeology has not yet solved this problem, nor indeed that of the 'reservoir between the two walls' (Isa. xxii. 11) which is probably in the same region and which Simons identifies with the Birket el-Hamra as he does the 'old pool' (Isa. xxii. 11) mentioned with it.[49] The complex water tunnel (see above, p. 285) leading from one corner of the Birket el-Hamra first south-east, then south-west, and finally south-east again towards the valley, might have something to do with the conduit of Isaiah, as it is definitely of Iron Age II construction.[50] In that event, Birket el-Hamra might be the Upper Pool, and the Lower Pool might lie still undiscovered lower down the valley! Any theorizing at present, however, is highly precarious. Even the location of the 'two walls' is not clear; though presumably the 'gate between the two walls', by which Zedekiah sought to flee from Nebuchadrezzar to Jericho (2 Kings xxv. 4 f. = Jer. lii. 7 f.), refers to the same landmark.[51] These walls could perhaps most easily be thought of as a double protection of some vulnerable sector near the point of the eastern ridge, perhaps just within the mouth of the central valley, or, if the city wall along the Kidron side of the ridge and the one on the central valley slope came together at a somewhat acute angle at the apex of the ridge, that triangle of land might have become known as the area 'between the walls'; or again it might refer to the 'stairs of the city of David' (see below, p. 292) which led to a small postern gate between two walls, according to Weill's reconstruction. In view of the less-accurate methods of interpretation in his day, it is not clear how many of the walls Weill discovered on the Kidron slope of Ophel near the southern end are actually defensive walls and how many housing terraces. Owing to the neglect of ceramic chronology there was always the tendency to pre-date, but Weill may be correct in attributing a cave full of dismembered corpses which he discovered here to the effects of the Assyrian siege of Sennacherib, though Vincent prefers to attribute the mass grave to Nebuchadrezzar's attack.[52] But to return to the question of the 'two walls'. Owing to the non-occupation of the lower part of the south-western hill at this period, they could not, if defensive, have been parallel walls either right across the mouth of the central valley or along each flank of it, as often depicted.

Both Hezekiah and Manasseh are said to have built new city walls (2 Chron. xxxii. 5, xxxiii. 14), but the tracing of these and the various other features mentioned in the Old Testament is more a matter of topographical deduction than of archaeology, except that, as stated above (p. 289), an Iron Age wall has been discovered parallel to but inside the western Turkish wall of the Old City, and this might mark the enclosure of a new city quarter—possibly the *mišneh* where Huldah lived (2 Kings xxii. 14), though the extent and location of this 'second quarter' is a much debated question. A midden deposit of seventh-century B.C. pottery has also been discovered in the same area.[53]

Nehemiah has left us perhaps the most complete topographical description of Old Testament Jerusalem that we have; on a few points archaeology has helped to pinpoint his description. The 'stairs of the city of David' (Neh. xii. 37; cf. iii. 15) have been identified fairly certainly by Weill at the southern apex of the eastern ridge. The staircase was cut in a gulley leading down from the top of the scarp into the valley; it passed through a gap 9 or 10 feet wide and ended in a small gate (see above, p. 291). Weill's reconstruction shows the city wall here as forming an archway over the staircase.[54] Nehemiah alone mentions the staircase, but it is clearly older than Canal II (see above, p. 283) which cuts it; it might therefore be at least Davidic.[55]

On his tour of inspection along the slopes of the Kidron valley Nehemiah saw that the destruction of Jerusalem's walls by Nebuchadrezzar had made progress so impossible that, we are told, he turned back (Neh. ii. 14 f.). Consequently, instead of seeking to rebuild the city wall near the foot of the slope or the collapsed terraces of houses on the slope, as inhabited by the citizens of populous pre-exilic Jerusalem, he ran the line of his wall along the crest of the ridge above.[56] No evidence for a pre-exilic wall along this line has been found, according to modern dating methods, and it has been pointed out that, whereas in most sections of Nehemiah's rebuilding of the defences references are given to gates or towers of the pre-exilic wall, here the references are keyed to private dwelling houses.[57]

For the succeeding centuries scarcely any features can be pointed out until we come to the considerable building activities of the expansionist Maccabees whose period, however, lies beyond our limit. In some ways archaeological investigation in Jerusalem may appear disappointing or meagre in its results, but that is largely because we know so much already that we are working to a very different scale here from elsewhere in Palestine. Furthermore, continuous occupation of the site has its own drawbacks, and though today the attitude of officialdom and citizen may be much more enlightened than in, say, the days of Warren, the winning back of more of those treasures of sacred history still lying thickly below the surface is likely to be a race against time and the building boom.

D. R. AP-THOMAS

NOTES

1. G. A. Smith, *Jerusalem, etc.*, 25th ed., i, 1931, p. 8, n. 2.
2. See L. Koehler and W. Baumgartner, *Lex. in V.T. Libros*, p. 404; A. Alt, *K.S.*, iii, 1959, p. 306; W. F. Albright, *B.A.S.O.R.* 83, 1941, p. 34.
3. For this meaning, see H. S. Nyberg, *A.R.W.* xxxv, 1938, p. 352; S. Krauss, *P.E.Q.*, 1945, p. 25.
4. G. A. Smith, op. cit., p. 14; M. Noth, *The History of Israel*, 2nd ed., 1960, p. 190; *I.D.B.*, ii. 844, § 2.
5. Cf. J. Garstang, *The Foundations of Bible History: Joshua Judges*, 1931, pp. 75 ff.
6. *P.E.Q.*, 1962, pp. 82, 84 f.
7. *J.O.T.*, pp. 64–67.
8. *Notes on the Survey and some of the most remarkable localities and buildings in and about Jerusalem.*
9. *Excavations at Jerusalem, 1894–1897,* 1898.
10. *Underground Jerusalem: Discoveries on the Hill of Ophel,* 1909–11; also published in a French version.
11. *J.A.T.*
12. For the convenience of readers who wish to pursue any point further, references to Simons's book (*J.O.T.*) have been frequently inserted here. He also has a good sketch of the history of Jerusalem excavation with a copious bibliography, pp. 29 ff.
13. *La Cité de David.*
14. *P.E.Q.*, 1962, pp. 79 f.
15. Ibid. 1964, p. 13.
16. See ibid., 1962 ff.
17. Publications of smaller-scale investigations and of incidental discoveries which cannot be noticed here are included in the 'Concise Bibliography of Excavations in Palestine—Jerusalem', *Q.D.A.P.* i, 1932, pp. 163–99, and in P. Thomsen, *Die Palästina-Literatur*, whose later volumes may be consulted for more recent publications, as may *Die Zeitschriftenschau für Bibelwissenschaft und Grenzgebiete*, published

annually, for articles appearing in journals only. There is also the 'Elenchus Bibliographicus' published annually in *Biblica*.

18. J. Garrow Duncan, *Digging up Biblical History*, i, 1931, pp. 14–17.

19. Illustrated in Ruth Amiran, *The Ancient Pottery of Eretz Yisrael*, 1963 (Hebrew), table 11, p. 73, nos. 8, 9, 12, corresponding to nos. 3, 4, 10 in the *Palestine Museum Bulletin*, 3, pl. iv.

20. *P.E.Q.*, 1964, pp. 11 f., 18.

21. Cf. *C.A.H.*, 2nd ed., I, xxi, 1965, §§ v–vii, fasc. 29, pp. 55, 58; but cf. also ibid. II, xxvi (*a*), 1965, § ii, fasc. 31, pp. 8 f.

22. Ibid., fasc. 29, pp. 37 ff.

23. *J.A.T.* iii, p. 632 n.; for a plan and fuller description see *J.O.T.*, pp. 165–8.

24. *P.E.Q.*, 1964, p. 8; cf. 1962, p. 82.

25. *J.O.T.*, pp. 187, 190.

26. *I.D.B.*, ii, p. 849; *J.O.T.*, p. 187.

27. For a plan of the tunnel of Hezekiah and other lesser ones, see *J.O.T.*, p. 174, fig. 23, and on a much larger scale and with much more dimensional detail, *J.A.T.*, pl. lxv.

28. For a translation of the inscription, see *D.O.T.T.*, pp. 210 ff.

29. Scholars have often debated the reason for this but the obvious explanation does not seem to have been mentioned. The whole inscription would naturally be chalked or painted on the space first; the engraver would then, just as obviously, begin with the lowest line, so as not to obscure with the falling dust and chips the letters he still had to carve. Why he did not finish we shall never know; maybe, with the onset of the Assyrian foe (2 Kings xviii. 17), there were more pressing tasks for stonemasons (2 Chron. xxxii. 8).

30. *P.E.Q.*, 1965, p. 15.

31. Ibid. pl. via.

32. Ibid. pp. 15 f.

33. Ibid. 1963, pp. 12 f.

34. Ibid. 1965, p. 12.

35. *J.O.T.*, pp. 243 ff.

36. *P.E.Q.*, 1963, p. 16; cf. W. F. Albright, *The Archaeology of Palestine*, 1960, p. 126; *P.E.Q.*, 1963, pl. viii*b*.

37. Ibid. p. 17.

38. *J.O.T.*, p. 206; W. F. Albright, op. cit., p. 160 and pl. 26.

39. *P.E.Q.*, 1964, p. 9; ibid., 1965, p. 14.

40. See *J.O.T.*, pp. 400, 417, for references to Josephus, especially *Ant.* xv. 398 ff. and *War*, i. 401, v. 189 ff., and to other sources.

41. Ibid., pp. 67, 143.

42. Ibid., pp. 347 f.

43. Ibid., pp. 253–6.

44. Ibid., pp. 231–4.

45. *P.E.Q.*, 1965, pp. 10, 25.

46. C. Singer, *A History of Technology*, i, 1954, p. 260.

47. e.g. *Oxford Bible Atlas*, ed. H. G. May, 1962, pp. 80 f.

48. *P.E.Q.*, 1965, pp. 15 f.
49. *J.O.T.*, pp. 191 f.
50. *P.E.Q.*, 1965, pp. 16 f.
51. *J.O.T.*, pp. 127 f.
52. Ibid., pp. 83 f., 94 f.
53. *P.E.Q.*, 1965, p. 20.
54. *J.O.T.*, pp. 95–98, 104 f.; figs. 10, 13, 14, and pl. xii. 2.
55. Ibid., p. 98.
56. *P.E.Q.*, 1963, pl. vii*b*.
57. Ibid., 1963 p. 15; 1965, p. 12.

BIBLIOGRAPHY

(Works mentioned in the body of the essay are not listed here)

Avi-Yonah, M. (ed.). *Sepher Yerushalayim (The Book of Jerusalem)*, i, 1956.

Parrot, A. *The Temple of Jerusalem*, 1957.

Stafford Wright, J. *The Building of the Second Temple*, 1958.

LACHISH

I N the summer of 1932 James Leslie Starkey secured the interest of Sir Henry Wellcome in his project to excavate at Tell
ed-Duweir, a site which among its other attractions had not
been investigated before. H. Dunscombe Colt also promised support, and further grants were forthcoming from Sir Robert Mond
and Sir Charles Marston. The Wellcome–Colt Archaeological
Research Expedition was in the field by October of that same
year, having obtained the necessary permit from the then Department of Antiquities, Government of Palestine, under British
Mandate. In 1933 Mr. Colt withdrew, and after Sir Henry's death
in 1936 Sir Charles Marston undertook to bear half the costs of the
field-work and his name was included in that of the expedition.

From 1932 to 1938 the Wellcome–Marston Expedition spent
an average of six months in the year at the site under Starkey's
leadership, which came to a tragic end with his murder in January
1938. He was succeeded for the three months which remained of
the season by Lankester Harding, Starkey's colleague for many
years, who was at that time Chief Inspector of Antiquities in
Jordan, and by Charles H. Inge. By then there had been six seasons
in the field without a break, and it was considered essential to
suspend work and concentrate on publication. The Trustees of the
late Sir Henry Wellcome (now the Wellcome Trust) therefore
instructed the members of the expedition then available to write
the reports and to obtain expert help where necessary. No work
was possible between 1940 and 1945, but the task was accomplished
by 1958, despite other delays. Names of assistants in the field and
of contributors to the text are given in the introductions to the four
volumes.[1]

i. Identity of the Site

In 1878 Conder proposed Tell Hesy as the site of Lachish in
preference to Robinson's choice of Umm Lakis, an entirely late
settlement in the plain, which he had visited between 1841–56.[2]
Conder's identification was upheld by Petrie,[3] on the evidence of

Onomasticon, and accepted somewhat guardedly by Bliss, who found a cuneiform tablet on the site mentioning Zimrida, king of Lachish.[4] The identity of Tell Hesy and Lachish remained un-challenged until Albright questioned it in 1929. After proposing Tell ed-Duweir as the site, which lies half-way between Jerusalem and Gaza, he continued:

> The Onomasticon[5] states that Lachish was a village in the seventh mile from Eleutheropolis to the Negeb (Daroma). The general location suits the Biblical references to the place remarkably well. . . . Tell ed-Duweir is easily four times as large as Tell el-Ḥesī, which is altogether too small to represent an important Jewish town like Lachish. Moreover, Tell el-Ḥesī is nearly twice as far away from Beit Djibrin as is allowed by Onomasticon for Lachish. . . .[6]

Further corroboration of this view was supplied by Garstang.[7] Since the excavations of 1932–8, and despite some initial doubts, the identification of Tell ed-Duweir with Lachish is now generally accepted.

ii. *Peoples of the Middle Bronze Age, c. 2100–1550 B.C.*

Though the occupation of the site now known as Tell ed-Duweir goes back at least to the eighth millennium B.C., its interest for readers of the Old Testament begins about 2000 B.C. The nucleus of the first settlement was, as always in Palestine, due to a good water-supply, and for centuries a widely spread troglodytic com-munity lived in cave-dwellings and had apparently no need of communal defence. But about the middle of the third millennium B.C. some threat or catastrophe occurred which caused the popula-tion to abandon that way of life and to congregate within the closer confines of an isolated spur, now raised to double its original height above the valley by the ruins of successive cities built upon it. The caves no longer needed by the living were soon reused for disposal of the dead; the bodies and many offerings were stacked together.

The next major change took place towards the end of the third millennium B.C. at Tell ed-Duweir and at most other sites on the Syro-Palestinian littoral. The dead were buried in single graves and few pots were placed with them, chiefly flat-based jars, beakers, and bowls, partly made on the wheel. The only other

objects with the essential containers of food and drink were an
occasional dagger or javelin. Little is yet known about living conditions on the tell at this time, but it appears to have been deserted,
and no stone buildings have come to light. Recovery from the
catastrophe was especially slow at Tell ed-Duweir, and, so far as
the excavations have shown up to the present, there was no significant reoccupation of the site before the middle of the eighteenth
century B.C.

Soundings on the tell itself were not sufficiently advanced by
1938 to present a full picture of the occupation levels, though it is
clear that the city by about 1750 B.C. was surrounded by a bank or
earthwork, which sloped down to a corresponding fosse or ditch.
Therefore the information which the site can offer about the
patriarchal period between the nineteenth and sixteenth centuries
B.C. comes from tombs, concentrated near the north-west corner
of the tell, but there is no way at present of isolating the patriarchal
group or groups from the other complex ethnic movements of the
Middle Bronze Age in Palestine. Though the Old Testament presents a clear picture of the Abrahamic way of life, its semi-nomadic
character could have left few of the normal traces on which the
archaeologist depends. A careful reading of the texts, however,
may indicate how the incoming tribes compared with or differed
from the settled population, as seen in their burial customs exposed in excavations.

The Middle Bronze Age people of the foothills soon reverted to
burial in cave-tombs, cut in soft limestone, wherever they could
not interfere with full use of agricultural land, but the bodies
were not so crowded in them as they had been at Jericho. The
greater rainfall on the western slopes facing the Mediterranean
had destroyed the perishable goods, and, apart from the pottery
vessels for food and drink and slats of bone from decorated boxes,
little else survived. The pottery shapes had changed once more, the
most striking feature being the extinction of the flat-based water
or beer jar and its replacement by a pear-shaped vessel with two
handles which lay on its side, unless provided with a ring-stand,
suggesting perhaps a change-over to a wine-drinking community.
Personal belongings were confined to short bronze or copper
daggers, no more deadly than a kitchen knife, and a metal pin to
secure the robe worn by both sexes on the left shoulder. We know

that these people were at least semi-literate and in touch with Egypt from the number of scarab-seals which they owned, often set in copper rings, and variously inscribed with hieroglyphic signs and symbols and most intricate designs. Very occasionally the scarab-seal was set in gold or electrum, but otherwise there is no evidence that men or women wore other jewellery of any kind.

Compare this picture with the story of Abraham. He bought the cave of Machpelah from Ephron the Hittite, who dwelt among the children of Heth at Hebron, for a burying-place (Gen. xxiii). In doing so he was following the practice of both elements in that community, or possibly he was adopting it for the first time. To this extent the pictures agree, but Abraham's position must have been exceptional for any period in southern Palestine before the sixteenth century B.C. for the wealth of silver and gold he is said to have possessed. In the same area the bestowal of betrothal presents of ear-(or nose-)rings and bracelets on Rebekah would be ana-chronistic before that period, though it is possible that different customs prevailed in the Upper Mesopotamian city of Nahor (Gen. xxiv. 22), not far east of Harran.[8] In this respect the ornaments of the Abrahamic tribes are in contrast to the lack of personal orna-ments from burials at Lachish and elsewhere during the earlier part of the Middle Bronze Age. The one exception in southern Palestine is to be found during the sixteenth or fifteenth century B.C. at Tell el-'Ajjul, where both gold and silver were plentiful, most cunningly worked into bangles, ear-(or nose-)rings, and into fillets for the hair. Other sites seem to be somewhat deserted over the same period, but the rubbish around the first two build-ings of the Fosse Temple at Lachish contained parts of ear-rings and pendants which can be attributed to that time.[9] Though ear-or nose-rings (Hebrew *nezem*) were accepted in Isaac's day as suitable gifts for an intended bride, his son Jacob called them all in as idolatrous symbols of strange gods and 'hid them under the oak which was by Shechem' (Gen. xxxv. 4).

iii. *A Provincial Capital in the Egyptian Empire*, c. *1550–1200 B.C.*

The northern campaigns of Tuthmosis III in the early fifteenth century B.C. brought stability to Lachish, a higher living standard, and closer relations with Egypt than ever before, as witnessed by scarabs of almost all the kings of the Eighteenth Dynasty. But the contact did not seem to extend to the religious beliefs of the people, and the Fosse Temple continued in use right up to the twelfth century B.C. The three superimposed buildings are especially rewarding for the light they shed on religious rites and practices. The sanctuary was twice rebuilt, each time it was enlarged and extra rooms were added, until it was finally destroyed by fire with the last offerings and the ritual vessels still in position round the shrine.[10] The lowest building of the three was founded on the filled-in fosse surrounding the earthwork near the north-west corner of the city above. It was therefore not the principal cult centre of the city, which would have presumably held a more commanding position, though its growth through more than three centuries confirms its popular appeal and its acceptance by Egyptians, who sent gifts to the shrine.[11] The only possible remains of a tangible object of worship recovered from the last of the three shrines are two ivory fragments, a carefully modelled right hand, and the inlay of an eye, both about three-quarters life-size.[12] It is worth examining the plans and construction of the three buildings and the temple furniture and offerings found in them in relation to Mosaic Law, which was largely a codification of established custom.[13]

The principal feature in each of the three buildings under review was an altar at the south end of the sanctuary. In the first phase the plan was tripartite made wholly of clay or mud, and in the second phase a smaller altar and a bench behind it were built up of small stones. Within the lifetime of the third and last building two further phases of the shrine were observed. In the first, the narrow bench of Structure II became a large white plastered platform built of earth or stone, and in the second an altar of mud bricks was built against the front of the platform or shrine, approached by three steps on the west side (Pl. XIII). The stones used in all three buildings were rough undressed boulders, except for the round column bases. In respect of the undressed stone, the method of construction follows the precepts of the Mosaic Code, though the provision of steps to an altar was prohibited (Exod. xx. 24 ff.). The reason that unhewn stone was specified in building altars seems to have been that iron tools were not to be used in shaping them (Joshua viii. 31; cf. 1 Kings vi. 7). No fragments of iron were found anywhere near the Fosse Temple, though it is unlikely

PLATE XIII

General view of Lachish, looking south-west across third and last building of Fosse Temple. In front of raised platform is a square altar; on right three steps lead to it. A small hearth occupies central position between stone column bases. In foreground one of many rubbish pits around the temple

that iron came into common use at Lachish before the beginning of the eleventh century B.C., when the building was already in ruins.

From the vast number of pottery bowls and other vessels found in and around the temple, there can be no doubt that the deposit of offerings was the main business of the cult. They were laid out in rows on the benches in the sanctuary, often containing animal bones; they were stored in cupboards in the east wall, and dozens lay around the shrine of Structure III. In the ante-room there was a specially large collection of bowls, which could perhaps be bought by those who needed them. There were over a hundred pottery lamps within the precincts, but strangely enough more than half of these came from Structure II or associated pits. Charred spouts on most of these lamps showed that they had been used, though there is nothing in the Mosaic Code to suggest that they fulfilled more than the practical purpose of lighting the sanctuary at eventide.

Unusual vessels which held a special place in the service of the cult were the great bin to the left of the altar, found almost full of animal bones, and the tubular stand to the right of it, on which a bowl with pierced hole in its base had been placed, either for the drink offering or for ablutions (Exod. xxxix. 39, xl. 30 ff.). They belonged to the last building, but other large jars with base missing sunk in the floor of the earliest building probably served a similar purpose. Though the hearths associated with Structures II and III showed signs of burning, they were too small to have been of practical use in preparation of the burnt offering (Lev. i. 3–7). The directions for the meat offering of fine flour (Lev. ii. 1–10) specify that it could be baked in an oven (Hebrew tannûr) or a pan (Hebrew maḥabaṯ) or a frying-pan (Hebrew marḥešeṯ). Ovens were found in the vicinity of the temple, and a flat 'bread-plate' was set up intact against the side of the altar in Structure I.[14] But the most convincing parallel between the cult practices in the Fosse Temple and the ordinances of Mosaic Law is to be found in the bones of the animals brought for sacrifice. They were all very young, and practically all the identifiable bones were metacarpals of the right foreleg of sheep or goat, in fact the right shoulder (Hebrew šôḳ) prescribed as the portion for the priest in the peace-offering (Lev. vii. 32).[15]

Judging from the state of the sanctuary, where no one had cleared the offerings away after the last service, the end came suddenly, and on the mound itself the ground near the chief buildings was littered with broken painted pottery, scraps of gold leaf, and smashed alabaster vases embedded in ash. This wholesale destruction marks the end of the Bronze Age at Lachish and at many other places as well. The date of this important event is not yet established with certainty, but the evidence from Lachish is very similar to the indications from other sites. There was a scarab-seal of Ramesses II (*c.* 1304–1237 B.C.), considered by some to be the Pharaoh of the Oppression, but nothing to commemorate his son Merneptah, whose victory stele specifically refers to Israel as a subjugated people.[16] Yet the city was still in commission forty years later, because a scarab of Ramesses III was picked up in the same area,[17] and it was this king who repulsed the 'Sea Peoples', though he could not prevent the Philistines among them from settling on the Palestinian coastal plain early in the twelfth century B.C.

If the Philistines or their associates were responsible for the destruction of Lachish at a time when the stronghold was still garrisoned by Egyptian troops, it would be basic military tactics to reduce a fortress in their rear. On the other hand, the Egyptians themselves may have burnt it in a punitive raid, or as a result of a scorched-earth policy in the path of the invading northerners, for which there is some literary evidence.[18] Another possibility is more attractive to students of the Old Testament, for whom the date of Joshua is still unsolved. Joshua certainly took Lachish in his first campaign, in which he was opposed by an Amorite confederacy of usually divided city states, led in the face of common danger by the king of Jerusalem. But they were no match for the Israelites, and Japhia, king of Lachish, was slain with four other kings at Makkedah (Joshua x). But unfortunately this solution cannot stand, for the text states categorically that among all the cities which Joshua took 'Israel burned none of them, save Hazor only; that did Joshua burn' (Joshua xi. 13). It is therefore impossible to name the aggressor, and it is unlikely that the date will be narrowed within the margin already achieved on the archaeological evidence, that is to say, some time during the first decades of the twelfth century B.C.

iv. *Joshua–Judges: the Lost Centuries*, c. *1200–900 B.C.*

There is nothing at present to suggest that the Philistines actually settled on the mound at Lachish, though two tombs cut in the counterscarp of the disused fosse contained broken 'slipper-shaped' coffins, associated with the 'Sea Peoples'.[19] But otherwise the lack of all the usual signs of human occupation and the absence on the tell of characteristic decorated pottery is perhaps the most eloquent witness to the virtual desertion of the site for more than a century. Even so, the most striking discovery which may date from the time of David was one isolated tomb chamber, containing two principal burials and burnished pottery in a new style strongly influenced by metal techniques. Confirming the advent of a new step forward in technology, iron knives accompanied the dead man, and a large iron trident lay within the threshold of the tomb, apparently left there after the funeral feast. According to 1 Sam. ii. 13 f. tridents were also used in the preparation of sacrifices, when 'the priest's servant came, while the flesh was in seething, with a fleshhook (Hebrew *mazlēḡ*) of three teeth in his hand; and he struck it into the pan, or kettle, or caldron, or pot; all that the fleshhook brought up the priest took therewith'. Y. Yadin illustrates the Lachish trident in a recent book and quotes his father's opinion that this type of weapon is to be identified with the Hebrew word *ṣinnôr* (R.V. 'watercourse', A.V. 'gutter', 2 Sam. v. 8).[20]

The Old Testament does not refer to Lachish in the reign of David, and he is not known to have fortified places outside his new capital, Jerusalem; indeed, there are few traces of excavated buildings which can be attributed to his reign.[21] However, Yadin considers that casemate walls may have been built in David's time, and he has established that this type of fortification, consisting of a double wall, linked by cross walls, dividing the space between them into small chambers, was employed by Solomon in building the defences of key outposts at Hazor, Megiddo, and Gezer. It is known that these walls at Megiddo were destroyed by Sheshonq (Shishak), king of Egypt, in his campaign dated to the fifth year of Rehoboam (c. 925 B.C.; cf. 1 Kings xiv. 25). Excavations have shown that they were built solid with salients and recesses. The practical reason Yadin gives for this radical change in the methods of fortification is the employment of a powerful battering ram.[22]

v. *Rehoboam–Zedekiah. Kingdom of Judah*, c. *900–600 B.C.*

It appears that Rehoboam was not slow to take preventive action against this new form of attack, for he built fifteen cities for defence in Judah on the division of the kingdom, including Lachish (2 Chron. xi. 5–10), and it is significant that the earliest Iron Age wall so far examined on the site is built on the new plan— a solid brick wall on stone foundations, 6 metres thick.[23] It has only been seen in a trial cut on the west side of the tell and in the area of the city gate, but it seems to have continued in use for two centuries until the destruction of the city by Hezekiah.[24] Within the fortifications, the ruin of the Bronze Age palace was enclosed in a solid block or platform of large stone, the outer face laid in even courses, forming a magnificent structure which survives to a considerable height. The earth and rubble-filled interior possibly illustrates the meaning of the mysterious Hebrew word *millô* such as David built at Jerusalem, for both the Hebrew word and its Assyrian equivalent (*mulū, tamlū*) can be translated 'filling'.[25] The plan of the first block was 32 metres square, agreeing with the architectural system of plans based on the square, practised on a larger scale in the Solomonic buildings of Jerusalem.[26] At a later stage the square was extended to more than twice its previous length.

Between 900–700 B.C. Lachish was one of the largest and most important cities in Judah, where Amaziah thought to find shelter for himself from a conspiracy in Jerusalem, 'but they sent after him to Lachish, and slew him there' (2 Kings xiv. 19). To this period also belongs the curious reference in Micah—'Bind the chariot to the swift steed, O inhabitant of Lachish: she was the beginning of sin to the daughter of Zion; for the transgressions of Israel were found in thee' (i. 13)—but what these were neither the site nor the Old Testament has revealed. The climax of the city's history came in 700 B.C., when, after the capture of the Israelite capital in 722 B.C., Sennacherib came up against the fenced cities of Judah and took them, as a prelude to his intended onslaught on Jerusalem (2 Kings xviii; Isa. xxxvi). The Chronicler adds in parenthesis 'now he was before Lachish and all his power with him' (2 Chron. xxxii. 9). Once more in its long history the city was taken and burnt, and there are many signs of damage and destruction among the houses and around the walls.[27] To the Assyrians also the capture of Lachish was the climax of their campaign commemorated in the royal palace of Nineveh by a series of reliefs; to students of the Old Testament they illustrate as no words could do the bare statement of the Chronicler.[28]

Nevertheless, the city wall of Lachish was soon rebuilt in stone on the stump of the destroyed wall of brick, either early in the seventh century B.C., when the city was controlled by an Assyrian governor,[29] or when Manasseh on his return from captivity renounced the idolatries of his earlier years, built a wall round Ophel, and put captains of war in all the fenced cities of Judah (2 Chron. xxxiii. 11–14). His son Josiah, 'while he was yet young', carried religious reform still further by destroying the sacred groves and breaking the graven images (2 Chron. xxxiv. 3; 2 Kings xxiii. 8). It is therefore likely that the pottery figurines of the mother goddess and other cult models of furniture found in tombs at Lachish and elsewhere belong to the half-century before the accession of Josiah, and they suggest that idolatrous practices had gained ground during the period of Assyrian control.[30] Though the fortifications were renewed, few houses seem to have been built within the wall, where open space may have been needed for troop movements. But up against the ruined east wall of the palace a row of ramshackle rooms provide all that is known so far of life in the city during the seventh century B.C. Though the rooms were small and poorly built, two inscriptions were found in them, one of which had been written on the shoulder of a large jar. It begins with the word *btš'yt* 'in the ninth', which could be explained as an abbreviated form of 'in the ninth year', and a confirmation of the historic date in the ninth year of Zedekiah when Nebuchadrezzar laid final siege to Jerusalem, which led to its fall two years later (2 Kings xxv. 1 f.; Jer. xxxix. 1 f.).

In the burnt guardroom near the city gate eighteen inscribed potsherds had already been recovered in 1936. They were addressed by a subordinate to the governor of the city, and they report on fulfilment of his orders. These Lachish letters, as they are now called, are of paramount importance in providing independent witness to the kind of Hebrew language and script Judaeans were using in the time of Jeremiah, the language being in all essentials identical with the Hebrew of the Old Testament. The epistolary style and the prevalence of proper names familiar from the Old Testament should be studied in detail from the documents themselves and the many studies devoted to them.[31] Ostracon III provides the first occurrence in non-Biblical texts of the Hebrew word for 'prophet' (nāḇî'), and it has opened up much speculation as to his identity.[32]

Ostracon IV supplies the first external evidence for the use of fire signals (Hebrew maś'ēṯ) in ancient Israel, a method of long-distance communication in use at Mari on the Middle Euphrates as early as 2000 B.C. at times of military and political crisis. The last sentence reads: 'And [my lord] will know that we are watching for the signals of Lachish, according to all the signs which my lord hath given, for we cannot see Azekah.' The words reaffirm a link, temporarily suspended for a reason we can only guess, forged between the two cities in the tenth century B.C., when with thirteen others they were fortified by Rehoboam (2 Chron. xi. 5–10). Recording events of the seventh–sixth centuries B.C., the book of Jeremiah sets them apart once more—'When the king of Babylon's army fought against Jerusalem, and against all the cities of Judah that were left, against Lachish and against Azekah; for these alone remained of the cities of Judah as fenced cities' (xxxiv. 7). No doubt both suffered the same fate. There is certainly evidence of two attacks on Lachish closely following each other, the first probably in the ninth year of Zedekiah before Jerusalem was besieged, the second perhaps after the fall of the capital two years later, when the chief buildings were deliberately burnt and the walls broken down (2 Kings xxv. 9 f.).

vi. *Return from Captivity*, c. 600–330 B.C.

The governorship of Gedaliah, left in charge by the Babylonians of the poor and the tillers of the soil, was soon ended by assassination (2 Kings xxv. 25), but even this short period is represented at Lachish by a clay sealing bearing his name and a title 'He who is over the house', reserved for the highest in the land.[33] The city is mentioned yet again with Azekah, when both were resettled on the return from captivity (Neh. xi. 30), but it never regained its former place as one of the chief cities of Judah.

O. TUFNELL

NOTES

1. See the Bibliography.
2. *P.E.F.Q.S.*, 1878, p. 20.
3. W. F. M. Petrie, *Tell el Hesy (Lachish)*, 1891, p. 18.
4. F. J. Bliss, *A Mound of Many Cities*, 1894, p. 139.
5. Eusebius, *Onomastica Sacra* (P. de Lagarde, 1887, p. 274/135, 22).
6. W. F. Albright, *Z.A.W.* vi, 1929, p. 3, n. 2.
7. J. Garstang, *Joshua Judges*, 1931, pp. 172 f.
8. R. de Vaux, *R.B.* lxxii, 1965, p. 10.
9. *Lachish II*, p. 65, pl. xxvi. 1–21.
10. Ibid., pls. vi–vii.
11. Ibid., p. 70, pl. xxxii. 39; p. 75, pl. xiv.
12. Ibid., p. 61, pl. xvi. 7–8.
13. R. de Vaux, op. cit., p. 22.
14. *Lachish II*, pl. iii. 4, pl. liv, 338.
15. Op. cit., pp. 93 f.
16. *D.O.T.T.*, p. 139.
17. *Lachish IV*, p. 97.
18. *A.N.E.T.*, p. 262.
19. *Lachish IV*, pp. 131 f., pls. 45. 3, 46.
20. Y. Yadin, *The Art of Warfare in Biblical Lands*, 1963, p. 268.
21. W. F. Albright, *The Archaeology of Palestine* (Pelican Books), 1954, p. 122.
22. Y. Yadin, op. cit., pp. 287–90.
23. *Lachish III*, pp. 87, 102, pl. 109. The ninth-century wall at Megiddo was also 6 metres wide and of similar construction, Y. Yadin, op. cit., p. 323.
24. *Lachish III*, p. 102; see the layer of burning *c.* 700 B.C. between Levels III and II.
25. Ibid., pp. 52, 80.
26. R. P. S. Hubbard, *P.E.Q.*, 1966, pp. 131 f.; cf. *Lachish III*, p. 79, pl. 110.
27. *Lachish III*, pp. 55 f.
28. *A.N.E.P.*, figs. 371–4.
29. *Lachish III*, p. 41.
30. Ibid., pp. 374 f., pls. 27–32.
31. *D.O.T.T.*, pp. 212–17.
32. See D. Winton Thomas, '*The Prophet*' in the Lachish Ostraca, 1946; 'Again "The Prophet" in the Lachish Ostraca', *Von Ugarit nach Qumran, Festschrift für Otto Eissfeldt* (ed. J. Hempel and L. Rost, 1958), pp. 244–9.
33. *D.O.T.T.*, pp. 223 f.

BIBLIOGRAPHY

THOMAS, D. WINTON. 'Letters from Lachish', *D.O.T.T.*, pp. 212–17.
TORCZYNER, H. *Lachish I (Tell ed-Duweir)*. *The Lachish Letters*, 1938.

TUFNELL, O., INGE, C. H., and HARDING, L. *Lachish II (Tell ed-Duweir).
The Fosse Temple*, 1940.

—— *Lachish III (Tell ed-Duweir). The Iron Age* (vol. i, text, ii plates),
1953.

—— *Lachish IV (Tell ed-Duweir). The Bronze Age* (vol. i, text, ii plates),
1958.

MEGIDDO

MEGIDDO has been described as the most important archaeological site in Palestine, revealing an almost continuous
history of the country from the fourth millennium to the
fourth century B.C. Situated on a low pass in the Carmel range, it
was a great fortress city owing its importance to its strategic position astride the coastal routes from Egypt and the Mediterranean
in the south, to Syria, Phoenicia, and Mesopotamia in the north.
It dominated the plain of Esdraelon.

The summit of the oval-shaped mound generally agreed to be
Megiddo, whose modern name is Tell el-Mutesellim, covers about
13 acres and its slopes another 13 acres. The depth of debris was
about 16·5 metres, in which the excavators differentiated twenty
strata. A good spring, 'Ain el-Kubbi, is adjacent to the site.

Excavations began in 1903, directed by G. Schumacher for the
Deutsche Orient-Gesellschaft, and continued for two years. Many
valuable discoveries were published, but dumps from trench digging were left on the surface, and consequently later single finds
in surface strata cannot be reliably dated. In 1925 the Oriental
Institute of Chicago, under the guidance of J. H. Breasted,
planned a costly excavation, to last five years. It was equipped with
the most modern scientific instruments then available, including
extending ladders and cameras attached to captive balloons, and
its aim was to remove completely each successive stratum.[1] After
a trial dig the whole mound was purchased, and work began on the
eastern slope to prepare ground for dumping an enormous quantity of soil. The excavations were directed by C. S. Fisher (1925–7),
P. L. O. Guy (1927–35), and G. Loud (1935–9).

Four strata were completely removed and part of Stratum V.
But the plan was too ambitious for available finance, and in 1935
a new five-year plan was made. Trial trenches 6 metres wide were
dug in selected areas, three of them being later extended to about
25 × 40 metres; a large area of the lower slopes was also excavated,
and the results arranged in a sequence of stages. The three excavated areas were—AA in the north by the city gate unearthed the

walls of the Strata VIII–VIIA palace and was continued to Stratum XIII, dated about the eighteenth century B.C. BB on the east was enlarged to include the whole of the temple area and then, in a smaller section, went through Stratum XX to bed-rock, *c.* 4000 B.C. CC on the south, after going through successive strata of houses, reached the mud-brick city wall of Strata XIII–XII and was then abandoned. Later both AA and BB were enlarged to link with the original Schumacher trench in DD.

The site was seldom totally destroyed and abandoned, but partial destructions entailed constant rebuilding, so that strata are often difficult to distinguish. This fact, coupled with frequent change of directors and personnel and the long history of the excavations, during which there have been great advances in the knowledge of pottery sequence, have combined to make many of the conclusions reached controversial.

In 1960 Y. Yadin redug the remains of the solid wall by the northern gate to compare wall and gateway with those found at Hazor and Gezer. Records of the excavations have been reconsidered, and conclusions drawn by the excavators modified in the light of discoveries made at other sites, particularly by Kathleen M. Kenyon and G. E. Wright.

i. *Chalcolithic*

The small size of the area (BB) excavated to bed-rock prevents any complete picture of the earliest occupation of Megiddo. A natural cave 3 × 5 metres had been used as a dwelling by a people who had bone and flint tools and weapons but no pottery. They were agriculturalists, using flint sickle teeth, hunters using flint javelin heads; they domesticated animals, as cave drawings show, and used long, slender-shaped bones with a hole pierced at one end, probably for weaving, as at Teleilat Ghassul before 3500 B.C.[2] The lowest stratum (XX) shows movement from caves to surface houses. There was considerable occupation. Mud-brick houses were built on foundations of rubble or long, thin, stone slabs laid on the rock surface, and were probably first circular, then apsidal, and later rectangular. Rock-cut pits were used for storage, and the presence of twin pits connected by a channel suggests olive-oil presses. The pottery, though rough and underfired, is already in a developed form, and there is no sequence to show development

from more primitive manufactures; clearly a people of some skill
have arrived. Stratum XX is earlier than anything found on the
slopes of the tell, and is regarded as Middle Chalcolithic.
There seems to have been no unoccupied period between Strata
XX and XIX, which began *c.* 3200 B.C., and was a thin stratum, but
the village has now been enclosed by a wall, and early planning is
seen in rows of rooms with mud-brick walls on a single paved
area. Evidence now comes also from the slopes, where Stages 7–5
and part of 4 are contemporaneous with this stratum; here tombs
show Megiddo as already a meeting-place, both negroid and
mediterranean types being found. The old Chalcolithic culture
persisted, but the sudden introduction from the north of Esdraelon
ware shows the arrival of newcomers. This ware is grey, burnished,
well fired in closed ovens. It has local characteristics at Megiddo,
which appears to have been a centre from which it spread through
Palestine. It dies out at the end of Stratum XIX and Stage 4 on the
slopes. There is evidence that copper was used in Stage 4, but
bronze appears later at Megiddo than at Teleilat Ghassul. There is
important evidence of religious observance in this period. A rectangular room 4 metres wide and 12 long, before continuing beyond
the excavated area, contained against the long wall opposite the
entrance a rectangular mud-brick altar 0·92 metres high, surfaced
with lime plaster, and approached by a low step. In front of it
were a low mound, perhaps to hold a vessel, and flat stones projecting to the same height from the floor at irregular intervals. The
altar had later been enlarged to 4·1 × 1·6 metres. At the rear of the
shrine a heavy mud-brick defensive wall 3·2 metres thick separated
this area from the rest of the town; the area remained sacred for
about 2,000 years, till the end of Stratum VII. On the stones of
the pavement in front of the shrine—one of the earliest yet found
in Palestine—were scratched excellent drawings of human and
animal figures, similar drawings being found on pottery in Stage 5.
Goats, dogs, and deer are represented, as well as a lyre player. The
excavators had difficulty in differentiating the pottery in these
lowest strata, and accurate dating has not always been possible,
pottery parallel to sherds which at other sites are regarded as
Neolithic, Ghassulian, Chalcolithic, and Esdraelon ware being
confused. But a firm date is established for Stratum XIX because
some pottery fragments bear the impressions of cylinder seals

comparable to those found at Jamdat-Naṣr (Mesopotamia) and
there dated *c.* 3200–2800 B.C. In a field nearby was found a basalt
male figurine, whose analogies are Early Bronze or Neolithic. It is
interesting that this image is male, for later the female pre-
dominates. In a tomb was found a limestone fragment with incised
decoration, possibly part of a female figurine.

ii. *The Early Bronze Age*

A general use of fine red burnished ware, partly wheel-made,
supersedes the grey of Stratum XIX. Strata XVIII–XVI are
called by G. M. Shipton true Early Bronze, and cover the third
millennium B.C. They are contemporaneous with the remaining
Stages (4–1) on the slopes. Objects from Egypt, Syria, and Mesopotamia, as well as a great variety of new forms of pottery, testify to
the presence of traders at Megiddo, and show that the coastal
plain was already a corridor for traffic between Asia and Africa.
A jug of hard, thin ware, well burnished and with red slip, parallel
to 'metallic' ware found at Abydos in the First Dynasty (founded
c. 3100 B.C.), dates Stratum XVIII, as does also comb decoration
on pottery in Stage 4. New influences are also seen in rectangular
houses of mud-brick or stone and storage pits, showing considerable increase in population and advance in urban life. The excavators dated in this stratum the most massive wall found on the site,
calling it a city wall. Originally 4–5 metres wide, it was doubled
and was still standing to a height of 4 metres, partly because in
Strata XVII and XVI it was the retaining wall for a terrace built
out to enlarge the area; the Stratum XVII town was thus more
level, and buildings did not need to follow the contours of the rock.
An impressive structure, partly excavated, was built over the remains of the Stratum XIX 'temple' in the 'sacred area'. At the
highest point of Stratum XVII in this area were the lowest courses
of an oval stone structure, 10 × 8·7 metres in diameter, which had
been destroyed to this level, rebuilt as more circular, 8 metres in
diameter, in Stratum XVI, and continued on the same exact site
through Stratum XIV. Its height above the Stratum XVII oval
base was 1·4 metres. Debris of pottery and animal bones at its base
show it to have been an altar. It is surrounded by a wall with one
narrow opening from a passage leading from the street, and in
Stratum XVII the altar is too close to the wall to allow movement

around it; this is, however, possible in Strata XVI–XIV, where the altar, built of selected stone rubble of one size and type, was approached by a flight of steps. Clearly it was a forerunner of altars on high places condemned by Israel's prophets, and it is of interest that, although the altar conforms to the law of Exod. xx. 25, forbidding the use of hewn stone, it breaks the law of the next verse, forbidding approach by steps. There are no indications of the form of religion practised, no cult objects, with the possible exception of pottery models of chariot wheels, nor were there figurines of deities; but a series of rooms in Strata XVII and XVI east and west of the altar area suggests the growth of religious institutions in the Early Bronze Age. There is close continuity between Strata XVII and XVI. The excavators found them sometimes difficult to distinguish, and it has even been suggested that much of Stratum XVII was really foundations of Stratum XVI.

Megiddo appears to have been exceptional in its burial customs. The early practice here as elsewhere was multiple burials in caves or rock-cut tombs. One such cave, earlier used domestically, contained remains of fourteen bodies and was used through the EB and early IA ages, the two periods being separated by a rock fall and a long period of disuse. The bones were not in order and had either been disturbed or put in as bones, not as bodies. Some bones of the EB deposit were burnt on the upper surface, that is, after being put into their present position, a feature not found elsewhere in this period. Burial chambers at the foot of rock-cut shafts had an unusual form. In one instance a square shaft 2 metres deep with footholes in its side led to three small chambers coated with lime plaster; the chambers had been reused, and again the bones were in disorder. The constructional form of these shaft tombs is not found elsewhere in Palestine, showing building skill and sophistication, suggesting that the historical pattern here is not necessarily the same as at some other cities, which were destroyed by nomadic, non-urban invaders at the close of the EB period. Moreover, in the Megiddo tombs of this period the group of pottery as a whole is unique in Palestine, probably influenced from north-eastern Syria. Some is imported, some is comparable to that dated EB IV at other sites, but, as L. H. Vincent states, the pottery sequence at Megiddo does not appear to be applicable to all Palestine. Wright, following W. F. Albright, dates Strata XVII to XVI in the twenty-eighth to the twenty-sixth centuries B.C., not, as the excavators, 2500–1950 B.C., and states that the city was evidently destroyed and not reoccupied, at least in the area excavated, for some five centuries. He is followed by J. Bright,[3] and more cautiously by J. Gray.[4] This destruction they link with nomadic Amorites. But the excavators do not appear to have noted evidence of a general destruction nor a gap of such length in occupation.

iii. *The Patriarchal Period*

Strata XV–XI cover the MB period, and initiate the 'Canaanite' culture widespread through Phoenicia and Palestine. They are the background of the patriarchal stories in the Old Testament. Stratum XVI had ended in destruction and Stratum XV soon afterwards was built directly on its ruins. A prosperous age began at Megiddo, and its material remains provide the best source in Palestine for the history of this period. The district, though its cultural links were with the north, appears to have been influenced, if not loosely controlled, by Egypt; in Stratum XV was found part of a broken statue of Thuthotep, high priest at Heliopolis in the nineteenth century B.C.[5] There are no inscriptions to indicate language or names of new invaders, but there is considerable evidence to suggest that Megiddo was not left untouched by the various waves of people concerned in the Hyksos movement from north and east, through Syria and Palestine to Egypt. 'Influence from the north, perhaps by a trading medium, but allied to the Hyksos type of culture, was permeating the country in advance of the true Hyksos period'.[6] Such influence is shown in building activity, changes in pottery and burial customs, and in the introduction of bronze toggle-pins and weapons. The new pottery of this MB period, found at Megiddo and elsewhere, is finer than before, entirely wheelmade on a fast wheel, highly burnished with red slip. It is of interest that there is very little evidence of Khirbet Kerak ware, as though the particular ethnic movement from the north, through Syria and Anatolia, which it represented, had spent its force before it reached Megiddo.

It is generally agreed that much disturbance through the whole MB period was caused by the movements of people connected with the Hyksos, and it is natural that methods of burial were not uniform, some tombs being single, some communal. New types of shaft tombs appear. Burials within the occupied area of the tell become much more frequent. Only thirteen tombs belonging to the whole of the MB period have been found on the slopes, but 187 in the occupied areas excavated. In the later part of the period burials were often close to, or under the floors of, houses. Through the whole period jar burials of infants occur. Much care was devoted to furnishing the dead with what was thought necessary, so that their graves yield a rich variety of pottery forms found nowhere else in Palestine at this time, these too showing links with the Hyksos type of culture. Further evidence of Hyksos influence is shown in the fortifications at Megiddo. A well-built city wall is protected at its base outside by a limestone glacis (Stratum XIII) characteristic of Hyksos sites. There is a sloping ramp parallel to the wall leading up to an outer gateway, giving access to a court where there is a right-angled turn towards an inner gateway. The unsettled state of the country is indicated by the fact that in Stratum XII the wall is made twice as thick, and in Stratum XI, while the glacis persists, interior buttresses strengthen the wall.

There was considerable building activity in the sacred area, but the circular altar continued in use through Strata XV and XIV. Most important was the discovery in Stratum XV of three almost identical temples near it. Each temple consisted of a large altar room 9 × 14 metres, whose side walls projected 5 metres to form a porch with a roof supported by columns on strong foundations and with cup depressions near their bases; there was a small side-room for each temple. Their altars differed. One was a large rectangular mud-brick construction, another was a much smaller stone altar approached by four steps. There was no indication of the deity or deities worshipped, nor of different usages of the altars in the three temples and the great circular altar at their rear. The construction of the temples and their roofed porches is comparable to that found in Troy II[7] and in megaron-type houses of the Bronze Age, which also had the arrangement of a large room juxtaposed to a small ante-room.[8] Some scholars argue from the presence of three temples that a triad of deities was worshipped, and refer to a similar possibility at Tell ed-Duweir (Lachish); but possibly one temple was later than the other two, and so, as at Beth-shean and Tell en-Naṣbeh, the two supposedly earlier temples may have been devoted to a god and goddess.

In Stratum XIV only one of the three temples remained, rebuilt on a much smaller scale as though to give access to a priest only; a niche, probably for a figurine, replaced the altar. But the foundations of the fortress temple of Stratum VIII went down into Stratum XIV, and destroyed much of the sacred area. The circular open-air altar was for the first time covered by new buildings in Stratum XIII. In Stratum XI the city is divided into two parts by the temple buildings. At the end of Stratum XI the city seems to have been partially destroyed, but immediately rebuilt, and the same Canaanite culture continues into Stratum X. It lasted till the twelfth century B.C. At the beginning of this long MB period there was evidence of the presence of forerunners of the Hyksos; towards its close, Hurrians and Ḫabiru appear, who were probably ancestors of the Hebrews.

iv. *Canaanite Megiddo* (c. *1550–1150 B.C.*)

The same city plan as was found in Stratum XI continues, showing there was no complete destruction by the Egyptian monarchs of the Eighteenth Dynasty who expelled the Hyksos from Egypt. But the archaeology of Megiddo still reflects unsettled conditions such as are seen in the rest of the country during this Late Bronze period, with evidence of partial destruction, rebuilding at various times, and new fortifications built to meet new dangers. Some rebuilding may have been necessary because earlier work was of poor construction. Material from all four trenches now helps to illuminate the city's history.

The most important discovery of this period at Megiddo is its pottery, from which the chronological sequence of LB pottery in Palestine has been constructed. Other cities such as Jericho and Tell Beit Mirsim lay desolate at times during this period, their cultural sequence being broken, whereas at Megiddo there is evidence of political defeat but not of catastrophic breaks in culture. Much interesting pottery comes from the tell and from tombs, the earliest examples from Stratum X, the most abundant and artistic from Stratum IX, and debased forms from Stratum VIII. Well-made vases, finished in light buff, are decorated in black and red with line patterns enclosing lively figures of birds, animals, and fish, often with the Tree of Life motif. The curious arrangement of creatures round this Tree sometimes suggests that the painter is referring to well-known mythical themes—'the subjects are deeply imbedded in a lore that is seen frequently to supersede all laws of artistic composition'.[9] The Tree seems to be a symbol of nourishment, and in one instance tubes lead from its branches down to the mouths of fish. Later, in IA pottery, the Tree occurs only in a highly stylized form, but the Old Testament shows that cultic use of trees continued (2 Sam. v. 24; 1 Kings vi. 29). The painted pottery at Megiddo has individual characteristics and seems to be the work of an itinerant artist or to come from one workshop, that began in Megiddo c. 1550 B.C., later moving south.[10] The painter and his school were, however, in the mainstream of Near Eastern culture, similar bichrome pottery being widespread from Egypt and Cyprus to Mesopotamia, evidence of big ethnic movements. At Megiddo it does not replace the normal Hyksos pottery but is found with it, suggesting that the people involved were closely concerned in the Hyksos migrations, perhaps a last great wave from the north before the Egyptian conquest of Palestine under the Eighteenth Dynasty. Archaeologists connect the decorative style of this pottery with the Hurrians, who, through the excavations at Nuzi, are shown to be linked with the patriarchal stories.

A similar influence is shown in the sudden appearance at Megiddo of figurines in bronze and pottery, a pottery rattle too heavy for a child's plaything and probably used in ritual dancing (cf. Judges xxi. 21), and pottery shrines and offering stands, indicating a religious revolution introduced from this source. Outstanding is a bronze statuette of the god Resheph, showing Hittite influence. A pottery female figurine without side-locks, Syro-Hittite rather than Egyptian, also suggests a Hurrian element in the Hyksos movements. Possibly Rachel's action over the teraphim (Gen. xxxi. 17–35), together with information about Hurrian laws gathered from Nuzi, may indicate that the teraphim of the story also derive from Hurrian sources. Megiddo yields examples of goddess figures of the usual Astarte type, both of the plaque (Stratum VIII) and of the rounded kind. A pregnant figurine, and the placing of figurines in tombs, are probably to be connected with fertility cults; this applies also to the presence of bronze and pottery bovine figurines. What may be a Babylonian liver model used for divination was assigned to Stratum VII.

In Stratum X a new fortification system included a city-gate, typical of the time, built of carefully fitted hewn stone covering a rubble interior, and containing two chambers formed by pairs of piers projecting from the sides of the entrance passage. It remained in use through Stratum VII. A new group of buildings in a well chosen position near the north gate became a palace, being restored several times before its final destruction at the end of Stratum VIIA. There was undoubtedly dislocation of life as Hyksos domination came to an end and the Hurrian–Ḫabiru invasions, reflected in the Tell el-Amarna letters, took place, but that this rebuilding at Megiddo was normal improvement is shown by the very slight rise in floor level between Strata X and VIIB, whereas the great rise between Strata VIIB and VIIA suggests that Stratum VII is divided by a violent destruction.

There is evidence of general prosperity in Stratum IX, which contains many late Hyksos scarabs and much jewellery. The house plan develops to an arrangement of rooms round an inner courtyard, streets are wider, and there are storage pits. At this time Megiddo was the centre of Canaanite opposition to Egyptian advance, as attested by the lively record on the temple walls at Karnak of the victory of Tuthmosis III,[11] c. 1468 B.C. There is a vivid account of the direct Egyptian approach up the pass from the south, panic-stricken chieftains outside the walls abandoning horses and costly chariots, and being hauled by their garments into the city while the Egyptians loitered to loot the treasure. The seven months' siege was followed by abject surrender, and the huge list of booty— slaves, gold, silver, turquoise, lapis lazuli, and ivory—clearly reveals the wealth and variety of Canaanite culture. Further evidence of this wealth is found in Stratum VIII: 'under the floor of an unimportant room . . . the excavators struck a rich hoard of precious objects. . . . The beauty of some of these articles is quite extraordinary. This hoard is beyond doubt one of the finest collections of artistic objects yet found in Bronze-Age Palestine.'[12] The hoard, revealing the art both of Egypt and Mesopotamia, included gold and lapis lazuli beads, glass scarabs set in gold, an electrum finger ring, a gold bowl and head-band, twin gold heads with disk crowns, stone and gold cosmetic jars, and some ivory, showing Phoenician styles.

Prosperity is seen too in the presence of functional rooms in the enlarged palace, one of them evidently an ablution room paved with sea shells; there are two large stone vessels for washing and a drain leading to a sump. An impressive building which continued in use till the end of Stratum VII was a fortress temple, comparable to the temple of El-berith found at Shechem (Judges ix. 46 ff.). A large rectangular room, $21\frac{1}{2} \times 16\frac{1}{2}$ metres, a single room 11×9 metres with a niche later replaced by a platform or altar opposite the doorway, projecting wings at each end (perhaps a portico), are all of excellent masonry, and the strength of the walls suggests that these may have had a mud-brick upper story; the model pottery shrines also suggest this. There is no inner sanctum. The large main hall would allow all worshippers to be in the presence of the deity.

Possibly related to Stratum VIII is a remarkable discovery[13] made by shepherds in the debris of the American excavations—a cuneiform tablet bearing forty lines of the Gilgamesh epic, the Babylonian story with which the Old Testament account of the Flood shows close contacts.[14] Similar tablets at Tell el-Amarna, contemporary with Stratum VIII, were used in the scribal schools, but it is at least possible that the Gilgamesh story was known in Palestine at this time, and that the invading Israelites learned it from the people of the land. Relationship between Megiddo and the scribal schools is seen in a satirical letter of the time of Ramesses II, testing knowledge by the question 'Let me know the way to pass Megiddo'.[15]

It is known from the Amarna tablets that for some years after the battle of Megiddo the city remained loyal to Egypt and resisted Ḫabiru invaders; a prince of Megiddo, Biridya, tells how he organized forced labour (Hebrew *mas*, as in Gen. xlix. 15) in the plains of Esdraelon.[16] But it may have become involved in the great rebellion of 1293 B.C., and the destruction with which Stratum VIII ends may have been caused by the punitive campaign of Ramesses II. Immediate rebuilding on similar plans without a cultural break followed in Stratum VII. An interesting addition to the palace was a three-roomed basement treasury, where was a collection of ivories, about 200 pieces incised and carved. Some bore hieroglyphic inscriptions: three mention Kerker, woman singer of the god Ptah in the palace of the prince of Ashkelon; another, a pen-case, belonged to a messenger of Ramesses III. A scarab of this monarch was found elsewhere in Stratum VII.

What is probably the earliest piece shows a Hittite king beneath a sun disk; he wears Anatolian dress and is supported by sphinxes. Hittite power in Megiddo was dominant between 1350 and 1300 B.C., so that it is possible that the whole collection may be dated between 1350 and 1150 B.C. Though there are renderings of Egyptian motifs and Assyrian affinities, the bulk of the collection is 'definitely an expression of local art . . . Canaanite Phoenician'.[17] Clearly the Megiddo of Stratum VII held out longer than other cities against the barbarian flood; its end can be dated c. 1150 B.C. by a bronze statue base of Ramesses VI found in the debris.

According to the excavators, the most outstanding achievement of the occupiers of this last fortified Canaanite city of Megiddo, in this disturbed twelfth century B.C., is its new water system, similar to those found in other Palestinian cities, and showing considerable scientific and engineering skill and experience, as well as much social organization of labour. Water must have been earlier available inside the city, which had withstood the siege of Tuthmosis III and the later Ḥabiru attacks, and from earliest times it was available at the foot of the slopes outside. At one source a spring by the use of many generations was deepened to a cave, and continually enlarged, probably by repeated cleaning. Perhaps as early as the fifteenth century B.C.[18] a covered gallery was constructed leading down the slope in the direction of the cave, which was probably protected by a guard. That the method became inadequate is shown by the skeleton of the last guard; this was found lying on a floor which covered debris which cannot be dated earlier than Stratum VII. Soon afterwards a shaft was dug down through the layers of previous cities, and a tunnel pierced from both directions linked the foot of the shaft with the cave. Steps cut round the sides of the shaft enabled water to be fetched in safety. Later this system was modified, by a much less skilled engineer, so that water could be drawn up from a sump at the base. It has been suggested that the instrument used to measure the required depth of the shaft was similar to the levelling device 'found at Thebes in the tomb of the Egyptian architect Sennozem (XIX–XXth dynasty)',[19] which would show that Megiddo was under Egyptian influence at the time, possibly a further connexion with Ramesses VI. There is no evidence to show whether Stratum VII was destroyed by Egyptians, Philistines, or Israelites, but here the fortified Canaanite city ended. The Stratum VI city, poorly built, remained Canaanite, as its pottery and cult objects show, but brooches instead of pins, and an iron knife and dagger, show that a new age has begun. The temple and sacred area have disappeared, but there is clear evidence of fertility worship, the kind of religion condemned by the Old Testament prophets. Elaborate pottery incense- or offering-bowls are fitted into the tops of tall stands with windows at the sides, decorated with lotus leaves and crude mother goddesses. One complete *kernos* ring supports a gazelle head, amphorae, pomegranates, doves, and a cup. Even during this short occupation there was another destruction, and probably the conditions reflected in this stratum are referred to in Judges i. 27 f., where Megiddo is described as remaining Canaanite till Israel grew stronger. The final destruction *c.* 1100 B.C. was accompanied by fierce burning, and the site appears to have lain unoccupied for many years, perhaps the period when caravans ceased, peasantry ceased, and travellers had to keep to the by-ways (Judges v. 6). Deborah's battle with Sisera took place 'in Taanach by the waters of Megiddo' (Judges v. 19), as though the great city no longer existed.

v. *The Israelite Period*

The sudden appearance everywhere in Stratum V of a different pottery, hand-burnished and covered with red wash, together with complete lack of Canaanite ceramic culture, show the settlement of a different people; but no complete change in religion is reflected in cult objects.

The first occupation (Stratum VB), scanty and poorly built, with no fortifications, large buildings, or sacred area, suggests that a peasant people made use of the Canaanite ruins. Only one Philistine sherd was found, and possibly Israelites settled here in the early days of David's reign. Later (Stratum VA) the whole mound was covered by buildings, possibly on a plan like that of other Israelite cities of the period, houses near the edge of the mound arranged radially, with an inner road dividing them from the central part of the city. Fresh digging by Yadin has shown that Strata VA–IVB represent a continuous occupation in the Solomonic period (the same mason's mark had been found in both strata) and an earlier fortified city beneath that containing the stables and

solid wall previously called 'Solomonic'. Yadin discovered, constructed as at Hazor and Gezer (1 Kings ix. 15), a lower casemate
wall, bonded to the magnificent six-chambered gate with two
towers, which had been correctly ascribed by the excavators to
Solomon, and which Albright[20] had compared with the Jerusalem
temple gate of Ezek. xl. 5 ff. He also found at the same level,
partly under the stables, a fine northern fort, containing Solomonic
hand-burnished pottery, and dominating the approach to the city
gate; the excavators had already uncovered a southern fort or
palace, perhaps occupied by Baana (1 Kings iv. 12). At the gate
is a small open courtyard approached by steps and containing
benches. In the Old Testament Solomon is credited with chariot
cities, 1,400 chariots (1 Kings x. 26) and 4,000 stalls for horses
(2 Chron. ix. 25; 1 Kings v. 6, R.V. iv. 26, 40,000); and his trade and
wealth are attested by his purchase of chariots (1 Kings v. 6, R.V.
iv. 26). But Megiddo is not named as a chariot city and his stables
at Megiddo have not yet been found. Much of the sacred area of
this period may have been obliterated by the foundations of the
fortress temple of Stratum IVA, but close to these foundations
were found in Stratum V two impressive buildings, one containing
upright stones, not structural in position, with cupmarks, regarded
as *maṣṣēḇôt* and associated with the worship of the male deity.
A primitive horned limestone altar (Exod. xxvii. 2; 1 Kings ii. 28),
the earliest found at Megiddo, lay in Stratum V beneath the
stables of Stratum IVA. Cult objects were not confined to the
sacred area, but were found in most rooms, suggesting household
shrines (Judges xvii. 4). A bronze stand showing Syro-Hittite influence has on each side a worshipper before a deity, and may be
compared with the bronze stands in Solomon's temple (1 Kings vii.
27-37). There are pottery bowls discoloured by fire, possibly used
as lamps (1 Sam. iii. 3); one offering-stand had fitted to its top
a bowl of the cup and saucer type, a hole from the cup into the
saucer leading into a long aperture running the length of the hollow
stand. Pottery chariot wheels were found and, as in previous strata,
many pottery female figurines, of which one displays chin- and
back-veils, associated in the Old Testament with prostitution
(Gen. xxxviii. 14). The same figure holds across the left breast
a round object, perhaps a tambourine for the sacred dance, or a cake
(Jer. vii. 18, xliv. 19). Two figurines, one from the sacred area,

represent pregnant mother goddesses, all suggesting continuation of the fertility cults. Zoomorphic vessels, common in the Iron Age, were also found in the sacred area, but are not necessarily connected with the cult.

The city (Strata VA–IVB) was destroyed *c*. 926 B.C. probably by Shishak (Pharaoh Sheshonq) (1 Kings xiv. 25 ff.; 2 Chron. xii. 2 ff.); part of a stele of this Egyptian monarch was found at Megiddo, and he mentions this city on the walls of the temple of Amun at Karnak in a list of his conquests.[21] There was apparently no long gap in occupation before Stratum IVA, in which stones from the Solomonic buildings were reused, and walls still standing to a considerable height were incorporated. In its pottery and type of building this city closely resembled Samaria, built by Omri at the beginning of the ninth century B.C. The pottery is wheel-burnished and with a light wash. Above the Solomonic casemate wall was erected a city wall with insets and offsets, built of large blocks of well-cut stone, also laid in a header-and-stretcher pattern, some stones across the thickness of the wall and adjoining ones laid lengthways. The insets were later filled in with rubble to make a solid wall. The great gate, bonded to the city wall, became four-chambered. The top of the mound was entirely covered by public buildings; domestic structures may have existed on the slopes outside.

Occupying a fifth of the site were the stables, now assigned to the period of Ahab.[22] They could accommodate about 480 horses, as well as chariots, and in addition there was a small unit near the palace for about twelve horses, perhaps officers' chargers, or for veterinary service. Stone pillars with tie-holes served for tethering horses and for roof supports. Between them were mangers hollowed out of limestone blocks, and between the lines of horses were spaces for chariots. No trace was found of harness or equipment. An inscription of Shalmaneser III states that at the battle of Qarqar, 853 B.C., Ahab provided 2,000 chariots.[23] The architect of the stable complex and palace may have been Egyptian, for their measurements seem based on the Egyptian cubit.[24] Before the construction of the stable unit, the water system was cleared, and the silt, containing late eleventh-century B.C. and Solomonic sherds, was used for levelling the site. At the same time masonry steps covered the rock-cut steps at the foot of the shaft. One large public building is described as a 'temple fortress', and its construction evidently resembled that of Solomon's temple at Jerusalem (1 Kings vii. 12), having 'three rows of hewn stone, and a row of cedar beams', probably surmounted by a mud-brick structure. There is some disagreement as to whether it was a secular or religious building, but its strength, together with its number of cult objects, suggests that it served both purposes, like the temple of Stratum VIII. One room, found by Schumacher, contained two *maṣṣēḇôt*, one with cupmark, one with a depression at the top, a stone table, a stone with a circular depression, and a layer of charcoal and animal remains. There was a large courtyard giving access to a number of rooms for temple personnel, and two rooms perhaps for the common people, which may be compared with the twin temples for a god and goddess at Tell en-Naṣbeh.

Pottery shrines of yellow and grey ware, covered with light red wash, typical of Stratum IVA pottery, were found near the temple. They were decorated with roof moulding and characteristic Palestinian volutes, recalling the Proto-Ionic capitals and the persistent Tree of Life theme. They have openings for doors and windows, and perhaps pigeon-holes for sacred birds, and may have been models of the actual temple building. One reconstructed model shows a female sphinx, with human head and lion body crowned with a tiara, standing at each corner; the art is indigenous rather than Egyptian. An unplaced fragment has a male sphinx with conical head-dress, and possibly the snake motif. Five Proto-Ionic capitals apparently belonged to this building, and also three limestone horned altars, of more developed form than the one found in Stratum V, but, like it, too small for animal sacrifice. The six-pointed 'star of David', incised on the wall of the room containing the *maṣṣēḇôt*, is a further indication of the fertility cult—it was also found at Tell eṣ-Ṣafi incised on a plaque of a nude mother-goddess. There is no definite change in cult objects, pottery figurines continuing from previous strata.

The city was destroyed, and the temple looted and burned, perhaps in the Syrian wars (2 Kings xiii. 3–7), or by Tiglath-Pileser III in 734 B.C. (2 Kings xv. 19). There was then a gap in occupation, and Stratum III (c. 760–650 B.C.) is dated in the prosperous days of Jeroboam II. A seal of Shabaka (c. 715–702 B.C.) was found in it, and to it is assigned a lion seal of Shemaʿ, servant of Jeroboam.[25] In this period Assyria governed Galilee from Megiddo,[26] and during this long occupation, which extended into Stratum II (till *c.* 600 B.C.), there were frequent repairs and replanning. The layout of the streets, unusual in Palestine, may be Assyrian; the buildings, mainly domestic, were arranged in blocks as 'back-to-back' houses. The usual IA ovens and drains with settling sumps continue through Strata II and I, and buildings are mainly of rubble, not ashlar stone. There was a double gateway, of a plan common in the Near East and showing Syro-Hittite influence, comparable to gates at Carchemish and Antioch. The only notable building was in the central area. Five steps led down to a sunken room flanked by side-chambers and containing on either side a bench, with a pottery bath sunk in the floor against the wall. Later additions were two large structures, one square, one circular and containing a large flat stone, perhaps a platform. A scaraboid seal found on the surface shows Egyptian influence. There is a locust in the lower section, and in the upper a winged griffin wearing the double crown of Egypt, with the Hebrew letters *ḥmn*, probably a reference to sun worship. Schumacher found another seal inscribed 'belonging to Asaph',[27] the name of a recorder in the time of Hezekiah (2 Kings xviii. 18).

Cult objects similar to those found in preceding strata continue. A pottery incense altar, much decorated, and a damaged limestone altar, probably horned, were found, and also a lamp to take seven wicks. There were three steatite censers, two with rope decoration and a conventional hand motif.[28] An interesting bovine skull, its horns still in position, bore traces of red wash. Perhaps it had been used in the bull cult (1 Kings xxii. 11). Clearly connected with fertility worship are pottery female figurines, the pregnant mother goddess being represented as well as the figure holding a tambourine or a cake; several come from the same mould. A limestone and a pottery phallus have obviously similar significance. A pottery leg is possibly an amulet, and chariot wheels are thought to be votive objects symbolizing the presence of the deity, as in 2 Kings ii. 11, vi. 17. Two male figurines seem furnished with bovine ears. There were also animal and human figurines whose purpose is in doubt, and equine figures were more numerous after the ninth century B.C.

In the seventh century B.C. stairs were built from the top of the tell down to a place where the masonry of the water shaft was broken. Later, in the Persian period, further steps were added above these. At some time a large wooden platform was erected over the original well, so that water could be drawn up through holes in it. Transition to Stratum II appears in general rebuilding, perhaps due to the reforms of Josiah. The city wall was restored but abandoned at the end of this period, which lasted only fifty years, and ended perhaps when Josiah was slain by Pharaoh Necho (2 Kings xxiii. 29 f.). Small houses, linked with a massive palace-fortress, were of the village rather than of the town type, and lasted till the fourth century B.C. The great pit or silo came to an end in this stratum. A sherd inscribed 'belonging to Yo'[29] suggests syncretism between the religion of Yahweh and the continuing indigenous cults. There were found a censer, female pottery figurines, one from an ancient mould, a misshapen pregnant mother-goddess, and bovine and equine pottery figures. The final occupation, Stratum I (c. 600–350 B.C.), yielded only scattered remains of the Babylonian and Persian periods, without any change in cult objects; there were remains of human and animal figurines, a pottery chariot wheel, and a solid bronze bull mounted on a platform.

The latest reference to Megiddo in the Old Testament contains evidence of the same religious syncretism—'In that day shall there be a great mourning in Jerusalem, as the mourning of Hadadrimmon in the valley of Megiddon' (Zech. xii. 11), probably a reference to ritual weeping connected with Hadad, god of storm, and Rimmon, chief god of Damascus.[30] Rev. xvi. 16 refers to 'the place which is called in Hebrew Har-Magedon' ('the hill of Megiddo').

J. N. SCHOFIELD

NOTES

1. *Antiquity* vi, 1932, pp. 148 ff.
2. G. Loud, *Megiddo II*, p. 140.
3. *A History of Israel*, 1962, p. 37.
4. *The Canaanites*, 1964, p. 28.
5. *A.J.S.L.* lviii, 1941, pp. 225 ff.
6. R. M. Engberg and G. M. Shipton, p. 77 (see Bibliography).
7. W. Dörpfeld, *Troja und Ilion*, i, 1902, p. 81, fig. 23.
8. W. Lamb, *Excavations at Thermi in Lesbos*, 1936, pp. 49 ff.
9. L. H. Vincent, *Syria* v, 1924, pp. 81 ff.

10. W. A. Heurtley, *Q.D.A.P.* viii, 1938, pp. 21 ff.
11. *A.N.E.T.*, pp. 235 f.
12. W. F. Albright, *B.A.S.O.R.* 68, 1937, p. 23.
13. See *B.A.* xviii, 1955, p. 44.
14. Cf. *D.O.T.T.*, pp. 17–26.
15. *A.N.E.T.*, p. 477.
16. Ibid., p. 485.
17. G. Loud, *The Megiddo Ivories* (O.I.P. 52, 1939), p. 11.
18. A. G. Barrois, *Syria* xviii, 1937, p. 244.
19. R. S. Lamon, *The Megiddo Water System* (O.I.P. 32, 1935), p. 15.
20. *A.J.A.* liii, 1949, pp. 213 ff.
21. *A.N.E.T.*, pp. 242 f., 263 f.
22. *B.A.* xxiii, 1960, pp. 67 ff.
23. *A.N.E.T.*, p. 279.
24. R. B. Y. Scott, *B.A.* xxii, 1959, p. 26.
25. See S. A. Cook, *P.E.Q.*, 1904, pp. 287 ff.; *D.O.T.T.*, pp. 220 f.; A. Reifenberg, *Ancient Hebrew Seals*, 1950, p. 27.
26. *A.N.E.T.*, p. 294; 2 Kings xv. 29 f.
27. See S. A. Cook, *The Religion of Ancient Palestine in the light of Archaeology* (Schweich Lectures 1925), 1930, p. 56.
28. W. F. Albright compares Num. vii. 50 (H. G. May, *Material Remains of the Megiddo Cult*, O.I.P. 26, 1935, p. 19).
29. *A.J.S.L.* 1, 1933–4, pp. 10 ff.
30. The Pesh. reads 'mourning for the son of Amon', that is, Josiah; see *A.N.E.T.*, p. 139.

BIBLIOGRAPHY

ALT, A. 'Megiddo im Übergang vom kanaanäischen zum israelitischen Zeitalter, *K.S.* i, 1944, pp. 256 ff.
—— 'Die assyrische Provinz Megiddo und ihr späteres Schicksal', ibid., ii, 1953, pp. 374 ff.
BARROIS, A. G. 'Les Installations hydrauliques de Megiddo', *Syria* xviii, 1937, pp. 237 ff.
CROWFOOT, J. W. 'Megiddo—A Review', *P.E.Q.*, 1940, pp. 132–47.
ENGBERG, R. M. 'Historical analysis of archaeological evidence: Megiddo and the Song of Deborah', *B.A.S.O.R.* 78, 1940, pp. 4–7.
—— and SHIPTON, G. M. *Notes on the Chalcolithic and Early Bronze Age Pottery of Megiddo* (S.A.O.C. 10, 1934).
FISHER, C. S. *The Excavation of Armageddon* (O.I.C. 4, 1929).
GUY, P. L. O. *New Light from Armageddon* (O.I.C. 9, 1931).
—— and ENGBERG, R. M. *Megiddo Tombs* (O.I.P. 33, 1938).
HOWIE, C. G. 'The east gate of Ezekiel's Temple Enclosure and the Solomonic gateway of Megiddo', *B.A.S.O.R.* 117, 1950, pp. 13 ff.
KENYON, K. M. 'Some notes on the Early Middle Bronze Strata of Megiddo', *Eretz Israel* v, 1928, pp. 51 ff.

LAMON, R. S. *The Megiddo Water System* (O.I.P. 32, 1935).

—— and SHIPTON, G. M. *Megiddo I: Seasons of 1925–34, Strata I–V* (O.I.P. 42, 1939).

LOUD, G. *The Megiddo Ivories* (O.I.P. 52, 1939).

—— *Megiddo II: Seasons of 1935–1939* (O.I.P. 62, 1948).

MAY, H. G. *Material Remains of the Megiddo Cult* (O.I.P. 26, 1935).

NELSON, H. H. *The Battle of Megiddo*, 1913.

SCHUMACHER, G., and STEUERNAGEL, C. *Tell el-Mutesellim*, i, 1908.

SHIPTON, G. M. *Notes on the Megiddo Pottery of Strata VI–XX* (S.A.O.C. 17, 1939).

WATZINGER, C. *Tell el-Mutesellim*, ii, 1929.

WRIGHT, G. E. 'The discoveries at Megiddo, 1935–9', *B.A.R.* ii, 1964, pp. 225 ff.

—— 'The problem of the transition between Chalcolithic and Bronze Age', *Eretz Israel* v, 1958, pp. 37 ff.

YADIN, Y. 'New light on Solomon's Megiddo', *B.A.R.* ii, 1964, pp. 240 ff.

MIZPAH

MIZPAH of Benjamin (Joshua xviii. 26; 1 Kings xv. 22, etc.), which was for a short time the capital of Judah, is probably to be identified with Tell en-Naṣbeh. We shall deal first with the problem of identification, and next with the important epigraphic material which the site has yielded.

Tell en-Naṣbeh, about 8 miles north of Jerusalem, lies near the boundary between the kingdoms of Judah and Israel, leading to Shechem and Samaria. It occupies the summit of a large hill, some 784 metres high, which stands in practical isolation and affords magnificent views, particularly towards the west and south. Indeed, it dominates all the heights as far south as the northern hills of Jerusalem, but not the hills towards the north and the east. The great north–south road, which runs beside Tell en-Naṣbeh, follows closely the watershed between the Mediterranean and the Jordan valley, and was of paramount importance not only as a link between Judah and Samaria, but also as a line of communication between Judah and Syria, and the northern regions, as far as Mesopotamia.

The American explorer Edward Robinson refers to this site in his journal of 15 May 1838,[1] but he does not mention it by name. He himself did not visit the site, but his companion, Eli Smith, climbed the hill and found there foundations of a tower, 'heaps of unwrought stones' and 'fragments of pottery strewed about'. Although some surface surveys were made, no excavation was undertaken before 1926. In that year a systematic excavation was begun by W. F. Badè on behalf of the Palestine Institute of the Pacific School of Religion, Berkeley, California. The excavations were carried out during five seasons (1926, 1927, 1929, 1932, and 1935), but Badè died in 1936, before the complete records were published.

i. *Settlement at the Site*

Before the end of the Chalcolithic period there was almost no occupation at Tell en-Naṣbeh. In the Early Bronze Age the site was inhabited, but subsequent settlers, possessing some degree of civilization, destroyed all surface evidence of occupation. However, a number of tombs and caves provide unmistakable evidence. Moreover, some Iron Age tombs also have Early Bronze Age deposits. But the small number of caves, about twenty in all, containing such deposits—covering a period of over a thousand years —indicates that the population in that period was somewhat sparse. The following periods—Middle Bronze and Late Bronze, corresponding mainly to the Hyksos period and that of the Egyptian hegemony—are not represented at all in the archaeological remains of the site. There is not much evidence either for the beginning of the Iron Age or of Philistine influence. Indeed, the great mass of material discovered at Tell en-Naṣbeh belongs to the period of the Hebrew settlement (c. 1100–400 B.C.). Occupation before the Solomonic period appears to have been slight.

In the middle period of Iron Age I and in Iron Age II and III there was a definite increase in population as well as in prosperity, as is clearly shown by some relatively rich tombs. Prosperity is also suggested by the development in architecture, by the number of cisterns and silos, by dye-plants, spinning whorls, loom weights, and presses for wine and oil. Numerous beads of semi-precious stones, eyelet pins, fibulae, bangles, and other metal jewellery, not to mention metal utensils and implements, point to a certain standard of luxury. It is difficult to assess the chronology of all the finds, but it would seem that at least some of the pottery goes back to the Solomonic period. On the other hand, the magnificent wall is generally dated after the division of the kingdom, that is, in Iron Age II. As time went on the city expanded beyond its walls.

It seems that in the fifth century B.C. the population of the city declined, but fragments of imported Greek ware, of inferior quality, indicate that the small Judaean country had commercial relations with Athens in her most glorious period. Of the Greek ware, only one object, unique in Palestine, is 'Clazomenian', or Eastern Greek; all the rest are Attic. Occupation of the site under Alexander's successors was slight, and the part played by the then small city during the Maccabaean war is obscure. But even in Hellenistic–Roman times there seems to have been a military watch-tower on the hill. At the end of its history, however, Tell en-Naṣbeh was no more than a small unwalled village.

ii. *Identification of the Site*

Mizpah appears in the Old Testament as a place for assembly (Judges xx. 1, 3, xxi. 1, 5; 1 Sam. vii. 5, etc.); it was visited by Samuel in his official circuit (1 Sam. vii. 16); its importance increased notably with its fortification by King Asa (1 Kings xv. 22); it became Gedaliah's capital, and there he and his entourage were slain by Ishmael (Jer. xli. 1 ff.); in 1 Macc. iii. 46 it is referred to as an ancient Hebrew sanctuary, which, during the Maccabaean war, was the scene of an inspiring assembly under Judas Maccabaeus. The importance of this ancient city has produced a variety of theories as to its identification. According to some scholars,[2] who follow Edward Robinson's lead, Nebi Samwil, which crowns an imposing height, 4½ miles north-west of Jerusalem, and which is the traditional burial place of Samuel, is the Old Testament Mizpah. The archaeological evidence from Nebi Samwil has, however, been regarded as decisive against the identification of it with Mizpah, and the linguistic equation Naṣbeh—Mizpah has been upheld,[3] though not by all scholars.[4] Tell en-Naṣbeh has further been identified with the Old Testament Beeroth,[5] and also with Ataroth Archi or Addar[6] (cf. Joshua xvi. 2, 5, xviii. 13). All in all, however, the balance of probability is in favour of its identification with Mizpah.[7] Abbé Raboisson[8] in 1897 was apparently the first to suggest this identification, and it was made also, quite independently, by C. R. Conder at about the same time.[9]

In his thorough investigation of the whole problem J. Muilenburg rightly emphasizes the importance of 1 Kings xv. 16–22,[10] which refer to the strong measures taken by Baasha, king of Israel, against Asa, king of Judah, and the latter's counter-measures, resulting in the fortification of Geba and Mizpah. One of these two towns was in all probability situated near the main north road; it was Geba (modern Jeba') which lies 'at a crucial point on the famous Michmash road'. Mizpah is accordingly most probably to be identified with Tell en-Naṣbeh—'It closes the narrow pass to the north, it affords an admirable view of the road leading to the south, and for a fortress it is far superior in its location to Ramah.'[11] It has been argued, however, that Gibeah (Tell el-Ful) would have been the fortress near the main road, while Nebi Samwil would be Mizpah.[12] From the strategic viewpoint Muilenburg's view seems the more probable. Some support for it may be seen in the tragic events in Judah following the destruction of the Temple in 587 B.C., when Mizpah became the capital of Judah under the governor, Gedaliah (Jer. xl f.). The reason for the choice of Mizpah was most probably a political–strategical one, and in this respect Tell en-Naṣbeh has a great advantage over Nebi Samwil.[13] Another indirect reference for the identification with Mizpah is the story of Ishmael, the murderer of Gedaliah, who, the day after the assassination, saw a procession of some eighty men from Shechem, Shiloh, and Samaria on their way to Jerusalem to present offerings in the Temple. Ishmael invited them to see Gedaliah and killed most of them. Topographically, Tell en-Naṣbeh would fit the circumstances much better than Nebi Samwil or any other site.[14]

The more strictly archaeological evidence may now be considered. According to C. C. McCown, the evidence 'brilliantly supports the identification of Mizpah with Tell en-Naṣbeh. The city begins as a Hebrew village in the twelfth or certainly the eleventh century. At a time which the archaeological evidence cannot fix within a century, but which certainly may have been about 900 B.C., the time of Asa, one of the strongest walls yet found in Palestine was built around it.'[15] It is true, however, that its gate opens to the north and not the south, and it has been held that it is incredible that the Mizpah which Asa fortified against Baasha of Israel should not have had a gate opening southward toward Jerusalem.[16] On the other hand, the ceramic evidence places it indisputably in the southern kingdom.[17] This is particularly true of the *lmlk* stamps on jar handles (see below), whereas Beth-el, only 3 miles away to the north, has yielded not a single such stamp. Archaeological evidence also indicates that Tell en-Naṣbeh was occupied even into Maccabaean times, and this occupation may relate to Mizpah mentioned in 1 Macc. iii. 46. Finally, the problem of the jar handle stamps inscribed *mṣp*, or rather *mṣh*, calls for consideration, and will be discussed below.

iii. *The Ancient City*

The fortification of the ancient city consisted of two walls and two strong towers, probably of the *miḡdāl* type. The inner, and older, city wall, which may be attributed to Iron Age I, or to the beginning of Iron Age II, was not as strong as some contemporary city walls. It was a rubble wall, built of stones and laid in clay mortar, whose extent has not been fully determined. There are remains around the southern end of the tell, but, with frequent long interruptions, the wall can still be followed on the west and around the north end. The western tower probably also belongs to Iron Age I. It was 8·40 metres wide and 9·50 metres long on the south side to 10·20 metres on the north side. The walls were founded on bed-rock and were of very strong construction. The tower enclosed two rooms about 5·75 metres long; one of them was a rectangle 1·50 metres wide, the other was 1·50 metres wide at the eastern and 1·75 metres at the western end. The northern tower, unlike the western, was irregular in its plan and construction, and in its south-eastern corner was apparently connected with the inner wall. On the north-west it is over 9 metres long, on the south-west about 8·50 metres; its width is about 7 metres, and its walls are 1·60–2·50 metres thick. One of the rooms is about 1·70×3·10 metres; the other is 3 metres long and 1·20–2 metres wide. This tower may also be assigned to Iron Age I.

Of particular interest is the impressive stone wall, which, it is generally agreed, is to be assigned to the end of Iron Age I. In its entire circumference it measured about 660 metres, enclosing some 32,000 square metres. On the west side its base was 770 metres above sea level, on the southern end 782 metres. There was no methodical plan of construction, and there are also differences in the masonry and thickness of the wall. It is possible that, like the wall at Jerusalem under Nehemiah, this wall too may have been built by groups of men with different building traditions and varying skill. On the northern end it appears that the builders had first excavated a wide trench, carried down to bed-rock, and this they filled to a height of 2 metres with loose, mostly small, rocks. Upon this bed the wall was built with courses of large stones laid with clay mortar. Along the outside a buttress wall was built. On the south the bottom foundation consisted of a platform of immense rocks, a metre or more in thickness and projecting a foot or two beyond its face. The wall throughout was built of limestone rock, laid in clay mortar. The thickness of the wall varies greatly; in some places it is 3·50 to 3·70 metres, but it is generally over 4 metres. While it is impossible to determine its exact height, it has been estimated that it was 8–10 metres above street level inside the wall and 12–14 metres above bed-rock. There was also a wide fosse and moat.

Nine or ten rectangular towers were constructed as part of the wall. They were built at turns in the wall or in the course of long straight stretches, but not, for nearly 100 metres, at the north end. The bases of the towers were protected by extensive buttress walls. The structures vary in thickness from 6 to 9 metres; their length, in nearly all cases, is 9·50 to 10 metres. Strangely enough, no remains of a city gate towards the south have come to light, but far to the north, on the east side of the tell, remains of a strong city-gate and gate-tower 9·40 metres thick have been discovered. Moreover, traces have been found of an earlier city-gate.

The greatest length of the city, measured from the outside of the walls, was about 265 metres, the greatest width about 160 metres. The highest spot of the hill was just over 784 metres. The south-west and north-west sectors especially, and parts of the east and west sides of the hill, were the most populated. It must be emphasized that there was only one city-gate, the great gate in the north-east, from which a street ran to the west. South of the gate there was a considerable open space, probably the market-place.

The houses represent a considerable variety of structure, but reveal no very high architectural skill. They were mostly enclosures with stone walls to secure protection from the elements. Certain houses, however, were more carefully constructed, and show a highly developed architectural tradition. There are three tripartite four-room buildings, rectangular in shape and of almost the same size, 10 × 12 or 13 metres. They consist of three long rooms, lying side by side and forming an almost perfect square, and a fourth room, approximately the same size, which ran across their ends. The central room, about 3 metres wide, was always the largest. When, in 1927, the first of these buildings was discovered, it was generally assumed that it was an early Hebrew sanctuary. It is now believed, however, that the buildings were either storehouses, or perhaps the dwellings of wealthier people. In some of the buildings remains of stairways and of second floors have been discovered.

iv. *Epigraphic Discoveries*

Seventy-nine scarabs were found in the tombs, of which by far the largest number (forty-one) came from Tomb 32. In another tomb there were five, but none of value except a cylinder seal (see below). Two specimens are amongst the most delicately worked ever discovered. Twenty-nine specimens were found on the mound, scattered through the area where dwellings or silos remained. There is also a rectangular piece of steatite with hieroglyphics on both sides. Three or four scarabs can be assigned to the Twenty-fifth Dynasty (*c.* 715–664 B.C.). Egyptian influence must accordingly have continued down to that time. On the mound itself only one scarab was found, which may tentatively be assigned to the Nineteenth Dynasty or later, possibly even as late as *c.* 1000 B.C. Their workmanship varies greatly, but with one or two exceptions, the carving displays no artistic merit, though it does illustrate cultural connexions. In hardly a single case are the hieroglyphs correctly written; it is evident that such objects were imported in blank and that the inscription was added by a local craftsman. The cylinder seal referred to above is artistically superior to many found in Palestine and elsewhere. It is about 25 millimetres in length and 13 in diameter. One of the many peculiar pieces is an irregular fragment of bone which carries on one side a carved inscription with hitherto unidentified characters. The Hebraist thinks the Egyptologist should interpret it; the Egyptologist believes the characters to be Hebrew.

One of the most interesting and most puzzling discoveries was made in Berkeley in August 1942. While some supposedly unimportant metal fragments were being cleaned, a portion of a heavily encrusted circlet (?) of bronze came out clean with a remarkably clear-cut cuneiform inscription. The fragment is a flat piece of bronze about a millimetre thick and 11 millimetres wide, curving on an outside diameter of about 16 centimetres. The inscription contains the curious expression *šar kiššati* 'king of the universe', and its date is *c.* 800–650 B.C.[18]

Very few Greek inscriptions have been found, and it is possible that these have nothing to do with the ancient Tell en-Naṣbeh, but belong to Khirbet esh-Shuweikeh.[19] One is a bone amulet inscribed in ink of the late Roman or Byzantine period which was enclosed in a metal case, probably of lead. The bone is 78 millimetres long and the case 90 millimetres. There are apparently eight lines—the upper two may be purely decorative—which are divided into four columns. Not all the characters can be deciphered.

One lamp carries a 'Light of Christ' inscription, written by a person who knew neither Greek nor the Greek alphabet, and a fragment of another bears a totally corrupt Greek inscription.

Only about twenty pre-Arabic coins have been found, and these are probably connected not with ancient Tell en-Naṣbeh, but with campers or temporary squatters on the mound. The oldest is an imitation of the early Attic bronze tetradrachm (406–393 B.C.). Another is a coin of Ptolemy II Philadelphus (285–247 B.C.) from the Tyre mint. Four Ptolemaic and three or four Seleucid coins were found, as well as five of Alexander Jannaeus (103–76 B.C.) or John Hyrcanus (135–104 B.C.), one of Herod Archelaus (4 B.C.– A.D. 6) and seven of Roman procurators. These coins prove conclusively that shortly after the beginning of the Ptolemaic period the mound must have been practically abandoned.[20]

Of much greater significance for Old Testament study are the Early Hebrew inscriptions, which may be divided into different groups. The seven fragmentary graffiti are mainly inscribed portions of jars or bowls, fragments of jar handles, and so on. The inscriptions were scratched either before or after the firing of the utensil. The earliest, c. 1000 B.C., contains only the letters *lḥ* 'belonging to Ḥ . . .'. Another, c. 750 B.C., may be read '[to Netha]nyo and to Samakh[yo]'. Two other fragments—one, perhaps of the third century B.C., does not seem to be Early Hebrew— contain parts of proper names; in one the name Yiddo may be read (cf. 1 Chron. xxvii. 21). The most interesting Early Hebrew graffito, also fragmentary, may contain the name Marsarzērukin, which may mean 'The Crown-prince [has established] posterity', and would testify to Assyrian influence in the eighth–ninth centuries B.C., the probable date of the inscription.[21]

Amongst the smaller objects there is a beautiful seal inscribed *ly'znyhw 'bd hmlk* 'belonging to Jaazaniah, slave (minister) of the king'. Jaazaniah is perhaps the royal officer referred to in 2 Kings xxv. 23 and Jer. xl. 8. This Jaazaniah was one of the commanders associated with Ishmael who killed Gedaliah at Mizpah. Beneath the inscription there is a representation of a fighting cock, which is the earliest Palestinian representation of this fowl. It fills a gap in our knowledge of the life of ancient Israel, for, since cocks are not mentioned in the Old Testament, it has been generally believed they were not known in Palestine in Old Testament times.

Undoubtedly the most significant of the Tell en-Naṣbeh inscriptions is the group of jar-handle stamps. That stamps inscribed
with *lmlk* 'belonging to the king' ('royal') were found at Tell en-
Naṣbeh indicates that this was a Judaean city. Moreover, and this
point is of importance, since no such impressions have come from
Beth-el, which is only 3 miles away, it may be assumed that the
boundary between Judah and Samaria ran to the north of Tell
en-Naṣbeh and to the south of Beth-el. Considering that Tell
en-Naṣbeh was a small town, the number of *lmlk* stamps is remarkable. Eighty-six in number, they are second only to those
discovered at Lachish (Tell ed-Duweir), and the number of impressions belonging to class iii (see below) is by far the highest
amongst the collections from all Palestinian sites. The 'royal'
stamps are oval in form, and contain a four- or two-winged symbol
with an inscription in two lines, one above the figure, reading
lmlk, and one below the figure, reading *ḥbrn*, *škh*, *z(y)p*, and *mmšt*.
These are references to the cities Hebron, Sokoh, and Ziph, but
the last (*mmšt*) is still not identified. It is now generally accepted
that the following three stylistical, palaeographical, and chronological classes of stamps may be distinguished—(i) the four-
winged type, representing the flying scarab or beetle with the
inscription in a more archaic character, dating probably about 700
B.C., perhaps in the reign of Hezekiah; (ii) a similar figure, but in
a completely stylized form, with the inscription in a slightly later
style, perhaps belonging to the time of Manasseh (687–642 B.C.);
(iii) the two-winged figure representing the winged sun-disk, or
rather, the winged flying scroll, or a crested bird, perhaps belonging to the period of Josiah and his successors (640–587 B.C.).[22]

When in January 1869 Charles Warren discovered in Jerusalem,
at the south-east angle of the Haram area, at a depth of 50 feet,
eight jar handles, of which seven bore the two-winged figure with
the 'royal' inscription, the script was considered to be Phoenician,
and even later the names were regarded either as proper names, for
example, 'Of the king Sokoh', or place-names, for example, 'Of the
king of Sokoh', and the stamps were dated as early as the fourteenth century B.C. or as late as 400 B.C., or even later. Nowadays
about 600 'royal' jar-handle impressions are known, and they can
now be dated with greater certainty, and their dates help to fix the
chronology of the archaeological strata in which they were found.

The Tell en-Naṣbeh collection of 'royal' impressions is characterized by another feature which has already been referred to. Seventy-one belong to class iii, and only sixteen to classes i and ii, whereas at Lachish (Tell ed-Duweir), for instance, the numbers are respectively 45 and 265. This great preponderance of class iii stamps at Tell en-Naṣbeh fits in well with this site if it is in fact Mizpah. The *lmlk* jars were probably not employed for tax collection, but for household use. If they had been used for tax collection, one would expect that their remains would have been found near the governor's residence, one of the large houses by the city gate.[23] In fact they were found in greatest numbers where the houses were most crowded. Household use might well be the explanation. With regard to the place-names in the inscriptions, while Hebron, for instance, appears in about 63 per cent. of the specimens found at Lachish (Tell ed-Duweir), it appears in only about 15 per cent. of those found at Tell en-Naṣbeh; *mmšt* occurs in about 2 per cent in the case of Lachish, but about 27 per cent in the legible 'royal' stamps found at Tell en-Naṣbeh. One may wonder what, if any, historical–geographical conclusions may be drawn from these proportions.

About ten impressions of post-exilic date come within the *yhd* group, some, however, not with complete certainty. The stamps of this group were once read *yhw*, and, together with the *yh* stamps, were regarded as 'divine' impressions. They have, however, been identified as *yhd*, Yehûd stamps, of the small autonomous state of Judah in the Persian period.[24] Eight jar-handle stamps bear the impression *yh*. In some other stamps, which may belong to this group, the letters are not quite clear. Only one stamp appears to come within the *yršlm* 'Jerusalem' group.[25]

The group of *mṣp* or *mṣh* impressions is the most exciting of all. Twenty-eight post-exilic impressions belong to this group, which is almost exclusive to Tell en-Naṣbeh. Only one such stamp has been found elsewhere, at Jericho. The first letter is certainly *mêm*, and the second is most probably *ṣādê*; the third is, however, uncertain. It is generally read as *h*, but *p* has been suggested.[26] In the latter case, the inscription *mṣp* (Miṣpah, Mizpah) would provide the strongest argument for the identification of the site, but palaeographically this particular reading is not satisfactory. Nor is the reading *mṣh* completely satisfactory. What would it signify? It is most unlikely that the jars with this stamp were intended for Pesaḥ wine for the feast of *maṣṣôṭ* 'unleavened bread'.[27] It is difficult to see why such a stamp should be exclusive, or nearly so, to Tell en-Naṣbeh. The same question might be asked if the inscription were read Moṣah (in Benjamin, Joshua xviii. 26). The most probable explanation seems to be that this inscription, coming from the transitional period (the period of transition from Early Hebrew characters to Aramaic–Square Hebrew script) may easily contain scribal confusions. On the other hand, if, as is highly probable, the particular letter is *hē*, the inscription *mṣh* is very likely an abbreviation of *mṣph* (Miṣpah, Mizpah).[28]

As to private jar-handle stamps, there are three impressions, possibly from two different specimens, of a seal bearing the inscription *lšbnt/šḥr*. The stamp is of the common oval shape, divided lengthwise by a double line, with the letters *lšbn* above and *tšḥr* below, the two names being separated by a small oblique stroke. The interpretation could be 'belonging to Shebnath [son or daughter of] Šaḥar'. Shebnath may be a feminine name, the counterpart of Shebna. Of the two other impressions, one, partly broken, can be read 'Ahaziah [son of] Mattaniah'. Of the second stamp only the double line and two uncertain letters are still visible.

Only three inscribed weights, belonging to the late pre-exilic period, come from Tell en-Naṣbeh. Two bear very clear inscriptions, both being marked *nṣp* (*neṣep-*). The third is not so clear, but the inscription *pym* (*pîm*) is certain. Since these weights have been discussed recently by the present writer, and the importance of the *pîm* weight for the understanding of 1 Sam. xiii. 21 has been shown,[29] it is not necessary to treat them more fully here.

With the discovery of the 'royal' stamps the study of the Early Hebrew alphabet (all the letters of the 'royal' stamps are Early Hebrew) has been significantly advanced. The other jar-handle stamps are of particular importance for the study of the transitional period (from Early Hebrew to Square Hebrew script) of Hebrew palaeography. We refer particularly to the *yhd*, *yh*, and the *mṣp/h* impressions, all of the post-exilic period. The *yhd* stamp, for instance, is a true representative of this transition, the *yôd* being practically Early Hebrew, the *dāleth* being Aramaic–Square Hebrew (in the Early Hebrew alphabet the letter would be *wāw*, as it was formerly believed to be), and the *hē* presents several forms which can be classified into six definite types.[30] This classification is highly interesting as it concerns also the *yh* and the *mṣh/p* stamps. The different types provide a kind of summary of the process of the early development of the Square Hebrew alphabet. At the same time the unskilled workmanship in some cases must not be overlooked. Until much more material, both in Judah and elsewhere, becomes available, the exact origin and early development of the Square Hebrew alphabet must remain a puzzle.[31] It may be emphasized that the material already available, scarce though it may be, demands much more thorough study than it has received hitherto.

D. DIRINGER

NOTES

1. *Biblical Researches, etc.* i. 1856, p. 575.

2. e.g. R. Kittel, *Stud. zur hebr. Archäologie*, 1908, p. 138; G. A. Smith, *Historical Geography of the Holy Land*, 25th ed., 1931, p. 120; P. Lohmann, *Z.D.P.V.* xli, 1918, pp. 117–57.

3. *R.B.* xix, 1922, pp. 376–402, xxi, 1924, pp. 637 f.

4. See, for example, W. F. Albright, *J.P.O.S.* iii, 1923, pp. 120 f.; C. C. McCown, *Tell en-Naṣbeh*, i, 1947, pp. 43 f.

5. W. F. Albright, *A.A.S.O.R.* iv, 1924, Appendix 1, pp. 90–111; J. Garstang, *Joshua Judges*, 1931, pp. 164 f.

6. W. F. Albright, *B.A.S.O.R.* 35, 1929, p. 4. The identification of Tell en-Naṣbeh with Ataroth Archi or Addar has also been proposed by L. Heidet, *Dict. de la Bible*, Supp. i, 1928, cols. 664 ff., as well as by A. Jirku, *J.P.O.S.* viii, 1928, pp. 187 ff. H. W. Hertzberg, *Z.A.W.* vi, 1929, pp. 161–96, argues that Mizpah was a great sanctuary in Benjamin, but Tell en-Naṣbeh cannot qualify as that Old Testament centre, lying as it does outside the tribe of Benjamin. Only Nebi Samwil is, he believes, a possibility; Tell en-Naṣbeh would be Beeroth, which, after its destruction, became Ataroth. See also W. F. Albright, *J.B.L.* lviii, 1939, pp. 179 f., and *J.Q.R.* xxii, 1931–2, pp. 415 f.

7. See especially G. Dalman, *P.J.B.* xxi, 1925, pp. 58–89; E. Baumann, *Z.D.P.V.* xxxiv, 1911, pp. 119–37; A. Alt, *P.J.B.* vi, 1910, pp. 46–62. Later, however, Alt changed his view and identified Mizpah with el-Bireh and Gibeon with Tell en-Naṣbeh, *P.J.B.* xxii, 1926, pp. 10 ff., 33, 39 ff. F.-M. Abel (*Géographie de la Palestine*, ii, 1938, pp. 30 f., 86, 92, 388 ff.), P. Thomsen (*Reallex. d. Vorgesch.* xiii, 1919, cols. 248 ff.) and J. Hempel (*Z.A.W.* vi, 1929, pp. 68 ff.) also favour the identification of Tell en-Naṣbeh with Mizpah.

8. *Les Maspeh*, 1897; see also L. H. Vincent, *R.B.* viii, 1899, pp. 315 f.

9. *P.E.F.Q.S.*, 1898, p. 169.
10. *Tell en-Naṣbeh*, i, 1947, pp. 28 ff.
11. Ibid., especially pp. 13–49.
12. *A.A.O.S.* iv, 1924, pp. 38 f.
13. *Tell en-Naṣbeh*, i, p. 31.
14. Ibid., pp. 34 ff. Muilenburg also deals with the remaining Old Testament and other literary sources concerning Mizpah, including Neh. iii. 7, 15–19, 1 Macc. iii. 46, Josephus, and Eusebius, but none of the references are of real help.
15. Ibid., p. 58.
16. *J.B.L.* lviii, 1939, pp. 179 f.
17. *Tell en-Naṣbeh*, i, pp. 54, 58.
18. Ibid., pp. 151 f.
19. Ibid., p. 173.
20. Ibid., p. 174.
21. Ibid., pp. 43 f.
22. Ibid., pp. 156–61. See also D. Diringer, *B.A.* xii, 1949, pp. 70–86, and *Lachish III*, pp. 340–7.
23. *Tell en-Naṣbeh*, i, p. 205.
24. E. L. Sukenik, *J.P.O.S.* xiv, 1934, pp. 178–84, xv, 1935, pp. 341 ff.
25. *Tell en-Naṣbeh*, i, p. 164.
26. Particularly C. C. Torrey; see *Tell en-Naṣbeh*, i, p. 166, n. 45.
27. Ibid., p. 167 and n. 49.
28. H. L. Ginsberg, *B.A.S.O.R.* 109, 1948, pp. 20 ff.
29. *D.O.T.T.*, pp. 229 f. See further W. R. Lane, *B.A.S.O.R.* 164, 1961, pp. 21 ff.
30. *Tell en-Naṣbeh*, i, pp. 170 f.
31. Ibid., p. 171.

BIBLIOGRAPHY

ABEL, F.-M. *Géographie de la Palestine*, ii, 1938.
ALBRIGHT, W. F. 'The site of Mizpah in Benjamin', *J.P.O.S.* iii, 1923, pp. 110–21.
—— 'Mizpah and Beeroth', *A.A.S.O.R.* iv, 1924, Appendix 1, pp. 90–111.
—— 'New Israelite and Pre-Israelite sites: the spring trip of 1929', *B.A.S.O.R.* 35, 1929, p. 4.
—— 'Recent works on the topography and archaeology of Jerusalem', *J.Q.R.* xxii, 1931–2, pp. 412–6.
—— *The Archaeology of Palestine and the Bible*, 3rd ed., 1935.
—— *Archaeology and the Religion of Israel*, 3rd ed., 1953.
BADÈ, W. F. *Excavations at Tell en-Naṣbeh, 1926 and 1927: A Preliminary Report*, 1928.
—— *Manual of Excavation in the Near East*, 1934.

BAUMANN, E. 'Die Lage von Mizpa in Benjamin', *Z.D.P.V.* xxxiv, 1911, pp. 119–37.

DALMAN, G. 'Die Nordstraße Jerusalems', *P.J.B.* xxi, 1925, pp. 58–89.

—— *Jerusalem und sein Gelände*, 1938.

GINSBERG, H. L. 'MMŠT and MṢH', *B.A.S.O.R.* 109, 1948, pp. 20 ff.

HEIDET, L. *Dictionnaire de la Bible.* Supp. 1, 1928, cols. 664 ff.

HEMPEL, J. "Aṭaroṯ-'Addar', *Z.D.P.V.* liii, 1930, pp. 233–6.

HERTZBERG, H. W. 'Mizpa', *Z.A.W.* vi, 1929, pp. 161–96.

McCOWN, C. C. *et al. Tell en-Naṣbeh*, i, ii, 1947.

MUILENBURG, J. 'Survey of the literature on Tell en-Naṣbeh', *Tell en-Naṣbeh*, i, 1947, pp. 13–22.

—— 'The literary sources bearing on the question of identification', ibid., pp. 23–44.

—— 'The history of Mizpah of Benjamin', ibid., pp. 45–49.

RABOISSON, ABBÉ. *Les Maspeh*, 1897.

ROBINSON, E. *Biblical Researches in Palestine and the adjacent regions: a Journal of Travels in the Years 1838 and 1852* (1856).

SAMARIA

THE name Samaria (Hebrew *šōmᵉrôn*, modern Sebasṭîyeh) is used in the Old Testament in reference both to the city which was made the new capital of the northern kingdom by Omri *c.* 880 B.C., and to the region more or less closely associated with it. Although we are here concerned primarily with the city itself, some reference must also be made to the region of which, for a considerable part of the period, the city was the administrative centre. It is situated at a strategic point in the centre of Palestine, built upon a hill reaching a height of about 300 feet above the surrounding valley and about 1,400 feet above sea level (Pl. XIV).[1] The hill, according to 1 Kings xvi. 24, was purchased by Omri from a man named Shemer for two talents of silver. The city was apparently designed to replace the capital at Tirzah, and certainly offered considerable advantages, being in a rich and fertile area and commanding lines of communication in three directions—west to the coastal plain through various valleys, north to Dothan, and thence to both Megiddo and Jezreel (a second important centre, virtually another capital, of the northern kingdom, cf. 1 Kings xxi; 2 Kings ix), and east to the ancient Shechem, from which the roads run further via Tirzah to the Jordan and south to Beth-el and Jerusalem.

The excavation of the site has been undertaken on a considerable scale, first in 1908–10 by the Harvard expedition led by G. A. Reisner and C. S. Fisher, an expedition which indicated the richness of the material available, but suffered because of the difficulty at that time of correctly interpreting the evidence of the stratification. Fuller investigation was made in 1931–5 by an expedition in which the Palestine Exploration Fund, the British Academy, the British School of Archaeology in Jerusalem, the Hebrew University, and Harvard University all combined for three seasons, the fourth being limited to the British members. Even this expedition was inevitably limited by the present occupation of so much of the area by gardens and olive-groves, and many problems remained unsolved. Much light was, however, shed by both series of excavations on the history of the site, and on the stages of its development under the Israelite kings and later, and in particular the ivories and ostraca discovered provided important evidence.

The impression given by the Old Testament record is that there had been no previous settlement on the hill. But it is probable that there was some occupation at a much earlier date (third millennium B.C.), and that, when Omri bought the hill, there was a small village on it. The pottery associated with periods I and II compares very closely with pottery from the tenth and early ninth centuries B.C. elsewhere,[2] and is probably to be regarded as earlier than the building activities of Omri and Ahab. It is not clear how this information is to be related to the reported purchase from Shemer. The name *šōmᵉrôn* itself perhaps means 'watch-post', and the Old Testament derivation from Shemer may therefore be a piece of popular tradition. A connexion has also been suggested with Shamir in Judges. x. 2. But it is also possible that Shemer was the name of the clan centred on the settlement, or that of the owner of a family estate. A. Alt's interpretation of the matter is worthy of consideration, namely, that the city, on a site acquired as a personal possession of the royal house, became a kind of royal city state within the kingdom, and more particularly a Canaanite centre in contrast to the more definitely Israelite centre at Jezreel.[3] Certainly there is much in its subsequent history to show that it was a place often occupied by elements alien to the main Israelite population of the north, though it is unlikely that it was in any sense purely Canaanite.

The establishment of the capital here by Omri was an event of great significance, and the excavations have shown the importance of the building operations—the creation of a royal quarter on the summit—in which he and his successors were engaged. Probably, since Omri is unlikely to have reigned long after the move of the capital, the work was largely carried out by Ahab. The palace and fortifications which are to be assigned to this first period occupied the top of the hill. The palace itself was not large; it followed the normal plan of rooms around a central courtyard, with additional rooms to north and south. The walls of palace and city were constructed with regular and careful alignment of the stones. There is evidence of walls further out too, indicating that the Israelite city covered a relatively large area. Omri's significance politically is

PLATE XIV

General view of Samaria, from east-south-east

shown by the references in Assyrian documents describing the founder of the next dynasty, Jehu, as 'son of Omri' (*mar-ḫumri*), and the country continued to be described as the 'territory of Omri' (*mat-ḫumri*) or 'house of Omri' (*bit-ḫumri*) on into the succeeding century.[4]

Ahab, according to 1 Kings xvi. 32, set up 'an altar for Baal in the house of Baal, which he had built in Samaria'. This is associated with his marriage with Jezebel of Tyre, and may represent an act of courtesy to his foreign wife (cf. 1 Kings xi. 7 f.); or it may indicate the recognition of Canaanite religious interests in this royal centre. The shrine was subsequently destroyed by Jehu (2 Kings x. 18–28), and the numbers involved, as also the numbers of prophets mentioned in the time of Ahab (1 Kings xviii. 22), strongly suggest that the worshippers were more than a small group of associates of the queen. No evidence of this shrine has been discovered, nor of the shrine which presumably contained 'the calf of Samaria' (Hos. viii. 5 f.) in the next century, probably this latter a royal shrine of Yahweh like those established at Dan and Beth-el by Jeroboam I (1 Kings xii. 28 f.). 'The pool of Samaria' (1 Kings xxii. 38) may perhaps be associated with one which was discovered within the royal buildings, but much more significant is the evidence which sheds light both on 'the ivory house' built by Ahab (1 Kings xxii. 39) and on 'the houses of ivory' and 'beds of ivory' (Amos iii. 15, vi. 4; cf. also Ps. xlv. 9, R.V. 8) in the period of Jeroboam II. There is some doubt about the precise dating of the large number of ivories discovered—many of them appear to have suffered in the final capture of the city in 722 B.C.—but it seems not improbable that some derive from the period of Ahab and others from the reigns of succeeding kings down through the eighth century.[5] The forms of Hebrew letters on the backs of some may well point to the earlier period.

The variety of themes illustrated on the ivories is indicative of the wealth of the kingdom, particularly during the reign of Jeroboam II, and also of the influence in Israel of religious symbols from the outside world. Some of the plaques have Egyptian themes depicting Horus and other deities; others have animals such as lions and stags; one has the 'woman at the window', almost certainly a religious symbol; others have flower decorations of various kinds. Such ivories were used to decorate the furniture, as is definitely known from the bed discovered at Ras Shamra in 1952,[6] and perhaps also for wall panels; they indicate the wealth which the upper classes enjoyed, no doubt as a result of the rich commercial life of Samaria. The style of the ivories is Phoenician and they may be of foreign manufacture, but the fact that some are unfinished suggests that craftsmen from abroad had also been brought to Samaria. It is possible that some of the ivories of similar type found in the palace of Sargon II at Khorsabad were plunder from Samaria, but this is merely supposition. Other indications of trade and prosperity are to be seen in the vessels of glass and alabaster from the site. Reflections of the social and religious conditions in Samaria in the middle of the eighth century B.C. are to be found in Amos (iii. 9 ff., iv. 1 ff., vi. 1 ff., viii. 14) and Hosea (vii. 1, viii. 5 f., x. 5 ff., xiv. 1, R.V. xiii. 16).[7]

During the period of wars with the Aramaean kingdom of Damascus there was more than one siege (cf. 1 Kings xx. 1 ff.; 2 Kings vi. 24 ff.); Aramaean domination was at one period such that markets for Aramaean traders could be established in Samaria (1 Kings xx. 34). No precise evidence of these points has been found, but further rebuilding on the site took place during the century following the period of Ahab. Perhaps in the period of Jehu and his immediate successor there was built a substantial wall of the casemate type, nearly thirty-three feet wide at the most vulnerable point of the site, though this has also been associated with the period of Jeroboam II. It gives some indication of the strength of the city and may help to explain why the later siege by the Assyrians lasted three years (725–722 B.C.), though a contributory cause could have been the insufficiency of the army deployed by the Assyrians against the city. The indications of the final capture are also clear enough in evidence of destruction, particularly by fire.

A considerable number of ostraca was found on the site, providing important evidence for the use of writing and the development of the forms of letters in the ancient Hebrew script. These are to be dated perhaps to the reign of Jeroboam II, or alternatively to that of Menahem.[8] They apparently provide records of taxes in kind, and they follow a fairly regular pattern, giving a date, the place of origin, the name of the official or of the owner of the estate,[9] and the name of the contributor.[10] The names, some compounded with the divine title *ba'al*, for example, *Abiba'al*, others with *yau* or *yō*, for example, *Ŝᵉmaryau*, show that Yahweh could be quite properly described by the title *ba'al*, though it is possible that alien religious practice is also indicated in this (Hos. ii. 18 f., R.V. 16 f.). Other divine titles also appear. The places mentioned appear all to be from the region fairly near Samaria, which would perhaps suggest that this indicates the gathering of contributions from one district in a way comparable to that organized for the whole land in the reign of Solomon (1 Kings iv. 7). It has also been suggested that these are contributions from the lessees of royal properties.[11]

The kingdom of Israel was reduced in size during the Assyrian advances; the areas of Megiddo, Dor, and Gilead were formed into separate provinces and only a small area around Samaria remained to the last king Hoshea,[12] put on the throne or confirmed there by Tiglath-pileser III in *c.* 729 B.C.[13] Intrigues with Egypt provided the occasion for Assyrian intervention (2 Kings xvii. 4, which refers to 'So king of Egypt', who has been variously identified; but perhaps the text should be read as 'to Sais (city), to the king of Egypt'). The Assyrian records provide clear statements concerning the conquest of the city and of the deportation of leading members of the population—'I surrounded and captured the city of Samaria; 27,290 of the people who dwelt in it I took away as prisoners'.[14] The Old Testament narrative contains a comparable statement (2 Kings xvii. 6), and this disaster to Samaria is also a theme of contemporary prophecy (cf. Isa. xxviii. 1 ff. (ix. 7 ff., R.V. 8 ff.), Mic. i. 5 ff.).

Some uncertainty, however, exists with regard to the actual capture of the city which is claimed by Sargon II.[15] A fuller investigation of the evidence suggests that it may have been Shalmaneser V (*c.* 727–722 B.C.) who actually captured the city, as the Old Testament implies in 2 Kings xvii. 6, xviii. 10. According to this evidence, the city was invested in 725 B.C. and fell in August/September 722. Shalmaneser died in December 722 B.C., and the capture of the city was subsequently utilized to fill out the first year of Sargon's reign in which he did not campaign in the west. This would fit well too with the evidence of a rebellion in which Samaria was involved in 721 B.C., for it is commonly the case that the advent of a new ruler brings upheavals.[16] Sargon II claims further that he 'restored the city of Samaria and made [it] more habitable than before'.[17]

The condition of the city after the Assyrian conquest is little known from the site itself, apart from indications of unimportant buildings on the summit. Later rebuilders, in the Hellenistic age, dug deep to lay the foundations of their buildings and must have destroyed earlier constructions. But both the Old Testament evidence and certain confirmatory statements from external records indicate its continued importance, now as a centre of administration for the Assyrian province of *Samerina*. 2 Kings xvii speaks of the settlement of colonists, as does Sargon—'I brought into it people from the countries conquered by my own hands'; and he refers to his appointment of 'my official . . . as district-governor'.[18] Shortly after, in 721 B.C. as we have seen, there was a rebellion against Sargon in which Samaria was involved.[19]

The Old Testament account picturesquely describes the difficulties of the settlers; they did not fear Yahweh and a plague of lions is attributed to this. It was perhaps the devastation of the land which, by reducing the population, allowed an increase in the number of lions, but other causes are equally possible. As a result a priest of Yahweh was sent and established at Beth-el to give proper religious guidance. The settlers of various nationalities also established their own religious practices, making gods which they 'put . . . in the houses of the high places which the Samaritans had made' (2 Kings xvii. 29). The names of the deities in question are listed and provide some information about the settlers. The cities from which they came are probably all Babylonian and Elamite, and so too the deities associated with them, though the names have become somewhat obscured in the Hebrew text.[20] It is said further that they worshipped Yahweh alongside their own gods, and that this continued down to the time at which the record was compiled. Unless this statement is additional to the original narrative—a piece of later anti-Samaritan polemic—the date of it cannot be much later than 561 B.C., the date of the last event recorded in 2 Kings xxv. 27–30. Indications of further settlements of foreigners (perhaps, but not certainly, in Samaria) are to be found in Ezra iv. 2, which refers to the period of Esar-haddon (681–669 B.C.), and in iv. 9 f., which refers to settlers in the period of Osnappar (Ashurbanipal, *c*. 669–627 B.C.), a list being given in this latter case of the peoples involved. The implication of the first of these statements is that these settlers too had adopted the worship of Yahweh, but that, presumably because of their continued acceptance of their own gods, they were regarded as aliens by the strict Yahwists of Jerusalem at the time of the rebuilding of the temple after the exile.

The statements regarding the settlers clearly refer only to a group of foreigners. No certainty exists as to how far intermarriage took place with the local inhabitants, for many of these no doubt remained after the Assyrian deportations. Subsequently there are indications of Yahweh worshippers from Shiloh, Shechem, and Samaria going on pilgrimage to the ruined shrine at Jerusalem, some time after its destruction in 587 B.C. (Jer. xli. 4 f.), with no suggestion that they were foreigners and every likelihood that they were representatives of the continuing tradition of faithful adherence to Yahweh in the area of the old northern kingdom. The evidence of the passage in 2 Kings xvii has, however, often been used to suggest that here is the origin of the Samaritan religious community, in spite of the fact that the later evidence indicates the Samaritans as a group of religious conservatives, upholding the purity of their tradition as they have continued to do down to the present day. The matter is confused both by the subsequent anti-Samaritan attitudes of the Jewish community, understandable in view of their common inheritance, and by the sole occurrence in the Old Testament in 2 Kings xvii. 29 of the word 'Samaritans'. But it is clear that the word here simply means 'people of Samaria', probably with reference to the whole area, though possibly with reference only to the city. The application of this name to the Samaritan religious community is likely to be of much later date, though there is no precise information about this. The Samaritans described themselves as *shamerim* 'keepers' (of the Law),[21] Hebrew *šômᵉrîm*, which may have been deliberately twisted into *šômᵉrônîm* 'Samaritans' as a nickname, perhaps intended to suggest their alien origin, or perhaps a reflection of their contacts with the civil authorities in the provincial centre of Samaria. This community was in any case more closely connected with Shechem than with Samaria.

Samaria remained the centre of the province during the Assyrian period.[22] As Assyrian power declined, the position of its governors must have become uncertain. No reference is made to such a governor in the period when Josiah moved north and came to control some not inconsiderable part of the centre of the land (2 Kings xxiii. 15–20), including Beth-el and other cities of Samaria (the province). But the same provincial organization reappears under the Babylonians, and was carried further under the Persians. It is not improbable that from the time of Gedaliah's assassination (2 Kings xxv. 25; Jer. xli), Judah was placed under the control of the governor in Samaria and continued to be in this position until the time of Nehemiah. Zerubbabel is described as 'governor' (peḥāh, Hag. i. 1, ii. 2, 21), but the term may well be used loosely to describe his function as commissioner charged with the task of rebuilding the temple, rather than as independent governor of a separate area. The term is not so used of him in Ezra iii f., nor is it used of Sheshbazzar in Ezra i.

At the time of the rebuilding of the temple (Ezra iv. 1–5, but cf. above), again at a time in the reign of Artaxerxes (presumably Artaxerxes I), when an attempt was made to rebuild the walls (Ezra iv. 6–23), and yet again in the time of Nehemiah (Neh. ii. 19, etc.), it would appear that the opposition came from the governor in Samaria or from the descendants of those who had been settled there after the Assyrian conquest. This may imply some measure of control, and in the last of these examples the claim to such control appears fairly evident. The Jews in Elephantine at the end of the fifth century B.C. were writing both to the authorities in Jerusalem and to the sons of Sanballat in Samaria, and this suggests that the position was still as it had been, or that any change was not yet fully recognized.[23] Underlying these circumstances there may be reason to suspect a much greater significance of Samaria for the Jewish community in and around Jerusalem than appears directly in the Old Testament record.

Sanballat I, as he must now be named (cf. below), appears clearly to have been governor in Samaria. His name 'Sin (moon-god) gives life' no more indicates that he was an adherent of Babylonian religion than do the names Zerubbabel or Sheshbazzar or Abed-nego; his sons were named Delaiah and Shelemiah, and he was related by marriage to the high priestly family (Neh. xiii. 28). Papyri, about forty in number, recently discovered in a cave north of Jericho,[24] but deriving from Samaria so far as their con-

tents are sufficiently preserved to indicate provenance, reveal some
of the business and legal affairs of the community there during the
fourth century B.C., a period concerning which very little is known.
They deal with sale and manumission of slaves, contracts, and
loans and the like. They also indicate that there were probably at
least two further governors named Sanballat, perhaps in each case
with another name intervening, giving a sequence Sanballat I,
Delaiah, Sanballat II, Hananiah (the name appears in the papyri),
Sanballat III. Josephus, whose account of the period is clearly
tendentious, may have confused these various personages, though
there may be some element of historical truth in his linking of the
priesthood of the Samaritans with Manasseh, son-in-law of one of
the Sanballats. He describes Sanballat as a Cuthite, of the alien
stock from Assyrian times.[25] There are indications on the site of
Samaria of a laid-out garden or orchard on the summit, perhaps
associated with a governor's residence of this period.

The period of Alexander the Great's invasions of the east may
have complicated the position. Samaria was one of the few places
in the Palestinian area which had to be taken by force, and it
was made into a Macedonian colony. There are some indications
of a subsequent insurrection and the execution and exile of some of
its people on Alexander's return from Egypt.[26] The older fortifications of the city were reused at this time, but strengthened by the
addition of round towers, clearly discovered in the course of the
excavations, though the precise date of these developments is not
absolutely clear. The city continued to be important, now as
a centre of Greek culture. A third-century shrine of Isis beneath
the later temple of Kore (belonging to the Roman period) reveals
its cosmopolitan religious life, a natural development from the
earlier situation. As an alien centre in a land which still boasted
many adherents of Yahweh, it was an understandable aim of the
Jewish rulers of the second century B.C. that they should endeavour
to control it, and it was besieged for a year and destroyed by John
Hyrcanus c. 107 B.C. He had earlier and quite independently
destroyed the Samaritan temple on Mount Gerizim (128 B.C.).

The situation was clarified with the intervention of Rome under
Pompey in 63 B.C. The city and its environs were attached to the
Roman province of Syria and thus made independent of the Jewish
state. The city itself was considerably restored by Gabinius

between 57 and 55 B.C., and its inhabitants called themselves 'Gabinians' in recognition of this. Subsequently the whole area was reorganized and welded into one as the kingdom of Herod the Great. Samaria, where he had married Mariamne in 37 B.C., was given to him by Augustus in 30 B.C., and entered upon a new period of prosperity and development as a city in Hellenistic style, with temples, theatre, forum, stadium, and other marks of status, being renamed by Herod as Sebaste (Greek *sebastos* = Augustus) in honour of the Roman ruler. A temple dedicated to Augustus was built over the area once occupied by the palace of Omri and Ahab. Veterans of the Roman campaigns were settled there, and when subsequently, in the Jewish War of A.D. 66–70, there was destruction, the Herodian buildings could nevertheless be restored, and the city enjoyed great prosperity again, particularly in the second and third centuries A.D. The larger part of the Roman remains is likely to be from this later period when the city covered an area of some 160 acres.

During the New Testament period the region of Samaria had, like Judaea, come first under the rule of Herod's son Archelaus, and from A.D. 6 onwards under a Roman procurator. The area of Samaria was visited by Jesus (Luke ix. 52, xvii. 11; John iv) though he forbade his disciples to go there (Matt. x. 5, but not the parallels in Luke and Mark), but there are no indications of any contact with the notably Hellenistic city, nor does it seem likely that the early church had any contact with it, though there was Christian activity in the region (cf. Acts i. 8, viii. 1, 4 ff.). The area came under Herod Agrippa I from A.D. 41–44 but then reverted to direct Roman control.

P. R. ACKROYD

NOTES

1. For a description, see G. A. Smith, *The Historical Geography of the Holy Land*, 25th ed., 1931, pp. 344 ff.

2. Cf. W. F. Albright, *B.A.S.O.R.* 150, 1958, p. 22; Y. Aharoni and R. Amiran, *I.E.J.* viii, 1958, pp. 171–80, see pp. 178 ff.; G. E. Wright, *B.A.S.O.R.* 155, 1959, pp. 20 f., *B.A.* xxii, 1959, pp. 76 f.

3. A. Alt, *V.T.* i, 1951, pp. 10 f. = *K.S.* ii, 1953, pp. 123 f., *Der Stadtstaat Samaria*, 1954 = *K.S.* iii, 1959, pp. 258–302. Cf. J. Gray, *I and II Kings*, 1964, p. 331, and the criticisms of Alt by G. E. Wright, *J.N.E.S.* xv, 1956, pp. 124 f., and *B.A.* xxii, 1959, p. 69, n. 2.

4. *D.O.T.T.*, pp. 47 f., 51 f.; *A.N.E.T.*, pp. 280 f., 283 f.

5. On the dating problems, cf. A. Parrot, *Samaria*, 1958, pp. 69 f., and footnotes giving references to the literature.

6. Cf. C. F. A. Schaeffer, *Syria* xxxi, 1954, pp. 51 ff. and pls. vii–x.

7. Other passages may well refer to conditions there, though Samaria is not actually named.

8. On the dating, cf. Parrot, op. cit., p. 77, and notes. For the later date, cf. Y. Yadin, *Scripta Hierosolymitana* (ed. C. Rabin), viii, 1961, pp. 9–25, and criticisms by Y. Aharoni, *I.E.J.* xii, 1962, pp. 67 ff.

9. On this, cf. Y. Yadin, *I.E.J.* ix, 1959, pp. 184–7, and the discussion in *I.E.J.* xii, 1962, pp. 62–69.

10. *D.O.T.T.*, pp. 206 f.; *A.N.E.T.*, p. 321.

11. Cf. M. Noth, *Z.D.P.V.* i, 1927, pp. 211–44, see pp. 219 ff., and *The History of Israel*, rev. ed., 1960, pp. 213 f., 237. For criticism of this view, cf. literature mentioned in note 9, *supra*.

12. *A.N.E.T.*, p. 283.

13. *D.O.T.T.*, p. 55; *A.N.E.T.*, p. 284.

14. *D.O.T.T.*, p. 60; *A.N.E.T.*, pp. 284 f.

15. *D.O.T.T.*, pp. 59 ff.; *A.N.E.T.*, pp. 284 f.

16. On the whole question, cf. H. Tadmor, *J.C.S.* xii, 1958, pp. 22–40, 77–100, see pp. 31, 33–40; W. W. Hallo, *B.A.* xxiii, 1960, pp. 34–61, see p. 51.

17. *D.O.T.T.*, p. 60.

18. Ibid., p. 60; *A.N.E.T.*, p. 284.

19. *D.O.T.T.*, p. 61; *A.N.E.T.*, p. 285.

20. Cf. G. R. Driver, *Eretz-Israel* v, pp. 16*–20*, see pp. 18*–20*.

21. Cf. J. Macdonald, *The Theology of the Samaritans*, 1964, pp. 22, 203, 272.

22. Cf. M. Noth, *The History of Israel*, rev. ed., 1960, p. 263.

23. *D.O.T.T.*, pp. 262 ff.; *A.N.E.T.*, p. 492.

24. F. M. Cross, *B.A.* xxvi, 1963, pp. 109–21.

25. Cf. Josephus, *Ant.* xi, sections 297–312, and H. H. Rowley, *B.J.R.L.* xxxviii, 1955–6, pp. 166–98 = *Men of God*, 1963, pp. 246–76, and 'The Samaritan schism in legend and history', in *Israel's Prophetic Heritage* (ed. B. W. Anderson and W. Harrelson), 1962, pp. 208–22.

26. Cf. the discussion of the evidence by G. E. Wright, *H.T.R.* lv, 1962, pp. 357–66.

BIBLIOGRAPHY

CROWFOOT, J. W., CROWFOOT, G. M., and SUKENIK, E. L. *Samaria-Sebaste I: Early Ivories from Samaria*, 1938.

—— KENYON, K. M., and SUKENIK, E. L. *Samaria-Sebaste II: The Buildings at Samaria*, 1942.

—— CROWFOOT, G. M., and KENYON, K. M. *Samaria-Sebaste III: The Objects from Samaria*, 1957.

KENYON, K. M. *Archaeology in the Holy Land*, 2nd ed., 1965; see index 'Samaria'.

PARROT, A. *Samaria: The Capital of the Kingdom of Israel* (E. Tr. S. H. Hooke), 1958. A useful bibliography is included.

REISNER, G. A., FISHER, C. S., and LYON, D. G. *Harvard Excavations at Samaria 1908–10*, 2 vols., 1924.

WRIGHT, G. E. 'Israelite Samaria and Iron Age Chronology', *B.A.S.O.R.* 155, 1959, pp. 13–29.

—— 'Samaria', *B.A.* xxii, 1959, pp. 67–78.

SHECHEM

i. *Location and Extra-Biblical Reference to the City*

BEFORE 1913-14 scholars generally assumed that the ruins of this Old Testament city[1] existed beneath modern Nablus. The latter, descended from Neapolis, a 'New City' founded by Vespasian in A.D. 72, is today the second largest city of Jordan, situated well within the pass between mounts Ebal and Gerizim, some 42 miles directly north of Jerusalem. The reason for this location goes back to Jerome who rejected earlier tradition which placed the city further east at the opening of the pass near 'Jacob's Well'.[2] Jerome was followed by no less a scholar than Edward Robinson, the father of modern Biblical topographical study, who also rejected the earlier tradition as uncritical speculation at the beginning of the age of Christian pilgrimage to the holy places.[3]

In the time of Constantine, the Church Father Eusebius, in his *Onomasticon* of Biblical places, and the Bordeaux Pilgrim who visited the Holy Land in A.D. 333, both placed Shechem at the eastern suburbs of Nablus between 'Jacob's Well' and the village of 'Askar. The earliest map of Palestine, in a mosaic floor of a mid-sixth century church at Madeba, gives the same location, and shows the traditional tomb of Joseph adjacent to the small village which the map depicts. These indications would lead us to the modern village of Balâṭah at the edge of which Muslim piety still preserves a place identified as the Tomb of Joseph. Yet the first modern scholar to identify ruins in this area as those of ancient Shechem was Hermann Thiersch who paused there for a day in 1903 because of tired horses.[4] He kept his discovery quiet, however, because he did not want a nation other than his own to act upon it.[5] Then in 1908 a bronze hoard was found in Balâṭah while a new house was being erected on the slopes of the tell to the north of the village. This hoard was purchased by F. Freiherr von Bissing for a museum in The Hague, where it attracted considerable attention.[6] It is not surprising then, that Ernst Sellin, after his successful excavations at Jericho with Carl Watzinger (1907–9), began work at Tell Belâṭah during the fall and spring of 1913–14. He followed a cyclopean city wall for some 60 metres on the mound's west side, when a massive three-entry gate was encountered and exposed. As a result of his work, he then wrote that there can be 'no doubt that the hill of Balatah represents the site of the Canaanite–Israelite Shechem'.[7] Eusebius and the Madeba Map were confirmed.

The mound at Balâṭah is comparatively small for the centre of one of the major Palestinian city states; it is only 10–12 acres in extent. It was created as a fortress to control its area and is unusual for the size and strength of its fortifications. For nearly 5 miles directly to the east and to the south a great L-shaped plain served as its bread-basket, while all major roads in north central Palestine pass by it. No less a scholar than A. Alt has acclaimed the site as the natural capital of Palestine, 'the uncrowned queen' of the country, while Jerusalem's paramount position is to be traced to the political and religious policies of King David rather than to the position accorded to it by nature.[8]

The earliest datable reference to the city is by an officer of the Egyptian Pharaoh, Sesostris III (c. 1878–1843 B.C.), who says that 'his majesty reached a foreign country of which the name was *skmm*. Then *skmm* fell, together with the wretched Retenu.'[9] A ruler of the city, Abesh-hadad, is mentioned as an enemy of Egypt in the Brussels group of Execration Texts, dating from the latter part of the Twelfth or from the Thirteenth Dynasty (c. 1800 B.C.).[10] In the period of the Tell el-Amarna letters of the first half of the fourteenth century B.C. the city was ruled by Lab'ayu who is the author of three of the letters,[11] while he or his sons are the subject of four additional letters.[12] Judging from these documents Shechem is the city state which controlled all territory of the hill-country between the city state of Megiddo on the north and those of Jerusalem and Gezer on the south. The vigour of the Shechem rulers is perhaps reflected by the hatred of their neighbours, evidently for their constant expansionist pressure. From the end of the Nineteenth Dynasty (late thirteenth century B.C.) there is an enigmatic reference to 'the mountain [or hill-country?] of Shechem' in Papyrus Anastasi I.[13] These extra-Biblical references from the period between the nineteenth and twelfth centuries B.C. suggest the importance of the Middle and Late Bronze Age city, which, like Samaria in the first millennium B.C., gave its name to its area.

ii. *The City of the Patriarchal Period (MB IIA–B)*

Between 1926 and 1934 new expeditions to the site were directed successively by E. Sellin, G. Walter, and H. Steckeweh, though the major work remains the credit of Sellin. Because of the failure of methodology, however, the basic problems of chronology and interpretation remained unsolved.[14] Between 1956 and 1966 a new expedition worked at the site which was sponsored by Drew University, McCormick Theological Seminary, and the American Schools of Oriental Research. Headed by G. Ernest Wright, its staff was composed mainly of young American scholars and graduate students whose chief concern was the clarification of the city's archaeological history. Success in this respect, together with the interpretation of what was found, has in turn led to a fresh handling of the Old Testament traditions concerning Shechem with surprising results.[15] First, we shall summarize the archaeological history during the Middle Bronze Age.

Although there was a sizeable Chalcolithic village during the fourth millennium B.C., the city of the historical period was a creation of new settlers of the 'Amorite' era of Middle Bronze IIA. The most detailed evidence comes from the sacred area on the tell's western side. Here not later than *c.* 1800 B.C. and before any known city walls had been erected, a vast earth-moving and levelling operation took place to prepare an area on the edge of the city for some public function. No certain evidence was discovered as to what that function was—unless we assume that it cannot be separated from the purpose the area served during the next six centuries when it was the site of a succession of temples. Because of these later buildings no attempt was made to clear a wide area to learn the nature of MB IIA structures. Yet we do know that one prominent feature was a large earthen podium, the sides of which were protected by stones to prevent erosion. It is perhaps useless to conjecture what it was used for, except that it confirms the public, rather than private, character of the area.

At the beginning of MB IIB, not later than the middle or third quarter of the eighteenth century B.C., the western area in question was enclosed by a city wall (Wall D) of brick on a stone socket, 6 cubits (2·50–2·75 metres) wide. Inside this fortification and separated from the rest of the city by a stout stone wall (No. 900), 5 cubits (c. 2·10–2·20 metres) wide, was a peculiar series of rooms which existed mainly on the north side of a large court which had within it a smaller court. The main entrance into the complex was to the south, and one was led north along a cobbled street beside enclosure Wall 900 at least 30 metres before a narrow passage-way led to an entrance into rooms and courts directly north of the great court. In the second building phase of the structure Wall D became solely the retaining wall for a vast earthen embankment which served as the mound's fortification during the Hyksos period. Including the width of Wall D and of the 5 metre high stone revetment (Wall C) on the outside, the width of this C fortification at its base was at least 37 metres.

The courtyard building maintained its basic character for a century through three major reconstructions. The most important spot within it and the pivot of the rebuildings appears to have been the location of the central court, the southern and eastern walls of which remained on the same lines while the arrangement of the northern rooms was changed in each rebuilding. The altars of the later temple were directly over the southern walls of the small court in question. Nothing was found within the buildings to suggest their purpose, except for two pillar bases at the centres of two adjacent small courts in the third building phase. These had no structural purpose and are most easily interpreted as sacred pillars (*maṣṣēḇôṯ*). Indirect suggestions are provided by the observation that architecturally the buildings make little sense as royal palaces, while subsequently their area is the courtyard of the great temple of El-berith (Judges ix. 46). Consequently, the interpretation of the structures as courtyard temples has commended itself, that is, as temples where the courts are the central feature of the architecture rather than a single building as the 'house' of deity. While it is known that such places of worship must have been widespread, archaeological examples have been known only from the Late Bronze Age at Beth-shean (Stratum IX, fourteenth century B.C.) and from the same period in Anatolia.[16] In the light of this interpretation the west side was the sacred area of Shechem throughout a long period until its destruction by Abimelech in the twelfth century B.C. (see below), and it must have been constructed as such even in its earliest period, MB IIA of the nineteenth–eighteenth centuries B.C.

Turning to the book of Genesis we find that Shechem plays a prominent role in patriarchal tradition. Jacob purchased a plot of ground near the city and built an altar for worship on it (Gen. xxxiii. 18 ff.). Abraham came to the *mākôm* (here assuredly meaning 'sacred area') of Shechem and erected there an altar (Gen. xii. 6 f.). In other words, as in the case of Beth-el, Mamre, and Beer-sheba, patriarchal association involved worship and the establishment of a cultic place. Both the Abrahamic and Jacob cycles of tradition claim this association for each patriarch. Indeed, the Jacob tradition would appear to claim the founding of Shechem's sacred area, even as it did the one at Beth-el (Gen. xxviii).

In Gen. xxxiv the city is spoken of as a person whose interactions with the family of Jacob involve two traditions: one of covenant, the first recorded treaty with a local group which permitted intermarriage; and one of conquest of the city, the latter perhaps being reflected also in the Hebrew of Gen. xlviii. 22. It has also been pointed out that the name of the people of Shechem, 'children of Hamor', actually must mean, on the basis of Mari evidence, 'people of the covenant', a treaty or confederation sealed by the slaughter of an ass.[17] If so, then covenant, confederation, or treaty is something which is a primary constituent of Shechem's earliest history.

Finally we note the specific allusion to a tree, 'the oak of Moreh' which evidently was in the *mākôm* or sacred area (Gen. xii. 6, cf. xxxv. 4), something to which we shall return. If we could be sure of the historicity of Jacob's founding of Shechem's sacred area, then we would have to date him to the nineteenth century B.C., the first part of the MB IIA period, when in the western sector the sacred area lay on the edge of the city before it was incorporated within city fortification. That the area of Shechem alluded to in the patriarchal stories is precisely the sacred area on the western side of the tell cannot be proved, but this surprisingly is strongly suggested by the continuity of cultic tradition there; we shall return to this subject below.

iii. *The City of the Fortress-Temple* (*MB IIC–IA I*)

About the middle of the seventeenth century B.C. the courtyard temple and C earthen embankment were replaced by new, huge, and unusual structures which have no precise parallel. Around the outer base of the embankment a cyclopean wall (Wall A) was erected. It had a vertical inner side, a battered exterior, and its full height, still preserved on the west and at least in places on the east, attained 8 to 10 metres. It was built course by course from the inside, and the top of the embankment was pulled down into the space between the two fortifications as the level rose. At the north-west a three-entry gate was constructed at a level near the top of the wall, so that its approach road must have been a ramp.

On the flat platform created where the earthen fortification had been a great rectangular building was erected in the sacred area. While its purpose and date were originally disputed, the stratification has solved the problem of date, while the altars and sacred stones to the east in the court over the courtyard temples now leave no doubt that the building was a temple which was erected in the same era as Wall A. It was a brick building on a stone foundation, the latter being completely preserved. It is 26·30 metres long by 21·20 metres wide, the side and rear walls of the *cella* being about 5·10 metres thick. These dimensions suggest that the builders were using the long or 'sacred' cubit mentioned in Ezek. xliii. 13 (*c.* 525 millimetres), and that the building was meant to be 50 × 40 × 10 cubits of this type. The entrance hall was 7 metres wide, and a single fluted stone column was set in a circular depression, 76 to 78 centimetres in diameter, prepared for it on a boulder set in the centre of the threshold. Other fluted column fragments, smaller in size, suggest that the roof of the *cella* was supported by them. These fluted stone column fragments, evidently of Egyptian inspiration, are the only examples of the type found in Western Asia from the Bronze Age.

During the same MB IIC period the city and temple were evidently seriously harmed by enemy action. The floor of the temple was then raised about 75 centimetres and the single column was eliminated in front by closing up one half of the entrance hall. Spaced so as to flank the new doorway exactly, two sacred standing stones (*maṣṣēḇôṯ*) were erected on the exterior close to the podium.

The brick foundations for the altar of this temple were identified in the court; it was probably square, the length of one side being slightly in excess of 3·50 metres. At about the same time the fortifications of the north and east sides of the tell were strengthened by the addition of Wall B and the East Gate. This was a brick wall on a stone socket, about 3·50 metres wide (8 cubits), which was erected on the remaining top of the C embankment, leaving a space of about 11 metres between it and Wall A, a space which was made into a glacis.

Only one other temple architecturally similar to this great rectangular one at Shechem has been found, even though it is not quite as large or massive. This was excavated at Megiddo. While the excavators there thought that their temple was not erected until Stratum VIII of the fourteenth century B.C., it is far more probable stratigraphically that its first phase dated from the same period as the Shechem structure, that is to the seventeenth and sixteenth centuries B.C. B. Mazar has argued in an unpublished article that the study of place-names suggests that the buildings belong to a class of *migdāl* or fortress-temples. When a town in Galilee is named Migdal-el (Joshua xix. 38), it makes sense only if the town derived its name from a fortress of the god El, a fortress that was also a temple (cf. also Migdal-gad in the Judaean lowlands and Migdol on the border of Egypt, Joshua xv. 37; Exod. xiv. 2). Penuel in Transjordan, another town with a precious patriarchal tradition (Gen. xxxii. 30 ff.), also had a *migdāl* in it, one which was destroyed only a short time before those of Shechem and Megiddo in the twelfth century B.C. (Judges viii. 8 f., 17). The fortress-like function of such a temple may possibly be illustrated by the story of Abimelech's siege of Thebez, modern Ṭūbâs, a dependency of Shechem (Judges ix. 50–55). After forcing his way into the city, he still had to capture the *migdāl* 'in the midst of the town', in which the inhabitants had taken refuge. While the English versions simply speak about the building as 'a strong tower', its Hebrew name *migdal-ʿōz* may well be that of a temple, since *ʿōz* is one of the commonest of divine epithets.

In the mid-sixteenth century B.C. Shechem was violently destroyed, along with all other Palestinian cities so far as they are known. There is evidence that there were two destructions of the city within a comparatively short time, perhaps one late in the reign of Pharaoh Amosis (*c.* 1570–1546 B.C.) and one early in the reign of Amenophis I (*c.* 1546–1526 B.C.), the first two kings of the Eighteenth Dynasty.[18]

After a gap in occupation the city was rebuilt, including the fortress-temple and the fortifications. A major change appears in the temple's plan. Its axis is shifted by 5 degrees south on the former *miḡdāl*'s foundations until it now faces 33° south of east. The walls are reduced in size from 10 long cubits thick to 4 (about 2·00 to 2·30 metres). The dimensions of the *cella* are now about 16 metres wide by 12·5 metres deep (about 30 × 24 long cubits), as against the first temple's *cella* of 11 metres wide by 13·50 metres in length. In other words, the new temple is basically a rectangular room with entrance on the long side, precisely like that of a majority of Canaanite temples of the third and second millennia B.C.

Temple 2, like Temple 1, had two phases, both of which used a portion of the Temple 1 rear wall as a podium to which three steps of stairs led. Belonging to the second phase (Temple 2b) there was the platform for a stone altar in the court which cannot be earlier than the latter part of the Bronze Age. Its dimensions were 2·20 metres long by 1·65 metres wide. Below it Sellin may have discovered the mud-brick foundations of the earlier altar of Temple 2a; he says its dimensions were 5·20 × 7·00 metres. Further east, 2·50 metres from, and in the same level of earth as the last altar, was a white stone monolith, its faces originally ground smooth, which was fitted into a socket cut for it in a huge rock. The stone, clearly a *maṣṣēḇāh*, had had its top broken off irregularly, so that its surviving height is only 1·45 metres on one side and 62 centimetres on the other. Its width is 1·48 metres and thickness 42 centimetres, or roughly 3 × 1 common cubits. There can be no doubt but that in the final phase of the temple's life both this and the two smaller sacred stones flanking the temple's doors were in place and visible. It is quite clear from the excavations that Bronze Age Shechem, like Bronze Age Megiddo, was not destroyed in the thirteenth century B.C., destructions which ended the Bronze Age at such sites as Lachish and Debir in the south (Joshua x. 31 f., 38 f.) and Hazor in Galilee (Joshua xi). Instead, both Shechem and Megiddo survived well into the twelfth century B.C. Only then were all Bronze Age structures destroyed in violent conflict.

Here follows, then, a summary of the stratification:

		Expedition stratum
Phase	*Date*	*(by Wall no.)*
Temenos 1	*c.* 1800–1750 B.C.	968

Massive fill and levelling of the area. First structures outside known fortifications. Platform 968.

Temenos 2	*c.* 1750–1725 B.C.	939

Simple courtyard temple and Streets 9–7 enclosed between City Wall D and *Temenos* Wall 900.

Temenos 3	*c.* 1725–1700 B.C.	902

Casemate-courtyard temple and Street 6. Wall C and the great 30-metre wide, earthen embankment between C and D. Major destruction.

Temenos 4	*c.* 1700–1675 B.C.	901

Pillar-courtyard temple and Streets 5–4. Wall 900 completely rebuilt. Wall D no longer visible when the 901 addition, Walls 912–27, was erected during the period.

Temenos 5	*c.* 1675–1650 B.C.	909–10

Enlarged courtyard temple built over edge of C Embankment, Streets 3–1. Silos built on Embankment.

Temenos 6	*c.* 1650–1600 B.C.	

Fortress-temple 1a, Wall A and North-west Gate.

Temenos 7	*c.* 1600–1550 B.C.	

Fortress-temple 1b with small *maṣṣēḇôṯ* on either side of entrance. Altar base with marl-brick edging. Wall B on east and north. East Gate.

Destructions (*c.* 1550–1540 B.C.) and gap in occupation (*c.* 1540–1450 B.C.)

Temenos 8	*c.* 1450–1200 B.C.	

Fortress-temple 2a, new brick altar, first phase of podium, repair and reuse of all fortifications. *Maṣṣēḇāh* 1 erected in this period or the next.

Temenos 9	*c.* 1200–1100 B.C.	

Fortress-temple 2b, marked by raising of floor and new altar of stone. All three sacred standing stones in use. Destruction and end of sacred area.

iv. *The Old Testament Tradition*

It now must be noted as a fact of paramount historical importance that there is no tradition of a conquest by Joshua of the area between Beth-el and the Esdraelon.[19] While by definite statement or implication we infer that Israel did not take the city states of Jerusalem and Gezer on the south and of Megiddo, Taanach, and Beth-shean on the north (cf. Judges i. 27, 29; Jerusalem was captured by David, 2 Sam. v. 7), nothing is said about warfare in relation to Shechem. Instead, there is a strong northern tradition about a covenant of 'all the tribes of Israel' at Shechem (Joshua xxiv),[20] and the time of this covenant is placed directly after the success in Benjamin and before the Judaean campaign (cf. Deut. xi. 26 ff.; Joshua viii. 30 ff.; cf. Deut. xxvii). From archaeological information we can say that Shechem controlled the whole territory between Beth-el and Megiddo, and that accordingly we must infer that the kingdom of Shechem, meaning the whole north-central hill-country, entered the Israelite tribal federation by treaty and not by conquest. At the same time the Old Testament story of Abimelech's destruction of Shechem provides a tradition that accounts for the archaeological fact of the demise of the Bronze Age city during the course of the twelfth century B.C. (Judges ix).

The Gideon–Abimelech stories (Judges vi–ix) would appear to represent the first movement toward kingship in Israel. This involved, in the case of Shechem, simply a return to the city state political pattern, either in independence of the authority of the tribal league centred in Shiloh, or within the league's framework. In any case, the movement was so counter to the covenant pattern of affairs in Israel that it is not surprising that the revolt against Abimelech led by Gaal ben-Ebed was successful. On the other hand, Abimelech's destruction of the city and his sowing it with salt is also understandable in the light of recent research which has shown that sowing with salt as a symbol of perpetual infertility was traditional custom which followed upon the breach of covenant.[21]

A special problem exists in the interpretation of Judges ix. After the story of Shechem's destruction and salting is concluded in verse 45, an additional paragraph (verses 46–49) is added, the interpretation of which has been much in dispute. Verse 46 reads: 'And when all the responsible citizens of Migdal-Shechem heard, they entered the ṣᵉrîaḥ of the Temple of El-berith.' There follows the story of the burning of the ṣᵉrîaḥ and the death of all the men and women in it. If verse 46, it has been argued, is read as continuous narrative, following verse 45, then the *Migdal-Shechem* cannot be in Shechem itself because the city has been destroyed.

PLATE XV

'Temple of El-berith' (Shechem). In centre foreground a portion of the temple's original court, with large sacred pillar re-erected where originally found. It belonged to Temple 2. Against the podium on left is a fragment of another pillar in its base, erected in period of Temple 1b. The base for another of the same date shown right centre. At bottom (foreground) excavations into the earlier courtyard temples

It is equally possible, however, that verses 46–49 are not meant to be read as a sequel to verse 45, but instead, in a manner typical of Hebrew narration, as an item of special importance, especially stressed, which narrates an occurrence *during* the destruction of the city. Less problems arise if the second interpretation is adopted.[22] *Migdal-Shechem* would thus be the name for the sacred area, which was the city's citadel (cf. the *migdāl* in Thebez, verse 51), while the special name of the temple was 'the house of the covenant God' (El-berith) (Pl. XV), and the *ṣᵉrîaḥ* in which the people took refuge was the towers of the temple.[23]

It was noted that in the Genesis traditions about Shechem, sacred area, covenant, and tree were present. Here in Judges ix the temple is named for 'the covenant God' (El-berith),[24] and Abimelech is made king by the oak (verse 6). Turning to Joshua xxiv we are reminded of the importance attached to this chapter in recent research as belonging to the primary covenant literature in the Old Testament.[25] There we are told that to commemorate the covenant, Joshua 'took a great stone and set it up there under the oak that was by [R.V. marg. 'in'] the sanctuary of the Lord' (verse 26). Here again we encounter sanctuary, covenant, and tree. These constant elements in three very different types of literature, each with its own history of transmission, suggest a continuity of cultic tradition connected with the sacred area of Shechem. Furthermore, since from the archaeological evidence the cultic symbols of the various covenants at Shechem appear to have been sacred pillars, it is difficult to dissociate the last and greatest of these stones from the tradition of Joshua's 'great stone'.

From the evidence surveyed above it is difficult to assume that the inhabitants of Shechem during the thirteenth and twelfth centuries B.C. were typical Canaanites, worshipping a Canaanite deity, as has often been assumed. If the covenant ceremony of Joshua xxiv took place in the sacred area, then that area had already been accepted by Yahwism. If so, then 'the Covenant God' (El-berith) of Shechem may represent one of the forms of 'the God of the Fathers' who was identified with Yahweh.

v. *Israelite Shechem*

Following the twelfth-century B.C. destruction of Shechem no occupational vigour has been found until Stratum X, the city of the Solomonic period from the second half of the tenth century B.C. It appears likely that Shechem, like Megiddo, Hazor, and Ramoth-gilead, was newly built as a provincial capital and administrative centre, in this case for the Solomonic province of 'Mount Ephraim'.[26] In early clan lists Shechem is listed among the clans of Manasseh (Num. xxvi. 31 ff.; Joshua xvii. 2; cf. 1 Chron. vii. 19), indicating that at first the city state was broken up, and the city and its adjoining lands were on the southern border of that tribal area. Beginning with the time of Solomon, however, Shechem as the administrative centre of 'Mount Ephraim' also served as the city of refuge and a Levitical city for its area (Joshua xx. 7, xxi. 21). During the late ninth or eighth century B.C. (Stratum IXA or VIII) a large government warehouse was erected on the ruins of the temple, indicating that the sacred area was never revived as such after Abimelech's destruction. A casemate reconstruction (Wall E) of Wall B was extended southward from the North-west Gate—which was reused—but though the new wall belongs to the general period, the precise date of its erection cannot now be ascertained (cf. 1 Kings xii. 25).

In spite of the secularization of the city's function, its old role as the chief religio-political centre of northern Israel meant that it was the place of assembly for the northerners who called Rehoboam to account and where they rejected his rule (1 Kings xii 1 ff). It was also chosen as the first capital of the northern kingdom (verse 25). Why Jeroboam left it within a short time for Penuel we do not know, unless we suppose that the ruined fortifications of the old Bronze Age site made new and strong fortification difficult. In any event, the city itself no longer played a prominent role in Israelite life, though the covenant ceremony of the blessings and curses was probably continued in its vicinity.[27]

The archaeological stratification of the Iron Age together with hypotheses concerning its interpretation are as follows:

Stratum X, the Solomonic city, was violently destroyed, presumably by Pharaoh Shishak in the fifth year of the reigns of Jeroboam and Rehoboam (1 Kings xiv. 25). Stratum IXA from the first part of the ninth century B.C. was a very solidly built city. This city was badly burned either as a result of an earthquake, or more probably as a result of the enemy action of Benhadad I of Damascus between c. 865 and 855 B.C. (1 Kings xx). Stratum IXB is the rebuilding of IXA, which in turn was destroyed by enemy action, probably by Hazael, c. 810 B.C. (cf. 2 Kings xii. 18, R.V. 17–xiii. 23), along with many of the towns of Israel. Stratum VIII represents the long and prosperous first half of the eighth century B.C. before the beginning of Israel's impoverishment and civil turmoil, occasioned by Assyrian pressure in the third quarter of the eighth century B.C. This last is the period of Stratum VII which was violently destroyed by the Assyrian army in the levelling of Israel in 724–723 B.C. During the seventh century B.C. the city of Stratum VI was an impoverished attempt to rebuild a town and even to repair the East Gate of the city. It suffered two destructions, however, and we do not have sufficient information to know the cause, unless it was the re-conquest of Israel by Josiah c. 628–622 B.C. (cf. 2 Chron. xxxiv. 6 f.). Equally or even more weak was the city of Stratum V belonging to the sixth (Jer. xl. 5) and early fifth centuries B.C. Judging from the date of the imported Greek pottery, this stratum lasted until c. 485–475 B.C., when the tell was abandoned for a century and a half.[28]

vi. *The City of the Samaritans*

At the end of the fourth century B.C. the city suddenly came to life again. It was quickly rebuilt on an extensive scale, and this included the repair of the fortifications and the preparation of a glacis on the eastern slope. This fact calls for an explanation. When taken together with the information in the new Samaritan scrolls,[29] it means that we must take seriously late information provided by Quintius Curtius, Eusebius, Jerome, and Syncellus, to the effect that Alexander the Great destroyed Samaria, the Samaritan capital, in 331 B.C. and gave it to a contingent of his Macedonian troops, who then settled there. The Samaritans, deprived of a capital, evidently returned to the abandoned Shechem and rebuilt it,[30] refortified it, and attempted to make it a rival of Jerusalem.

Life could not have been easy or undisturbed. At least four times in the course of a century there was disturbance which caused extensive rebuilding. Strata IVB and IVA extended from 331 B.C. to c. 250 B.C. Strata IIIA and IIIB, during which the fortifications, a new glacis, and the buildings of the city had to be rebuilt, lasted from c. 250 B.C. until c. 190 B.C. At this point the coins of the Ptolemaic rulers cease, and those of the Seleucids begin. But the city was not again fortified after the period of

Stratum III, even though it gives every evidence of being very prosperous with an extensive population. Josephus records the destruction of Shechem by John Hyrcanus (135–104 B.C.) at the same time in which he destroyed the Samaritan temple on mount Gerizim, *c.* 128 B.C.[31] If true, we should presumably credit him with the destruction of Stratum II. The reoccupation of the city was immediate and extended until shortly after 110 B.C., when the series of coins ceases on the tell. Perhaps Stratum I was destroyed by John Hyrcanus when he destroyed Samaria *c.* 107 B.C.[32] In any event, the last major event at the site was the transfer of a vast amount of earth from the mountain sides to cover over the surviving Wall A and north-west gate so that they could never again be used for fortification. The name of the site survived for some centuries, but thereafter was only a small village, like modern Balâṭah, by the excellent spring issuing from the base of Mount Gerizim.

G. ERNEST WRIGHT

NOTES

1. Hebrew *šᵉkem* 'shoulder', Greek Συχέμ, Σίκιμα.

2. Jerome, *Pilgrimage of the Holy Paula*, xvi; *Quaest. in Gen.*, cap. xlviii, no. 22.

3. E. Robinson and E. Smith, *Biblical Researches in Palestine: A Journal of Travels in the Year 1838*, ii, p. 292.

4. Quoted by J. Hempel from Thiersch's diary in *Z.A.W.* li, 1933, p. 157.

5. See Hempel, ibid., pp. 159–69, especially n. 3.

6. For the first detailed publication, see von Bissing's appendix to F. M. Th. Böhl's article on the excavations at the site in *Mededeelingen der Koninklijke Akad. van Wetenschappen*, Amsterdam, Afd. Letterkunde, Deel 62, Serie B, 1926, pp. 1–24. The museum in question has long since been closed and its collections dispersed. After a long search a member of the staff of the Drew-McCormick Archaeological Expedition discovered in 1964 that the bronze hoard from the 1908 discovery is now in the Archaeological Seminar of the University of Munich.

7. *Anzeiger der Kaiserl. Akad. der Wiss. in Wien*, Phil.-Hist. Klasse, 51 Jahrgang, 1914, vii, pp. 35–40, and xviii, pp. 204–7.

8. A. Alt, *Z.D.M.G.* lxxix, 1925, pp. 1–19 (reprinted in *K.S.* iii, 1959, pp. 243–57).

9. The Khu-Sebek inscription on a stele from Abydos: see J. Wilson, *A.N.E.T.*, p. 230. The second *m* is to be understood either as a dual ending or else the enclitic *ma*.

10. Ibid., p. 329. For the original publication, see G. Posener, *Princes et pays d'Asie et de Nubie*, 1940.

11. *E.A.* 252, 253, 254. For recent treatment, see E. F. Campbell, Appendix 2 in G. Ernest Wright, *Shechem, Biography of a Biblical City*, 1965, pp. 191–207; and E. F. Campbell, *The Chronology of the Amarna Letters*, 1964.

12. *E.A.* 244, 245, 250, 289.

13. *A.N.E.T.*, p. 477.

14. Only brief preliminary reports were published: see Sellin, *Z.D.P.V.* xlix, 1926, pp. 229–36, 304–20; l, 1927, pp. 205–11, 265–74; li, 1928, pp. 119–23; Welter, *Forschungen und Fortschritte*, iv, nos. 31–32 (1 and 10 Nov. 1928), pp. 316 f., 329; *Archäolog. Anzeiger*, 1932, iii/iv, cols. 289–314; Sellin and Steckeweh, *Z.D.P.V.* lxiv, 1941, pp. 1–20.

15. For preliminary reports of the Archaeological Director and members of his staff, see especially the issues of *B.A.S.O.R.* and *B.A.*, beginning in 1956. The fullest preliminary description and interpretation is G. Ernest Wright, *Shechem: The Biography of a Biblical City*, 1965, with seven appendixes on various technical matters by members of the staff.

16. See A. Rowe, *The Topography and History of Beth-Shan*, 1930, pp. 10–17, with plan in fig. 1 and photographs in pls. 16–22, though the author dates the stratum at least a century too early; and R. Naumann, *Architektur Kleinasiens*, 1955, pp. 389 ff. and figs. 475 f.

17. See W. F. Albright, *From the Stone Age to Christianity* (Anchor ed. 1957), p. 279; E. Mendenhall, *B.A.S.O.R.* 133, 1954, pp. 26–30; M. Noth, *Gesammelte Studien zum A.T.*, 1957, pp. 142–54; and F. Willesen, *V.T.* iv, 1954, pp. 216 f. The last mentioned also draws attention to a South Arabian inscription in which 'ass' designates covenant alliance.

18. If still lower dates for Amosis and Amenophis I are accepted as proposed by W. Helck, R. A. Parker, and W. F. Albright (cf. the last mentioned in *B.A.S.O.R.* 176, 1964, p. 44, n. 23), then the Egyptian reconquest of Palestine would be lowered to the period between *c.* 1535 and 1520 B.C. Helck's suggested dates for Amosis are 1552–1527 B.C. and for Amenophis I 1527–1507 B.C.: *Die Beziehungen Ägyptens zu Vorderasien im 3. und 2. Jahrtausend v. Chr.*, 1962, p. 99.

19. Joshua xii. 17 lists the kings of Tappuah and Hepher as having been defeated by Israel. These localities were dependencies of Shechem, but we have no other information which would enable us to make use of the tradition. Joshua xii appears to be a secondary compilation of all traditional successes ascribed to the conquest.

20. The LXX places the ceremony at Shiloh, rather than at Shechem. While this is probably an original reading of the LXX text tradition, it cannot be explained as other than secondary harmonization: see Wright, *Shechem*, p. 256, n. 19.

21. See S. Gevirtz, *V.T.* xiii, 1963, pp. 52–62; and F. C. Fensham, *B.A.* xxv, 1962, pp. 48 ff.

22. See Wright, *Shechem*, pp. 124–8.

23. For this meaning of the obscure Hebrew term and its defence by

citation of the translation of the Alexandrian family of Greek manuscripts and by cognate terms in classical Arabic and South Arabic, see Wright, *Shechem*, p. 127.

24. In Judges ix. 4 the deity is named Baal-berith, presumably a later change of the name at a time when the deity was considered a Canaanite idol (cf. Judges viii. 33).

25. Cf. M. Noth, *Das System der Zwölfstämme Israels*, 1930; cf. E. Nielsen, *Shechem, A Traditio-Historical Investigation*, 1955.

26. See G. Ernest Wright, *Eretz Israel* viii, 1967; *Shechem*, pp. 142 ff.

27. Cf. Deut. xxvii, xi. 26 ff.; Joshua viii. 30 ff. The fact that the city is not mentioned in these passages, but that the emphasis is placed upon the mountains, may suggest that these pericopes reflect the covenant ceremony as it was celebrated after the twelfth century B.C. destruction of the sacred area. Cf. also Deut. xxxi. 9–13: see E. Nielsen, *Shechem*, especially pp. 335 ff.

28. For more detail, see Wright, *Shechem*, pp. 144–69.

29. These are economic documents found in an almost inaccessible cave in the Wadi Daliyeh, north of Jericho, along with the skeletons of a large number of people, men, women, and children. They were from Samaria, evidently fugitives. Some of the documents are dated to the reign of Darius III (336–331 B.C.) when the governor of Samaria is mentioned by the family name Sanballat; see F. M. Cross, *B.A.* xxvi, 1963, pp. 110–21.

30. For more detail, see Wright, *Shechem*, pp. 170–84, and *H.T.R.* lv, 1962, pp. 357–66. The new information from Shechem and from the Samaria papyri has done much to clarify the interpretation of Josephus's story about the Samaritans, whom he also calls 'Shechemites', and the erection of their temple on mount Gerizim (*Ant.* xi. 302 ff.). Ecclus. l. 25 f. speaks of 'the foolish people that dwell in Sichem'.

31. *Ant.* xiii. 254 ff.

32. Ibid. xiii. 281; *The Jewish War*, i. 265.

BIBLIOGRAPHY

NIELSEN, E. *Shechem, A Traditio-Historical Investigation*, 1955.
WRIGHT, G. ERNEST. *Shechem, The Biography of a Biblical City*, 1965.

TIRZAH

THE ancient site of Tell el-Far'ah lies 7 miles to the north-east of Nablus; it is not to be confused with the site of the same name in southern Palestine, which was excavated by Flinders Petrie. Northern Tell el-Far'ah rises between two plentiful springs, 'Ain el-Far'ah and 'Ain ed-Dleib at the head of the Wady Far'ah, which is the only wide pass leading from the Jordan valley into the heart of Palestine. Two other natural roads lead from Tell el-Far'ah southwards towards Shechem (Nablus) and northwards towards Beth-shean. Tell el-Far'ah is then a strategic point, straddling a knot of communications, with plenty of water, and at the head of a fertile valley. The site was excavated by the École Archéologique Française de Jérusalem during nine seasons between 1946 and 1960. The best-preserved remains and the most important for archaeology are those of the Chalcolithic, the Early Bronze, and the Iron Ages. In accordance with the character of this volume, special attention will be given to the strata of the Israelite Period and to the evidence they provide for Old Testament studies, especially for the identification of Tell el-Far'ah with Tirzah, the first capital of the northern kingdom.

i. *Neolithic Age*

The earliest occupation of Tell el-Far'ah was in the Pre-Pottery Neolithic Age. Several pits and plastered floors were cleared, with bone and flint implements appearing akin to Jericho Pre-Pottery Neolithic B. It seems to have been a light and scattered occupation.

ii. *Chalcolithic Age*

Human dwelling on any considerable scale starts at Tell el-Far'ah with the appearance of pottery. In the preliminary reports all the strata with pottery were labelled 'Chalcolithic' and the name is kept here for convenience, but it is agreed that the lower 'Chalcolithic' stratum in Tell el-Far'ah is related to and contemporary with the Pottery Neolithic of other Palestinian sites, mostly Beth-shean XVIII and pits and Jericho VIII (Pottery Neolithic B).

Lower and Upper Chalcolithic have one important fact in com-mon—the lack of constructions. The dwellings were exclusively shallow pits surrounded by a small wall of mud mixed with broken pebbles. Such dwelling pits exist in many other contemporary sites in Palestine. In Upper Chalcolithic (= Kathleen M. Kenyon's Proto-Urban), bone and flint implements are still numerous but pottery has become plentiful, the two main classes of which are the grey-burnished and the red-burnished wares. These were taken as characteristic of an 'Esdraelon Culture', but are now found as far south as Jericho and the caves of the Jordan Desert. They are associated with a third kind of pottery—painted, which is found in greater quantities in central Palestine and was classified at the very beginning of the Early Bronze Age (EB IA). It is likely that these three types are of different origin and are not entirely contem-poraneous, but at Tell el-Far'ah they are found together in the same strata of the tell and, generally, in the tombs. These collec-tive tombs are either fairly big rooms hewn out of the rock or natural caves enlarged and evened off, in both cases with flint tools, the marks of which we can still trace. They have yielded the most important and most complete collection of vases and objects from the Upper Chalcolithic which has yet been found.

iii. *Early Bronze Age*

A sudden and complete change in dwelling conditions followed the end of the Chalcolithic Period. The pits were filled in with the broken pebbles of the mud walls, the surface was levelled, and houses were built. They were rectangular, with walls of two courses of stones and a superstructure of mud bricks, and slabs against the walls or in the axis of the room as bases of the wooden posts supporting the roof. They bordered on straight streets, equipped with drains collecting the waste water and bringing it into a sewer which led outside the settlement. From the very beginning (this is a correction of the statement made in the first preliminary reports) this settlement was enclosed by a rampart. It is best preserved on the western front, where it appears as a strong wall of mud-bricks, 8 feet wide, built upon a footing of three courses of stones. The pre-eminent feature of this rampart is a fortified gate with two towers projecting from the line of the wall. Also in that first phase there was a small sanctuary with a cult-room opening towards the east and a *cella*. Thus the elements of an urban culture were brought together and the village of huts or dwelling-pits of Chalcolithic times had become a city. The archaeological date is given by the pottery; it is the beginning of the Early Bronze Age proper (EB IB); the absolute date is *c.* 3100 B.C.

Such a transformation cannot be explained by an evolution on the spot; it marks and requires the arrival of a new population, with new techniques and traditions of an urban life already developed. This new population was the founder of the culture of the Early Bronze Age, which spread at that time over all Palestine, and continued until the last centuries of the third millennium B.C. At Tell el-Far'ah this period is represented by six successive strata. The general planning of the city remained the same, but the houses were rebuilt on the same lines, or with a different plan. The sanctuary was transformed after the first stage. In the third stage there was a pottery kiln, comprising a lower chamber for the fire and an upper chamber where the pots were stacked on a floor perforated by flues. This is the oldest potter's oven yet discovered in Palestine, and probably one of the earliest that existed in the country. It is interesting to find that this type of kiln with flues persisted for thousands of years; another one, from Roman times, was discovered at Khirbet Qumran.

After this third stage the northern line of the rampart was moved back a few metres to the south, where a rampart of stones was built. At the same time the western rampart of mud-bricks was reinforced with a stone wall. The varying fortunes during the history of the town can still be read at the city gate, which was successively burnt, repaired, raised, blocked, and then reopened during the Early Bronze Age. At the end of the fifth stage a part of the western rampart collapsed and enormous piles of bricks fell inside the city. The catastrophe affected only a limited area, and the inhabitants quickly re-established themselves on the ruins behind a much weaker defensive wall. This last stage was of short duration and Tell el-Far'ah was deserted.

Pottery and other small finds allow one to give an approximate dating for these stages. The first two stages may safely be dated

Early Bronze Age I, the third stage is transitional with Early
Bronze Age II, the last three stages still fall in Early Bronze Age
II. The pottery of Khirbet Kerak, which is the landmark for Early
Bronze Age III, is not represented, even by a single sherd. In
terms of absolute chronology this means that the Early Bronze
Age occupation at Tell el-Farʿah did not last much later than 2600
B.C. This abandonment has possible historical implications. Ras
el-ʿAin, at the source of the Jaffa river, was deserted, as was Tell
el-Farʿah, before the Early Bronze Age III phase. Then the move
became general and, during Early Bronze Age III or at the close
of this period, urban occupation stopped at Megiddo, Beth-shean,
Khirbet Kerak, Ai, and Jericho. It was the beginning of the Intermediate Early Bronze–Middle Bronze Period, a dark age, marked
by an eclipse of the urban civilization, and best explained by the
arrival of the semi-nomad Amorites. However, Tell el-Farʿah was
abandoned earlier than most of the other sites and was reoccupied
later than several of them. To the historical fact just mentioned
we must perhaps add the unhealthiness of the spot (malaria was
endemic until very recently) to explain the protracted abandonment of the site.

iv. *Middle and Late Bronze Ages*

The site was reoccupied in the nineteenth century B.C., during
the Middle Bronze Age IIA of the common nomenclature, the
Middle Bronze Age I of Kathleen M. Kenyon. The newcomers
were at first few in number and settled down under the protection
of the ruined fortifications of the Early Bronze Age. The occupation was sparse and the dead were buried in the open spaces left
between the houses inside the line of the then existing rampart.
Towards the end of the eighteenth century B.C. the population
increased and Tell el-Farʿah became again a true city. A new
rampart was erected, partly on the ruins of the Early Bronze Age
one, but enclosing only the western half of the tell. It was a stone
wall of varying thickness, which was later on protected on the
northern side by a glacis of boulders, and on the west by a large
glacis of red earth held in position by a solid wall. The city gate
was on the western line, as was the gate of the Early Bronze Age,
but at a different place. It was a rectangular room with two

thresholds, and was preceded by an open-air approach, which had to be entered at right angles to the gate. It remained in use, with minor changes, during the Middle Bronze, Late Bronze, and Iron Ages. In the first part of the Iron Age the gate-room had a bench against its western wall; this recalls the Old Testament texts which tell how the elders of a town would sit at the gate to settle the affairs of the community. In the stonework of the gate, near the base, was a niche with a jar containing the skeleton of a new-born child. This brings to mind the text of 1 Kings xvi. 34—'Hiel of Beth-el built Jericho; he laid its foundation at the cost of Abiram his first-born and set up its gates at the cost of his youngest son Segub.' But in the first place it is not certain that this text refers to a 'foundation-sacrifice', and secondly the jar-burial at Tell el-Farʿah may be later than the building of the gate.

The Middle Bronze Age strata have been badly preserved, but there is an interesting building; it is an underground sanctuary, apparently connected with a temple above, which has been entirely destroyed. It contained, with pottery of the eighteenth to six-teenth centuries B.C., bones of young pigs. Sacrifices of pigs offered to chthonic deities or in magic are attested elsewhere in the ancient Near East and seem to have penetrated into Israel, as late as the return from Exile (cf. Isa. lxv. 4, lxvi. 3, 17).

The Late Bronze Age strata were as much destroyed as those of the Middle Bronze Age. A building with a courtyard leading into a long room, or perhaps a hall with a colonnade, may have been a temple; a little statue of the goddess Hathor, made of bronze covered with silver leaf, was found in the building. The Late Bronze Age occupation continued until the middle of the thir-teenth century B.C., but cannot be dated accurately owing to the scarcity of the finds and to the uncertainty as to the beginning of the following stratum (see below). There is no positive argument for attributing this destruction to the Israelites, except for the mention of Tirzah (assuming that Tirzah is Tell el-Farʿah) at the end of the list of Canaanite kings supposed to have been defeated by Joshua (Joshua xii. 24). Moreover, the historical records of the Old Testament and archaeological evidence (Shechem, Dothan) suggest that the settlement of the Israelites in that area was achieved peacefully by some kind of understanding with the Canaanites.

v. *Stratum III* (*Israelite*)

Happily, the Israelite strata are far better preserved. Immediately above the ruins of the Late Bronze Age, houses appear which stand in an orderly fashion along well-marked streets. The plan is always the same; from the street one enters a courtyard, on each side of which are one or more rooms. All the houses follow more or

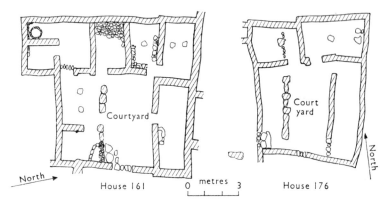

FIG. 8. Tirzah: Israelite houses (Stratum III)

less the same arrangement and have roughly the same dimensions (Fig. 8). Each represents the home of an Israelite family, and the very uniformity of the dwellings shows that there was no great social inequality among the inhabitants. This corresponds excellently with the social conditions of the period under David and Solomon and the first kings of the northern kingdom.

In fact, the objects found in the houses, pottery and conical seals, all date from the second half of the tenth century B.C. and the beginning of the ninth century. They belong to the last phase of this occupation, but this had been a long one, uninterrupted by large-scale destructions. Indeed, the houses were several times repaired or rebuilt on the same plan; the street level rose gradually by about 18 inches. This continuity makes it difficult to give a date, even an approximate one, for the beginning of this stratum.

From it came a little model sanctuary, similar to several others found in Cyprus, at Megiddo, and in Transjordan, dated to the tenth or ninth century B.C. They are pious household objects of the first Israelite period. When one entered the city, in the axis of the city gate one saw a square piece of masonry or platform and nearby a small stone basin. There seems to be no doubt that this platform was the support of a stone pillar, which was found in the last Israelite stratum at the same spot near a basin built up with slabs. This pillar was a *maṣṣēḇāh* and, with the basin, marked a place of worship at the entrance to the city. In fact it was a legacy from Canaanite times; already in the Middle Bronze Age strata, near the gate, there was a larger basin, very likely for ritual use. The *maṣṣēḇāh* was raised from one stratum to the other throughout the Israelite period, in spite of the prohibition of the Law and the condemnation of the prophets. This illustrates the permanence of religious customs and the syncretistic character of Yahweh's cult in the northern kingdom.

vi. *Intermediate Stratum*

Stratum III was brutally destroyed at the beginning of the ninth century B.C. Then, in some parts of the excavations, new buildings appeared. Cutting through what remained of the previous walls, running across courtyards and over streets, new walls were constructed on the floor level of the ruined stratum. In particular, one large building was planned, but never finished; it never rose above the foundations and the thresholds, which are visible. One dressed stone intended for the superstructure rested on the surface but was never placed in position. No floor level was associated with the construction.

Then Tell el-Farʿah was abandoned, it appears, for a short time. Life returned to the hill, though in a very small way. There are some remains of walls, later than the unfinished building, with pottery of the ninth century B.C.

vii. *Stratum II (Israelite)*

Occupation was far more intensive in this stratum. There was a large building near the city gate, with a paved courtyard, evidence of an upper floor, and a room full of broken jars. This must have been a public building, the residence of the governor and the centre of administration. Elsewhere was a group of attractive private houses. They followed the plan of the houses of the tenth century B.C., but they were a little larger and of superior construction; the plan was more regular, the walls built with two lines of stones, the stones better trimmed, and the corners well bonded (Fig. 9). This rich quarter was separated by a long straight wall from the poor quarter where smaller houses were huddled together, and where the techniques of an earlier age perpetuated themselves in a steady decline (Pl. XVI).

The wealth of pottery collected in the houses of both rich and poor, and a comparison with Samaria, Megiddo, and Hazor, leave no doubt about the date of this stratum; it belongs to the eighth century B.C. The juxtaposition of rich and poor houses, which contrasts with the uniformity of the dwellings in Stratum II, reflects a social evolution—the birth of an urban proletariat. It is a concrete illustration of the invectives of the prophets of those days—'Forasmuch therefore as ye trample upon the poor, and take exactions from him of wheat: ye have built houses of hewn stone, but ye shall not dwell in them' (Amos v. 11)—'For Israel hath forgotten his Maker . . . but I will send a fire upon his cities, and it shall devour the castles thereof' (Hos. viii. 14).

viii. *Stratum I* (*Assyrian*)

Indeed, Stratum II was destroyed and burnt and we can date the event exactly. Above the ruins and ashes rose a new stratum, much poorer, and a new kind of pottery appears in small quantities, which is clearly characterized by its clay, workmanship, and shape. It has been found also, in the same region, at Samaria and at Dothan, in one isolated site in the south, Tell Jemmeh, and in a tomb at Amman. It is not Palestinian, but it is identical with that which recent excavations at Nimrud have brought to light—along with the prototypes in metal work—in the palace of Sargon II, the conqueror of Samaria. It is Assyrian pottery, brought to Tell el-Far‘ah by the conquerors or by the colonists they installed there. The authors and the date of the destruction of the fine Israelite stratum are thus determined; Tell el-Far‘ah was captured by the Assyrians when they laid siege to Samaria in 723 B.C. (cf. 2 Kings xvii. 5). They dismantled the town, the city gate was blocked, and an unprotected entrance was cut in the rampart; Tell el-Far‘ah became literally an 'open city'. Life continued, but never again did the inhabitants know the same level of prosperity. Rather it

PLATE XVI

Rich quarter of Stratum II (Tirzah)

was a period of steady decline, and around 600 B.C. the site was finally abandoned. This decline is clearly the result of the general impoverishment of the northern kingdom under the foreign over-

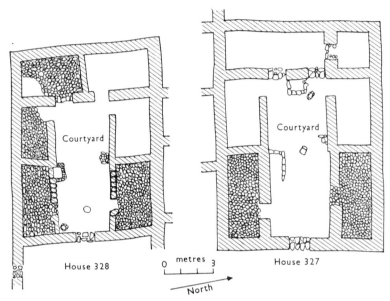

FIG. 9. Tirzah: rich Israelite houses (Stratum II)

lordship of the Assyrians. But this historical explanation does not seem a sufficient one for a total desertion and, once more, it is possible that another outbreak of malaria led the population to emigrate.

ix. *Tell el-Far'ah = Tirzah*

Tell el-Far'ah has been identified with various places mentioned in the Old Testament. G. Dalman,[1] followed by A. Alt,[2] suggested that it was Ophrah of the Abiezrites, the home of Gideon; F.-M. Abel[3] thought of the Beth-barah mentioned in Judges vii. 24. However, W. F. Albright proposed Tirzah, Jeroboam's capital.[4] He seems to have been proved right by the excavations; Tell el-Far'ah is the ancient Tirzah.

(*a*) Tirzah belonged to Manasseh, more precisely to the clan of Hepher (Num. xxvi. 33, xxvii. 1, xxxvi. 10; Joshua xvii. 3). Tell el-Far'ah is in the territory of the tribe of Manasseh. According to the same texts, Tirzah is one of the 'daughters' of Zelophehad, who were given an inheritance among the brethren of their father (Joshua xvii. 4). Two other 'daughters' of Zelophehad are Noah and Hoglah, two place-names mentioned in the Samaria ostraca. These documents tell us nothing more about Noah, but they do tell us that two villages, Yasit and Geba', were dependencies of Hoglah. Now it is quite certain that these two names are represented by the two modern villages of Yazid, 4 miles west of Tell el-Far'ah, and Jeba', 8 miles north-west of Tell el-Far'ah. The last 'daughter' of Zelophehad, Tirzah, must therefore lie in the same region, and the site of Tell el-Far'ah suits it perfectly.

(b) Tirzah, according to Joshua xii. 24, was a royal Canaanite city. During the Middle and Late Bronze Ages, Tell el-Far'ah, with its rampart and fortified city gate, was certainly an important city, the head of a small kingdom.

(c) Tirzah became the capital of the northern kingdom under Jeroboam I, according to a reference in the history of the death of Jeroboam's son (1 Kings xiv. 17). In any case Tirzah is mentioned as a royal residence under Baasha (1 Kings xv. 21, 33), and remained such until the founding of Samaria by Omri. It is admitted that nothing was found in Tell el-Far'ah which could be called the 'palace' of Jeroboam and his successors, but the Israelite city of Stratum III has not been entirely excavated, and it was a large city, with strong defences, and it could have been a capital.

(d) At the beginning of the ninth century B.C. Tirzah passed through a period of bloodshed; after two years reign Elah was assassinated by Zimri, after seven days Omri was proclaimed king by the army, besieged Tirzah, and took it. The usurper Zimri perished in the flames of the palace (1 Kings xvi. 17 f.). The most probable date is 885 B.C. This date fits in with the archaeological evidence for the destruction of Stratum III at Tell el-Far'ah.

(e) Omri reigned six years in Tirzah according to 1 Kings xvi. 23. The first four years were taken up with the struggle against his rival, Tibni (cf. 1 Kings xvi. 15, 22 f.), and two years later Omri decided to transfer his capital to the hill of Samaria, which he had just bought (1 Kings xvi. 23 f.). Only during these two years could Omri think of building in Tirzah, and the work was stopped when he moved to Samaria. In Tell el-Far'ah the vestiges of his activity are the constructions whose foundations reach down into Stratum III and which were left unfinished.

(*f*) The royal family, the officers and soldiers with their families and their servants all left with the king. It is also probable that many inhabitants of Tirzah, workmen and merchants, also left with the court. It is even possible, since Omri was to found his capital on a deserted hill, that he took with him all or part of the population of Tirzah. This would explain the poverty of the Intermediate Stratum at Tell el-Far‘ah, preceded perhaps by a short period of complete abandonment.

(*g*) However, during the period of prosperity of the kingdom of Israel, under Joash and Jeroboam II, Tirzah must have recovered some of its former life, and it is from there that Menahem marched to Samaria and seized the throne (2 Kings xv. 14). This flourishing period is represented at Tell el-Far‘ah by Stratum II, with its rich private houses and the large public building, perhaps the residence of Menahem, if the latter was actually governor of Tirzah. The destruction of Stratum II marks the invasion of 'all the land' by the Assyrians when they laid siege to Samaria in 723 B.C.

(*h*) Since the history of Tirzah is so closely linked with that of Samaria in the Old Testament it is important to see whether the same connexion can be found between the archaeology of Tell el-Far‘ah and that of Samaria. Stratum III at Tell el-Far‘ah, which comes to an end at the beginning of the ninth century B.C., is naturally not represented at Samaria, which was founded in 880 B.C. On the other hand, Periods I and II of Samaria (880–850 B.C.) have nothing corresponding at Tell el-Far‘ah; this would confirm an abandonment of Tell el-Far‘ah after Omri left Tirzah for Samaria. Contact begins during Samaria Period III (850–800 B.C.) and the Intermediate Stratum of Tell el-Far‘ah. In Samaria Periods IV and V, and especially during Samaria Period VI (800–722 B.C.), there is a perfect parallel with Tell el-Far‘ah Stratum II; the clay and the shape of the pottery are identical for both sites so that one could almost exchange the plates of the two publications. The same parallelism continues between Samaria VII (from 722 B.C. onwards) and Tell el-Far‘ah Stratum I; Assyrian pottery is found at both sites. Thus, not only does the archaeology of Tell el-Far‘ah fit in with the history of Tirzah as given by the Old Testament, but it dovetails into the archaeology of Samaria in the same way as the history of Tirzah dovetails into the history of Samaria.

Short of an epigraphic discovery which would provide demonstrable proof, archaeology has provided convincing arguments for the identification of Tell el-Far'ah with Tirzah. This identification is confirmed by geographical and historical considerations. Tell el-Far'ah faces east, towards Transjordan, where the Israelites had blood-brothers and where, under David, the opposition of Israel to Judah had been concentrated. It was a land where the kings of Israel first controlled vast territories which were threatened by the Aramaeans, the Ammonites, and the Moabites. Tell el-Far'ah was therefore a suitable site for the capital of the kingdom of Israel in its first period. Its communications with the south, however, are less satisfactory, and it was there that the kings of Israel soon had to defend their frontier against the kingdom of Judah (1 Kings xv. 16–22) and against the Philistines (1 Kings xv. 27, xvi. 15). Communications were still more difficult with the west, where the richest part of the kingdom lay, and with the north-west, where the way to Phoenicia and the ports for foreign trade lay open. Omri had been acclaimed as king by the army when it was camped before the Philistine town of Gibbethon (1 Kings xvi. 15 f.), and he did not forget the event. He wished also to lead Israel out of its isolation and to strengthen friendly relations with the Phoenicians, for the sake of trade and to protect himself against the Aramaean pressure which was already threatening in the east. All this goes to explain why he chose as his new capital the hill of Samaria, which was easy of access and yet easy to defend. It was nearer than Tirzah to the centre of the kingdom, with excellent communications towards the north, south, and west. Tell el-Far'ah looks eastwards, Samaria looks to the west. This contrast corresponds to the change in political orientation which marks the reign of Omri, and provides a last argument in favour of the identification of Tell el-Far'ah with Tirzah.

R. DE VAUX

NOTES

1. *P.J.B.* viii, 1913, pp. 31 f.
2. Ibid. xxiii, 1927, pp. 36 f., xxviii, 1932, pp. 40 f.
3. *Géographie de la Palestine*, ii, 1938, p. 268.
4. *J.P.O.S.* xi, 1931, pp. 241 f.

BIBLIOGRAPHY

Preliminary reports on the excavations in *R.B.* liv, 1947, pp. 394–433, 573–89; lv, 1948, pp. 544–80; lvi, 1949, pp. 102–38; lviii, 1951, pp. 393–430, 566–90; lix, 1952, pp. 551–83; lxii, 1955, pp. 541–89; lxiv, 1957, pp. 552–80; lxviii, 1961, pp. 393–430; lxix, 1962, pp. 212–53.

DE VAUX, R. 'The excavations at Tell el-Farʿah and the site of ancient Tirzah', *P.E.Q.*, 1956, pp. 125–40.

GRAY, J. 'Tell el-Farʿa by Nablus: a "Mother" in ancient Israel', ibid., 1952, pp. 110–13.

JOCHIMS, U. 'Thirza und die Ausgrabungen auf dem tell el Farʿa', *Z.D.P.V.* lxxvi, 1960, pp. 73–96.

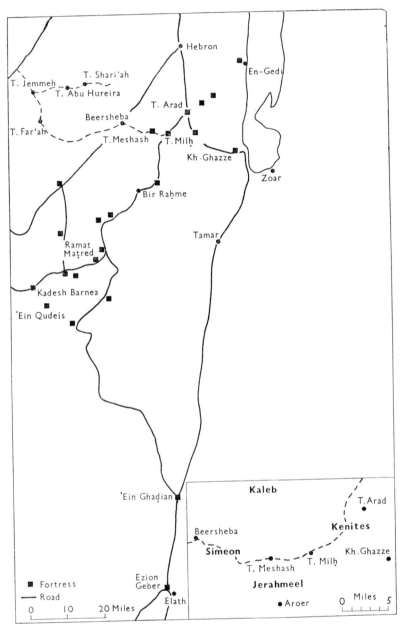

FIG. 10. Map of the Negeb

THE NEGEB

THE modern term Negeb includes all the southern part of Israel, from slightly north of Beer-sheba down to Elath, most of it a vast wilderness, especially in its most southern parts. The Old Testament term Negeb was used in a more restricted sense. The term, which means 'dry (land)', included only the semi-arid area to a distance of about 15 miles north and south of Beer-sheba, which is a kind of transitional area between the desert and the sown. In its northern part the average annual rainfall is 200–300 millimetres, which suffices for crops and especially for barley. Droughts, however, are frequent. South of Beer-sheba the rainfall decreases rapidly, and dry-farming becomes impossible. The southernmost parts, which become more and more real desert, are called *miḏbār* 'wilderness, desert' in the Old Testament, for example, Midbar Zin (Num. xx. 1) and Midbar Paran (Num. xiii. 26).

The dry climate and the proximity of the desert are serious obstacles to sedentary occupation, which flourished only during few and rather short periods. These obstacles, however, constitute a real advantage so far as the possibilities of archaeological research are concerned. The distinct gaps in occupation bring out much more clearly the rise and fall of civilizations than in other regions of the country. Many sites are rather small and short-lived, and it is therefore much easier to survey them and to connect building remains with surface pottery. Finally, the dry climate and the remoteness of the ruins have contributed greatly to their excellent state of preservation. Nowhere else in Palestine are ancient buildings preserved to such an extent. This makes it possible to map most of the buildings without elaborate excavations. In places where excavations have been carried out utensils were found in a remarkable state of preservation, including a good deal of inscribed material, which is so rare in Palestine. There is good reason to hope that the Negeb will in time become the main source of Hebrew inscriptions from the Old Testament period.

The main periods of occupation reoccurred in the Negeb about

once in a thousand years—the first in the transitional period from
the Chalcolithic to the Early Bronze Age (*c.* 3000 B.C.); the second
in the first stage of the Middle Bronze Age (MB I, *c.* 2100 B.C.);
and the third in the days of the monarchy (*c.* 1000 B.C. onwards).
The first two call only for a general description; our survey will
deal mainly with the third, which illuminates many Old Testament passages.

i. *The Proto-Historic Periods*

The beginning of sedentary occupation in the Negeb took place
in the latter part of the Chalcolithic Period, *c.* 3400 B.C. Settlements sprang up mainly along the major river beds of the Negeb,
where the main sources of water are to be found.[1] The occupants
gained their livelihood mainly from small cattle and seasonal
agriculture, but crafts also were developed to some extent,
especially copper, stone, and ivory working. They lived mainly in
unfortified villages, sometimes in underground dwellings cut into
the loess. They arrived suddenly, apparently in remarkable strength,
and disappeared as suddenly at the beginning of the Bronze Age
(*c.* 3200 B.C.). Most of the small settlements were deserted for
good; however, a century or two later, at the end of EB I, or the
beginning of EB II, a chain of settlements spread out in the
northern Negeb. It is doubtful if there was any continuity between
them and the older settlements, in spite of the fact that their culture and architecture exhibit features in common.

One of the major Early Bronze cities of the Negeb, perhaps the
greatest of them, has been excavated at Tell Arad.[2] It was surrounded by a stone wall, 2·3–2·5 metres thick, which enclosed an
area of more than 20 acres. At certain intervals there were projecting semicircular towers, similar to those discovered at Ai, Jericho,
and at Uruk in Mesopotamia from the same period. The houses
were well built and were of a special architectural type. The main
part consisted of one large, broad room, with the entrance at the
centre of the longer wall and benches all round. This type of
building is identical in plan with a Chalcolithic sanctuary discovered at En-gedi,[3] one of the most striking affinities between the
two cultures. The material remains provide evidence of a rich and
well-organized culture, and the utensils show clear connexions
with Egypt during the First Dynasty (*c.* 2900 B.C.). Egyptian

imported vessels were found at Arad and the beautiful so-called Abydos ware is most plentiful. It becomes clear that Tell Arad was one of the centres of the manufacture of this Palestino-Syrian pottery, which is chiefly known from First-Dynasty cemeteries in Egypt.

Remains of grain and large granaries show the importance of agriculture in the economy of the city, a fact of special interest in this now semi-arid area. Experience of recent years shows that a good harvest can be expected once in every three to four years. Were the many granaries perhaps intended to store grain over periods of drought? Not less interesting is the problem of water-supplies. There exists neither a spring nor a well at Tell Arad or nearby. Had the early inhabitants already mastered the technique of run-off water collection and storing similar to those used in later periods? Just as we still lack a clear answer to the question of the foundation and existence of so large a city in this remote region, so we may wonder too about the reason for its sudden disappearance. It was destroyed completely not later than *c.* 2700 B.C. after an existence of not more than 200 to 300 years, and it remained un-settled for the following one and a half millennia.

ii. *The Middle Bronze Age I*

Tell Arad did not experience the next wave of occupation which spread over the Negeb in the MB I period at the end of the third millennium B.C. This period too remains most enigmatic and has not yet been understood in a broader historical context. Various scholars have tried to connect it with the Abrahamic traditions of the Old Testament, mainly on the basis that this is the only pre-Israelite period of settlement in the Negeb.[4] However, all over Palestine this is a period of destruction and desolation with a semi-nomadic people roaming everywhere, and not a single settled and built-up town has been discovered to this day. This situation stands in striking contrast to the Old Testament narratives about Abraham and his age, which must come from a later period when most cities flourished once again. On the other hand, we hear nothing of an encounter of Abraham with a settled population in the Negeb,[5] and there seems therefore to be no basis whatever for connecting his age with the MB I settlement of the Negeb.

Settlements in this period are much more widespread than in the earlier one, and penetrate into the southern regions of the Negeb as far as the Sinai peninsula.[6] In the most northern part of the Negeb, however, as in the vicinity of Tell Arad, they are conspicuously lacking. It seems that these settlements penetrated into the fringes of the desert and even into the desert proper, while the fertile regions remained vast and desolate. They belong probably to the movement of tribes, which brought about this desolation, yet their attempt to settle just the desert still remains a riddle.

Most of their settlements look rather like temporary camps—tents, huts, and enclosures for small cattle. It is doubtful if they were used all the year round, and they possibly served only as winter encampments. Yet well-made pottery, which is to be found on the surface, and burial grounds, mainly on the peaks, with elaborate stone tumuli, show that they were not mere nomads. There exist also larger sites of this period with more solid and permanent structures. One of the most impressive of them has been located near Beer Yeroham (Bir Raḥme), about 20 miles south of Beer-sheba, and has been thoroughly studied and partly excavated.[7] It is situated on a high and steep hill and the houses are clustered all around, forming some kind of defence. The architecture displays some peculiar features, such as supporting pillars made of round stone slabs. Not only their knowledge of pottery and copper working but also their distinct architecture witness to their settled origins. At Beer Yeroham even two strata of occupation were observed, of which the earlier especially displays the features just mentioned. However, both occupations seem to have been short-lived, and they apparently came to an end as suddenly as they appeared. From the paucity of finds it seems that the inhabitants left peacefully, and this is probably true of most of the MB I settlements in the Negeb.

iii. The Late Bronze Age

Most of the Negeb and the southern deserts were apparently uninhabited in the MB II and LB Ages. Surveys and excavations south of Beer-sheba have not revealed a single find of the period between MB I and the Iron Age, that is, during most of the second millennium B.C. Remains of this period have come to light only in excavations in the westernmost fringes of the Negeb, at Tell el-Far'ah[8] and at Tell Jemmeh,[9] south-east of Gaza. These impressive mounds belong actually more to the coastal region than to the Negeb, and for this reason they are well known from Egyptian sources of the New Kingdom. Tell el-Far'ah is probably the Old Testament Sharuhen[10] (Joshua xix. 6), and Tell Jemmeh is probably Yurza of the Egyptian sources.[11]

A little further to the east is the large mound of Tell Abu Hureira, probably the Old Testament Gerar.[12] Traces of the MB II and LB periods have been discovered here and at the neighbouring Tell esh-Shari'ah, perhaps the Old Testament Ziklag, but they have not yet been excavated. On the other hand, at Tell es-Seba', the mound of Beer-sheba north-east of the modern town, no sherds of these periods have been found. As at Tell Arad there was apparently no settlement at Tell es-Seba' between the Chalcolithic period and the Iron Age. This does not contradict the narratives about Abraham and Isaac, who encamped at Beersheba after their departure from Gerar. On the contrary, from the city of Gerar they go to the area of Beer-sheba, which, as the archaeological survey has shown, was not settled in the patriarchal period.

Further to the east there are two mounds which were settled during the MB II and perhaps LB Ages, namely, Khirbet el-Meshash and Tell el-Milḥ. Both are situated on the same river-bed, overlooking abundant wells, which are still the main sources of water for the local bedouin. Only about 4 miles apart, their history was doubtless interlocked, as they were probably frequently rivals for the dominating place in the area. Since excavations have revealed that Tell Arad was unsettled during this period, it now becomes probable that Arad and Hormah were located at these two tells respectively. Hence their important role during the period of the conquest, as the main, and perhaps only, Canaanite centres in the eastern Negeb. We shall return to this problem at the end of our survey, while reviewing the topographical questions raised by the finds at Tell Arad.

iv. *The Iron Age*

Archaeological survey has shown that the establishment of the Israelite monarchy brought with it a heyday in the settlement of the Negeb. Several settlements probably antedate the tenth century B.C., but only few have been discovered hitherto. One of the most

interesting was recently excavated at Tell Esdar, just north of the
Old Testament Aroer, about 12 miles south-east of Beer-sheba.[13]
Its houses are arranged in a wide circle enclosing a broad empty
area in the centre. Though the walls are narrow, they are well
built, and their simple pottery, mostly storage jars and cooking
pots, belongs to the eleventh century B.C. This was probably one
of the cities of the Jerahmeelites or the Kenites, mentioned in the
days of Saul (1 Sam. xxx. 29), perhaps one of the daughter settlements of Aroer, which is mentioned in the same passage (verse 28).

A vast number of sites have been discovered belonging to the
tenth century B.C. onwards, mainly from Iron Age II. Especially in
the Negeb proper, that is, in the area about 15 miles north and
south of Beer-sheba, density of settlement reached apparently
a level never attained in any other period. The more than fifty sites
discovered here hitherto include probably most of 'the uttermost
cities of the tribe of the children of Judah toward the border of
Edom in the South (Hebrew *negeb*) . . . twenty and nine, with their
villages' (Joshua xv. 21–32). However, only few of them can be
identified with any certainty, because we lack additional information about most of them, and the preservation of names is very
rare in this region due to long gaps in occupation.

This is apparently the first period of major development of the
Negeb by a central authority, which is attested by the discovery
of many royal fortresses. These are not confined to the northern,
densely settled, part of the Negeb, but are to be found up to its
southernmost limits. The number of them discovered so far ex-
ceeds twenty, and undoubtedly many more will be found in future
surveys.[14] Their location points to their general purpose. Most of
them were built on the roads leading southwards to the Arabah,
Edom, Sinai, and Egypt. Their aim was to secure these important
trade routes of the kingdom, to guard the borders, and, of course,
the settlements and sources of water in the settled areas.

The general plan of most fortresses is visible even before
excavation. Almost all have rooms leaning against the outer wall
in the form of a casemate wall, surrounding a central courtyard.
Three main types can be distinguished:

(*a*) Rectangular fortresses about 40 × 50 metres with projecting
towers. This type has long been known, especially at Kadesh-
barnea,[15] and similar fortresses have been discovered recently at

Khirbet Ghazze and at Tell Arad.[16] They belong to the eighth–
seventh centuries B.C., and they were probably planned as major
fortresses at important junctions and places on the border.

(*b*) Oval or irregular fortresses without towers, of about the
same size, or even larger than the previous type. This kind
is known from 'Ein Qudeis (south of Kadesh-barnea = 'Ein
Qudeirat),[17] from 'Ein Ghadian on the road to Elath,[18] from a
fortress north-east of Bir Raḥme,[19] and recently from a site just
north of Sedeh Boqer.[20] They too belong to a larger and centrally
located type of fortress, and they are probably quite early, perhaps
from the tenth century B.C.

(*c*) A smaller, square fortress without towers, about 20 × 20
metres. This was the medium type, and several have been discovered, mainly on the roads to Kadesh-barnea and the southern
deserts.[21] They too may have been erected in the tenth century
B.C., but the exact dating of all these fortresses needs further
investigation.

Together with the fortresses a certain number of settlements
spread into the southern regions. Near most of the fortresses a
few houses of the same period are to be found, which may have
belonged to families of soldiers and merchants, who made a living
from passing caravans. In some instances these developed into real
villages, where husbandry and agriculture were pursued.[22] The
last is most surprising, because agriculture in these dry regions
is possible only through the collection of run-off water. Several
'farms', however, with pure Iron Age pottery, and especially
a whole village at Ramat Maṭred, about 70 miles south-west of
Beer-sheba, provide evidence that the settlers managed to irrigate
their fields and to collect a sufficient amount of water into rock-cut
or stone-built cisterns.[23] The settlement at Ramat Maṭred possessed well-built houses, connected with fenced and terraced
fields. It existed mainly in the tenth century B.C., guarded by
a chain of fortresses on the road nearby, and suffered destruction
at the end of the century, perhaps during the campaign of
Shishak.

The only Iron Age fortress which has been excavated hitherto
is the fortress of Tell Arad[24] and its finds throw much light on
a royal Judaean fortress and on the history of the Negeb in this
period.

v. *The Fortress at Tell Arad*

As stated above, Tell Arad remained in ruins from EB II to an early phase in the Iron Age. Most of the early city was never re-settled, and the new settlement was concentrated at its southern corner on an isolated hill-top.

The first settlement was an unfortified village of the eleventh century B.C., perhaps similar to that at Tell Esdar. However, not much of its plan has yet been revealed, since it is covered by 5–7 metres of later strata. These were made up mainly by fortresses, which occupied the site in the Iron Age and in later periods. Test pits on the lower slopes of the mound revealed structures and silos from different periods, and provide evidence of settlements which sprang up around the fortresses. However, almost nothing is known about their character and size, as the excavations were con-centrated mainly on the citadel hill. The following strata were un-covered here, including the later strata, which are outside the scope of the present study:

Stratum	Period	Approximate date	Type of settlement
I	Mameluke	Thirteenth century A.D. and later	Tombs
II	Early Arab	Seventh to eighth centuries A.D.	Khan
III	Roman	First century A.D.	Fortress
IV	Hellenistic	Third to second centuries B.C.	Tower
V	Persian	Fifth to fourth centuries B.C.	Fortress?
VI–XI	Iron Age II	Tenth to early sixth centuries B.C.	Fortresses
XII	Iron Age I	Eleventh to early tenth centuries B.C.	Village

Also on the high tell the Early Bronze Age strata were reached at the bottom; they have not been included in this table. Strata VI–XI comprise six Iron Age fortresses, which were erected at the site during the period of the monarchy. They were destroyed six times during a period of probably less than 400 years. Each destruc-tion level was marked by layers of ash and masses of broken pottery vessels and other utensils, a paradise for archaeologists and a clear indication of their sudden and violent capture. These frequent destructions are obviously due to the remote position of the fortresses on the border of the desert, and thanks to them this is now the best stratified site of Judah in Iron Age II.

The fortresses were of the larger type, including an area of about 50 × 50 metres, which is, of course, relatively small for an important archaeological site. The fortifications were exceptionally strong and well built, a fact which points to the importance of the places. The walls were constructed partially of well-cut and bossed ashlar masonry, found here for the first time in the Negeb. The type of fortification changed in the different levels. The first wall was of the casemate type. The area excavated at this level is still restricted, yet enough of its walls has been exposed to clarify its double (casemate) construction, with rooms between the two walls; and at least one projecting tower has been laid bare on its western side.

The second fortress was completely different. The earlier casemate wall was filled and overlaid by a solid wall, 3–4 metres thick, with small indentations about every 9–10 metres. The slopes, which became gradually steeper and higher, were strengthened by a beaten glacis, and a second wall, about 2 metres in breadth, was built below. These walls rank with the strongest Iron Age fortifications discovered so far in Palestine, and the proportions between the huge walls and the modest citadel are almost grotesque. This strong wall existed throughout four strata (X–VII), but in Strata VIII and VII, and perhaps also earlier in Stratum IX, it was further strengthened by walls and rooms of the casemate type built against it. In the last Iron Age stratum (VI) the solid wall was abandoned, and a fortress with casemate walls and projecting towers, similar to that at Kadesh-barnea, was built on top of it.

These alterations probably reflect the general tactics of warfare and techniques of fortification at this period. The trend to exchange the tenth-century B.C. casemate walls for thick and solid walls in the ninth century has been noted at various sites in Israel and Judah, for example, at Hazor, Megiddo, Tell en-Naṣbeh, and Ezion-geber.[25] It was brought about apparently by the catastrophes which befell the two kingdoms after their division, mainly by the campaign of Shishak, to which also Arad fell victim according to his inscription. The relatively weak (but cheap!) casemate walls

were unable to withstand the assault of a powerful army and seemed
to be inadequate against the battering ram and tunnelling beneath
the walls. The reversal to casemate walls in the eighth and seventh
centuries B.C. was due probably to the recognition that even the
thickest walls were of no avail against the overwhelming power of
great empires. Yet what could be the reason for building casemate rooms against the solid wall at Arad, which would hardly
add much strength to the wall 4 metres thick? The intention could
perhaps have been to enlarge the upper area of the wall in order
that more defenders and stronger structures (cf. 2 Chron. xxvi. 15)[26]
could be located there.

It has been possible to establish with considerable accuracy
dates for the six strata with the help of (a) the wealth of pottery
and other finds, (b) the plan of the different walls in comparison
with other places, (c) palaeographic examination of the inscribed
material, mainly ostraca, which were found in Strata X–VI,
(d) general historical considerations. We may refer here only to
major conclusions which can hardly be questioned. There is no
doubt that the first fortress belongs to the tenth century B.C. and is
probably Solomonic. Irregular hand burnish, common in the latter
part of the eleventh century B.C., appears in the earlier village
(Stratum XII). On the other hand, this must be the fortress
destroyed by Shishak, and therefore a date c. 945–924 B.C. for it is
virtually certain. As stated above, the casemate wall of Stratum XI
and the solid wall of Stratum X fit in excellently with their tenth–
ninth centuries B.C. dates. The last fortress (Stratum VI) was
destroyed at the end of the period of the First Temple (597 or 587
B.C.). This is obvious, not only from the pottery, but also from
Hebrew ostraca whose script resembles that of the Lachish ostraca.

The distribution of the remaining three strata (IX–VII) between
the ninth and seventh centuries B.C. leaves no great margin for
possible errors, and their dating is further narrowed down with the
help of palaeography and by general historical considerations.
Enemies waiting for an opportunity to sack the Israelite border
fortresses were never lacking, such as the Edomites and the various
nomads of the desert (cf., for example, 2 Kings xiii. 20; 2 Chron.
xxviii. 17). It is reasonable to assume that the six periods of building activity and the six destruction levels at Arad coincide with the
ups and downs in the history of the Negeb.

vi. *The Sanctuary*

Undoubtedly the most surprising discovery at Arad is an Israelite sanctuary, the first ever discovered in archaeological excavations. It occupied the north-western corner of the fortress, and its area of about 15 × 20 metres was quite a considerable part of it. It was divided into four successive parts surrounded by smaller rooms, the entrance in the east, the holy of holies in the west, and openings along its central axis. This is the essential plan of the Jerusalem temple according to the description in the Old Testament with its courtyard, porch, holy place, holy of holies (*ḥāṣēr, 'ûlām, hêkāl dᵉḇîr*), and stories round about. The direction of the building also corresponds with that of the Jerusalem temple and the Tabernacle. This is a most remarkable fact, because Canaanite temples discovered so far usually face east or north.

The size of the building and its rooms raises intricate questions which we can only briefly touch upon. In its first phase (Stratum XI) the holy place was 9 metres long and 2·6–2·7 metres broad. If we assume a cubit of 45 centimetres, we arrive at 20 × 6 cubits for its size. In the next phase (Stratum X) it was enlarged northward to a length of 10·5 metres. This obviously was due to some very special reason, because its layout now became asymmetric, the entrances being south of the centre. An examination of the new length leads to the surprising result that 10·5 metres may represent again exactly 20 cubits, if a large or 'royal' standard of 52·5 centimetres is assumed. Could it be that the official standard of the cubit was altered between the tenth and ninth centuries B.C.? This possibility may be hinted at in 2 Chron. iii. 3—'Now these are the foundations which Solomon laid for the building of the house of God. The length by cubits *after the first measure* was threescore cubits, and the *breadth twenty cubits*.' The breadth of the Temple, north to south, was therefore identical with that at Arad, and it was altered at Arad when the *measure* was altered.[27]

The holy of holies was merely a kind of a central niche, 3 × 3 cubits square (Pl. XVII*a*). Only the two inner parts were roofed over, the porch as well as the courtyard being open. The large altar of burnt offering stood in the north-western corner of the courtyard (Pl. XVII*b*). It was built of small unhewn stones (cf. Deut. xxvii. 5) plastered over. On its top was a large flint

slab, surrounded by plastered gutters. Its size was a square of
5×5 cubits, 3 cubits in height. It is hardly accidental that these
are precisely the measurements of the altar in the Tabernacle
(Exod. xxvii. 1). In the western part of the porch, on both sides
of the entrance into the holy place, two stone slabs were found,
which served probably as bases for pillars. A comparison of them
with the Old Testament Jachin and Boaz is obvious, and they add
support to the statement in 2 Chron. iii. 17 that these two pillars
were set up 'before the temple' (Hebrew *hêḵāl* 'holy place').[28]

On the steps leading up from the holy place to the holy of holies
two small altars were found, 30 and 51 centimetres high respectively. They are made of soft limestone, smoothly dressed, similar
to the Megiddo altars,[29] but without horns. In the flat depressions
on their upper surfaces were preserved traces of a burnt organic
substance, evidently animal fat. In the holy of holies there was
a slightly raised platform (*bāmāh*), and near it on the ground
a fallen stele (*maṣṣēḇāh*) was lying. This is a hard, well-dressed
limestone, 90 centimetres high, flat on its face, and rounded on its
back and at its ends, and traces of red paint were preserved on it.
Two much cruder slabs of flint were built into the wall of the holy
of holies and plastered over. They were probably *maṣṣēḇôṯ* of an
earlier stratum.

Among the small finds in the sanctuary the following deserve
special mention—a small bronze figurine of a lion, found near the
large altar in Stratum IX; two offering bowls, found on the base
of the altar in Stratum X (on both there are two incised signs, the
first being the ancient Hebrew letter *qôp*, while the second, in the
form of a trident, is probably a symbol); and several Hebrew
ostraca, found in one of the adjoining rooms in Stratum VIII. All
of them have one or two names written upon them, and it is remarkable that two of them have the names of well-known priestly
families, Meremoth and Pashhur (cf. Ezra viii. 33, x. 22).

The plan of the sanctuary and its contents leave no doubt that
this was an Israelite sanctuary dedicated to Yahweh. This view is
strengthened by the consideration that it was built as an integral
part of the royal fortress. It was actually built with the first
fortress (Stratum XI); it continued in existence, with repairs and
rebuildings, until Stratum VII; and it was finally destroyed by
the casemate wall of Stratum VI, which cuts straight through the

PLATE XVII

a. 'Holy of holies' of Israelite sanctuary (Tell Arad)

b. Altar of Israelite sanctuary (Tell Arad); the earlier, smaller altar below

middle of the holy place. The large altar, however, went out of use after Stratum VIII, and nothing was found in its place in Stratum VII.

Let us 'translate' its history into the language of our historical scheme. Its origins were Solomonic; it continued in existence up to the eighth or early seventh century B.C., yet its altar was ultimately neglected (in the days of Hezekiah? Cf. 2 Kings xviii. 4, 22); it was finally abandoned and deliberately destroyed when the last citadel was erected, evidently after Josiah's reforms.

In contrast with this the other part of the fortress served virtually the same purpose during all the periods of its existence, as far as can be deduced from those which have been excavated. The south-west corner opposite the sanctuary was occupied by a large storehouse. The gate was originally in the centre of the eastern side leading directly into the central courtyard. Later it was transferred to the northern side, leading into a corridor which passed between the storehouse and the sanctuary. The purpose of this transfer was perhaps to admit people to these two buildings who were not allowed to proceed to the rest of the fortress. West of the courtyard were various workshops, probably for metal working, pottery, and a perfume distillery. The southern side of the fortress was occupied by common rooms and houses. Here were the living quarters of the functionaries of the royal citadel, and here their archives, part of which have been found in the excavations, were deposited.

vii. *The Eliashib Archives*

Arad is unusually rich in inscribed material. The reasons are probably twofold—the better prospect of the preservation of ink in the dry climate, and the fact that this was a royal, military, administrative, and cultic centre in which a great deal of writing was done. All in all about 200 ostraca have been found, more than the total number unearthed in Palestine. Of course, not all are in the same state of preservation, and in some cases only single letters can be deciphered. Yet even these are important because they belong to different strata of the fortress. About half the ostraca bear inscriptions in Aramaic and belong to the Persian period (Stratum V, *c.* 400 B.C.). They come from refuse pits and were obsolete dockets, their contents being mainly the distribution of cereals, wine, oil, and money to specified persons. From them we learn that in this period too there was a military garrison at the place, which was organized in contingents called by the names of their commanders, similar to the custom in contemporary Elephantine. Thus a certain person is assigned 'to the contingent of 'Abdihay' (*ldgl 'bdhy*). Among his subordinates was a Jew called 'Aqabiah' (*'qbyh*).

The rest are Hebrew ostraca which came from Strata X–VI; they are to be dated accordingly from the ninth to the early sixth centuries B.C.[30] Though only few of them come from Strata X–VIII, they are of much interest. They are the earliest inscriptions in the ancient Hebrew cursive script which can be safely dated, and they may help to provide a more stable basis for the study of Hebrew palaeography. It now becomes quite clear that the Hebrew cursive script was already well established and developed in the ninth century B.C., and that it was remarkably different from the script of the Mesha inscription. The development which is generally attributed to the eighth–seventh centuries B.C. seems now to belong in reality to the ninth–seventh centuries B.C., and various Hebrew inscriptions have recently been dated too low.[31]

From the last fortress (Stratum VI) comes part of an archive which was found in one of the rooms of the southern casemate wall. It must be stressed once again that this is the same wall which cuts through the middle of the sanctuary. The fragments were discovered in a thick burnt layer and they belong to seventeen documents, nine of which are nearly complete. Most are addressed to a certain Eliashib (*'lyšb*), and contain brief orders to deliver certain amounts of goods to specified persons, mainly wine, flour, bread, and oil. He is required to take note of the date, and in one case the provisions are intended to last for four days. It is probable that these short letters were delivered by the persons mentioned in them and were kept in the archive as evidence for the delivery of the goods. This is especially clear from one letter addressed to a man called Nahum (*nhm*). He is ordered to go to the house of 'Eliashib son of Eshyahu' (*'lyšb bn 'šyhw*), to take from him one jar of oil and to send it sealed with his seal. On the other side of this ostracon there is a note in a different hand, to the effect that on a certain date Nahum has sent one jar of oil through 'the Kitti'. This note was doubtless written by Eliashib or his scribe, and the letter was kept in Eliashib's archives to testify to the fulfilment of the order. In several letters short memoranda and orders are added, again mainly to do with provisions, but also, it seems, with taxes and tithes. Who are the Kittim (*ktym*) who are mentioned in several letters? They receive allocations of wine and bread, but oil they were required to deliver sealed. In the Old Testament the name designates Greeks, inhabitants of the isles and coastlands (cf., for example, Gen. x. 4; Jer. ii. 10). We may suppose that they were Greek or Cypriot mercenaries serving in the Judaean fortresses of the Negeb.

One of the most interesting ostraca was written by a subordinate of Eliashib, as is indicated by its opening—'To my lord Eliashib, may Yahweh care for (inquire after) your health, and now . . .' ('*l 'dny. 'lyšb. yhwh yš'l lšlmk. w't*). He asks Eliashib to give various things to a certain Shemaryahu and 'to the Kerosi' (*lqrsy*). The latter is probably to be connected with one of the families of the temple servants (Nethinim), that is, the children of Keros (Ezra. ii. 44; Neh. vii. 47). Finally, he writes that a certain order of his lord has been fulfilled and 'he dwells in the house of Yahweh' (*byt yhwh. h' yšb*). Which temple ('house of Yahweh') is meant here? Certainly not that at Arad; its sanctuary was in ruins, and the letter was sent to Arad from some other place. It is improbable that at this late period a house of Yahweh existed besides the Jerusalem temple. This must mean that Eliashib's subordinate wrote from Jerusalem and had connexions with temple circles. The mention of the Kerosi points in the same direction.

What was the position of Eliashib? Was he merely in charge of the stores, or was he the commander of the fortress? The connexions with the temple suggest that he may have been in charge of the priestly Levite administration 'for all the business of the Lord, and for the service of the king' (1 Chron. xxvi. 30, cf. verse 32), which might have continued to act at Arad even after the abolition of the sanctuary. In this connexion it is interesting to note that Eliashib is the name of a well-known priestly family in the Old Testament (cf. Ezra x. 6; Neh. iii. 1).

Another surprising find adds to our information about Eliashib. A small room, adjacent to the Eliashib archive, but belonging to the earlier Stratum VII, was apparently a kind of treasury. It contained the following items—a hoard of unusually delicate Iron Age pottery of various types; a decorated bowl made of the shell of

Tridacna sqamosa;[32] two inscribed shekel weights; a hieratic ostracon; some Hebrew ostraca; and three Hebrew seals. One of the ostraca, which is well preserved, is a docket concerning the distribution of wheat (it is headed *ḥṭm* 'wheat') with a list of names and quantities. The three Hebrew seals found in the same corner are made of various precious stones and all three have the same inscription—*l'lyšb bn 'šyhw* 'belonging to Eliashib son of Eshyahu'.

Obviously these are the seals with which Eliashib or his functionaries sealed the oil jugs, as mentioned in the ostraca. It is interesting to note that he possessed more than one seal at the same time. Astonishingly enough these seals belong to an earlier stratum (VII) than the ostraca (Stratum VI). The script of the *ḥṭm* ostracon, which is distinctly earlier than that of the Eliashib ostraca, points in the same direction. Did Eliashib return to the place after its reconstruction, or was this one of his ancestors who served in the same capacity?

viii. *Arad and the History of the Negeb*

In addition to the light which the fortress of Arad throws on the history of the Judaean Negeb, two stimulating questions arise. First, how can we explain the erection of a 'house of Yahweh' in the royal fortress? And secondly, where was the Canaanite Arad mentioned in the Old Testament (Num. xxi. 1; Joshua xii. 14), of which no traces have been found at Tell Arad? We are well aware that these are intricate problems which need thorough study and which will undoubtedly be the subject of much debate. We may conclude with some brief observations upon them.

The identification of Israelite Arad with Tell Arad, borne out by the preservation of the name still known to Eusebius,[33] has been further strengthened by a bowl found in Stratum IX with the name Arad (*'rd*) scratched on it several times in ancient Hebrew letters. As mentioned above, the only Canaanite mounds in the vicinity seem to be Tell el-Milḥ and Khirbet el-Meshash, which fit in well with the Old Testament passages about Arad and Hormah.

Tell el-Milḥ is situated eight miles south-west of Tell Arad. How can we explain the transference of the name from one tell to another at such a distance even in the plains of the Negeb? We would suggest that a new fortress may have been set up beside the old one bearing the same name. This is borne out by the Shishak list, which mentions *two* fortresses named Arad in the Negeb— *hqrm-'rd- rbt- 'rd- nbt- yrhm* 'the fortresses Arad the great (Rabbat) and Arad of Beth Yeroham'. We may assume, therefore, that the new and important fortress at Tell Arad was called Arad Rabbat, while the ancient site was designated by the name of the Yeroham (Jerahmeel?) family which settled the place.

The reason for the duplication of the name may be the sanctuary. We have in the Old Testament an interesting passage which states that the Kenite Hobab family, which was related to Moses, settled in the Negeb of Arad (cf. Judges i. 16, LXX). B. Mazar is probably right in his view that the Old Testament emphasis on this special family and its relation to Moses provides a hint as to the important role it played in connexion with the worship of Yahweh at various places.[34]

We suggest, therefore, the following solution. The prominent hill of Tell Arad was chosen by the Hobab family as their central place of worship in the Negeb of Arad. This was a further reason why Solomon chose this place for his main fortress in the area, without changing its name. The traditional high place was converted into a sanctuary within the royal citadel, the priest perhaps being the honoured Kenite priests who traced their genealogy back to Moses (cf. Judges xviii. 30). The sanctuary was an important part of the royal citadel, which served as an administrative and military centre in this border region. Exactly the same motives apparently guided Jeroboam in the construction of his two main royal sanctuaries at Beth-el and Dan, both of them near the border of the kingdom and both venerated through ancient traditions.

The old tribal territories of the Negeb now become much clearer. Tell Arad was the centre of the Kenites, Tell el-Milh belonged to the Jerahmeelites, and Hormah (Tell el-Meshash) was in the territory of Simeon. On this basis a much more accurate and intelligible map of the different regions can be drawn, including the Negeb areas of Kaleb, the Kenites, the Jerahmeelites, and Simeon (cf. 1 Sam. xxvii. 10, xxx. 14, 29).

Y. AHARONI

NOTES

1. E. Macdonald, *et al.*, *Beth-Pelet II*, 1932; J. Perrot, *I.E.J.* v, 1955, pp. 17 ff.
2. Y. Aharoni, *B.J.P.E.S.* xxviii, 1964, pp. 153–64 (in Hebrew); Y. Aharoni and Ruth Amiran, *Archaeology* xvii, 1964, pp. 43 ff.
3. B. Mazar, *I.L.N.*, 13 April 1963, pp. 546 f.
4. N. Glueck, *Rivers in the Desert*, 1951, pp. 60–110; W. F. Albright, *B.A.S.O.R.* 163, 1961, pp. 36 ff.
5. Gerar is not in the Negeb proper and its history is different, as will be shown later.
6. N. Glueck, *A.A.S.O.R.* xviii–xix, 1939, pp. 264 ff.; *Rivers in the Desert*, pp. 60 ff.
7. B. Rothenberg, *God's Wilderness*, 1961, pp. 15 ff.; M. Kochavi, *B.J.P.E.S.* xxvii, 1963, pp. 284–92 (in Hebrew).
8. W. M. Flinders Petrie, *Beth-Pelet I*, 1930.
9. W. M. Flinders Petrie, *Gerar*, 1928.
10. W. F. Albright, *B.A.S.O.R.* 33, 1929, p. 7.
11. B. Mazar (Maisler), *B.J.P.E.S.* xvi, 1951, pp. 38–41 (in Hebrew); *P.E.Q.*, 1952, pp. 48–51.
12. Y. Aharoni, *I.E.J.* vi, 1956, pp. 26–32.
13. M. Kochavi, ibid. xiv, 1964, pp. 111 f. The name is new, and in the maps only the field name es-Sudar appears in the vicinity. The place was excavated because the new Beer-sheba–Dimona railroad had to cross it and it was mostly destroyed after excavation.
14. N. Glueck, *Rivers in the Desert*, pp. 173 ff. Y. Aharoni, in *Elath*, Jerusalem, 1963, pp. 54–73 (in Hebrew).
15. C. L. Woolley and T. E. Lawrence, *P.E.F.A.* iii, 1914, pp. 64 ff.
16. Y. Aharoni, *I.E.J.* vii, 1958, pp. 33–35; Y. Aharoni and Ruth Amiran, ibid. xiv, 1964, pp. 135 f.
17. Y. Aharoni *ap.* B. Rothenberg, op. cit., p. 138.
18. N. Glueck, *B.A.S.O.R.* 145, 1957, pp. 23 f.
19. Ibid., pp. 22 f.
20. Discovered by the southern team of the new archaeological survey of Israel, directed by R. Cohen, and not yet published.
21. *I.E.J.* viii, 1958, p. 239, fig. 5, x, 1960, pp. 103–9.
22. Ibid. viii, 1958, pp. 242 f.
23. Ibid. x, 1960, pp. 97–111.
24. Only trial excavations have been carried out at Kadesh-barnea (cf. M. Dothan, ibid. xv, 1965—in the press). Another one which has been excavated is the fortress of Ezion-geber (cf. N. Glueck, *B.A.S.O.R.* 71, 1938, pp. 3–17; 75, 1939, pp. 8–22; 79, 1940, pp. 2–18; 80, 1940, pp. 3–10; 82, 1941, pp. 3–11; *B.A.* xxviii, 1965, pp. 70–87), and it has much in common with the history of Arad.
25. Y. Yadin, *I.E.J.* viii, 1958, pp. 80 ff.; *The Art of Warfare in Biblical Lands*, 1963, pp. 326 f.
26. On this passage, cf. Yadin, ibid., loc. cit.

27. We may only hint at other changes which point to the same conclusions: the altar too was enlarged by about 35 centimetres between Strata XI and X; the width of the holy place was about 2·7 metres and 3·15 metres in Strata XI and VIII respectively, that is, six small and large cubits or one reed.

28. Incidentally such is the case also in the Canaanite–Phoenician prototypes of the Jerusalem temple, for example, the temple discovered in Hazor.

29. H. G. May, *Material Remains of the Megiddo Cult*, 1935, p. 126, pl. xii.

30. There are also a few Arab ostraca and one Greek ostracon.

31. Cf. F. M. Cross, *B.A.S.O.R.* 165, 1926, pp. 34 ff.

32. A fragment of a similar bowl had already been discovered in the first season, cf. *I.E.J.* xiv, 1964, pp. 137 f., pl. 37A.

33. *Onomasticon*, ed. E. Klostermann, 1904, p. 14, 2.

34. B. Mazar, *Ereṣ Yisra'el* vii, 1964, pp. 1–5 (in Hebrew); *J.N.E.S.* xxiv, 1965, pp. 297–303.

BIBLIOGRAPHY

AHARONI, Y. 'The Negeb of Judah', *I.E.J.* viii, 1958, pp. 26–38.

—— and AMIRAN, RUTH. 'Excavations at Tel Arad, Preliminary Report on the First Season, 1962', ibid. xiv, 1964, pp. 131–47.

—— —— 'Arad: a Biblical city in southern Palestine', *Archaeology* xvii, 1964, pp. 43–53.

—— —— 'Hebrew Ostraca from Tel Arad' *I.E.J.* xvi, 1966, pp. 1–7.

ALBRIGHT, W. F. 'Egypt and the early history of the Negeb', *J.P.O.S.* iv, 1924, pp. 131–61.

EVENARI, M., AHARONI, Y., et al. 'The ancient desert agriculture of the Negev', *I.E.J.* viii, 1958, pp. 231–68, x, 1960, pp. 97–111.

GLUECK, N. *Rivers in the Desert*, 1959.

KIRK, G. E. 'Archaeological exploration of the southern desert', *P.E.Q.* 1938, pp. 211–35.

—— 'The Negev or southern desert of Palestine', ibid., 1941, pp. 57–71.

ROTHENBERG, B., et al. *God's Wilderness*, 1961.

WOOLLEY, C. L., and LAWRENCE, T. E. *The Wilderness of Zin*, 1936.

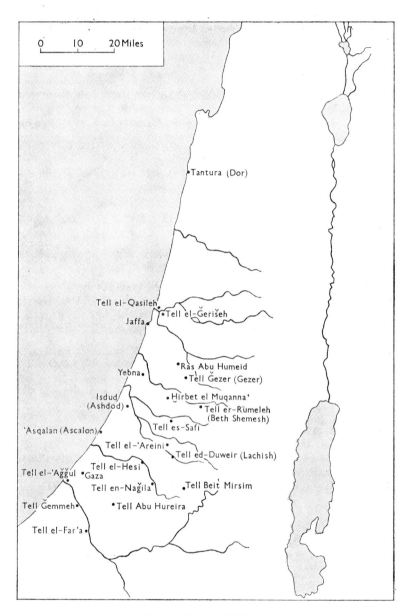

FIG. 11. Map of Philistia

PHILISTIA

THE name Philistia refers to the part of Palestine which was dominated by the Philistines in the period of the Israelite monarchy. This was the area of the coastal plain lying roughly between Jaffa in the north and the region some fifty miles to the south, beyond Gaza, where the desert which separates Palestine from Egypt begins.[1] The eastern boundary may be most conveniently defined as the junction between the alluvial coast plain and the limestone plateau called the Shephelah, which formed a buffer zone to the hill country of Judah.[2]

Philistia was an area of importance from early times, since one of the most convenient routes between Egypt and Syria passed through it.[3] From the early second millennium B.C. this part of the coast was also engaged in important sea trade. This is indicated by pottery recovered from the sea which shows a strong concentration off Philistia, especially opposite Ashkelon and Ashdod, and very little elsewhere south of Carmel, except off Tantura.[4]

There were a number of important cities in this area in ancient times, of which the best known are the five of the Philistine pentapolis, Ashdod, Ashkelon, Gaza, Ekron, and Gath. Others were Joppa,[5] Jabneel,[6] Gerar, and Sharuhen. Among the noteworthy neighbouring cities in the Shephelah were Gezer, Beth-shemesh, Lachish, and, at the southern end of the Judaean hills, Debir.

Significant sites which have been excavated in Philistia are, from north to south, Tell el-Qasileh,[7] Tell el-Ǧerišeh,[8] Isdûd,[9] Ḥirbet el-Muqanna',[10] Tell eṣ-Ṣâfi,[11] 'Askalan,[12] Tell el-'Areini,[13] Tell en-Naǧila,[14] Tell el-Ḥesi,[15] Gaza,[16] Tell el-'Aǧǧûl,[17] Tell Ǧemmeh,[18] and Tell el-Far'a.[19]

Unfortunately it is not always possible to equate the cities mentioned in the texts with these excavated sites. Those of which the identification is fairly well established are Ashdod = Isdûd, Ashkelon = 'Askalan, Gaza = modern Gaza, and it is probable that Jabneel = the unexcavated site Yebna. The two inland cities of the Philistine pentapolis, Ekron and Gath, have not been certainly identified. It has recently been argued that Ekron =

Khirbet el-Muqanna',[20] and after uncorroborative investigations at Tell el-'Areini,[21] an identification of Gath with Tell en-Naǧila has now been proposed.[22] The identification of Gath is complicated by the fact that such a common noun ('winepress') occurs in several place-names,[23] any of which might be quoted in abbreviated form.[24] Other suggested, but unsubstantiated, identifications are Gath-rimmon = Tell el-Ǧerišeh,[25] Libnah = Tell eṣ-Ṣâfi,[26] Eglon = Tell el-Ḥesi,[27] Gerar = Tell Abu Hureira,[28] Sharuhen = Tell el-Far'a,[29] Beth-eglaim = Tell el-'Aǧǧûl, and Yurza = Tell Ǧemmeh.[30]

Much of the coast of southern Palestine is today, and probably was in antiquity, backed by sand dunes, and of the five principal Philistine cities Ashkelon was the only one directly on the coast.[31] Ashdod, some $2\frac{1}{2}$ miles inland, had a port, Ašdōd-yām, Assyrian Asdudimmu, perhaps modern Minet el-Qal'a,[32] and Gaza, about 2 miles from the coast, probably used an open roadstead.[33]

The earliest significant settlement so far revealed in this part of Palestine dates from about the early fourth millennium B.C., when agricultural communities of a type similar to that known at Teleilat Ghassul in the Jordan valley are found at a number of sites.[34] The sequence of the transition from this culture to that of the Early Bronze Age is not yet clear,[35] but there is evidence that by the end of the fourth millennium there was contact with Egypt.[36] There was already a substantial settlement at Tell el-'Areini, and probably one at Tell Abu Hureira in the fourth millennium. It is not known whether these sites received, during this period, the names by which they were known in later times, or indeed who the people were who inhabited them, for although there is some evidence that there were Semitic speakers in Palestine in the third millennium,[37] they cannot be specifically defined as 'Canaanites'.[38] 'Canaanite' is a cultural term; from the point of view of race, or physical type, it is probable that by the fourth millennium Palestine was occupied by members of the Mediterranean division of the White or Caucasoid race, which continued to be the dominant type throughout ancient times.[39]

Towards the end of the third millennium B.C. there is evidence of the influx of new groups of peoples into Palestine. In the south this is especially attested in tombs at Tell el-'Aǧǧûl. It seems that the bearers of this culture were nomads who may have hovered on the desert fringes of the settled areas, before infiltrating.[40] It is possible that during this period, which is usually designated Middle Bronze Age I, there were indirect relations with the Aegean world through the intermediation of Cyprus,[41] the preliminary to later direct contacts.

The culture established in the early centuries of the second millennium B.C. continued with no major changes throughout most of the millennium. Egypt, united under the Twelfth Dynasty, now had influence and possibly control in Palestine,[42] and it is at about this period that the first glimpse of the ethnic[43] affiliations of the people of Syria-Palestine is afforded in the Execration Texts which give the names of some of the enemies of Egypt at this time.[44] Such names as can be identified indicate that already in this period many of the cities of Palestine bore the names which are familiar from later times. The only city of Philistia which is probably to be identified in these texts is Ashkelon.[45] It is possible to postulate a Semitic etymology for this name,[46] and it may here be observed that a Semitic etymology or morphology may likewise be argued for most of the place-names known later, and perhaps dating to this time or earlier, in this area of Palestine.[47] The personal names in these texts show that by the second millennium B.C. the area was occupied by north-west Semitic speakers.[48]

Though the material culture of Palestine continued in the same tradition, outside influences brought about innovations from time to time. From about 1750 B.C. (Middle Bronze IIB) new types of pottery appear alongside the established ones, and a new kind of fortification, consisting of a massive earth slope with plastered or stone-faced surface appears from north Syria to the Egyptian delta, and it has been argued that this development betrays the introduction of the war-chariot and the battering ram.[49] The sites of Tell el-Ġerišeh, Tell el-ʿAǧǧûl, and Tell el-Farʿa exhibit this new fortification, and at ʿAskalan a rampart enclosing an area of some 130 acres was erected, probably in this period.[50] It has been commonly concluded that these innovations are to be attributed to the Hyksos, Asiatics who came to control Egypt at about this time, but while these people were definable as foreigners to the Egyptians, it is probable that in Palestine they would have been regarded as an integral part of the population. Hyksos personal names suggest that, in addition to Semitic speakers, there were also people of originally Hurrian and possibly Indo-European speaking groups among them.[51] The pressure of Indo-European speakers from south Russia on Hurrian speakers south of the Caucasus is perhaps to be seen as the agency by which the horse-drawn chariot, and the mixed warriors who adopted it, were introduced into the Near East.[52] It is perhaps in this context that a horse burial at Tell el-ʿAǧǧûl is to be seen.[53] From a slightly later date at this site comes a rich find of gold jewellery which has some interesting parallels with late third millennium finds at Maikop in the Caucasus.[54]

There is some evidence of new racial elements in Palestine in this period. The Mediterranean type, characterized by long-heads, continued to predominate, but now a few round-headed individuals, of a type already known in Asia Minor and Europe, are recorded.[55]

In this period, the Middle Bronze Age, there is evidence, both archaeological[56] and textual, of extensive trade between Syria, Egypt, and Crete. It is probable that the names Kftyw, attested in Egyptian documents,[57] and Kaptara, in Babylonian documents,[58] at or by this period, are to be connected with Old Testament Caphtor, and identified with some part of the Aegean area, probably Crete.[59] One of the Mari documents records gifts from the king of Hazor to Kaptara and to a possible Carian in Ugarit,[60] and an inscription from Byblos indicates the presence of a Lycian in the court of the ruler there.[61]

This, the Middle Bronze Age, was probably the period of the Hebrew patriarchs.[62] It has recently been argued that there was a developed donkey caravan trade in the Near East which reached its peak in the nineteenth century B.C., and that Abraham was engaged in this trade, particularly in the sector between southern Palestine and Egypt, having a permanent residence in Gerar.[63] According to Genesis, Abraham was living at this time in the 'land of the Philistines',[64] and the ruler of Gerar in the time of Abraham and Isaac, whose name was Abimelech, is described as 'king of the Philistines'.[65] The reference here to 'Philistines' is generally regarded as an anachronism, since the name and the artefacts usually associated with these people are not attested until the closing centuries of the second millennium B.C.[66] The Philistines of this later period are known, however, to have been of

Aegean origin, and it is possible that the name was used in Genesis to refer to earlier people with Aegean affiliations. The name Abimelech, and that of his counsellor Ahuzzath, are Semitic, but the name of his army commander, Phicol, is non-Semitic and of uncertain connexions.[67]

In the sixteenth century Kamose, the last ruler of the Seventeenth Dynasty in Thebes, began a campaign, continued by his brother Amosis, first ruler of the Eighteenth Dynasty, which put an end to Hyksos dominion in Egypt. The Palestinian strong point of Sharuhen was besieged and destroyed,[68] and the Egyptian conquest of Palestine and much of Syria, which was finally completed by Tuthmosis III in the early fifteenth century, was begun.[69] Cities in south-west Palestine mentioned in the inscriptions of Tuthmosis III are Gaza, Joppa,[70] Beth-dagon, and Gezer. There are destruction levels at most excavated sites in Palestine which may be assigned to this period, and this point is taken conventionally as marking the beginning of the Late Bronze Age. South-west Palestine lay now for about a century under Egyptian administration. New pottery appears alongside the old. Imported Cypriote types are found,[71] and reciprocal trade is attested by a type known as Bichrome Ware from Cyprus, Cilicia, Syria, and Palestine.[72]

It was this period in the Aegean that saw the Late Helladic or Mycenaean culture of mainland Greece rival the long-standing Minoan civilization of Crete. Widespread trade links were established, and Late Helladic pottery is an important indication of this, and Late Helladic II sherds of about the fifteenth century B.C. have been found in south-west Palestine.[73]

There is not much direct evidence of Philistia in the texts in this period but in the fourteenth century there are new sources. At Ugarit, Ashdod and Ashkelon are mentioned as trading centres,[74] and the Amarna letters, which betray the weakening of Egyptian power in Asia, throw some light on the political and ethnic situation of the time. They include correspondence from the ruler of Ashkelon,[75] they mention Gath, Gaza and Joppa,[76] and they show in general that at this time, while the majority of rulers bore Semitic names, a certain number, including Widiya at Ashkelon,[77] were Indo-European, and a few Hurrian.[78] This shows the established results of the earlier migrations. It is probable that the

Egyptians had their main administrative centre of this area at Gaza and a less important one at Joppa,[79] and that the other cities vied with each other for advantage. Ḫabiru,[80] already known from earlier texts, are mentioned as troublesome raiders in the letters from Gezer,[81] and the ruler of Jerusalem reports that the inhabitants of Ashkelon have been assisting them with food.[82]

Another element in the Amarna correspondence indicates contacts with northern peoples. In a letter from Cyprus (Alašia) mention is made of piratical raids by people of the Lukku land,[83] or Lycians. From Byblos there is mention of Sherdana as settled and in service there,[84] and from Tyre a king of the Danuna is mentioned as if these were people settled in the area.[85] These three peoples, the Luka, Sherden, and Danuna, are the precursors of a group, comprising also the Aḳawasha, Tursha, Sheklesh, Weshesh, Peleset, and Tjekker, known collectively as the 'Sea Peoples', who in the following two centuries descended from the north and west upon the Levant coast and Egypt.[86] The origins of these people are uncertain and much debated. Connexions seem likely between the Sherden and Sardinia,[87] and possible between the Sheklesh and Sicily,[88] and the Tursha and the Etruscans,[89] but it is probable that these were subsequent to the movements of the late second millennium. The Luka are probably to be connected with western Anatolia and the area of later Lycia,[90] though they may have been on the move towards the east for some time,[91] and, if they are to be linked with the Luwian speakers, their forebears may have been there since the third millennium.[92] The Danuna seem to have been well established in the area of Cilicia and the Amq Plain, and were probably not part of the original movement.[93] The Sheklesh and Weshesh may have been Anatolian peoples,[94] and the Aḳawasha are sometimes equated with the Achaean (Mycenaean) Greeks,[95] though this identification is not universally accepted,[96] so the other 'Sea Peoples' are generally assumed, by association, to have come from the area of the Aegean. The Peleset and the Tjekker are not mentioned in the inscriptions until the twelfth century B.C.,[97] but it is possible that small contingents were present before they became prominent enough to be mentioned in the texts.[98]

Other evidence of continuing relations with the Aegean in the fourteenth century is provided by Late Helladic IIIA pottery from 'Askalan, Gaza, Tell el-'Aǧǧûl, and Tell Ǧemmeh.[99]

During the remainder of the fourteenth century B.C. there is little documentary evidence on Philistia, but at the end of the century Sethos I, the second king of the Nineteenth Dynasty, began the recovery of Egypt's lost Asiatic empire.[100] This led to contact with the Hittites, and in the account of the battle of Kadesh the records of Ramesses II name Lukku among those fighting with the Hittites, and Sherden, whom he had previously repulsed from Egypt, on the Egyptian side.[101]

Aegean contacts continued in the thirteenth century as is shown by finds of pottery in the Late Helladic IIIB style at 'Askalan, Tell el-Ḥesi, Tell el-'Aǧǧûl, Tell Ǧemmeh, and Tell el-Far'a,[102] and, though these may be only the products of trade, it has been suggested that a group of Cretan seals found near Gaza may imply a colony of craftsmen there.[103]

Ramesses' successor, Merneptah, had to face another invasion of 'Sea Peoples', but, as he indicates on a funerary stele, he was able to avert the danger.[104] At the end of this stele a passage typifies his pacifications in Asia with the names Hatti (eastern Asia Minor and north Syria), Canaan, Ashkelon, Gezer, Yanoam, Israel, and Hurru (Palestine and Syria). This may be no more than a rhetorical collocation of names, 'Canaan' and 'Hurru', for instance, probably overlapping, but there is other evidence that he did capture Gezer,[105] so that some encounter with Ashkelon also is possible. The date of the Exodus is not certainly known, but this inscription shows that the Israelites were now in Palestine though not yet in permanent settlements.[106]

From this time the Old Testament begins to bear again on the history of Palestine. The route of the Israelites from Egypt in the second half of the thirteenth century B.C. did not go by way of the 'Land of the Philistines'.[107] This probably refers to the vicinity of Gaza, where Caphtorim were settled,[108] and not to Philistia as a whole, the term 'Philistine' being used in the general sense of 'Aegean people'. This, the late Nineteenth Dynasty in Egypt, was a period of weakness when control in Palestine was not effective, but there is evidence that Sethos II may have maintained a garrison at Tell el-Far'a.[109]

The excavations at Isdûd have shown a violent destruction in about the middle of the thirteenth century B.C., possibly due to the Israelites,[110] which perhaps adds weight to the statement in

Judges i. 18 that Judah took Gaza, Ashkelon, and Ekron and their territories.[111]

In the Aegean area there is evidence of destruction and catastrophe at about the end of the thirteenth century, possibly as a result of the movements of peoples in central Europe.[112] The same causes must have set off other movements which brought about the destruction of the Hittite Empire and of cities in Syria and Palestine, including such sites as 'Askalan and Tell el-Far'a. At about this time Ramesses III had to meet a new onslaught of 'Sea Peoples', this time the Peleset and Tjekker being mentioned,[113] so that these destructions may be attributed to them.

Following the destructions in the Aegean area, the Late Helladic IIIB pottery, which was more or less uniform throughout its distribution, was replaced by a new style, Late Helladic IIIC, with many regional variations.[114] It extended to Cyprus, and in Philistia a new style appears in the early twelfth century which combines elements of this Late Helladic IIIC pottery of Cyprus with native Cypriote, Egyptian, and local Palestinian components.[115] The earliest known sherds of this ware were found at Tell el-Far'a in a building which is probably to be attributed to Sethos II, though it no doubt continued in use after his time,[116] so that it may be that the owners of this pottery were established there by the Egyptians. This pottery is found throughout the area known from later documents to have been occupied by the Philistines, and in deposits which can be dated to the twelfth and eleventh centuries, the main period of Philistine domination, so that there is good reason to identify it as Philistine pottery.[117] The recent excavations at Isdûd show that this site was fortified by the Philistines.[118] It seems that in most cases they simply took over conquered sites, though Ḥirbet el-Muqanna' and Tell Qasileh may have been new foundations.[119]

Valuable information on the Philistines at this time is provided in the triumphal relief carvings which adorn the mortuary temple of Ramesses III at Medînet Ḥābu. These show battle scenes involving warriors who can be identified as Peleset, Tjekker, and Sherden, the latter acting as mercenaries for the Egyptians.[120] The Peleset and Tjekker wear head-dresses consisting of a horizontal band with vertical bristles or feathers sticking up from it.[121] These have parallels in seventeenth- to sixteenth-century

PLATE XVIII

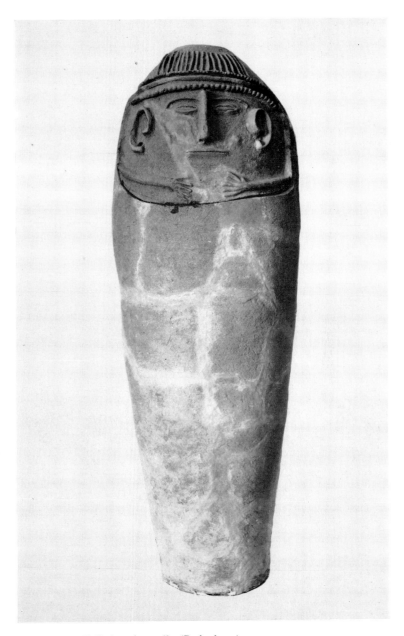

Philistine clay coffin (Beth-shean), *c.* 1200–1100 B.C.

Crete,[122] sixteenth-century Mycenae,[123] and thirteenth- to twelfth-century Cyprus.[124] Herodotus states that the Carians invented the helmet crest,[125] and that the Lycians wore (felt) caps ringed about with feathers[126] so that, although these statements cannot both be relevant, either would point to south-west Asia Minor. The Peleset and Tjekker as well as the Sherden are shown in ribbed corslets, kilts, and carrying round shields, long broadswords, and triangular daggers. Not all of these are of diagnostic value, but the swords, of which an actual example of about the twelfth century was found near Jaffa,[127] and daggers have parallels with the area of the Caucasus.[128] It has been suggested that the racial type depicted is northern long-head,[129] contrasting with the still-predominant Mediterranean long-heads of the Levant, and possibly suggesting an origin in central and south-east Europe or south Russia. This is very tenuous evidence, but it may suggest that the 'Sea-Peoples' included elements perhaps from south Russia who came into the region of the Aegean and western Anatolia, attracted other disparate elements to them, and then migrated by land and sea to the Near East. Such a view would not conflict with a possible equation of the name *pᵉlištîm* with *pelasgoi*,[130] vaguely defined by Greek authors as an early population group in the Aegean area, and with the statement in the Old Testament that the Philistines came from the coastlands (and islands) of Caphtor.[131]

During the twelfth and eleventh centuries, the period of the Judges, the Philistines, having settled, and possibly been settled as garrison troops by the Egyptians, in the area of Philistia,[132] expanded inland and threatened the Israelites in the hill country.

References in the Old Testament[133] indicate that the Philistines had a system of government based on the five main cities, Gaza, Ashkelon, Ashdod, Gath, and Ekron, each under the rule of a lord (*seren*), and a central shrine to their principal god Dagon at Ashdod.[134] The term *seren*[135] is probably cognate with Greek τύραννος 'tyrant',[136] and possibly hieroglyphic Hittite *tarwana*-'judge',[137] which points to an Aegean–West Anatolian origin, since τύραννος is probably a pre-Hellenic loan-word in Greek,[138] and the language of the Hittite hieroglyphics is probably related to Luwian and Lycian.[139]

The end of the second millennium B.C. was the period of the

transition from the Bronze to the Iron Age, and the Philistines, who may have learnt the technology in Anatolia, maintained a monopoly of iron working.[140]

A number of anthropoid clay coffins found at Beth-shean and Tell el-Far'a in association with Philistine pottery are probably to be connected with the Philistines. Such coffin burial may have been copied by mercenaries from Egyptian practices, for other examples are known from the eastern Delta and from Nubia.[141] On some of the Beth-shean examples the heads of the coffin lids are shown with the characteristic feather head-dress (Pl. XVIII). The distribution of these remains[142] illustrates the influence and spread of the Philistines. The story of Wen-Amun[143] shows that in the early eleventh century B.C. the Philistines' associates, the Tjekker, were engaged in profitable sea trade at Dor,[144] and the same is probably true of the Philistines themselves further south.

The Israelites suffered a severe defeat when the Philistines captured the ark, and, probably about the middle of the eleventh century, their religious centre at Shiloh was destroyed.[145] This was the period of the Philistines' greatest power. They controlled much of the plain of Esdraelon, the Shephelah, and the Negeb, and even parts of the Judaean hills. This was, however, the occasion for the emergence of Samuel, Saul, and finally David, who in a series of battles confined the Philistines to the coastal plain where they continued in reduced independence. David now employed Philistines and Cretans as a body-guard,[146] and these continued until the beginning of Solomon's reign,[147] but they are not mentioned after this, though a related group, Carians, were used in the ninth century.[148]

The narratives in Samuel suggest that by the time of the struggle with Israel the culture of the Philistines had become very much assimilated to that of the Canaanites. Three of their gods are mentioned, Dagon, Baal-zebub, and Ashtaroth with a temple at Beth-shean. These all have Semitic names and may have been adopted by the Philistines as the equivalents of some of their own deities. It is probable that Ashtaroth was a well-established deity in pre-Philistine Beth-shean, where the Philistines are unlikely to have been in more than garrison occupation.[149] Dagon was known, under the form Dagan, with weather and fertility aspects, from the third millennium in the Near East,[150] and Baal-zebub, whether the name is taken as it stands as 'Lord-Fly' or as a corruption of Baal-zebul 'Baal-Prince',[151] which has support in Ugaritic *zbl.b'l*,[152] has nothing that is not Near Eastern about it.

A possible clue to objects introduced into Palestine by the Philistines is to be found in loan-words in the Old Testament. The word for 'helmet', significantly spelt with an uncertain first consonant, *kôba'* and *ḳôba'*, which first appears in the account of Goliath's armour (1 Sam. xvii.), is perhaps cognate with Hittite *kupaḫi-* 'helmet, hat, head-dress',[153] and may refer to a new type, for helmets are attested in Mesopotamia at least from the third millennium and must have been known.

Another possible word is *'argaz*, which is used in one context only, describing the 'box' or 'chest' in which the Philistines placed the gold images which they returned with the captured ark (1 Sam. vi. 8, 11, 15). It is possible that this word is cognate with Hittite *ark-* 'to shut in' and Greek ἄρκος 'protection'.[154]

Among the names of the Philistines of this period, two have probable west Anatolian connexions: Goliath, spelt *golyat*, in which the element -*yat* may be cognate with -*wattaš* found in the names of western foes of the Hittites, and with -*uattes* in the names of Lydian kings of the seventh and sixth centuries B.C.;[155] and Achish, spelt *'āḳîš*, which is found in a list of what are described as *kftiw* names on an Egyptian school writing-board probably of the Eighteenth Dynasty,[156] and is possibly cognate with Anchises, the name, according to Homer,[157] of a Trojan, the father of Aeneas.

After their defeat by David, the Philistines were seldom a threat to the kings of the divided monarchy.[158] It is probable that some of their cities were taken by Sheshonq (Old Testament Shishak), first king of the Egyptian Twenty-first Dynasty, at the end of the tenth century,[159] but the main outside source of information for this period is the Assyrian inscriptions of the eighth and seventh centuries B.C.[160] Areas adjacent to Philistia became Assyrian provinces in the late eighth century—Dor in the time of Tiglath-pileser III,[161] and Samaria in Sargon's time[162]—but, except for Ashdod for a short time in the reigns of Sargon and Sennacherib,[163] the main Philistine cities remained, like Judah, independent kingdoms. They are, however, frequently mentioned as suffering from the campaigns of the Assyrians.[164] Gath seems to have declined in importance by this time. It is mentioned (*gi-im-tu*) as a conquest by Sargon in the late eighth century,[165] but, as it was sacked earlier in the century by Uzziah,[166] and soon thereafter the four Philistine cities are mentioned without it, and it is cited as an example of a city fallen low,[167] it may be that Sargon's conquest was of the site possibly to be identified with Ras Abu Ḥamid, and not the Philistine city.[168]

Several of the rulers of the Philistine cities are mentioned: Ḥanunu and Ṣil-Bel, of Gaza; Mitinti, Rukibtu, Šarruludari, Ṣidqa, and Mitinti, of Ashkelon; Azuri, Aḥimetu, Iamani, Mitinti, and Aḥimilki of Ashdod; and Padi and Ikausu, of Ekron.[169] The area is sometimes referred to by the Assyrians as Philistia,[170] but the rulers' names show that the tendency to adopt the local culture had gone a long way. Šarruludari is Assyrian,[171] but most of them can be interpreted as West-Semitic,[172] and though Ikausu is possibly a form of the name Achish,[173] Iamani, which has usually been taken, whether as a name or a gentilic, to signify 'a Greek',[174] may also be Semitic.[175] It seems indeed as though the inhabitants of Philistia at this time were hardly different, except in name, from the neighbouring peoples.

With the decline of Assyria in the late seventh century B.C., new movements were made for control in Palestine. The Egyptian Twenty-sixth (Saite) Dynasty king, Psammetichus I, is said to have taken Ashdod after a siege of unparalleled duration,[176] and his successor Necho II to have taken Gaza,[177] though from its position it may be guessed that it had already submitted to Psammetichus and then defected. It was not long, however, before Nebuchadrezzar appeared in the west, and having defeated Necho's forces at Carchemish in 605 B.C., the Babylonian Chronicle claims that he became master of all Syria-Palestine.[178] It may be that this campaign was what prompted an Aramaic letter from a Palestinian ruler, found at Saḳḳara, asking Pharaoh for help against the approaching Babylonians. The context suggests that the writer must have been in Philistia, possibly Ashkelon, but his name, 'Adon, and the language of the letter again betray no specifically Philistine elements.[179] At all events in 604 B.C. Nebuchadrezzar sacked Ashkelon,[180] and ration lists of his time from Babylon show that a number of Ashkelonite prisoners were living there.[181] Other prisoners or hostages in Babylon included the kings of Ashdod and Gaza.[182]

Already in the early part of the first millennium B.C. incense from
south Arabia was known in the Near East, and one of the principal
routes by which it was brought there was overland through the
Ḥiǧâz to Petra. This seems to have given some importance to Gaza
which became one of the staging points between Petra and Egypt
and Syria.[183] It is possible that the Saite king Apries retook Gaza
in the early sixth century,[184] but, if so, the Babylonian Chronicle
claims that it was in Babylonian hands again by the time of
Nabonidus.[185]

In 539 B.C. Cyrus the Persian took Babylon and formed it, with
Syria, Phoenicia, and Palestine, into the province of Babylon and
Ebir-nâri ('Across the River').[186] In the south-west, it seems that
the Nabataeans were in control of a stretch of coast from Gaza
southwards at the time of Cambyses' invasion of Egypt in 525
B.C.,[187] and according to Herodotus they paid no tribute when,
under Darius, they formed part, with Phoenicia, Palestine, and
Cyprus, of the fifth satrapy.[188]

It is probable that Eshmun'azar, king of Sidon, is to be dated
sometime in the Persian period. He claims in the inscription on his
sarcophagus that the 'Lord of Kings' had given him Dor and
Joppa.[189] These he describes, according to one possible rendering,
as 'mighty lands of Dagon',[190] which, if correct, implies a religious continuity in the area.[191] It is also possible that there was a
linguistic continuity, and that the Ashdodite language ('ašdôdît)
spoken by the children of Israelite mixed marriages in the time of
Nehemiah was still Philistine, though it may only have been some
local Semitic dialect.[192]

The place of Philistia in the incense trade continued to bring
many outside influences.[193] A fourth-century hoard of bronzes
from Ashkelon shows a marked Egyptian style,[194] and it seems
clear that Attic type coins were being struck at Gaza already in the
fifth century.[195] The extent of the incense trade may perhaps be
judged from the statement that, when Alexander the Great took
Gaza in 332 B.C., over 500 talents' weight of frankincense was
found there.[196] This trade continued in the ensuing Hellenistic
period, and there were coin mints at both Gaza and Ashkelon.[197]

The conquests of Alexander marked a turning-point in the Near
East, and the history of Philistia in the Hellenistic and subsequent
periods cannot be entered into here. The name 'Palestine', of

course, derives from that of the Philistines. It already appears in the form Παλαιστίνη in Herodotus (iii. 91), but it only replaced the earlier 'Judaea' after the suppression of the Second Jewish Revolt of A.D. 132–5, when the Romans wished to obscure the name.[198]

T. C. MITCHELL

NOTES

1. See map in R. J. Braidwood and G. R. Willey, *Courses Toward Urban Life*, 1962, p. 149, where J. Perrot shows the general limits of climatic zones, and with this cf. map, *J.B.L.* lxxv, 1956, p. 213.

2. D. Baly, *The Geography of the Bible*, 1957, pp. 138–47; G. Adam Smith, *The Historical Geography of the Holy Land*, 25th ed., 1931, pp. 169–98.

3. Baly, op. cit., pp. 112 f.; J. Garstang, *The Foundations of Bible History: Joshua Judges*, 1931, pp. 84 ff. In later times Gaza became important as a stage on the incense route from south Arabia via Petra; see A. Grohmann, *Arabien* (Müller, Handb. d. Altertumswiss. III. i. 3. 3. 4), 1963, p. 7, and n. 1.

4. D. Barag, *I.E.J.* xiii, 1963, pp. 13–19, and map, p. 14.

5. Joshua xix. 46.

6. Joshua xv. 11, probably to be identified with *yabneh*, 2 Chron. xxvi. 6.

7. B. Mazar, *I.E.J.* i, 1950–1, pp. 61–76, 125–40, 194–218; cf. *B.A.S.O.R.* 124, 1951, pp. 21–25.

8. E. L. Sukenik, *Q.D.A.P.* iv, 1935, pp. 208 f., vi, 1938, p. 225.

9. E. F. Campbell, *B.A.* xxvi, 1963, pp. 30 ff.; D. N. Freedman, *B.A.* ibid., pp. 134–9.

10. J. Naveh, *I.E.J.* viii, 1958, pp. 87–100, 165–70 (survey); Y. Aharoni, *P.E.Q.* xc, 1958, pp. 27–31; cf. B. Mazar, *I.E.J.* x, 1960, pp. 65 f.

11. F. J. Bliss and R. A. S. Macalister, *Excavations in Palestine during the Years 1898–1900*, 1902, pp. 28–43.

12. J. Garstang and W. J. Pythian Adams, *P.E.Q.* liii, 1921, pp. 12–16, 73–90, 162–9; liv, 1922, pp. 112–19; lv, 1923, pp. 60–84; lvi, 1924, pp. 24–35; Garstang, *Joshua Judges*, pp. 357–60.

13. S. Yeivin, *I.E.J.* vi, 1956, pp. 258 f.; vii, 1957, pp. 264 f.; viii, 1958, pp. 274–6; ix, 1959, pp. 269–71; x, 1960, pp. 122 f.; *First Preliminary Report on the Excavations at Tel 'Gath'. 1956–1958*, Jerusalem, 1961. The full name is given as Tell esh-Sheikh Aḥmad el-ʿAreini.

14. R. Bulow and R. A. Mitchell, *I.E.J.* xi, 1961, pp. 101–10.

15. W. M. Flinders Petrie, *Tell el-Hesi (Lakish)*, 1891; F. J. Bliss, *A Mound of Many Cities*, 1894.

16. J. Garstang, *P.E.Q.* lii, 1920, pp. 156 f.; W. J. Phythian Adams, *P.E.Q.* lv, 1923, pp. 11–36; see J. P. Peters, *P.E.Q.* liii, 1921, pp. 60 f.

17. W. M. Flinders Petrie *et al.*, *Ancient Gaza*, i–v, 1931–52; see W. F. Albright, *A.J.S.L.* lv, 1938, pp. 337–59.

18. W. J. Phythian Adams, *P.E.Q.* lv, 1923, pp. 140–6; W. M. Flinders Petrie, *Gerar*, 1928.

19. W. M. Flinders Petrie *et al.*, *Beth Pelet*, i–ii, 1930–2.

20. Naveh, *I.E.J.* viii, 1958, pp. 166–70; accepted by Mazar, *I.E.J.* x, 1960, pp. 65 f., *contra* Albright, *C.A.H.*, rev. ed., ii, ch. xxxiii, 1966, p. 26, n. 3.

21. Yeivin (*Tell 'Gath.' 1956–1958*, pp. 10 f.) has now proposed an identification of Tell el-'Areini with Mmšt (cf. *D.O.T.T.*, pp. 219 f.). Albright, however, still favours 'Areini (*C.A.H.* ii, ch. xxxiii, p. 26).

22. Bulow and Mitchell, *I.E.J.* xi, 1961, pp. 108 ff.; cf. *B.A.* xxvi, 1963, pp. 30 f.

23. W. Borée, *Die alten Ortsnamen Palästinas*, 1930, pp. 83 f.

24. As is argued by B. Mazar, *I.E.J.* iv, 1954, pp. 227–35, who proposes that Philistine Gath = 'Iraq el-Manshiyye, i.e. Tell el-'Areini which is nearby (cf. *B.A.S.O.R.* 17, 1925, p. 8), and that there was another Gath at Ras Abu Ḥamid in the southern Shephelah.

25. Mazar, *I.E.J.* iv, 1954, p. 227.

26. Garstang, *Joshua Judges*, pp. 392 f.; cf., however, Albright, *B.A.S.O.R.* 15, 1924, p. 9.

27. Ibid., 17, 1925, pp. 7 f.

28. Surveyed by D. Alon; see Y. Aharoni, *I.E.J.* vi, 1956, pp. 26–32; Albright, *B.A.S.O.R.* 163, 1961, p. 48.

29. Ibid., 33, 1929, p. 7; cf. Aharoni, *I.E.J.* vi, 1956, p. 31.

30. Ibid., p. 32, and map, p. 29. Yurza is mentioned in the Amarna letters (*E.A.* ii, p. 1350), but not in the Old Testament.

31. Cf., however, the suggestion of J. P. Peters (*P.E.Q.* liii, 1921, p. 61).

32. J. Kaplan, *I.E.J.* v, 1955, p. 118.

33. Cf., however, the negative results of a surface search for early remains at coastal Gaza (D. Mackenzie, *P.E.Q.* l, 1918, pp. 72–85).

34. R. North, *Ghassul 1960. Excavation Report*, 1961, pp. 42–70 *passim*, and map, p. 79.

35. See G. E. Wright, *B.A.N.E.*, pp. 81 f., 105, n. 44.

36. H. J. Kantor and W. F. Albright, *Chronologies in Old World Archaeology* (ed. R. W. Ehrich), 1965, pp. 7 ff., 27, 49 f.; S. Yeivin, *I.E.J.* x, 1960, pp. 193–203; Perrot (op. cit., p. 148) suggests that Palestine was a southern *cul-de-sac* until this period.

37. Albright, *B.A.N.E.*, p. 332; cf. G. Posener, *C.A.H.*, rev. ed., i, ch. xxi, 1965, p. 5.

38. See, for example, M. Noth, *The Old Testament World*, 1966, trans. from 4th German ed., 1964, pp. 50–53; Albright (*B.A.N.E.*, p. 332) considers that the name can be applied in this period.

39. Skeletal remains have not been comprehensively studied, and indeed the validity of such purely morphological criteria as cephalic index has been called in question (see, for example, R. L. Beals and H.

Hoijer, *An Introduction to Anthropology*, 1953, pp. 177 ff., and in general 169–74), but, pending new material, see M. Boule and H. V. Vallois, *Fossil Men*, 1957, pp. 345, 363, 380; W. M. Krogman, in H. H. von der Osten, *The Alishar Huyuk. Seasons of 1930–32*, part iii, 1937, table vi, facing p. 224.

40. K. M. Kenyon, *Archaeology in the Holy Land*, 2nd ed. 1965, ch. 6; Wright, *B.A.N.E.*, pp. 88 ff.

41. Amiram, *I.E.J.* x, 1960, p. 225; R. W. Hutchinson, *Prehistoric Crete*, 1962, p. 105; H. J. Kantor, *The Aegean and the Orient in the Second Millennium B.C.*, 1947, p. 18.

42. Alan Gardiner, *Egypt of the Pharaohs*, 1961, pp. 131 ff.

43. 'Ethnic' is here used in the sense of 'cultural', as manifested in this case by language, and not 'racial'. On present evidence the main physical type was still Mediterranean; see above, n. 39.

44. See W. Helck, *Die Beziehungen Ägyptens zu Vorderasien*, 1962, pp. 49–68, and map, p. 4; and J. A. Wilson, *A.N.E.T.*, pp. 328 f.

45. Helck, op. cit., pp. 52 f.; *A.N.E.T.*, p. 329.

46. Borée, op. cit., pp. 57, 70; also F. M. Cross and D. N. Freedman, *B.A.S.O.R.* 175, 1964, p. 49, and A. Goetze, *J.C.S.* xvi, 1962, p. 52, n. 27.

47. Borée, op. cit., s.v., pp. 23, 39, 59, 60, 65, 69 (with *B.A.S.O.R.* 175, 1964, pp. 48 ff.), 72, 76, 78, 79, 99, 100. Probable non-Semitic names in this region include *ṣiklag̱*, *lākîš*, and *šārûḥen* (pp. 116 f. and 119). For a proposed connexion between the name *ṣiklag̱* and that of the Tjekker, see G. A. Wainwright, *J.E.A.* xlvii, 1961, p. 77.

48. On the distinction between Canaanite and Amorite, see E. A. Speiser, *At the Dawn of Civilization* (ed. E. A. Speiser), 1964, pp. 162–9.

49. Y. Yadin, *B.A.S.O.R.* 137, 1955, pp. 23–32.

50. See plan in Garstang, *Joshua Judges*, p. 358.

51. I. J. Gelb, *Hurrians and Subarians*, 1944, p. 68; E. A. Speiser, *A.A.S.O.R.* xiii, 1933, pp. 46–52. It has been argued recently, however (e.g. Albright, *B.A.N.E.*, p. 335; J. Vercoutter in E. Cassin *et al.*, *Die altorient. Reiche*, i, 1965, pp. 357 f.), that many of the names previously considered Hurrian or Indo-European can be explained as Semitic.

52. S. Piggott, *Ancient Europe*, 1965, pp. 116 ff., 129–33, 141 f.; cf. H. Hencken, *Indo-European Languages and Archaeology* (American Anthropologist, 57, 6, 3, Memoir 84), 1955, pp. 42 ff.

53. Petrie, *Gaza*, i, pp. 4 f., pls. viii–ix, lvii.

54. Ibid. v, pp. 9 f.; iv, pls. xiii–xx; v, pls. A, B; vi–viii.

55. A. Hrdlička in P. L. O. Guy and R. M. Engberg, *Megiddo Tombs*, 1938, p. 192; Krogman in von der Osten, *Alishar. 1930–32*, iii, table vi facing p. 224.

56. e.g. Crete: B. Porter and R. L. B. Moss, *Topographical Bibliography of Ancient Egyptian Hieroglyphic Texts, Reliefs and Paintings*, vii, 1951, p. 405; Kantor, op. cit., p. 19 (n. 22); Egypt: Kantor, op. cit., pp. 19 f.; cf. pp. 18–19, 21–30, in Ehrich, op. cit., pp. 19–22, 27; Syria-Palestine: Porter and Moss, op. cit., vii, pp. 369–96 *passim*; A. Parrot, *Mission archéologique de Mari*, ii, *Le Palais*, ii, *Peintures murales*, 1958,

pp. 67 ff., 108 ff.; Y. Yadin, *Hazor*, i, 1958, pp. 123, 126; *Hazor*, ii, 1960, pp. 86, 91, 115 f. (cf. Malamat, *J.B.L.* lxxix, 1960, pp. 18 f.); Guy and Engberg, *Megiddo Tombs*, p. 49.

57. J. Vercoutter, *L'Égypte et le monde égéen préhellénique*, 1956, pp. 33-123.

58. From Mari (G. Dossin, *Syria* xx, 1939, pp. 111 f.; A. Pohl, *Orient.* xix, 1950, p. 509, xxxi, 1962, p. 147), and probably from Asshur (A. H. Sayce, *Essays in Aegean Archaeology Presented to Sir Arthur Evans* (ed. S. Casson), 1927, pp. 107 ff., with S. Smith, *Early History of Assyria*, 1928, p. 89).

59. See A. H. Gardiner, *Ancient Egyptian Onomastica*, 1947, i, pp. 202 f.; Vercoutter, *Égypte et monde égéen*, pp. 33-123, 369-95; cf., however, G. A. Wainwright; *Jahrb. für kleinasiat. Forschung*, xi, 1965, pp. 485 ff.

60. Pohl (reporting Dossin), *Orient.* xix, 1950, p. 509; see Malamat, *J.B.L.* lxxix, 1960, p. 19.

61. Albright, *B.A.S.O.R.* 155, 1959, pp. 33 f.; 176, 1964, pp. 38-44; 179, 1965, pp. 38-43.

62. For bibliography, see *B.A.N.E.*, p. 225, n. 2.

63. Albright, *B.A.S.O.R.* 163, 1961, pp. 36-54.

64. Gen. xxi. 34.

65. Gen. xxvi. 1, 8; see xxi. 32, xxvi. 15, 18.

66. e.g., J. Bright, *A History of Israel*, 1959, p. 73; E. A. Speiser, *Genesis*, 1964, p. 159.

67. For one suggestion, see Albright, *J.P.O.S.* iv, 1924, pp. 138 f., reading *pylk* < Egyptian *p'-rkw* 'the Lycian'.

68. *A.N.E.T.*, pp. 233 f.; Helck, op. cit., pp. 114 f.

69. *A.N.E.T.*, pp. 234-41, and list on pp. 242 f.

70. See also *A.N.E.T.*, pp. 22 f.

71. And indeed were probably known at the end of the Middle Bronze Age; see Wright, *B.A.N.E.*, pp. 91, 109, n. 82.

72. W. A. Heurtley, *Q.D.A.P.* viii, 1938, pp. 21-37.

73. F. H. Stubbings, *Mycenaean Pottery in the Levant*, 1951, pp. 55 f., and map i.

74. J. Nougayrol, *C.R.A.I.* (Jan.-Mar. 1956), p. 127; A. Rainey, *I.E.J.* xiii, 1963, pp. 43, 314; Freedman, *B.A.* xxvi, 1963, p. 136.

75. *E.A.*, nos. 320-6 (320 = *A.N.E.T.*, p. 490), *aš-qa-lu-na*.

76. *gi-im-ti* (*E.A.*, pp. 1311, 1574); *ḫa-za-ti*, *az-za-ti* (ibid., pp. 1342 f., 1575); *ia-pu*, *ia-a-pu* (ibid., pp. 1239, 1576).

77. *wi-id-ia*; see P. E. Dumont in R. T. O'Callaghan, *Aram Naharaim*, 1948, p. 153, no. 78.

78. Albright, *C.A.H.* ii, xx, pp. 12 ff.; Helck, op. cit., map on p. 622.

79. E. F. Campbell, *B.A.* xxiii, 1960, pp. 21 f.; Albright, *C.A.H.* ii, ch. xx, p. 7.

80. For bibliography, see Albright, *B.A.S.O.R.* 163, 1961, p. 54, n. 79.

81. *E.A.* nos. 298 f., though it may be that the term is used to refer to

outlaws in general without an ethnic significance (Campbell, *B.A.* xxiii, 1960, pp. 13 ff.).

82. Knudtzon, *E.A.*, no. 287 = *D.O.T.T.*, pp. 39 f. = *A.N.E.T.*, p. 488.

83. *E.A.*, no. 38: 10.

84. Ibid., nos. 81, 122, 123, cf., however, Albright, *A.J.A.* liv, 1950, p. 167, who argues that this is simply a form of a noun *šerdu* 'servitor'.

85. *E.A.*, no. 151; cf., however, Gardiner, *Onomastica*, i, p. 125*, who does not consider that this passage refers to the people later known by this name.

86. For summaries and bibliography, see Helck, op. cit., pp. 240–6; P. Mertens, *Chronique d'Égypte*, xxxv, 1960, pp. 65–88; E. Drioton and J. Vandier, *Les Peuples de l'orient méditerranéen*, ii, *L'Égypte*, 3rd ed., 1952, pp. 430–9, 450. The spellings of the names here used are those of Gardiner in *Onomastica* and *Pharaohs*.

87. See M. Guido, *Sardinia*, 1963, pp. 187–91; Albright, *A.J.A.* liv, 1950, p. 167, *B.A.N.E.*, p. 361, n. 102.

88. e.g. Gardiner, *Onomastica*, i, pp. 196 ff.*; but cf. Albright, *A.J.A.* liv, 1950, pp. 170 f., on connecting the Tjekker with Sicily.

89. M. Pallottino, *The Etruscans*, 1955, pp. 55 f.; Albright, *B.A.N.E.*, p. 361, n. 102.

90. Goetze, *Kleinasien*, pp. 180 f., and in general Gardiner, *Onomastica*, i, pp. 124*–7*.

91. Goetze, *Kleinasien*, p. 178.

92. Ibid., pp. 60 f.

93. See in general Gardiner, *Onomastica*, i, pp. 124*–7*; Albright, *A.J.A.* liv, 1950, pp. 170 ff.; identification with Greek *Danaoi* is rejected by D. Page, *History and the Homeric Iliad*, 1959, pp. 22 f.; Goetze, (*J.C.S.* xvi, 1962, pp. 50–54) argues that the name is Hurrian.

94. Ibid., p. 50.

95. e.g. Albright, *A.J.A.* liv, 1950, pp. 166 f.

96. See, for example, Page, op. cit., pp. 21 f.

97. See Macalister, *Philistines*, p. 24; Mertens, *Chronique d'Égypte*, xxxv, 1960, p. 72; Helck, op. cit., p. 243.

98. Cf. Pohl, *Orient.* xxxi, 1962, p. 148.

99. Stubbings, op. cit., pp. 66–68, and map ii.

100. His reliefs depict 'the [town] of Canaan', probably Gaza, as one of his first conquests; see Gardiner, *J.E.A.* vi, 1920, pp. 100, 103 f.; R. Lepsius, *Denkmäler aus Aegypt. und Aethiop.* iii, pl. 127a.

101. Convenient references in Mertens, op. cit., xxxv, 1960, pp. 71–75.

102. Stubbings, op. cit., pp. 84–86, and map iii.

103. See V. E. G. Kenna, *Cretan Seals*, 1960, pp. 65, 78, 151 f.; in general Albright, *J.P.O.S.* i, 1921, pp. 187–94.

104. Stele: *D.O.T.T.*, pp. 137–41 = *A.N.E.T.*, pp. 376 ff.

105. Gardiner, *Pharaohs*, p. 273.

106. See *D.O.T.T.*, pp. 140 f.; *A.N.E.T.*, p. 378, n. 18.

107. Exod. xiii. 17.

108. Deut. ii. 23, the *kaptōrîm* having dispossessed the Avvim 'who

dwelt in villages in the vicinity of Gaza'. For this sense of ʿaḏ see H. L. Ginsberg, *B.A.S.O.R.* 122, 1951, pp. 12 ff.; see also n. 103, above.

109. Albright, *C.A.H.* ii, ch. xxxiii, p. 27.

110. Freedman, *B.A.* xxvi, 1963, p. 136.

111. It may be that a lapse of time is to be understood between this verse and the next, and that the verbs used (18. . . . *lāḵaḏ* . . . 19. . . . *yāraš* . . .) indicate a quick conquest at first but a failure to take permanent possession.

112. See, for example, Piggott, *Ancient Europe*, pp. 157–60.

113. See Mertens, op. cit., xxxv, 1960, pp. 76 f. for references.

114. V. R. d'A. Desborough, *The Last Mycenaeans and their Successors*, 1964, pp. 22–25, 199 f.

115. A. Furumark, *The Mycenaean Pottery. Analysis and Classification*, 1941, p. 575; Desborough, *C.A.H.*, rev. ed., ii, ch. xxxvi, pp. 4 f.; T. Dothan, *Antiquity and Survival*, ii, 1957, pp. 152 ff.

116. Albright, *C.A.H.* ii, ch. xxxiii, p. 27; Furumark, *The Chronology of the Mycenaean Pottery*, 1941, p. 121.

117. Furumark, *Chronology*, pp. 118–22; Dothan, op. cit., pp. 151–64; Desborough, *Last Mycenaeans*, pp. 209–14; Albright, *A.A.S.O.R.* xii, 1932, pp. 53–56.

118. Freedman, *B.A.* xxvi, 1963, p. 136.

119. Aharoni, *I.E.J.* xi, 1961, p. 90.

120. H. H. Nelson *et al.*, *Medinet Habu*, I, *Earlier Historical Records of Ramses III*, 1930, especially pls. 32–44; II, *Later Historical Records* . . ., 1932, especially pl. 98.

121. J. A. Wilson (*J.N.E.S.* xxi, 1962, p. 70) suggests that it might have been pleated leather.

122. Phaistos Disc: Hutchinson, op. cit., pp. 66–70; for a recent attempt at decipherment, see B. Schwartz, *J.N.E.S.* xviii, 1959, pp. 105–12.

123. Warrior Vase: A. J. Evans, *The Palace of Minos*, iii, 1930, pp. 89–106, figs. 50–52, who here reverses his earlier view (i, p. 668), and argues that only a shock of hair is represented.

124. Ivory box from Enkomi: C. Decamps de Mertzenfeld, *Inventaire commenté des ivoires phéniciens*, 1954, pl. lxix, pp. 116 f.

125. i. 171.

126. vii. 92.

127. R. D. Barnett, *Illustrations of Old Testament History*, 1966, fig. 16 (p. 31), and pp. 29, 87.

128. R. Maxwell-Hyslop, *Iraq* viii, 1946, pp. 57–60.

129. Krogman in von der Osten, op. cit., p. 271.

130. Already suggested in the eighteenth century (Macalister, *Philistines*, p. 2) and now supported by new evidence, V. Georgiev, *Jahrb. für kleinasiat. Forschung*, i (1950–1), p. 137; J. Bérard, *Rev. arch.* xxxvii, 1951, p. 132.

131. Jer. xlvii. 4; Amos ix. 7. On *ʾī*, see R. Dussaud, *Anat. Stud.* vi, 1956, pp. 63 ff.

132. Aharoni, *I.E.J.* v, 1955, p. 122.

133. Joshua xiii. 3; Judges iii. 3, xvi. 5, 8, 18, 27, 30, etc.

134. See B. D. Rahtjen, *J.N.E.S.* xxiv, 1965, pp. 100–4, who suggests that the shrine was at Gaza until its destruction by Samson. On this episode, see Macalister, *Bible Sidelights from the Mound of Gezer*, 1906, pp. 127–38.

135. Only attested in the plural *s*^e*rānîm, sarnê.*

136. G. Bonfante, *A.J.A.* l. 1946, p. 258; Georgiev, op. cit., pp. 138 f.

137. I owe this observation to Mr. K. A. Kitchen; for the form, see E. Laroche, *Les Hiéroglyphes hittites,* i, 1960, pp. 197 f.

138. e.g. H. G. Liddell, R. Scott, and H. S. Jones, *A Greek–English Lexicon,* 1940, p. 1836; cf. M. Ellenbogen, *Foreign Words in the Old Testament,* 1962, pp. 126 f.

139. Goetze, *Kleinasien,* pp. 53–56; Gurney, *The Hittites,* rev. ed., p. 127.

140. 1 Sam. xiii. 19–22, on which see *D.O.T.T.,* p. 230, and in general G. E. Wright, *A.J.A.* xliii, 1939, pp. 458–63, *J.B.L.* lx, 1941, pp. 27–42; B. Mazar, *I.E.J.* v, 1955, p. 115.

141. Dothan, op. cit., ii, 1957, pp. 154–64; Wright, *B.A.* xxii, 1959, pp. 54–66. Pre-Philistine coffins from Lachish show that others besides the Philistines had adopted the practice.

142. See also Wright, *B.A.* xxii, 1959, pp. 56 f. and Albright, *C.A.H.* ii, ch. xxxiii, p. 27.

143. *A.N.E.T.,* pp. 25–29.

144. Where Philistine pottery has been found, see reference in Maisler, *I.E.J.* i, 1950–1, p. 126, n. 13.

145. H. Kjaer, *P.E.Q.* lxiii, 1931, pp. 74–78.

146. 2 Sam. viii. 18, xx. 23, in which *p*^e*lētî* is probably an analogical adaptation of *p*^e*lištî* to make it assonant with *k*^e*rētî.*

147. 1 Kings i. 38, 44.

148. 2 King's xi. 4, 19, *kārî.*

149. On a possible identification of this temple, see A. Rowe, *The Four Canaanite Temples of Beth-Shan,* part i, 1940, pp. 31–34.

150. See D. O. Edzard and M. H. Pope, *Wörterb. der Mythologie* (ed. H. W. Haussig), i, pp. 49 f., 276 ff. There is no evidence that Dagon had anything to do with fish.

151. As in, for example, Matt. xii. 24.

152. See Pope in Haussig, op. cit., i, p. 254.

153. E. Sapir, *J.A.O.S.* lvii, 1937, pp. 73–77; C. Rabin, *Orient.* xxxii, 1963, pp. 124 f.

154. Sapir, *J.A.O.S.* lvi, 1936, pp. 272–81. There are other foreign words in the vocabulary of the Old Testament which have possible cognates in Greek (see, for example, Macalister, *Philistines,* p. 80; C. H. Gordon, *Antiquity* xxx, 1956, pp. 23 f.); but there is no evidence that they had anything to do with the Philistines.

155. Albright, *C.A.H.* ii, ch. xxxiii, p. 30; Goetze, *Kleinasien,* p. 207; Herodotus, i. 16.

156. T. E. Peet, *Essays in Aegean Archaeology* (ed. S. Casson), pp. 90–99; Vercoutter, *Égypte et monde égéen*, pp. 45–50.

157. *Iliad*, v. 311 ff.

158. Summary in Macalister, *Philistines*, pp. 62 f.

159. Wright, *B.A.N.E.*, pp. 95 f.; B. Mazar, *V.T. Supp.* iv, 1957, pp. 57–66, especially 63.

160. See W. W. Hallo, *B.A.* xxiii, 1960, pp. 33–61 = (with revisions) *B.A.R.* ii, 1964, pp. 152–88.

161. E. Forrer, *Die Provinzeinteilung d. assyr. Reiches*, 1920, pp. 60 f.

162. Hallo, *B.A.* xxiii, 1960, pp. 51 f.

163. Tadmor, *J.C.S.* xii, 1958, pp. 83 f.; Forrer, op. cit., pp. 63 f.

164. See Hallo and indexes of *D.O.T.T.*, *A.N.E.T.*, and D. D. Luckenbill, *Ancient Records of Assyria and Babylonia*, i–ii, 1926–7.

165. *A.N.E.T.*, p. 286; cf. *D.O.T.T.*, p. 59.

166. 2 Chron. xxvi. 6, with Ashdod and Jabneh.

167. Amos i. 6 ff., vi. 2.

168. See above, n. 24, and Tadmor, *J.C.S.* xii, 1958, p. 83, n. 242.

169. *D.O.T.T.*, pp. 55–74 *passim*; *A.N.E.T.*, pp. 282–94 *passim*; K. L. Tallqvist, *Assyrian Personal Names*, 1918, s.v.

170. R. Boudou, *Orient.* xxxvi–xxxviii, 1929, pp. 137, 141; Tadmor, op. cit., p. 83, n. 235.

171. Tallqvist, op. cit., pp. 218 f.

172. For different views on Mitinti, see F. Bork, *A.f.O.* xiii, 1939–41, pp. 227 f.; Bonfante, *A.J.A.* l, 1946, pp. 254 f.; on Padi, Bonfante, ibid., p. 255.

173. e.g. Peet, *Essays in Aegean Archaeology* (ed. S. Casson), pp. 96 f.; if it is not to be read *i-ka-šam-su*, cf. *A.N.E.T.*, p. 294 n.

174. *D.O.T.T.*, p. 61; *A.N.E.T.*, p. 286; cf. Hallo, *B.A.* xxiii, 1960, p. 56, n. 129.

175. Tadmor, op. cit. xii, p. 80, n. 217.

176. Hdt. ii. 157, taking "Ἄζωτος = Ashdod; cf., however, on this siege, Gardiner, *Pharaohs*, p. 357. See also Hdt. i. 105.

177. Hdt. ii. 159, taking Κάδυτις = Gaza; cf., however, Gardiner, *Onomastica*, i, p. 191*.

178. D. J. Wiseman, *Chronicles of Chaldaean Kings*, 1956, pp. 25, 68 f., line 8; *D.O.T.T.*, p. 79.

179. *D.O.T.T.*, pp. 251–5, cf. 79 f.; J. Bright, *B.A.* xii, 1949, pp. 46–52; *K.A.I.*, no. 266; J. A. Fitzmyer, *Biblica* xlvi, 1965, pp. 41–55; Albright *ap.* Tadmor *I.E.J.* xi, 1961, p. 150.

180. Wiseman, op. cit., pp. 28, 68 f., lines 18 ff.; *D.O.T.T.*, p. 79; on the reading *iš-qi-il-lu-nu*, see Albright, *B.A.S.O.R.* 164, 1961, p. 20, n. 5, also J. D. Quinn, *B.A.S.O.R.* 164, 1961, pp. 19 f.

181. E. F. Weidner, *Mélanges syriens offerts à monsieur René Dussaud*, ii, 1939, p. 928; cf. *D.O.T.T.*, pp. 84 ff.; *A.N.E.T.*, p. 308. Among the prisoners were two sons of a king Aga' of Ashkelon, implying either that 'Adon of Ashkelon had been replaced by Aga', or that 'Adon's city was not Ashkelon (see Fitzmyer, op. cit., pp. 48 f.).

182. *A.N.E.T.*, p. 308, as well as King Jehoiachin of Judah (see references in n. 181).

183. See G. W. Van Beek, *B.A.* xxiii, 1960, pp. 69–95.

184. Wiseman, op. cit., p. 30, on the basis of Jer. xlvii. 1.

185. S. Langdon, *Die neubabylon. Königsinschriften*, 1912, pp. 220 f., lines 38 ff.

186. See O. Leuze, *Die Satrapieneinteilung in Syrien und im Zweistrom-lande* (Schrift. d. Königsberg. Gelehrt. Gesellsch., ii, 4), 1935, pp. 25 ff. Ebir-nâri appears in the Old Testament as *'ēḇer hannāhār* (Hebrew) and *ʿaḇar-nahʿrâ* (Aramaic) (Leuze, pp. 27 f.).

187. Hdt. iii. 4 f., *Τοῦ Ἀραβίου* = Nabataeans; on *Κάδυτις* = Gaza, however, cf. n. 177, above.

188. iii. 91; see Leuze, op. cit., pp. 105–8.

189. *A.N.E.T.*, p. 505; *K.A.I.*, no. 14. It seems unnecessary to place this monument as late as the Ptolemaic period. The Aramaic semantic equivalent (*mr' mlkn*) of *'dn mlkm* 'Lord of Kings', which is taken as an indication of late date, is found in the Saḳḳara letter cited above (*K.A.I.*, no. 266. 6). The phrase could quite well refer to a Persian king (so Leuze, op. cit., p. 225).

190. F. Rosenthal (*A.N.E.T.*, p. 505); many commentators, however, take *'rṣt dgn* as 'corn-land' (e.g., *K.A.I.* ii, pp. 20, 23); either interpretation is possible.

191. For other hints of religious continuity, see S. A. Cook, *The Religion of Ancient Palestine in the Light of Archaeology* (Schweich Lectures, 1925), 1930, pp. 180–6, and Macalister, *Philistines*, pp. 106–14.

192. Neh. xiii. 24; see, for example, Macalister, *Philistines*, pp. 66 f.; G. R. Driver, *The People and the Book* (ed. A. S. Peake), p. 74; D. Winton Thomas, *Record and Revelation* (ed. H. W. Robinson), 1938, p. 388 n.

193. See N. Glueck, *Deities and Dolphins*, 1966, pp. 69, 374; Sir William Tarn and G. T. Griffith, *Hellenistic Civilization*, 3rd ed., 1952, pp. 244 f.

194. J. H. Iliffe, *Q.D.A.P.* v, 1936, pp. 61–68.

195. G. F. Hill, *Catalogue of the Greek Coins of Palestine*, 1914, pp. lxxxiii–lxxxix, 176–81; B. V. Head, *Historia Numorum*, 2nd ed., 1911, p. 805.

196. Tarn and Griffith, op. cit., p. 260. Weight standards varied, but according to the Attic-Euboic system (1 talent = c. 36·86 kg.), this would amount to nearly two tons.

197. Hill, op. cit., pp. lxvi–lxxix, 143–68, and xlviii–lxiv, 104–40; Head, op. cit., pp. 804 f.

198. Noth, *World of the Old Testament*, pp. 7 ff.

BIBLIOGRAPHY

ALBRIGHT, W. F. *The Excavations of Tell Beit Mirsim I* (*A.A.S.O.R.* xii), 1932, pp. 53–58.

—— 'The Sea Peoples in Palestine', *C.A.H.*, 2nd ed., ii, ch. xxxiii, 1966, pp. 24–33.

BÉRARD, J. 'Philistins et Préhellénes', *Rev. arch.* xxxvii, 1951, pp. 129–42.

DOTHAN, T. 'Archaeological reflections on the Philistine problem', *Antiquity and Survival*, ii, 1957, pp. 151–64.

EISSFELDT, O. 'Philister', *Paulys Real-Encyclop. d. classisch. Altertumswiss.*, new ed., ed. G. Wissowa *et al.*, xxxviii, 1938, 2390–401.

FURUMARK, A. 'Philistine ware', *The Chronology of Mycenaean Pottery*, 1941, pp. 118–21.

GARDINER, A. H. 'Prst', *Ancient Egyptian Onomastica. Text*, i, 1947, pp. 200*–5*.

GEORGIEV, V. 'Sur l'origine et la langue des Pélasges, des Philistins, des Danaens et des Achéens', *Jahrb. für kleinasiat. Forschung*, i, 1950, pp. 136–41.

GORDON, C. H. 'The role of the Philistines', *Antiquity* xxx, 1956, pp. 22–26.

GRANT, E. 'The Philistines', *J.B.L.* lv, 1936, pp. 175–94.

MACALISTER, R. A. S. *The Philistines. Their History and Institutions*, 1914, reprint 1965.

MAZAR, B. 'The Philistines and the rise of Israel and Tyre', *Proceed. of the Israel Acad. of Sciences and Humanities*, I, 7, 1964.

RAHTJEN, B. D. 'Philistine and Hebrew amphictyonies', *J.N.E.S.* xxiv, 1965, pp. 100–4.

TADMOR, H. 'Philistia under Assyrian rule', *B.A.* xxix, 1966, pp. 86–102.

WRIGHT, G. E. 'Philistine coffins and mercenaries', ibid. xxii, 1959, pp. 53–66.

—— 'Fresh evidence for the Philistine Story', ibid. xxix, 1966, pp. 70–86.

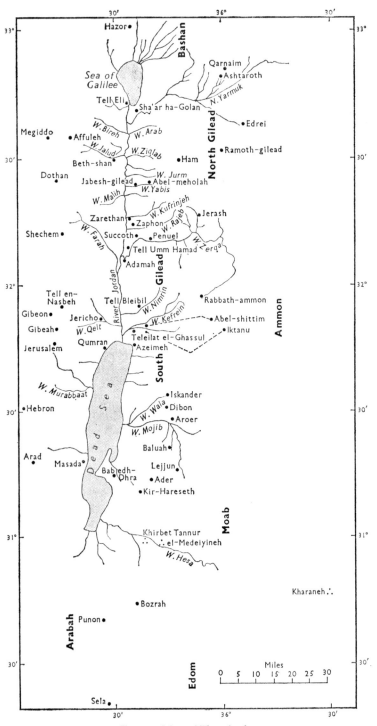

FIG. 12. Map of Transjordan

TRANSJORDAN

TRANSJORDAN and Cisjordan, which have sometimes been called Eastern and Western Palestine, are sharply separated by the north–south trough of the Jordan valley, the Dead Sea depression, and the Wadi Arabah reaching down to the north shore of the Gulf of Aqabah (the eastern arm of the Red Sea). These three divisions are part of a much longer rift that extends from Asia Minor to the East African lakes. The Old Testament knows Transjordan as 'the Other Side of the Jordan, towards the rising of the sun' (Joshua xii. 1).

Most of Transjordan consists of a long, more or less rectangular, broken, upland plateau, slashed into distinctive segments by a series of east–west perennial streams. Its western sides descend precipitously to the Jordan–Dead Sea–Arabah rift. On its eastern desert side there is an almost imperceptible slope to the broad, extremely shallow, Wadi Sirhan that reaches from Azrak in the north to Jauf in Arabia to the south. At fairly numerous places the water-table in the Wadi Sirhan is close to the surface.

Rising in the area separating the Desert from the Sown near the eastern side of the Transjordanian plateau, the streams cut their way deeply across the country to empty either into the Jordan river or the Dead Sea. Among them are the Wadi Yarmuk in the north, the Wadi Zerqa in the centre, and the Wadi Hesban in the south. Below them are the Wadi Mojib and the Wadi Hesa, which empty into the Dead Sea. Most of them are known by name in the Old Testament and figure frequently in its accounts. The Zerqa is the Old Testament Jabbok, the Mojib is the Arnon, and the Hesa is the Old Testament Zered. With the exception of the Yarmuk, whose volume equals that of the Jordan when it meets it south of the Lake of Galilee, all these streams are smaller than the Jordan to whose flood they contribute. The beds in which they flow all the year round are at the bottom of canyons which become deeper and steeper as the waters cut their way westward. East–west tracks parallel the tops of the plateaux above them. A modern north–south road crosses from one end of the country to another, zigzagging up and down their sides, and extending from Damascus in the north to Aqabah in the south. It was preceded by Trajan's Road, parts of which can still be seen, and before that by the 'King's Highway' (Num. xx. 14–21). A section of an important east–west road can still be seen going down from Kerak (Kir of Moab) to the peninsula of the Lisan on the east side of the Dead Sea.

The streams on the east side of the Jordan are larger, more numerous, and more valuable than those on the west side, and water the valley into the greenness which made Lot call it a garden of God (Gen. xiii. 10). Between the Yarmuk and the Jabbok are the perennial streams of the Wadis Arab, Ziqlab, Jurm, Yabis (Jabesh-gilead), Kufrinji, and Rajeb. Beyond them, south of the Jabbok, are the Nimrin, Kefrein, Rameh, and Azeimeh, the latter, however, emptying into the Dead Sea. The Old Testament names of all but one of these streams elude us. The knowledge of their existence, however, makes understandable the fact that the Jordan Valley was the home of some of the earliest settlements of man anywhere in the Near East. Nearly ten millennia ago a formidable city existed at Jericho. A settlement with Early Neolithic pottery has been found, for example, at Sha'ar ha-Golan, near the outlet of the Yarmuk into the Jordan, dating approximately between 4500 and 4250 B.C., occupying a position between Early Pottery Neolithic Jericho IX and Late Pottery Neolithic Jericho VIII. And in the hill-country above the east side of the Jordan valley the waters of these streams, together with those of numerous springs, wells, and cisterns, sustained hundreds of settlements in some widely separated periods. Tell Eli, near Sha'ar ha-Golan, and located to the south-east of the Sea of Galilee, dates from Early Pottery Neolithic (Jericho IX) of the first half of the fifth millennium B.C. to the Chalcolithic of the first two-thirds of the fourth millennium B.C.

Between the Jabbok and the Nimrin on the east side of the Jordan valley is an arid region about 16 miles long, with neither springs nor streams to relieve its dryness. The Romans and Byzantines, however, tapped underground water sources by sinking a series of vertical shafts to the underground water-table, connecting them by a horizontal shaft and thus bringing to a particular garden area a constant stream of water laboriously collected. Water-collecting devices of this type, called *qanat* or *fuqara*, are still in use in many places in the modern Near East.

Evidence of the existence of early civilization in the Jordan
valley and in the hill-country above it is furnished by megalithic
dolmens found, among other places, in the foothills east of Tell
Damieh (Old Testament Adamah) near the confluence of the Jabbok and the Jordan, and in the foothills above the Plains of Moab
at the north-east end of the Dead Sea. Dolmen fields can be
found or are known to have existed along much of the length of
the Transjordan plateau, along its western slopes, and in the valleys
bordering the Jordan river and the Dead Sea. They extend north
into Syria and west into Palestine. Used for tombs, they probably
date back originally to the sixth millennium B.C.

Several miles to the north-west, north-north-west of Tell
Damieh, is a large Chalcolithic–Early Bronze IA site called
Khirbet Umm Hamad Sherqi, with great masses of sherds belonging to the last 500 years of the fourth millennium B.C. Next to it
are the remains of Khirbet Umm Hamad Gharbi, with extensive
pottery remains belonging particularly to Middle Bronze I. Still
further to the north-north-west is the imposing mound of Tell
Deir 'Alla (probably Old Testament Succoth; Gen. xxxiii. 16 f.;
1 Kings vii. 45 f.). Excavations there in recent years by H. J.
Franken[1] have revealed the presence of an advanced metallurgical
industry for the smelting and casting of iron and copper both prior
to and during and after the times of Solomon (cf. 1 Kings vii.
45 f.; 2 Chron. iv. 17). Also discovered by Franken at Tell Deir
'Alla were three clay tablets bearing inscriptions in a hitherto
unknown script.[2]

Excavations at Tell es-Sa'idiyeh by J. B. Pritchard have
yielded results confirming its identification with Old Testament
Zarethan. It is located on the south side of the Wadi Kufrinji near its
west end, and was occupied as early as the late Chalcolithic–Early
Bronze II periods, extending from the thirty-fifth to the twenty-
sixth centuries B.C., and also in Israelite times. The Israelite period
city of Tell es-Sa'idiyeh was surrounded by a strong casemate fortification wall. It also possessed an underground water tunnel, related
to the type found in Jerusalem, Gezer, Megiddo, and Kir of Moab
(Kerak), for example, giving the inhabitants safe access to a secure
water-supply inside the fortifications even under siege conditions.

The Old Testament names of most of the ancient sites in the
Jordan valley, and particularly of the largest number of them

located on the more fertile and well-watered east side of the valley belonging to Transjordan, will never be known. Some thirty-five ancient settlements on the east side of the Jordan valley, datable by pottery remains on their surfaces, can be assigned to the Iron Age I–II period. The Old Testament writers were probably familiar with the locations, names, and histories of most of these sites, as well as of the contemporary and earlier ones on the west side of the Jordan valley, but they did not choose to list all of them. Indeed, on the east side they mentioned only nine of them. The Old Testament editors were not interested in writing an historical geography or an onomasticon of the Holy Land. In general, they mention only such places, peoples, and events as fitted in with the theological motivation of Sacred Writ. Sometimes the original Old Testament name is retained in the modern one, such as Tell Damieh (Adamah), with its location and pottery remains fitting in with the Old Testament description. At other times it becomes necessary to attempt to identify ancient sites with Old Testament place-names on the basis of agreement of the archaeological circumstances with Old Testament information.

The identification of Tell es-Sa'idiyeh with Old Testament Zarethan and of Tell Deir 'Alla with Old Testament Succoth has been mentioned. It is possible also to identify the locations of Jabesh-gilead with Tell el-Meqbereh–Tell Abu Kharaz, and of Abel-meholah with Tell el-Maqlub on the Wadi Yabis. In 1 Kings xvii. 1 there is reference to 'Elijah the Tishbite of the inhabitants of Gilead'. It should probably read 'Elijah the Jabeshite from Jabesh-gilead'. The brook Cherith where Elijah hid (1 Kings xvii. 1 f.) may well have been one of the easternmost branches of the Wadi Yabis, whose beginnings rise in the eastern desert. Elisha, too, to whom Elijah had been bidden to transfer the mantle of prophecy, was also a North Gileadite from Abel-meholah on the river Jabesh-gilead (Wadi Yabis), some miles to the east of Jabesh-gilead (1 Kings xix. 16, 19 ff.).

The men of Jabesh-gilead long remembered the kindness Saul had shown them in saving them from the Ammonites, who at one time pressed their power as far west as the Jordan (1 Sam. xi. 1–13, xxxi. 3–10). Another North Gileadite was Jephthah, who too once saved Israel from Ammon, losing his only child, his daughter, as a result of an unbreakable vow he had made in that connexion, and being forced also to defeat the ungrateful Ephraimites, who resented the victory to which they had not contributed (Judges xi. 22–40, xii. 1–6). And many other incidents figuring in the annals of the Old Testament took place in Gilead and more particularly at sites by the Jabbok. Ish-baal (Ish-bosheth), Saul's crippled son, took refuge at Mahanaim (2 Sam. ii. 8 f.), and later on David took refuge there from his son Absalom (2 Sam. xvii. 27 ff.).

It is possible to identify Old Testament Zaphon with Tell Qos on the north side of the Wadi Rajeb, and Penuel with Tell-edh-Dhahab on the Jabbok, and to make several other identifications which seem certain on the basis of agreement between archaeological and Old Testament evidence. Thus in North Gilead, for example, archaeological exploration and excavation have resulted in the identification of Tell Ramith with the Old Testament Ramoth-gilead. Other certain identifications, which may be mentioned at random, of ancient sites in the highlands of Transjordan, are of modern Amman with Old Testament Rabbah, the capital of Ammon, Hesban with Heshbon, Dhiban with Dibon, Kerak with Kir-hareseth, Buseirah in Edom with Bozrah, and Feinan in the Wadi Arabah with Punon. Hundreds of other ancient sites which can definitely be dated by reliable archaeological criteria cannot possibly be identified with Old Testament names, because they are not mentioned in the Old Testament.

i. *Edom*

It has been seen that the main divisions of Transjordan stem from east–west canyons of the perennial streams that cross it, emptying either into the Jordan or into the Dead Sea. The southernmost of these canyons is the Old Testament river Zered (Wadi Hesa), which empties into the south-east end of the Dead Sea. The Zered marked the northern limit of ancient Edom. Its territory extended southward for about 100 miles to the Gulf of Aqabah, and was bounded on the west side by the Wadi Arabah and on the east side by the desert. It is into the desert of the Wadi Hismeh which forms the southern part of Edom and connects with Arabia that the Wadi Yitm extends. The path through it leads from the south-east side of the Wadi Arabah to the base of the Neqb esh-Shtar of the Edomite hill-country, overlooking the Hismeh desert.

The 'King's Highway' followed this route northward to Syria. The Wadi Hismeh, Wadi Ramm, and Wadi Yitm, parts of the kingdom of Old Testament Edom, were largely uninhabited or even fortified except in Nabataean times, and were controlled by armed forces of the Edomite kingdom. Its base of power rested in the highlands of Edom extending for about 70 miles northward from the southern edge of the Jebel Shera overlooking the Neqb esh-Shtar and the Wadi Hismeh and terminating at the line of the great canyon of the river Zered.

The archaeological survey of Edom and of the rest of Trans-jordan revealed that during much of the period between the thirteenth and sixth centuries B.C. in Iron Age I–II, Edom, Moab, Ammon, and the Amorite kingdoms of Gilead were highly advanced and strongly organized. The highlands of Transjordan were then dotted with well-built stone villages and towns. The borders of their kingdoms were fortified by strong fortresses, built usually on eminences, and commanding a view of each other, or being able to signal to each other by smoke or fire by day or night.

Within its main boundaries, Edom in the Iron Age was a thriving, prosperous, civilized kingdom, filled with cities and towns and villages, with its economy based on intensive agriculture, animal husbandry, trade, and to a certain degree industry. The Edomites, as well as the Israelites, may have exploited the ores of the Wadi Arabah at various times. Through the Kenizzites, to whom they were related (Gen. xv. 19, xxxvi. 10 f., 42), the Edomites probably had connexions with the Kenites, and learned from them, as did the Israelites, both the locations of the copper in the Wadi Arabah and the methods of exploiting them and smelting and refining it. That the Kenites were at home in Edom is indicated by Balaam's punning proverb with regard to the Kenites in Num. xxiv. 21— 'Everlasting is thy habitation and set in the Rock (*sela‘*) is thy nest (*ḳēn*)'. The literature of the Edomites may have been of no mean order, if one may draw inferences from the background of the book of Job, even as one can definitely determine much about the Moabites from the ninth century B.C. Mesha stele, and from the reused twelfth century B.C. Egyptianized stele from Balu‘ah found south of the Wadi Mojib. The wealth of the Transjordanian kingdoms in the Iron Age even under eventual Assyrian domination may be judged from the tribute paid to Esar-haddon. Edom paid 12 manas of silver in comparison with 10 manas paid by Judah; Ammon paid 2 manas of gold, Moab paid one. The reality of these kingdoms was very substantial, however scanty the literary remains and memories of their existence have chanced to be.

The archaeological evidence based on extensive surface explorations and some excavations have demonstrated that the military power of Edom and Moab and the other Transjordanian kingdoms of the Iron Age depended both upon a well-worked-out system of fortifications and upon solid economic strength. The passage in Amos i. 12, referring to Bozrah and Teman as being evidently in the northern and southern parts of Edom respectively, suggests the relative positions of Buseirah in the north, which is to be identified with Bozrah, and Tawilan in the south near Petra, which is to be identified with the Teman of that verse.

The Edomites were devoted to the gods and goddesses of fertility. Townspeople and peasants had in their houses crude pottery figurines representing the deities whose goodwill they sought. Thus near Buseirah (Bozrah) was found a ninth–eighth century B.C. pottery figurine of a fertility goddess, wearing a lamp as a crown and holding in her hands some sacred object.

The Edomite and other Transjordanian pottery of the thirteenth–sixth centuries B.C. in itself bespeaks a highly developed civilization. Much of the ware is similar to contemporary ware in Cisjordan. There are, however, sufficient differences to compel individual classification. The distinctiveness of some of the Edomite, Moabite, and Ammonite pottery, for example, may be ascribed to influences emanating from Syria and Assyria via the trade route that indeed in all ages has followed the line of the 'King's Highway' (Num. xx. 17, xxi. 22). The orientation of Edom, Moab, Ammon, and Gilead, because of cultural, topographical, and geographical reasons, may be said to be directed more from north to south than from east to west, that is, mainly from Syria to Arabia rather than from the Mediterranean to the eastern desert.

There is no archaeological evidence to dispute the Old Testament account that the Israelites begged the Edomites and Moabites in vain for permission to travel along the 'King's Highway' through their kingdoms. The Israelites were compelled to go around these kingdoms. Finally they succeeded in forcing their way westward to the Jordan along the north side of the Naḥal Arnon (Wadi Mojib), which at that time was the southern part of the territory of Sihon, king of the Amorites. Had the Exodus through southern Transjordan taken place before the thirteenth century B.C., the Israelites would have found neither Edomite nor Moabite kingdoms, well organized and well fortified, whose rulers could have given or withheld permission to go through their territories. The political organization of Edom and the other Transjordanian kingdoms of the Iron Age was apparently more organized than that of the Israelites, who long maintained their loose confederation based on the amphictyonic principle. The Edomites on the other hand, to judge from the account in Gen. xxxi. 31, had eight Edomite kings before the Israelites had a king.

The name of Esau is connected with the term Edom (Gen. xxxvi. 1), just as the name Edom, meaning 'red' or 'reddish', is connected with the red pottage for which Esau exchanged his birthright with Jacob (Gen. xxv. 30, xxxvi. 1, 8, 19). It is also connected in similar popular etymology with the ruddiness of Esau at the time of his birth (Gen. xxv. 25), even as the wooded hills of Seir (Joshua xi. 17, xii. 7) facing Mount Halak ('smooth' mountain) of Israel is brought into relationship with the hairiness of Esau as contrasted with the smoothness of Jacob (Gen. xxvii. 11). The possibility that Edomite power once extended into parts of southern Palestine and of Sinai is suggested by a number of Old Testament verses which definitely locate Edom-Seir on the west side of the Arabah. All these verses (Deut. i. 2, 44, xxxiii. 1; Joshua xi. 17, xii. 7; 1 Chron. iv. 42 f.; Judges v. 4 f.; Hab. iii. 3), however, in their present form must be dated to the exilic period or later. They reflect the Idumaean settlement in southern Palestine which the author of Deut. xxiii. 8, R.V. 7, probably had in mind, meaning those Idumaeans who had been Judaized and had become Yahweh worshippers. The general attitude of the Old Testament to the Edomites is one of unmitigated hostility, although Zephaniah and Zechariah do not include Edom among the nations that are doomed. Egyptian records from the temple of Ramesses II at Luxor do associate Edom and Seir, and seem to confirm the history of settlement in Edom and Moab as established through archaeological undertakings.

The Wadi Arabah with its minerals, having also access to the trade of Arabia and the commerce of the Red Sea, served perhaps as the main cause of the bitter and protracted warfare between Israel and Edom. The rich routes of commerce coming from Arabia led northward to Damascus, westward to Gaza and Egypt, and eastward to the Euphrates and the Persian Gulf. The prosperous periods in the history of the United Kingdom and of Judah and Edom seem to have a direct relationship to the periods in which they controlled the Arabah and its copper mines and a port on the Gulf of Aqabah. The copper mines in the Wadi Arabah (Deut. viii. 9) furnish the explanation of one of the chief sources of Solomon's wealth. The ores mined and smelted there were sent in part to his port and store-city and industrial and caravan centre of Ezion-geber to be turned into manufactured articles and to be used as export articles in his Tarshish fleet (1 Kings ix. 26, x. 11, 22; 2 Chron. viii. 17 f.) that sailed regularly to Ophir and back.

The working of the copper mines in the Wadi Arabah by Solomon followed David's conquest and enslavement of the Edomites (2 Sam. viii. 13 ff.; 1 Kings xi. 15 f.). In addition to serving as one of his merchants' main export items, some of the Wadi Arabah copper may have been used in the construction of Solomon's temple and palace in Jerusalem, after being fashioned into suitable forms in the Jordan valley by Hiram (1 Kings ix. 10).

ii. *Tell el-Kheleifeh* (*Ezion-geber: Elath*)

The progress of the bitter and protracted struggle between Israel or Judah and Edom can be correlated with the development, destruction, abandonment, reoccupation, and final disappearance from history of the port and store-city and industrial and caravan centre of the Ezion-geber founded by Solomon. It is to be identified, as first suggested by F. Frank, with the small low mound of Tell el-Kheleifeh, located approximately in the centre of the north shore of the Gulf of Aqabah. Its position approximates to the description in 1 Kings ix. 26 of Ezion-geber's being 'beside Eloth, on the shore of the Red Sea, in the land of Edom'. When the Israelites of the Exodus reached the north shore of the gulf, an Ezion-geber was already in existence. All traces of it have disappeared. The pottery remains found on the surfaces of Tell el-Kheleifeh date from the tenth to the fifth centuries B.C., spanning the history of both Ezion-geber and the Elath which succeeded it on the same site. It seems certain that only Solomon possessed the

ability, authority, wealth, and power to build Ezion-geber anew.
The excavations undertaken there in 1938–40 by the American
Schools of Oriental Research, the Smithsonian Institution, and the
American Philosophical Society, seem to have confirmed the
identification of the site.

The central location of Tell el-Kheleifeh in the middle of the
southern end of the Wadi Arabah, its possession of the first drink-
able water, however brackish, as one comes from the western side
of the north shore of the Gulf of Aqabah, and the fact that the
shoreline immediately in front of it is free of rocks, so that small
boats could have been drawn up on it or anchored close to it, add
up to the sum of its natural advantages.

The first building excavated at the north-west corner of the
site had two rows of horizontal apertures in the walls of its three
small square rooms and three long rectangular rooms. When the
debris had been cleared the drafts of air entering through the
apertures in the outer north wall could be felt emerging through
the apertures in the outer south wall, the length of the building
removed. It had originally been thought that the apertures served
as flue-holes during Period I of this structure, which was conceived
by the excavator as serving as an advanced type of smelter-refinery.
Through these apertures or flue-holes, it was opined, the strong
winds from the north-north-west entered into the furnace rooms
of this so-called 'smelter' to furnish a natural draft to fan the flames.
The excavator, Nelson Glueck, had previously visited and dated
by surface pottery finds many of the copper-mining and smelting
sites on both sides of the Wadi Arabah (some of which had already
been visited by others, among them notably F. Frank) especially
to the times of Solomon and his successors. He had called them
'King Solomon's Mines', and had attributed, as he still does, a
considerable part of Solomon's wealth to his exploitation of the
mineral resources of the Wadi Arabah. It seemed natural thus, when
the pronounced apertures became visible in the fire-hardened
brick walls of the first building excavated at Tell el-Kheleifeh, to
consider them as flue-holes of a copper-smelter and refinery.

It has now become apparent, however, that these apertures
were not intended as flue-holes or as ventilation channels or any
other purpose. They resulted from the decay and/or burning of
wooden cross-beams laid across the mud-brick walls of the

PLATE XIX

a. Crude, hand-made Iron Age II ware (Ezion-geber)

b. Seal signet ring of Jotham (Ezion-geber)

structure for bonding or anchoring purposes. Some of the wooden beams were inserted also laterally and vertically into the walls, which were then plastered over with a mud coating, hiding the ends or sides of the bonding timbers from sight. Examples of this kind of construction of mud-brick walls have been found at Zenjirli, Boğazköy, Tell Tainat, Tell Halaf, Troy, and Knossos, for example. The use of timber joists for bonding purposes in stone walls has been attested to by finds in Samaria. This type of construction seems to be reflected in the description in 1 Kings vi. 36. At ancient Jericho numerous horizontal lacing timbers were employed in several stages in the walls of the town. Striking parallels to the apertures at Ezion-geber are furnished by the 'granary' at Mohenjo-daro.

Aside from the fact that the inner and outer faces of the walls of the main building at the north-west corner of Tell el-Kheleifeh were covered with a coating of mud plaster in the initial Period I, a mud-brick rampart or glacis was built against it in the same period, negating the possible use of any apertures or flues for draft or ventilation purposes. The excavator believes now that this structure was designed as a citadel, and was also employed, as others have suggested, as a storehouse and/or granary, and that indeed Solomon's Ezion-geber served in a comparatively modest way as the southernmost of the fortified district and chariot cities that Solomon built in elaborate fashion at Hazor, Megiddo, and Gezer (1 Kings ix. 15–17, 19).

Industrial and metallurgical operations definitely did take place, however, at Ezion-geber, as evidenced by the finding in the excavations of some copper slag, and remains of a hand-bellows furnace. Numerous fragments of copper implements and vessels were found, which, however, by themselves furnish no proof of industrial operations. There was, however, little slag compared to the great masses of slag marking numerous Late Iron Age I and Early Iron Age II copper-mining and smelting sites in the Wadi Arabah, where also mining and smelting activities were carried on in Middle Bronze Age I and still earlier in late Chalcolithic times.

In the excavations of Tell el-Kheleifeh a coarse, handmade type of pottery was found that at the time was completely new in pottery of the Iron Age (Pl. XIXa). The excavator briefly considered them to be pottery crucibles, but soon abandoned this idea when it became apparent from his archaeological explorations of the Negeb how widespread this type of pottery was in the Negeb and the Wadi Arabah, as well as in the various periods of occupation of Ezion-geber. It is believed that this crude, handmade ware, often marked by mat bases and knob or horn or ledge handles, was the handiwork of Kenites, Rechabites, Calebites, Jerahmeelites, and related inhabitants of the Negeb and the Wadi Arabah. It will be remembered that it was the Kenites who introduced the Israelites into the art of metallurgy. Together with this crude ware there were found more familiar types of Iron Age I and II wheelmade wares, some of which had regional differences characteristic of Edomite, Moabite, Ammonite, and Amorite Iron Age Transjordan pottery.

The citadel storehouse of Ezion-geber I, with its supporting glacis, was located not quite in the centre of a square enclosed by a casemate wall, each of whose outer sides was 45 metres in length, divided into three salients and two recesses, each 9 metres in length. Ezion-geber I may have been destroyed by Shishak (Pharaoh Sheshonq) in the fifth year of Rehoboam (1 Kings xiv. 25 f.; 2 Chron. xii. 2 ff.). At the beginning of Period II a completely new series of massive fortification walls of mud-brick was erected around and partly over the ruins of Ezion-geber I. It consisted of a double wall, with a glacis bonded into each one, and a dry moat between them, and a massive city gateway with three pairs of doors and two opposite sets of guardrooms between them. It is much similar to the massive gateway of city IV (IVA) of Megiddo which Y. Yadin has shown was built long after the time of Solomon, perhaps by Ahab.

It is possible that Period II of Ezion-geber represents a reconstruction by Jehoshaphat of Judah (c. 870–848 B.C.). He was the one who made the abortive attempt to revive the sea trade between Ezion-geber and Arabia and Africa that had flourished during the reign of Solomon (1 Kings xxii. 49, R.V. 48; 2 Chron. xx. 36 f.). As a result of the subsequent economic decline, coupled with the growing political weakness of Judah, the importance of Ezion-geber seems to have declined. At any rate, after the time of Jehoshaphat it is no longer mentioned in the Old Testament.

Ezion-geber may have been destroyed again during the successful rebellion of the Edomites against his son Jehoram (Joram) (2 Kings viii. 20 ff.; 2 Chron. xxi. 8 ff.), shortly after the middle of

the ninth century B.C. They were, however, not powerful enough
to rebuild it, and were probably not strong enough to renew copper
mining and smelting on a large scale in the Wadi Arabah. Nor
apparently was their economic and military strength sufficient to
enable them to build a fleet of ships of their own and emulate the
foreign trade activities of Solomon.

About half a century later, the Edomites again lost their independence to the Judaeans under Amaziah (c. 796–767 B.C.). He
captured their great stronghold of Sela which he renamed Joktheel
(2 Kings xiv. 7; 2 Chron. xxv. 11 f.). Ezion-geber remains un-
mentioned in the Old Testament and there is no reference to an
Elath of that time. It was first during the reign of his very capable
son Uzziah (Azariah, c. 767–740 B.C.), who 'built towers in the
wilderness (the Negeb) and hewed out many cisterns' (2 Chron.
xxvi. 10), that the name of Elath appears again. It is written that
he 'built Elath and restored it to Judah' (2 Kings xiv. 22; 2 Chron.
xxvi. 1 f.). This occurred probably early in his reign, shortly after
the first quarter of the eighth century B.C. It may be identified
with Period III of Tell el-Kheleifeh.

Nearly seventy years had passed between the destruction of
Ezion-geber and the rebuilding over its ruins of a new city, with
which in the interval the name of Elath may have become
associated. It preserved thus the name of the original Eloth (1 Kings
ix. 26) that at the time of the Exodus and later may have existed
further east, either near or on the site of modern Aqabah. In any
event, the occupational history of Tell el-Kheleifeh as determined
by the excavations there encompasses the histories both of Ezion-
geber and Elath as delineated in the Old Testament from the time
of Solomon onwards, and it spans the period between the tenth
and fifth–fourth centuries B.C.

In the Period III city a seal signet ring was found bearing
the inscription 'belonging to Jotham' (Pl. XIX*b*).[3] It may have
belonged to the governor of Elath ruling in the name of Jotham,
king of Judah, the successor of Uzziah. Underneath the inscription is a horned ram, and in front of it an object that N. Avigad
has identified as a bellows. The representation of the bellows
seems to testify to the continuation of metallurgical activities first
inaugurated on a large scale by Solomon in the Wadi Arabah and
of related industrial activities at Ezion-geber.

After the time of Uzziah and Jotham, Elath was to change hands once more. Taking advantage of the distress of Uzziah's son Ahaz, during the Syro-Ephraimite war in 733 B.C., the Edomites regained control of Elath. 2 Kings xvi. 6 has been emended to read: 'At that time the king of Edom restored Elath to Edom and drove out all the Judaeans from Elath; whereupon the Edomites came to Elath and dwelt there unto this day.'

The Edomites subsequently rebuilt Elath, which had been considerably damaged when they recaptured it from the Judaeans. Their substantial new city, which contained the largest collections of pottery found on the site, is represented by Period IV at Tell el-Kheleifeh. With its several sub-periods, it lasted from about the end of the eighth century to about the end of the sixth century B.C. The freedom regained by Edom from Ahaz was never again threatened by Judah, which was not strong enough thereafter to dispute Edom's control over the Arabah and Elath.

Stamped on the handles of a series of jars belonging to the first phase of Period IV, which probably extended well into the seventh century B.C., was an Edomite inscription reading—'Belonging to Ḳausanal, the servant of the king'. The first part of the theophorous name Ḳausanal or Ḳosanal, namely Ḳaus or Ḳos, is that of a well-known Edomite and subsequently Nabataean deity, and occurs also in the Old Testament (Ezra ii. 53; Neh. vii. 55). One of the Edomite kings who paid homage and tribute to Tiglath-pileser III at Damascus was named Kaushmalaku.[4] Belonging also to the Edomite city of Period IV were fragments of a large jar, which was probably used for transporting incense and spices from Arabia. On two of its fragments were incised the first South Arabic letters of the Minaean script thus far discovered in a controlled excavation in greater Palestine. Other finds were made in the course of the excavations showing connexions with Egypt, among others being a small faience bead representing a Bubastite cat.

The Babylonian conquest brought an end to the independence not only of Judah but also of Edom and to Edomite rule over the Elath of Period IV. It was destroyed before the end of the sixth century B.C. A new industrial city of Period V was built over it, which lasted from near the end of the sixth or from early in the fifth century B.C., mainly under Persian administration. Trade on an extensive scale was still carried on with Arabia as evidenced by Aramaic ostraca, including wine receipts. And goods were exchanged between both countries and Greece, as indicated by fragments of fifth–fourth centuries B.C. black-glazed Greek pottery. Tell el-Kheleifeh was abandoned thereafter, and the subsequent Nabataean settlement was located further to the east, at Aila, close to present-day Aqabah.

By the fourth century B.C. the Nabataeans had so heavily infiltrated Edom and Moab (with many of the former inhabitants gradually becoming Nabataeanized, and others, particularly the Edomites, becoming known as Idumaeans moving into the northern Negeb and southern Judaea) that they were able to establish Petra as their central bastion and trade centre and were able to resist attacks from Syria.

iii. *Gaps in the History of Settlement*

Before the advent of the Edomites and Moabites and other contemporary peoples of Iron Ages I–II in Transjordan, much of the land was largely empty of civilized settlement for more than half a millennium. In other words, from the end of Middle Bronze Age I to the very beginning of Iron Age I, most of Transjordan was peopled largely by bedouin. The same phenomenon characterizes the sedentary, civilized history also of the Negeb, and probably also of Sinai. In general it may be said in this connexion that the history of the Negeb is more bound up with the history of Transjordan, south of the Jabbok, than it seems to be with that of the rest of Cisjordan to the north of the Negeb. The Middle Bronze Age II and Late Bronze Age civilizations that were known in the Jordan valley and in Palestine north of the Negeb, and that existed in the northern part of Transjordan in North Gilead, did not flourish, with few exceptions, in Edom, Moab, Ammon, and South Gilead. It is significant in this connexion that neither the Egyptian lists of towns nor the Tell el-Amarna tablets refer to Eastern Palestine in the period extending from the twentieth to the thirteenth centuries B.C. Edom and Seir are first mentioned in the records of Ramesses II (*c.* 1304–1237 B.C.). It may further be mentioned in this connexion that there are no archaeological traces of the Horites in either the hill-country of Edom, or in the Wadi Arabah, or in the Negeb, unless under Horites are to be understood purely nomadic groups, such as the Edomites must have found and conquered when they entered southern Transjordan (Gen. xiv. 6, xxxvi. 21 f.; Deut. ii. 12).

The statement that south of North Gilead, that is, south of the Jabbok river (Wadi Zerqa), there is a break in the history of sedentary occupation of Transjordan applying to the southern kingdom of the Amorites and to the kingdoms of Ammon, Moab, and Edom, need not significantly be modified by the discovery of several Middle Bronze Age IIB tombs in Amman and, 2 miles outside of Amman, of a small shrine or temple standing completely by itself and containing a considerable amount of pottery of the Late Bronze Age period. With regard to the Middle Bronze Age IIB tombs in Amman, it is known that nomads and semi-nomads buried their dead in tombs (cf. Gen. xxiii). It has been suggested with regard to the Late Bronze Age tomb outside Amman that it was built and used by a nomadic or semi-nomadic people who had control of caravan trade stemming from the west in general and coming from the Aegean region in particular. F. Cross's suggestion that this Late Bronze Age shrine might be an amphictyonic sanctuary fits in with the idea of the nomadic or semi-nomadic character of the people who built it.

The occupation, abandonment, and reoccupation of lands like Edom and Moab cannot be explained by popular theories of precipitation cycles rendering human habitation in these areas progressively impossible. Although all the variables making for the establishment and destruction and disappearance of widely separated periods of civilization cannot be ascertained for Edom, Moab, and other parts of Transjordan, the chief explanation both for periods of intensive settlement and extensive abandonment of these countries is to be found in political and economic, or, in a word, in human factors rather than in major, permanent, climatic changes.

There is clear evidence of late fourth millennium B.C. Chalcolithic settlements in Edom and in the Wadi Arabah, and a Pre-Pottery Neolithic village of the first part of the seventh millennium B.C. has been excavated by Diana Kirkbride at Baida near Petra. An advanced civilization belonging to the Middle Bronze I period existed between the twenty-first and nineteenth centuries B.C. in Transjordan, the Wadi Arabah, the Negeb, and Sinai, as has been archaeologically demonstrated. Its destruction was sudden and catastrophic. It simply disappeared from off the face of the earth. The presence and disappearance of this civilization authenticates the general validity of the background of Gen. xiv. 5 ff. of how the eastern kings led by Chedorlaomer conquered all Transjordan. They subdued and destroyed one after another all the fortified sites which lay in their path from Ashteroth and Ham at the northern end to El-Paran at the southern end of the territory which later on became known as Edom. It is known that the Egyptian Sinuhe visited ancient Kedem, east of the Jordan, at the beginning of the twentieth century B.C., but, besides the veiled references in Gen. xiv, there are no literary records dealing with the occupation of Transjordan in this Middle Bronze I period. Its existence has been fully demonstrated by the discovery of numerous Middle Bronze Age I sites, which were destroyed at the end of that period, and most of which were never again reoccupied. When the Edomites and others came across these sites, they could hardly have recognized them as ancient places of dwelling of civilized settlers who made pottery distinctively characteristic of their period. The Old Testament record of the existence of this Middle Bronze Age I civilization as reflected particularly in Gen. xiv must be attributed to the phenomenon of historical memory.

iv. *Moab*

The boundaries of Moab in the Iron Age were fully as strongly fortified as those of Edom, and it seems clear that both kingdoms were sufficiently entrenched at the time of the advent of the Israelites of the Exodus to be able to deny the Israelites permission to pass through their territories and force them to go around them. The western boundary of Moab was formed by the Dead Sea, the southern by the great canyon of the Naḥal Zered (Wadi Hesa), the eastern by the desert. The northern boundary of Moab at the time of the Exodus was marked by the impressive canyon of the Naḥal Arnon (Wadi Mojib). This part of the rolling Moabite plateau was some 35 miles long from north to south and some 25 miles wide, with precipitous slopes on all sides except the east side which merged with the desert. The plateau is about 3,000 feet above sea level. Originally the northern boundary of Moab extended to the east–west line of the Wadi Hesban (Heshbon), which, under the name of the Wadi Kefrein, joins the Wadi Rameh flowing east–west to the south of it to empty into the Jordan river several miles above the northern end of the Dead Sea. Num. xxi. 26–30 informs us that the 'first' king of Moab had been defeated by Sihon, king of the Amorites, who had established his residence at Heshbon. Ruling over the southern half of Gilead extending from the river Jabbok southward, he had conquered, or perhaps reconquered, that part of Moabite territory which extended from the Wadi Hesban (Naḥal Heshbon) southward as far as the Naḥal Arnon. The greatest extent of Moab thus at one time from north to south was about 60 miles.

The original northern border of Moab extending west–east from near the northern end of the Dead Sea was subsequently to mark the northern limit of the southern part of the Nabataean kingdom in southern Transjordan. The northern part of the Nabataean kingdom in the Hauran was connected with the Arabian part (which formed a continuation of the southern Transjordan part) through the Wadi Sirhan. No Nabataean pottery seems to occur in the Syrian part of the Nabataean kingdom or in the Wadi Sirhan, in contrast to its ubiquitous appearance in the rest of the Nabataean kingdom, including probably the north Arabian section, whose chief Nabataean city was Meda'in Salih.

While the Edomite and Moabite kingdoms were too formidable for the Israelites to cope with at the time of their arrival, they did succeed in entering and conquering the kingdom of Sihon, which extended then south–north from the Arnon to the Jabbok (Judges xi. 22). This territory between the Arnon and the Jabbok forming South Gilead was allotted to Reuben and Gad (Num. xxi. 21–30, xxxii. 39), who constructed, or reconstructed, many cities in the southern half of this area (Num. xxxii. 34–48, 1–4; Joshua xiii. 24–27).

The history of civilized, sedentary occupation of Moab in Iron Age I–II between the thirteenth and sixth centuries B.C. parallels that of Edom, with intermittent warfare taking place between Judah or Israel and Moab. Old Testament tradition in 2 Kings iii. 27 relates how Mesha of Moab frightened off the attacking forces of Joram of Israel and Jehoshaphat of Judah, and saved his capital city of Kir-hareseth through the dreadful expedient of sacrificing his eldest son on its outer fortification wall. Regaining ultimately the freedom of his country from Ahab of Israel, Mesha caused to be inscribed the so-called Mesha stele commemorating the event.[5] It is the longest single literary document outside the Old Testament dealing with the history of Palestine and Transjordan in the Iron Age. This ninth-century B.C. stele, together with the twelfth-century one, adapted from a much earlier menhir, found at Balu'ah, south of the Arnon, whose inscribed lines are unfortunately so worn as to be illegible, give an indication of the literary wealth that may yet be discovered when numerous Moabite sites of the Iron Age are excavated.

The fertile lands of the rolling Moabite plateau supported extensive agriculture and provided grazing for great flocks and herds of domesticated animals. Before Mesha regained the independence of Moab, he was required to deliver annually to the king of Israel 'the wool of an hundred thousand lambs, and of an hundred thousand rams' (2 Kings iii. 4). The technique of digging cisterns and making them impermeable with coats of slaked lime, which was perfected in the Iron Age, contributed greatly to the economy of the kingdoms on both sides of the Jordan rift.

The god Chemosh, whom Mesha mentions in his stele, and numerous pottery figurines found on the surfaces of Moabite sites, indicate that the Moabite religion was much similar to that of contemporary Transjordan and of much of Cisjordan too. The strong fortifications, found not only along the Moabite frontiers but in the interior of the land, testify to advanced construction skills. Moabite pottery of Iron Age I–II is closely related to contemporary Edomite and Ammonite pottery, as has already been seen.

Archaeological exploration and excavation have shown that Moab was inhabited by a sedentary, civilized population between the thirteenth and sixth centuries B.C. A fallow period ensued during which bedouin ruled the land. The Nabataeans who infiltrated Edom and Moab thereafter were able to establish themselves as the dominant power in these lands by the fourth century B.C., and henceforth to increase their power and create a kingdom which was absorbed finally into the Roman Provincia Arabia in A.D. 106.

Preceding the Iron Age I–II occupation of the land there was

a Middle Bronze I period of occupation, with a gap extending between the two periods, characteristic of the history of Transjordan
south of the Jabbok river. An earlier period of civilized settlement
has been found to exist in the Plains of Moab (Num. xxxiii. 48 f.)
in the Chalcolithic and early parts of the Early Bronze periods. The
dolmens found there and elsewhere in Transjordan and Cisjordan
probably belong to the Neolithic period, not later than the sixth
millennium B.C. The great standing pillars of stone, called menhirs,
sometimes set up in rows or circles, found at such places as Khirbet
Iskander, Lejjun, and Ader in Moab, may belong to the period
of the end of the third millennium B.C. occupation of these sites.
Contemporary with them may be the two Moabite stelae of
Shihon and Balu'ah, the latter reused in the twelfth century B.C.
Others of smaller size, such as those found at the great sanctuary
of Bab edh-Dhra' on the east side of the Dead Sea, may belong to
the period between the twenty-third and nineteenth centuries
B.C., as do the Cities of the Plain located south of the peninsula,
extending into it on the east side, called the Lisan (Gen. xiii. 12).

In the well-watered Plains of Moab were located important
Old Testament cities of Iron Age I–II, located at strategic sites
and guarding the emergence from the hills of the perennial streams
of the Wadi Nimrin, the Wadi Kefrein, the Wadi er-Rameh
(which, two-thirds of the way across the valley, runs into the
Wadi Kefrein and which is known in the hills as the Wadi Hesban),
and the Wadi Azeimeh. From north to south in the Plains of Moab,
these towns were known in the Old Testament as Beth-nimrah
(to be identified with Tell Bleibil), Abel-shittim (Tell Hammam),
Beth-haram (Tell Iktanu), and Beth-jeshimoth (Tell Azeimeh).

v. *Kingdoms of Sihon and Ammon*

The territory of Sihon, king of the Amorites, extended south–
north from the Arnon to the Jabbok. The first part of the Jabbok,
commencing in Rabbath-Ammon and flowing more or less northward before bending westward towards the Jordan, formed also the
east boundary of the territory of Sihon and at the same time the
west boundary of the kingdom of Ammon (Judges xi. 22; Joshua
xii. 2 f.). The western side of the kingdom of Sihon consisted of a
corridor on the east side of the Jordan, extending between the
east half of the northern side of the Dead Sea and the east side of

the southern end of the Sea of Chinnereth (Joshua xii. 3; Deut. iii. 16 f.). The area that later on was to become known as Peraea was located in this corridor.

The original Ammonite kingdom consisted of a small, strongly fortified, fairly fertile strip along the east side of the south–north stretch of the Naḥal Jabbok (Wadi Zerqa) and reached eastward to the desert. South and south-west of Amman were also found some important fortifications which may have belonged to the Ammonite kingdom. When Israel conquered Sihon, it is said that they took his land 'from the Arnon to [both stretches of] the Jabbok—as far [east] as the territory of the Ammonites, whose boundary was strong' (Num. xxi. 24; Deut. ii. 19, 37).

Among the most striking of Ammonite fortifications were strongly built circular towers of megalithic construction, which either alone, or usually in conjunction with rectangular or square fortifications, also built of large blocks of stone, provided the defences of the Ammonite kingdom and particularly of the approaches to their capital city of Rabbath-Ammon. These megalithic structures seem to have been built in the Iron I period and to have been utilized also during the Iron II period of the Ammonite kingdom.

That the Ammonite Iron Age kingdom had a vigorous cultural history is indicated by important tomb finds both inside and immediately outside of Rabbath-Ammon. Inscriptions, anthropoid pottery coffins, horse-and-rider figurines, several complete small stone sculptures, one bearing on its base in old Aramaic characters the inscription 'Yaraḥ'azar, head of the cavalry', almost life-size torsos of limestone statues into which the heads were separately inserted, inscribed seals, excellent pottery with clear relationships to other Iron Age I–II Transjordan wares, some of which revealed clear Phoenician, Syrian, and Assyrian influences, testify to the cultural achievements of the Ammonites in Iron Age I–II and particularly in Iron Age II.

The occupational history of the kingdom of Ammon and the kingdom of Sihon parallels that of Moab and Edom. Some of the sites along the Naḥal Jabbok show an occupational history extending from about the twenty-third to the middle of the eighteenth centuries B.C., followed by a blank period lasting till the thirteenth century B.C., while south of it there is a gap in the history of sedentary occupation between the middle of the nineteenth and the

G g

beginning of the thirteenth centuries B.C. The Naḥal Jabbok formed a boundary line between South Gilead and North Gilead and between South Gilead and Ammon.

vi. *Gilead*

The term Gilead is used loosely in the Old Testament. In Num. xxxii. 33 the territory assigned to Gad, Reuben, and half the tribe of Manasseh, includes the kingdoms of Sihon, king of the Amorites, and of Og, king of Bashan, comprising all the territory between the Arnon river and the Yarmuk and beyond. In 2 Kings x. 33 the word Gilead is employed for the whole of this territory as well as for part of it. The phrase '*all the land of Gilead*' thus also includes a part called *Gilead*, which is obviously north of the Jabbok.

In Deut. iii. 16 f. we read that Gilead includes the territory between the Jabbok and the Arnon, which was given to Reuben and Gad (cf. Joshua xii. 2, xiii. 24–27), in addition to the Jordan river corridor extending to the Sea of Chinnereth. In Deut. iii. 12 there is the statement that *half of Mount Gilead* was given to Reuben and Gad (cf. Num. xxi. 20–30). And in Num. xxxii. 39 it is stated that the land of *Gilead* is to be given to Gad and Reuben. It cannot be more than the south half of Gilead between the Arnon and the Jabbok. Num. xxxii. 34–38 mentions the cities built by Gad and Reuben. They are limited to the southern half of South Gilead, namely to the originally Moabite territory between the Naḥal Arnon and the Naḥal Heshbon, which Sihon incorporated into his kingdom before the advent of the Israelites.

The rest of Gilead, which is known just by that name, is coupled with Bashan, to include the territory between the Jabbok and the Yarmuk and beyond, belonging to the kingdom of Og and assigned to half of the tribe of Manasseh (Deut. iii. 13; Joshua xiii. 30 f.). The *Rest of Gilead* is also called *Half of Gilead* (Joshua xiii. 31), or simply *Gilead* (Joshua xvii. 1, 5; Num. xxxii. 39–42; 2 Kings x. 33). This part of Gilead, belonging to the kingdom of Og, may be designated as *North Gilead*.

North Gilead represents the richest part of the lands of Transjordan. It is blessed with a rainfall of from 28 to 32 inches a year. This explains the existence of so comparatively many perennial streams descending from the fertile highlands westward to the Jordan. Going northward from the Jabbok they are, as has previously been mentioned, the Wadis Kufrinji, Yabis, Jurm, Ziqlab, Tayibeh, and Arab. Some important tributaries of the Yarmuk also rise in North Gilead, as do others on the north side of the Yarmuk canyon in the land of Bashan.

Between the Jabbok and the Yarmuk rivers, North Gilead extends south–north for about 35 miles. The land of Bashan north of the Yarmuk reaches to Mount Hermon and eastward to the northern slopes of the Hauran and to the city of Salecah. On its west side it extends south–north for about 35 miles and on its east side for about 50 miles. Like North Gilead, and even more so, Bashan is a rich land, open to the rains from the west. It was full of cities or settlements in ancient times, marked by long records of unbroken occupation, with no gaps paralleling those in the history of civilized sedentary settlement from the Jabbok river southward in Transjordan. Among its main cities were Ashtaroth (Tell Ashtarah), the capital of Og, Karnaim (Sheikh Sa'ad), which, in the Old Testament (Gen. xiv. 5) has been joined with Ashtaroth, although they are two separate places, and Edrei (modern Der'ah) near the beginning of the east–west line of the Wadi Yarmuk. It was at Edrei that the Israelites defeated Og, whose territory of Bashan and North Gilead was assigned to half the tribe of Manasseh (Deut. i. 4, iii. 1–14). Og's territory passed from David to Solomon, was then lost during the Syrian wars, to be regained by Jeroboam II (2 Kings xiv. 25). From the time of Tiglath-pileser III (2 Kings xv. 29) it passed into foreign control.

In North Gilead and in Bashan artificial city hills (*tulul*) make their appearance, in contradistinction to their absence in the rest of Transjordan. The various periods of gaps in the history of civilized, sedentary settlement in Transjordan south of the Jabbok made it impossible for accretions of foundation ruins of a series of cities built on top of each other to pile up in practically unbroken succession throughout the centuries and thus form the *tulul*. A small tell such as that of Tell el-Kheleifeh could be formed representing one age, namely that of Iron Age I–II, but not a tell containing within its structure evidence of settlements extending, for example, from the beginning of the Early Bronze Age to, and through, and beyond Iron Age I–II. Within this framework can be placed such a site as Tell Ashtarah (Ashtaroth) on the north side of the Yarmuk, as ascertained by W. F. Albright in his archaeological explorations. The history of civilized, sedentary occupation of North Gilead and Bashan is more closely related to that of the Jordan valley than to the rest of Transjordan south of the Jabbok river. Excavations of some of the sites just below the Jabbok river may yet reveal that their history goes back to the beginnings of the Early Bronze Age. Indeed, much more scientific archaeological excavation of ancient sites in Transjordan needs to be undertaken, such as that by P. Lapp at Ramoth-gilead (Tell er-Ramith), and by others of the American Schools of Oriental Research, at Dhiban (Dibon) in Moab. Numerous sites of pre-historic periods, identifiable by worked flint tools of the Palaeolithic to the Neolithic periods, exist in Transjordan, as evidenced by finds, among numerous other places, at Khirbet Kharaneh, Azrak, the Wadi Dhobai, Kilwa, and Sha'ar ha-Golan.

NELSON GLUECK

NOTES

1. See *V.T.* x, 1960, pp. 386–93, xi, 1961, pp. 361–72, xii, 1962, pp. 378–82, xiv, 1964, pp. 377 ff.
2. Ibid. xv, 1965, pp. 150 ff.; A. van den Branden, ibid., pp. 129–50.
3. See *D.O.T.T.*, pp. 224 f.; N. Avigad, *B.A.S.O.R.* 163, 1961, pp. 18–22.
4. *A.N.E.T.*, p. 282.
5. See *D.O.T.T.*, pp. 195–8.

BIBLIOGRAPHY

ABEL, F.-M. *Géographie de la Palestine*, 2 vols. (1933, 1938).
ALBRIGHT, W. F. *The Archaeology of Palestine*, 1954.
BALY, D. *The Geography of the Bible: a study in historical geography*, 1957.
—— *Geographical Companion to the Bible*, 1963.
BENNETT, C. M. 'Fovilles d'Umm el-Biyara. Rapport préliminaire,' *R.B.* lxiii, 1966, pp. 372–403.
BLAKE, G. S. *The Mineral Resources of Palestine and Transjordan*, 1930.
FRANK, F. 'Aus der Arabah', *Z.D.P.V.* lvii, 1934, pp. 208–78.
GLUECK, NELSON. *The Other Side of the Jordan*, 1940.
—— *The River Jordan*, 1946.
—— *Explorations in Eastern Palestine I–IV*, *A.A.S.O.R.* xiv, 1934, xv, 1935, xviii–xix, 1939, xxv–xxviii, 1951.
—— *Rivers in the Desert*, 1959.
—— *Deities and Dolphins*, 1965.
—— 'Ezion-geber', *B.A.* xxviii, 1965, pp. 70–87.

HARDING, G. L. *Antiquities of Jordan*, 1959.

IONIDES, M. G., and BLAKE, G. S. *Report on the Water Resources of Transjordan*, 1939.

KITCHEN, K. A. 'Ramesses II in Transjordan', in 'Asiatic Wars of Ramesses II', *J.E.A.*, 1964, pp. 63–70.

LANDES, G. M. 'The material civilization of the Ammonites', *B.A.* xxiv, 1961, pp. 66–86.

RHOTERT, H. *Transjordanien: Vorgeschichtliche Forschungen*, 1938.

ROTHENBERG, B. 'Ancient copper industries in the Western Arabah', *P.E.Q.*, 1962, pp. 5–71.

SMITH, G. A. *The Historical Geography of the Holy Land*, 25th ed., 1931.

WRIGHT, G. E. *Biblical Archaeology*, 1962.

—— and FILSON, F. V. *The Westminster Historical Atlas to the Bible*, 1958.

GENERAL BIBLIOGRAPHY

ABEL, F.-M. *Géographie de la Palestine*, 2 vols., 1933, 1938.
ALBRIGHT, W. F. *The Archaeology of Palestine and the Bible*, 1932.
—— *The Archaeology of Palestine* (Pelican Books), 1954.
—— *Archaeology and the Religion of Israel*, 3rd ed., 1953.
—— *From the Stone Age to Christianity*, 2nd ed., 1957.
—— 'The Old Testament and the archaeology of Palestine', *O.T.M.S.*, pp. 1–26.
—— 'The Old Testament and the archaeology of the Ancient East', ibid., pp. 27–47.
—— 'The archaeology of the Ancient Near East', in Peake's *Commentary on the Bible*, ed. M. Black and H. H. Rowley, 1962, pp. 58–65.
BALY, D. *The Geography of the Bible: a study in historical geography*, 1957.
BARROIS, A.-G. *Manuel d'archéologie biblique*, i, 1939, ii, 1953.
BENZINGER, I. *Hebräische Archäologie*, 3rd rev. ed., 1927.
BURROWS, M. *What Mean these Stones? The Significance of Archaeology for Biblical Studies*, 1957.
CONTENAU, G. *Manuel d'archéologie orientale depuis les origines jusqu'à l'époque d'Alexandre*, i–iv, 1927–47.
COOK, S. A. *The Religion of Ancient Palestine in the Light of Archaeology* (Schweich Lectures, 1925), 1930.
DE VAUX, R. *Ancient Israel, its Life and Institutions*, 1961.
DRIVER, G. R. *Semitic Writing: From Pictograph to Alphabet* (Schweich Lectures, 1944), rev. ed., 1954.
FINEGAN, J. *Light from the Ancient Past; the Archaeological Background of Judaism and Christianity*, 2nd ed., 1959.
GALLING, K. *Biblisches Reallexicon*, 1937.
GRAY, J. *Archaeology and the Old Testament World*, 1962.
—— 'The archaeology of Palestine—11. The Biblical period', in Peake's *Commentary on the Bible*, ed. M. Black and H. H. Rowely, 1962, pp. 50–57.
GROLLENBERG, L. H. *Atlas of the Bible*, trans. and ed. by J. M. H. Reid and H. H. Rowley, 1956.
KENYON, KATHLEEN M. 'The archaeology of Palestine—1. Prehistoric and early phases', in Peake's *Commentary on the Bible*, ed. M. Black and H. H. Rowley, 1962, pp. 42–49.
—— *Archaeology in the Holy Land*, 2nd ed., 1965.
MAY, H. G. (ed.). *Oxford Bible Atlas*, 1962.
McCOWN, C. C. *The Ladder of Progress in Palestine*, 1943.
NOTH, M. *The Old Testament World*, 1966.
PRITCHARD, J. B. *Archaeology and the Old Testament*, 1958.

PRITCHARD, J. B. *The Ancient Near East: An Anthology of Texts and Pictures*, 1958 (an abridgement of *A.N.E.P.* and *A.N.E.T.*).

ROWLEY, H. H. 'Recent discovery and the patriarchal age', *B.J.R.L.* xxxii, 1949–50, pp. 44–79. (Reprinted in *The Servant of the Lord and other Essays on the Old Testament*, 1952, pp. 271–305.)

SCHAEFFER, C. F. A. *Stratigraphie comparée et chronologie de l'Asie occidentale, IIIe et IIe millénaires*, 1948.

SIMONS, J. *The Geographical and Topographical Texts of the Old Testament: A Concise Commentary in xxxii Chapters*, 1959.

SMITH, G. A. *The Historical Geography of the Holy Land*, 25th ed., 1931.

THOMAS, D. WINTON (ed.). *Documents from Old Testament Times*, 1958.

THOMPSON, J. A. *The Bible and Archaeology*, 1962.

UNGER, M. F. *Archaeology and the Old Testament*, 1954.

WATZINGER, C. *Denkmäler Palästinas: eine Einführung in die Archäologie des Heiligen Landes*, 2 vols., 1933–5.

WISEMAN, D. J. 'Archaeology', in *The New Bible Dictionary*, ed. J. D. Douglas *et al.*, 1962, pp. 60–76.

WRIGHT, G. E. 'Archaeology and Old Testament Studies', *J.B.L.* lxxvii, 1958, pp. 39–51.

—— 'The Archaeology of Palestine', in *The Bible and the Ancient Near East (Essays in honor of William Foxwell Albright)*, ed. G. E. Wright, 1961, pp. 73–112.

—— *Biblical Archaeology*, rev. ed., 1962.

—— *An Introduction to Biblical Archaeology*, 1960.

—— and FILSON, F. V. (ed.). *The Westminster Historical Atlas to the Bible*, 5th ed., 1958.

YEIVIN, S. *A Decade of Archaeology in Israel, 1948–1958*, 1960.

INDEXES

(a) BIBLICAL REFERENCES

(b) GENERAL

I i

Salem, 277, 282.
Ṣaliḥ, Kh., 183.
Salonen, A., 98.
Salt, sowing with, 364.
Samakh(yo), 336.
Samaria, 64, 66, 150, 179 f., 323, 329,
  332, 337, 343 ff., 357, 367 f., 370,
  378, 380 ff., 415, 439; pool of, 345;
  papyri from, 367, 370; a Mace-
  donian colony, 351.
Samaritans, 349, 367, 370.
Samânum, 141.
Samerina, 66, 348.
Šamši-Adad, 79.
Samson, 133, 163, 424; and Herakles,
  150.
Samuel, 125, 331, 414.
s/šananu, 133.
Sanballat, family name of, 370; sons
  of, 350.
Sanballat I, 350, 351.
Sanballat II, 351.
Sanballat III, 351.
Sanctuary(-ies), 373, 375 f., 386,
  395 ff., 402, 444, 448.
ṣāpāh, 163.
Ṣaphon, 148, 150, 163.
Sapir, E., 424.
Saps, 130.
Sapsi, 133.
šar kiššati, 335.
Sarah, Sarai, 75, 76, 127.
Sardinia, 410.
Sargon II, 54, 59, 64, 66 ff., 85, 346 ff.,
  378, 415 f.
Sargon of Agade, 53, 119, 136 f.
Šarri-il, 153.
Šarruludari, of Ashkelon, 416.
šarrum, 245.
šārûhen, 420.
Šauška, 131.
Saussha(ta)tar, 123.
Sayce, A. H., 14, 18, 421.
šbn, 176.
šbnt, 339.
Schaefer, H., 22.
Schaeffer, C. F. A. 99, 149, 151, 162 ff.,
  167, 196, 216, 253.
Scheil, V., 56.
Schick, C., 279.
Schmidt, W., 166.
Schnabel, P., 100.

Schneider, N., 101.
School(s), an Egyptian, 415; scribal,
  319.
Schulman, R., 133.
Schumacher, G., 309, 324 f., 328.
Schwartz, B., 423.
Scott, R. B. Y., 327, 424.
Scribes, apprentice, 151; of Alalakh,
  129.
Script, ancient Hebrew, 305, 339 f.,
  346, 398, 400; Aramaic square,
  339 f.; old Aramaic, 449; Phoeni-
  cian, 337; South Arabic, 442;
  Minaean, 442.
Scythians, 186; occupation of Beth-
  shean by, 188.
Scythopolis (Beth-shean), 186.
Sea, Baal against the, 158 f.
Sea-and-River, Ba'al's victory over,
  147.
'Sea' of Solomon's temple, 252.
'Sea Peoples', 22, 109, 124, 185, 195,
  215, 302 f., 410 ff.
Seals, cylinder, 311; late Mitannian
  type, 252; Mitannian, 192; on pot-
  tery, 204; on documents, 151 f.;
  use of, at Alalakh, 130; dynastic, of
  Kings of Ugarit, 153; Cretan, 411;
  Hebrew, 400; 'private', at Arad,
  184; from Beth-haccherem, 173;
  post-exilic, 338; sealing of clay at
  Lachish, 306.
Sebaste (Samaria), 352.
Sebasṭîyeh, see Samaria.
Sedeh Boqer, 391.
ṣedek, 282.
Segal, J. B., 72, 99 f.
Segub, son of Hiel, 375.
sᵉgullāh, 134.
Seir (Edom), 80, 436, 443.
Sela, 433, 441.
Selamiyah, 70.
Seleucids, 186, 367.
Sellin, E., 275, 355, 357, 369.
Semechonitis, Lake (= Lake Huleh),
  246.
šemeš, 197.
Semitic and Aegean traditions, mutual
  influence of, 150.
Semnah stele, 124.
Sennacherib, 42, 47, 68, 178, 203, 217,
  291, 304, 415.

PRINTED IN GREAT BRITAIN
AT THE UNIVERSITY PRESS, OXFORD
BY VIVIAN RIDLER
PRINTER TO THE UNIVERSITY